# The
# NEW
# TESTAMENT
## for
## Latter-day
## Saint
## Families

# The
# *NEW*
# *TESTAMENT*
## for
## *Latter-day*
## *Saint*
## *Families*

## Illustrated King James Version
## with Helps for Children

——— GENERAL EDITOR ———
## Thomas R. Valletta

——— ASSOCIATE EDITORS ———

| | | | |
|---|---|---|---|
| Bruce L. Andreason | Richard O. Christensen | Brian D. Garner | Dennis H Leavitt |
| Randall C. Bird | John L. Fowles | Gordon B. Holbrook | George R. Sims |

## Illustrated by Robert T. Barrett

Bookcraft
Salt Lake City, Utah

Library of Congress Catalog Card Number: 98-73233

ISBN 1-57008-530-7

First Printing, 1998

Printed in the United States of America

Color separations by WHN, Salt Lake City, Utah
Printed at Inland Press, Menomonee Falls, Wisconsin

*Christ as a child*

*For the children*

# CONTENTS

# INTRODUCTION

## TO THE YOUNG READER

Welcome to *The New Testament for Latter-day Saint Families!* This edition of the New Testament was designed especially for families with young readers. It will help you read, understand, and think about the scriptures in exciting new ways.

You will notice right away there are many beautiful pictures and drawings to help you understand what you are reading.

In addition to the pictures, several other kinds of help can be found on every page. Whenever you see a verse number that is **colored red**, look for the following kinds of help at the bottom of the page:

• Many words that may be hard to understand are **colored blue**. That means you will find help for those words at the bottom of that page next to this picture: 🔖 In some cases these word helps are definitions of the hard words, but most often they are replacement words to help you understand what the verse means.

• Sometimes a verse is worth a closer look. Next to the picture of the magnifying glass you will find helpful explanations about the meaning of a verse or about the history, the people, or the customs that make that verse interesting. 🔍

• Heavenly Father has told us many things in the Book of Mormon, the Doctrine and Covenants, and the Pearl of Great Price that make the New Testament much easier to understand. Prophets and apostles in our day also teach us many things to help us understand the scriptures better. Next to the picture of a sun you will find more light from modern prophets and modern scriptures. (Note that whenever a reference to a non-scriptural source is given in the text, the full publication information for that source can be found in the "Sources Cited" section at the back of the book.) ☀️

• Sometimes the best way to understand the scriptures is to ponder them. To *ponder* the scriptures means to stop and think and pray about

what you are reading so that Heavenly Father can help you learn what he wants you to learn. Next to this picture at the bottom of the page you will find some thoughts and questions that will help you ponder what you are reading. 🔄

Heavenly Father wants you to understand his plan for you. His plan is taught in the scriptures. The helps mentioned above are just some of the ways this book will help you understand and love the scriptures.

## A WORD TO PARENTS

*The New Testament for Latter-day Saint Families* is different from the many other editions of the Bible available today. The purpose of this book is not to offer a rewriting of the New Testament in modern language but rather to help the young reader learn to read and appreciate the beauty of the King James Version. As such it is designed to complement and not replace the 1979 LDS edition of the King James Bible.

Elder Bruce R. McConkie declared: "As far as the Bibles of the world are concerned, the King James Version is so far ahead of all others that there is little comparison. . . . It is the Bible that came into being to prepare the way for the translation of the Book of Mormon and to set a literary pattern and standard for the revelations in the Doctrine and Covenants. It is the official Bible of the Church." (*Sermons and Writings of Bruce R. McConkie,* p. 288.)

In addition to the helpful features mentioned under the heading "To the Young Reader" above, this edition of the New Testament provides several other kinds of help for your family:

• A **glossary** helps explain difficult terms and concepts, such as *Pharisee* and *Gentile*. Words found in the glossary are **colored pink** in the text.

• A **pronunciation guide** helps readers recognize and pronounce some of the difficult names and words.

- **Book introductions** provide help in understanding the setting and purpose of every New Testament book.

- **Chapter introductions** provide a brief overview of each chapter in simple English. They also offer suggestions regarding important things to look for to give purpose to family members' reading.

- **Topic headings** are provided in the text whenever the subject changes. These headings help the young reader follow the flow of the chapter without getting lost.

Teaching our young people to read and understand the King James Version will better prepare them to participate in Primary, Sunday School and seminary classes, missions, and every other aspect of Church service.

President Gordon B. Hinckley said: "Read to your children. Read the story of the Son of God. Read to them from the New Testament. Read to them from the Book of Mormon. It will take time, and you are very busy, but it will prove to be a great blessing in your lives as well as in their lives. And there will grow in their hearts a great love for the Savior of the world, the only perfect man who walked the earth. He will become to them a very real living being, and His great atoning sacrifice, as they grow to manhood and womanhood, will take on a new and more glorious meaning in their lives." ("Messages of Inspiration from President Hinckley," p. 2.)

# KINDS OF HELPS FOUND IN
## *THE NEW TESTAMENT FOR LATTER-DAY SAINT FAMILIES*

**Chapter introductions give a brief overview of each chapter.**

**Book introductions give background help for each book.**

**Topic headings help you see when the subject changes.**

**When you see a verse with a red number, it means that you will find additional help for understanding that verse at the bottom of the page.**

**If a word is colored pink it means that you will find an explanation of that word in the Glossary at the back of the book.**

**If a word is colored blue it means that word is explained at the bottom of the page.**

**The sun picture tells you that this help provides more light from modern scriptures or modern prophets.**

**The magnifying glass means that here you will find information about the meaning of a verse or about the history, the people, or the customs that make the verse interesting.**

**The question mark means that here you will find some thoughts and some questions that will help you ponder what you are reading.**

---

THE EPISTLE OF PAUL THE APOSTLE TO THE
# ROMANS

*The book of Romans is a letter written by the Apostle Paul to the Saints living in Rome to prepare them for his visit to them. He wrote the letter about A.D. 57 while staying in Corinth (see Acts 20:2-3).*

### CHAPTER 1

*Paul was a fearless missionary. Notice what he says that shows his courage.*

**PAUL LONGS TO PREACH THE GOSPEL TO THE SAINTS IN ROME**

1 PAUL, a servant of Jesus Christ, called to be an apostle, separated unto the gospel of God,

2 (Which he had promised afore by his prophets in the holy scriptures,)

3 Concerning his Son Jesus Christ our Lord, which was made of the seed of David according to the flesh;

4 And declared to be the Son of God with power, according to the spirit of holiness, by the resurrection from the dead:

5 By whom we have received grace and apostleship for obedience to the faith among all nations, for his name:

6 Among whom are ye also the called of Jesus Christ:

7 To all that be in Rome, beloved of God, called to be saints: Grace to you and peace from God our Father, and the Lord Jesus Christ.

8 ¶ First, I thank my God through Jesus Christ for you all, that your faith is spoken of throughout the whole world.

9 For God is my witness, whom I serve with my spirit in the gospel of his Son, that without ceasing I make mention of you always in my prayers;

10 Making request, if by any means now at length I might have a prosperous journey by the will of God to come unto you.

11 For I long to see you, that I may impart unto you some spiritual gift, to the end ye may be established;

12 That is, that I may be comforted together with you by the mutual faith both of you and me.

13 Now I would not have you ignorant, brethren, that oftentimes I purposed to come unto you, (but was let hitherto,) that I might have some fruit among you also, even as among other Gentiles.

14 I am debtor both to the Greeks, and to the Barbarians; both to the wise, and to the unwise.

15 So, as much as in me is, I am ready to preach the gospel to you that are at Rome also.

16 ¶ For I am not ashamed of the gospel of Christ: for it is the power of God unto salvation to every one that believeth; to the Jew first, and also to the Greek.

---

1:1   Apostles are "special witnesses of the name of Christ in all the world" (D&C 107:23).

1:1   *separated*—set apart

1:2   *afore*—before

1:2-4   The prophets taught that Jesus would be born of the seed or lineage of King David (see Matthew 22:42) and also be the Son of God (see Luke 1:35).

1:5   The Joseph Smith Translation tells us that Paul became an Apostle of Jesus Christ "through obedience, and faith in his name" (JST, Romans 1:5).

1:9   Paul prayed "without ceasing" for the Saints. How does it make you feel to know that the leaders of the Church pray for you?

1:11   *impart*—give
*established*—strengthened

1:13   *let hitherto*—prevented until now
*some fruit*—converts

1:14   *debtor*—one who owes

Greeks were civilized people known for their wisdom. To them, everyone else was barbaric, or uncivilized. Paul had been blessed by both the civilized and the uncivilized (see Acts 28:2).

1:16   Paul was not ashamed to share his testimony of Jesus Christ. How do you feel about sharing your testimony?

---

  = Word Help    = A Closer Look

  = More Light    = Ponder This

Words in pink are explained in the Glossary.

# THE GOSPEL ACCORDING TO
# ST. MATTHEW*

*Matthew, also known as Levi, son of Alphaeus, was a hated tax collector who, having been converted to the gospel, became an Apostle of Jesus Christ. He wrote his Gospel as a testimony to the Jews that Jesus Christ was the fulfillment of the Law and the Prophets. (See LDS Bible Dictionary, s.v. "Matthew," p. 729.)*

## CHAPTER 1

*The birth of Jesus Christ had been prophesied by many prophets long before it happened. Look for how Jesus' birth exactly fulfills these prophecies.*

### JESUS CHRIST'S FAMILY HISTORY IS GIVEN

1 THE book of the generation of Jesus Christ, the son of David, the son of Abraham.

2 Abraham begat Isaac; and Isaac begat Jacob; and Jacob begat Judas and his brethren;

3 And Judas begat Phares and Zara of Thamar; and Phares begat Esrom; and Esrom begat Aram;

4 And Aram begat Aminadab; and Aminadab begat Naasson; and Naasson begat Salmon;

5 And Salmon begat Booz of Rachab; and Booz begat Obed of Ruth; and Obed begat Jesse;

6 And Jesse begat David the king; and David the king begat Solomon of her that had been the wife of Urias;

7 And Solomon begat Roboam; and Roboam begat Abia; and Abia begat Asa;

8 And Asa begat Josaphat; and Josaphat begat Joram; and Joram begat Ozias;

9 And Ozias begat Joatham; and Joatham begat Achaz; and Achaz begat Ezekias;

10 And Ezekias begat Manasses; and Manasses begat Amon; and Amon begat Josias;

11 And Josias begat Jechonias and his brethren, about the time they were carried away to Babylon:

12 And after they were brought to Babylon, Jechonias begat Salathiel; and Salathiel begat Zorobabel;

13 And Zorobabel begat Abiud; and Abiud begat Eliakim; and Eliakim begat Azor;

14 And Azor begat Sadoc; and Sadoc begat Achim; and Achim begat Eliud;

15 And Eliud begat Eleazar; and Eleazar begat Matthan; and Matthan begat Jacob;

16 And Jacob begat Joseph the husband of Mary, of whom was born Jesus, who is called Christ.

17 So all the generations from Abraham to David are fourteen generations; and from David until the carrying away into Babylon are fourteen generations; and from the carrying away into Babylon unto Christ are fourteen generations.

---

\* The Joseph Smith Translation changes the title of this book from "The Gospel According to St. Matthew" to "The Testimony of St. Matthew."

1:1 David was one of the greatest kings of Israel and had been promised that the Messiah would be his descendant. Jesus Christ was his descendant, the promised Messiah and rightful king of Israel. Abraham, one of the great prophets in the Old Testament, had received a promise that Jesus Christ would descend from him (see Genesis 22:18).

1:2 **begat**—was the ancestor of

1:11 The Jews were defeated in 587 B.C. by the Babylonians and carried captive from the land of Israel to the land of Babylon.

1:16 *Christ* is a Greek word meaning "the Anointed One"; the Hebrew word with the same meaning is *Messiah* (see LDS Bible Dictionary, s.v. "Christ," p. 633).

1:17 The family history of Jesus Christ is important because, among other reasons, it shows that Jesus fulfilled Old Testament promises. The promises said that the Savior would be a son of Abraham and of King David (see 2 Samuel 7:12-16; Isaiah 9:6-7).

---

|  |  |  |  |
|---|---|---|---|
| = Word Help | | = A Closer Look | |
| = More Light | | = Ponder This | |

Words in pink are explained in the Glossary.

## JESUS CHRIST IS BORN

18 ¶ Now the birth of Jesus Christ was on this wise: When as his mother Mary was espoused to Joseph, before they came together, she was found with child of the Holy Ghost.

19 Then Joseph her husband, being a just man, and not willing to make her a publick example, was minded to put her away privily

20 But while he thought on these things, behold, the angel of the Lord appeared unto him in a dream, saying, Joseph, thou son of David, fear not to take unto thee Mary thy wife: for that which is conceived in her is of the Holy Ghost.

21 And she shall bring forth a son, and thou shalt call his name JESUS: for he shall save his people from their sins.

22 Now all this was done, that it might be fulfilled which was spoken of the Lord by the prophet, saying,

23 Behold, a virgin shall be with child, and shall bring forth a son, and they shall call his name Emmanuel, which being interpreted is, God with us.

24 Then Joseph being raised from sleep did as the angel of the Lord had bidden him, and took unto him his wife:

25 And knew her not till she had brought forth her firstborn son: and he called his name JESUS.

## CHAPTER 2

*Wise men search for the Christ child, but King Herod, fearful of a new king, seeks to kill the child. Look for how Heavenly Father protects baby Jesus.*

### THE WISE MEN ARE LED BY A STAR

1 ¶ NOW when Jesus was born in Bethlehem of Judaea in the days of Herod the king, behold, there came wise men from the east to Jerusalem,

2 Saying, Where is he that is born King of the Jews? for we have seen his star in the east, and are come to worship him.

3 When Herod the king had heard these things, he was troubled, and all Jerusalem with him.

4 And when he had gathered all the chief priests and scribes of the people together, he demanded of them where Christ should be born.

5 And they said unto him, In Bethlehem of Judaea: for thus it is written by the prophet,

6 And thou Bethlehem, in the land of Juda, art not the least among the princes of Juda: for out of thee shall come a Governor, that shall rule my people Israel.

7 Then Herod, when he had privily called the wise men, enquired of them diligently what time the star appeared.

---

1:18    ¶—When this symbol is shown at the beginning of a verse, it means a new paragraph or a new direction in thought or story is beginning.
**espoused**—promised to be married
**came together**—were married

Jesus was the son of Mary and God the Father. He was conceived by the power of the Holy Ghost. (See Luke 1:32, 35.)

1:19    **make her a publick example**—embarrass her
**was minded to put her away privily**—wanted to end their engagement privately, secretly

1:21    *Jesus* is the Greek form of the name *Joshua,* meaning "the Lord saves" (see LDS Bible Dictionary, s.v. "Jesus," p. 713).

1:22    This refers to the prophet Isaiah. The passage cited is in Isaiah 7:14.

1:23    **virgin**—an unmarried person who is pure, chaste, and virtuous

1:25    **knew her not**—had no intimate relations with her

2:1    It has been suggested that these wise men "were actually prophets on a divine errand" (LDS Bible Dictionary, s.v. "Wise Men of the East," p. 789). Herod was the king of the Jews, but he led under the protection of the Romans, who ruled the land of Israel at this time (see LDS Bible Dictionary, s.v. "Herod," pp. 700-701).

2:2    The Joseph Smith Translation changes "King of the Jews" to "Messiah of the Jews." *Messiah* is a Hebrew word meaning "the Anointed One." *Christ* is the Greek word meaning "the Anointed One."

2:4    The chief priests and scribes were Jewish religious leaders and teachers.

2:5    This verse refers to a prophecy from the Old Testament prophet named Micah (see Micah 5:2). *Bethlehem* means "house of bread." Jesus, who was born in Bethlehem, is the "Bread of Life" (see John 6:48).

2:7    **privily**—privately

*Just as the prophet Micah had foretold, the Savior was born in the village of Bethlehem.*

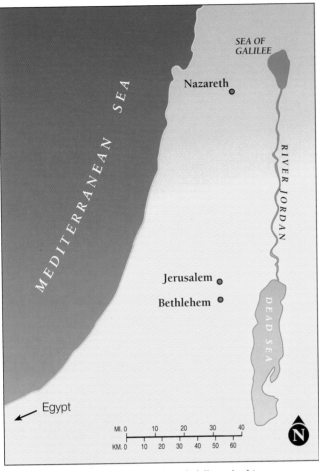

*Important places in the childhood of Jesus*

10 When they saw the star, they rejoiced with exceeding great joy.

11 And when they were come into the house, they saw the young child with Mary his mother, and fell down, and worshipped him: and when they had opened their treasures, they presented unto him gifts; gold, and frankincense, and myrrh.

## JOSEPH AND HIS FAMILY ESCAPE INTO EGYPT

12 And being warned of God in a dream that they should not return to Herod, they departed into their own country another way.

13 ¶ And when they were departed, behold, the angel of the Lord appeareth to Joseph in a dream, saying, Arise, and take the young child and his mother, and flee into Egypt, and be thou there until I bring thee word: for Herod will seek the young child to destroy him.

14 When he arose, he took the young child and his mother by night, and departed into Egypt:

15 And was there until the death of Herod: that it might be fulfilled which was spoken of the Lord by the prophet, saying, Out of Egypt have I called my son.

16 ¶ Then Herod, when he saw that he was mocked of the wise men, was exceeding wroth, and sent forth, and slew all the children that were in Bethlehem, and in all the coasts thereof, from two years old and under, according to the time which he had diligently enquired of the wise men.

17 Then was fulfilled that which was spoken by Jeremy the prophet, saying,

18 In Rama was there a voice heard, lamentation, and weeping, and great mourning, Rachel weeping for her children, and would not be comforted, because they are not.

19 ¶ But when Herod was dead, behold, an angel of

8 And he sent them to Bethlehem, and said, Go and search diligently for the young child; and when ye have found him, bring me word again, that I may come and worship him also.

9 ¶ When they had heard the king, they departed; and, lo, the star, which they saw in the east, went before them, till it came and stood over where the young child was.

---

2:11    The Wise Men did not come the night of Jesus' birth. They came later when Jesus was a "young child" in a "house." Gold, frankincense, and myrrh were ideal gifts for the baby Jesus. Tradition says that gold, as king of metals, was appropriate for a king. Frankincense, an ingredient used in temple worship and sacrifices, was ideal for a priest. Myrrh, used for preparing the dead, symbolized Jesus' future suffering and death to atone for all mankind.

2:13    What do you learn about Joseph in this verse? Why do you think he was a good and obedient man?

2:15    This verse refers to a prophecy from the Old Testament prophet Hosea (see Hosea 11:1).

2:16    **mocked**—fooled, not treated like a king
**exceeding wroth**—very angry

2:17    **Jeremy**—the Old Testament prophet Jeremiah. See Jeremiah 31:15.

2:18    Rama was a city located near Jerusalem. Rachel was a wife of Jacob (Israel) and mother of Joseph. She was one of the great women of the Old Testament. Rachel died while giving birth to Benjamin and was buried near Bethlehem (see Genesis 35:16-20). In this verse, Matthew reminds us of the prophecy of Jeremiah, that this great mother in Israel would be heard weeping and mourning for her children "because they are not."

*One of the Wise Men with the young child Jesus*

*To protect Jesus, Joseph and Mary took him to live for a time in Egypt, where a large number of Jews lived during this period.*

the Lord appeareth in a dream to Joseph in Egypt,

20 Saying, Arise, and take the young child and his mother, and go into the land of Israel: for they are dead which sought the young child's life.

21 And he arose, and took the young child and his mother, and came into the land of Israel.

22 But when he heard that Archelaus did reign in Judaea in the room of his father Herod, he was afraid to go thither: notwithstanding, being warned of God in a dream, he turned aside into the parts of Galilee:

23 And he came and dwelt in a city called Nazareth: that it might be fulfilled which was spoken by the prophets, He shall be called a Nazarene

## CHAPTER 3

*One of the greatest of the prophets, John the Baptist, came to earth with a very specific mission. Look for what John the Baptist did to prepare the way for Jesus Christ.*

### JOHN THE BAPTIST TEACHES REPENTANCE AND BAPTISM

1 ¶ IN those days came John the Baptist, preaching in the wilderness of Judaea,

2 And saying, Repent ye: for the kingdom of heaven is at hand.

3 For this is he that was spoken of by the prophet Esaias, saying, The voice of one crying in the wilderness, Prepare ye the way of the Lord, make his paths straight.

4 And the same John had his raiment of camel's hair, and a leathern girdle about his loins; and his meat was locusts and wild honey.

5 Then went out to him Jerusalem, and all Judaea, and all the region round about Jordan,

6 And were baptized of him in Jordan, confessing their sins.

7 ¶ But when he saw many of the Pharisees and Sadducees come to his baptism, he said unto them, O generation of vipers, who hath warned you to flee from the wrath to come?

8 Bring forth therefore fruits meet for repentance:

9 And think not to say within yourselves, We have Abraham to our father: for I say unto you, that God is able of these stones to raise up children unto Abraham.

10 And now also the axe is laid unto the root of the trees: therefore every tree which bringeth not forth good fruit is hewn down, and cast into the fire.

---

2:22  **thither**—there

2:23  **Nazarene**—a person from the city of Nazareth

The Joseph Smith Translation adds the following to what, in the King James Version, is the end of Matthew 2: "And it came to pass that Jesus grew up with his brethren, and waxed strong, and waited upon the Lord for the time of his ministry to come. And he served under his father, and he spake not as other men, neither could he be taught; for he needed not that any man should teach him. And after many years, the hour of his ministry drew nigh." (JST, Matthew 3:24-26.)

3:1  John the Baptist was a cousin of Jesus Christ (see Luke 1:36).

How did John the Baptist receive the priesthood? (See D&C 84:26-28.) John the Baptist later conferred the Aaronic Priesthood upon Joseph Smith (see D&C 13). Do you know anyone who holds the Aaronic Priesthood today?

3:2  John the Baptist prepared people for Jesus Christ by calling them to repentance. A person must repent to be forgiven of his sins. How does repentance prepare people to believe in Jesus Christ? What effect can belief in Jesus Christ have on your ability to repent?

The phrase "kingdom of heaven" is used several ways throughout the scriptures. Often it means the celestial kingdom. Sometimes it refers to the Lord's true church on the earth. Other times it refers to the government over which Jesus Christ will reign during the Millennium. In this verse it seems to refer to the Church. (See Bruce R. McConkie, *Mormon Doctrine*, pp. 417-18.)

3:3  *Esaias* is the Greek name for *Isaiah*. See Isaiah 40:3.

3:4  **raiment**—clothing
**girdle**—belt
**loins**—waist                          *Wild locust*

3:7  The Pharisees and Sadducees were religious and political leaders of the Jews.

**generation of vipers**—people who are dangerous like snakes
**wrath**—judgments of God

3:8  **fruits meet for repentance**—things people can do to show they are trying to repent

3:9  Does it matter who our faithful ancestors are if we refuse to follow their righteous example?

3:10  **hewn**—cut

11 I indeed baptize you with water unto repentance: but he that cometh after me is mightier than I, whose shoes I am not worthy to bear: he shall baptize you with the Holy Ghost, and with fire:

12 Whose fan is in his hand, and he will throughly purge his floor, and gather his wheat into the garner; but he will burn up the chaff with unquenchable fire.

### JESUS IS BAPTIZED

13 ¶ Then cometh Jesus from Galilee to Jordan unto John, to be baptized of him.

14 But John forbad him, saying, I have need to be baptized of thee, and comest thou to me?

15 And Jesus answering said unto him, Suffer it to be so now: for thus it becometh us to fulfil all righteousness. Then he suffered him.

16 And Jesus, when he was baptized, went up straightway out of the water: and, lo, the heavens were opened unto him, and he saw the Spirit of God descending like a dove, and lighting upon him:

17 And lo a voice from heaven, saying, This is my beloved Son, in whom I am well pleased.

## CHAPTER 4

*When we resist temptation, we gain power to do God's work. Watch for what Jesus does to overcome Satan's temptations.*

### JESUS FASTS AND IS TEMPTED BY SATAN

1 ¶ THEN was Jesus led up of the Spirit into the wilderness to be tempted of the devil.

2 And when he had fasted forty days and forty nights, he was afterward an hungred.

---

3:11    The Joseph Smith Translation changes this verse to read: "I indeed baptize you with water, *upon* your repentance" (JST, Matthew 3:38; emphasis added).

**he that cometh after me**—John is testifying of Jesus Christ
**bear**—carry

3:12    **throughly purge**—completely clean
**garner**—storehouse
**chaff**—portion of the wheat that is not edible
**unquenchable fire**—fire that cannot be put out

3:14    **forbad him**—said he would not baptize him

3:15    **Suffer**—let or allow
**Then he suffered him**—John baptized Jesus

Jesus was perfect, but he still had to be baptized (see 2 Nephi 31:4-12). Why do you think this was necessary? Have you been baptized yet? How does baptism help you?

3:16    What do you find in this verse that shows Jesus was baptized by immersion?

Joseph Smith taught that when the Holy Ghost came to Jesus, John also saw a dove. "The sign of the dove was instituted before the creation of the world, a witness for the Holy Ghost, and the devil cannot come in the sign of a dove. . . . The Holy Ghost cannot be transformed into a dove; but the sign of a dove was given to John to signify the truth of the deed, as the dove is an emblem or token of truth and innocence." (*The Teachings of Joseph Smith,* p. 202.)

3:16-17    The Godhead is Heavenly Father, Jesus Christ, and the Holy Ghost. How many members of the Godhead were at the baptism of Jesus?

4:1    The Joseph Smith Translation changes the phrase "to be tempted of the devil" to read, "to be with God."

*The Judean Wilderness, where, after his baptism, Jesus went to fast and to commune with God*

4:1-11    Satan tempted Jesus with hunger, pride, and riches. What are you tempted with? How can Jesus' example help you overcome temptations?

4:2    The Joseph Smith Translation teaches that Jesus "communed," or talked, with God as he fasted (see JST, Matthew 4:2).

*Setting an example of obedience and humility for all people, Jesus was baptized by John.*

3 And when the tempter came to him, he said, If thou be the Son of God, command that these stones be made bread.

4 But he answered and said, It is written, Man shall not live by bread alone, but by every word that proceedeth out of the mouth of God.

5 Then the devil taketh him up into the holy city, and setteth him on a pinnacle of the temple,

6 And saith unto him, If thou be the Son of God, cast thyself down: for it is written, He shall give his angels charge concerning thee: and in their hands they shall bear thee up, lest at any time thou dash thy foot against a stone.

7 Jesus said unto him, It is written again, Thou shalt not tempt the Lord thy God.

8 Again, the devil taketh him up into an exceeding high mountain, and sheweth him all the kingdoms of the world, and the glory of them;

9 And saith unto him, All these things will I give thee, if thou wilt fall down and worship me.

10 Then saith Jesus unto him, Get thee hence, Satan: for it is written, Thou shalt worship the Lord thy God, and him only shalt thou serve.

11 Then the devil leaveth him, and, behold, angels came and ministered unto him.

## JESUS BEGINS HIS MINISTRY

12 ¶ Now when Jesus had heard that John was cast into prison, he departed into Galilee;

13 And leaving Nazareth, he came and dwelt in Capernaum, which is upon the sea coast, in the borders of Zabulon and Nephthalim:

14 That it might be fulfilled which was spoken by Esaias the prophet, saying,

15 The land of Zabulon, and the land of Nephthalim, by the way of the sea, beyond Jordan, Galilee of the Gentiles;

16 The people which sat in darkness saw great light; and to them which sat in the region and shadow of death light is sprung up.

17 From that time Jesus began to preach, and to say, Repent: for the kingdom of heaven is at hand.

## JESUS CALLS MEN TO FOLLOW HIM

18 ¶ And Jesus, walking by the sea of Galilee, saw two brethren, Simon called Peter, and Andrew his brother, casting a net into the sea: for they were fishers.

19 And he saith unto them, Follow me, and I will make you fishers of men.

20 And they straightway left their nets, and followed him.

21 And going on from thence, he saw other two brethren, James the son of Zebedee, and John his brother, in a ship with Zebedee their father, mending their nets; and he called them.

22 And they immediately left the ship and their father, and followed him.

23 ¶ And Jesus went about all Galilee, teaching in their synagogues, and preaching the gospel of the kingdom, and healing all manner of sickness and all manner of disease among the people.

---

4:3-6 Why do you think Satan began the first two temptations by saying, "If thou be the Son of God"? Remembering that you are a child of God will help you be stronger than the temptations that come into your life.

4:4-10 In these verses Jesus quotes scriptures to help him fight temptation. He recites Deuteronomy 8:3, 6:16, and then 6:13. How can scriptures help us when we are tempted?

4:4 **proceedeth**—comes

4:5, 8 The Joseph Smith Translation shows that it was the "Spirit," not Satan, that put Jesus on the pinnacle of the temple and then on the top of a mountain.

4:5 **holy city**—Jerusalem
**pinnacle**—tower

4:6 **charge concerning thee**—the assignment to protect Jesus

4:10 **hence**—away

4:11 **ministered unto**—cared for

4:14 When Jesus dwelt in Capernaum, it fulfilled a prophecy of Isaiah (see Isaiah 9:1-2).

4:15 *Gentiles* is a word that means "nations." It refers to those not of the family of Israel or who do not believe in the God of Israel. (See LDS Bible Dictionary, s.v. "Gentile," pp. 679-80.)

4:17 How would knowing that the Church of Jesus Christ was on the earth help a person want to repent?

4:19 **fishers of men**—missionaries and teachers of the gospel

4:20 **straightway**—immediately

4:23 **synagogues**—Jewish places of worship

*Andrew and Peter approaching Christ*

24 And his fame went throughout all Syria: and they brought unto him all sick people that were taken with divers diseases and torments, and those which were possessed with devils, and those which were lunatick, and those that had the palsy; and he healed them.

25 And there followed him great multitudes of people from Galilee, and from Decapolis, and from Jerusalem, and from Judaea, and from beyond Jordan.

# CHAPTER 5

*The Sermon on the Mount contains some of Jesus' most important teachings. See what the Savior would have you do to become perfect.*

## JESUS TEACHES THE BEATITUDES

1 ¶ AND seeing the multitudes, he went up into a mountain: and when he was set, his disciples came unto him:

2 And he opened his mouth, and taught them, saying,

3 ¶ Blessed are the poor in spirit: for theirs is the kingdom of heaven.

4 Blessed are they that mourn: for they shall be comforted.

5 Blessed are the meek: for they shall inherit the earth.

6 Blessed are they which do hunger and thirst after righteousness: for they shall be filled.

7 Blessed are the merciful: for they shall obtain mercy.

8 Blessed are the pure in heart: for they shall see God.

9 Blessed are the peacemakers: for they shall be called the children of God.

10 Blessed are they which are persecuted for righteousness' sake: for theirs is the kingdom of heaven.

11 Blessed are ye, when men shall revile you, and persecute you, and shall say all manner of evil against you falsely, for my sake.

12 Rejoice, and be exceeding glad: for great is your reward in heaven: for so persecuted they the prophets which were before you.

## JESUS COMPARES THE LAW OF MOSES WITH THE GOSPEL OF JESUS CHRIST

13 ¶ Ye are the salt of the earth: but if the salt have lost his savour, wherewith shall it be salted? it is thenceforth good for nothing, but to be cast out, and to be trodden under foot of men.

14 Ye are the light of the world. A city that is set on an hill cannot be hid.

15 Neither do men light a candle, and put it under a bushel, but on a candlestick; and it giveth light unto all that are in the house.

16 Let your light so shine before men, that they may see your good works, and glorify your Father which is in heaven.

---

4:24 **divers**—many different
**torments**—pains
**lunatick**—mentally ill
**had the palsy**—were physically disabled

5:2 Following this verse, the Joseph Smith Translation adds Jesus' teaching that those who believe and follow the words of the Savior and of his servants by humbling themselves and being baptized will receive the Holy Ghost and a forgiveness of sins (see JST, Matthew 5:3–4).

5:3 **poor in spirit**—humble

The Joseph Smith Translation changes this verse to: "Blessed are the poor in spirit, who come unto me; for theirs is the kingdom of heaven" (JST, Matthew 5:5).

5:4 **mourn**—feel sad

5:5 **meek**—gentle, forgiving, and kindly
**inherit**—get, receive

5:6 The Joseph Smith Translation adds that those people who "hunger and thirst after righteousness"

shall be "filled with the Holy Ghost" (JST, Matthew 5:8).

5:8 The pure in heart "are those among the saints who in full measure are free from sin. Purity of heart is a figure for purity of soul." (Bruce R. McConkie, *A New Witness for the Articles of Faith*, p. 492.)

How can a person's heart become more pure? (See 1 Peter 1:22 and Mosiah 4:2.)

5:10 **persecuted**—hurt or made to suffer

5:11 **revile you**—speak evil against you

5:13–16 The Savior often compared simple objects that people understood to spiritual truths. How do the comparisons Jesus made in these verses help you better understand spiritual truths?

5:13 **savour**—flavor
**trodden**—stepped on

5:15 **bushel**—basket or bowl

*Sermon on the Mount*

17 ¶ Think not that I am come to destroy the law, or the prophets: I am not come to destroy, but to fulfil.

18 For verily I say unto you, Till heaven and earth pass, one jot or one tittle shall in no wise pass from the law, till all be fulfilled.

19 Whosoever therefore shall break one of these least commandments, and shall teach men so, he shall be called the least in the kingdom of heaven: but whosoever shall do and teach them, the same shall be called great in the kingdom of heaven.

20 For I say unto you, That except your righteousness shall exceed the righteousness of the scribes and Pharisees, ye shall in no case enter into the kingdom of heaven.

21 ¶ Ye have heard that it was said by them of old time, Thou shalt not kill; and whosoever shall kill shall be in danger of the judgment:

22 But I say unto you, That whosoever is angry with his brother without a cause shall be in danger of the judgment: and whosoever shall say to his brother, Raca, shall be in danger of the council: but whosoever shall say, Thou fool, shall be in danger of hell fire.

23 Therefore if thou bring thy gift to the altar, and there rememberest that thy brother hath ought against thee;

24 Leave there thy gift before the altar, and go thy way; first be reconciled to thy brother, and then come and offer thy gift.

25 Agree with thine adversary quickly, whiles thou art in the way with him; lest at any time the adversary deliver thee to the judge, and the judge deliver thee to the officer, and thou be cast into prison.

26 Verily I say unto thee, Thou shalt by no means come out thence, till thou hast paid the uttermost farthing.

27 ¶ Ye have heard that it was said by them of old time, Thou shalt not commit adultery:

28 But I say unto you, That whosoever looketh on a woman to lust after her hath committed adultery with her already in his heart.

29 And if thy right eye offend thee, pluck it out, and cast it from thee: for it is profitable for thee that one of thy members should perish, and not that thy whole body should be cast into hell.

30 And if thy right hand offend thee, cut it off, and cast it from thee: for it is profitable for thee that one of thy members should perish, and not that thy whole body should be cast into hell.

31 It hath been said, Whosoever shall put away his wife, let him give her a writing of divorcement:

32 But I say unto you, That whosoever shall put away his wife, saving for the cause of fornication, causeth her to commit adultery: and whosoever shall marry her that is divorced committeth adultery.

33 ¶ Again, ye have heard that it hath been said by them of old time, Thou shalt not forswear thyself, but shalt perform unto the Lord thine oaths:

---

5:17   "The law" is the law of Moses, which the children of Israel had been commanded to follow since the days of Moses (see LDS Bible Dictionary, s.v. "Law of Moses," pp. 722-23).

5:18   **one jot or one tittle**—the smallest part

5:20   Scribes were men who taught the scriptures. They were sometimes called lawyers. (See LDS Bible Dictionary, s.v. "Scribe," p. 770.)

5:21   The phrase "Ye have heard" in verses 21, 27, 33, 38, and 43 introduces parts of the law of Moses that Jesus then compares with His higher law.

5:22   The Joseph Smith Translation leaves out the phrase "without a cause" (see JST, Matthew 5:24).

   **Raca**—fool
   **be in danger of the council**—likely be judged and punished

5:24   **be reconciled**—become friends again

5:25   **adversary**—enemy

5:26   **paid the uttermost farthing**—paid all that the law requires

5:27   **adultery**—misuse of the sacred creative powers; that is, use of these powers with someone other than your husband or wife

5:28   **lust after**—desire in a sinful way

5:29-
30   The Joseph Smith Translation helps us understand these verses by adding the following sentence: "And now this I speak, a parable concerning your sins; wherefore, cast them from you, that ye may not be hewn down and cast into the fire" (JST, Matthew 5:34). In other words, parts of the body, such as an eye or a hand, are compared to our sins.

5:29   **offend thee**—makes you sin
   **profitable**—better
   **thy members**—the parts of your body

5:31   **put away**—divorce

5:32   **fornication**—misuse of the sacred creative powers; that is, use of these powers between people who are not married

5:33   **forswear thyself**—break your promise

34 But I say unto you, Swear not at all; neither by heaven; for it is God's throne:

35 Nor by the earth; for it is his footstool: neither by Jerusalem; for it is the city of the great King.

36 Neither shalt thou swear by thy head, because thou canst not make one hair white or black.

37 But let your communication be, Yea, yea; Nay, nay: for whatsoever is more than these cometh of evil.

38 ¶ Ye have heard that it hath been said, An eye for an eye, and a tooth for a tooth:

39 But I say unto you, That ye resist not evil: but whosoever shall smite thee on thy right cheek, turn to him the other also.

40 And if any man will sue thee at the law, and take away thy coat, let him have thy cloke also.

41 And whosoever shall compel thee to go a mile, go with him twain.

42 Give to him that asketh thee, and from him that would borrow of thee turn not thou away.

43 ¶ Ye have heard that it hath been said, Thou shalt love thy neighbour, and hate thine enemy.

44 But I say unto you, Love your enemies, bless them that curse you, do good to them that hate you, and pray for them which despitefully use you, and persecute you;

45 That ye may be the children of your Father which is in heaven: for he maketh his sun to rise on the evil and on the good, and sendeth rain on the just and on the unjust.

46 For if ye love them which love you, what reward have ye? do not even the publicans the same?

47 And if ye salute your brethren only, what do ye more than others? do not even the publicans so?

48 Be ye therefore perfect, even as your Father which is in heaven is perfect.

# CHAPTER 6

*Living the commandments for the right reasons is important to our spiritual growth. As you read this chapter, look for ways you can improve in doing good for the right reasons.*

## JESUS TEACHES ABOUT GIVING

1 ¶ TAKE heed that ye do not your alms before men, to be seen of them: otherwise ye have no reward of your Father which is in heaven.

2 Therefore when thou doest thine alms, do not sound a trumpet before thee, as the hypocrites do in the synagogues and in the streets, that they may have glory of men. Verily I say unto you, They have their reward.

3 But when thou doest alms, let not thy left hand know what thy right hand doeth:

4 That thine alms may be in secret: and thy Father which seeth in secret himself shall reward thee openly.

## JESUS TEACHES ABOUT PRAYER

5 ¶ And when thou prayest, thou shalt not be as the hypocrites are: for they love to pray standing in the synagogues and in the corners of the streets, that they may be seen of men. Verily I say unto you, They have their reward.

---

5:34 **Swear not at all**—Do not make promises in the name of someone or something that is honored

5:38 Under the law of Moses, if a wrong was done to someone, a punishment or price equal to the wrongful act was to be paid by the person who did wrong (see Leviticus 24:20).

5:40 **coat**—inner garment (similar to a shirt)
**cloke**—outer garment (similar to a robe, shawl, or toga)

5:41 **twain**—two

5:44 **despitefully use**—abuse

5:45 **just**—righteous

5:46 Publicans were Jews who were disliked because they collected taxes for the Romans.

5:47 **salute**—greet, say hello to

5:48 It is really possible to become perfect like Heavenly Father, with the help of Jesus Christ (see Moroni 10:32-33). Why do you want to become perfect like your Heavenly Father? Why do you think Jesus wants you to become like Heavenly Father?

6:1 **Take heed**—Be careful
**alms**—gifts or kind deeds

6:2 **hypocrites**—people who pretend to be good when they are not

6:3-4 What kind deeds have you done for others? What are some reasons you are kind to others?

6:5-6 What did Jesus teach about prayer that could make your prayers better?

6 But thou, when thou prayest, enter into thy closet, and when thou hast shut thy door, pray to thy Father which is in secret; and thy Father which seeth in secret shall reward thee openly.

7 But when ye pray, use not vain repetitions, as the heathen do: for they think that they shall be heard for their much speaking.

8 Be not ye therefore like unto them: for your Father knoweth what things ye have need of, before ye ask him.

9 ¶ After this manner therefore pray ye: Our Father which art in heaven, Hallowed be thy name.

10 Thy kingdom come. Thy will be done in earth, as it is in heaven.

11 Give us this day our daily bread.

12 And forgive us our debts, as we forgive our debtors.

13 And lead us not into temptation, but deliver us from evil: For thine is the kingdom, and the power, and the glory, for ever. Amen.

14 For if ye forgive men their trespasses, your heavenly Father will also forgive you:

15 But if ye forgive not men their trespasses, neither will your Father forgive your trespasses.

## JESUS TEACHES THE LAW OF THE FAST

16 ¶ Moreover when ye fast, be not, as the hypocrites, of a sad countenance: for they disfigure their faces, that they may appear unto men to fast. Verily I say unto you, They have their reward.

17 But thou, when thou fastest, anoint thine head, and wash thy face;

18 That thou appear not unto men to fast, but unto thy Father which is in secret: and thy Father, which seeth in secret, shall reward thee openly.

## THE DISCIPLES OF CHRIST SEEK FIRST THE KINGDOM OF GOD

19 ¶ Lay not up for yourselves treasures upon earth, where moth and rust doth corrupt, and where thieves break through and steal:

20 But lay up for yourselves treasures in heaven, where neither moth nor rust doth corrupt, and where thieves do not break through nor steal:

21 For where your treasure is, there will your heart be also.

22 The light of the body is the eye: if therefore thine eye be single, thy whole body shall be full of light.

23 But if thine eye be evil, thy whole body shall be full of darkness. If therefore the light that is in thee be darkness, how great is that darkness!

24 No man can serve two masters: for either he will hate the one, and love the other; or else he will hold to the one, and despise the other. Ye cannot serve God and mammon.

25 ¶ Therefore I say unto you, Take no thought for your life, what ye shall eat, or what ye shall drink; nor yet for your body, what ye shall put on. Is not the life more than meat, and the body than raiment?

26 Behold the fowls of the air: for they sow not, neither do they reap, nor gather into barns; yet your heavenly Father feedeth them. Are ye not much better than they?

---

6:7 **vain repetitions**—words that you do not mean and that you say over and over
**heathen**—people who do not believe in the true and living God

6:9 **Hallowed**—Sacred and holy

6:12 The Joseph Smith Translation changes this verse to read, "And forgive us our trespasses [sins], as we forgive those who trespass against us" (JST, Matthew 6:13).

6:13 The Joseph Smith Translation changes this verse to read, "And suffer us not to be led into temptation" (JST, Matthew 6:14).

6:16 **fast**—go without food or drink for spiritual reasons
**disfigure their faces**—change their faces to look sad

6:19 **corrupt**—ruin

6:21 What are some treasures or blessings you can have and love forever?

6:22 The Joseph Smith Translation makes it clear that your eye should be single "to the glory of God" (JST, Matthew 6:22). This means that all you do should be aimed toward God and his work.

6:24 **mammon**—worldly riches

Everyone has to decide whether or not to serve God (see Joshua 24:15). What have you decided?

6:25 **raiment**—clothes

6:26 **sow**—plant
**reap**—harvest

27 Which of you by taking thought can add one cubit unto his stature?

28 And why take ye thought for raiment? Consider the lilies of the field, how they grow; they toil not, neither do they spin:

29 And yet I say unto you, That even Solomon in all his glory was not arrayed like one of these.

30 Wherefore, if God so clothe the grass of the field, which to day is, and to morrow is cast into the oven, shall he not much more clothe you, O ye of little faith?

31 Therefore take no thought, saying, What shall we eat? or, What shall we drink? or, Wherewithal shall we be clothed?

32 (For after all these things do the Gentiles seek:) for your heavenly Father knoweth that ye have need of all these things.

33 But seek ye first the kingdom of God, and his righteousness; and all these things shall be added unto you.

34 Take therefore no thought for the morrow: for the morrow shall take thought for the things of itself. Sufficient unto the day is the evil thereof.

## CHAPTER 7

*This is the last chapter of the Sermon on the Mount. Notice what promises Jesus Christ makes to those who are obedient to Heavenly Father.*

### JESUS TEACHES HOW TO JUDGE RIGHTEOUSLY

1 ¶ JUDGE not, that ye be not judged.

2 For with what judgment ye judge, ye shall be judged: and with what measure ye mete, it shall be measured to you again.

3 And why beholdest thou the mote that is in thy brother's eye, but considerest not the beam that is in thine own eye?

4 Or how wilt thou say to thy brother, Let me pull out the mote out of thine eye; and, behold, a beam is in thine own eye?

5 Thou hypocrite, first cast out the beam out of thine own eye; and then shalt thou see clearly to cast out the mote out of thy brother's eye.

6 Give not that which is holy unto the dogs, neither cast ye your pearls before swine, lest they trample them under their feet, and turn again and rend you.

### JESUS TEACHES THE NEED TO ASK, SEEK, AND KNOCK

7 ¶ Ask, and it shall be given you; seek, and ye shall find; knock, and it shall be opened unto you:

8 For every one that asketh receiveth; and he that seeketh findeth; and to him that knocketh it shall be opened.

9 Or what man is there of you, whom if his son ask bread, will he give him a stone?

---

6:27 **cubit**—about eighteen inches
**stature**—height

6:28 **toil**—work

6:29 Solomon was a great and wealthy king of ancient Israel (see 1 Kings 10:4-7).

6:31 **Wherewithal**—With what

6:33 The Joseph Smith Translation begins this verse with the addition, "Wherefore, seek not the things of this world but seek ye first to build up the kingdom of God" (JST, Matthew 6:38).

7:1 The Joseph Smith Translation adds to this verse that we should not judge "unrighteously . . . but judge righteous judgment" (JST, Matthew 7:2).

7:2 What is the difference between righteous and unrighteous judging?

**measure**—amount
**mete**—give

7:3 **mote**—small speck
**considerest**—see

7:6 **rend**—tear

The Joseph Smith Translation explains that the pearls Jesus speaks about are the mysteries (sacred truths) of the kingdom of God. Sacred truths should not be shared with people who are not spiritually prepared. (See JST, Matthew 7:9-11.)

Why would it be unwise to bear your testimony to friends who were not spiritually prepared?

7:7 What is the difference between asking, seeking, and knocking when trying to obtain answers to our questions?

7:7-8 Heavenly Father loves us and will give answers to those who come to him in sincere prayer (see James 1:5).

10 Or if he ask a fish, will he give him a serpent?

11 If ye then, being evil, know how to give good gifts unto your children, how much more shall your Father which is in heaven give good things to them that ask him?

## JESUS WARNS AGAINST FALSE PROPHETS

12 ¶ Therefore all things whatsoever ye would that men should do to you, do ye even so to them: for this is the law and the prophets.

13 Enter ye in at the strait gate: for wide is the gate, and broad is the way, that leadeth to destruction, and many there be which go in thereat:

14 Because strait is the gate, and narrow is the way, which leadeth unto life, and few there be that find it.

15 ¶ Beware of false prophets, which come to you in sheep's clothing, but inwardly they are ravening wolves.

16 Ye shall know them by their fruits. Do men gather grapes of thorns, or figs of thistles?

17 Even so every good tree bringeth forth good fruit; but a corrupt tree bringeth forth evil fruit.

18 A good tree cannot bring forth evil fruit, neither can a corrupt tree bring forth good fruit.

19 Every tree that bringeth not forth good fruit is hewn down, and cast into the fire.

20 Wherefore by their fruits ye shall know them.

## JESUS TEACHES OBEDIENCE

21 ¶ Not every one that saith unto me, Lord, Lord, shall enter into the kingdom of heaven; but he that doeth the will of my Father which is in heaven.

22 Many will say to me in that day, Lord, Lord, have we not prophesied in thy name? and in thy name have cast out devils? and in thy name done many wonderful works?

23 And then will I profess unto them, I never knew you: depart from me, ye that work iniquity.

24 Therefore whosoever heareth these sayings of mine, and doeth them, I will liken him unto a wise man, which built his house upon a rock:

25 And the rain descended, and the floods came, and the winds blew, and beat upon that house; and it fell not: for it was founded upon a rock.

26 And every one that heareth these sayings of mine, and doeth them not, shall be likened unto a foolish man, which built his house upon the sand:

27 And the rain descended, and the floods came, and the winds blew, and beat upon that house; and it fell: and great was the fall of it.

28 And it came to pass, when Jesus had ended these sayings, the people were astonished at his doctrine:

29 For he taught them as one having authority, and not as the scribes.

---

7:11    Why should you never be afraid to pray to our Heavenly Father?

7:12    **the law and the prophets**—the law of Moses and the teachings of the prophets of the Old Testament

     This is sometimes called the "Golden Rule." What have you noticed about how people usually treat you when you are nice to them?

7:13    **strait**—narrow
**broad**—wide

*Thorns*

7:14    **life**—eternal life

7:15    **ravening**—mean and hungry

7:17    **corrupt**—rotten

7:19    **hewn**—cut

7:20    **by their fruits ye shall know them**—you can know whether they are good or bad by what they do

7:21    Following this verse, the Joseph Smith Translation adds: "For the day soon cometh, that men shall come before me to judgment, to be judged according to their works" (JST, Matthew 7:31).

7:24    **I will liken him unto**—I will say that he is like

7:25    **founded**—built

*The regions of Galilee and Phoenicia*

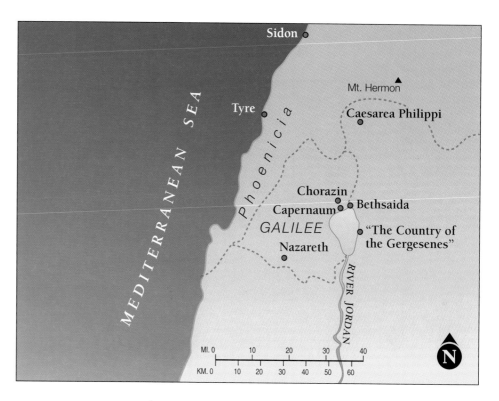

## CHAPTER 8

*Jesus Christ has power over all things. Watch for how many different kinds of miracles Jesus performs.*

### JESUS HEALS A LEPER

1 ¶ WHEN he was come down from the mountain, great multitudes followed him.

2 And, behold, there came a leper and worshipped him, saying, Lord, if thou wilt, thou canst make me clean.

3 And Jesus put forth his hand, and touched him, saying, I will; be thou clean. And immediately his leprosy was cleansed.

4 And Jesus saith unto him, See thou tell no man; but go thy way, shew thyself to the priest, and offer the gift that Moses commanded, for a testimony unto them.

### JESUS HEALS A SOLDIER'S SERVANT

5 ¶ And when Jesus was entered into Capernaum, there came unto him a centurion, beseeching him,

6 And saying, Lord, my servant lieth at home sick of the palsy, grievously tormented.

7 And Jesus saith unto him, I will come and heal him.

8 The centurion answered and said, Lord, I am not worthy that thou shouldest come under my roof: but speak the word only, and my servant shall be healed.

9 For I am a man under authority, having soldiers under me: and I say to this man, Go, and he goeth; and to another, Come, and he cometh; and to my servant, Do this, and he doeth it.

10 When Jesus heard it, he marvelled, and said to them that followed, Verily I say unto you, I have not found so great faith, no, not in Israel.

---

8:2   **leper**—a person with leprosy (*leprosy* being a word used for many different skin diseases and infections)

**clean**—free from the disease

How does the phrase "thou canst make me clean" show that this man had faith in Jesus Christ? Why is having faith such an important part of receiving blessings from the Lord?

8:4   **shew**—This word is pronounced the same way as the word *show* and has the same meaning; *shew* is simply an old spelling of *show*.

8:5   **centurion**—a Roman military officer

8:6   **grievously tormented**—greatly pained

11 And I say unto you, That many shall come from the east and west, and shall sit down with Abraham, and Isaac, and Jacob, in the kingdom of heaven.

12 But the children of the kingdom shall be cast out into outer darkness: there shall be weeping and gnashing of teeth.

13 And Jesus said unto the centurion, Go thy way; and as thou hast believed, so be it done unto thee. And his servant was healed in the selfsame hour.

### JESUS HEALS PETER'S WIFE'S MOTHER AND OTHERS

14 ¶ And when Jesus was come into Peter's house, he saw his wife's mother laid, and sick of a fever.

15 And he touched her hand, and the fever left her: and she arose, and ministered unto them.

16 When the even was come, they brought unto him many that were possessed with devils: and he cast out the spirits with his word, and healed all that were sick:

17 That it might be fulfilled which was spoken by Esaias the prophet, saying, Himself took our infirmities, and bare our sicknesses.

### SOME PEOPLE WANT TO FOLLOW JESUS

18 ¶ Now when Jesus saw great multitudes about him, he gave commandment to depart unto the other side.

19 And a certain scribe came, and said unto him, Master, I will follow thee whithersoever thou goest.

20 And Jesus saith unto him, The foxes have holes, and the birds of the air have nests; but the Son of man hath not where to lay his head.

21 And another of his disciples said unto him, Lord, suffer me first to go and bury my father.

22 But Jesus said unto him, Follow me; and let the dead bury their dead.

### JESUS CALMS THE SEA

23 ¶ And when he was entered into a ship, his disciples followed him.

24 And, behold, there arose a great tempest in the sea, insomuch that the ship was covered with the waves: but he was asleep.

25 And his disciples came to him, and awoke him, saying, Lord, save us: we perish.

26 And he saith unto them, Why are ye fearful, O ye of little faith? Then he arose, and rebuked the winds and the sea; and there was a great calm.

27 But the men marvelled, saying, What manner of man is this, that even the winds and the sea obey him!

### JESUS HAS POWER OVER EVIL SPIRITS

28 ¶ And when he was come to the other side into the country of the Gergesenes, there met him two possessed with devils, coming out of the tombs, exceeding fierce, so that no man might pass by that way.

29 And, behold, they cried out, saying, What have we to do with thee, Jesus, thou Son of God? art thou come hither to torment us before the time?

---

8:11    Jesus prophesied that many people "from the east and west" would enter the kingdom of heaven. These people are not of the family of Israel but will come to the Lord and believe the truth. (See Luke 13:28-29.)

8:12    **children of the kingdom**—people who are of the family of Israel
**gnashing**—grinding; expressing pain and grief

8:17    This is a prophecy by the Old Testament prophet Isaiah (see Isaiah 53:3-5).

   **infirmities**—sicknesses or weaknesses

8:19    **withersoever**—wherever

8:20    "In the language of Adam, Man of Holiness is [Heavenly Father's] name, and the name of his Only Begotten is the Son of Man, even Jesus Christ" (Moses 6:57).

8:21    **disciples**—followers
**suffer**—let

8:22    Jesus' words "let the dead bury their dead" teach us that no other care in our lives should get in the way of following the Savior. What do people sometimes let become more important in their lives than following Jesus?

8:24    **tempest**—storm

8:26    **rebuked**—commanded

8:28    The Joseph Smith Translation changes the words "two possessed with devils" to "a man possessed with devils." With this change, Matthew's account agrees with Mark 5:2 and Luke 8:27.

   **possessed with**—taken over by
**exceeding fierce**—very dangerous

8:29    **art thou come hither**—have you come here
**torment**—punish, trouble

   In this verse "the time" refers to the final judgment, at which time devils will be cast into outer darkness.

30 And there was a good way off from them an herd of many swine feeding.

31 So the devils besought him, saying, If thou cast us out, suffer us to go away into the herd of swine.

32 And he said unto them, Go. And when they were come out, they went into the herd of swine: and, behold, the whole herd of swine ran violently down a steep place into the sea, and perished in the waters.

33 And they that kept them fled, and went their ways into the city, and told every thing, and what was befallen to the possessed of the devils.

34 And, behold, the whole city came out to meet Jesus: and when they saw him, they besought him that he would depart out of their coasts.

# CHAPTER 9

*This chapter is filled with examples of Jesus' power to perform miracles. In the last three verses Jesus expresses a desire for more helpers with his work. As you read this chapter, look for reasons Jesus wants help with his mission.*

## JESUS FORGIVES AND HEALS A MAN

1 ¶ AND he entered into a ship, and passed over, and came into his own city.

2 And, behold, they brought to him a man sick of the palsy, lying on a bed: and Jesus seeing their faith said unto the sick of the palsy; Son, be of good cheer; thy sins be forgiven thee.

3 And, behold, certain of the scribes said within themselves, This man blasphemeth.

4 And Jesus knowing their thoughts said, Wherefore think ye evil in your hearts?

5 For whether is easier, to say, Thy sins be forgiven thee; or to say, Arise, and walk?

6 But that ye may know that the Son of man hath power on earth to forgive sins, (then saith he to the sick of the palsy,) Arise, take up thy bed, and go unto thine house.

7 And he arose, and departed to his house.

8 But when the multitudes saw it, they marvelled, and glorified God, which had given such power unto men.

## JESUS CHRIST CALLS MATTHEW TO FOLLOW HIM

9 ¶ And as Jesus passed forth from thence, he saw a man, named Matthew, sitting at the receipt of custom: and he saith unto him, Follow me. And he arose, and followed him.

10 And it came to pass, as Jesus sat at meat in the house, behold, many publicans and sinners came and sat down with him and his disciples.

11 And when the Pharisees saw it, they said unto his disciples, Why eateth your Master with publicans and sinners?

12 But when Jesus heard that, he said unto them, They that be whole need not a physician, but they that are sick.

13 But go ye and learn what that meaneth, I will have mercy, and not sacrifice: for I am not come to call the righteous, but sinners to repentance.

14 ¶ Then came to him the disciples of John, saying, Why do we and the Pharisees fast oft, but thy disciples fast not?

15 And Jesus said unto them, Can the children of the bridechamber mourn, as long as the bridegroom is with them? but the days will come, when the bridegroom shall be taken from them, and then shall they fast.

---

8:32 In this verse, Jesus casts out the evil spirits. Elsewhere in the chapter he calms the sea and heals the sick. How much power does Jesus Christ have? Does he have the power to help you solve your problems?

8:33 **was befallen**—had happened

9:2 The Joseph Smith Translation adds to the end of this verse, "go thy way and sin no more."

9:3 Blasphemy is the sin of claiming to be like God or speaking evil of God. Of all people on earth, Jesus was the only one who could claim to be like God and not be guilty of blasphemy.

9:6 What did Jesus do to prove that he had power to forgive the man's sins? Why is it important for you to know that Jesus has such power?

9:9 **sitting at the receipt of custom**—seated at the place where taxes were taken

9:11-13 The Pharisees thought Jesus was wrong to eat with people who were sinful. Jesus explained that just as doctors serve the sick, he visited the sinful to help them repent.

9:12 **whole**—healthy
**physician**—doctor

9:14 **disciples of John**—followers of John the Baptist

9:15 **children of the bridechamber**—wedding guests who are friends of the groom

A "bridegroom" was a man engaged to be or already married. In this case the word is used to refer to Jesus Christ and his covenants with members of his church.

16 No man putteth a piece of new cloth unto an old garment, for that which is put in to fill it up taketh from the garment, and the rent is made worse.

17 Neither do men put new wine into old bottles: else the bottles break, and the wine runneth out, and the bottles perish: but they put new wine into new bottles, and both are preserved.

## TWO GREAT MIRACLES ARE PERFORMED

18 ¶ While he spake these things unto them, behold, there came a certain ruler, and worshipped him, saying, My daughter is even now dead: but come and lay thy hand upon her, and she shall live.

19 And Jesus arose, and followed him, and so did his disciples.

20 And, behold, a woman, which was diseased with an issue of blood twelve years, came behind him, and touched the hem of his garment:

21 For she said within herself, If I may but touch his garment, I shall be whole.

22 But Jesus turned him about, and when he saw her, he said, Daughter, be of good comfort; thy faith hath made thee whole. And the woman was made whole from that hour.

23 And when Jesus came into the ruler's house, and saw the minstrels and the people making a noise,

24 He said unto them, Give place: for the maid is not dead, but sleepeth. And they laughed him to scorn.

25 But when the people were put forth, he went in, and took her by the hand, and the maid arose.

26 And the fame hereof went abroad into all that land.

## JESUS HEALS TWO BLIND MEN

27 ¶ And when Jesus departed thence, two blind men followed him, crying, and saying, Thou Son of David, have mercy on us.

28 And when he was come into the house, the blind men came to him: and Jesus saith unto them, Believe ye that I am able to do this? They said unto him, Yea, Lord.

29 Then touched he their eyes, saying, According to your faith be it unto you.

30 And their eyes were opened; and Jesus straitly charged them, saying, See that no man know it.

31 But they, when they were departed, spread abroad his fame in all that country.

## JESUS HEALS A MAN WHO COULD NOT SPEAK

32 As they went out, behold, they brought to him a dumb man possessed with a devil.

33 And when the devil was cast out, the dumb spake: and the multitudes marvelled, saying, It was never so seen in Israel.

34 But the Pharisees said, He casteth out devils through the prince of the devils.

## JESUS TEACHES AND LOVES THE PEOPLE

35 ¶ And Jesus went about all the cities and villages, teaching in their synagogues, and preaching the gospel of the kingdom, and healing every sickness and every disease among the people.

---

9:16  The Joseph Smith Translation shows that at this point the Pharisees asked Jesus a question that is now missing from the Bible. They asked why Jesus did not accept them as righteous, since they lived the law of Moses. He replied that if they had really obeyed the law, they would have accepted him, because he was the one who gave the law in the first place.

9:20  **was diseased with an issue of blood**—had been bleeding

9:23  **minstrels**—people who play musical instruments

9:25  **put forth**—made to leave the room.

9:30  **straitly charged them**—told them strongly

9:32  **dumb man**—a man who could not talk **possessed with**—taken over by

9:34  Why did the Pharisees continue to refuse to believe in Jesus even after all of these miracles? (See D&C 63:7-12.)

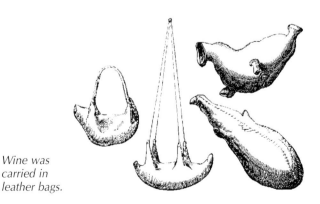

*Wine was carried in leather bags.*

36 But when he saw the multitudes, he was moved with compassion on them, because they fainted, and were scattered abroad, as sheep having no shepherd.

37 Then saith he unto his disciples, The harvest truly is plenteous, but the labourers are few;

38 Pray ye therefore the Lord of the harvest, that he will send forth labourers into his harvest.

## CHAPTER 10

*Jesus calls other men to help in spreading the message of the gospel. Notice ways the Twelve Apostles help with the Lord's work.*

### JESUS CALLS THE TWELVE APOSTLES

1 ¶ AND when he had called unto him his twelve disciples, he gave them power against unclean spirits, to cast them out, and to heal all manner of sickness and all manner of disease.

2 Now the names of the twelve apostles are these; The first, Simon, who is called Peter, and Andrew his brother; James the son of Zebedee, and John his brother;

3 Philip, and Bartholomew; Thomas, and Matthew the publican; James the son of Alphaeus, and Lebbaeus, whose surname was Thaddaeus;

4 Simon the Canaanite, and Judas Iscariot, who also betrayed him.

### THE TWELVE PREACH THE GOSPEL

5 ¶ These twelve Jesus sent forth, and commanded them, saying, Go not into the way of the Gentiles, and into any city of the Samaritans enter ye not:

6 But go rather to the lost sheep of the house of Israel.

7 And as ye go, preach, saying, The kingdom of heaven is at hand.

8 Heal the sick, cleanse the lepers, raise the dead, cast out devils: freely ye have received, freely give.

9 Provide neither gold, nor silver, nor brass in your purses,

10 Nor scrip for your journey, neither two coats, neither shoes, nor yet staves: for the workman is worthy of his meat.

11 And into whatsoever city or town ye shall enter, enquire who in it is worthy; and there abide till ye go thence.

12 And when ye come into an house, salute it.

13 And if the house be worthy, let your peace come upon it: but if it be not worthy, let your peace return to you.

14 And whosoever shall not receive you, nor hear your words, when ye depart out of that house or city, shake off the dust of your feet.

15 Verily I say unto you, It shall be more tolerable for the land of Sodom and Gomorrha in the day of judgment, than for that city.

---

9:36   *moved with compassion*—filled with love

9:37   What kind of harvest is Jesus referring to in this verse? Who are the laborers who help with this harvest? How can you prepare to be a laborer for the Lord? (See D&C 4:1-7.)

10:1   *disciples*—followers of Jesus Christ

10:4   *betrayed him*—gave Jesus to his enemies so they could kill him

Jesus Christ called twelve Apostles. Do you know the names of the twelve Apostles today?

10:5   Samaritans were the people who lived in Samaria after the Assyrians conquered the northern kingdom of Israel. The Jews hated them because, among other reasons, the Samaritans were part Gentile and also had mixed true religion with false religion. (See LDS Bible Dictionary, s.v. "Samaritans," p. 768.) The Savior loved the Samaritans, as he does all people (see Luke 10:33;

John 4:9-10; and 2 Nephi 26:33). He declared that one day Samaria would be open to missionary work (see Mark 16:15; Acts 1:8; Acts 8:25).

10:10   *scrip*—food bag
*staves*—walking sticks
*the workman is worthy of his meat*—someone who works deserves to be fed

10:12   *salute it*—greet the people who live there

10:15   *It shall be more tolerable*—the punishment will be less

Sodom and Gomorrah were two Old Testament cities destroyed by the Lord because of their wickedness (see Genesis 19:24-25).

16 ¶ Behold, I send you forth as sheep in the midst of wolves: be ye therefore wise as serpents, and harmless as doves.

## JESUS WARNS OF DANGER AHEAD FOR THE APOSTLES

17 But beware of men: for they will deliver you up to the councils, and they will scourge you in their synagogues;

18 And ye shall be brought before governors and kings for my sake, for a testimony against them and the Gentiles.

19 But when they deliver you up, take no thought how or what ye shall speak: for it shall be given you in that same hour what ye shall speak.

20 For it is not ye that speak, but the Spirit of your Father which speaketh in you.

21 And the brother shall deliver up the brother to death, and the father the child: and the children shall rise up against their parents, and cause them to be put to death.

22 And ye shall be hated of all men for my name's sake: but he that endureth to the end shall be saved.

23 But when they persecute you in this city, flee ye into another: for verily I say unto you, Ye shall not have gone over the cities of Israel, till the Son of man be come.

24 The disciple is not above his master, nor the servant above his lord.

25 It is enough for the disciple that he be as his master, and the servant as his lord. If they have called the master of the house Beelzebub, how much more shall they call them of his household?

26 Fear them not therefore: for there is nothing covered, that shall not be revealed; and hid, that shall not be known.

## THE LORD BLESSES THOSE WHO FOLLOW HIM

27 What I tell you in darkness, that speak ye in light: and what ye hear in the ear, that preach ye upon the housetops.

28 And fear not them which kill the body, but are not able to kill the soul: but rather fear him which is able to destroy both soul and body in hell.

29 Are not two sparrows sold for a farthing? and one of them shall not fall on the ground without your Father.

30 But the very hairs of your head are all numbered.

31 Fear ye not therefore, ye are of more value than many sparrows.

32 Whosoever therefore shall confess me before men, him will I confess also before my Father which is in heaven.

33 But whosoever shall deny me before men, him will I also deny before my Father which is in heaven.

34 Think not that I am come to send peace on earth: I came not to send peace, but a sword.

35 For I am come to set a man at variance against his father, and the daughter against her mother, and the daughter in law against her mother in law.

36 And a man's foes shall be they of his own household.

37 He that loveth father or mother more than me is not worthy of me: and he that loveth son or daughter more than me is not worthy of me.

38 And he that taketh not his cross, and followeth after me, is not worthy of me.

39 He that findeth his life shall lose it: and he that loseth his life for my sake shall find it.

40 He that receiveth you receiveth me, and he that receiveth me receiveth him that sent me.

---

10:17 **scourge**—whip

10:22 **for my name's sake**—because you testify of me

10:25 **Beelzebub**—Satan

10:28 **soul**—spiritual part of a person

10:29 **farthing**—cent and a half

The Joseph Smith Translation makes it clear that a sparrow "shall not fall on the ground without" Heavenly Father knowing it (see JST, Matthew 10:26).

10:34 Here the word *sword* represents the trouble that those who accept the gospel are sometimes subjected to, even on occasion by their own families.

10:36 **foes**—enemies

10:36-39 Why do you think the Lord wants us to put him first in our lives? How does loving God help us love our family more? What is wrong with putting other priorities before God in our lives?

10:38 **taketh not his cross**—does not do the things the Lord wants him to do in this life

41 He that receiveth a prophet in the name of a prophet shall receive a prophet's reward; and he that receiveth a righteous man in the name of a righteous man shall receive a righteous man's reward.

42 And whosoever shall give to drink unto one of these little ones a cup of cold water only in the name of a disciple, verily I say unto you, he shall in no wise lose his reward.

## CHAPTER 11

*Jesus' teachings bring happiness and hope. As you read this chapter, look for ways that the Savior can help you in your life.*

### JESUS CHRIST PRAISES JOHN THE BAPTIST

1 ¶ AND it came to pass, when Jesus had made an end of commanding his twelve disciples, he departed thence to teach and to preach in their cities.

2 Now when John had heard in the prison the works of Christ, he sent two of his disciples,

3 And said unto him, Art thou he that should come, or do we look for another?

4 Jesus answered and said unto them, Go and shew John again those things which ye do hear and see:

5 The blind receive their sight, and the lame walk, the lepers are cleansed, and the deaf hear, the dead are raised up, and the poor have the gospel preached to them.

6 And blessed is he, whosoever shall not be offended in me.

### JESUS TESTIFIES OF JOHN THE BAPTIST

7 ¶ And as they departed, Jesus began to say unto the multitudes concerning John, What went ye out into the wilderness to see? A reed shaken with the wind?

8 But what went ye out for to see? A man clothed in soft raiment? behold, they that wear soft clothing are in kings' houses.

9 But what went ye out for to see? A prophet? yea, I say unto you, and more than a prophet.

10 For this is he, of whom it is written, Behold, I send my messenger before thy face, which shall prepare thy way before thee.

11 Verily I say unto you, Among them that are born of women there hath not risen a greater than John the Baptist: notwithstanding he that is least in the kingdom of heaven is greater than he.

12 And from the days of John the Baptist until now the kingdom of heaven suffereth violence, and the violent take it by force.

13 For all the prophets and the law prophesied until John.

14 And if ye will receive it, this is Elias, which was for to come.

15 He that hath ears to hear, let him hear.

### JESUS GIVES A WARNING TO THOSE WHO REJECT THE GOSPEL MESSAGE

16 ¶ But whereunto shall I liken this generation? It is like unto children sitting in the markets, and calling unto their fellows,

---

10:41 What kind of reward might we receive by following the living prophet?

11:3 Why would John send two of his disciples to visit Jesus Christ? John the Baptist wanted his disciples to begin following and serving the Savior (see Bruce R. McConkie, *Doctrinal New Testament Commentary* 1:261).

11:6 **not be offended in me**—not be ashamed to believe and follow Jesus Christ

11:7 A reed is a tall, slender plant that bends and waves in the slightest breeze.

11:9-11 "How is it that John was considered one of the greatest prophets? . . . First. He was entrusted with a divine mission of preparing the way before the face of the Lord. . . . Secondly. He was entrusted with the important mission . . . to baptize the Son of Man. . . . Thirdly. John, at that time, was the only legal administrator . . . holding the keys of power." (*The Teachings of Joseph Smith*, pp. 353, 354.)

11:11 The Prophet Joseph Smith taught that when Jesus referred to "he that is least in the kingdom of heaven" he was referring to himself (see *The Teachings of Joseph Smith*, p. 354).

11:14 Elias is a title for someone who goes first to prepare the way for another. John the Baptist prepared the way before Jesus Christ, and so he was an Elias. (See LDS Bible Dictionary, s.v. "Elias," p. 663.)

11:15 **He that hath ears to hear**—Those who are willing to hear, listen, and obey

11:16 **liken**—compare
**fellows**—friends

17 And saying, We have piped unto you, and ye have not danced; we have mourned unto you, and ye have not lamented.

18 For John came neither eating nor drinking, and they say, He hath a devil.

19 The Son of man came eating and drinking, and they say, Behold a man gluttonous, and a winebibber, a friend of publicans and sinners. But wisdom is justified of her children.

20 Then began he to upbraid the cities wherein most of his mighty works were done, because they repented not:

21 Woe unto thee, Chorazin! woe unto thee, Bethsaida! for if the mighty works, which were done in you, had been done in Tyre and Sidon, they would have repented long ago in sackcloth and ashes.

22 But I say unto you, It shall be more tolerable for Tyre and Sidon at the day of judgment, than for you.

23 And thou, Capernaum, which art exalted unto heaven, shalt be brought down to hell: for if the mighty works, which have been done in thee, had been done in Sodom, it would have remained until this day.

24 But I say unto you, That it shall be more tolerable for the land of Sodom in the day of judgment, than for thee.

## COME UNTO JESUS CHRIST

25 ¶ At that time Jesus answered and said, I thank thee, O Father, Lord of heaven and earth, because thou hast hid these things from the wise and prudent, and hast revealed them unto babes.

26 Even so, Father: for so it seemed good in thy sight.

27 All things are delivered unto me of my Father: and no man knoweth the Son, but the Father; neither knoweth any man the Father, save the Son, and he to whomsoever the Son will reveal him.

28 Come unto me, all ye that labour and are heavy laden, and I will give you rest.

29 Take my yoke upon you, and learn of me; for I am meek and lowly in heart: and ye shall find rest unto your souls.

30 For my yoke is easy, and my burden is light.

# CHAPTER 12

*Jesus is accused of not keeping the Sabbath day holy; and his miracles are explained away as the power of Satan. As you read this chapter, look for why the wicked seem to try so hard to reject the truth.*

---

11:17  **piped**—played music
**lamented**—felt sad

11:19  **a man gluttonous**—someone who eats great amounts of food
**winebibber**—person who drinks great amounts of wine

11:20  **upbraid**—scold

11:21  **Woe**—Sorrow and suffering

Chorazin and Bethsaida were wicked cities where people of the family of Israel lived.

Tyre and Sidon were wicked cities where people who were not of the family of Israel lived.

In Bible times, when people wanted to repent, they would often wear rough clothes called sackcloth and put cold ashes from a fire on their heads. In this way they would show the Lord how humble and repentant they were.

11:28-  Wooden yokes were worn by teams of
29  animals. Oxen yoked together shared the load. Jesus promises to share our load and work beside us.

What are some things in your heart that worry you, sadden you, or make you feel like they are too heavy for you to carry? How has Jesus Christ offered to help you with these concerns?

*A heavy yoke was used to help oxen work together.*

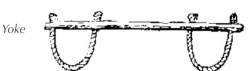

*Yoke*

## Jesus Heals on the Sabbath

1 ¶ AT that time Jesus went on the sabbath day through the corn; and his disciples were an hungred, and began to pluck the ears of corn, and to eat.

2 But when the Pharisees saw it, they said unto him, Behold, thy disciples do that which is not lawful to do upon the sabbath day.

3 But he said unto them, Have ye not read what David did, when he was an hungred, and they that were with him;

4 How he entered into the house of God, and did eat the shewbread, which was not lawful for him to eat, neither for them which were with him, but only for the priests?

5 Or have ye not read in the law, how that on the sabbath days the priests in the temple profane the sabbath, and are blameless?

6 But I say unto you, That in this place is one greater than the temple.

7 But if ye had known what this meaneth, I will have mercy, and not sacrifice, ye would not have condemned the guiltless.

8 For the Son of man is Lord even of the sabbath day.

9 And when he was departed thence, he went into their synagogue:

10 And, behold, there was a man which had his hand withered. And they asked him, saying, Is it lawful to heal on the sabbath days? that they might accuse him.

11 And he said unto them, What man shall there be among you, that shall have one sheep, and if it fall into a pit on the sabbath day, will he not lay hold on it, and lift it out?

12 How much then is a man better than a sheep? Wherefore it is lawful to do well on the sabbath days.

13 Then saith he to the man, Stretch forth thine hand. And he stretched it forth; and it was restored whole, like as the other.

14 ¶ Then the Pharisees went out, and held a council against him, how they might destroy him.

15 But when Jesus knew it, he withdrew himself from thence: and great multitudes followed him, and he healed them all;

16 And charged them that they should not make him known:

17 That it might be fulfilled which was spoken by Esaias the prophet, saying,

18 Behold my servant, whom I have chosen; my beloved, in whom my soul is well pleased: I will put my spirit upon him, and he shall shew judgment to the Gentiles.

19 He shall not strive, nor cry; neither shall any man hear his voice in the streets.

20 A bruised reed shall he not break, and smoking flax shall he not quench, till he send forth judgment unto victory.

21 And in his name shall the Gentiles trust.

## Jesus' Power Is from Heavenly Father

22 ¶ Then was brought unto him one possessed with a devil, blind, and dumb: and he healed him, insomuch that the blind and dumb both spake and saw.

23 And all the people were amazed, and said, Is not this the son of David?

24 But when the Pharisees heard it, they said, This fellow doth not cast out devils, but by Beelzebub the prince of the devils.

---

*An ear of corn was a head of wheat.*

12:1   corn—grain
pluck—pick

12:4   shewbread—bread, like the sacrament, that was blessed and placed in the temple; pronounced "SHOW-bread"

12:8   Jesus Christ is the "Lord even of the sabbath day." He commanded that we keep it holy, and he taught us how to worship on that special day. From the Savior's example, what should be done on the Sabbath day?

12:10   withered—crippled, deformed

12:15   withdrew himself from thence—went away from there

12:18   Matthew 12:18-21 is a prophecy of Isaiah about the Savior (see Isaiah 42:1-4).

12:22   dumb—unable to speak

12:24   Beelzebub—Satan

25 And Jesus knew their thoughts, and said unto them, Every kingdom divided against itself is brought to desolation; and every city or house divided against itself shall not stand:

26 And if Satan cast out Satan, he is divided against himself; how shall then his kingdom stand?

27 And if I by Beelzebub cast out devils, by whom do your children cast them out? therefore they shall be your judges.

28 But if I cast out devils by the Spirit of God, then the kingdom of God is come unto you.

29 Or else how can one enter into a strong man's house, and spoil his goods, except he first bind the strong man? and then he will spoil his house.

30 He that is not with me is against me; and he that gathereth not with me scattereth abroad.

## JESUS TELLS OF THE SIN AGAINST THE HOLY GHOST

31 Wherefore I say unto you, All manner of sin and blasphemy shall be forgiven unto men: but the blasphemy against the Holy Ghost shall not be forgiven unto men.

32 And whosoever speaketh a word against the Son of man, it shall be forgiven him: but whosoever speaketh against the Holy Ghost, it shall not be forgiven him, neither in this world, neither in the world to come.

33 Either make the tree good, and his fruit good; or else make the tree corrupt, and his fruit corrupt: for the tree is known by his fruit.

34 O generation of vipers, how can ye, being evil, speak good things? for out of the abundance of the heart the mouth speaketh.

35 A good man out of the good treasure of the heart bringeth forth good things: and an evil man out of the evil treasure bringeth forth evil things.

36 But I say unto you, That every idle word that men shall speak, they shall give account thereof in the day of judgment.

37 For by thy words thou shalt be justified, and by thy words thou shalt be condemned.

## THE WICKED SEEK SIGNS

38 ¶ Then certain of the scribes and of the Pharisees answered, saying, Master, we would see a sign from thee.

39 But he answered and said unto them, An evil and adulterous generation seeketh after a sign; and there shall no sign be given to it, but the sign of the prophet Jonas:

40 For as Jonas was three days and three nights in the whale's belly; so shall the Son of man be three days and three nights in the heart of the earth.

41 The men of Nineveh shall rise in judgment with this generation, and shall condemn it: because they repented at the preaching of Jonas; and, behold, a greater than Jonas is here.

42 The queen of the south shall rise up in the judgment with this generation, and shall condemn it: for she came from the uttermost parts of the earth to hear the wisdom of Solomon; and, behold, a greater than Solomon is here.

43 When the unclean spirit is gone out of a man, he walketh through dry places, seeking rest, and findeth none.

---

12:25 **desolation**—ruin and destruction

12:29 **spoil his goods**—take away his things

12:32 "The testimony of the Holy Ghost is the strongest testimony that can be given. It is better than a personal visit. It is for this reason that the Savior said that all manner of sin and blasphemy against the Holy Ghost could not be forgiven." (Joseph Fielding Smith, *Doctrines of Salvation* 3:153-54.)

12:34 **generation of vipers**—people who are dangerous like snakes

The phrase "abundance of the heart" refers to what a person is really like inside and to the things that person loves. Elder Bruce R. McConkie explained: "Man will be judged by his words. (Alma 12:14.) They reveal what is in his heart." (*Mormon Doctrine*, p. 373.)

12:36 **idle**—thoughtless

12:37 **justified**—shown to be righteous

12:38 **sign**—miracle or wonder

12:39 **adulterous generation**—an unfaithful and immoral people

12:39-40 Jonah's experience in the belly of the fish for three days and nights is likened to Jesus Christ's three days of burial in the tomb while his spirit would go to the spirit world. Can you think of any other experiences of prophets that can be likened to the Savior's life, death, and resurrection?

12:40 Jesus would be "in the heart of the earth," meaning buried in a tomb, for three days and nights before he would be resurrected.

44 Then he saith, I will return into my house from whence I came out; and when he is come, he findeth it empty, swept, and garnished.

45 Then goeth he, and taketh with himself seven other spirits more wicked than himself, and they enter in and dwell there: and the last state of that man is worse than the first. Even so shall it be also unto this wicked generation.

### JESUS DEFINES THE FAMILY OF CHRIST

46 ¶ While he yet talked to the people, behold, his mother and his brethren stood without, desiring to speak with him.

47 Then one said unto him, Behold, thy mother and thy brethren stand without, desiring to speak with thee.

48 But he answered and said unto him that told him, Who is my mother? and who are my brethren?

49 And he stretched forth his hand toward his disciples, and said, Behold my mother and my brethren!

50 For whosoever shall do the will of my Father which is in heaven, the same is my brother, and sister, and mother.

# CHAPTER 13

*See why Jesus spoke in parables and how parables effectively teach the gospel.*

### JESUS GIVES THE PARABLE OF THE SOWER AND THE SEED

1 ¶ THE same day went Jesus out of the house, and sat by the sea side.

2 And great multitudes were gathered together unto him, so that he went into a ship, and sat; and the whole multitude stood on the shore.

3 And he spake many things unto them in parables, saying, Behold, a sower went forth to sow;

4 And when he sowed, some seeds fell by the way side, and the fowls came and devoured them up:

5 Some fell upon stony places, where they had not much earth: and forthwith they sprung up, because they had no deepness of earth:

6 And when the sun was up, they were scorched; and because they had no root, they withered away.

7 And some fell among thorns; and the thorns sprung up, and choked them:

8 But other fell into good ground, and brought forth fruit, some an hundredfold, some sixtyfold, some thirtyfold.

9 Who hath ears to hear, let him hear.

10 And the disciples came, and said unto him, Why speakest thou unto them in parables?

11 He answered and said unto them, Because it is given unto you to know the mysteries of the kingdom of heaven, but to them it is not given.

12 For whosoever hath, to him shall be given, and he

---

12:44    *garnished*—put in order

12:45    The Joseph Smith Translation makes it clear that verses 43-45 are in response to a question from the scribes about why the sin against the Holy Ghost cannot be forgiven (see JST, Matthew 12:37-38).

12:48-   We have many families we can belong to.
50       We are born into an important family in this life and are also children of our Heavenly Father. Jesus taught about another family that we become part of as we live his gospel.

13:3     *parables*—earthly stories with heavenly or spiritual meaning
         *sower*—someone who plants seeds

13:5     *forthwith*—immediately

13:6     *withered away*—dried up

13:9     Do you have ears that hear spiritually? Are you in tune with the Holy Ghost?

13:10-   What reason did Jesus give for teaching in
15       parables? (See also LDS Bible Dictionary, s.v.

*Sowing, or planting, seeds*

"Parables," pp.740-41.) How do parables help you learn the gospel?

13:11-   "Mysteries of the kingdom" are the sacred
12       truths of the gospel. Jesus said they should not be given to those who refuse to obey them. The Book of Mormon adds that those who hear and obey will be given more truth. Those who will not hear and obey will lose even the little truth they had. (See Alma 12:9-11.)

shall have more abundance: but whosoever hath not, from him shall be taken away even that he hath.

13 Therefore speak I to them in parables: because they seeing see not; and hearing they hear not, neither do they understand.

14 And in them is fulfilled the prophecy of Esaias, which saith, By hearing ye shall hear, and shall not understand; and seeing ye shall see, and shall not perceive:

15 For this people's heart is waxed gross, and their ears are dull of hearing, and their eyes they have closed; lest at any time they should see with their eyes, and hear with their ears, and should understand with their heart, and should be converted, and I should heal them.

16 But blessed are your eyes, for they see: and your ears, for they hear.

17 For verily I say unto you, That many prophets and righteous men have desired to see those things which ye see, and have not seen them; and to hear those things which ye hear, and have not heard them.

18 Hear ye therefore the parable of the sower.

19 When any one heareth the word of the kingdom, and understandeth it not, then cometh the wicked one, and catcheth away that which was sown in his heart. This is he which received seed by the way side.

20 But he that received the seed into stony places, the same is he that heareth the word, and anon with joy receiveth it;

21 Yet hath he not root in himself, but dureth for a while: for when tribulation or persecution ariseth because of the word, by and by he is offended.

22 He also that received seed among the thorns is he that heareth the word; and the care of this world, and the deceitfulness of riches, choke the word, and he becometh unfruitful.

23 But he that received seed into the good ground is he that heareth the word, and understandeth it; which also beareth fruit, and bringeth forth, some an hundredfold, some sixty, some thirty.

## JESUS GIVES THE PARABLE OF THE WHEAT AND THE TARES

24 ¶ Another parable put he forth unto them, saying, The kingdom of heaven is likened unto a man which sowed good seed in his field:

25 But while men slept, his enemy came and sowed tares among the wheat, and went his way.

26 But when the blade was sprung up, and brought forth fruit, then appeared the tares also.

27 So the servants of the householder came and said unto him, Sir, didst not thou sow good seed in thy field? from whence then hath it tares?

28 He said unto them, An enemy hath done this. The servants said unto him, Wilt thou then that we go and gather them up?

29 But he said, Nay; lest while ye gather up the tares, ye root up also the wheat with them.

30 Let both grow together until the harvest: and in the time of harvest I will say to the reapers, Gather ye together first the tares, and bind them in bundles to burn them: but gather the wheat into my barn.

## JESUS GIVES THE PARABLES OF THE MUSTARD SEED AND THE LEAVEN

31 Another parable put he forth unto them, saying, The kingdom of heaven is like to a grain of mustard seed, which a man took, and sowed in his field:

32 Which indeed is the least of all seeds: but when it is grown, it is the greatest among herbs, and becometh a tree, so that the birds of the air come and lodge in the branches thereof.

---

13:14 *perceive*—see or understand

13:15 *waxed*—grown
*gross*—fat or thick, meaning unable to understand
*dull of hearing*—unable to hear easily

13:18- Jesus explains the parable of the sower and
23 says that there are four kinds of soil where the seed is planted. If the seed is the word of God in this parable, what would the soil be? In which of the four groups would you include yourself?

13:20 *anon*—immediately

13:21 *dureth*—remains true

13:22 *deceitfulness*—lies

13:25 Tares are poisonous plants that look very much like wheat until they are fully grown.

13:27 *whence*—where

13:30 The Joseph Smith Translation changes the order of the harvest. The reapers (those who bring in the harvest) are to gather "first the wheat into my barn; and the tares are bound in bundles to be burned" (JST, Matthew 13:29).

33 Another parable spake he unto them; The kingdom of heaven is like unto leaven, which a woman took, and hid in three measures of meal, till the whole was leavened.

34 All these things spake Jesus unto the multitude in parables; and without a parable spake he not unto them:

35 That it might be fulfilled which was spoken by the prophet, saying, I will open my mouth in parables; I will utter things which have been kept secret from the foundation of the world.

## JESUS GIVES THE MEANING OF THE PARABLE OF THE WHEAT AND THE TARES

36 Then Jesus sent the multitude away, and went into the house: and his disciples came unto him, saying, Declare unto us the parable of the tares of the field.

37 He answered and said unto them, He that soweth the good seed is the Son of man;

38 The field is the world; the good seed are the children of the kingdom; but the tares are the children of the wicked one;

39 The enemy that sowed them is the devil; the harvest is the end of the world; and the reapers are the angels.

40 As therefore the tares are gathered and burned in the fire; so shall it be in the end of this world.

41 The Son of man shall send forth his angels, and they shall gather out of his kingdom all things that offend, and them which do iniquity;

42 And shall cast them into a furnace of fire: there shall be wailing and gnashing of teeth.

43 Then shall the righteous shine forth as the sun in the kingdom of their Father. Who hath ears to hear, let him hear.

## JESUS GIVES THE PARABLES OF THE TREASURE, THE PEARL, THE GOSPEL NET, AND THE NEW AND OLD THINGS

44 ¶ Again, the kingdom of heaven is like unto treasure hid in a field; the which when a man hath found, he hideth, and for joy thereof goeth and selleth all that he hath, and buyeth that field.

45 Again, the kingdom of heaven is like unto a merchant man, seeking goodly pearls:

46 Who, when he had found one pearl of great price, went and sold all that he had, and bought it.

47 Again, the kingdom of heaven is like unto a net, that was cast into the sea, and gathered of every kind:

48 Which, when it was full, they drew to shore, and sat down, and gathered the good into vessels, but cast the bad away.

49 So shall it be at the end of the world: the angels shall come forth, and sever the wicked from among the just,

50 And shall cast them into the furnace of fire: there shall be wailing and gnashing of teeth.

51 Jesus saith unto them, Have ye understood all these things? They say unto him, Yea, Lord.

52 Then said he unto them, Therefore every scribe which is instructed unto the kingdom of heaven is like unto a man that is an householder, which bringeth forth out of his treasure things new and old.

53 ¶ And it came to pass, that when Jesus had finished these parables, he departed thence.

## THE PEOPLE IN HIS OWN COUNTRY DO NOT BELIEVE JESUS

54 And when he was come into his own country, he taught them in their synagogue, insomuch that they were astonished, and said, Whence hath this man this wisdom, and these mighty works?

55 Is not this the carpenter's son? is not his mother called Mary? and his brethren, James, and Joses, and Simon, and Judas?

56 And his sisters, are they not all with us? Whence then hath this man all these things?

57 And they were offended in him. But Jesus said unto them, A prophet is not without honour, save in his own country, and in his own house.

58 And he did not many mighty works there because of their unbelief.

---

13:33 *leaven*—yeast
*leavened*—raised

13:42 *gnashing*—grinding; expressing pain and grief

13:45 *merchant man*—man who buys and sells things

13:49 *sever*—separate

13:57 Many people from the town where Jesus grew up rejected him because they remembered him as the carpenter's son and as a member of Mary's family. Why is it sometimes easier to honor and respect someone you know less well? Is there ever a danger of our not fully respecting or honoring someone's call to a Church position because we are so close to the person?

# CHAPTER 14

*Jesus lived to serve Heavenly Father's children. In this chapter look for experiences that show how much the Savior loves all people.*

## JOHN THE BAPTIST IS KILLED

1 ¶ AT that time Herod the tetrarch heard of the fame of Jesus,

2 And said unto his servants, This is John the Baptist; he is risen from the dead; and therefore mighty works do shew forth themselves in him.

3 For Herod had laid hold on John, and bound him, and put him in prison for Herodias' sake, his brother Philip's wife.

4 For John said unto him, It is not lawful for thee to have her.

5 And when he would have put him to death, he feared the multitude, because they counted him as a prophet.

6 But when Herod's birthday was kept, the daughter of Herodias danced before them, and pleased Herod.

7 Whereupon he promised with an oath to give her whatsoever she would ask.

8 And she, being before instructed of her mother, said, Give me here John Baptist's head in a charger.

9 And the king was sorry: nevertheless for the oath's sake, and them which sat with him at meat, he commanded it to be given her.

10 And he sent, and beheaded John in the prison.

11 And his head was brought in a charger, and given to the damsel: and she brought it to her mother.

12 And his disciples came, and took up the body, and buried it, and went and told Jesus.

## JESUS FEEDS FIVE THOUSAND

13 ¶ When Jesus heard of it, he departed thence by ship into a desert place apart: and when the people had heard thereof, they followed him on foot out of the cities.

14 And Jesus went forth, and saw a great multitude, and was moved with compassion toward them, and he healed their sick.

15 And when it was evening, his disciples came to him, saying, This is a desert place, and the time is now past; send the multitude away, that they may go into the villages, and buy themselves victuals.

16 But Jesus said unto them, They need not depart; give ye them to eat.

17 And they say unto him, We have here but five loaves, and two fishes.

18 He said, Bring them hither to me.

19 And he commanded the multitude to sit down on the grass, and took the five loaves, and the two fishes, and looking up to heaven, he blessed, and brake, and gave the loaves to his disciples, and the disciples to the multitude.

20 And they did all eat, and were filled: and they took up of the fragments that remained twelve baskets full.

21 And they that had eaten were about five thousand men, beside women and children.

## JESUS CALMS THE STORM

22 ¶ And straightway Jesus constrained his disciples to get into a ship, and to go before him unto the other side, while he sent the multitudes away.

23 And when he had sent the multitudes away, he

---

14:1 Herod the tetrarch, who was also called Herod Antipas, was one of the rulers over the Jews (see LDS Bible Dictionary, s.v. "Herod," pp. 700-701).

14:2 **do shew forth themselves in him**—are done by him

14:4 For more information on what Herod Antipas did to break the law, see LDS Bible Dictionary, s.v. "Herod," p. 701.

14:7 **an oath**—a solemn promise

14:8 **charger**—large plate

14:10 **beheaded**—cut off the head of

14:11 **damsel**—girl

14:12 John the Baptist was resurrected and came to Joseph Smith and Oliver Cowdery in 1829 and gave them the Aaronic Priesthood. What do you think happened to Herod Antipas after he died?

14:14 **compassion**—deep love

14:15 **victuals**—food

14:18 **hither**—here

14:20 **fragments that remained**—pieces that were not eaten

14:22 **constrained**—directed or told

*The miracle known as the feeding of the five thousand showed Jesus' power over the elements and bore witness to the people that he was the Messiah, the Son of God.*

*Christ walking on the water with Peter*

went up into a mountain apart to pray: and when the evening was come, he was there alone.

24 But the ship was now in the midst of the sea, tossed with waves: for the wind was contrary.

25 And in the fourth watch of the night Jesus went unto them, walking on the sea.

26 And when the disciples saw him walking on the sea, they were troubled, saying, It is a spirit; and they cried out for fear.

27 But straightway Jesus spake unto them, saying, Be of good cheer; it is I; be not afraid.

28 And Peter answered him and said, Lord, if it be thou, bid me come unto thee on the water.

29 And he said, Come. And when Peter was come down out of the ship, he walked on the water, to go to Jesus.

30 But when he saw the wind boisterous, he was afraid; and beginning to sink, he cried, saying, Lord, save me.

31 And immediately Jesus stretched forth his hand, and caught him, and said unto him, O thou of little faith, wherefore didst thou doubt?

32 And when they were come into the ship, the wind ceased.

33 Then they that were in the ship came and worshipped him, saying, Of a truth thou art the Son of God.

34 ¶ And when they were gone over, they came into the land of Gennesaret.

35 And when the men of that place had knowledge of him, they sent out into all that country round about, and brought unto him all that were diseased;

---

14:24 **midst**—middle
**contrary**—blowing them away from where they were going

14:25 The fourth watch of the night was from three to six in the morning (see LDS Bible Dictionary, s.v. "Watches," p. 788).

14:27 **straightway**—immediately

14:28 **bid**—invite

14:30 Have you ever been afraid as Peter was at this time? Whom did Peter turn to for help and courage? How can you show your faith and rely on the Savior when you need help?

**boisterous**—getting stronger

14:32 **ceased**—stopped

36 And besought him that they might only touch the hem of his garment: and as many as touched were made perfectly whole.

## CHAPTER 15

*We can love things that are good and helpful or things that are bad and harmful. Notice what the Pharisees, a Gentile woman, and Jesus loved.*

### JESUS TEACHES ABOUT WHAT MAKES US UNCLEAN

1 ¶ THEN came to Jesus scribes and Pharisees, which were of Jerusalem, saying,

2 Why do thy disciples transgress the tradition of the elders? for they wash not their hands when they eat bread.

3 But he answered and said unto them, Why do ye also transgress the commandment of God by your tradition?

4 For God commanded, saying, Honour thy father and mother: and, He that curseth father or mother, let him die the death.

5 But ye say, Whosoever shall say to his father or his mother, It is a gift, by whatsoever thou mightest be profited by me;

6 And honour not his father or his mother, he shall be free. Thus have ye made the commandment of God of none effect by your tradition.

7 Ye hypocrites, well did Esaias prophesy of you, saying,

8 This people draweth nigh unto me with their mouth, and honoureth me with their lips; but their heart is far from me.

9 But in vain they do worship me, teaching for doctrines the commandments of men.

10 ¶ And he called the multitude, and said unto them, Hear, and understand:

11 Not that which goeth into the mouth defileth a man; but that which cometh out of the mouth, this defileth a man.

12 Then came his disciples, and said unto him, Knowest thou that the Pharisees were offended, after they heard this saying?

13 But he answered and said, Every plant, which my heavenly Father hath not planted, shall be rooted up.

14 Let them alone: they be blind leaders of the blind. And if the blind lead the blind, both shall fall into the ditch.

15 Then answered Peter and said unto him, Declare unto us this parable.

16 And Jesus said, Are ye also yet without understanding?

17 Do not ye yet understand, that whatsoever entereth in at the mouth goeth into the belly, and is cast out into the draught?

18 But those things which proceed out of the mouth come forth from the heart; and they defile the man.

19 For out of the heart proceed evil thoughts, murders, adulteries, fornications, thefts, false witness, blasphemies:

20 These are the things which defile a man: but to eat with unwashen hands defileth not a man.

### JESUS HEALS THE DAUGHTER OF A GENTILE WOMAN

21 ¶ Then Jesus went thence, and departed into the coasts of Tyre and Sidon.

22 And, behold, a woman of Canaan came out of the same coasts, and cried unto him, saying, Have mercy on me, O Lord, thou Son of David; my daughter is grievously vexed with a devil.

---

14:36 **besought**—begged

15:2 **transgress**—break

The traditions of the elders were unwritten laws added by men and not God. Many Jewish leaders thought their traditions were more important than the laws of God.

15:3-6 For help understanding these verses, see for Mark 7:9-13.

15:7 *Esaias* is the Greek name for *Isaiah*. See Isaiah 29:13.

15:11 **defileth a man**—makes a man unclean

Do the things you say often show people what is in your heart? Jesus taught that speaking evil words is worse than eating with dirty hands (see Matthew 15:19-20). Have you ever said anything that hurt someone? How did this make you feel?

15:13 **rooted up**—pulled up by the roots, as in weeding a garden

15:17 **is cast out into the draught**—leaves the body. That is, what is eaten passes through the body and passes away; it does not dirty the soul.

15:22 Canaan is an area near Galilee where many lived who were not of the family of Israel (see LDS Bible Dictionary, s.v. "Canaan," p. 629).

**vexed**—troubled

23 But he answered her not a word. And his disciples came and besought him, saying, Send her away; for she crieth after us.

24 But he answered and said, I am not sent but unto the lost sheep of the house of Israel.

25 Then came she and worshipped him, saying, Lord, help me.

26 But he answered and said, It is not meet to take the children's bread, and to cast it to dogs.

27 And she said, Truth, Lord: yet the dogs eat of the crumbs which fall from their masters' table.

28 Then Jesus answered and said unto her, O woman, great is thy faith: be it unto thee even as thou wilt. And her daughter was made whole from that very hour.

29 ¶ And Jesus departed from thence, and came nigh unto the sea of Galilee; and went up into a mountain, and sat down there.

30 And great multitudes came unto him, having with them those that were lame, blind, dumb, maimed, and many others, and cast them down at Jesus' feet; and he healed them:

31 Insomuch that the multitude wondered, when they saw the dumb to speak, the maimed to be whole, the lame to walk, and the blind to see: and they glorified the God of Israel.

### JESUS MIRACULOUSLY FEEDS FOUR THOUSAND PEOPLE

32 Then Jesus called his disciples unto him, and said, I have compassion on the multitude, because they continue with me now three days, and have nothing to eat: and I will not send them away fasting, lest they faint in the way.

33 And his disciples say unto him, Whence should we have so much bread in the wilderness, as to fill so great a multitude?

34 And Jesus saith unto them, How many loaves have ye? And they said, Seven, and a few little fishes.

35 And he commanded the multitude to sit down on the ground.

36 And he took the seven loaves and the fishes, and gave thanks, and brake them, and gave to his disciples, and the disciples to the multitude.

37 And they did all eat, and were filled: and they took up of the broken meat that was left seven baskets full.

38 And they that did eat were four thousand men, beside women and children.

39 And he sent away the multitude, and took ship, and came into the coasts of Magdala.

## CHAPTER 16

*True followers of Jesus Christ know and accept him. As you read this chapter note how Peter knew that Jesus was the Christ and how the Savior blessed Peter.*

### JESUS WARNS THE UNBELIEVING JEWS

1 ¶ THE Pharisees also with the Sadducees came, and tempting desired him that he would shew them a sign from heaven.

2 He answered and said unto them, When it is evening, ye say, It will be fair weather: for the sky is red.

3 And in the morning, It will be foul weather to day: for the sky is red and lowring. O ye hypocrites, ye can discern the face of the sky; but can ye not discern the signs of the times?

---

15:23 **besought**—implored or begged

15:24 Jesus' answer to the Gentile woman makes it clear that his mortal ministry was primarily to preach to the house of Israel (see also Matthew 10:5). Missionary work to those not of the house of Israel would begin later (see Acts 10).

15:26 The Greek word for *dogs* here means "little dogs" or pet dogs. Pet dogs (meaning the Gentiles) do get fed, but not before the children (meaning the house of Israel). Jesus blesses the Gentile woman's daughter because of her unusual faith.

15:30 **maimed**—injured

15:32 Why did Jesus miraculously multiply the bread and fishes to feed the four thousand? The scripture says that he had compassion on the people.

Compassion is love and deep concern. Do you ever feel compassion for others?

15:37 After the miraculous meal, the disciples gathered up seven basketfuls of broken pieces that were left over. What are some things you learn from the disciples' gathering up the leftovers?

16:1 **tempting**—testing

After all of the miracles that Jesus had already done, do you think the Pharisees and Sadducees would have been convinced by anything? What do you think they were actually hoping to see?

16:3 **lowring**—dark, gloomy
**discern**—figure out

4 A wicked and adulterous generation seeketh after a sign; and there shall no sign be given unto it, but the sign of the prophet Jonas. And he left them, and departed.

## Jesus Warns of Evil Teachings

5 ¶ And when his disciples were come to the other side, they had forgotten to take bread.

6 Then Jesus said unto them, Take heed and beware of the leaven of the Pharisees and of the Sadducees.

7 And they reasoned among themselves, saying, It is because we have taken no bread.

8 Which when Jesus perceived, he said unto them, O ye of little faith, why reason ye among yourselves, because ye have brought no bread?

9 Do ye not yet understand, neither remember the five loaves of the five thousand, and how many baskets ye took up?

10 Neither the seven loaves of the four thousand, and how many baskets ye took up?

11 How is it that ye do not understand that I spake it not to you concerning bread, that ye should beware of the leaven of the Pharisees and of the Sadducees?

12 Then understood they how that he bade them not beware of the leaven of bread, but of the doctrine of the Pharisees and of the Sadducees.

## Peter Testifies That Jesus Is the Christ

13 ¶ When Jesus came into the coasts of Caesarea Philippi, he asked his disciples, saying, Whom do men say that I the Son of man am?

14 And they said, Some say that thou art John the Baptist: some, Elias; and others, Jeremias, or one of the prophets.

15 He saith unto them, But whom say ye that I am?

16 And Simon Peter answered and said, Thou art the Christ, the Son of the living God.

17 And Jesus answered and said unto him, Blessed art thou, Simon Bar-jona: for flesh and blood hath not revealed it unto thee, but my Father which is in heaven.

18 And I say also unto thee, That thou art Peter, and upon this rock I will build my church; and the gates of hell shall not prevail against it.

19 And I will give unto thee the keys of the kingdom of heaven: and whatsoever thou shalt bind on earth shall be bound in heaven: and whatsoever thou shalt loose on earth shall be loosed in heaven.

20 Then charged he his disciples that they should tell no man that he was Jesus the Christ.

---

16:6    Jesus used the term *leaven*, or yeast, to represent "the doctrine of the Pharisees and of the Sadducees" (Matthew 16:12). A little leaven (yeast) mixed in bread dough will change all the dough and make it spoil more quickly. The sin, corruption, and hypocrisy of the wicked Jewish leaders were like leaven; their wrongdoing was causing many other people to sin.

16:13    Caesarea Philippi was north of Galilee in an area in which many people worshipped false gods. Some have wondered if it was being in this area of false religion that prompted Jesus to ask his followers, "Whom do men say that I the Son of man am?"

16:16-17    Man had not convinced Peter that Jesus was the Christ. True revelation from Heavenly Father was the source of Peter's testimony. Do you believe that Jesus is the Christ? How can you strengthen your testimony?

16:17    ***Bar-jona***—son of Jonah; another name for Peter, who was also called Simon Peter and Cephas

16:18    Jesus promised Peter that the Church of Jesus Christ would be built upon the "rock," which is

*Caves or alcoves that contain shrines to false gods can be seen today at Caesarea Philippi.*

revelation (see *The Teachings of Joseph Smith*, p. 575).

16:19    The "keys of the kingdom of heaven" are special powers or authority. These keys are the right of presidency. Peter, James, and John received these keys from Jesus Christ. (See D&C 27:12-13; 128:20.)

21 ¶ From that time forth began Jesus to shew unto his disciples, how that he must go unto Jerusalem, and suffer many things of the elders and chief priests and scribes, and be killed, and be raised again the third day.

22 Then Peter took him, and began to rebuke him, saying, Be it far from thee, Lord: this shall not be unto thee.

23 But he turned, and said unto Peter, Get thee behind me, Satan: thou art an offence unto me: for thou savourest not the things that be of God, but those that be of men.

## JESUS COMMANDS US TO FOLLOW HIM

24 ¶ Then said Jesus unto his disciples, If any man will come after me, let him deny himself, and take up his cross, and follow me.

25 For whosoever will save his life shall lose it: and whosoever will lose his life for my sake shall find it.

26 For what is a man profited, if he shall gain the whole world, and lose his own soul? or what shall a man give in exchange for his soul?

27 For the Son of man shall come in the glory of his Father with his angels; and then he shall reward every man according to his works.

28 Verily I say unto you, There be some standing here, which shall not taste of death, till they see the Son of man coming in his kingdom.

## CHAPTER 17

*In this chapter Jesus' chief Apostles receive powerful instruction in both heavenly and earthly matters. Look for what the Apostles might have learned from Jesus about revelation, faith, and respect for law.*

### JESUS TAKES PETER, JAMES, AND JOHN UP THE MOUNT OF TRANSFIGURATION

1 ¶ AND after six days Jesus taketh Peter, James, and John his brother, and bringeth them up into an high mountain apart,

2 And was transfigured before them: and his face did shine as the sun, and his raiment was white as the light.

3 And, behold, there appeared unto them Moses and Elias talking with him.

4 Then answered Peter, and said unto Jesus, Lord, it is good for us to be here: if thou wilt, let us make here three tabernacles; one for thee, and one for Moses, and one for Elias.

---

16:21 🔍 The elders, chief priests, and scribes were Jewish religious leaders and teachers.

16:21-23 🔍 Peter loved Jesus and did not want him to be killed. He did not understand that Jesus chose to give his life to save all of us. If Peter stopped Jesus from dying, he would be helping Satan. Jesus chastised Peter.

16:23 📖 **savourest not**—do not desire

16:24 🔥 The Joseph Smith Translation explains that to take up our "cross" means to keep the commandments and stay away from everything that is unholy or evil (see JST, Matthew 16:26).

🔄 What does it mean to follow Jesus? What can you do to be a better follower?

16:26 🔄 The question Jesus asks in this verse is a good question to ask yourself if you ever feel tempted to do something wrong. Is anything worth more to you than your eternal happiness? Eternal happiness and joy are what Jesus Christ offers you.

17:1-13 🔍 See the helps for Luke 9:28-36.

17:1 🔍 Mountains have often been the location of

very sacred experiences. The Old Testament prophet Isaiah referred to "the house of the God of Jacob" as "the mountain of the Lord" (Isaiah 2:3).

17:2-3 🔥 To be transfigured is to have "a special change in appearance . . . by the power of God. This divine transformation is from a lower to a higher state; it results in a more exalted, impressive, and glorious condition." (Bruce R. McConkie, *Mormon Doctrine*, p. 803.) At this time Elijah and Moses strengthened, encouraged, comforted, and supported Jesus as he prepared for the future sufferings he would experience during the Atonement (see James E. Talmage, *Jesus the Christ*, p. 373).

17:2 📖 **raiment**—clothing

17:3 📖 **Elias**—in this verse it is the Greek name of the prophet Elijah

🔥 Joseph Smith learned in a revelation that Peter, James, and John were also shown the transfiguration of the earth that will take place at the Millennium (see D&C 63:21).

17:4 📖 **tabernacles**—tents or small huts

5 While he yet spake, behold, a bright cloud over-shadowed them: and behold a voice out of the cloud, which said, This is my beloved Son, in whom I am well pleased; hear ye him.

6 And when the disciples heard it, they fell on their face, and were sore afraid.

7 And Jesus came and touched them, and said, Arise, and be not afraid.

8 And when they had lifted up their eyes, they saw no man, save Jesus only.

9 And as they came down from the mountain, Jesus charged them, saying, Tell the vision to no man, until the Son of man be risen again from the dead.

10 And his disciples asked him, saying, Why then say the scribes that Elias must first come?

11 And Jesus answered and said unto them, Elias truly shall first come, and restore all things.

12 But I say unto you, That Elias is come already, and they knew him not, but have done unto him whatso-ever they listed. Likewise shall also the Son of man suffer of them.

13 Then the disciples understood that he spake unto them of John the Baptist.

## JESUS HEALS A BOY WHO HAS AN EVIL SPIRIT

14 ¶ And when they were come to the multitude, there came to him a certain man, kneeling down to him, and saying,

15 Lord, have mercy on my son: for he is lunatick, and sore vexed: for ofttimes he falleth into the fire, and oft into the water.

16 And I brought him to thy disciples, and they could not cure him.

17 Then Jesus answered and said, O faithless and perverse generation, how long shall I be with you? how long shall I suffer you? bring him hither to me.

18 And Jesus rebuked the devil; and he departed out of him: and the child was cured from that very hour.

19 Then came the disciples to Jesus apart, and said, Why could not we cast him out?

20 And Jesus said unto them, Because of your unbe-lief: for verily I say unto you, If ye have faith as a grain of mustard seed, ye shall say unto this mountain, Remove hence to yonder place; and it shall remove; and nothing shall be impossible unto you.

21 Howbeit this kind goeth not out but by prayer and fasting.

22 ¶ And while they abode in Galilee, Jesus said unto them, The Son of man shall be betrayed into the hands of men:

23 And they shall kill him, and the third day he shall be raised again. And they were exceeding sorry.

## JESUS PAYS THE TEMPLE TAX BY WAY OF A MIRACLE

24 ¶ And when they were come to Capernaum, they that received tribute money came to Peter, and said, Doth not your master pay tribute?

25 He saith, Yes. And when he was come into the house, Jesus prevented him, saying, What thinkest thou, Simon? of whom do the kings of the earth take custom or tribute? of their own children, or of strangers?

26 Peter saith unto him, Of strangers. Jesus saith unto him, Then are the children free.

27 Notwithstanding, lest we should offend them, go thou to the sea, and cast an hook, and take up the fish

---

17:5 ☼ The Prophet Joseph Smith taught that Peter, James, and John were also transfigured and that Moses and Elias gave them priesthood keys (see *The Teachings of Joseph Smith,* p. 504).

17:6 🅦 *sore*—very, greatly

17:11- ☼ The Joseph Smith Translation explains that
13 *Elias,* besides being the Greek form of *Elijah,* is also a mission or calling. An Elias is someone called to prepare the way for the Savior. John the Baptist was an Elias. (See JST, Matthew 17:10-14; see also LDS Bible Dictionary, s.v. "Elias," p. 663.)

17:12 🅦 *listed*—wanted

17:15 🅦 *is lunatick, and sore vexed*—suffers from seizures

17:17 🅦 *perverse*—turned aside from the right path

17:20 🔎 A mustard seed is one of the smallest seeds (see Matthew 13:31-32).

17:20- 🔁 Have you ever felt discouraged by problems
21 you face? How do the Savior's words "If ye have faith as a grain of mustard seed, . . . nothing shall be impossible unto you" make you feel? What can you do to strengthen your faith? (See verse 21.)

17:24 🔎 This tribute, used for the temple upkeep, was a tax of two days' wages. Every male Israelite twenty years of age and older was required to pay it every year. (See Exodus 30:13.)

17:26- 🔁 Jesus explained that he did not have to pay the
27 tax, but he instructed Peter to pay it anyway. What was Jesus teaching Peter? Why did Jesus go about paying the tax in such a miraculous manner?

that first cometh up; and when thou hast opened his mouth, thou shalt find a piece of money: that take, and give unto them for me and thee.

# CHAPTER 18

*As you read this chapter, see what kind of people will go to the celestial kingdom.*

## JESUS PRESENTS THE PRINCIPLE OF BECOMING AS A LITTLE CHILD

1 ¶ AT the same time came the disciples unto Jesus, saying, Who is the greatest in the kingdom of heaven?

2 And Jesus called a little child unto him, and set him in the midst of them,

3 And said, Verily I say unto you, Except ye be converted, and become as little children, ye shall not enter into the kingdom of heaven.

4 Whosoever therefore shall humble himself as this little child, the same is greatest in the kingdom of heaven.

5 And whoso shall receive one such little child in my name receiveth me.

6 But whoso shall offend one of these little ones which believe in me, it were better for him that a millstone were hanged about his neck, and that he were drowned in the depth of the sea.

7 ¶ Woe unto the world because of offences! for it must needs be that offences come; but woe to that man by whom the offence cometh!

8 Wherefore if thy hand or thy foot offend thee, cut them off, and cast them from thee: it is better for thee to enter into life halt or maimed, rather than having two hands or two feet to be cast into everlasting fire.

9 And if thine eye offend thee, pluck it out, and cast it from thee: it is better for thee to enter into life with one eye, rather than having two eyes to be cast into hell fire.

10 Take heed that ye despise not one of these little ones; for I say unto you, That in heaven their angels do always behold the face of my Father which is in heaven.

## JESUS GIVES THE PARABLE OF THE LOST SHEEP

11 For the Son of man is come to save that which was lost.

12 How think ye? if a man have an hundred sheep, and one of them be gone astray, doth he not leave the ninety and nine, and goeth into the mountains, and seeketh that which is gone astray?

13 And if so be that he find it, verily I say unto you, he rejoiceth more of that sheep, than of the ninety and nine which went not astray.

14 Even so it is not the will of your Father which is in heaven, that one of these little ones should perish.

## JESUS TEACHES HOW TO RESPOND WHEN SOMEONE SINS AGAINST YOU

15 ¶ Moreover if thy brother shall trespass against thee, go and tell him his fault between thee and him alone: if he shall hear thee, thou hast gained thy brother.

16 But if he will not hear thee, then take with thee one or two more, that in the mouth of two or three witnesses every word may be established.

17 And if he shall neglect to hear them, tell it unto the church: but if he neglect to hear the church, let him be unto thee as an heathen man and a publican.

---

18:2-6 When asked who was greatest in the kingdom of heaven, why would Jesus place a little child in the middle of the people? Why do you feel Jesus liked little children so much?

18:3 **converted**—changed

18:8 **halt or maimed**—crippled

18:8-9 Why does Jesus say to cut off a hand or foot? The Joseph Smith Translation explains that "a man's hand is his friend, and his foot, also; and a man's eye, are they of his own household" (JST, Matthew 18:9).

18:11 The Joseph Smith Translation adds an important phrase at the end of this verse: "and to call sinners to repentance; but these little ones have no need of repentance, and I will save them."

18:12 **be gone astray**—wander, leave the path

Who are Heavenly Father's sheep and how do some get lost? If you had a hundred sheep, and one got lost, would you leave the ninety-nine to go after the one? Why?

18:13 Have you ever found something very important to you after searching for a long time? How did you feel when you found it?

18:15 **trespass**—sin

18:17 **heathen**—person who was not of the family of Israel and who did not believe in the God of Israel

18 Verily I say unto you, Whatsoever ye shall bind on earth shall be bound in heaven: and whatsoever ye shall loose on earth shall be loosed in heaven.

19 Again I say unto you, That if two of you shall agree on earth as touching any thing that they shall ask, it shall be done for them of my Father which is in heaven.

20 For where two or three are gathered together in my name, there am I in the midst of them.

21 ¶ Then came Peter to him, and said, Lord, how oft shall my brother sin against me, and I forgive him? till seven times?

22 Jesus saith unto him, I say not unto thee, Until seven times: but, Until seventy times seven.

### JESUS GIVES THE PARABLE OF THE UNMERCIFUL SERVANT

23 Therefore is the kingdom of heaven likened unto a certain king, which would take account of his servants.

24 And when he had begun to reckon, one was brought unto him, which owed him ten thousand talents.

25 But forasmuch as he had not to pay, his lord commanded him to be sold, and his wife, and children, and all that he had, and payment to be made.

26 The servant therefore fell down, and worshipped him, saying, Lord, have patience with me, and I will pay thee all.

27 Then the lord of that servant was moved with compassion, and loosed him, and forgave him the debt.

28 But the same servant went out, and found one of his fellowservants, which owed him an hundred pence: and he laid hands on him, and took him by the throat, saying, Pay me that thou owest.

29 And his fellowservant fell down at his feet, and

besought him, saying, Have patience with me, and I will pay thee all.

30 And he would not: but went and cast him into prison, till he should pay the debt.

31 So when his fellowservants saw what was done, they were very sorry, and came and told unto their lord all that was done.

32 Then his lord, after that he had called him, said unto him, O thou wicked servant, I forgave thee all that debt, because thou desiredst me:

33 Shouldest not thou also have had compassion on thy fellowservant, even as I had pity on thee?

34 And his lord was wroth, and delivered him to the tormentors, till he should pay all that was due unto him.

35 So likewise shall my heavenly Father do also unto you, if ye from your hearts forgive not every one his brother their trespasses.

## CHAPTER 19

*In this chapter a rich young man asks the Savior, "What good thing shall I do, that I may have eternal life?" As you read, look for important direction from the Lord that would answer this question.*

### JESUS CHRIST TEACHES THE IMPORTANCE OF MARRIAGE AND AVOIDING DIVORCE

1 ¶ AND it came to pass, that when Jesus had finished these sayings, he departed from Galilee, and came into the coasts of Judaea beyond Jordan;

2 And great multitudes followed him; and he healed them there.

3 ¶ The Pharisees also came unto him, tempting him, and saying unto him, Is it lawful for a man to put away his wife for every cause?

---

18:22 **Until seventy times seven**— represents an endless number of times

18:23 **would take account of his servants**—decided to collect the money his servants owed him

18:23-35 We should forgive others because God forgives us. Jesus Christ said, "Ye ought to forgive one another; for he that forgiveth not his brother his trespasses standeth condemned before the Lord; for there remaineth in him the greater sin" (D&C 64:9).

18:24 **ten thousand talents**—millions (maybe billions) of dollars in our currency

18:27 This is a parable about the Lord's willingness to forgive us of our sins. How does this parable make you feel toward Jesus?

18:28 One pence (often called a penny) was a laborer's pay for about one day's work (see Matthew 20:2). A hundred pence would be the pay for about three months' labor.

18:34 **tormentors**—people who hurt or torture others

19:3 **put away**—divorce

4 And he answered and said unto them, Have ye not read, that he which made them at the beginning made them male and female,

5 And said, For this cause shall a man leave father and mother, and shall cleave to his wife: and they twain shall be one flesh?

6 Wherefore they are no more twain, but one flesh. What therefore God hath joined together, let not man put asunder.

7 They say unto him, Why did Moses then command to give a writing of divorcement, and to put her away?

8 He saith unto them, Moses because of the hardness of your hearts suffered you to put away your wives: but from the beginning it was not so.

9 And I say unto you, Whosoever shall put away his wife, except it be for fornication, and shall marry another, committeth adultery: and whoso marrieth her which is put away doth commit adultery.

10 His disciples say unto him, If the case of the man be so with his wife, it is not good to marry.

11 But he said unto them, All men cannot receive this saying, save they to whom it is given.

12 For there are some eunuchs, which were so born from their mother's womb: and there are some eunuchs, which were made eunuchs of men: and there be eunuchs, which have made themselves eunuchs for the kingdom of heaven's sake. He that is able to receive it, let him receive it.

## JESUS WELCOMES CHILDREN

13 ¶ Then were there brought unto him little children, that he should put his hands on them, and pray: and the disciples rebuked them.

14 But Jesus said, Suffer little children, and forbid them not, to come unto me: for of such is the kingdom of heaven.

15 And he laid his hands on them, and departed thence.

## JESUS ANSWERS A YOUNG MAN'S QUESTION ABOUT ETERNAL LIFE

16 ¶ And, behold, one came and said unto him, Good Master, what good thing shall I do, that I may have eternal life?

17 And he said unto him, Why callest thou me good? there is none good but one, that is, God: but if thou wilt enter into life, keep the commandments.

18 He saith unto him, Which? Jesus said, Thou shalt do no murder, Thou shalt not commit adultery, Thou shalt not steal, Thou shalt not bear false witness,

19 Honour thy father and thy mother: and, Thou shalt love thy neighbour as thyself.

20 The young man saith unto him, All these things have I kept from my youth up: what lack I yet?

21 Jesus said unto him, If thou wilt be perfect, go and sell that thou hast, and give to the poor, and thou shalt have treasure in heaven: and come and follow me.

22 But when the young man heard that saying, he went away sorrowful: for he had great possessions.

## JESUS USES THE EXAMPLE OF A CAMEL AND THE EYE OF A NEEDLE

23 ¶ Then said Jesus unto his disciples, Verily I say unto you, That a rich man shall hardly enter into the kingdom of heaven.

24 And again I say unto you, It is easier for a camel to go through the eye of a needle, than for a rich man to enter into the kingdom of God.

---

19:4-5 Jesus is quoting from Genesis 1:27 and 2:24.

19:5 **cleave**—be united
**they twain**—the two

19:6 **put asunder**—separate

19:8 "Divorce is not part of the Gospel plan and has been introduced because of the hardness of heart and unbelief of the people" (Joseph Fielding Smith, *The Way to Perfection*, p. 240).

19:9 **fornication**—misuse of the sacred creative powers; that is, use of these powers between people who are not married
**adultery**—misuse of the sacred creative powers; that is, use of these powers with someone who is not your husband or wife

19:12 **eunuchs**—men without ability to become fathers

19:14 Should grown-ups act like children? Is there a difference between being childish and childlike?

19:17-19 Do you recognize the commandments that the Savior lists? Do you feel that these commandments were important to Jesus? Do you feel that they are still important today?

19:18 **bear false witness**—lie

19:22 **great possessions**—much property

19:24-26 Could a camel go through the eye of a needle? Why would Jesus use this example to show the difficulty of a rich man's getting to heaven? Can anyone, rich or poor, get into heaven without the power of God?

*Jesus Christ loved children.*

25 When his disciples heard it, they were exceedingly amazed, saying, Who then can be saved?

26 But Jesus beheld them, and said unto them, With men this is impossible; but with God all things are possible.

27 Then answered Peter and said unto him, Behold, we have forsaken all, and followed thee; what shall we have therefore?

28 And Jesus said unto them, Verily I say unto you, That ye which have followed me, in the regeneration when the Son of man shall sit in the throne of his glory, ye also shall sit upon twelve thrones, judging the twelve tribes of Israel.

29 And every one that hath forsaken houses, or brethren, or sisters, or father, or mother, or wife, or children, or lands, for my name's sake, shall receive an hundredfold, and shall inherit everlasting life.

30 But many that are first shall be last; and the last shall be first.

# CHAPTER 20

*What do a parable, a mother's request, and a dramatic healing of two blind men have in common? As you read this chapter find the answer in the importance Jesus places on selfless, loving service.*

## JESUS GIVES THE PARABLE OF THE WORKERS IN THE FIELD

1 ¶ FOR the kingdom of heaven is like unto a man that is an householder, which went out early in the morning to hire labourers into his vineyard.

2 And when he had agreed with the labourers for a penny a day, he sent them into his vineyard.

3 And he went out about the third hour, and saw others standing idle in the marketplace,

4 And said unto them; Go ye also into the vineyard, and whatsoever is right I will give you. And they went their way.

5 Again he went out about the sixth and ninth hour, and did likewise.

6 And about the eleventh hour he went out, and found others standing idle, and saith unto them, Why stand ye here all the day idle?

7 They say unto him, Because no man hath hired us. He saith unto them, Go ye also into the vineyard; and whatsoever is right, that shall ye receive.

8 So when even was come, the lord of the vineyard saith unto his steward, Call the labourers, and give them their hire, beginning from the last unto the first.

9 And when they came that were hired about the eleventh hour, they received every man a penny.

10 But when the first came, they supposed that they should have received more; and they likewise received every man a penny.

11 And when they had received it, they murmured against the goodman of the house,

12 Saying, These last have wrought but one hour, and thou hast made them equal unto us, which have borne the burden and heat of the day.

13 But he answered one of them, and said, Friend, I do thee no wrong: didst not thou agree with me for a penny?

14 Take that thine is, and go thy way: I will give unto this last, even as unto thee.

15 Is it not lawful for me to do what I will with mine own? Is thine eye evil, because I am good?

16 So the last shall be first, and the first last: for many be called, but few chosen.

## JESUS TELLS OF HIS CRUCIFIXION AND RESURRECTION

17 ¶ And Jesus going up to Jerusalem took the twelve disciples apart in the way, and said unto them,

---

19:27  **forsaken all**—given up or sacrificed much

19:28  The Joseph Smith Translation changes *regeneration* to *resurrection*.

20:1  **householder**—landowner

20:2  A "penny a day" was considered a day's pay for a day's work in Jesus' time.

20:8  **hire**—day's pay

20:11  **murmured**—complained

20:12  **wrought**—worked

20:14  **Take that thine is**—Take what you have been paid

20:15  **Is thine eye evil, because I am good?**—Are you jealous, because I am generous?

20:17-19  Why does Jesus again take time to prepare the Apostles for his betrayal, death, and resurrection? He had done so at least twice before already (see Matthew 16:21-23 and Matthew 17:22-23). Do you think the Apostles really understood all that the Savior was telling them?

18 Behold, we go up to Jerusalem; and the Son of man shall be betrayed unto the chief priests and unto the scribes, and they shall condemn him to death,

19 And shall deliver him to the Gentiles to mock, and to scourge, and to crucify him: and the third day he shall rise again.

### Jesus Teaches His Disciples the Importance of Service

20 ¶ Then came to him the mother of Zebedee's children with her sons, worshipping him, and desiring a certain thing of him.

21 And he said unto her, What wilt thou? She saith unto him, Grant that these my two sons may sit, the one on thy right hand, and the other on the left, in thy kingdom.

22 But Jesus answered and said, Ye know not what ye ask. Are ye able to drink of the cup that I shall drink of, and to be baptized with the baptism that I am baptized with? They say unto him, We are able.

23 And he saith unto them, Ye shall drink indeed of my cup, and be baptized with the baptism that I am baptized with: but to sit on my right hand, and on my left, is not mine to give, but it shall be given to them for whom it is prepared of my Father.

24 And when the ten heard it, they were moved with indignation against the two brethren.

25 But Jesus called them unto him, and said, Ye know that the princes of the Gentiles exercise dominion over them, and they that are great exercise authority upon them.

26 But it shall not be so among you: but whosoever will be great among you, let him be your minister;

27 And whosoever will be chief among you, let him be your servant:

28 Even as the Son of man came not to be ministered unto, but to minister, and to give his life a ransom for many.

29 ¶ And as they departed from Jericho, a great multitude followed him.

### Jesus Heals Two Blind Men

30 And, behold, two blind men sitting by the way side, when they heard that Jesus passed by, cried out, saying, Have mercy on us, O Lord, thou Son of David.

31 And the multitude rebuked them, because they should hold their peace: but they cried the more, saying, Have mercy on us, O Lord, thou Son of David.

32 And Jesus stood still, and called them, and said, What will ye that I shall do unto you?

33 They say unto him, Lord, that our eyes may be opened.

34 So Jesus had compassion on them, and touched their eyes: and immediately their eyes received sight, and they followed him.

## CHAPTER 21

*Jesus Christ spent one last week in Jerusalem before he was crucified. He entered the city in such a way that his true followers recognized him as king and Lord. Read this story as if you were there and think about whether you would have recognized that Jesus was truly your Savior.*

### Jesus Enters Jerusalem Triumphantly

1 ¶ AND when they drew nigh unto Jerusalem, and were come to Bethphage, unto the mount of Olives, then sent Jesus two disciples,

2 Saying unto them, Go into the village over against you, and straightway ye shall find an ass tied, and a colt with her: loose them, and bring them unto me.

3 And if any man say ought unto you, ye shall say, The Lord hath need of them; and straightway he will send them.

---

20:22   According to Elder Bruce R. McConkie, the phrase "to drink of the cup that I shall drink of" means " 'to do the things which my lot in life requires of me.' " Elder McConkie indicates further that the phrase "to be baptized with the baptism that I am baptized with" means " 'to follow my course, suffer persecution, be rejected of men, and finally be slain for the truth's sake.' " (*Doctrinal New Testament Commentary* 1:566.)

20:24   **indignation**—anger

20:25   **princes of the Gentiles**—rulers of the nations
**dominion**—power

20:28   **ransom**—payment

20:34   Jesus could touch the eyes of the blind and they could see again. What did these two men do that shows their spiritual eyes were opened also?

21:1   **drew nigh**—came near

21:2   **over against you**—in front of you
**ass**—donkey
**colt**—young donkey

*Christ's triumphal entry*

4 All this was done, that it might be fulfilled which was spoken by the prophet, saying,

5 Tell ye the daughter of Sion, Behold, thy King cometh unto thee, meek, and sitting upon an ass, and a colt the foal of an ass.

6 And the disciples went, and did as Jesus commanded them,

7 And brought the ass, and the colt, and put on them their clothes, and they set him thereon.

8 And a very great multitude spread their garments in the way; others cut down branches from the trees, and strawed them in the way.

9 And the multitudes that went before, and that followed, cried, saying, Hosanna to the Son of David: Blessed is he that cometh in the name of the Lord; Hosanna in the highest.

10 And when he was come into Jerusalem, all the city was moved, saying, Who is this?

11 And the multitude said, This is Jesus the prophet of Nazareth of Galilee.

## JESUS CLEANSES THE TEMPLE AGAIN

12 ¶ And Jesus went into the temple of God, and cast out all them that sold and bought in the temple, and overthrew the tables of the moneychangers, and the seats of them that sold doves,

13 And said unto them, It is written, My house shall be called the house of prayer; but ye have made it a den of thieves.

---

21:4-5    Ancient prophets foretold Jesus' entering Jerusalem on a colt (see Zechariah 9:9).

21:8    **garments**—outer clothing, or cloaks

     Such displays of respect and honor were reserved only for kings and conquerors (see 2 Kings 9:13).

21:8-11    How would you have reacted had you been there to greet Jesus riding into town as a king?

21:9    **Hosanna**—Save now! or Save, we pray!

21:12-13    Jesus protected the holiness of the temple. President Ezra Taft Benson said that a temple is "the closest place to heaven on earth—[it is] the house of the Lord" (*The Teachings of Ezra Taft Benson*, p. 253).

14 And the blind and the lame came to him in the temple; and he healed them.

15 And when the chief priests and scribes saw the wonderful things that he did, and the children crying in the temple, and saying, Hosanna to the Son of David; they were sore displeased,

16 And said unto him, Hearest thou what these say? And Jesus saith unto them, Yea; have ye never read, Out of the mouth of babes and sucklings thou hast perfected praise?

17 And he left them, and went out of the city into Bethany; and he lodged there.

## JESUS CURSES THE BARREN FIG TREE

18 ¶ Now in the morning as he returned into the city, he hungered.

19 And when he saw a fig tree in the way, he came to it, and found nothing thereon, but leaves only, and said unto it, Let no fruit grow on thee henceforward for ever. And presently the fig tree withered away.

20 And when the disciples saw it, they marvelled, saying, How soon is the fig tree withered away!

21 Jesus answered and said unto them, Verily I say unto you, If ye have faith, and doubt not, ye shall not only do this which is done to the fig tree, but also if ye shall say unto this mountain, Be thou removed, and be thou cast into the sea; it shall be done.

22 And all things, whatsoever ye shall ask in prayer, believing, ye shall receive.

## JESUS TEACHES OF HIS AUTHORITY BY TELLING TWO PARABLES

23 ¶ And when he was come into the temple, the chief priests and the elders of the people came unto him as he was teaching, and said, By what authority doest thou these things? and who gave thee this authority?

24 And Jesus answered and said unto them, I also will ask you one thing, which if ye tell me, I in like wise will tell you by what authority I do these things.

25 The baptism of John, whence was it? from heaven, or of men? And they reasoned with themselves, saying, If we shall say, From heaven; he will say unto us, Why did ye not then believe him?

26 But if we shall say, Of men; we fear the people; for all hold John as a prophet.

27 And they answered Jesus, and said, We cannot tell. And he said unto them, Neither tell I you by what authority I do these things.

28 ¶ But what think ye? A certain man had two sons; and he came to the first, and said, Son, go work to day in my vineyard.

29 He answered and said, I will not: but afterward he repented, and went.

30 And he came to the second, and said likewise. And he answered and said, I go, sir: and went not.

31 Whether of them twain did the will of his father? They say unto him, The first. Jesus saith unto them, Verily I say unto you, That the publicans and the harlots go into the kingdom of God before you.

32 For John came unto you in the way of righteousness, and ye believed him not: but the publicans and the harlots believed him: and ye, when ye had seen it, repented not afterward, that ye might believe him.

33 ¶ Hear another parable: There was a certain householder, which planted a vineyard, and hedged it round about, and digged a winepress in it, and built a tower, and let it out to husbandmen, and went into a far country:

34 And when the time of the fruit drew near, he sent his servants to the husbandmen, that they might receive the fruits of it.

35 And the husbandmen took his servants, and beat one, and killed another, and stoned another.

36 Again, he sent other servants more than the first: and they did unto them likewise.

---

21:14   Did you know you must be worthy to attend the temple? What does it mean to be worthy? Are you planning on going to the temple someday?

21:16   **sucklings**—infant children

21:19-   A fruit tree full of leaves looks nice, but if it
20   has no fruit it is "barren." A barren tree cannot save people from starving. Many people in Jesus' day believed in a religion that did not feed them spiritually. By cursing this tree Jesus warned his disciples about the wickedness of "barren" religions (see Matthew 7:15-20).

21:20   **withered away**—dried up and dead

21:23-   How sincere were those who asked about
27   Jesus' authority? Why do you think he answered their question the way he did?

21:31   **twain**—two

21:33   **householder**—landowner
  **let it out to husbandmen**—rented the property to some men to care for it

37 But last of all he sent unto them his son, saying, They will reverence my son.

38 But when the husbandmen saw the son, they said among themselves, This is the heir; come, let us kill him, and let us seize on his inheritance.

39 And they caught him, and cast him out of the vineyard, and slew him.

40 When the lord therefore of the vineyard cometh, what will he do unto those husbandmen?

41 They say unto him, He will miserably destroy those wicked men, and will let out his vineyard unto other husbandmen, which shall render him the fruits in their seasons.

42 Jesus saith unto them, Did ye never read in the scriptures, The stone which the builders rejected, the same is become the head of the corner: this is the Lord's doing, and it is marvellous in our eyes?

43 Therefore say I unto you, The kingdom of God shall be taken from you, and given to a nation bringing forth the fruits thereof.

44 And whosoever shall fall on this stone shall be broken: but on whomsoever it shall fall, it will grind him to powder.

45 And when the chief priests and Pharisees had heard his parables, they perceived that he spake of them.

46 But when they sought to lay hands on him, they feared the multitude, because they took him for a prophet.

## CHAPTER 22

*Jesus knew that the things of this world could keep us from heaven. In this chapter look for ways that the Savior teaches that heavenly blessings are more important than earthly cares.*

### JESUS RECOUNTS THE PARABLE OF THE MARRIAGE OF THE KING'S SON

1 ¶ AND Jesus answered and spake unto them again by parables, and said,

2 The kingdom of heaven is like unto a certain king, which made a marriage for his son,

3 And sent forth his servants to call them that were bidden to the wedding: and they would not come.

4 Again, he sent forth other servants, saying, Tell them which are bidden, Behold, I have prepared my dinner: my oxen and my fatlings are killed, and all things are ready: come unto the marriage.

5 But they made light of it, and went their ways, one to his farm, another to his merchandise:

6 And the remnant took his servants, and entreated them spitefully, and slew them.

7 But when the king heard thereof, he was wroth: and he sent forth his armies, and destroyed those murderers, and burned up their city.

8 Then saith he to his servants, The wedding is ready, but they which were bidden were not worthy.

9 Go ye therefore into the highways, and as many as ye shall find, bid to the marriage.

10 So those servants went out into the highways, and gathered together all as many as they found, both bad and good: and the wedding was furnished with guests.

11 And when the king came in to see the guests, he saw there a man which had not on a wedding garment:

12 And he saith unto him, Friend, how camest thou in hither not having a wedding garment? And he was speechless.

13 Then said the king to the servants, Bind him hand and foot, and take him away, and cast him into outer darkness; there shall be weeping and gnashing of teeth.

---

21:38    An heir is a child who inherits a parent's possessions (see Romans 8:16-17). In this parable the heir refers to Jesus Christ, who should have been respected by the people but was rejected and killed like many other prophets.

21:45    **perceived**—understood or sensed

21:46    The Joseph Smith Translation adds several sentences to the end of this chapter that teach that the stone mentioned in verses 42 and 44 refers to Jesus Christ.

22:2-14    The parable in verses 2-14 is a story that teaches about the end of the world. As you read this parable think of the king as Heavenly Father, the son as Jesus Christ, and the wedding dinner as Jesus Christ's second coming.

22:5    **made light of it**—paid no attention
**merchandise**—business

22:6    **entreated them spitefully, and slew them**—treated them badly and killed them.

22:11-13    Why was one man cast out? "He had accepted the invitation (the gospel); joined with the true worshipers (come into the true Church); but had not put on the robes of righteousness" (Bruce R. McConkie, *Doctrinal New Testament Commentary* 1:598). Only those who are actually righteous will be acceptable to God when Jesus Christ comes again (see Revelation 19:7-9).

14 For many are called, but few are chosen.

## JESUS IS QUESTIONED ABOUT PAYING TAXES TO CAESAR

15 ¶ Then went the Pharisees, and took counsel how they might entangle him in his talk.

16 And they sent out unto him their disciples with the Herodians, saying, Master, we know that thou art true, and teachest the way of God in truth, neither carest thou for any man: for thou regardest not the person of men.

17 Tell us therefore, What thinkest thou? Is it lawful to give tribute unto Caesar, or not?

18 But Jesus perceived their wickedness, and said, Why tempt ye me, ye hypocrites?

19 Shew me the tribute money. And they brought unto him a penny.

20 And he saith unto them, Whose is this image and superscription?

21 They say unto him, Caesar's. Then saith he unto them, Render therefore unto Caesar the things which are Caesar's; and unto God the things that are God's.

22 When they had heard these words, they marvelled, and left him, and went their way.

## JESUS IS QUESTIONED ABOUT MARRIAGE AND THE RESURRECTION

23 ¶ The same day came to him the Sadducees, which say that there is no resurrection, and asked him,

24 Saying, Master, Moses said, If a man die, having no children, his brother shall marry his wife, and raise up seed unto his brother.

25 Now there were with us seven brethren: and the first, when he had married a wife, deceased, and, having no issue, left his wife unto his brother:

26 Likewise the second also, and the third, unto the seventh.

27 And last of all the woman died also.

28 Therefore in the resurrection whose wife shall she be of the seven? for they all had her.

29 Jesus answered and said unto them, Ye do err, not knowing the scriptures, nor the power of God.

30 For in the resurrection they neither marry, nor are given in marriage, but are as the angels of God in heaven.

31 But as touching the resurrection of the dead, have ye not read that which was spoken unto you by God, saying,

32 I am the God of Abraham, and the God of Isaac, and the God of Jacob? God is not the God of the dead, but of the living.

33 And when the multitude heard this, they were astonished at his doctrine.

## JESUS IS QUESTIONED ABOUT THE GREATEST COMMANDMENT

34 ¶ But when the Pharisees had heard that he had put the Sadducees to silence, they were gathered together.

---

22:14 Jesus Christ has invited everyone to come unto him (see 2 Nephi 26:33). What are you doing about your invitation to come unto Christ?

22:15 *entangle*—trap

22:16 The Herodians were a group of Jews who wanted members of King Herod's family to be their rulers (see LDS Bible Dictionary, s.v. "Herodians," pp. 701-2).

*neither carest thou for any man*—that is to say, Jesus treated everyone the same. He didn't favor the rich or ignore the poor.

22:17 *give tribute unto Caesar*—pay taxes to the Romans.

22:17-21 The question the Herodians asked was meant to be a trap for Jesus. If he said the Jews should pay taxes to Rome, the Jews would be angry because they hated the Romans. If he said they should not pay, the Romans could arrest him for rebelling against their authority.

22:20 *image and superscription*—picture and title

22:25 *deceased*—died

*Caesar's Roman coin*

22:28 The Sadducees did not even believe in the resurrection (see verse 23), and they made up this story only to make fun of the idea of life after death.

22:30 Are there marriages in heaven? Marriages and families can last forever. Jesus said that people do not get married in the next life because marriages that continue after death must be performed by the holy priesthood here in this life (see D&C 132:15-19).

35 Then one of them, which was a lawyer, asked him a question, tempting him, and saying,

36 Master, which is the great commandment in the law?

37 Jesus said unto him, Thou shalt love the Lord thy God with all thy heart, and with all thy soul, and with all thy mind.

38 This is the first and great commandment.

39 And the second is like unto it, Thou shalt love thy neighbour as thyself.

40 On these two commandments hang all the law and the prophets.

## "WHAT THINK YE OF CHRIST?"

41 ¶ While the Pharisees were gathered together, Jesus asked them,

42 Saying, What think ye of Christ? whose son is he? They say unto him, The Son of David.

43 He saith unto them, How then doth David in spirit call him Lord, saying,

44 The LORD said unto my Lord, Sit thou on my right hand, till I make thine enemies thy footstool?

45 If David then call him Lord, how is he his son?

46 And no man was able to answer him a word, neither durst any man from that day forth ask him any more questions.

## CHAPTER 23

*The word* HYPOCRITE *usually means one who pretends to be religious when he is not. As you read this chapter, note how Jesus feels about hypocrites.*

### JESUS CONDEMNS THE SCRIBES AND PHARISEES

1 ¶ THEN spake Jesus to the multitude, and to his disciples,

2 Saying, The scribes and the Pharisees sit in Moses' seat:

3 All therefore whatsoever they bid you observe, that observe and do; but do not ye after their works: for they say, and do not.

4 For they bind heavy burdens and grievous to be borne, and lay them on men's shoulders; but they themselves will not move them with one of their fingers.

5 But all their works they do for to be seen of men: they make broad their phylacteries, and enlarge the borders of their garments,

---

22:35-40   The Pharisees also came to test Jesus by asking him which commandment was most important. Jesus gave the same answer he has given in all ages (see Deuteronomy 6:5; Leviticus 19:18; D&C 59:5-6).

22:40   **the law and the prophets**—the law of Moses and the teachings of the prophets of the Old Testament

How do you think the world would be different if everyone really loved God and if they loved others as much as they love themselves?

22:42-45   Christ is the son, or descendant, of David through his mother, Mary (see Matthew 1:1). But Jesus is also David's "Lord" because God is Jesus' father. Jesus Christ has the power to save us because he is the Son of God.

22:46   **durst**—dared

23:2   **Moses' seat**—an official chair in the Jewish synagogues that indicated judgment and instruction

23:3   The Joseph Smith Translation clarifies Jesus' statement to the multitude concerning the scribes and Pharisees: "All, therefore, whatsoever they bid you observe, they will make you observe and do; for they are ministers of the law, and they make themselves your judges" (JST, Matthew 23:2).

23:5   What does it mean to "make broad their phylacteries, and enlarge the borders of their garments"? Phylacteries were small leather boxes that contained strips of paper on which were written four passages of the law of Moses. These boxes were fastened by a leather strap to the forehead and to the left arm. This was done to remind the wearer of the duty of keeping the commands of God in the head and in the heart (see Exodus 13:9, 16). The Pharisees widened (made broad) their phylacteries as a show of their spirituality. For the same reason they enlarged the borders, or fringes, of the garments that Moses had commanded them to wear (see Numbers 15:38).

*Phylacteries are small boxes that contain scripture passages written on paper.*

6 And love the uppermost rooms at feasts, and the chief seats in the synagogues,

7 And greetings in the markets, and to be called of men, Rabbi, Rabbi.

8 But be not ye called Rabbi: for one is your Master, even Christ; and all ye are brethren.

9 And call no man your father upon the earth: for one is your Father, which is in heaven.

10 Neither be ye called masters: for one is your Master, even Christ.

11 But he that is greatest among you shall be your servant.

12 And whosoever shall exalt himself shall be abased; and he that shall humble himself shall be exalted.

13 ¶ But woe unto you, scribes and Pharisees, hypocrites! for ye shut up the kingdom of heaven against men: for ye neither go in yourselves, neither suffer ye them that are entering to go in.

14 Woe unto you, scribes and Pharisees, hypocrites! for ye devour widows' houses, and for a pretence make long prayer: therefore ye shall receive the greater damnation.

15 Woe unto you, scribes and Pharisees, hypocrites! for ye compass sea and land to make one proselyte, and when he is made, ye make him twofold more the child of hell than yourselves.

16 Woe unto you, ye blind guides, which say, Whosoever shall swear by the temple, it is nothing; but whosoever shall swear by the gold of the temple, he is a debtor!

17 Ye fools and blind: for whether is greater, the gold, or the temple that sanctifieth the gold?

18 And, Whosoever shall swear by the altar, it is nothing; but whosoever sweareth by the gift that is upon it, he is guilty.

19 Ye fools and blind: for whether is greater, the gift, or the altar that sanctifieth the gift?

20 Whoso therefore shall swear by the altar, sweareth by it, and by all things thereon.

21 And whoso shall swear by the temple, sweareth by it, and by him that dwelleth therein.

22 And he that shall swear by heaven, sweareth by the throne of God, and by him that sitteth thereon.

23 Woe unto you, scribes and Pharisees, hypocrites! for ye pay tithe of mint and anise and cummin, and have omitted the weightier matters of the law, judgment, mercy, and faith: these ought ye to have done, and not to leave the other undone.

24 Ye blind guides, which strain at a gnat, and swallow a camel.

25 Woe unto you, scribes and Pharisees, hypocrites! for ye make clean the outside of the cup and of the platter, but within they are full of extortion and excess.

26 Thou blind Pharisee, cleanse first that which is within the cup and platter, that the outside of them may be clean also.

27 Woe unto you, scribes and Pharisees, hypocrites! for ye are like unto whited sepulchres, which indeed appear beautiful outward, but are within full of dead men's bones, and of all uncleanness.

---

23:7  **Rabbi**—a title used by Jewish people to address their teachers

23:9  The Joseph Smith Translation changes this passage to read: "And call no one your creator upon the earth, or your heavenly Father; for one is your creator and heavenly Father, even he who is in heaven" (JST, Matthew 23:6).

23:13  **woe**—suffering or grief

23:14  **damnation**—condemnation

23:15  **compass**—go over

23:23  **mint and anise and cummin**—sweet-smelling but insignificant plants
**weightier matters**—more important things

23:23-29  Which is more important—what's on the inside or what's on the outside? "Lips can speak honeyed words while hearts are black and foul. These men could pay tithes and make gifts for show and pray on street corners in the stance of humility while stiff with pride." (Spencer W. Kimball, *Humility,* p. 6.)

23:24  Can you picture a person who strains a tiny insect out of a drink, only to end up swallowing a giant, filthy camel? Can you imagine a person who is afraid of making tiny and insignificant mistakes but couldn't care less about committing ugly and evil sins?

The Joseph Smith Translation adds an important phrase at the end of this passage: "who make yourselves appear unto men that ye would not commit the least sin, and yet ye yourselves, transgress the whole law" (JST, Matthew 23:21).

23:27  The phrase "whited sepulchres" refers to the whitewashed tombs of the Jews. This was done each year before the Passover, both to beautify them and to mark the spots so as to prevent anyone from passing over them and becoming "unclean" according to the Jews' interpretation of the law of Moses (see Numbers 19:16).

28 Even so ye also outwardly appear righteous unto men, but within ye are full of hypocrisy and iniquity.

29 Woe unto you, scribes and Pharisees, hypocrites! because ye build the tombs of the prophets, and garnish the sepulchres of the righteous,

30 And say, If we had been in the days of our fathers, we would not have been partakers with them in the blood of the prophets.

31 Wherefore ye be witnesses unto yourselves, that ye are the children of them which killed the prophets.

32 Fill ye up then the measure of your fathers.

33 Ye serpents, ye generation of vipers, how can ye escape the damnation of hell?

34 ¶ Wherefore, behold, I send unto you prophets, and wise men, and scribes: and some of them ye shall kill and crucify; and some of them shall ye scourge in your synagogues, and persecute them from city to city:

35 That upon you may come all the righteous blood shed upon the earth, from the blood of righteous Abel unto the blood of Zacharias son of Barachias, whom ye slew between the temple and the altar.

36 Verily I say unto you, All these things shall come upon this generation.

## JESUS MOURNS FOR JERUSALEM

37 O Jerusalem, Jerusalem, thou that killest the prophets, and stonest them which are sent unto thee, how often would I have gathered thy children together, even as a hen gathereth her chickens under her wings, and ye would not!

38 Behold, your house is left unto you desolate.

39 For I say unto you, Ye shall not see me henceforth, till ye shall say, Blessed is he that cometh in the name of the Lord.

## CHAPTER 24

*In this chapter Jesus tells his followers of awful destruction that will come in the future. As you read, look for the causes of these horrible events.*

### JERUSALEM AND THE TEMPLE WILL BE DESTROYED

1 ¶ AND Jesus went out, and departed from the temple: and his disciples came to him for to shew him the buildings of the temple.

---

23:28 **iniquity**—sin

23:33 **generation of vipers**—people who are dangerous like snakes

23:37 What does Jesus mean by saying, "How often would I have gathered thy children together, even as a hen gathereth her chickens under her wings, and ye would not"? How does a mother hen gather her little chicks? Could you imagine the baby chicks refusing to go to their mother? How and why would Heavenly Father's children refuse to gather together?

23:37-39 What was going to happen to Jerusalem? Like Jesus, Jerusalem would suffer indignities, anguish, and death (see D&C 45:18-19).

23:38 **desolate**—empty, lonely

When Jesus stated: "Your house is left unto you desolate," he may have been referring to the temple. In the next few verses, Matthew 24:1-2, Jesus declares concerning the temple: "There shall not be left here one stone upon another, that shall not be thrown down." This is a particularly sad prophecy when one considers that Jesus had earlier referred to the temple as his Father's house and even as his own house (see John 2:16 and Matthew 21:13).

*A view of Jerusalem today from the Mount of Olives*

2 And Jesus said unto them, See ye not all these things? verily I say unto you, There shall not be left here one stone upon another, that shall not be thrown down.

## CHURCH MEMBERS WILL BE HATED, PERSECUTED, AND DECEIVED

3 And as he sat upon the mount of Olives, the disciples came unto him privately, saying, Tell us, when shall these things be? and what shall be the sign of thy coming, and of the end of the world?

4 ¶ And Jesus answered and said unto them, Take heed that no man deceive you.

5 For many shall come in my name, saying, I am Christ; and shall deceive many.

6 And ye shall hear of wars and rumours of wars: see that ye be not troubled: for all these things must come to pass, but the end is not yet.

7 For nation shall rise against nation, and kingdom against kingdom: and there shall be famines, and pestilences, and earthquakes, in divers places.

8 All these are the beginning of sorrows.

9 Then shall they deliver you up to be afflicted, and shall kill you: and ye shall be hated of all nations for my name's sake.

10 And then shall many be offended, and shall betray one another, and shall hate one another.

11 And many false prophets shall rise, and shall deceive many.

12 And because iniquity shall abound, the love of many shall wax cold.

13 But he that shall endure unto the end, the same shall be saved.

14 And this gospel of the kingdom shall be preached in all the world for a witness unto all nations; and then shall the end come.

## STAND IN THE HOLY PLACE

15 When ye therefore shall see the abomination of desolation, spoken of by Daniel the prophet, stand in the holy place, (whoso readeth, let him understand:)

16 Then let them which be in Judaea flee into the mountains:

17 Let him which is on the housetop not come down to take any thing out of his house:

18 Neither let him which is in the field return back to take his clothes.

19 And woe unto them that are with child, and to them that give suck in those days!

20 But pray ye that your flight be not in the winter, neither on the sabbath day:

21 For then shall be great tribulation, such as was not since the beginning of the world to this time, no, nor ever shall be.

22 And except those days should be shortened, there should no flesh be saved: but for the elect's sake those days shall be shortened.

---

24:2 In a revelation to Joseph Smith in which the Lord repeated the message given to the Twelve Apostles anciently, Jesus said that the destruction of the temple would come suddenly like a thief in the night (see D&C 45:15-21).

24:3 The Joseph Smith Translation explains that "the end of the world" means "the destruction of the wicked" (JST, Matthew 24:4).

24:4 *deceive you*—lead you away from the truth

24:7 *pestilences*—diseases
*divers*—several

24:12 *iniquity shall abound*—wickedness and sin will increase

24:14 The manner in which the material of Matthew 24 is organized in the Joseph Smith Translation helps us understand that this passage refers to the restoration of the gospel and of the Church in the last days (see JST, Matthew 24:32).

Who is responsible to preach the gospel "in all the world for a witness unto all nations"? What can you do now to teach the gospel to others?

24:15 Speaking to the Old Testament prophet Daniel, a messenger from the Lord warned of a day when there would come "the abomination that maketh desolate" (Daniel 11:31; 12:11). An abomination is something that is horrible and wicked. Desolation is ruin and destruction. The Savior warned that some horrible events, brought on by wickedness, would happen at Jerusalem.

"The counsel that the saints should then 'stand in the holy place' means that they should assemble together where they could receive prophetic guidance" (Bruce R. McConkie, *The Mortal Messiah* 3:430).

24:21 *tribulation*—trial and trouble

24:22 The elect are the faithful Saints who hear the Lord's voice and follow him (see D&C 29:7).

## Many Will Be Deceived Before the Second Coming of Jesus Christ

23 Then if any man shall say unto you, Lo, here is Christ, or there; believe it not.

24 For there shall arise false Christs, and false prophets, and shall shew great signs and wonders; insomuch that, if it were possible, they shall deceive the very elect.

25 Behold, I have told you before.

26 Wherefore if they shall say unto you, Behold, he is in the desert; go not forth: behold, he is in the secret chambers; believe it not.

## Jesus Christ Will Come Again in Great Power and Glory

27 For as the lightning cometh out of the east, and shineth even unto the west; so shall also the coming of the Son of man be.

28 For wheresoever the carcase is, there will the eagles be gathered together.

29 Immediately after the tribulation of those days shall the sun be darkened, and the moon shall not give her light, and the stars shall fall from heaven, and the powers of the heavens shall be shaken:

30 And then shall appear the sign of the Son of man in heaven: and then shall all the tribes of the earth mourn, and they shall see the Son of man coming in the clouds of heaven with power and great glory.

31 And he shall send his angels with a great sound of a trumpet, and they shall gather together his elect from the four winds, from one end of heaven to the other.

32 ¶ Now learn a parable of the fig tree; When his branch is yet tender, and putteth forth leaves, ye know that summer is nigh:

33 So likewise ye, when ye shall see all these things, know that it is near, even at the doors.

34 Verily I say unto you, This generation shall not pass, till all these things be fulfilled.

35 Heaven and earth shall pass away, but my words shall not pass away.

## When Shall Jesus Christ Come Again?

36 But of that day and hour knoweth no man, no, not the angels of heaven, but my Father only.

37 But as the days of Noe were, so shall also the coming of the Son of man be.

38 For as in the days that were before the flood they were eating and drinking, marrying and giving in marriage, until the day that Noe entered into the ark,

39 And knew not until the flood came, and took them all away; so shall also the coming of the Son of man be.

40 Then shall two be in the field; the one shall be taken, and the other left.

41 Two women shall be grinding at the mill; the one shall be taken, and the other left.

---

24:24    Elder Harold B. Lee taught: "Unless every member of this church gains for himself an unshakable testimony of the divinity of this church, he will be among those who will be deceived" (*The Teachings of Harold B. Lee*, p. 132).

24:27    The Joseph Smith Translation changes this verse to say: "For as the light of the morning cometh out of the east, and shineth even unto the west, and covereth the whole earth; so shall also the coming of the Son of man be."

24:28    This verse tells of the gathering of Israel in the last days. "The carcass is the body of the Church to which the eagles, who are Israel, shall fly to find nourishment" (Bruce R. McConkie, *Doctrinal New Testament Commentary* 1:648).

24:29    The Joseph Smith Translation helps us under-stand that the signs given in this verse will be fulfilled in the very last days, just prior to the second coming of Jesus Christ (see JST, Matthew 24:33-36).

24:30    What is the "sign of the Son of man"? According to the Prophet Joseph Smith, when this sign appears in the heavens many "will say it is a planet, a comet, &c. But the Son of Man will come as the sign of the coming of the Son of Man, which will be as the light of the morning cometh out of the east." When this sign is given, however, it will be known to and identified by the prophet of God on earth. (See *The Teachings of Joseph Smith*, pp. 624, 633.)

24:31    **from the four winds**—from every direction

24:36    Although no man knows the day nor the hour of the Savior's return, "whoso treasureth up [the] word, shall not be deceived" (Joseph Smith—Matthew 1:37).

24:37    "As it [the Flood] was a real drowning, there will be a real burning at this next great event when the end of the world comes, and the wicked will be burned" (*The Teachings of Spencer W. Kimball*, p. 441).

24:41    **grinding at the mill**—making grain into flour

42 Watch therefore: for ye know not what hour your Lord doth come.

43 But know this, that if the goodman of the house had known in what watch the thief would come, he would have watched, and would not have suffered his house to be broken up.

44 Therefore be ye also ready: for in such an hour as ye think not the Son of man cometh.

### JESUS SPEAKS OF THE FAITHFUL SERVANT AND THE EVIL SERVANT

45 Who then is a faithful and wise servant, whom his lord hath made ruler over his household, to give them meat in due season?

46 Blessed is that servant, whom his lord when he cometh shall find so doing.

47 Verily I say unto you, That he shall make him ruler over all his goods.

48 But and if that evil servant shall say in his heart, My lord delayeth his coming;

49 And shall begin to smite his fellowservants, and to eat and drink with the drunken;

50 The lord of that servant shall come in a day when he looketh not for him, and in an hour that he is not aware of,

51 And shall cut him asunder, and appoint him his portion with the hypocrites: there shall be weeping and gnashing of teeth.

## CHAPTER 25

*In this chapter Jesus tells three parables and includes teachings on how to prepare for his second coming. See what the Savior says you can do to prepare for his second coming.*

### JESUS GIVES THE PARABLE OF THE TEN VIRGINS

1 ¶ THEN shall the kingdom of heaven be likened unto ten virgins, which took their lamps, and went forth to meet the bridegroom.

2 And five of them were wise, and five were foolish.

3 They that were foolish took their lamps, and took no oil with them:

4 But the wise took oil in their vessels with their lamps.

5 While the bridegroom tarried, they all slumbered and slept.

6 And at midnight there was a cry made, Behold, the bridegroom cometh; go ye out to meet him.

---

24:42 Why would Heavenly Father want you to always be prepared for the second coming of Jesus Christ?

24:43 **goodman of the house**—owner of the house
**in what watch**—in what time of the night

24:44 How can we prepare and be "ready" for the second coming of Jesus?

24:45 **meat in due season**—food at the proper time

24:49 **smite**—hit

24:51 **cut him asunder**—cut him in two or cut him off, meaning to punish him severely
**appoint him his portion**—assign him his place
**weeping and gnashing of teeth**—crying and great sorrow

25:1 The Joseph Smith Translation adds some important words at the beginning of this parable: "And then, at that day, before the Son of man comes, the kingdom of heaven shall be likened unto ten virgins . . ."

25:1-13 The Lord told Joseph Smith that this parable was about His second coming. He described the

*An oil lamp*

wise virgins who had oil as members of the Church who had "received the truth" and "taken the Holy Spirit for their guide" (D&C 45:56-57).

25:1 A "bridegroom" was a man engaged to be or already married. In this case the word is used to refer to Jesus Christ and his covenants with members of his church.

25:5 **tarried**—was slow in coming

7 Then all those virgins arose, and trimmed their lamps.

8 And the foolish said unto the wise, Give us of your oil; for our lamps are gone out.

9 But the wise answered, saying, Not so; lest there be not enough for us and you: but go ye rather to them that sell, and buy for yourselves.

10 And while they went to buy, the bridegroom came; and they that were ready went in with him to the marriage: and the door was shut.

11 Afterward came also the other virgins, saying, Lord, Lord, open to us.

12 But he answered and said, Verily I say unto you, I know you not.

13 Watch therefore, for ye know neither the day nor the hour wherein the Son of man cometh.

## JESUS GIVES THE PARABLE OF THE TALENTS

14 ¶ For the kingdom of heaven is as a man travelling into a far country, who called his own servants, and delivered unto them his goods.

15 And unto one he gave five talents, to another two, and to another one; to every man according to his several ability; and straightway took his journey.

16 Then he that had received the five talents went and traded with the same, and made them other five talents.

17 And likewise he that had received two, he also gained other two.

18 But he that had received one went and digged in the earth, and hid his lord's money.

19 After a long time the lord of those servants cometh, and reckoneth with them.

20 And so he that had received five talents came and brought other five talents, saying, Lord, thou deliveredst unto me five talents: behold, I have gained beside them five talents more.

21 His lord said unto him, Well done, thou good and faithful servant: thou hast been faithful over a few things, I will make thee ruler over many things: enter thou into the joy of thy lord.

22 He also that had received two talents came and said, Lord, thou deliveredst unto me two talents: behold, I have gained two other talents beside them.

23 His lord said unto him, Well done, good and faithful servant; thou hast been faithful over a few things, I will make thee ruler over many things: enter thou into the joy of thy lord.

24 Then he which had received the one talent came and said, Lord, I knew thee that thou art an hard man, reaping where thou hast not sown, and gathering where thou hast not strawed:

25 And I was afraid, and went and hid thy talent in the earth: lo, there thou hast that is thine.

26 His lord answered and said unto him, Thou wicked and slothful servant, thou knewest that I reap where I sowed not, and gather where I have not strawed:

27 Thou oughtest therefore to have put my money to the exchangers, and then at my coming I should have received mine own with usury.

28 Take therefore the talent from him, and give it unto him which hath ten talents.

29 For unto every one that hath shall be given, and he shall have abundance: but from him that hath not shall be taken away even that which he hath.

30 And cast ye the unprofitable servant into outer

---

25:7 *trimmed their lamps*—prepared their lamps for lighting

25:12 The Joseph Smith Translation changes this passage to read: "But he answered and said, Verily I say unto you, Ye know me not."

25:13 Jesus Christ has promised he will come again one day. When he does, everyone will be judged and the wicked will be sent away. But, according to D&C 45:57, "they that are wise and have received the truth, and have taken the Holy Spirit for their guide, and have not been deceived—verily I say unto you, they shall not be hewn down and cast into the fire, but shall abide the day." When Jesus Christ comes again, will you be among the wise? How can you prepare now?

25:15 *talents*—A talent is an amount of money, one talent being equal to more than a thousand dollars in today's currency.

25:19 *reckoneth with them*—asked them to tell what they had done with their talents

25:26 *slothful*—lazy

25:27 *exchangers*—bankers
*usury*—interest

Notice how pleased the Lord was with those who increased their talents. If talents are compared to gifts, how can you improve upon and increase your gifts from the Lord?

25:30 *unprofitable*—useless

darkness: there shall be weeping and gnashing of teeth.

## JESUS GIVES THE PARABLE OF THE SHEEP AND THE GOATS

31 ¶ When the Son of man shall come in his glory, and all the holy angels with him, then shall he sit upon the throne of his glory:

32 And before him shall be gathered all nations: and he shall separate them one from another, as a shepherd divideth his sheep from the goats:

33 And he shall set the sheep on his right hand, but the goats on the left.

34 Then shall the King say unto them on his right hand, Come, ye blessed of my Father, inherit the kingdom prepared for you from the foundation of the world:

35 For I was an hungred, and ye gave me meat: I was thirsty, and ye gave me drink: I was a stranger, and ye took me in:

36 Naked, and ye clothed me: I was sick, and ye visited me: I was in prison, and ye came unto me.

37 Then shall the righteous answer him, saying, Lord, when saw we thee an hungred, and fed thee? or thirsty, and gave thee drink?

38 When saw we thee a stranger, and took thee in? or naked, and clothed thee?

39 Or when saw we thee sick, or in prison, and came unto thee?

40 And the King shall answer and say unto them, Verily I say unto you, Inasmuch as ye have done it unto one of the least of these my brethren, ye have done it unto me.

41 Then shall he say also unto them on the left hand, Depart from me, ye cursed, into everlasting fire, prepared for the devil and his angels:

42 For I was an hungred, and ye gave me no meat: I was thirsty, and ye gave me no drink:

43 I was a stranger, and ye took me not in: naked, and ye clothed me not: sick, and in prison, and ye visited me not.

44 Then shall they also answer him, saying, Lord, when saw we thee an hungred, or athirst, or a stranger, or naked, or sick, or in prison, and did not minister unto thee?

45 Then shall he answer them, saying, Verily I say unto you, Inasmuch as ye did it not to one of the least of these, ye did it not to me.

46 And these shall go away into everlasting punishment: but the righteous into life eternal.

## CHAPTER 26

*What Jesus did for us in Gethsemane and on the cross is the most important thing that has ever happened. As you read this chapter, look for how aware Jesus was of his approaching suffering and crucifixion.*

## A PLOT IS FORMED TO BETRAY AND KILL JESUS

1 ¶ AND it came to pass, when Jesus had finished all these sayings, he said unto his disciples,

2 Ye know that after two days is the feast of the passover, and the Son of man is betrayed to be crucified.

3 Then assembled together the chief priests, and the scribes, and the elders of the people, unto the palace of the high priest, who was called Caiaphas,

4 And consulted that they might take Jesus by subtilty, and kill him.

5 But they said, Not on the feast day, lest there be an uproar among the people.

6 ¶ Now when Jesus was in Bethany, in the house of Simon the leper,

---

25:33 The sheep, who represent the righteous, are placed at the right hand, the place of honor.

25:35-40 Jesus taught that when we help others we are really helping him (see King Benjamin's similar teaching in Mosiah 2:17).

25:40 Who was the last person you helped? If helping others is like serving Jesus, why is it important to help others often?

26:2 The yearly Feast of the Passover reminded Israel how the Lord "passed over" their ancestors' homes and spared the firstborn of the Israelites while the firstborn of the Egyptians died. It also reminded them how the Lord delivered their ancestors from slavery in Egypt. (See Exodus 12:3-14.) The lamb that was killed each Passover was to remind the people that a Savior would someday come to deliver them. Why do you think Heavenly Father allowed Jesus Christ, "the Lamb of God," to be crucified during the time of Passover?

26:3 Caiaphas was a wicked high priest who helped in the plot to kill Jesus Christ.

26:4 *by subtilty*—in secret and with trickery

7 There came unto him a woman having an alabaster box of very precious ointment, and poured it on his head, as he sat at meat.

8 But when his disciples saw it, they had indignation, saying, To what purpose is this waste?

9 For this ointment might have been sold for much, and given to the poor.

10 When Jesus understood it, he said unto them, Why trouble ye the woman? for she hath wrought a good work upon me.

11 For ye have the poor always with you; but me ye have not always.

12 For in that she hath poured this ointment on my body, she did it for my burial.

13 Verily I say unto you, Wheresoever this gospel shall be preached in the whole world, there shall also this, that this woman hath done, be told for a memorial of her.

14 ¶ Then one of the twelve, called Judas Iscariot, went unto the chief priests,

15 And said unto them, What will ye give me, and I will deliver him unto you? And they covenanted with him for thirty pieces of silver.

16 And from that time he sought opportunity to betray him.

## THE LAST SUPPER IS HELD

17 ¶ Now the first day of the feast of unleavened bread the disciples came to Jesus, saying unto him, Where wilt thou that we prepare for thee to eat the passover?

18 And he said, Go into the city to such a man, and say unto him, The Master saith, My time is at hand; I will keep the passover at thy house with my disciples.

19 And the disciples did as Jesus had appointed them; and they made ready the passover.

20 Now when the even was come, he sat down with the twelve.

21 And as they did eat, he said, Verily I say unto you, that one of you shall betray me.

22 And they were exceeding sorrowful, and began every one of them to say unto him, Lord, is it I?

23 And he answered and said, He that dippeth his hand with me in the dish, the same shall betray me.

24 The Son of man goeth as it is written of him: but woe unto that man by whom the Son of man is betrayed! it had been good for that man if he had not been born.

25 Then Judas, which betrayed him, answered and said, Master, is it I? He said unto him, Thou hast said.

26 ¶ And as they were eating, Jesus took bread, and blessed it, and brake it, and gave it to the disciples, and said, Take, eat; this is my body.

27 And he took the cup, and gave thanks, and gave it to them, saying, Drink ye all of it;

28 For this is my blood of the new testament, which is shed for many for the remission of sins.

29 But I say unto you, I will not drink henceforth of this fruit of the vine, until that day when I drink it new with you in my Father's kingdom.

30 And when they had sung an hymn, they went out into the mount of Olives.

31 ¶ Then saith Jesus unto them, All ye shall be offended because of me this night: for it is written, I will smite the shepherd, and the sheep of the flock shall be scattered abroad.

---

26:7 This ointment was an expensive perfume. Pouring it upon the Savior's head was an act of love, respect, and honor.

26:8 *they had indignation*—they were upset

26:10 *wrought*—done

26:13 *for a memorial of her*—in memory of her

26:15 Thirty pieces of silver was the common price of a slave. How does it make you feel to know that Judas turned against Jesus for thirty pieces of silver?

26:17 The Feast of Unleavened Bread took place immediately after the Feast of the Passover, and the two feasts were often considered as one. The Feast of Unleavened Bread commemorated the exodus of Israel out of Egypt. (See Exodus 12 and Leviticus 23:5-6.)

26:23-25 Jesus knew that Judas would be the one to betray him.

26:26 The Joseph Smith Translation changes "this is my body" to "this is in remembrance of my body."

26:26-28 The sacrament was served for the first time at the Last Supper. What did Jesus say the bread and drink represented? Whom should we think about during the sacrament? Notice that Jesus said he would be giving his life for the remission of sins—in other words, he would die so that we could be forgiven of all our sins.

26:28 *new testament*—new covenant

26:29 *fruit of the vine*—wine

*The Last Supper*

32 But after I am risen again, I will go before you into Galilee.

33 Peter answered and said unto him, Though all men shall be offended because of thee, yet will I never be offended.

34 Jesus said unto him, Verily I say unto thee, That this night, before the cock crow, thou shalt deny me thrice.

35 Peter said unto him, Though I should die with thee, yet will I not deny thee. Likewise also said all the disciples.

## JESUS SUFFERS IN THE GARDEN OF GETHSEMANE

36 ¶ Then cometh Jesus with them unto a place called Gethsemane, and saith unto the disciples, Sit ye here, while I go and pray yonder.

37 And he took with him Peter and the two sons of Zebedee, and began to be sorrowful and very heavy.

38 Then saith he unto them, My soul is exceeding sorrowful, even unto death: tarry ye here, and watch with me.

39 And he went a little further, and fell on his face, and prayed, saying, O my Father, if it be possible, let this cup pass from me: nevertheless not as I will, but as thou wilt.

40 And he cometh unto the disciples, and findeth them asleep, and saith unto Peter, What, could ye not watch with me one hour?

41 Watch and pray, that ye enter not into temptation: the spirit indeed is willing, but the flesh is weak.

42 He went away again the second time, and prayed, saying, O my Father, if this cup may not pass away from me, except I drink it, thy will be done.

43 And he came and found them asleep again: for their eyes were heavy.

44 And he left them, and went away again, and prayed the third time, saying the same words.

45 Then cometh he to his disciples, and saith unto them, Sleep on now, and take your rest: behold, the hour is at hand, and the Son of man is betrayed into the hands of sinners.

46 Rise, let us be going: behold, he is at hand that doth betray me.

## JESUS CHRIST IS BETRAYED BY JUDAS

47 ¶ And while he yet spake, lo, Judas, one of the twelve, came, and with him a great multitude with swords and staves, from the chief priests and elders of the people.

48 Now he that betrayed him gave them a sign, saying, Whomsoever I shall kiss, that same is he: hold him fast.

49 And forthwith he came to Jesus, and said, Hail, master; and kissed him.

50 And Jesus said unto him, Friend, wherefore art thou come? Then came they, and laid hands on Jesus, and took him.

51 And, behold, one of them which were with Jesus stretched out his hand, and drew his sword, and struck a servant of the high priest's, and smote off his ear.

52 Then said Jesus unto him, Put up again thy sword into his place: for all they that take the sword shall perish with the sword.

53 Thinkest thou that I cannot now pray to my Father, and he shall presently give me more than twelve legions of angels?

---

26:34 *thrice*—three times

*The Garden of Gethsemane*

26:37-38 Can you find the words that describe how difficult Christ's suffering was?

26:39 To do someone's "will" is to do what that person wants. Whose will did Jesus do? Whose will should you obey? President Howard W. Hunter gave some advice that will help: "We should at every opportunity ask ourselves, 'What would Jesus do?' and then be more courageous to act upon the answer" (*The Teachings of Howard W. Hunter*, p. 43).

26:53 Jesus could have called many legions, or armies, of angels to save him. But he knew he must be taken and killed in order to fulfill Heavenly Father's plan so that we could be saved in heaven.

54 But how then shall the scriptures be fulfilled, that thus it must be?

55 In that same hour said Jesus to the multitudes, Are ye come out as against a thief with swords and staves for to take me? I sat daily with you teaching in the temple, and ye laid no hold on me.

56 But all this was done, that the scriptures of the prophets might be fulfilled. Then all the disciples forsook him, and fled.

### Jesus Is Arrested and Put on Trial

57 ¶ And they that had laid hold on Jesus led him away to Caiaphas the high priest, where the scribes and the elders were assembled.

58 But Peter followed him afar off unto the high priest's palace, and went in, and sat with the servants, to see the end.

59 Now the chief priests, and elders, and all the council, sought false witness against Jesus, to put him to death;

60 But found none: yea, though many false witnesses came, yet found they none. At the last came two false witnesses,

61 And said, This fellow said, I am able to destroy the temple of God, and to build it in three days.

62 And the high priest arose, and said unto him, Answerest thou nothing? what is it which these witness against thee?

63 But Jesus held his peace. And the high priest answered and said unto him, I adjure thee by the living God, that thou tell us whether thou be the Christ, the Son of God.

64 Jesus saith unto him, Thou hast said: nevertheless I say unto you, Hereafter shall ye see the Son of man sitting on the right hand of power, and coming in the clouds of heaven.

65 Then the high priest rent his clothes, saying, He hath spoken blasphemy; what further need have we of witnesses? behold, now ye have heard his blasphemy.

66 What think ye? They answered and said, He is guilty of death.

67 Then did they spit in his face, and buffeted him; and others smote him with the palms of their hands,

68 Saying, Prophesy unto us, thou Christ, Who is he that smote thee?

### Peter Denies Knowing Jesus Christ

69 ¶ Now Peter sat without in the palace: and a damsel came unto him, saying, Thou also wast with Jesus of Galilee.

70 But he denied before them all, saying, I know not what thou sayest.

71 And when he was gone out into the porch, another maid saw him, and said unto them that were there, This fellow was also with Jesus of Nazareth.

72 And again he denied with an oath, I do not know the man.

73 And after a while came unto him they that stood by, and said to Peter, Surely thou also art one of them; for thy speech bewrayeth thee.

74 Then began he to curse and to swear, saying, I know not the man. And immediately the cock crew.

75 And Peter remembered the word of Jesus, which said unto him, Before the cock crow, thou shalt deny me thrice. And he went out, and wept bitterly.

## CHAPTER 27

*As you read, notice the ways different people reacted to Jesus' trials and crucifixion. Which people showed their love for Jesus even after he died?*

### Judas Hangs Himself

1 ¶ WHEN the morning was come, all the chief priests and elders of the people took counsel against Jesus to put him to death:

2 And when they had bound him, they led him away, and delivered him to Pontius Pilate the governor.

3 Then Judas, which had betrayed him, when he saw that he was condemned, repented himself, and brought again the thirty pieces of silver to the chief priests and elders,

4 Saying, I have sinned in that I have betrayed the innocent blood. And they said, What is that to us? see thou to that.

---

26:63  *adjure thee*—command you under oath

26:65  *rent*—tore

26:67  *buffeted*—struck

26:73  *bewrayeth thee*—reveals you

26:74  *cock crew*—rooster crowed

27:2  By Roman law, the Jews did not have authority to put anyone to death. In order to have Jesus crucified, the Jews had to take him to Pontius Pilate, the Roman governor.

27:4  *see thou to that*—that is your problem

5 And he cast down the pieces of silver in the temple, and departed, and went and hanged himself.

6 And the chief priests took the silver pieces, and said, It is not lawful for to put them into the treasury, because it is the price of blood.

7 And they took counsel, and bought with them the potter's field, to bury strangers in.

8 Wherefore that field was called, The field of blood, unto this day.

9 Then was fulfilled that which was spoken by Jeremy the prophet, saying, And they took the thirty pieces of silver, the price of him that was valued, whom they of the children of Israel did value;

10 And gave them for the potter's field, as the Lord appointed me.

## JESUS IS TRIED BEFORE PILATE

11 ¶ And Jesus stood before the governor: and the governor asked him, saying, Art thou the King of the Jews? And Jesus said unto him, Thou sayest

12 And when he was accused of the chief priests and elders, he answered nothing.

13 Then said Pilate unto him, Hearest thou not how many things they witness against thee?

14 And he answered him to never a word; insomuch that the governor marvelled greatly.

15 Now at that feast the governor was wont to release unto the people a prisoner, whom they would.

16 And they had then a notable prisoner, called Barabbas.

17 Therefore when they were gathered together, Pilate said unto them, Whom will ye that I release unto you? Barabbas, or Jesus which is called Christ?

18 For he knew that for envy they had delivered him.

19 When he was set down on the judgment seat, his wife sent unto him, saying, Have thou nothing to do with that just man: for I have suffered many things this day in a dream because of him.

20 But the chief priests and elders persuaded the multitude that they should ask Barabbas, and destroy Jesus.

21 The governor answered and said unto them, Whether of the twain will ye that I release unto you? They said, Barabbas.

22 Pilate saith unto them, What shall I do then with Jesus which is called Christ? They all say unto him, Let him be crucified.

23 And the governor said, Why, what evil hath he done? But they cried out the more, saying, Let him be crucified.

24 When Pilate saw that he could prevail nothing, but that rather a tumult was made, he took water, and washed his hands before the multitude, saying, I am innocent of the blood of this just person: see ye to it.

25 Then answered all the people, and said, His blood be on us, and on our children.

26 ¶ Then released he Barabbas unto them: and when he had scourged Jesus, he delivered him to be crucified.

## THE SOLDIERS ABUSE JESUS

27 Then the soldiers of the governor took Jesus into the common hall, and gathered unto him the whole band of soldiers.

28 And they stripped him, and put on him a scarlet robe.

29 And when they had platted a crown of thorns, they put it upon his head, and a reed in his right hand: and they bowed the knee before him, and mocked him, saying, Hail, King of the Jews!

30 And they spit upon him, and took the reed, and smote him on the head.

31 And after that they had mocked him, they took the robe off from him, and put his own raiment on him, and led him away to crucify him.

---

27:11 **Thou sayest**—I am just what you say

27:15 **the governor was wont**—it was the governor's custom

27:18 **for envy they had delivered him**—Jesus was arrested because the Jewish leaders were jealous of him

27:21 **Whether of the twain**—Which of the two

27:24 **tumult**—riot

27:25 When the Jews cried out, "His blood be on us, and on our children," they had no idea how horrible the results would be. Less than forty years later Jerusalem was destroyed, thousands were killed, and the remaining Jews were scattered. (See 2 Nephi 10:3-6.)

27:28-31 Why did Jesus allow himself to be so abused and then crucified? (See Alma 7:11-13.) What does this teach you about his love for you personally?

27:29 **platted**—twisted together or woven

*Christ and Pilate*

## JESUS IS CRUCIFIED

32 And as they came out, they found a man of Cyrene, Simon by name: him they compelled to bear his cross.

33 ¶ And when they were come unto a place called Golgotha, that is to say, a place of a skull,

34 They gave him vinegar to drink mingled with gall: and when he had tasted thereof, he would not drink.

35 And they crucified him, and parted his garments, casting lots: that it might be fulfilled which was spoken by the prophet, They parted my garments among them, and upon my vesture did they cast lots.

36 And sitting down they watched him there;

37 And set up over his head his accusation written, THIS IS JESUS THE KING OF THE JEWS.

38 Then were there two thieves crucified with him, one on the right hand, and another on the left.

39 And they that passed by reviled him, wagging their heads,

40 And saying, Thou that destroyest the temple, and buildest it in three days, save thyself. If thou be the Son of God, come down from the cross.

41 Likewise also the chief priests mocking him, with the scribes and elders, said,

42 He saved others; himself he cannot save. If he be the King of Israel, let him now come down from the cross, and we will believe him.

43 He trusted in God; let him deliver him now, if he will have him: for he said, I am the Son of God.

44 The thieves also, which were crucified with him, cast the same in his teeth.

45 Now from the sixth hour there was darkness over all the land unto the ninth hour.

46 And about the ninth hour Jesus cried with a loud voice, saying, Eli, Eli, lama sabachthani? that is to say, My God, my God, why hast thou forsaken me?

47 Some of them that stood there, when they heard that, said, This man calleth for Elias.

48 And straightway one of them ran, and took a spunge, and filled it with vinegar, and put it on a reed, and gave him to drink.

49 The rest said, Let be, let us see whether Elias will come to save him.

50 ¶ Jesus, when he had cried again with a loud voice, yielded up the ghost.

51 And, behold, the veil of the temple was rent in twain from the top to the bottom; and the earth did quake, and the rocks rent;

52 And the graves were opened; and many bodies of the saints which slept arose,

53 And came out of the graves after his resurrection, and went into the holy city, and appeared unto many.

54 Now when the centurion, and they that were with him, watching Jesus, saw the earthquake, and those things that were done, they feared greatly, saying, Truly this was the Son of God.

55 And many women were there beholding afar off, which followed Jesus from Galilee, ministering unto him:

56 Among which was Mary Magdalene, and Mary the mother of James and Joses, and the mother of Zebedee's children.

## JESUS IS BURIED

57 ¶ When the even was come, there came a rich man of Arimathaea, named Joseph, who also himself was Jesus' disciple:

---

27:34 **vinegar . . . mingled with gall**—a pain-killing drug

27:35 Just as was prophesied in Psalm 22:18, the soldiers gambled over who would get Jesus' clothing.

27:39 **reviled him, wagging their heads**—insulted and mocked him, shaking their heads

27:40-42 These men used the same mocking words, "If thou be the Son of God," that the devil used when he tried to tempt Jesus as recorded in Matthew 4:3, 6. Would they really have been converted if Jesus had come down from the cross?

27:44 **cast the same in his teeth**—insulted him with the same words

27:45 The twelve daylight hours for the Jews began at sunrise. The sixth hour was twelve noon, and the ninth hour was three P.M.

27:50 The Joseph Smith Translation shows that just before he died, Jesus said, "Father it is finished, thy will is done" (JST, Matthew 27:54).

27:51 **rent in twain**—torn in two

27:52-53 After Jesus' resurrection many righteous people who had died were also resurrected. They showed themselves to many of the faithful in Jerusalem as proof of the resurrection. (See also 3 Nephi 23:9-11.)

58 He went to Pilate, and begged the body of Jesus. Then Pilate commanded the body to be delivered.

59 And when Joseph had taken the body, he wrapped it in a clean linen cloth,

60 And laid it in his own new tomb, which he had hewn out in the rock: and he rolled a great stone to the door of the sepulchre, and departed.

61 And there was Mary Magdalene, and the other Mary, sitting over against the sepulchre.

## SOLDIERS GUARD THE TOMB

62 Now the next day, that followed the day of the preparation, the chief priests and Pharisees came together unto Pilate,

63 Saying, Sir, we remember that that deceiver said, while he was yet alive, After three days I will rise again.

64 Command therefore that the sepulchre be made sure until the third day, lest his disciples come by night, and steal him away, and say unto the people, He is risen from the dead: so the last error shall be worse than the first.

65 Pilate said unto them, Ye have a watch: go your way, make it as sure as ye can.

66 So they went, and made the sepulchre sure, sealing the stone, and setting a watch.

## CHAPTER 28

*One of the greatest events in all history was the resurrection of Jesus Christ. Because of his resurrection, all of us will live again with glorious resurrected bodies. Enjoy reading about this beautiful part of the gospel and the events surrounding it.*

### HE IS RISEN!

1 ¶ IN the end of the sabbath, as it began to dawn toward the first day of the week, came Mary Magdalene and the other Mary to see the sepulchre.

2 And, behold, there was a great earthquake: for the angel of the Lord descended from heaven, and came and rolled back the stone from the door, and sat upon it.

3 His countenance was like lightning, and his raiment white as snow:

4 And for fear of him the keepers did shake, and became as dead men.

5 And the angel answered and said unto the women, Fear not ye: for I know that ye seek Jesus, which was crucified.

6 He is not here: for he is risen, as he said. Come, see the place where the Lord lay.

7 And go quickly, and tell his disciples that he is risen from the dead; and, behold, he goeth before you into

---

27:60 **tomb**—burial place for the dead

**sepulchre**—burial place for the dead (same Greek word as *tomb*)

*Jesus was buried in a tomb similar to this one. A stone like the one seen here was placed in front of the opening.*

27:64 **be made sure**—be made secure

27:66 **setting a watch**—placing soldiers to guard the tomb

28:1 Why is "the first day of the week" so important? "Because Jesus came forth from the grave on the first day of the week, to commemorate [honor] that day and to keep in remembrance the glorious reality of the resurrection, the ancient apostles, as guided by the Spirit, changed the Sabbath to Sunday" (Bruce R. McConkie, *Doctrinal New Testament Commentary* 1:841).

28:2 The Joseph Smith Translation says "two angels" descended from heaven.

28:4 **keepers**—guards

*Three women at the tomb*

Galilee; there shall ye see him: lo, I have told you.

8 And they departed quickly from the sepulchre with fear and great joy; and did run to bring his disciples word.

## WOMEN SEE THE RESURRECTED LORD

9 And as they went to tell his disciples, behold, Jesus met them, saying, All hail. And they came and held him by the feet, and worshipped him.

10 Then said Jesus unto them, Be not afraid: go tell my brethren that they go into Galilee, and there shall they see me.

## THE SOLDIERS ACCEPT BRIBES

11 ¶ Now when they were going, behold, some of the watch came into the city, and shewed unto the chief priests all the things that were done.

12 And when they were assembled with the elders, and had taken counsel, they gave large money unto the soldiers,

13 Saying, Say ye, His disciples came by night, and stole him away while we slept.

14 And if this come to the governor's ears, we will persuade him, and secure you.

15 So they took the money, and did as they were taught: and this saying is commonly reported among the Jews until this day.

## THE APOSTLES ARE SENT TO ALL THE WORLD

16 ¶ Then the eleven disciples went away into Galilee, into a mountain where Jesus had appointed them.

17 And when they saw him, they worshipped him: but some doubted.

18 And Jesus came and spake unto them, saying, All power is given unto me in heaven and in earth.

19 Go ye therefore, and teach all nations, baptizing them in the name of the Father, and of the Son, and of the Holy Ghost:

20 Teaching them to observe all things whatsoever I have commanded you: and, lo, I am with you alway, even unto the end of the world. Amen.

---

28:9 *All hail*—Greetings! or Rejoice!

28:9-10 The first mortals to see the resurrected Jesus were women. How important are women in Heavenly Father's plan? How would you have felt if you had been in their place?

28:11 *watch*—guards
*shewed*—This word is pronounced the same way as the word *showed* and has the same meaning; *shewed* is simply an old spelling of *showed*.

28:13 If the guards had been asleep, how would they know what happened to the Savior's body? Why would they say that people stole the body of Jesus while they slept?

28:14 *secure you*—keep you out of trouble

28:16 Why were there only eleven disciples at this time?

28:19 Whom does the Lord send today to help "teach all nations"? What can you do to help the missionary effort?

28:20 How long did Jesus promise to be with us? How can this promise help us each day of our lives?

# THE GOSPEL ACCORDING TO
# ST. MARK*

*The Gospel of St. Mark is the shortest and most action-filled of the four Gospels. Written by Mark, probably with the help of the Apostle Peter, this testimony seems directed to a gentile audience. (See LDS Bible Dictionary, s.v. "Gospels," p. 683; and s.v. "Mark," p. 728.)*

## CHAPTER 1

*Mark begins his testimony with the opening scenes of the Savior's mortal ministry. Look for how Jesus Christ began his mortal ministry.*

### JESUS IS BAPTIZED BY JOHN THE BAPTIST

1 THE beginning of the gospel of Jesus Christ, the Son of God;

2 As it is written in the prophets, Behold, I send my messenger before thy face, which shall prepare thy way before thee.

3 The voice of one crying in the wilderness, Prepare ye the way of the Lord, make his paths straight.

4 John did baptize in the wilderness, and preach the baptism of repentance for the remission of sins.

5 And there went out unto him all the land of Judaea, and they of Jerusalem, and were all baptized of him in the river of Jordan, confessing their sins.

6 And John was clothed with camel's hair, and with a girdle of a skin about his loins; and he did eat locusts and wild honey;

7 And preached, saying, There cometh one mightier than I after me, the latchet of whose shoes I am not worthy to stoop down and unloose.

8 I indeed have baptized you with water: but he shall baptize you with the Holy Ghost.

9 ¶ And it came to pass in those days, that Jesus came from Nazareth of Galilee, and was baptized of John in Jordan.

10 And straightway coming up out of the water, he saw the heavens opened, and the Spirit like a dove descending upon him:

11 And there came a voice from heaven, saying, Thou art my beloved Son, in whom I am well pleased.

### JESUS IS TAKEN INTO THE WILDERNESS FOR FORTY DAYS

12 And immediately the Spirit driveth him into the wilderness.

13 And he was there in the wilderness forty days, tempted of Satan; and was with the wild beasts; and the angels ministered unto him.

### JESUS CALLS DISCIPLES TO FOLLOW HIM

14 ¶ Now after that John was put in prison, Jesus came into Galilee, preaching the gospel of the kingdom of God,

---

\*    ![] The Joseph Smith Translation changes the title of this book from "The Gospel According to St. Mark" to "The Testimony of St. Mark."

1:4    ![] **remission of sins**—forgiveness of sins

1:6    ![] **girdle of a skin about his loins**—leather belt around his waist

1:7    ![] Why do you think John felt unworthy to undo Jesus' shoes?

1:12    ![] The Joseph Smith Translation changes "the Spirit driveth him into the wilderness" to "the Spirit took him into the wilderness" (JST, Mark 1:10).

1:13    ![] The Joseph Smith Translation changes "tempted of Satan" to "Satan seeking to tempt him" (JST, Mark 1:11).

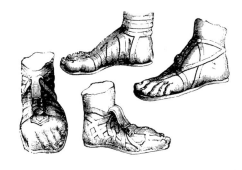

*The "shoes" mentioned in Mark 1:7 were sandals, and the "latchet" refers to the strap or straps that fastened the sandal onto a person's foot.*

| | | | |
|---|---|---|---|
| ![] = Word Help | | ![] = A Closer Look | |
| ![] = More Light | | ![] = Ponder This | |
| Words in pink are explained in the Glossary. | | | |

*John the Baptist in the wilderness*

15 And saying, The time is fulfilled, and the kingdom of God is at hand: repent ye, and believe the gospel.

16 Now as he walked by the sea of Galilee, he saw Simon and Andrew his brother casting a net into the sea: for they were fishers.

17 And Jesus said unto them, Come ye after me, and I will make you to become fishers of men.

18 And straightway they forsook their nets, and followed him.

19 And when he had gone a little further thence, he saw James the son of Zebedee, and John his brother, who also were in the ship mending their nets.

20 And straightway he called them: and they left their father Zebedee in the ship with the hired servants, and went after him.

### JESUS CASTS AN EVIL SPIRIT OUT OF A MAN

21 And they went into Capernaum; and straightway on the sabbath day he entered into the synagogue, and taught.

22 And they were astonished at his doctrine: for he taught them as one that had authority, and not as the scribes.

23 ¶ And there was in their synagogue a man with an unclean spirit; and he cried out,

24 Saying, Let us alone; what have we to do with thee, thou Jesus of Nazareth? art thou come to destroy us? I know thee who thou art, the Holy One of God.

25 And Jesus rebuked him, saying, Hold thy peace, and come out of him.

26 And when the unclean spirit had torn him, and cried with a loud voice, he came out of him.

27 And they were all amazed, insomuch that they questioned among themselves, saying, What thing is this? what new doctrine is this? for with authority commandeth he even the unclean spirits, and they do obey him.

28 And immediately his fame spread abroad throughout all the region round about Galilee.

### JESUS HEALS MANY PEOPLE

29 ¶ And forthwith, when they were come out of the synagogue, they entered into the house of Simon and Andrew, with James and John.

30 But Simon's wife's mother lay sick of a fever, and anon they tell him of her.

31 And he came and took her by the hand, and lifted her up; and immediately the fever left her, and she ministered unto them.

32 And at even, when the sun did set, they brought unto him all that were diseased, and them that were possessed with devils.

33 And all the city was gathered together at the door.

34 And he healed many that were sick of divers diseases, and cast out many devils; and suffered not the devils to speak, because they knew him.

35 And in the morning, rising up a great while before day, he went out, and departed into a solitary place, and there prayed.

36 And Simon and they that were with him followed after him.

---

1:15 "Generally speaking, the kingdom of God on the earth is the Church. It is a preparation for the greater kingdom—the celestial or kingdom of heaven." (LDS Bible Dictionary, s.v. "Kingdom of Heaven," p. 721.)

1:16-20 What would you be willing to leave behind if Jesus asked you to follow him?

1:18 **straightway**—immediately

1:21 **synagogue**—a Jewish place of worship

1:23-45 By what power did Jesus heal so many people? By what power are people healed today?

1:25 **Hold thy peace**—Be quiet

1:26 **torn**—shaken

1:29 **forthwith**—immediately

1:30 **anon**—immediately

1:34 **divers**—several kinds of

1:35 **a solitary place**—a place where he could be alone

*This ancient synagogue in Nazareth dates back to about the time of Christ.*

37 And when they had found him, they said unto him, All men seek for thee.

38 And he said unto them, Let us go into the next towns, that I may preach there also: for therefore came I forth.

39 And he preached in their synagogues throughout all Galilee, and cast out devils.

## JESUS HEALS A MAN WITH LEPROSY

40 ¶ And there came a leper to him, beseeching him, and kneeling down to him, and saying unto him, If thou wilt, thou canst make me clean.

41 And Jesus, moved with compassion, put forth his hand, and touched him, and saith unto him, I will; be thou clean.

42 And as soon as he had spoken, immediately the leprosy departed from him, and he was cleansed.

43 And he straitly charged him, and forthwith sent him away;

44 And saith unto him, See thou say nothing to any man: but go thy way, shew thyself to the priest, and offer for thy cleansing those things which Moses commanded, for a testimony unto them.

45 But he went out, and began to publish it much, and to blaze abroad the matter, insomuch that Jesus could no more openly enter into the city, but was without in desert places: and they came to him from every quarter.

## CHAPTER 2

*As you read this chapter, see how Jesus feels about sinners.*

## JESUS FORGIVES AND HEALS A PARALYZED MAN

1 ¶ AND again he entered into Capernaum after some days; and it was noised that he was in the house.

2 And straightway many were gathered together, insomuch that there was no room to receive them, no, not so much as about the door: and he preached the word unto them.

3 And they come unto him, bringing one sick of the palsy, which was borne of four.

4 And when they could not come nigh unto him for the press, they uncovered the roof where he was: and when they had broken it up, they let down the bed wherein the sick of the palsy lay.

5 When Jesus saw their faith, he said unto the sick of the palsy, Son, thy sins be forgiven thee.

6 But there were certain of the scribes sitting there, and reasoning in their hearts,

7 Why doth this man thus speak blasphemies? who can forgive sins but God only?

8 And immediately when Jesus perceived in his spirit that they so reasoned within themselves, he said unto them, Why reason ye these things in your hearts?

9 Whether is it easier to say to the sick of the palsy, Thy sins be forgiven thee; or to say, Arise, and take up thy bed, and walk?

10 But that ye may know that the Son of man hath power on earth to forgive sins, (he saith to the sick of the palsy,)

11 I say unto thee, Arise, and take up thy bed, and go thy way into thine house.

12 And immediately he arose, took up the bed, and went forth before them all; insomuch that they were all amazed, and glorified God, saying, We never saw it on this fashion.

---

1:38   *for therefore came I forth*—for this is why I came

1:40   *leper*—a person with leprosy (*leprosy* being a word used for many different skin diseases and infections)
*beseeching*—begging
*clean*—pure and well

1:41   *compassion*—love

1:44   *shew*—This word is pronounced the same way as the word *show* and has the same meaning; *shew* is simply an old spelling of *show*.
*offer for thy cleansing those things which Moses commanded*—offer the sacrifices commanded in the law of Moses

1:45   *blaze abroad*—tell everyone
*quarter*—part of the land

2:1    *it was noised*—people heard

2:3    *sick of the palsy*—physically disabled
*borne of four*—carried by four people

2:4    *nigh unto him for the press*—near him because of the crowd of people

2:5-12   If you make a mistake, who can you turn to for forgiveness and help? How has Jesus helped you overcome your mistakes in the past?

## MATTHEW FOLLOWS JESUS

13 ¶ And he went forth again by the sea side; and all the multitude resorted unto him, and he taught them.

14 And as he passed by, he saw Levi the son of Alphaeus sitting at the receipt of custom, and said unto him, Follow me. And he arose and followed him.

## JESUS CAME TO HELP SINNERS

15 And it came to pass, that, as Jesus sat at meat in his house, many publicans and sinners sat also together with Jesus and his disciples: for there were many, and they followed him.

16 And when the scribes and Pharisees saw him eat with publicans and sinners, they said unto his disciples, How is it that he eateth and drinketh with publicans and sinners?

17 When Jesus heard it, he saith unto them, They that are whole have no need of the physician, but they that are sick: I came not to call the righteous, but sinners to repentance.

18 ¶ And the disciples of John and of the Pharisees used to fast: and they come and say unto him, Why do the disciples of John and of the Pharisees fast, but thy disciples fast not?

19 And Jesus said unto them, Can the children of the bridechamber fast, while the bridegroom is with them? as long as they have the bridegroom with them, they cannot fast.

20 But the days will come, when the bridegroom shall be taken away from them, and then shall they fast in those days.

21 No man also seweth a piece of new cloth on an old garment: else the new piece that filled it up taketh away from the old, and the rent is made worse.

22 And no man putteth new wine into old bottles: else the new wine doth burst the bottles, and the wine is spilled, and the bottles will be marred: but new wine must be put into new bottles.

## JESUS IS THE LORD (MASTER) OF THE SABBATH

23 And it came to pass, that he went through the corn fields on the sabbath day; and his disciples began, as they went, to pluck the ears of corn.

24 And the Pharisees said unto him, Behold, why do they on the sabbath day that which is not lawful?

25 And he said unto them, Have ye never read what David did, when he had need, and was an hungred, he, and they that were with him?

26 How he went into the house of God in the days of Abiathar the high priest, and did eat the shewbread, which is not lawful to eat but for the priests, and gave also to them which were with him?

27 And he said unto them, The sabbath was made for man, and not man for the sabbath:

28 Therefore the Son of man is Lord also of the sabbath.

# CHAPTER 3

*Jesus heals many, calls his Apostles, and teaches the gospel. Watch for how and why Jesus is criticized for doing what Heavenly Father would have him do.*

## JESUS HEALS A MAN ON THE SABBATH DAY

1 ¶ AND he entered again into the synagogue; and there was a man there which had a withered hand.

2 And they watched him, whether he would heal him on the sabbath day; that they might accuse him.

---

2:13 **resorted**—went

2:14 Levi is another name for Matthew (see Matthew 9:9).

**receipt of custom**—place where tax collectors sat to collect taxes

2:15 Publicans were Jews who were disliked because they collected taxes for the Romans.

2:16-17 Jesus heals sinners just as a doctor helps sick people. What kind of people need doctors? Why does everyone need Jesus' help?

2:18 The disciples of John were followers of John the Baptist.

2:19 **children of the bridechamber**—people who are invited to a wedding (the expression is used to refer to Jesus' followers)

**bridegroom**—man getting married (in this case the word is used to refer to Jesus)

2:26 Temple workers had let David and his men eat some of the blessed bread that was used in the temple because they were so hungry (see 1 Samuel 21:1-6).

2:28 The Joseph Smith Translation changes this passage to read: "Wherefore the Sabbath was given unto man for a day of rest; and also that man should glorify God, and not that man should not eat; for the Son of man [Jesus] made the Sabbath day, therefore the Son of man is Lord [Master] also of the Sabbath" (JST, Mark 2:26-27).

3:1 **withered**—deformed; crippled

*Christ healing the man with the withered hand*

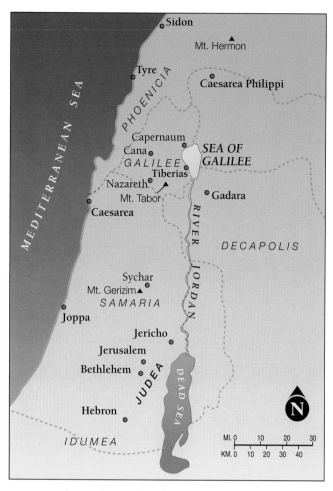

*The Holy Land at the time of the Savior*

3 And he saith unto the man which had the withered hand, Stand forth.

4 And he saith unto them, Is it lawful to do good on the sabbath days, or to do evil? to save life, or to kill? But they held their peace.

5 And when he had looked round about on them with anger, being grieved for the hardness of their hearts, he saith unto the man, Stretch forth thine hand.

And he stretched it out: and his hand was restored whole as the other.

6 And the Pharisees went forth, and straightway took counsel with the Herodians against him, how they might destroy him.

## JESUS HEALS MANY PEOPLE

7 But Jesus withdrew himself with his disciples to the sea: and a great multitude from Galilee followed him, and from Judaea,

8 And from Jerusalem, and from Idumaea, and from beyond Jordan; and they about Tyre and Sidon, a great multitude, when they had heard what great things he did, came unto him.

9 And he spake to his disciples, that a small ship should wait on him because of the multitude, lest they should throng him.

10 For he had healed many; insomuch that they pressed upon him for to touch him, as many as had plagues.

11 And unclean spirits, when they saw him, fell down before him, and cried, saying, Thou art the Son of God.

12 And he straitly charged them that they should not make him known.

## TWELVE APOSTLES ARE CALLED AND ORDAINED

13 ¶ And he goeth up into a mountain, and calleth unto him whom he would: and they came unto him.

14 And he ordained twelve, that they should be with him, and that he might send them forth to preach,

15 And to have power to heal sicknesses, and to cast out devils:

16 And Simon he surnamed Peter;

17 And James the son of Zebedee, and John the brother of James; and he surnamed them Boanerges, which is, The sons of thunder:

18 And Andrew, and Philip, and Bartholomew, and Matthew, and Thomas, and James the son of

3:4   **held their peace**—did not speak

How would you answer these questions from the Savior? What kinds of activities are good to do on the Sabbath?

3:5   Jesus was angry because of the Pharisees' "inability to see how appropriate a healing on the Sabbath day was" (Neal A. Maxwell, *Sermons Not Spoken*, p. 87).

**grieved**—sad

3:6   Pharisees were religious and political leaders of the Jews.

The Herodians were a group of Jews who wanted members of King Herod's family to be their rulers.

3:9   **throng**—crowd

3:10   **plagues**—sicknesses

3:12   **straitly charged**—strongly told

3:14–18   Who were the Twelve Apostles? What did Jesus ask them to do? Do you know who the Twelve Apostles are today?

Alphaeus, and Thaddaeus, and Simon the Canaanite,

19 And Judas Iscariot, which also betrayed him: and they went into an house.

20 And the multitude cometh together again, so that they could not so much as eat bread.

21 And when his friends heard of it, they went out to lay hold on him: for they said, He is beside himself.

## JESUS RESPONDS TO THOSE WHO CALL HIM SATAN

22 ¶ And the scribes which came down from Jerusalem said, He hath Beelzebub, and by the prince of the devils casteth he out devils.

23 And he called them unto him, and said unto them in parables, How can Satan cast out Satan?

24 And if a kingdom be divided against itself, that kingdom cannot stand.

25 And if a house be divided against itself, that house cannot stand.

26 And if Satan rise up against himself, and be divided, he cannot stand, but hath an end.

27 No man can enter into a strong man's house, and spoil his goods, except he will first bind the strong man; and then he will spoil his house.

28 Verily I say unto you, All sins shall be forgiven unto the sons of men, and blasphemies wherewith soever they shall blaspheme:

29 But he that shall blaspheme against the Holy Ghost hath never forgiveness, but is in danger of eternal damnation:

30 Because they said, He hath an unclean spirit.

## JESUS' FAMILY LOOK FOR HIM

31 ¶ There came then his brethren and his mother, and, standing without, sent unto him, calling him.

32 And the multitude sat about him, and they said unto him, Behold, thy mother and thy brethren without seek for thee.

33 And he answered them, saying, Who is my mother, or my brethren?

34 And he looked round about on them which sat about him, and said, Behold my mother and my brethren!

35 For whosoever shall do the will of God, the same is my brother, and my sister, and mother.

# CHAPTER 4

*Jesus was a teacher. In this chapter he teaches with parables. As you read them, look for their meanings and how they can help you.*

## JESUS GIVES THE PARABLE OF THE SOWER

1 ¶ AND he began again to teach by the sea side: and there was gathered unto him a great multitude, so that he entered into a ship, and sat in the sea; and the whole multitude was by the sea on the land.

2 And he taught them many things by parables, and said unto them in his doctrine,

3 Hearken; Behold, there went out a sower to sow:

4 And it came to pass, as he sowed, some fell by the way side, and the fowls of the air came and devoured it up.

5 And some fell on stony ground, where it had not much earth; and immediately it sprang up, because it had no depth of earth:

6 But when the sun was up, it was scorched; and because it had no root, it withered away.

7 And some fell among thorns, and the thorns grew up, and choked it, and it yielded no fruit.

---

3:19    **betrayed him**—turned Jesus over to his enemies

3:21    **He is beside himself**—He is out of his mind

3:22    **Beelzebub**—Satan

3:27    **spoil**—rob or plunder

3:28-29    The Joseph Smith Translation makes it clear that all sins that are repented of will be forgiven, except blasphemy against the Holy Ghost (see JST, Mark 3:21-25).

3:29    **blaspheme against the Holy Ghost**—"willfully [deny] Christ after having received a perfect knowledge of him from the Holy Ghost" (LDS Bible Dictionary, s.v. "Blasphemy," p. 626)

3:31    **without**—outside

3:35    Every member of a family has certain responsibilities. What should we do to be part of the family of Jesus Christ?

4:2    A parable is a simple story that teaches a principle of the gospel. The word *parable* in Greek means "a setting side by side" or a comparison of one thing to another. (See LDS Bible Dictionary, s.v. "Parables," pp. 740-41.)

     What is Jesus' doctrine? (See 3 Nephi 11:37-40.)

4:3    **sower**—someone who plants seeds

4:4    **way side**—side of the road

8 And other fell on good ground, and did yield fruit that sprang up and increased; and brought forth, some thirty, and some sixty, and some an hundred.

9 And he said unto them, He that hath ears to hear, let him hear.

10 And when he was alone, they that were about him with the twelve asked of him the parable.

11 And he said unto them, Unto you it is given to know the mystery of the kingdom of God: but unto them that are without, all these things are done in parables:

12 That seeing they may see, and not perceive; and hearing they may hear, and not understand; lest at any time they should be converted, and their sins should be forgiven them.

13 And he said unto them, Know ye not this parable? and how then will ye know all parables?

14 The sower soweth the word.

15 And these are they by the way side, where the word is sown; but when they have heard, Satan cometh immediately, and taketh away the word that was sown in their hearts.

16 And these are they likewise which are sown on stony ground; who, when they have heard the word, immediately receive it with gladness;

17 And have no root in themselves, and so endure but for a time: afterward, when affliction or persecution ariseth for the word's sake, immediately they are offended.

18 And these are they which are sown among thorns; such as hear the word,

19 And the cares of this world, and the deceitfulness of riches, and the lusts of other things entering in, choke the word, and it becometh unfruitful.

20 And these are they which are sown on good ground; such as hear the word, and receive it, and bring forth fruit, some thirtyfold, some sixty, and some an hundred.

## JESUS GIVES AND EXPLAINS MORE PARABLES TO HIS DISCIPLES

21 ¶ And he said unto them, Is a candle brought to be put under a bushel, or under a bed? and not to be set on a candlestick?

22 For there is nothing hid, which shall not be manifested; neither was any thing kept secret, but that it should come abroad.

23 If any man have ears to hear, let him hear.

24 And he said unto them, Take heed what ye hear: with what measure ye mete, it shall be measured to you: and unto you that hear shall more be given.

25 For he that hath, to him shall be given: and he that hath not, from him shall be taken even that which he hath.

26 And he said, So is the kingdom of God, as if a man should cast seed into the ground;

27 And should sleep, and rise night and day, and the seed should spring and grow up, he knoweth not how.

28 For the earth bringeth forth fruit of herself; first the blade, then the ear, after that the full corn in the ear.

29 But when the fruit is brought forth, immediately he putteth in the sickle, because the harvest is come.

30 And he said, Whereunto shall we liken the kingdom of God? or with what comparison shall we compare it?

31 It is like a grain of mustard seed, which, when it is sown in the earth, is less than all the seeds that be in the earth:

---

4:10　　The Joseph Smith Translation tells us that Jesus explained the meaning of his parables only to those "that believed in him" (JST, Mark 4:9).

4:11　　*mystery of the kingdom of God*—sacred truths of the gospel

4:12　　*perceive*—understand

4:14-20　　In this parable Jesus compares how different people react to the gospel. Some are overwhelmed by Satan (v. 15); some lose their faith because of trials (vv. 16-17); some love the things of the world more than the gospel (vv. 18-19). What happens to those who "hear the word, and receive it"? (v. 20)

4:17　　*they are offended*—they stumble spiritually, reject the word of God

4:19　　*deceitfulness of riches*—misleading attraction of wealth

How can riches mislead or lie to us? See the example of the rich young ruler who thought he desired eternal life but couldn't give up his riches to follow the Son (see Mark 10:17-22).

*lusts of*—evil desires for

4:22　　*manifested*—revealed or made known

4:24　　*measure*—amount
*mete*—give

4:30　　*Whereunto shall we liken the kingdom of God?*—What can we say the Church of Jesus Christ is like?

*Christ stilling the storm*

32 But when it is sown, it groweth up, and becometh greater than all herbs, and shooteth out great branches; so that the fowls of the air may lodge under the shadow of it.

33 And with many such parables spake he the word unto them, as they were able to hear it.

34 But without a parable spake he not unto them: and when they were alone, he expounded all things to his disciples.

## JESUS CALMS THE SEA

35 ¶ And the same day, when the even was come, he saith unto them, Let us pass over unto the other side.

36 And when they had sent away the multitude, they took him even as he was in the ship. And there were also with him other little ships.

37 And there arose a great storm of wind, and the waves beat into the ship, so that it was now full.

38 And he was in the hinder part of the ship, asleep on a pillow: and they awake him, and say unto him, Master, carest thou not that we perish?

39 And he arose, and rebuked the wind, and said unto the sea, Peace, be still. And the wind ceased, and there was a great calm.

40 And he said unto them, Why are ye so fearful? how is it that ye have no faith?

41 And they feared exceedingly, and said one to another, What manner of man is this, that even the wind and the sea obey him?

---

4:32 **herbs**—plants

4:34 **expounded**—explained the meaning of

4:40-41 Have you ever been afraid as Jesus' disciples were at this time? How has Jesus helped you when you were afraid?

# CHAPTER 5

*In this chapter, note the different ways Jesus Christ blesses people.*

## JESUS COMMANDS DEVILS TO LEAVE A MAN

1 ¶ AND they came over unto the other side of the sea, into the country of the Gadarenes.

2 And when he was come out of the ship, immediately there met him out of the tombs a man with an unclean spirit,

3 Who had his dwelling among the tombs; and no man could bind him, no, not with chains:

4 Because that he had been often bound with fetters and chains, and the chains had been plucked asunder by him, and the fetters broken in pieces: neither could any man tame him.

5 And always, night and day, he was in the mountains, and in the tombs, crying, and cutting himself with stones.

6 But when he saw Jesus afar off, he ran and worshipped him,

7 And cried with a loud voice, and said, What have I to do with thee, Jesus, thou Son of the most high God? I adjure thee by God, that thou torment me not.

8 For he said unto him, Come out of the man, thou unclean spirit.

9 And he asked him, What is thy name? And he answered, saying, My name is Legion: for we are many.

10 And he besought him much that he would not send them away out of the country.

11 Now there was there nigh unto the mountains a great herd of swine feeding.

12 And all the devils besought him, saying, Send us into the swine, that we may enter into them.

13 And forthwith Jesus gave them leave. And the unclean spirits went out, and entered into the swine: and the herd ran violently down a steep place into the sea, (they were about two thousand;) and were choked in the sea.

14 And they that fed the swine fled, and told it in the city, and in the country. And they went out to see what it was that was done.

15 And they come to Jesus, and see him that was possessed with the devil, and had the legion, sitting, and clothed, and in his right mind: and they were afraid.

16 And they that saw it told them how it befell to him that was possessed with the devil, and also concerning the swine.

17 And they began to pray him to depart out of their coasts.

18 And when he was come into the ship, he that had been possessed with the devil prayed him that he might be with him.

19 Howbeit Jesus suffered him not, but saith unto him, Go home to thy friends, and tell them how great things the Lord hath done for thee, and hath had compassion on thee.

20 And he departed, and began to publish in

---

5:2　**tombs**—burial places for the dead
　　　**an unclean spirit**—the spirit of a devil

5:4　**plucked asunder**—pulled apart

5:7　**adjure**—beg

5:11　**swine**—pigs

5:11-　The Prophet Joseph Smith taught: "All beings
13　who had bodies have power over those who have not. The devil has no power over us only as we permit him." (*The Teachings of Joseph Smith*, p. 184.) Elder LeGrand Richards said: "It is so desirable to have a body that these evil spirits, who had forfeited the right to bodies of their own, were even willing to enter the bodies of swine" (*A Marvelous Work and A Wonder*, p. 293).

5:16　**how it befell**—what happened

5:17　**depart out of their coasts**—leave their land

5:19　This man, who had been so blessed by Jesus Christ, wanted to stay with the Savior. Jesus told him instead to go home and tell his family and friends of his great blessings. What blessings do you have that you can share with others?

5:20　**publish**—tell

Decapolis how great things Jesus had done for him: and all men did marvel.

## JESUS HEALS A WOMAN AND RAISES A GIRL FROM DEATH

21 ¶ And when Jesus was passed over again by ship unto the other side, much people gathered unto him: and he was nigh unto the sea.

22 And, behold, there cometh one of the rulers of the synagogue, Jairus by name; and when he saw him, he fell at his feet,

23 And besought him greatly, saying, My little daughter lieth at the point of death: I pray thee, come and lay thy hands on her, that she may be healed; and she shall live.

24 And Jesus went with him; and much people followed him, and thronged him.

25 And a certain woman, which had an issue of blood twelve years,

26 And had suffered many things of many physicians, and had spent all that she had, and was nothing bettered, but rather grew worse,

27 When she had heard of Jesus, came in the press behind, and touched his garment.

28 For she said, If I may touch but his clothes, I shall be whole.

29 And straightway the fountain of her blood was dried up; and she felt in her body that she was healed of that plague.

30 And Jesus, immediately knowing in himself that virtue had gone out of him, turned him about in the press, and said, Who touched my clothes?

31 And his disciples said unto him, Thou seest the multitude thronging thee, and sayest thou, Who touched me?

32 And he looked round about to see her that had done this thing.

33 But the woman fearing and trembling, knowing what was done in her, came and fell down before him, and told him all the truth.

34 And he said unto her, Daughter, thy faith hath made thee whole; go in peace, and be whole of thy plague.

35 ¶ While he yet spake, there came from the ruler of the synagogue's house certain which said, Thy daughter is dead: why troublest thou the Master any further?

36 As soon as Jesus heard the word that was spoken, he saith unto the ruler of the synagogue, Be not afraid, only believe.

37 And he suffered no man to follow him, save Peter, and James, and John the brother of James.

38 And he cometh to the house of the ruler of the synagogue, and seeth the tumult, and them that wept and wailed greatly.

39 And when he was come in, he saith unto them, Why make ye this ado, and weep? the damsel is not dead, but sleepeth.

40 And they laughed him to scorn. But when he had put them all out, he taketh the father and the mother of the damsel, and them that were with him, and entereth in where the damsel was lying.

41 And he took the damsel by the hand, and said unto her, Talitha cumi; which is, being interpreted, Damsel, I say unto thee, arise.

42 And straightway the damsel arose, and walked; for she was of the age of twelve years. And they were astonished with a great astonishment.

43 And he charged them straitly that no man should know it; and commanded that something should be given her to eat.

# CHAPTER 6

*This chapter contains some miracles of Jesus Christ, but it also contains the sad story of his being rejected in his own hometown of Nazareth. Look for how the faith of the people affects the blessings they can receive from the Lord.*

---

5:22-43   🔁 Today we have the priesthood of God. This is the same power Jesus used to heal people. Have you or someone you know ever had a blessing by the power of the priesthood?

5:24   📖 **thronged him**—pushed in tightly around Jesus

5:25   📖 **had an issue of blood**—had been bleeding

5:26   📖 **physicians**—doctors

5:29   📖 **plague**—disease

5:30   📖 **virtue**—power

5:34   🔁 In whom did this woman have faith? How can increasing your faith in Jesus Christ help your life improve?

5:38   📖 **tumult**—noisy and upset people

5:39   📖 **Why make ye this ado**—Why do you act in this noisy way
**damsel**—young girl

5:41   📖 **which is, being interpreted**—which means

## JESUS' OWN FRIENDS AND FAMILY DO NOT BELIEVE IN HIM

1 ¶ AND he went out from thence, and came into his own country; and his disciples follow him.

2 And when the sabbath day was come, he began to teach in the synagogue: and many hearing him were astonished, saying, From whence hath this man these things? and what wisdom is this which is given unto him, that even such mighty works are wrought by his hands?

3 Is not this the carpenter, the son of Mary, the brother of James, and Joses, and of Juda, and Simon? and are not his sisters here with us? And they were offended at him.

4 But Jesus said unto them, A prophet is not without honour, but in his own country, and among his own kin, and in his own house.

5 And he could there do no mighty work, save that he laid his hands upon a few sick folk, and healed them.

6 And he marvelled because of their unbelief. And he went round about the villages, teaching.

## THE TWELVE ARE SENT ON MISSIONS

7 ¶ And he called unto him the twelve, and began to send them forth by two and two; and gave them power over unclean spirits;

8 And commanded them that they should take nothing for their journey, save a staff only; no scrip, no bread, no money in their purse:

9 But be shod with sandals; and not put on two coats.

10 And he said unto them, In what place soever ye enter into an house, there abide till ye depart from that place.

11 And whosoever shall not receive you, nor hear you, when ye depart thence, shake off the dust under your feet for a testimony against them. Verily I say unto you, It shall be more tolerable for Sodom and Gomorrha in the day of judgment, than for that city.

12 And they went out, and preached that men should repent.

13 And they cast out many devils, and anointed with oil many that were sick, and healed them.

## HEROD ORDERS JOHN THE BAPTIST KILLED

14 ¶ And king Herod heard of him; (for his name was spread abroad:) and he said, That John the Baptist was risen from the dead, and therefore mighty works do shew forth themselves in him.

15 Others said, That it is Elias. And others said, That it is a prophet, or as one of the prophets.

16 But when Herod heard thereof, he said, It is John, whom I beheaded: he is risen from the dead.

17 For Herod himself had sent forth and laid hold upon John, and bound him in prison for Herodias' sake, his brother Philip's wife: for he had married her.

---

6:2 **wrought**—worked

6:4 **kin**—family

6:4-5 Why do you think the people of Nazareth and Jesus' own brothers and sisters did not believe he was the Son of God? How did this lack of faith affect his ability to work mighty miracles among them?

6:7 The Lord also said in our day that "ye shall go forth in the power of my Spirit, preaching my gospel, two by two, in my name" (D&C 42:6).

6:8 **scrip**—bag for food or clothing

6:9 **be shod with**—have on their feet

6:10 **abide**—stay

6:11 **It shall be more tolerable**—The punishment will be less

6:14-29 Why do you think Herod was so afraid of Jesus and John the Baptist?

6:15 *Elias* is the Greek word for *Elijah*. Elias is also a title for someone who goes first to prepare the way for another. John the Baptist prepared the way before Jesus Christ and so he was an Elias. (See LDS Bible Dictionary, s.v. "Elias," p. 663.)

*Nazareth as it appears today*

18 For John had said unto Herod, It is not lawful for thee to have thy brother's wife.

19 Therefore Herodias had a quarrel against him, and would have killed him; but she could not:

20 For Herod feared John, knowing that he was a just man and an holy, and observed him; and when he heard him, he did many things, and heard him gladly.

21 And when a convenient day was come, that Herod on his birthday made a supper to his lords, high captains, and chief estates of Galilee;

22 And when the daughter of the said Herodias came in, and danced, and pleased Herod and them that sat with him, the king said unto the damsel, Ask of me whatsoever thou wilt, and I will give it thee.

23 And he sware unto her, Whatsoever thou shalt ask of me, I will give it thee, unto the half of my kingdom.

24 And she went forth, and said unto her mother, What shall I ask? And she said, The head of John the Baptist.

25 And she came in straightway with haste unto the king, and asked, saying, I will that thou give me by and by in a charger the head of John the Baptist.

26 And the king was exceeding sorry; yet for his oath's sake, and for their sakes which sat with him, he would not reject her.

27 And immediately the king sent an executioner, and commanded his head to be brought: and he went and beheaded him in the prison,

28 And brought his head in a charger, and gave it to the damsel: and the damsel gave it to her mother.

29 And when his disciples heard of it, they came and took up his corpse, and laid it in a tomb.

## JESUS TEACHES AND FEEDS FIVE THOUSAND

30 ¶ And the apostles gathered themselves together unto Jesus, and told him all things, both what they had done, and what they had taught.

31 And he said unto them, Come ye yourselves apart into a desert place, and rest a while: for there were many coming and going, and they had no leisure so much as to eat.

32 And they departed into a desert place by ship privately.

33 And the people saw them departing, and many knew him, and ran afoot thither out of all cities, and outwent them, and came together unto him.

34 And Jesus, when he came out, saw much people, and was moved with compassion toward them, because they were as sheep not having a shepherd: and he began to teach them many things.

35 And when the day was now far spent, his disciples came unto him, and said, This is a desert place, and now the time is far passed:

36 Send them away, that they may go into the country round about, and into the villages, and buy themselves bread: for they have nothing to eat.

37 He answered and said unto them, Give ye them to eat. And they say unto him, Shall we go and buy two hundred pennyworth of bread, and give them to eat?

38 He saith unto them, How many loaves have ye? go and see. And when they knew, they say, Five, and two fishes.

39 And he commanded them to make all sit down by companies upon the green grass.

40 And they sat down in ranks, by hundreds, and by fifties.

41 And when he had taken the five loaves and the two fishes, he looked up to heaven, and blessed, and brake the loaves, and gave them to his disciples to set before them; and the two fishes divided he among them all.

42 And they did all eat, and were filled.

43 And they took up twelve baskets full of the fragments, and of the fishes.

44 And they that did eat of the loaves were about five thousand men.

---

6:22   *damsel*—girl

6:25   *charger*—large plate

6:26   *oath's*—sacred promise's

6:29   *corpse*—body

6:31   *leisure*—free time

6:33   *outwent*—got there before

6:34   *compassion*—love

The Joseph Smith Translation explains that Jesus and his disciples had hoped to go to a place where they could be alone. Jesus gave up his chance to be alone in order to spend his time with the people. What does this teach us about Jesus' love and concern for others?

6:37   A "pennyworth of bread" was equal to the average person's pay for a day's labor.

6:39   *by companies*—in groups

6:40   *ranks*—groups

*Loaves and fishes*

## JESUS WALKS ON THE WATER

45 ¶ And straightway he constrained his disciples to get into the ship, and to go to the other side before unto Bethsaida, while he sent away the people.

46 And when he had sent them away, he departed into a mountain to pray.

47 And when even was come, the ship was in the midst of the sea, and he alone on the land.

48 And he saw them toiling in rowing; for the wind was contrary unto them: and about the fourth watch of the night he cometh unto them, walking upon the sea, and would have passed by them.

49 But when they saw him walking upon the sea, they supposed it had been a spirit, and cried out:

50 For they all saw him, and were troubled. And immediately he talked with them, and saith unto them, Be of good cheer: it is I; be not afraid.

6:45 *straightway he constrained*—immediately he commanded

6:48 *contrary unto*—against

The fourth watch of the night was from three to six in the morning (see LDS Bible Dictionary, s.v. "Watches," p. 788).

51 And he went up unto them into the ship; and the wind ceased: and they were sore amazed in themselves beyond measure, and wondered.

52 For they considered not the miracle of the loaves: for their heart was hardened.

53 And when they had passed over, they came into the land of Gennesaret, and drew to the shore.

## JESUS HEALS MANY PEOPLE

54 And when they were come out of the ship, straightway they knew him,

55 And ran through that whole region round about, and began to carry about in beds those that were sick, where they heard he was.

56 And whithersoever he entered, into villages, or cities, or country, they laid the sick in the streets, and besought him that they might touch if it were but the border of his garment: and as many as touched him were made whole.

## CHAPTER 7

*The Pharisees accused Jesus of breaking their traditional rules. As you read this chapter, watch for what Jesus said was more important than the "tradition of the elders."*

## WHAT MAKES A PERSON UNCLEAN BEFORE GOD?

1 ¶ THEN came together unto him the Pharisees, and certain of the scribes, which came from Jerusalem.

2 And when they saw some of his disciples eat bread with defiled, that is to say, with unwashen, hands, they found fault.

3 For the Pharisees, and all the Jews, except they wash their hands oft, eat not, holding the tradition of the elders.

4 And when they come from the market, except they wash, they eat not. And many other things there be, which they have received to hold, as the washing of cups, and pots, brasen vessels, and of tables.

5 Then the Pharisees and scribes asked him, Why walk not thy disciples according to the tradition of the elders, but eat bread with unwashen hands?

6 He answered and said unto them, Well hath Esaias prophesied of you hypocrites, as it is written, This people honoureth me with their lips, but their heart is far from me.

7 Howbeit in vain do they worship me, teaching for doctrines the commandments of men.

8 For laying aside the commandment of God, ye hold the tradition of men, as the washing of pots and cups: and many other such like things ye do.

9 And he said unto them, Full well ye reject the commandment of God, that ye may keep your own tradition.

10 For Moses said, Honour thy father and thy mother; and, Whoso curseth father or mother, let him die the death:

11 But ye say, If a man shall say to his father or mother, It is Corban, that is to say, a gift, by whatsoever thou mightest be profited by me; he shall be free.

12 And ye suffer him no more to do ought for his father or his mother;

13 Making the word of God of none effect through your tradition, which ye have delivered: and many such like things do ye.

14 And when he had called all the people unto him, he said unto them, Hearken unto me every one of you, and understand:

---

6:51-52 🔁 These verses say that the disciples were amazed at this miracle because they "considered not the miracle of the loaves." Are there wonderful events and people in your own life that you have not thought much about?

7:1 🔍 Scribes were men who taught the scriptures. They were sometimes called lawyers.

7:3 🔍 The "tradition of the elders" referred to unwritten laws added by men, not God. Many Jewish leaders thought their traditions were more important than the commandments of God.

7:6 📖 **hypocrites**—people who pretend to be good when they are not

7:7 📖 **Howbeit in vain do they worship me**—Nevertheless their worshiping me does them no good

7:9 🔁 These people rejected the commandments because of their own traditions. What kinds of traditions today prevent people from keeping the commandments?

7:9-13 🔍 Some Jews avoided their duty to take care of their elderly parents by claiming that the money that would have been given to their parents had instead been promised to God. Such a gift was called "Corban." They believed such a promise was more sacred than God's commandment to honor their parents. (See LDS Bible Dictionary, s.v. "Corban," p. 650.)

7:12 📖 **ought**—anything

15 There is nothing from without a man, that entering into him can defile him: but the things which come out of him, those are they that defile the man.

16 If any man have ears to hear, let him hear.

17 And when he was entered into the house from the people, his disciples asked him concerning the parable.

18 And he saith unto them, Are ye so without understanding also? Do ye not perceive, that whatsoever thing from without entereth into the man, it cannot defile him;

19 Because it entereth not into his heart, but into the belly, and goeth out into the draught, purging all meats?

20 And he said, That which cometh out of the man, that defileth the man.

21 For from within, out of the heart of men, proceed evil thoughts, adulteries, fornications, murders,

22 Thefts, covetousness, wickedness, deceit, lasciviousness, an evil eye, blasphemy, pride, foolishness:

23 All these evil things come from within, and defile the man.

## Jesus Casts Out a Devil

24 ¶ And from thence he arose, and went into the borders of Tyre and Sidon, and entered into an house, and would have no man know it: but he could not be hid.

25 For a certain woman, whose young daughter had an unclean spirit, heard of him, and came and fell at his feet:

26 The woman was a Greek, a Syrophenician by nation; and she besought him that he would cast forth the devil out of her daughter.

27 But Jesus said unto her, Let the children first be filled: for it is not meet to take the children's bread, and to cast it unto the dogs.

28 And she answered and said unto him, Yes, Lord: yet the dogs under the table eat of the children's crumbs.

29 And he said unto her, For this saying go thy way; the devil is gone out of thy daughter.

30 And when she was come to her house, she found the devil gone out, and her daughter laid upon the bed.

## Jesus Heals a Deaf Man

31 ¶ And again, departing from the coasts of Tyre and Sidon, he came unto the sea of Galilee, through the midst of the coasts of Decapolis.

32 And they bring unto him one that was deaf, and had an impediment in his speech; and they beseech him to put his hand upon him.

33 And he took him aside from the multitude, and put his fingers into his ears, and he spit, and touched his tongue;

34 And looking up to heaven, he sighed, and saith unto him, Ephphatha, that is, Be opened.

35 And straightway his ears were opened, and the string of his tongue was loosed, and he spake plain.

36 And he charged them that they should tell no man: but the more he charged them, so much the more a great deal they published it;

37 And were beyond measure astonished, saying, He hath done all things well: he maketh both the deaf to hear, and the dumb to speak.

---

7:15   *defile him*—make a person unclean or evil

The Joseph Smith Translation explains that it is not food which makes us spiritually unclean but the things that come "out of the heart" (see JST, Mark 7:15).

7:18   *perceive*—see or understand

7:19   *goeth out into the draught*—passes through the body and passes away

7:22   *covetousness*—wanting what others own and even being willing to break any commandment to obtain it

*lasciviousness*—immoral desires leading to misuse of the sacred creative powers

7:24   The Joseph Smith Translation adds that although Jesus wanted to be alone, he would not tell the people to go away because he loved all men (see JST, Mark 7:22-23).

7:26   *besought*—begged

7:27   See for Matthew 15:24.

7:32   *had an impediment in his speech*—could not speak clearly

# CHAPTER 8

*Miracles come as a result of faith. In this chapter notice the way Jesus uses miracles to teach his disciples about faith.*

## JESUS MIRACULOUSLY FEEDS FOUR THOUSAND

1 ¶ IN those days the multitude being very great, and having nothing to eat, Jesus called his disciples unto him, and saith unto them,

2 I have compassion on the multitude, because they have now been with me three days, and have nothing to eat:

3 And if I send them away fasting to their own houses, they will faint by the way: for divers of them came from far.

4 And his disciples answered him, From whence can a man satisfy these men with bread here in the wilderness?

5 And he asked them, How many loaves have ye? And they said, Seven.

6 And he commanded the people to sit down on the ground: and he took the seven loaves, and gave thanks, and brake, and gave to his disciples to set before them; and they did set them before the people.

7 And they had a few small fishes: and he blessed, and commanded to set them also before them.

8 So they did eat, and were filled: and they took up of the broken meat that was left seven baskets.

9 And they that had eaten were about four thousand: and he sent them away.

## JESUS TEACHES HIS DISCIPLES TO BEWARE OF THE LEAVEN OF THE PHARISEES

10 ¶ And straightway he entered into a ship with his disciples, and came into the parts of Dalmanutha.

11 And the Pharisees came forth, and began to question with him, seeking of him a sign from heaven, tempting him.

12 And he sighed deeply in his spirit, and saith, Why doth this generation seek after a sign? verily I say unto you, There shall no sign be given unto this generation.

13 And he left them, and entering into the ship again departed to the other side.

14 Now the disciples had forgotten to take bread, neither had they in the ship with them more than one loaf.

15 And he charged them, saying, Take heed, beware of the leaven of the Pharisees, and of the leaven of Herod.

16 And they reasoned among themselves, saying, It is because we have no bread.

17 And when Jesus knew it, he saith unto them, Why reason ye, because ye have no bread? perceive ye not yet, neither understand? have ye your heart yet hardened?

18 Having eyes, see ye not? and having ears, hear ye not? and do ye not remember?

19 When I brake the five loaves among five thousand, how many baskets full of fragments took ye up? They say unto him, Twelve.

20 And when the seven among four thousand, how many baskets full of fragments took ye up? And they said, Seven.

---

*Looking down onto the Plain of Gennesaret (where the feeding of the four thousand took place), with a view of the western side of the Sea of Galilee*

8:2   **compassion on**—love for

8:3   **divers**—some

8:12   **generation**—group of people

8:14-16   Often when Jesus speaks about spiritual truths, his disciples think he is talking about physical things. How hard is it, sometimes, to understand spiritual truths? What can you do to better understand spiritual truths?

8:15   Just as leaven (yeast) causes bread dough to grow larger, the teachings of the Pharisees would cause wickedness to become greater in the people who believed them.

8:17   **perceive**—see

8:19   **fragments**—pieces

21 And he said unto them, How is it that ye do not understand?

## JESUS HEALS A BLIND MAN

22 ¶ And he cometh to Bethsaida; and they bring a blind man unto him, and besought him to touch him.

23 And he took the blind man by the hand, and led him out of the town; and when he had spit on his eyes, and put his hands upon him, he asked him if he saw ought.

24 And he looked up, and said, I see men as trees, walking.

25 After that he put his hands again upon his eyes, and made him look up: and he was restored, and saw every man clearly.

26 And he sent him away to his house, saying, Neither go into the town, nor tell it to any in the town.

## PETER TESTIFIES OF CHRIST

27 ¶ And Jesus went out, and his disciples, into the towns of Caesarea Philippi: and by the way he asked his disciples, saying unto them, Whom do men say that I am?

28 And they answered, John the Baptist: but some say, Elias; and others, One of the prophets.

29 And he saith unto them, But whom say ye that I am? And Peter answereth and saith unto him, Thou art the Christ.

30 And he charged them that they should tell no man of him.

31 And he began to teach them, that the Son of man must suffer many things, and be rejected of the elders, and of the chief priests, and scribes, and be killed, and after three days rise again.

32 And he spake that saying openly. And Peter took him, and began to rebuke him.

33 But when he had turned about and looked on his disciples, he rebuked Peter, saying, Get thee behind me, Satan: for thou savourest not the things that be of God, but the things that be of men.

34 And when he had called the people unto him with his disciples also, he said unto them, Whosoever will come after me, let him deny himself, and take up his cross, and follow me.

35 For whosoever will save his life shall lose it; but whosoever shall lose his life for my sake and the gospel's, the same shall save it.

36 For what shall it profit a man, if he shall gain the whole world, and lose his own soul?

37 Or what shall a man give in exchange for his soul?

38 Whosoever therefore shall be ashamed of me and of my words in this adulterous and sinful generation; of him also shall the Son of man be ashamed, when he cometh in the glory of his Father with the holy angels.

# CHAPTER 9

*Jesus wants us to follow his example. In this chapter look for what Jesus did to show us who he is and what we must do to be like him.*

## JESUS IS TRANSFIGURED

1 ¶ AND he said unto them, Verily I say unto you, That there be some of them that stand here, which shall not taste of death, till they have seen the kingdom of God come with power.

2 And after six days Jesus taketh with him Peter, and

---

8:23 **ought**—anything

8:29 If Jesus asked you who you thought he was, what would you say?

8:33 **thou savourest not**—you love not

8:34 The Joseph Smith Translation explains that to take up our "cross" means to keep the commandments and stay away from everything that is unholy or evil (see JST, Matthew 16:26).

8:38 What would you say to help someone who was ashamed of Jesus Christ's church and his teachings?

Following this passage, the Joseph Smith Translation adds: "And they shall not have part in that resurrection when he cometh. For verily I say unto you, That he shall come; and he that layeth down his life for my sake and the gospel's, shall come

with him, and shall be clothed with his glory in the cloud, on the right hand of the Son of man." (JST, Mark 8:42-43.)

9:2 The Joseph Smith Translation adds that just before Jesus took them up the mountain, Peter, James, and John asked him many questions about what he taught them (see JST, Mark 9:1).

9:2-4 To be transfigured is to have "a special change in appearance . . . by the power of God. This divine transformation is from a lower to a higher state; it results in a more exalted, impressive, and glorious condition." (Bruce R. McConkie, *Mormon Doctrine*, p. 803.) At this time Elijah and Moses strengthened, encouraged, comforted, and supported Jesus as he prepared for the future sufferings he would experience during the Atonement (see James E. Talmage, *Jesus the Christ*, p. 373).

James, and John, and leadeth them up into an high mountain apart by themselves: and he was transfigured before them.

3 And his raiment became shining, exceeding white as snow; so as no fuller on earth can white them.

4 And there appeared unto them Elias with Moses: and they were talking with Jesus.

5 And Peter answered and said to Jesus, Master, it is good for us to be here: and let us make three tabernacles; one for thee, and one for Moses, and one for Elias.

6 For he wist not what to say; for they were sore afraid.

7 And there was a cloud that overshadowed them: and a voice came out of the cloud, saying, This is my beloved Son: hear him.

8 And suddenly, when they had looked round about, they saw no man any more, save Jesus only with themselves.

9 And as they came down from the mountain, he charged them that they should tell no man what things they had seen, till the Son of man were risen from the dead.

10 And they kept that saying with themselves, questioning one with another what the rising from the dead should mean.

11 And they asked him, saying, Why say the scribes that Elias must first come?

12 And he answered and told them, Elias verily cometh first, and restoreth all things; and how it is written of the Son of man, that he must suffer many things, and be set at nought.

13 But I say unto you, That Elias is indeed come, and they have done unto him whatsoever they listed, as it is written of him.

## JESUS HEALS A BOY POSSESSED BY AN EVIL SPIRIT

14 ¶ And when he came to his disciples, he saw a great multitude about them, and the scribes questioning with them.

15 And straightway all the people, when they beheld him, were greatly amazed, and running to him saluted him.

16 And he asked the scribes, What question ye with them?

17 And one of the multitude answered and said, Master, I have brought unto thee my son, which hath a dumb spirit;

18 And wheresoever he taketh him, he teareth him: and he foameth, and gnasheth with his teeth, and pineth away: and I spake to thy disciples that they should cast him out; and they could not.

19 He answereth him, and saith, O faithless generation, how long shall I be with you? how long shall I suffer you? bring him unto me.

20 And they brought him unto him: and when he saw him, straightway the spirit tare him; and he fell on the ground, and wallowed foaming.

21 And he asked his father, How long is it ago since this came unto him? And he said, Of a child.

22 And ofttimes it hath cast him into the fire, and into the waters, to destroy him: but if thou canst do any thing, have compassion on us, and help us.

23 Jesus said unto him, If thou canst believe, all things are possible to him that believeth.

24 And straightway the father of the child cried out, and said with tears, Lord, I believe; help thou mine unbelief.

25 When Jesus saw that the people came running together, he rebuked the foul spirit, saying unto him,

---

9:3    **fuller**—a person whose business was making clothes clean and white

9:6    **wist**—knew

9:7    Heavenly Father called Jesus Christ his "beloved" Son. Why do you think Heavenly Father loves Jesus so much? (See John 8:29.)

9:9    "In the language of Adam, Man of Holiness is [Heavenly Father's] name, and the name of his Only Begotten is the Son of Man, even Jesus Christ" (Moses 6:57).

9:12    The Joseph Smith Translation changes the word *restoreth* in this passage to *prepareth*. John the Baptist came as an Elias to prepare the way for Jesus Christ.

9:13    The Joseph Smith Translation adds that Elias (meaning John the Baptist) testified of Jesus but that the people did not believe him (see JST, Mark 9:11).

9:17    **a dumb spirit**—a spirit that makes it so he cannot speak

9:22-24    How important is faith in receiving blessings from Heavenly Father? Who can help us have more faith?

Thou dumb and deaf spirit, I charge thee, come out of him, and enter no more into him.

26 And the spirit cried, and rent him sore, and came out of him: and he was as one dead; insomuch that many said, He is dead.

27 But Jesus took him by the hand, and lifted him up; and he arose.

28 And when he was come into the house, his disciples asked him privately, Why could not we cast him out?

29 And he said unto them, This kind can come forth by nothing, but by prayer and fasting.

30 ¶ And they departed thence, and passed through Galilee; and he would not that any man should know it.

31 For he taught his disciples, and said unto them, The Son of man is delivered into the hands of men, and they shall kill him; and after that he is killed, he shall rise the third day.

32 But they understood not that saying, and were afraid to ask him.

## THE DISCIPLES ARGUE ABOUT WHO IS THE GREATEST

33 And he came to Capernaum: and being in the house he asked them, What was it that ye disputed among yourselves by the way?

34 But they held their peace: for by the way they had disputed among themselves, who should be the greatest.

35 And he sat down, and called the twelve, and saith unto them, If any man desire to be first, the same shall be last of all, and servant of all.

36 And he took a child, and set him in the midst of them: and when he had taken him in his arms, he said unto them,

37 Whosoever shall receive one of such children in my name, receiveth me: and whosoever shall receive me, receiveth not me, but him that sent me.

38 And John answered him, saying, Master, we saw one casting out devils in thy name, and he followeth not us: and we forbade him, because he followeth not us.

39 But Jesus said, Forbid him not: for there is no man which shall do a miracle in my name, that can lightly speak evil of me.

40 For he that is not against us is on our part.

41 ¶ For whosoever shall give you a cup of water to drink in my name, because ye belong to Christ, verily I say unto you, he shall not lose his reward.

## STAY AWAY FROM PEOPLE WHO WOULD LEAD YOU TO SIN

42 And whosoever shall offend one of these little ones that believe in me, it is better for him that a millstone were hanged about his neck, and he were cast into the sea.

43 And if thy hand offend thee, cut it off: it is better for thee to enter into life maimed, than having two hands to go into hell, into the fire that never shall be quenched:

---

9:26   *rent him sore*—shook him wildly

9:29   How does fasting and prayer build spiritual power? President Ezra Taft Benson said, "Fasting can help clear up the mind and strengthen the body and the spirit. . . . It should be coupled with prayer and meditation." (*The Teachings of Ezra Taft Benson*, p. 331.)

9:33   *disputed*—argued about

9:36-  What do you think it is about little children
37     that Jesus loves so much?

9:37   The Joseph Smith Translation changes this passage to read: "Whosoever shall humble himself like one of these children, and receiveth me, ye shall receive in my name" (JST, Mark 9:34).

9:43-  The Joseph Smith Translation explains that the
48     Lord is using *hand, foot,* and *eye* to represent

A millstone is a large stone used for grinding grain into flour.

people. In other words, if a brother, a friend, or a leader tries to get us to do wicked things, we should stay away from them. (See JST, Mark 9:40-48.)

44 Where their worm dieth not, and the fire is not quenched.

45 And if thy foot offend thee, cut it off: it is better for thee to enter halt into life, than having two feet to be cast into hell, into the fire that never shall be quenched:

46 Where their worm dieth not, and the fire is not quenched.

47 And if thine eye offend thee, pluck it out: it is better for thee to enter into the kingdom of God with one eye, than having two eyes to be cast into hell fire:

48 Where their worm dieth not, and the fire is not quenched.

49 For every one shall be salted with fire, and every sacrifice shall be salted with salt.

50 Salt is good: but if the salt have lost his saltness, wherewith will ye season it? Have salt in yourselves, and have peace one with another.

# CHAPTER 10

*Jesus' disciples ask, "Who then can be saved?" (Mark 10:26.) As you read this chapter look for different ways in which Jesus answers this question.*

## JESUS TEACHES ABOUT MARRIAGE AND DIVORCE

1 ¶ AND he arose from thence, and cometh into the coasts of Judaea by the farther side of Jordan: and the people resort unto him again; and, as he was wont, he taught them again.

2 And the Pharisees came to him, and asked him, Is it lawful for a man to put away his wife? tempting him.

3 And he answered and said unto them, What did Moses command you?

4 And they said, Moses suffered to write a bill of divorcement, and to put her away.

5 And Jesus answered and said unto them, For the hardness of your heart he wrote you this precept.

6 But from the beginning of the creation God made them male and female.

7 For this cause shall a man leave his father and mother, and cleave to his wife;

8 And they twain shall be one flesh: so then they are no more twain, but one flesh.

9 What therefore God hath joined together, let not man put asunder.

10 And in the house his disciples asked him again of the same matter.

11 And he saith unto them, Whosoever shall put away his wife, and marry another, committeth adultery against her.

12 And if a woman shall put away her husband, and be married to another, she committeth adultery.

## JESUS BLESSES THE LITTLE CHILDREN

13 ¶ And they brought young children to him, that he should touch them: and his disciples rebuked those that brought them.

14 But when Jesus saw it, he was much displeased, and said unto them, Suffer the little children to come unto me, and forbid them not: for of such is the kingdom of God.

15 Verily I say unto you, Whosoever shall not receive the kingdom of God as a little child, he shall not enter therein.

16 And he took them up in his arms, put his hands upon them, and blessed them.

## JESUS COUNSELS THE RICH YOUNG MAN

17 ¶ And when he was gone forth into the way, there came one running, and kneeled to him, and asked him, Good Master, what shall I do that I may inherit eternal life?

18 And Jesus said unto him, Why callest thou me good? there is none good but one, that is, God.

19 Thou knowest the commandments, Do not commit adultery, Do not kill, Do not steal, Do not bear false witness, Defraud not, Honour thy father and mother.

20 And he answered and said unto him, Master, all these have I observed from my youth.

---

9:44, 46, 48 — These verses symbolize the terrible suffering of those who refuse to repent and to keep the commandments (see Bruce R. McConkie, *Mormon Doctrine*, p. 308).

10:1 **thence**—there
**resort**—came

10:2 **put away**—divorce

10:4 **suffered**—allowed

10:5 **precept**—commandment

10:7 **cleave**—be joined

10:9 **put asunder**—separate or divide

10:11 **adultery**—misuse of the sacred creative powers; that is, use of these powers with someone other than your husband or wife

10:13 **rebuked**—scolded

10:14 **Suffer**—Allow

10:16 What would it mean to you to have Jesus "put his hands upon" you and bless you?

10:19 **bear false witness**—lie
**Defraud**—Cheat

*Christ and the rich young ruler*

21 Then Jesus beholding him loved him, and said unto him, One thing thou lackest: go thy way, sell whatsoever thou hast, and give to the poor, and thou shalt have treasure in heaven: and come, take up the cross, and follow me.

22 And he was sad at that saying, and went away grieved: for he had great possessions.

## WITH GOD ALL THINGS ARE POSSIBLE

23 And Jesus looked round about, and saith unto his disciples, How hardly shall they that have riches enter into the kingdom of God!

24 And the disciples were astonished at his words. But Jesus answereth again, and saith unto them, Children, how hard is it for them that trust in riches to enter into the kingdom of God!

25 It is easier for a camel to go through the eye of a needle, than for a rich man to enter into the kingdom of God.

26 And they were astonished out of measure, saying among themselves, Who then can be saved?

27 And Jesus looking upon them saith, With men it is impossible, but not with God: for with God all things are possible.

28 Then Peter began to say unto him, Lo, we have left all, and have followed thee.

29 And Jesus answered and said, Verily I say unto you, There is no man that hath left house, or brethren, or sisters, or father, or mother, or wife, or children, or lands, for my sake, and the gospel's,

30 But he shall receive an hundredfold now in this time, houses, and brethren, and sisters, and mothers, and children, and lands, with persecutions; and in the world to come eternal life.

31 But many that are first shall be last; and the last first.

## JESUS FORETELLS HIS OWN DEATH AND RESURRECTION

32 ¶ And they were in the way going up to Jerusalem; and Jesus went before them: and they were amazed; and as they followed, they were afraid. And he took again the twelve, and began to tell them what things should happen unto him,

33 Saying, Behold, we go up to Jerusalem; and the Son of man shall be delivered unto the chief priests, and unto the scribes; and they shall condemn him to death, and shall deliver him to the Gentiles:

34 And they shall mock him, and shall scourge him, and shall spit upon him, and shall kill him: and the third day he shall rise again.

## JESUS TEACHES HIS DISCIPLES ABOUT THE GREATNESS OF SERVING

35 And James and John, the sons of Zebedee, come unto him, saying, Master, we would that thou shouldest do for us whatsoever we shall desire.

36 And he said unto them, What would ye that I should do for you?

37 They said unto him, Grant unto us that we may sit, one on thy right hand, and the other on thy left hand, in thy glory.

38 But Jesus said unto them, Ye know not what ye ask: can ye drink of the cup that I drink of? and be baptized with the baptism that I am baptized with?

39 And they said unto him, We can. And Jesus said unto them, Ye shall indeed drink of the cup that I drink of; and with the baptism that I am baptized withal shall ye be baptized:

40 But to sit on my right hand and on my left hand is not mine to give; but it shall be given to them for whom it is prepared.

41 And when the ten heard it, they began to be much displeased with James and John.

42 But Jesus called them to him, and saith unto them, Ye know that they which are accounted to rule over the Gentiles exercise lordship over them; and their great ones exercise authority upon them.

43 But so shall it not be among you: but whosoever will be great among you, shall be your minister:

44 And whosoever of you will be the chiefest, shall be servant of all.

---

10:22 Why was it so hard for this rich young man to follow Jesus?

10:26 *out of measure*—greatly

10:27 The Joseph Smith Translation reveals that Jesus said that those "who trust in God and leave all for my sake" can be saved, while those who "trust in riches" cannot be saved (JST, Mark 10:26).

10:33 *Gentiles* is a word that means "nations." It describes those not of the family of Israel or not believing in the God of Israel.

10:38 See for Matthew 20:22.

10:42 *accounted to rule*—thought to be rulers *great ones*—rulers or leaders

10:43 *minister*—servant

45 For even the Son of man came not to be ministered unto, but to minister, and to give his life a ransom for many.

### JESUS HEALS BLIND BARTIMAEUS

46 ¶ And they came to Jericho: and as he went out of Jericho with his disciples and a great number of people, blind Bartimaeus, the son of Timaeus, sat by the highway side begging.

47 And when he heard that it was Jesus of Nazareth, he began to cry out, and say, Jesus, thou Son of David, have mercy on me.

48 And many charged him that he should hold his peace: but he cried the more a great deal, Thou Son of David, have mercy on me.

49 And Jesus stood still, and commanded him to be called. And they call the blind man, saying unto him, Be of good comfort, rise; he calleth thee.

50 And he, casting away his garment, rose, and came to Jesus.

51 And Jesus answered and said unto him, What wilt thou that I should do unto thee? The blind man said unto him, Lord, that I might receive my sight.

52 And Jesus said unto him, Go thy way; thy faith hath made thee whole. And immediately he received his sight, and followed Jesus in the way.

## CHAPTER 11

*Mark wrote much in this chapter about the last week in the life of Christ. As you read, see what Jesus taught the people during this time.*

### JESUS ENTERS JERUSALEM TRIUMPHANTLY

1 ¶ AND when they came nigh to Jerusalem, unto Bethphage and Bethany, at the mount of Olives, he sendeth forth two of his disciples,

2 And saith unto them, Go your way into the village over against you: and as soon as ye be entered into it, ye shall find a colt tied, whereon never man sat; loose him, and bring him.

3 And if any man say unto you, Why do ye this? say ye that the Lord hath need of him; and straightway he will send him hither.

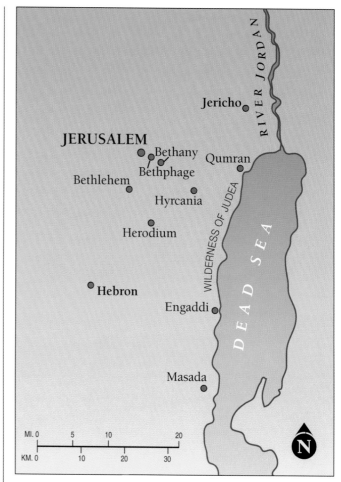

*Jerusalem and surrounding area*

4 And they went their way, and found the colt tied by the door without in a place where two ways met; and they loose him.

5 And certain of them that stood there said unto them, What do ye, loosing the colt?

6 And they said unto them even as Jesus had commanded: and they let them go.

7 And they brought the colt to Jesus, and cast their garments on him; and he sat upon him.

8 And many spread their garments in the way: and others cut down branches off the trees, and strawed them in the way.

9 And they that went before, and they that followed, cried, saying, Hosanna; Blessed is he that cometh in the name of the Lord:

---

10:45 ↻ All of us sin. Jesus came into the world to pay the ransom, or the price, for our sins so that we can be free of them. How do you feel about Jesus' paying so high a price to save you from your sins?

11:1-11 See helps for Matthew 21:1-11 for additional guidance in understanding Jesus' triumphal entry into Jerusalem.

10 Blessed be the kingdom of our father David, that cometh in the name of the Lord: Hosanna in the highest.

11 And Jesus entered into Jerusalem, and into the temple: and when he had looked round about upon all things, and now the eventide was come, he went out unto Bethany with the twelve.

## JESUS CURSES A FIG TREE

12 ¶ And on the morrow, when they were come from Bethany, he was hungry:

13 And seeing a fig tree afar off having leaves, he came, if haply he might find any thing thereon: and when he came to it, he found nothing but leaves; for the time of figs was not yet.

14 And Jesus answered and said unto it, No man eat fruit of thee hereafter for ever. And his disciples heard it.

## JESUS CLEANSES THE TEMPLE

15 ¶ And they come to Jerusalem: and Jesus went into the temple, and began to cast out them that sold and bought in the temple, and overthrew the tables of the moneychangers, and the seats of them that sold doves;

16 And would not suffer that any man should carry any vessel through the temple.

17 And he taught, saying unto them, Is it not written, My house shall be called of all nations the house of prayer? but ye have made it a den of thieves.

18 And the scribes and chief priests heard it, and sought how they might destroy him: for they feared him, because all the people was astonished at his doctrine.

19 And when even was come, he went out of the city.

---

11:10   Many people recognized Jesus as the Messiah or King by throwing their garments (robes or cloaks) in front of him as he entered the city. They also shouted a psalm that recognized Jesus as Messiah (see Psalm 118:26).

11:11   During this last week of his life, Jesus often spent the evenings at the home of Lazarus, Mary, and Martha. They lived in Bethany. (See Matthew 21:17.)

11:12   **on the morrow**—the next day; in this case, it was Monday

11:13-14   Fig trees generally produce edible buds in March, leaves in April, and full fruit later on. This tree had leaves, which would cause one to hope that it would also have food. This tree had nothing but leaves.

11:14   What do you think Jesus was teaching when he cursed the fig tree? How can the fig tree be compared to a person who pretends to be someone that he really is not? See 🔍 for Matthew 21:19-20.

11:15   Why didn't Jesus want people to buy and sell goods in the temple? Are there activities that you can think of that may not be wrong or bad but that are not reverent enough to be done in a church or temple?

Not only was the outer court of the temple crowded with those that bought and sold items, but there were tables of money changers who overcharged for exchanging Roman and other foreign money for special temple coins that could buy animals to be sacrificed.

11:16   **vessel**—item to sell

*The withered fig tree was a testimony of Jesus' power over nature.*

*Figs normally appear on the tree before the leaves do.*

## THE CURSED FIG TREE IS DRIED UP

20 And in the morning, as they passed by, they saw the fig tree dried up from the roots.

21 And Peter calling to remembrance saith unto him, Master, behold, the fig tree which thou cursedst is withered away.

22 And Jesus answering saith unto them, Have faith in God.

23 For verily I say unto you, That whosoever shall say unto this mountain, Be thou removed, and be thou cast into the sea; and shall not doubt in his heart, but shall believe that those things which he saith shall come to pass; he shall have whatsoever he saith.

24 Therefore I say unto you, What things soever ye desire, when ye pray, believe that ye receive them, and ye shall have them.

25 And when ye stand praying, forgive, if ye have ought against any: that your Father also which is in heaven may forgive you your trespasses.

26 But if ye do not forgive, neither will your Father which is in heaven forgive your trespasses.

## JEWISH LEADERS QUESTION JESUS' AUTHORITY

27 ¶ And they come again to Jerusalem: and as he was walking in the temple, there come to him the chief priests, and the scribes, and the elders,

28 And say unto him, By what authority doest thou these things? and who gave thee this authority to do these things?

29 And Jesus answered and said unto them, I will also ask of you one question, and answer me, and I will tell you by what authority I do these things.

30 The baptism of John, was it from heaven, or of men? answer me.

31 And they reasoned with themselves, saying, If we shall say, From heaven; he will say, Why then did ye not believe him?

32 But if we shall say, Of men; they feared the people: for all men counted John, that he was a prophet indeed.

33 And they answered and said unto Jesus, We cannot tell. And Jesus answering saith unto them, Neither do I tell you by what authority I do these things.

## CHAPTER 12

*After Jesus tells the parable of the wicked husbandmen, several people try to question him in order to catch him making a mistake. Notice how Jesus answers these questions and also how unsuccessful the wicked are in trying to trap him.*

## JESUS GIVES THE PARABLE OF THE WICKED HUSBANDMEN

1 ¶ AND he began to speak unto them by parables. A certain man planted a vineyard, and set an hedge about it, and digged a place for the winefat, and built a tower, and let it out to husbandmen, and went into a far country.

2 And at the season he sent to the husbandmen a servant, that he might receive from the husbandmen of the fruit of the vineyard.

3 And they caught him, and beat him, and sent him away empty.

4 And again he sent unto them another servant; and at him they cast stones, and wounded him in the head, and sent him away shamefully handled.

5 And again he sent another; and him they killed, and many others; beating some, and killing some.

---

11:23-24   Can you think of anyone you know or have read about who has this amount of faith? (See Ether 12:30 and Jacob 4:6.) Which do you think would take more faith in your life, moving a mountain or living all the commandments? Which of these do you feel would make Heavenly Father happiest?

11:25-26   The Lord has said, "I, the Lord, will forgive whom I will forgive, but of you it is required to forgive all men" (D&C 64:10).

11:27   The chief priests, scribes, and elders were Jewish religious leaders and teachers.

12:1   **winefat**—container to hold the juice from the vineyard's fruit

**let it out to husbandmen**—rented the property to some men to care for it

12:2-6   The vineyard represents the world. The servants in this parable represent ancient prophets who were rejected.

*A scribe*

6 Having yet therefore one son, his wellbeloved, he sent him also last unto them, saying, They will reverence my son.

7 But those husbandmen said among themselves, This is the heir; come, let us kill him, and the inheritance shall be ours.

8 And they took him, and killed him, and cast him out of the vineyard.

9 What shall therefore the lord of the vineyard do? he will come and destroy the husbandmen, and will give the vineyard unto others.

10 And have ye not read this scripture; The stone which the builders rejected is become the head of the corner:

11 This was the Lord's doing, and it is marvellous in our eyes?

12 And they sought to lay hold on him, but feared the people: for they knew that he had spoken the parable against them: and they left him, and went their way.

## JESUS IS QUESTIONED ABOUT PAYING TAXES TO CAESAR

13 ¶ And they send unto him certain of the Pharisees and of the Herodians, to catch him in his words.

14 And when they were come, they say unto him, Master, we know that thou art true, and carest for no man: for thou regardest not the person of men, but teachest the way of God in truth: Is it lawful to give tribute to Caesar, or not?

15 Shall we give, or shall we not give? But he, knowing their hypocrisy, said unto them, Why tempt ye me? bring me a penny, that I may see it.

16 And they brought it. And he saith unto them, Whose is this image and superscription? And they said unto him, Caesar's.

17 And Jesus answering said unto them, Render to Caesar the things that are Caesar's, and to God the things that are God's. And they marvelled at him.

## JESUS IS QUESTIONED ABOUT MARRIAGE AND THE RESURRECTION

18 ¶ Then come unto him the Sadducees, which say there is no resurrection; and they asked him, saying,

19 Master, Moses wrote unto us, If a man's brother die, and leave his wife behind him, and leave no children, that his brother should take his wife, and raise up seed unto his brother.

20 Now there were seven brethren: and the first took a wife, and dying left no seed.

21 And the second took her, and died, neither left he any seed: and the third likewise.

22 And the seven had her, and left no seed: last of all the woman died also.

23 In the resurrection therefore, when they shall rise, whose wife shall she be of them? for the seven had her to wife.

24 And Jesus answering said unto them, Do ye not

---

12:6-9 An heir is a child who inherits a parent's possessions. In this parable the heir refers to Jesus Christ, who should have been respected by the people but was rejected and killed like many other prophets.

12:10 "By quoting . . . the Messianic prophecy about the stone which the builders rejected becoming the head of the corner (Ps. 118:22-23), Jesus was announcing himself as the promised Messiah" (Bruce R. McConkie, *Doctrinal New Testament Commentary* 1:595).

12:13 **to catch him in his words**—trick him into saying something so that they could falsely accuse him

An heir The Herodians were a group of Jews who wanted members of King Herod's family to be their rulers (see LDS Bible Dictionary, s.v. "Herodians," pp. 701-2).

12:14 **carest for no man**—treat everyone the same; don't favor the rich or ignore the poor
**give tribute to Caesar**—pay taxes to the Romans

12:15 The question the Herodians asked was meant to be a trap for Jesus. If he said the Jews should pay taxes to Rome, the Jews would be angry because they hated the Romans. If he said they should not pay, the Romans could arrest him for rebelling against their authority.

**their hypocrisy**—that they were only pretending to be sincere and to be interested in Jesus' opinions

12:16 **image and superscription**—picture and title

12:18 Sadducees were religious and political leaders of the Jews.

12:18-27 The Sadducees did not even believe in the resurrection. They made up this story only to trap Jesus with his own words.

12:24-25 Marriages and families can last forever. Jesus said that people do not get married in the next life because marriages that continue after death must be performed by the holy priesthood here in this life (see D&C 132:15-19).

therefore err, because ye know not the scriptures, neither the power of God?

25 For when they shall rise from the dead, they neither marry, nor are given in marriage; but are as the angels which are in heaven.

26 And as touching the dead, that they rise: have ye not read in the book of Moses, how in the bush God spake unto him, saying, I am the God of Abraham, and the God of Isaac, and the God of Jacob?

27 He is not the God of the dead, but the God of the living: ye therefore do greatly err.

### Jesus Is Questioned About the Greatest Commandment

28 ¶ And one of the scribes came, and having heard them reasoning together, and perceiving that he had answered them well, asked him, Which is the first commandment of all?

29 And Jesus answered him, The first of all the commandments is, Hear, O Israel; The Lord our God is one Lord:

30 And thou shalt love the Lord thy God with all thy heart, and with all thy soul, and with all thy mind, and with all thy strength: this is the first commandment.

31 And the second is like, namely this, Thou shalt love thy neighbour as thyself. There is none other commandment greater than these.

32 And the scribe said unto him, Well, Master, thou hast said the truth: for there is one God; and there is none other but he:

33 And to love him with all the heart, and with all the understanding, and with all the soul, and with all the strength, and to love his neighbour as himself, is more than all whole burnt offerings and sacrifices.

34 And when Jesus saw that he answered discreetly, he said unto him, Thou art not far from the kingdom of God. And no man after that durst ask him any question.

35 ¶ And Jesus answered and said, while he taught in the temple, How say the scribes that Christ is the Son of David?

36 For David himself said by the Holy Ghost, The LORD said to my Lord, Sit thou on my right hand, till I make thine enemies thy footstool.

37 David therefore himself calleth him Lord; and whence is he then his son? And the common people heard him gladly.

38 And he said unto them in his doctrine, Beware of the scribes, which love to go in long clothing, and love salutations in the marketplaces,

39 And the chief seats in the synagogues, and the uppermost rooms at feasts:

40 Which devour widows' houses, and for a pretence make long prayers: these shall receive greater damnation.

### A Poor Widow Gives All She Has to the Lord

41 ¶ And Jesus sat over against the treasury, and beheld how the people cast money into the treasury: and many that were rich cast in much.

42 And there came a certain poor widow, and she threw in two mites, which make a farthing.

43 And he called unto him his disciples, and saith unto them, Verily I say unto you, That this poor widow hath cast more in, than all they which have cast into the treasury:

44 For all they did cast in of their abundance; but she of her want did cast in all that she had, even all her living.

---

12:28-33   The scribes also tested Jesus by asking him which commandment was most important. Jesus gave the same answer he has given in all ages (see Deuteronomy 6:5; Leviticus 19:18; D&C 59:5–6).

12:30-31   What are the greatest of all of the commandments? What are you doing to live these commandments?

12:34   **discreetly**—wisely

12:40   **devour widows' houses**—take away the property of poor widows

12:41   **treasury**—place where money donated to the temple was kept

12:42   **mites . . . farthing**—units of money worth very little

12:43-44   Even though it was not much money, this widow gave all she had. Which do you think is more important to the Lord, how much we give or how much we sacrifice in order to give?

*The widow cast in all that she had.*

## CHAPTER 13

*In this chapter Jesus prophesies of events in two different time periods: the destruction of Jerusalem soon after his mortal ministry, and the signs leading up to his second coming. Look for similarities between the events of each time.*

### JESUS PROPHESIES THE DESTRUCTION OF JERUSALEM AND HIS SECOND COMING

1 ¶ AND as he went out of the temple, one of his disciples saith unto him, Master, see what manner of stones and what buildings are here!

2 And Jesus answering said unto him, Seest thou these great buildings? there shall not be left one stone upon another, that shall not be thrown down.

3 And as he sat upon the mount of Olives over against the temple, Peter and James and John and Andrew asked him privately,

4 Tell us, when shall these things be? and what shall be the sign when all these things shall be fulfilled?

5 ¶ And Jesus answering them began to say, Take heed lest any man deceive you:

6 For many shall come in my name, saying, I am Christ; and shall deceive many.

7 And when ye shall hear of wars and rumours of wars, be ye not troubled: for such things must needs be; but the end shall not be yet.

8 For nation shall rise against nation, and kingdom against kingdom: and there shall be earthquakes in divers places, and there shall be famines and troubles: these are the beginnings of sorrows.

9 But take heed to yourselves: for they shall deliver you up to councils; and in the synagogues ye shall be beaten: and ye shall be brought before rulers and kings for my sake, for a testimony against them.

10 And the gospel must first be published among all nations.

11 But when they shall lead you, and deliver you up, take no thought beforehand what ye shall speak, neither do ye premeditate: but whatsoever shall be given you in that hour, that speak ye: for it is not ye that speak, but the Holy Ghost.

12 Now the brother shall betray the brother to death, and the father the son; and children shall rise up against their parents, and shall cause them to be put to death.

13 And ye shall be hated of all men for my name's sake: but he that shall endure unto the end, the same shall be saved.

14 ¶ But when ye shall see the abomination of desolation, spoken of by Daniel the prophet, standing where it ought not, (let him that readeth understand,) then let them that be in Judaea flee to the mountains:

15 And let him that is on the housetop not go down into the house, neither enter therein, to take any thing out of his house:

16 And let him that is in the field not turn back again for to take up his garment.

17 But woe to them that are with child, and to them that give suck in those days!

18 And pray ye that your flight be not in the winter.

19 For in those days shall be affliction, such as was not from the beginning of the creation which God created unto this time, neither shall be.

20 And except that the Lord had shortened those days, no flesh should be saved: but for the elect's sake, whom he hath chosen, he hath shortened the days.

21 And then if any man shall say to you, Lo, here is Christ; or, lo, he is there; believe him not:

22 For false Christs and false prophets shall rise, and shall shew signs and wonders, to seduce, if it were possible, even the elect.

23 But take ye heed: behold, I have foretold you all things.

---

13:1 In the Joseph Smith Translation the text for Mark 13 is the same as that for Matthew 24. It might be helpful to see the notes that are included with Matthew 24 in this book, as well as study Joseph Smith—Matthew in the Pearl of Great Price.

13:5 **Take heed lest any man deceive you**—Watch carefully so that no one can lie to you or lead you astray

13:8 **divers places**—many different places

13:9 **councils**—local rulers

**for a testimony against them**—as witnesses to them of Jesus Christ

13:10 **published**—taught or preached

13:14 See the notes given for Matthew 24:15.

13:14-19 The destruction of Jerusalem will come suddenly. A woman who is expecting a baby or must carry an infant may not be able to get away fast enough.

13:20 Who are the "elect" that God has chosen in the last days? (See D&C 29:1-2, 7-8.)

13:22 **seduce**—lead away, deceive

24 ¶ But in those days, after that tribulation, the sun shall be darkened, and the moon shall not give her light,

25 And the stars of heaven shall fall, and the powers that are in heaven shall be shaken.

26 And then shall they see the Son of man coming in the clouds with great power and glory.

27 And then shall he send his angels, and shall gather together his elect from the four winds, from the uttermost part of the earth to the uttermost part of heaven.

28 ¶ Now learn a parable of the fig tree; When her branch is yet tender, and putteth forth leaves, ye know that summer is near:

29 So ye in like manner, when ye shall see these things come to pass, know that it is nigh, even at the doors.

30 Verily I say unto you, that this generation shall not pass, till all these things be done.

31 Heaven and earth shall pass away: but my words shall not pass away.

32 But of that day and that hour knoweth no man, no, not the angels which are in heaven, neither the Son, but the Father.

33 Take ye heed, watch and pray: for ye know not when the time is.

34 For the Son of man is as a man taking a far journey, who left his house, and gave authority to his servants, and to every man his work, and commanded the porter to watch.

35 Watch ye therefore: for ye know not when the master of the house cometh, at even, or at midnight, or at the cockcrowing, or in the morning:

36 Lest coming suddenly he find you sleeping.

37 And what I say unto you I say unto all, Watch.

# CHAPTER 14

*Near the end of his mortal life, Jesus was surrounded by friends and enemies. As you read this chapter, look for his friends and enemies and how they treated him.*

## A WOMAN ANOINTS JESUS WITH OIL

1 ¶ AFTER two days was the feast of the passover, and of unleavened bread: and the chief priests and the scribes sought how they might take him by craft, and put him to death.

2 But they said, Not on the feast day, lest there be an uproar of the people.

3 And being in Bethany in the house of Simon the leper, as he sat at meat, there came a woman having an alabaster box of ointment of spikenard very precious; and she brake the box, and poured it on his head.

4 And there were some that had indignation within themselves, and said, Why was this waste of the ointment made?

5 For it might have been sold for more than three hundred pence, and have been given to the poor. And they murmured against her.

6 And Jesus said, Let her alone; why trouble ye her? she hath wrought a good work on me.

7 For ye have the poor with you always, and whensoever ye will ye may do them good: but me ye have not always.

---

13:30   A "generation" is all the people born and living at the same time. The Joseph Smith Translation explains that it is the generation in which the signs appear that will not pass away until all the signs are fulfilled (see JST, Mark 13:39 and Joseph Smith—Matthew 1:34).

13:32-36   How will knowing what will happen before Jesus Christ comes again help us prepare for that great day?

14:1   The Feast of the Passover was held each year by the Jews to remember the night the destroying angel passed over the children of Israel and slew the firstborn of Egypt. It was a time to celebrate their release from Egyptian bondage. Every year at Passover a male lamb was killed to remind the people that a Savior would someday come to deliver them. (See Exodus 12.)

*take him by craft*—arrest him by trickery or dishonesty

14:3   *an alabaster box of ointment of spikenard very precious*—an expensive container filled with very expensive oil

14:3-5   The ointment with which this woman so lovingly honored Jesus was worth "three hundred pence," or about a year's wages. Why would she give such an expensive gift? What gift could you give the Savior that would show you love him?

14:4   *had indignation*—were very displeased

14:4-5   The Gospel of John identifies Judas Iscariot as the disciple who complained that this woman wasted the expensive ointment on Jesus (see John 12:4-6).

14:6   *wrought*—done

8 She hath done what she could: she is come aforehand to anoint my body to the burying.

9 Verily I say unto you, Wheresoever this gospel shall be preached throughout the whole world, this also that she hath done shall be spoken of for a memorial of her.

## Judas Conspires to Betray the Lord

10 And Judas Iscariot, one of the twelve, went unto the chief priests, to betray him unto them.

11 And when they heard it, they were glad, and promised to give him money. And he sought how he might conveniently betray him.

## The Last Supper Is Held

12 ¶ And the first day of unleavened bread, when they killed the passover, his disciples said unto him, Where wilt thou that we go and prepare that thou mayest eat the passover?

13 And he sendeth forth two of his disciples, and saith unto them, Go ye into the city, and there shall meet you a man bearing a pitcher of water: follow him.

14 And wheresoever he shall go in, say ye to the goodman of the house, The Master saith, Where is the guestchamber, where I shall eat the passover with my disciples?

15 And he will shew you a large upper room furnished and prepared: there make ready for us.

16 And his disciples went forth, and came into the city, and found as he had said unto them: and they made ready the passover.

17 And in the evening he cometh with the twelve.

18 And as they sat and did eat, Jesus said, Verily I say unto you, One of you which eateth with me shall betray me.

19 And they began to be sorrowful, and to say unto him one by one, Is it I? and another said, Is it I?

20 And he answered and said unto them, It is one of the twelve, that dippeth with me in the dish.

21 The Son of man indeed goeth, as it is written of him: but woe to that man by whom the Son of man is betrayed! good were it for that man if he had never been born.

## Jesus Introduces the Sacrament

22 And as they did eat, Jesus took bread, and blessed, and brake it, and gave to them, and said, Take, eat: this is my body.

23 And he took the cup, and when he had given thanks, he gave it to them: and they all drank of it.

24 And he said unto them, This is my blood of the new testament, which is shed for many.

25 Verily I say unto you, I will drink no more of the fruit of the vine, until that day that I drink it new in the kingdom of God.

## Jesus Predicts Peter's Denial

26 And when they had sung an hymn, they went out into the mount of Olives.

27 And Jesus saith unto them, All ye shall be offended because of me this night: for it is written, I will smite the shepherd, and the sheep shall be scattered.

28 But after that I am risen, I will go before you into Galilee.

29 But Peter said unto him, Although all shall be offended, yet will not I.

30 And Jesus saith unto him, Verily I say unto thee, That this day, even in this night, before the cock crow twice, thou shalt deny me thrice.

31 But he spake the more vehemently, If I should die

---

14:8  It was common for the Jews to prepare bodies for burial in this manner. By accepting her anointing, Jesus again testified that he was going to die soon.

14:9  *for a memorial of*—in memory of

14:10  *betray him*—turn against him and deliver him to another

14:10-11  In contrast to the woman who honored Jesus with expensive ointment, Judas agrees to betray him to his enemies for a price. According to Matthew the price was thirty pieces of silver (see Matthew 26:14-16), which was the price of a slave.

14:19  Jesus told his Apostles that one of them would betray him. Most people would ask, "Who is it?" Why do you think the Apostles asked instead, "Is it I?"

14:22-25  Just prior to Jesus' suffering in Gethsemane he introduced the ordinance of the sacrament to his disciples. The Joseph Smith Translation adds, "As oft as ye do this ordinance, ye will remember me" (JST, Mark 14:24). We too should remember Jesus as we partake of the bread and water.

14:30  *thrice*—three times

14:31  *vehemently*—emphatically, strongly

*The Last Supper*

with thee, I will not deny thee in any wise. Likewise also said they all.

## JESUS SUFFERS IN THE GARDEN OF GETHSEMANE

32 ¶ And they came to a place which was named Gethsemane: and he saith to his disciples, Sit ye here, while I shall pray.

33 And he taketh with him Peter and James and John, and began to be sore amazed, and to be very heavy;

34 And saith unto them, My soul is exceeding sorrowful unto death: tarry ye here, and watch.

35 And he went forward a little, and fell on the ground, and prayed that, if it were possible, the hour might pass from him.

36 And he said, Abba, Father, all things are possible unto thee; take away this cup from me: nevertheless not what I will, but what thou wilt.

37 And he cometh, and findeth them sleeping, and saith unto Peter, Simon, sleepest thou? couldest not thou watch one hour?

38 Watch ye and pray, lest ye enter into temptation. The spirit truly is ready, but the flesh is weak.

39 And again he went away, and prayed, and spake the same words.

40 And when he returned, he found them asleep again, (for their eyes were heavy,) neither wist they what to answer him.

41 And he cometh the third time, and saith unto them, Sleep on now, and take your rest: it is enough, the hour is come; behold, the Son of man is betrayed into the hands of sinners.

42 Rise up, let us go; lo, he that betrayeth me is at hand.

## JUDAS ISCARIOT BETRAYS JESUS

43 ¶ And immediately, while he yet spake, cometh Judas, one of the twelve, and with him a great multitude with swords and staves, from the chief priests and the scribes and the elders.

44 And he that betrayed him had given them a token, saying, Whomsoever I shall kiss, that same is he; take him, and lead him away safely.

45 And as soon as he was come, he goeth straightway to him, and saith, Master, master; and kissed him.

46 And they laid their hands on him, and took him.

47 And one of them that stood by drew a sword, and smote a servant of the high priest, and cut off his ear.

48 And Jesus answered and said unto them, Are ye come out, as against a thief, with swords and with staves to take me?

---

14:32    *Gethsemane* means "oil press." It is the place where Jesus Christ (*Christ* meaning "the Anointed One") felt the pressing weight of the sins of the whole world.

14:32-
42    "The pain and suffering, the triumph [victory] and grandeur [greatness], of the atonement took place primarily in Gethsemane. It was there Jesus took upon himself the sins of the world on conditions of repentance." (Bruce R. McConkie, *Doctrinal New Testament Commentary* 1:774.)

*In a press such as this one, olives are crushed in order to make oil.*

14:33    **sore amazed**—astonished
**very heavy**—depressed

The Joseph Smith Translation says that the Apostles were "sore amazed" and "very heavy" and that they wondered if Jesus was really the Messiah (see JST, Mark 14:36).

14:37-
38    When Jesus found his disciples asleep, he expressed his understanding of their situation with the words, "The spirit truly is ready, but the flesh is weak." He asked them to pray for additional help. Are there times when you have felt the need to pray that you will be able to make the right choice?

14:40    **neither wist they**—neither did they know

14:43    **staves**—wooden clubs

14:44    **token**—sign

14:44-
45    In Jesus' day, greeting another person with a kiss was a sign of deep friendship. When Judas betrayed the Savior with a kiss it was a serious betrayal of trust. How would it make you feel if you had a friend betray you as Judas betrayed the Savior?

*After betraying the Savior, Judas came to realize that he had done an awful thing and he tried to return the money given to him by the chief priests and elders. These Jewish leaders did not care that Judas now felt bad. (See Matthew 27:3-10.)*

49 I was daily with you in the temple teaching, and ye took me not: but the scriptures must be fulfilled.

50 And they all forsook him, and fled.

51 And there followed him a certain young man, having a linen cloth cast about his naked body; and the young men laid hold on him:

52 And he left the linen cloth, and fled from them naked.

### Jesus Is Falsely Accused by the Chief Priests and Elders

53 ¶ And they led Jesus away to the high priest: and with him were assembled all the chief priests and the elders and the scribes.

54 And Peter followed him afar off, even into the palace of the high priest: and he sat with the servants, and warmed himself at the fire.

55 And the chief priests and all the council sought for witness against Jesus to put him to death; and found none.

56 For many bare false witness against him, but their witness agreed not together.

57 And there arose certain, and bare false witness against him, saying,

58 We heard him say, I will destroy this temple that is made with hands, and within three days I will build another made without hands.

59 But neither so did their witness agree together.

60 And the high priest stood up in the midst, and asked Jesus, saying, Answerest thou nothing? what is it which these witness against thee?

61 But he held his peace, and answered nothing. Again the high priest asked him, and said unto him, Art thou the Christ, the Son of the Blessed?

14:50   *forsook him*—left him alone

62 And Jesus said, I am: and ye shall see the Son of man sitting on the right hand of power, and coming in the clouds of heaven.

63 Then the high priest rent his clothes, and saith, What need we any further witnesses?

64 Ye have heard the blasphemy: what think ye? And they all condemned him to be guilty of death.

65 And some began to spit on him, and to cover his face, and to buffet him, and to say unto him, Prophesy: and the servants did strike him with the palms of their hands.

## THREE TIMES PETER DENIES KNOWING CHRIST

66 ¶ And as Peter was beneath in the palace, there cometh one of the maids of the high priest:

67 And when she saw Peter warming himself, she looked upon him, and said, And thou also wast with Jesus of Nazareth.

68 But he denied, saying, I know not, neither understand I what thou sayest. And he went out into the porch; and the cock crew.

69 And a maid saw him again, and began to say to them that stood by, This is one of them.

70 And he denied it again. And a little after, they that stood by said again to Peter, Surely thou art one of them: for thou art a Galilaean, and thy speech agreeth thereto.

71 But he began to curse and to swear, saying, I know not this man of whom ye speak.

72 And the second time the cock crew. And Peter called to mind the word that Jesus said unto him, Before the cock crow twice, thou shalt deny me thrice. And when he thought thereon, he wept.

## CHAPTER 15

*The last days of the Savior's mortal life confirm his greatness and provide an example for all of his disciples to follow. Watch for those qualities demonstrated*

*by Jesus that would be good for us to make a part of our lives.*

## JESUS IS JUDGED BY PILATE

1 ¶ AND straightway in the morning the chief priests held a consultation with the elders and scribes and the whole council, and bound Jesus, and carried him away, and delivered him to Pilate.

2 And Pilate asked him, Art thou the King of the Jews? And he answering said unto him, Thou sayest it.

3 And the chief priests accused him of many things: but he answered nothing.

4 And Pilate asked him again, saying, Answerest thou nothing? behold how many things they witness against thee.

5 But Jesus yet answered nothing; so that Pilate marvelled.

## BARABBAS IS SET FREE INSTEAD OF JESUS CHRIST

6 Now at that feast he released unto them one prisoner, whomsoever they desired.

7 And there was one named Barabbas, which lay bound with them that had made insurrection with him, who had committed murder in the insurrection.

8 And the multitude crying aloud began to desire him to do as he had ever done unto them.

9 But Pilate answered them, saying, Will ye that I release unto you the King of the Jews?

10 For he knew that the chief priests had delivered him for envy.

11 But the chief priests moved the people, that he should rather release Barabbas unto them.

12 And Pilate answered and said again unto them, What will ye then that I shall do unto him whom ye call the King of the Jews?

13 And they cried out again, Crucify him.

14 Then Pilate said unto them, Why, what evil hath he done? And they cried out the more exceedingly, Crucify him.

---

14:63-64  The "renting," or tearing, of clothes was a sign of deep feelings of grief or anger. The high priest was angry that Jesus said He was the Son of God. If Jesus were not really the Son of God, He would have been guilty of the sin of blasphemy.

14:65  **buffet**—hit

14:72  In Matthew's account of this story we are told that Peter wept "bitterly" (see Matthew 26:75).

15:1  The Jewish leaders had no power to carry out a death sentence, so they took Jesus to Pontius Pilate, who had this authority from Rome. Pilate, a

high-ranking Roman official, is sometimes referred to as governor (see Matthew 27:2).

15:2  **Thou sayest it**—Yes

15:6  **that feast**—the Feast of the Passover

15:7  Barabbas, whose name means "son of the father," was a terrorist and murderer.

**insurrection**—rebellion

15:8  **to do as he had ever done unto them**—to release a prisoner as he had done at every Passover

15 ¶ And so Pilate, willing to content the people, released Barabbas unto them, and delivered Jesus, when he had scourged him, to be crucified.

## JESUS IS MOCKED BY THE SOLDIERS

16 And the soldiers led him away into the hall, called Praetorium; and they call together the whole band.

17 And they clothed him with purple, and platted a crown of thorns, and put it about his head,

18 And began to salute him, Hail, King of the Jews!

19 And they smote him on the head with a reed, and did spit upon him, and bowing their knees worshipped him.

20 And when they had mocked him, they took off the purple from him, and put his own clothes on him, and led him out to crucify him.

## JESUS IS CRUCIFIED

21 And they compel one Simon a Cyrenian, who passed by, coming out of the country, the father of Alexander and Rufus, to bear his cross.

22 ¶ And they bring him unto the place Golgotha, which is, being interpreted, The place of a skull.

23 And they gave him to drink wine mingled with myrrh: but he received it not.

24 And when they had crucified him, they parted his garments, casting lots upon them, what every man should take.

25 And it was the third hour, and they crucified him.

26 And the superscription of his accusation was written over, THE KING OF THE JEWS.

27 And with him they crucify two thieves; the one on his right hand, and the other on his left.

28 And the scripture was fulfilled, which saith, And he was numbered with the transgressors.

29 And they that passed by railed on him, wagging their heads, and saying, Ah, thou that destroyest the temple, and buildest it in three days,

30 Save thyself, and come down from the cross.

31 Likewise also the chief priests mocking said among themselves with the scribes, He saved others; himself he cannot save.

32 Let Christ the King of Israel descend now from the cross, that we may see and believe. And they that were crucified with him reviled him.

33 ¶ And when the sixth hour was come, there was darkness over the whole land until the ninth hour.

34 And at the ninth hour Jesus cried with a loud voice, saying, Eloi, Eloi, lama sabachthani? which is, being interpreted, My God, my God, why hast thou forsaken me?

35 And some of them that stood by, when they heard it, said, Behold, he calleth Elias.

36 And one ran and filled a spunge full of vinegar, and put it on a reed, and gave him to drink, saying, Let alone; let us see whether Elias will come to take him down.

37 And Jesus cried with a loud voice, and gave up the ghost.

38 And the veil of the temple was rent in twain from the top to the bottom.

39 And when the centurion, which stood over against him, saw that he so cried out, and gave up the ghost, he said, Truly this man was the Son of God.

40 There were also women looking on afar off: among whom was Mary Magdalene, and Mary the mother of James the less and of Joses, and Salome;

41 (Who also, when he was in Galilee, followed him, and ministered unto him;) and many other women which came up with him unto Jerusalem.

---

15:15 **content**—calm and please

**scourged him**—beat him with a leather whip that had metal and sharp pieces of bone tied to it

15:17 Purple was considered a royal color worn by kings.

**platted**—twisted together or wove

15:23 **myrrh**—a perfume that was also used as flavoring

*A scourge (or whip)*

15:24 See for Matthew 27:35.

15:26 **superscription of his accusation**—sign indicating the crime he was charged with

15:32 **reviled**—mocked and insulted

15:37 **gave up the ghost**—died

15:38 Elder Bruce R. McConkie said: "As to the rending of the veil of the temple, it was the one thing that would symbolize, in power, the end of the old Jewish dispensation and the beginning of the new Christian day" (*The Mortal Messiah* 4:229).

## JESUS IS BURIED

42 ¶ And now when the even was come, because it was the preparation, that is, the day before the sabbath,

43 Joseph of Arimathaea, an honourable counsellor, which also waited for the kingdom of God, came, and went in boldly unto Pilate, and craved the body of Jesus.

44 And Pilate marvelled if he were already dead: and calling unto him the centurion, he asked him whether he had been any while dead.

45 And when he knew it of the centurion, he gave the body to Joseph.

46 And he bought fine linen, and took him down, and wrapped him in the linen, and laid him in a sepulchre which was hewn out of a rock, and rolled a stone unto the door of the sepulchre.

47 And Mary Magdalene and Mary the mother of Joses beheld where he was laid.

## CHAPTER 16

*Jesus Christ was resurrected! As you read this glorious account, notice how many people he appeared to and what he taught them.*

## JESUS CHRIST IS RESURRECTED

1 ¶ AND when the sabbath was past, Mary Magdalene, and Mary the mother of James, and Salome, had bought sweet spices, that they might come and anoint him.

2 And very early in the morning the first day of the week, they came unto the sepulchre at the rising of the sun.

3 And they said among themselves, Who shall roll us away the stone from the door of the sepulchre?

4 And when they looked, they saw that the stone was rolled away: for it was very great.

5 And entering into the sepulchre, they saw a young man sitting on the right side, clothed in a long white garment; and they were affrighted.

6 And he saith unto them, Be not affrighted: Ye seek Jesus of Nazareth, which was crucified: he is risen; he is not here: behold the place where they laid him.

7 But go your way, tell his disciples and Peter that he goeth before you into Galilee: there shall ye see him, as he said unto you.

8 And they went out quickly, and fled from the sepulchre; for they trembled and were amazed: neither said they any thing to any man; for they were afraid.

## JESUS APPEARS TO HIS DISCIPLES AND ASCENDS TO HEAVEN

9 ¶ Now when Jesus was risen early the first day of the week, he appeared first to Mary Magdalene, out of whom he had cast seven devils.

10 And she went and told them that had been with him, as they mourned and wept.

11 And they, when they had heard that he was alive, and had been seen of her, believed not.

12 After that he appeared in another form unto two of them, as they walked, and went into the country.

13 And they went and told it unto the residue: neither believed they them.

---

15:44   Pilate marveled that Jesus was already dead, since death by crucifixion usually took a long time, sometimes days.

15:46   *sepulchre*—burial place for the dead (same Greek word as *tomb*)

16:1   These women showed love for Jesus by caring for his body, using sweet-smelling spices.

16:2   The Jewish Sabbath was on Saturday. Jesus was resurrected on the first day of the week, which was Sunday. We now worship on that sacred day (see D&C 59:10).

16:3   *sepulchre*—burial place for the dead (same Greek word as *tomb*)

16:4   The Joseph Smith Translation adds that there were two angels there as witnesses of Jesus' resurrection (see JST, Mark 16:3).

16:5, 6   *affrighted*—afraid

16:6   When Jesus was resurrected, his spirit and his physical body were reunited (see D&C 76:22-23). Because of his resurrection each of us will live again with glorious resurrected bodies (see Alma 11:43-44).

16:12   This other appearance happened on the road to Emmaus (see Luke 24:13-35).

16:13   *residue*—rest of them

*Christ appears to the Apostles after the Resurrection.*

14 ¶ Afterward he appeared unto the eleven as they sat at meat, and upbraided them with their unbelief and hardness of heart, because they believed not them which had seen him after he was risen.

15 And he said unto them, Go ye into all the world, and preach the gospel to every creature.

16 He that believeth and is baptized shall be saved; but he that believeth not shall be damned.

17 And these signs shall follow them that believe; In my name shall they cast out devils; they shall speak with new tongues;

18 They shall take up serpents; and if they drink any deadly thing, it shall not hurt them; they shall lay hands on the sick, and they shall recover.

19 ¶ So then after the Lord had spoken unto them, he was received up into heaven, and sat on the right hand of God.

20 And they went forth, and preached every where, the Lord working with them, and confirming the word with signs following. Amen.

---

16:14    At this time there were only eleven Apostles. After Judas betrayed Jesus he took his own life (see Matthew 27:5).

**upbraided them with their unbelief**—scolded the Apostles for not believing

16:15    This is an important commandment that Jesus Christ gives to his followers. President Spencer W. Kimball asked that "every member [be] a missionary" (see *The Teachings of Spencer W. Kimball,* pp. 551-52, 585). How could you help do missionary work?

16:16    **damned**—stopped in going further

16:17    **speak with new tongues**—be able to speak another language with God's help

16:18    Modern disciples have this same promise of protection and of power to perform miracles (see D&C 84:64-73).

16:19-
20    When people become missionaries, they do not work alone. According to these verses, who works with them? Have you ever felt the Lord's help when you did missionary work?

# THE GOSPEL ACCORDING TO
# ST. LUKE*

*The Gospel of St. Luke was written by Luke, a son of Gentile parents and a student of medicine who became "a messenger of Jesus Christ" (JST, Luke 1:1). This book is his testimony of Jesus Christ as the Savior of both Jew and Gentile.*

## CHAPTER 1

*This chapter is mainly about the birth of John the Baptist. As you read, look for the miraculous events leading to his birth and why his life would be important.*

### LUKE EXPLAINS WHY HE IS WRITING HIS TESTIMONY

1 FORASMUCH as many have taken in hand to set forth in order a declaration of those things which are most surely believed among us,

2 Even as they delivered them unto us, which from the beginning were eyewitnesses, and ministers of the word;

3 It seemed good to me also, having had perfect understanding of all things from the very first, to write unto thee in order, most excellent Theophilus,

4 That thou mightest know the certainty of those things, wherein thou hast been instructed.

### ZACHARIAS IS PROMISED A SON

5 ¶ There was in the days of Herod, the king of Judaea, a certain priest named Zacharias, of the course of Abia: and his wife was of the daughters of Aaron, and her name was Elisabeth.

6 And they were both righteous before God, walking in all the commandments and ordinances of the Lord blameless.

7 And they had no child, because that Elisabeth was barren, and they both were now well stricken in years.

8 And it came to pass, that while he executed the priest's office before God in the order of his course,

9 According to the custom of the priest's office, his lot was to burn incense when he went into the temple of the Lord.

10 And the whole multitude of the people were praying without at the time of incense.

11 And there appeared unto him an angel of the Lord standing on the right side of the altar of incense.

12 And when Zacharias saw him, he was troubled, and fear fell upon him.

13 But the angel said unto him, Fear not, Zacharias: for thy prayer is heard; and thy wife Elisabeth shall bear thee a son, and thou shalt call his name John.

---

\* 🔆 The Joseph Smith Translation changes the title of this book from "The Gospel According to St. Luke" to "The Testimony of St. Luke."

1:1 📝 **a declaration**—an account

1:2 🔎 Luke is referring to those disciples who actually saw some of the events occur and then told others about them or wrote down their testimonies. Both Matthew and John, for example, were Apostles of Jesus Christ. They wrote about what they saw.

1:5 🔎 In the time of Christ, only men who were descendants of Aaron held the Aaronic Priesthood. Aaron was the brother of Moses. Both parents of John the Baptist were descendants of Aaron (see LDS Bible Dictionary, s.v. "John the Baptist," pp. 714-15). Zacharias was of the "course of Abia," which was like a priesthood quorum whose members had certain duties at times in the temple.

1:7 📝 **barren**—unable to have children

1:8 🔆 The Joseph Smith Translation changes the word *course* to *priesthood.*

📝 **executed the priest's office**—did his priesthood duties

1:8-10 🔎 Zacharias was selected to burn incense in the temple while everyone worshiped outside. "Only once in a lifetime could a man enjoy this privilege, and he was ever afterwards called 'rich'" (J. R. Dummelow, ed., *A Commentary on the Holy Bible,* p. 737).

---

| 📝 = Word Help | 🔎 = A Closer Look |
|---|---|
| 🔆 = More Light | 🔄 = Ponder This |

Words in pink are explained in the Glossary.

*Luke writes the story of Jesus' birth.*

14 And thou shalt have joy and gladness; and many shall rejoice at his birth.

15 For he shall be great in the sight of the Lord, and shall drink neither wine nor strong drink; and he shall be filled with the Holy Ghost, even from his mother's womb.

16 And many of the children of Israel shall he turn to the Lord their God.

17 And he shall go before him in the spirit and power of Elias, to turn the hearts of the fathers to the children, and the disobedient to the wisdom of the just; to make ready a people prepared for the Lord.

18 And Zacharias said unto the angel, Whereby shall I know this? for I am an old man, and my wife well stricken in years.

19 And the angel answering said unto him, I am Gabriel, that stand in the presence of God; and am sent to speak unto thee, and to shew thee these glad tidings.

20 And, behold, thou shalt be dumb, and not able to speak, until the day that these things shall be performed, because thou believest not my words, which shall be fulfilled in their season.

21 And the people waited for Zacharias, and marvelled that he tarried so long in the temple.

22 And when he came out, he could not speak unto them: and they perceived that he had seen a vision in the temple: for he beckoned unto them, and remained speechless.

23 And it came to pass, that, as soon as the days of his ministration were accomplished, he departed to his own house.

24 And after those days his wife Elisabeth conceived, and hid herself five months, saying,

25 Thus hath the Lord dealt with me in the days wherein he looked on me, to take away my reproach among men.

## MARY LEARNS SHE WILL BE THE MOTHER OF THE SON OF GOD

26 ¶ And in the sixth month the angel Gabriel was sent from God unto a city of Galilee, named Nazareth,

27 To a virgin espoused to a man whose name was Joseph, of the house of David; and the virgin's name was Mary.

28 And the angel came in unto her, and said, Hail, thou that art highly favoured, the Lord is with thee: blessed art thou among women.

29 And when she saw him, she was troubled at his saying, and cast in her mind what manner of salutation this should be.

30 And the angel said unto her, Fear not, Mary: for thou hast found favour with God.

31 And, behold, thou shalt conceive in thy womb, and bring forth a son, and shalt call his name JESUS.

32 He shall be great, and shall be called the Son of the Highest: and the Lord God shall give unto him the throne of his father David:

33 And he shall reign over the house of Jacob for ever; and of his kingdom there shall be no end.

34 Then said Mary unto the angel, How shall this be, seeing I know not a man?

35 And the angel answered and said unto her, The Holy Ghost shall come upon thee, and the power of the Highest shall overshadow thee: therefore also that holy thing which shall be born of thee shall be called the Son of God.

---

1:17 *Elias* is a title for someone who goes first to prepare the way for another. John the Baptist prepared the way before Jesus Christ and so he was an Elias. (See LDS Bible Dictionary, s.v. "Elias," p. 663.)

1:19 **shew**—This word is pronounced the same way as the word *show* and has the same meaning; *shew* is simply an old spelling of *show*.
**these glad tidings**—this good news

The Prophet Joseph Smith taught that the angel Gabriel was Noah, the Old Testament prophet (see *The Teachings of Joseph Smith,* p. 19).

1:22 **beckoned**—motioned with his arms

1:23 **ministration**—priesthood duties

1:25 **reproach**—shame

1:27 **virgin**—an unmarried person who is pure, chaste, and virtuous
**espoused**—promised to be married

1:29 **salutation**—greeting

1:31 The name *Jesus* means "God is help" or "Savior" (see LDS Bible Dictionary, s.v. "Jesus," p. 713).

*The angel announces to Mary the coming birth of Christ.*

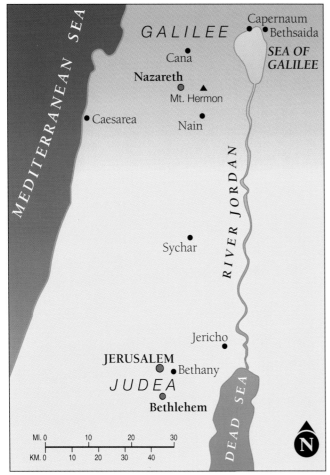

*Important places connected with the birth and childhood of Jesus*

36 And, behold, thy cousin Elisabeth, she hath also conceived a son in her old age: and this is the sixth month with her, who was called barren.

37 For with God nothing shall be impossible.

38 And Mary said, Behold the handmaid of the Lord; be it unto me according to thy word. And the angel departed from her.

## MARY VISITS ELISABETH

39 ¶ And Mary arose in those days, and went into the hill country with haste, into a city of Juda;

40 And entered into the house of Zacharias, and saluted Elisabeth.

41 And it came to pass, that, when Elisabeth heard the salutation of Mary, the babe leaped in her womb; and Elisabeth was filled with the Holy Ghost:

42 And she spake out with a loud voice, and said, Blessed art thou among women, and blessed is the fruit of thy womb.

43 And whence is this to me, that the mother of my Lord should come to me?

44 For, lo, as soon as the voice of thy salutation sounded in mine ears, the babe leaped in my womb for joy.

45 And blessed is she that believed: for there shall be a performance of those things which were told her from the Lord.

46 And Mary said, My soul doth magnify the Lord,

47 And my spirit hath rejoiced in God my Saviour.

48 For he hath regarded the low estate of his handmaiden: for, behold, from henceforth all generations shall call me blessed.

49 For he that is mighty hath done to me great things; and holy is his name.

50 And his mercy is on them that fear him from generation to generation.

51 He hath shewed strength with his arm; he hath scattered the proud in the imagination of their hearts.

52 He hath put down the mighty from their seats, and exalted them of low degree.

53 He hath filled the hungry with good things; and the rich he hath sent empty away.

54 He hath holpen his servant Israel, in remembrance of his mercy;

55 As he spake to our fathers, to Abraham, and to his seed for ever.

---

1:38  *handmaid*—woman servant; or a devoted woman

How did Mary's reaction to the angel's message compare with Zacharias's reaction? (See Luke 1:18.) Why do you think they reacted so differently?

1:42  *the fruit of thy womb*—the unborn baby Jesus

1:43  *whence*—how

1:45  *performance*—fulfillment

1:48  *estate*—place
*henceforth*—now on

1:51  *shewed*—This word is pronounced the same way as the word *showed* and has the same meaning; *shewed* is simply an old spelling of *showed*.

1:52  *exalted*—raised

1:54  *holpen*—helped

56 And Mary abode with her about three months, and returned to her own house.

## John the Baptist Is Born

57 ¶ Now Elisabeth's full time came that she should be delivered; and she brought forth a son.

58 And her neighbours and her cousins heard how the Lord had shewed great mercy upon her; and they rejoiced with her.

59 And it came to pass, that on the eighth day they came to circumcise the child; and they called him Zacharias, after the name of his father.

60 And his mother answered and said, Not so; but he shall be called John.

61 And they said unto her, There is none of thy kindred that is called by this name.

62 And they made signs to his father, how he would have him called.

63 And he asked for a writing table, and wrote, saying, His name is John. And they marvelled all.

64 And his mouth was opened immediately, and his tongue loosed, and he spake, and praised God.

65 And fear came on all that dwelt round about them: and all these sayings were noised abroad throughout all the hill country of Judaea.

66 And all they that heard them laid them up in their hearts, saying, What manner of child shall this be! And the hand of the Lord was with him.

67 ¶ And his father Zacharias was filled with the Holy Ghost, and prophesied, saying,

68 Blessed be the Lord God of Israel; for he hath visited and redeemed his people,

69 And hath raised up an horn of salvation for us in the house of his servant David;

70 As he spake by the mouth of his holy prophets, which have been since the world began:

71 That we should be saved from our enemies, and from the hand of all that hate us;

72 To perform the mercy promised to our fathers, and to remember his holy covenant;

73 The oath which he sware to our father Abraham,

74 That he would grant unto us, that we being delivered out of the hand of our enemies might serve him without fear,

75 In holiness and righteousness before him, all the days of our life.

76 And thou, child, shalt be called the prophet of the Highest: for thou shalt go before the face of the Lord to prepare his ways;

77 To give knowledge of salvation unto his people by the remission of their sins,

78 Through the tender mercy of our God; whereby the dayspring from on high hath visited us,

79 To give light to them that sit in darkness and in the shadow of death, to guide our feet into the way of peace.

80 And the child grew, and waxed strong in spirit, and was in the deserts till the day of his shewing unto Israel.

# CHAPTER 2

*Heavenly Father wanted people to know that Jesus was very special. Watch for how many people bore testimony that the baby Jesus was the Savior.*

## Jesus Christ Is Born

1 ¶ AND it came to pass in those days, that there went out a decree from Caesar Augustus, that all the world should be taxed.

---

1:57    **be delivered**—have her baby

1:59    Circumcision was first revealed to Abraham. It was an ordinance for boys who were eight days old to show they were God's covenant children. The Joseph Smith Translation indicates that it was also to remind the Lord's people that baptism was not necessary until the age of eight (see JST, Genesis 17:11-12).

1:61    **kindred**—family

1:65    **noised abroad**—talked about everywhere

1:66    **laid them up**—remembered them

1:69    "An horn of salvation" is someone who has power to save the people. Horns (like those of a powerful bull) were a symbol of power (see 1 Samuel 2:1, 10; Psalm 18:2; Psalm 132:17). Jesus Christ is the power by which salvation comes.

1:73    **oath which he sware**—promise which he made

1:78-79    The "dayspring" is the sun that comes up in the morning bringing light and life to the earth. "Christ is the dayspring from on high" (Bruce R. McConkie, *Doctrinal New Testament Commentary* 1:88).

2:1    **a decree**—an order
**taxed**—counted

   Caesar Augustus was the emperor or king of the Roman Empire. The armies of Rome had conquered the land of Israel and many other countries.

*No room in the inn*

2 (And this taxing was first made when Cyrenius was governor of Syria.)

3 And all went to be taxed, every one into his own city.

4 And Joseph also went up from Galilee, out of the city of Nazareth, into Judaea, unto the city of David, which is called Bethlehem; (because he was of the house and lineage of David:)

5 To be taxed with Mary his espoused wife, being great with child.

6 And so it was, that, while they were there, the days were accomplished that she should be delivered.

7 And she brought forth her firstborn son, and wrapped him in swaddling clothes, and laid him in a manger; because there was no room for them in the inn.

## ANGELS APPEAR TO THE SHEPHERDS AND ANNOUNCE JESUS' BIRTH

8 ¶ And there were in the same country shepherds abiding in the field, keeping watch over their flock by night.

9 And, lo, the angel of the Lord came upon them, and the glory of the Lord shone round about them: and they were sore afraid.

10 And the angel said unto them, Fear not: for, behold, I bring you good tidings of great joy, which shall be to all people.

11 For unto you is born this day in the city of David a Saviour, which is Christ the Lord.

12 And this shall be a sign unto you; Ye shall find the babe wrapped in swaddling clothes, lying in a manger.

13 And suddenly there was with the angel a multitude of the heavenly host praising God, and saying,

14 Glory to God in the highest, and on earth peace, good will toward men.

15 And it came to pass, as the angels were gone away from them into heaven, the shepherds said one to another, Let us now go even unto Bethlehem, and see this thing which is come to pass, which the Lord hath made known unto us.

16 And they came with haste, and found Mary, and Joseph, and the babe lying in a manger.

17 And when they had seen it, they made known abroad the saying which was told them concerning this child.

18 And all they that heard it wondered at those things which were told them by the shepherds.

19 But Mary kept all these things, and pondered them in her heart.

20 And the shepherds returned, glorifying and praising God for all the things that they had heard and seen, as it was told unto them.

## BABY JESUS IS RECOGNIZED IN THE TEMPLE

21 ¶ And when eight days were accomplished for the circumcising of the child, his name was called JESUS, which was so named of the angel before he was conceived in the womb.

---

2:4    *lineage*—family

2:6    *be delivered*—have the baby

2:7    The Joseph Smith Translation changes the last part of this verse to read, "There was none to give room for them in the inns" (JST, Luke 2:7). In other words, there was more than one place where the Jews would not make room for the birth of their Savior.

2:8    *abiding*—living

2:10   *tidings*—news

2:13   *heavenly host*—angels of heaven

2:16   *came with haste*—hurried

2:17   *made known abroad*—told many people

Can you imagine how you would have felt had you seen the baby Jesus? What would you have wanted to do for him?

2:19   What "things" do you think Mary thought about? Why?

2:21   *accomplished*—over
*was conceived in the womb*—began to grow inside his mother

The name *Jesus* means "God is help" or "Savior" (see LDS Bible Dictionary, s.v. "Jesus," p. 713). How has Jesus been a help or Savior to you?

*In a shepherd's field like this, an angel announced the birth of the true Shepherd.*

*"And they . . . found Mary, and Joseph, and the babe lying in a manger."*

22 And when the days of her purification according to the law of Moses were accomplished, they brought him to Jerusalem, to present him to the Lord;

23 (As it is written in the law of the Lord, Every male that openeth the womb shall be called holy to the Lord;)

24 And to offer a sacrifice according to that which is said in the law of the Lord, A pair of turtledoves, or two young pigeons.

25 ¶ And, behold, there was a man in Jerusalem, whose name was Simeon; and the same man was just and devout, waiting for the consolation of Israel: and the Holy Ghost was upon him.

26 And it was revealed unto him by the Holy Ghost, that he should not see death, before he had seen the Lord's Christ.

27 And he came by the Spirit into the temple: and when the parents brought in the child Jesus, to do for him after the custom of the law,

28 Then took he him up in his arms, and blessed God, and said,

29 Lord, now lettest thou thy servant depart in peace, according to thy word:

30 For mine eyes have seen thy salvation,

31 Which thou hast prepared before the face of all people;

32 A light to lighten the Gentiles, and the glory of thy people Israel.

33 And Joseph and his mother marvelled at those things which were spoken of him.

34 And Simeon blessed them, and said unto Mary his mother, Behold, this child is set for the fall and rising again of many in Israel; and for a sign which shall be spoken against;

35 (Yea, a sword shall pierce through thy own soul also,) that the thoughts of many hearts may be revealed.

36 And there was one Anna, a prophetess, the daughter of Phanuel, of the tribe of Aser: she was of a great age, and had lived with an husband seven years from her virginity;

37 And she was a widow of about fourscore and four years, which departed not from the temple, but served God with fastings and prayers night and day.

38 And she coming in that instant gave thanks likewise unto the Lord, and spake of him to all them that looked for redemption in Jerusalem.

39 And when they had performed all things according to the law of the Lord, they returned into Galilee, to their own city Nazareth.

## JESUS TEACHES IN THE TEMPLE

40 And the child grew, and waxed strong in spirit, filled with wisdom: and the grace of God was upon him.

41 ¶ Now his parents went to Jerusalem every year at the feast of the passover.

42 And when he was twelve years old, they went up to Jerusalem after the custom of the feast.

43 And when they had fulfilled the days, as they returned, the child Jesus tarried behind in Jerusalem; and Joseph and his mother knew not of it.

44 But they, supposing him to have been in the company, went a day's journey; and they sought him among their kinsfolk and acquaintance.

45 And when they found him not, they turned back again to Jerusalem, seeking him.

46 And it came to pass, that after three days they found him in the temple, sitting in the midst of the doctors, both hearing them, and asking them questions.

47 And all that heard him were astonished at his understanding and answers.

48 And when they saw him, they were amazed: and

---

2:22-24 🔍 "Purification" was a cleansing ceremony required by the law of Moses (see Leviticus 12).

2:25 🔍 The "consolation of Israel" was the Savior, who would come to Israel and bring them comfort and peace.

2:32 🔍 *Gentiles* is a word that means "nations." It describes those not of the family of Israel or those who do not believe in the God of Israel.

2:37 📝 **fourscore and four years**—eighty-four years

2:38 📝 **for redemption**—to be saved from their sins and from death

2:40 📝 **waxed**—became

2:41 🔍 The Feast of the Passover was an important Jewish celebration and a reminder that the angel of death "passed over" the children of Israel when the firstborn children of Egypt all died (see LDS Bible Dictionary, s.v. "Feasts," pp. 672-74).

2:46 📝 **doctors**—teachers

🕊 The Joseph Smith Translation tells us that the doctors "were hearing [Jesus], and asking him questions" (JST, Luke 2:46).

2:48 🔄 What do you learn about Mary's and Joseph's love for Jesus from Luke 2:48?

*The long-awaited promise is fulfilled: Simeon sees the Savior of Israel.*

his mother said unto him, Son, why hast thou thus dealt with us? behold, thy father and I have sought thee sorrowing.

49 And he said unto them, How is it that ye sought me? wist ye not that I must be about my Father's business?

50 And they understood not the saying which he spake unto them.

51 And he went down with them, and came to Nazareth, and was subject unto them: but his mother kept all these sayings in her heart.

52 And Jesus increased in wisdom and stature, and in favour with God and man.

# CHAPTER 3

*John the Baptist prepared the way for the Savior. Look for important gospel truths that John taught.*

## JOHN THE BAPTIST TEACHES AND BAPTIZES

1 ¶ NOW in the fifteenth year of the reign of Tiberius Caesar, Pontius Pilate being governor of Judaea, and Herod being tetrarch of Galilee, and his brother Philip tetrarch of Ituraea and of the region of Trachonitis, and Lysanias the tetrarch of Abilene,

2 Annas and Caiaphas being the high priests, the word of God came unto John the son of Zacharias in the wilderness.

3 And he came into all the country about Jordan, preaching the baptism of repentance for the remission of sins;

4 As it is written in the book of the words of Esaias the prophet, saying, The voice of one crying in the wilderness, Prepare ye the way of the Lord, make his paths straight.

5 Every valley shall be filled, and every mountain and hill shall be brought low; and the crooked shall be made straight, and the rough ways shall be made smooth;

6 And all flesh shall see the salvation of God.

7 Then said he to the multitude that came forth to be baptized of him, O generation of vipers, who hath warned you to flee from the wrath to come?

8 Bring forth therefore fruits worthy of repentance, and begin not to say within yourselves, We have Abraham to our father: for I say unto you, That God is able of these stones to raise up children unto Abraham.

9 And now also the axe is laid unto the root of the trees: every tree therefore which bringeth not forth good fruit is hewn down, and cast into the fire.

10 And the people asked him, saying, What shall we do then?

11 He answereth and saith unto them, He that hath two coats, let him impart to him that hath none; and he that hath meat, let him do likewise.

12 Then came also publicans to be baptized, and said unto him, Master, what shall we do?

13 And he said unto them, Exact no more than that which is appointed you.

---

2:49 **wist ye not**—don't you understand

Who was Jesus' actual Father? (See Luke 1:35.) What "business" did Heavenly Father want Jesus to do?

2:52 **stature**—size and strength

3:1-2 The men listed in verses 1 and 2 were the most powerful political and religious leaders of the Jews. Why do you think the "word of God" did not come to them but to John the Baptist, who lived in the wilderness?

3:3 **remission**—forgiveness

3:4-6 *Esaias* is the Greek name of *Isaiah*. John the Baptist is referring to an Isaiah passage (see Isaiah 40:3-5).

3:4 The Joseph Smith Translation adds that John testified that Jesus Christ would come to save the house of Israel and the Gentiles and to bring to pass the resurrection of the dead (see JST, Luke 3:4-11).

3:7 **generation of vipers**—people who are dangerous like poisonous snakes
**wrath**—judgments of God

3:8 **fruits worthy of repentance**—things people do to show they have repented of their sins

The Joseph Smith Translation explains that because the Jews were children of Abraham, they thought they were the only people who would be saved, even if they did not repent (see JST, Luke 3:13).

3:9 **hewn**—cut

3:10-14 Three different groups of people asked John what they should do to be saved. What do you learn from the truths he taught them that could help you be saved?

3:12 Publicans were Jews who were disliked because they collected taxes for the Romans.

3:13 **Exact**—Collect

14 And the soldiers likewise demanded of him, saying, And what shall we do? And he said unto them, Do violence to no man, neither accuse any falsely; and be content with your wages.

15 ¶ And as the people were in expectation, and all men mused in their hearts of John, whether he were the Christ, or not;

16 John answered, saying unto them all, I indeed baptize you with water; but one mightier than I cometh, the latchet of whose shoes I am not worthy to unloose: he shall baptize you with the Holy Ghost and with fire:

17 Whose fan is in his hand, and he will throughly purge his floor, and will gather the wheat into his garner; but the chaff he will burn with fire unquenchable.

18 And many other things in his exhortation preached he unto the people.

19 But Herod the tetrarch, being reproved by him for Herodias his brother Philip's wife, and for all the evils which Herod had done,

20 Added yet this above all, that he shut up John in prison.

## JESUS IS BAPTIZED

21 ¶ Now when all the people were baptized, it came to pass, that Jesus also being baptized, and praying, the heaven was opened,

22 And the Holy Ghost descended in a bodily shape like a dove upon him, and a voice came from heaven, which said, Thou art my beloved Son; in thee I am well pleased.

## JESUS' FAMILY HISTORY IS LISTED

23 And Jesus himself began to be about thirty years of age, being (as was supposed) the son of Joseph, which was the son of Heli,

24 Which was the son of Matthat, which was the son of Levi, which was the son of Melchi, which was the son of Janna, which was the son of Joseph,

25 Which was the son of Mattathias, which was the son of Amos, which was the son of Naum, which was the son of Esli, which was the son of Nagge,

26 Which was the son of Maath, which was the son of Mattathias, which was the son of Semei, which was the son of Joseph, which was the son of Juda,

27 Which was the son of Joanna, which was the son of Rhesa, which was the son of Zorobabel, which was the son of Salathiel, which was the son of Neri,

28 Which was the son of Melchi, which was the son of Addi, which was the son of Cosam, which was the son of Elmodam, which was the son of Er,

29 Which was the son of Jose, which was the son of Eliezer, which was the son of Jorim, which was the son of Matthat, which was the son of Levi,

30 Which was the son of Simeon, which was the son of Juda, which was the son of Joseph, which was the son of Jonan, which was the son of Eliakim,

31 Which was the son of Melea, which was the son of Menan, which was the son of Mattatha, which was the son of Nathan, which was the son of David,

32 Which was the son of Jesse, which was the son of Obed, which was the son of Booz, which was the son of Salmon, which was the son of Naasson,

33 Which was the son of Aminadab, which was the son of Aram, which was the son of Esrom, which was the son of Phares, which was the son of Juda,

34 Which was the son of Jacob, which was the son of Isaac, which was the son of Abraham, which was the son of Thara, which was the son of Nachor,

35 Which was the son of Saruch, which was the son of Ragau, which was the son of Phalec, which was the son of Heber, which was the son of Sala,

*Wind was used to help separate the wheat from the chaff.*

3:15 *mused*—wondered

3:17 *purge*—clean

3:18 *exhortation*—talk or sermon

3:19 *reproved*—told to repent

3:22 Why was Heavenly Father so pleased with his Son, Jesus? Is he pleased with you when you keep the commandments?

3:23 Some people thought Jesus was the son of Joseph. How can people come to know that Jesus is the Son of God?

36 Which was the son of Cainan, which was the son of Arphaxad, which was the son of Sem, which was the son of Noe, which was the son of Lamech,

37 Which was the son of Mathusala, which was the son of Enoch, which was the son of Jared, which was the son of Maleleel, which was the son of Cainan,

38 Which was the son of Enos, which was the son of Seth, which was the son of Adam, which was the son of God.

# CHAPTER 4

*In this chapter Jesus begins his mission to teach the people. See what he does to show that he is the promised Savior.*

## JESUS IS TEMPTED BY THE DEVIL

1 ¶ AND Jesus being full of the Holy Ghost returned from Jordan, and was led by the Spirit into the wilderness,

2 Being forty days tempted of the devil. And in those days he did eat nothing: and when they were ended, he afterward hungered.

3 And the devil said unto him, If thou be the Son of God, command this stone that it be made bread.

4 And Jesus answered him, saying, It is written, That man shall not live by bread alone, but by every word of God.

5 And the devil, taking him up into an high mountain, shewed unto him all the kingdoms of the world in a moment of time.

6 And the devil said unto him, All this power will I give thee, and the glory of them: for that is delivered unto me; and to whomsoever I will I give it.

7 If thou therefore wilt worship me, all shall be thine.

8 And Jesus answered and said unto him, Get thee behind me, Satan: for it is written, Thou shalt worship the Lord thy God, and him only shalt thou serve.

9 And he brought him to Jerusalem, and set him on a pinnacle of the temple, and said unto him, If thou be the Son of God, cast thyself down from hence:

10 For it is written, He shall give his angels charge over thee, to keep thee:

11 And in their hands they shall bear thee up, lest at any time thou dash thy foot against a stone.

12 And Jesus answering said unto him, It is said, Thou shalt not tempt the Lord thy God.

13 And when the devil had ended all the temptation, he departed from him for a season.

---

3:38   In the Joseph Smith Translation the last part of this passage reads, "…which was the son of Adam, who was formed of God, and the first man upon the earth" (JST, Luke 3:45; see also Moses 6:22).

4:2   The Joseph Smith Translation tells us that the devil came to tempt Jesus after His forty-day fast (see JST, Luke 4:2).

4:3–13   In Luke 4:3-13, the devil tempts Jesus, and Jesus overcomes the temptations. How did Jesus use the scriptures to help him overcome those temptations? What do you learn from his example?

4:5   The Joseph Smith Translation says that it was the Spirit that took Jesus up "into a high mountain," not the devil (see JST, Luke 4:5).

4:8   The name *Satan* means "adversary" or "enemy." Satan is the enemy of all good and of all of God's children who want to be good (see LDS Bible Dictionary, s.v. "Devil," p. 656).

4:9   The Joseph Smith Translation again explains that "the Spirit brought [Jesus] to Jerusalem, and set him on a pinnacle of the temple. And the devil came unto him . . ." (JST, Luke 4:9.)

4:11   *dash*—strike or hit

4:13   Elder David O. McKay said that the three kinds of temptations Jesus experienced are the same kinds of temptations we face today: (1) we are tempted to do things that our bodies hunger for; (2) we are tempted by pride to do things that prove how great we are; and (3) we are tempted to do things that are wrong so that we can get the riches and powers of the world (see *Gospel Ideals*, pp. 154-55).

*The pinnacle of the temple was a high, steep place. (The structures shown here are part of the model city of ancient Jerusalem at the Holyland Hotel, Jerusalem.)*

## Jesus Is Rejected by the People in Nazareth

14 ¶ And Jesus returned in the power of the Spirit into Galilee: and there went out a fame of him through all the region round about.

15 And he taught in their synagogues, being glorified of all.

16 And he came to Nazareth, where he had been brought up: and, as his custom was, he went into the synagogue on the sabbath day, and stood up for to read.

17 And there was delivered unto him the book of the prophet Esaias. And when he had opened the book, he found the place where it was written,

18 The Spirit of the Lord is upon me, because he hath anointed me to preach the gospel to the poor; he hath sent me to heal the brokenhearted, to preach deliverance to the captives, and recovering of sight to the blind, to set at liberty them that are bruised,

19 To preach the acceptable year of the Lord.

20 And he closed the book, and he gave it again to the minister, and sat down. And the eyes of all them that were in the synagogue were fastened on him.

21 And he began to say unto them, This day is this scripture fulfilled in your ears.

22 And all bare him witness, and wondered at the gracious words which proceeded out of his mouth. And they said, Is not this Joseph's son?

23 And he said unto them, Ye will surely say unto me this proverb, Physician, heal thyself: whatsoever we have heard done in Capernaum, do also here in thy country.

24 And he said, Verily I say unto you, No prophet is accepted in his own country.

25 But I tell you of a truth, many widows were in Israel in the days of Elias, when the heaven was shut up three years and six months, when great famine was throughout all the land;

26 But unto none of them was Elias sent, save unto Sarepta, a city of Sidon, unto a woman that was a widow.

27 And many lepers were in Israel in the time of Eliseus the prophet; and none of them was cleansed, saving Naaman the Syrian.

28 And all they in the synagogue, when they heard these things, were filled with wrath,

29 And rose up, and thrust him out of the city, and led him unto the brow of the hill whereon their city was built, that they might cast him down headlong.

30 But he passing through the midst of them went his way,

## Jesus Casts Out Devils and Heals Many People

31 ¶ And came down to Capernaum, a city of Galilee, and taught them on the sabbath days.

32 And they were astonished at his doctrine: for his word was with power.

33 And in the synagogue there was a man, which had a spirit of an unclean devil, and cried out with a loud voice,

34 Saying, Let us alone; what have we to do with thee, thou Jesus of Nazareth? art thou come to destroy us? I know thee who thou art; the Holy One of God.

35 And Jesus rebuked him, saying, Hold thy peace, and come out of him. And when the devil had thrown him in the midst, he came out of him, and hurt him not.

36 And they were all amazed, and spake among themselves, saying, What a word is this! for with authority and power he commandeth the unclean spirits, and they come out.

37 And the fame of him went out into every place of the country round about.

38 And he arose out of the synagogue, and entered into Simon's house. And Simon's wife's mother was taken with a great fever; and they besought him for her.

---

4:15   Synagogues were Jewish places of worship.

4:22   The people where Jesus grew up thought Jesus was only the son of Joseph and Mary. They did not believe he was the Son of God. (See John 6:42.)

4:23   **proverb**—saying

4:26   To learn more about the story of Elijah and the widow, see 1 Kings 17:8-16.

4:27   **lepers**—people with leprosy (*leprosy* being a word used for many different skin diseases and infections)

  To learn more about the story of Elisha and Naaman, see 2 Kings 5:1-19.

4:28   **wrath**—anger

4:29   **headlong**—headfirst

4:35   **rebuked**—scolded
**Hold thy peace**—Be quiet

4:36   Why do you think evil spirits always obey Jesus? Does Jesus have the power to help you overcome the devil?

4:38   **besought**—begged

39 And he stood over her, and rebuked the fever; and it left her: and immediately she arose and ministered unto them.

40 Now when the sun was setting, all they that had any sick with divers diseases brought them unto him; and he laid his hands on every one of them, and healed them.

41 And devils also came out of many, crying out, and saying, Thou art Christ the Son of God. And he rebuking them suffered them not to speak: for they knew that he was Christ.

42 And when it was day, he departed and went into a desert place: and the people sought him, and came unto him, and stayed him, that he should not depart from them.

43 And he said unto them, I must preach the kingdom of God to other cities also: for therefore am I sent.

44 And he preached in the synagogues of Galilee.

# CHAPTER 5

*This chapter contains many examples of Jesus' divinity. Look for reasons why some people believe that Jesus is the Son of God and some do not.*

## JESUS CALLS SOME DISCIPLES TO BE FISHERS OF MEN

1 ¶ AND it came to pass, that, as the people pressed upon him to hear the word of God, he stood by the lake of Gennesaret,

2 And saw two ships standing by the lake: but the fishermen were gone out of them, and were washing their nets.

3 And he entered into one of the ships, which was Simon's, and prayed him that he would thrust out a little from the land. And he sat down, and taught the people out of the ship.

4 Now when he had left speaking, he said unto Simon, Launch out into the deep, and let down your nets for a draught.

5 And Simon answering said unto him, Master, we have toiled all the night, and have taken nothing: nevertheless at thy word I will let down the net.

6 And when they had this done, they inclosed a great multitude of fishes: and their net brake.

7 And they beckoned unto their partners, which were in the other ship, that they should come and help them. And they came, and filled both the ships, so that they began to sink.

8 When Simon Peter saw it, he fell down at Jesus' knees, saying, Depart from me; for I am a sinful man, O Lord.

9 For he was astonished, and all that were with him, at the draught of the fishes which they had taken:

10 And so was also James, and John, the sons of Zebedee, which were partners with Simon. And Jesus said unto Simon, Fear not; from henceforth thou shalt catch men.

11 And when they had brought their ships to land, they forsook all, and followed him.

## JESUS HEALS A LEPER

12 ¶ And it came to pass, when he was in a certain city, behold a man full of leprosy: who seeing Jesus fell on his face, and besought him, saying, Lord, if thou wilt, thou canst make me clean.

13 And he put forth his hand, and touched him, saying, I will: be thou clean. And immediately the leprosy departed from him.

14 And he charged him to tell no man: but go, and shew thyself to the priest, and offer for thy cleansing, according as Moses commanded, for a testimony unto them.

---

4:40   *divers*—various

4:41   *suffered*—allowed

5:1   *lake of Gennesaret*—Sea of Galilee

5:3   Simon is another name for Peter. He is also called Cephas. (See John 1:40-42.)

5:4   *for a draught*—to catch fish

5:5   Why do you think Simon Peter was willing to do what Jesus told him to do?

5:11   *forsook all*—left everything behind

Peter, James, and John left everything behind to follow Jesus. What does this story teach you about these men?

5:12   *clean*—well

5:14   From the days of Moses, lepers who were healed had to go to holders of the priesthood, offer certain sacrifices, and have the priesthood holders prove they were healed of leprosy (see Leviticus 14:2).

*Simon Peter mending and washing his fishing nets*

15 But so much the more went there a fame abroad of him: and great multitudes came together to hear, and to be healed by him of their infirmities.

## JESUS FORGIVES AND HEALS A MAN WITH PALSY

16 And he withdrew himself into the wilderness, and prayed.

17 ¶ And it came to pass on a certain day, as he was teaching, that there were Pharisees and doctors of the law sitting by, which were come out of every town of Galilee, and Judaea, and Jerusalem: and the power of the Lord was present to heal them.

18 And, behold, men brought in a bed a man which was taken with a palsy: and they sought means to bring him in, and to lay him before him.

19 And when they could not find by what way they might bring him in because of the multitude, they went upon the housetop, and let him down through the tiling with his couch into the midst before Jesus.

20 And when he saw their faith, he said unto him, Man, thy sins are forgiven thee.

21 And the scribes and the Pharisees began to reason, saying, Who is this which speaketh blasphemies? Who can forgive sins, but God alone?

---

5:15    *infirmities*—sicknesses

5:16-   How does this miracle show that Jesus has
26      power to forgive sins?

5:18    *taken with a palsy*—physically disabled

5:19    *tiling*—roof coverings

5:21    Blasphemy is the sin of claiming to be like God or speaking evil of God. Of all people on earth, Jesus was the only one who could claim to be like God and not be guilty of blasphemy.

22 But when Jesus perceived their thoughts, he answering said unto them, What reason ye in your hearts?

23 Whether is easier, to say, Thy sins be forgiven thee; or to say, Rise up and walk?

24 But that ye may know that the Son of man hath power upon earth to forgive sins, (he said unto the sick of the palsy,) I say unto thee, Arise, and take up thy couch, and go into thine house.

25 And immediately he rose up before them, and took up that whereon he lay, and departed to his own house, glorifying God.

26 And they were all amazed, and they glorified God, and were filled with fear, saying, We have seen strange things to day.

## JESUS HAS COME TO HEAL SINNERS

27 ¶ And after these things he went forth, and saw a publican, named Levi, sitting at the receipt of custom: and he said unto him, Follow me.

28 And he left all, rose up, and followed him.

29 And Levi made him a great feast in his own house: and there was a great company of publicans and of others that sat down with them.

30 But their scribes and Pharisees murmured against his disciples, saying, Why do ye eat and drink with publicans and sinners?

31 And Jesus answering said unto them, They that are whole need not a physician; but they that are sick.

32 I came not to call the righteous, but sinners to repentance.

33 And they said unto him, Why do the disciples of John fast often, and make prayers, and likewise the disciples of the Pharisees; but thine eat and drink?

34 And he said unto them, Can ye make the children of the bridechamber fast, while the bridegroom is with them?

35 But the days will come, when the bridegroom shall be taken away from them, and then shall they fast in those days.

36 And he spake also a parable unto them; No man putteth a piece of a new garment upon an old; if otherwise, then both the new maketh a rent, and the piece that was taken out of the new agreeth not with the old.

37 And no man putteth new wine into old bottles; else the new wine will burst the bottles, and be spilled, and the bottles shall perish.

38 But new wine must be put into new bottles; and both are preserved.

39 No man also having drunk old wine straightway desireth new: for he saith, The old is better.

---

5:22   **perceived their thoughts**—knew what they were thinking

5:23   The Joseph Smith Translation changes verse 23 to read, "Does it require more power to forgive sins than to make the sick rise up and walk?" (JST, Luke 5:23.)

5:27   Levi is also known as Matthew (see Matthew 9:9).

     **receipt of custom**—place where taxes were collected

5:29-32   Some people act as if they are better than others. What do you learn from Jesus' example about how to treat other people?

5:31   **whole**—well

5:31-32   Jesus likens what a physician can do for a sick person to what He can do for a sinner. How does this comparison help you want to repent of your sins?

5:34   **children of the bridechamber**—wedding guests who are friends of the groom

     A "bridegroom" was a man engaged to be or already married. In this case the word is used to refer to Jesus Christ and his covenants with members of his church (see LDS Bible Dictionary, s.v. "Marriage," pp. 728-29).

5:36   **parable**—story that has deep spiritual meanings
     **rent**—tear

5:36-38   The purpose of this parable was to teach why Jesus did not try to adapt his gospel to the corrupted religious organizations of his day. He was not there to reform but to restore. (See Bruce R. McConkie, *Mortal Messiah* 2:62.)

5:39   **straightway**—immediately

# CHAPTER 6

*This chapter includes important events and teachings of the Savior. He heals the sick, calls his Apostles, and teaches gospel truths. Look for the truths that Jesus Christ teaches, both by his example and by his words.*

## JESUS HEALS ON THE SABBATH DAY

1 ¶ AND it came to pass on the second sabbath after the first, that he went through the corn fields; and his disciples plucked the ears of corn, and did eat, rubbing them in their hands.

2 And certain of the Pharisees said unto them, Why do ye that which is not lawful to do on the sabbath days?

3 And Jesus answering them said, Have ye not read so much as this, what David did, when himself was an hungred, and they which were with him;

4 How he went into the house of God, and did take and eat the shewbread, and gave also to them that were with him; which it is not lawful to eat but for the priests alone?

5 And he said unto them, That the Son of man is Lord also of the sabbath.

6 And it came to pass also on another sabbath, that he entered into the synagogue and taught: and there was a man whose right hand was withered.

7 And the scribes and Pharisees watched him, whether he would heal on the sabbath day; that they might find an accusation against him.

8 But he knew their thoughts, and said to the man which had the withered hand, Rise up, and stand forth in the midst. And he arose and stood forth.

9 Then said Jesus unto them, I will ask you one thing; Is it lawful on the sabbath days to do good, or to do evil? to save life, or to destroy it?

10 And looking round about upon them all, he said unto the man, Stretch forth thy hand. And he did so: and his hand was restored whole as the other.

11 And they were filled with madness; and communed one with another what they might do to Jesus.

## JESUS CHOOSES TWELVE APOSTLES

12 ¶ And it came to pass in those days, that he went out into a mountain to pray, and continued all night in prayer to God.

13 And when it was day, he called unto him his disciples: and of them he chose twelve, whom also he named apostles;

14 Simon, (whom he also named Peter,) and Andrew his brother, James and John, Philip and Bartholomew,

15 Matthew and Thomas, James the son of Alphaeus, and Simon called Zelotes,

16 And Judas the brother of James, and Judas Iscariot, which also was the traitor.

## JESUS DECLARES BLESSINGS FOR RIGHTEOUS PEOPLE AND WOES FOR WICKED PEOPLE

17 And he came down with them, and stood in the plain, and the company of his disciples, and a great multitude of people out of all Judaea and Jerusalem, and from the sea coast of Tyre and Sidon, which came to hear him, and to be healed of their diseases;

18 And they that were vexed with unclean spirits: and they were healed.

19 And the whole multitude sought to touch him: for there went virtue out of him, and healed them all.

20 ¶ And he lifted up his eyes on his disciples, and said, Blessed be ye poor: for yours is the kingdom of God.

21 Blessed are ye that hunger now: for ye shall be

---

6:1 **plucked the ears of corn**—picked the heads of grain

6:3-4 The Pharisees believed it was wrong to pick grain on the Sabbath (see for Mark 7:3). Jesus used the story of David's eating the temple shewbread to teach that God's rules are more important than man's rules (see 1 Samuel 21:1-6).

6:4 **shewbread**—bread, like the sacrament, that was blessed and placed in the temple; pronounced "SHOW-bread"

6:5 See for Mark 2:28.

6:6 **withered**—crippled, deformed

6:7 **an accusation against him**—something he did that was against the law

6:11 What kind of people would be "filled with madness" (rage) at the healing of a person by the Savior? Are there people who fight against the gospel and the Lord's servants today?

6:13 A disciple of Jesus is one who follows Him. An Apostle, however, is a disciple with a special calling and authority (see D&C 27:12 and 107:23).

6:18 **vexed**—troubled

6:19 **virtue**—power

filled. Blessed are ye that weep now: for ye shall laugh.

22 Blessed are ye, when men shall hate you, and when they shall separate you from their company, and shall reproach you, and cast out your name as evil, for the Son of man's sake.

23 Rejoice ye in that day, and leap for joy: for, behold, your reward is great in heaven: for in the like manner did their fathers unto the prophets.

24 But woe unto you that are rich! for ye have received your consolation.

25 Woe unto you that are full! for ye shall hunger. Woe unto you that laugh now! for ye shall mourn and weep.

26 Woe unto you, when all men shall speak well of you! for so did their fathers to the false prophets.

## JESUS TELLS HOW TO LIVE THE GOSPEL

27 ¶ But I say unto you which hear, Love your enemies, do good to them which hate you,

28 Bless them that curse you, and pray for them which despitefully use you.

29 And unto him that smiteth thee on the one cheek offer also the other; and him that taketh away thy cloke forbid not to take thy coat also.

30 Give to every man that asketh of thee; and of him that taketh away thy goods ask them not again.

31 And as ye would that men should do to you, do ye also to them likewise.

32 For if ye love them which love you, what thank have ye? for sinners also love those that love them.

33 And if ye do good to them which do good to you, what thank have ye? for sinners also do even the same.

34 And if ye lend to them of whom ye hope to receive, what thank have ye? for sinners also lend to sinners, to receive as much again.

35 But love ye your enemies, and do good, and lend, hoping for nothing again; and your reward shall be great, and ye shall be the children of the Highest:

for he is kind unto the unthankful and to the evil.

36 Be ye therefore merciful, as your Father also is merciful.

37 ¶ Judge not, and ye shall not be judged: condemn not, and ye shall not be condemned: forgive, and ye shall be forgiven:

38 Give, and it shall be given unto you; good measure, pressed down, and shaken together, and running over, shall men give into your bosom. For with the same measure that ye mete withal it shall be measured to you again.

39 And he spake a parable unto them, Can the blind lead the blind? shall they not both fall into the ditch?

40 The disciple is not above his master: but every one that is perfect shall be as his master.

41 And why beholdest thou the mote that is in thy brother's eye, but perceivest not the beam that is in thine own eye?

42 Either how canst thou say to thy brother, Brother, let me pull out the mote that is in thine eye, when thou thyself beholdest not the beam that is in thine own eye? Thou hypocrite, cast out first the beam out of thine own eye, and then shalt thou see clearly to pull out the mote that is in thy brother's eye.

43 For a good tree bringeth not forth corrupt fruit; neither doth a corrupt tree bring forth good fruit.

44 For every tree is known by his own fruit. For of thorns men do not gather figs, nor of a bramble bush gather they grapes.

45 A good man out of the good treasure of his heart bringeth forth that which is good; and an evil man out of the evil treasure of his heart bringeth forth that which is evil: for of the abundance of the heart his mouth speaketh.

46 And why call ye me, Lord, Lord, and do not the things which I say?

47 Whosoever cometh to me, and heareth my sayings, and doeth them, I will shew you to whom he is like:

---

6:22    *reproach*—say evil things about

6:24    *woe*—grief or sorrow
     *consolation*—comfort

6:27-49   In verses 27-49, Jesus teaches higher laws of the gospel. How would you be different if you lived these higher laws? How would your family be different if they all did?

6:37-38   The Lord will judge us the same way we judged others, and he will bless us just as much as we blessed others (see D&C 1:10).

6:41    *mote*—small sliver
     *beam*—big piece of wood

6:42    *hypocrite*—person who pretends to be good when he or she is not

6:45    *abundance*—fulness

*Area of Galilee, where Jesus healed many*

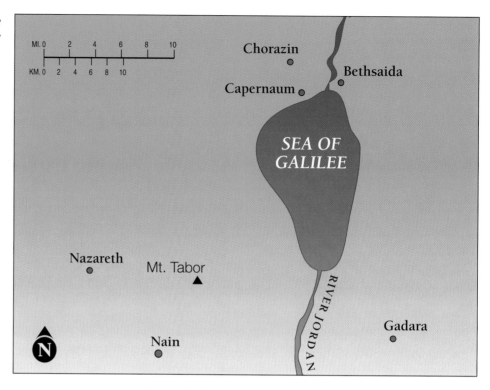

48 He is like a man which built an house, and digged deep, and laid the foundation on a rock: and when the flood arose, the stream beat vehemently upon that house, and could not shake it: for it was founded upon a rock.

49 But he that heareth, and doeth not, is like a man that without a foundation built an house upon the earth; against which the stream did beat vehemently, and immediately it fell; and the ruin of that house was great.

## CHAPTER 7

*Jesus' life was one of loving service and example. Watch for ways people's lives are changed when Jesus comes near them.*

### JESUS HEALS THE CENTURION'S SERVANT

1 ¶ NOW when he had ended all his sayings in the audience of the people, he entered into Capernaum.

2 And a certain centurion's servant, who was dear unto him, was sick, and ready to die.

3 And when he heard of Jesus, he sent unto him the elders of the Jews, beseeching him that he would come and heal his servant.

4 And when they came to Jesus, they besought him instantly, saying, That he was worthy for whom he should do this:

5 For he loveth our nation, and he hath built us a synagogue.

6 Then Jesus went with them. And when he was now not far from the house, the centurion sent friends to him, saying unto him, Lord, trouble not thyself: for I am not worthy that thou shouldest enter under my roof:

7 Wherefore neither thought I myself worthy to come unto thee: but say in a word, and my servant shall be healed.

8 For I also am a man set under authority, having under me soldiers, and I say unto one, Go, and he goeth; and to another, Come, and he cometh; and to my servant, Do this, and he doeth it.

9 When Jesus heard these things, he marvelled at him, and turned him about, and said unto the people that followed him, I say unto you, I have not found so great faith, no, not in Israel.

10 And they that were sent, returning to the house, found the servant whole that had been sick.

### JESUS RAISES A WIDOW'S SON FROM THE DEAD

11 ¶ And it came to pass the day after, that he went into a city called Nain; and many of his disciples went with him, and much people.

---

6:48   **vehemently**—strongly

How is not doing what is right like building your house on dirt or sand? How would that kind of a house hold up in a terrible storm? How is living the commandments like building your house on a rock?

7:2   A "centurion" was a Roman military officer who was in charge of one hundred soldiers (see LDS Bible Dictionary, s.v. "Centurion," p. 632).

7:3   **beseeching**—begging

7:8   **set under authority**—placed under others' authority or power

12 Now when he came nigh to the gate of the city, behold, there was a dead man carried out, the only son of his mother, and she was a widow: and much people of the city was with her.

13 And when the Lord saw her, he had compassion on her, and said unto her, Weep not.

14 And he came and touched the bier: and they that bare him stood still. And he said, Young man, I say unto thee, Arise.

15 And he that was dead sat up, and began to speak. And he delivered him to his mother.

16 And there came a fear on all: and they glorified God, saying, That a great prophet is risen up among us; and, That God hath visited his people.

17 And this rumour of him went forth throughout all Judaea, and throughout all the region round about.

## JESUS TESTIFIES OF HIMSELF AND OF JOHN THE BAPTIST

18 And the disciples of John shewed him of all these things.

19 ¶ And John calling unto him two of his disciples sent them to Jesus, saying, Art thou he that should come? or look we for another?

20 When the men were come unto him, they said, John Baptist hath sent us unto thee, saying, Art thou he that should come? or look we for another?

21 And in that same hour he cured many of their infirmities and plagues, and of evil spirits; and unto many that were blind he gave sight.

22 Then Jesus answering said unto them, Go your way, and tell John what things ye have seen and heard; how that the blind see, the lame walk, the lepers are cleansed, the deaf hear, the dead are raised, to the poor the gospel is preached.

23 And blessed is he, whosoever shall not be offended in me.

24 And when the messengers of John were departed, he began to speak unto the people concerning John, What went ye out into the wilderness for to see? A reed shaken with the wind?

25 But what went ye out for to see? A man clothed in soft raiment? Behold, they which are gorgeously apparelled, and live delicately, are in kings' courts.

26 But what went ye out for to see? A prophet? Yea, I say unto you, and much more than a prophet.

27 This is he, of whom it is written, Behold, I send my messenger before thy face, which shall prepare thy way before thee.

28 For I say unto you, Among those that are born of women there is not a greater prophet than John the Baptist: but he that is least in the kingdom of God is greater than he.

29 And all the people that heard him, and the publicans, justified God, being baptized with the baptism of John.

30 But the Pharisees and lawyers rejected the counsel of God against themselves, being not baptized of him.

31 And the Lord said, Whereunto then shall I liken the men of this generation? and to what are they like?

32 They are like unto children sitting in the marketplace, and calling one to another, and saying, We have piped unto you, and ye have not danced; we have mourned to you, and ye have not wept.

---

7:13    **compassion on**—sympathy for, love for

7:13-16  According to verse 13, why did Jesus Christ raise the widow's son? What was the reaction of those who saw this miracle? How do you think you would have felt if you had been there to see Jesus raise this man from the dead?

7:14    **bier**—stretcher upon which dead people were carried to their graves

7:16    The word *fear* in Greek can sometimes mean *reverence* (see LDS Bible Dictionary, s.v. "Fear," p. 672).

7:17    **this rumour of him**—the things people said about Jesus

7:19    John the Baptist wanted his disciples to ask Jesus if He was the promised Messiah. John asked them to do this so they would learn who Jesus was and follow him. (See Bruce R. McConkie, *Doctrinal New Testament Commentary* 1:261.)

7:25    **raiment**—clothing
        **gorgeously apparelled**—beautifully dressed
        **live delicately**—live in luxury

7:28    "He that is least in the kingdom" refers to Jesus Christ (see *The Teachings of Joseph Smith*, p. 354).

7:31-35  Jesus compared the Jews to children who are not happy no matter how you try to please them. They rejected John the Baptist because he would not eat and drink with them. Then they rejected Jesus, saying he ate and drank too much and with the wrong people. Do you ever let looking for faults in other Church members get in the way of your spiritual growth?

7:32    **piped**—played music

33 For John the Baptist came neither eating bread nor drinking wine; and ye say, He hath a devil.

34 The Son of man is come eating and drinking; and ye say, Behold a gluttonous man, and a winebibber, a friend of publicans and sinners!

35 But wisdom is justified of all her children.

## JESUS FORGIVES A WOMAN OF HER SINS

36 ¶ And one of the Pharisees desired him that he would eat with him. And he went into the Pharisee's house, and sat down to meat.

37 And, behold, a woman in the city, which was a sinner, when she knew that Jesus sat at meat in the Pharisee's house, brought an alabaster box of ointment,

38 And stood at his feet behind him weeping, and began to wash his feet with tears, and did wipe them with the hairs of her head, and kissed his feet, and anointed them with the ointment.

39 Now when the Pharisee which had bidden him saw it, he spake within himself, saying, This man, if he were a prophet, would have known who and what manner of woman this is that toucheth him: for she is a sinner.

40 And Jesus answering said unto him, Simon, I have somewhat to say unto thee. And he saith, Master, say on.

41 There was a certain creditor which had two debtors: the one owed five hundred pence, and the other fifty.

42 And when they had nothing to pay, he frankly forgave them both. Tell me therefore, which of them will love him most?

43 Simon answered and said, I suppose that he, to whom he forgave most. And he said unto him, Thou hast rightly judged.

44 And he turned to the woman, and said unto Simon, Seest thou this woman? I entered into thine house, thou gavest me no water for my feet: but she hath washed my feet with tears, and wiped them with the hairs of her head.

45 Thou gavest me no kiss: but this woman since the time I came in hath not ceased to kiss my feet.

46 My head with oil thou didst not anoint: but this woman hath anointed my feet with ointment.

47 Wherefore I say unto thee, Her sins, which are many, are forgiven; for she loved much: but to whom little is forgiven, the same loveth little.

48 And he said unto her, Thy sins are forgiven.

49 And they that sat at meat with him began to say within themselves, Who is this that forgiveth sins also?

50 And he said to the woman, Thy faith hath saved thee; go in peace.

## CHAPTER 8

*Jesus teaches that the faith people have in him affects how he can use his power to bless their lives. Look for what the Savior does to bless the lives of others with his power.*

## JESUS TEACHES WITH PARABLES

1 ¶ AND it came to pass afterward, that he went throughout every city and village, preaching and shewing the glad tidings of the kingdom of God: and the twelve were with him,

2 And certain women, which had been healed of evil spirits and infirmities, Mary called Magdalene, out of whom went seven devils,

3 And Joanna the wife of Chuza Herod's steward, and Susanna, and many others, which ministered unto him of their substance.

---

7:34   *a gluttonous man*—someone who eats great amounts of food
**winebibber**—person who drinks great amounts of wine

7:37-38   This ointment was a kind of oil that contained soothing medicine or perfume. When this woman washed, dried, and anointed the Savior's feet, it was an act of love, respect, and honor.

7:39   *bidden him*—invited him to dinner

7:41   *creditor*—someone who lends people money
**debtors**—people who owe money

7:48   How do you think Jesus' statement made the woman feel? What would you be willing to do to have Jesus say this to you?

8:1   *tidings*—news

The phrase "kingdom of God" is used several ways throughout the scriptures. Often it means the celestial kingdom. Sometimes it refers to the Lord's true church on the earth. Other times it refers to the government over which Jesus Christ will reign during the Millennium. (See Bruce R. McConkie, *Mormon Doctrine*, pp. 415-17.)

8:2   *infirmities*—sicknesses

4 ¶ And when much people were gathered together, and were come to him out of every city, he spake by a parable:

5 A sower went out to sow his seed: and as he sowed, some fell by the way side; and it was trodden down, and the fowls of the air devoured it.

6 And some fell upon a rock; and as soon as it was sprung up, it withered away, because it lacked moisture.

7 And some fell among thorns; and the thorns sprang up with it, and choked it.

8 And other fell on good ground, and sprang up, and bare fruit an hundredfold. And when he had said these things, he cried, He that hath ears to hear, let him hear.

9 And his disciples asked him, saying, What might this parable be?

10 And he said, Unto you it is given to know the mysteries of the kingdom of God: but to others in parables; that seeing they might not see, and hearing they might not understand.

11 Now the parable is this: The seed is the word of God.

12 Those by the way side are they that hear; then cometh the devil, and taketh away the word out of their hearts, lest they should believe and be saved.

13 They on the rock are they, which, when they hear, receive the word with joy; and these have no root, which for a while believe, and in time of temptation fall away.

14 And that which fell among thorns are they, which, when they have heard, go forth, and are choked with cares and riches and pleasures of this life, and bring no fruit to perfection.

15 But that on the good ground are they, which in an honest and good heart, having heard the word, keep it, and bring forth fruit with patience.

16 No man, when he hath lighted a candle, covereth it with a vessel, or putteth it under a bed; but setteth it on a candlestick, that they which enter in may see the light.

17 For nothing is secret, that shall not be made manifest; neither any thing hid, that shall not be known and come abroad.

18 Take heed therefore how ye hear: for whosoever hath, to him shall be given; and whosoever hath not, from him shall be taken even that which he seemeth to have.

## Jesus' Family Visits Him

19 Then came to him his mother and his brethren, and could not come at him for the press.

20 And it was told him by certain which said, Thy mother and thy brethren stand without, desiring to see thee.

21 And he answered and said unto them, My mother and my brethren are these which hear the word of God, and do it.

## Jesus Calms the Sea

22 ¶ Now it came to pass on a certain day, that he went into a ship with his disciples: and he said unto them, Let us go over unto the other side of the lake. And they launched forth.

23 But as they sailed he fell asleep: and there came down a storm of wind on the lake; and they were filled with water, and were in jeopardy.

24 And they came to him, and awoke him, saying, Master, master, we perish. Then he arose, and rebuked the wind and the raging of the water: and they ceased, and there was a calm.

25 And he said unto them, Where is your faith? And they being afraid wondered, saying one to another, What manner of man is this! for he commandeth even the winds and water, and they obey him.

## Jesus Casts Out a Legion of Devils

26 And they arrived at the country of the Gadarenes, which is over against Galilee.

---

8:4-15   See helps for Matthew 13:1-23

8:5      **way side**—side of the road
         **devoured**—ate

8:6      **withered away**—dried up

8:10     **mysteries**—sacred truths

8:14     **fruit**—good deeds

8:17     **manifest**—known

8:19     **press**—crowd of people

8:21     According to this verse, how does one become part of Jesus' family?

8:23     The Joseph Smith Translation changes the latter part of this verse to read, "…and they were filled with fear, and were in danger" (JST, Luke 8:23).

8:25     What happens to your fear when you increase in faith?

27 And when he went forth to land, there met him out of the city a certain man, which had devils long time, and ware no clothes, neither abode in any house, but in the tombs.

28 When he saw Jesus, he cried out, and fell down before him, and with a loud voice said, What have I to do with thee, Jesus, thou Son of God most high? I beseech thee, torment me not.

29 (For he had commanded the unclean spirit to come out of the man. For oftentimes it had caught him: and he was kept bound with chains and in fetters; and he brake the bands, and was driven of the devil into the wilderness.)

30 And Jesus asked him, saying, What is thy name? And he said, Legion: because many devils were entered into him.

31 And they besought him that he would not command them to go out into the deep.

32 And there was there an herd of many swine feeding on the mountain: and they besought him that he would suffer them to enter into them. And he suffered them.

33 Then went the devils out of the man, and entered into the swine: and the herd ran violently down a steep place into the lake, and were choked.

34 When they that fed them saw what was done, they fled, and went and told it in the city and in the country.

35 Then they went out to see what was done; and came to Jesus, and found the man, out of whom the devils were departed, sitting at the feet of Jesus, clothed, and in his right mind: and they were afraid.

36 They also which saw it told them by what means he that was possessed of the devils was healed.

37 Then the whole multitude of the country of the Gadarenes round about besought him to depart from them; for they were taken with great fear: and he went up into the ship, and returned back again.

38 Now the man out of whom the devils were departed besought him that he might be with him: but Jesus sent him away, saying,

39 Return to thine own house, and shew how great things God hath done unto thee. And he went his way, and published throughout the whole city how great things Jesus had done unto him.

### JESUS BLESSES TWO PEOPLE

40 ¶ And it came to pass, that, when Jesus was returned, the people gladly received him: for they were all waiting for him.

41 And, behold, there came a man named Jairus, and he was a ruler of the synagogue: and he fell down at Jesus' feet, and besought him that he would come into his house:

42 For he had one only daughter, about twelve years of age, and she lay a dying. But as he went the people thronged him.

43 And a woman having an issue of blood twelve years, which had spent all her living upon physicians, neither could be healed of any,

44 Came behind him, and touched the border of his garment: and immediately her issue of blood stanched.

45 And Jesus said, Who touched me? When all denied, Peter and they that were with him said, Master, the multitude throng thee and press thee, and sayest thou, Who touched me?

46 And Jesus said, Somebody hath touched me: for I perceive that virtue is gone out of me.

47 And when the woman saw that she was not hid, she came trembling, and falling down before him, she declared unto him before all the people for what cause she had touched him, and how she was healed immediately.

48 And he said unto her, Daughter, be of good comfort: thy faith hath made thee whole; go in peace.

---

8:27   *tombs*—burial places for the dead

8:28   Elder LeGrand Richards explained how the devils knew Jesus. "No one needed to introduce the Savior" because the devils had known the Savior in the premortal existence (See Conference Report, October 1949, p. 52.)

   *beseech*—beg

8:32   *swine*—pigs
   *suffer them to*—let them

8:39   *published*—told people

8:42   *thronged*—crowded around

8:43   *having an issue of blood*—who had been bleeding

8:44   *stanched*—stopped

8:46   *virtue*—power

8:48   According to this verse, was the woman healed because of touching Jesus' clothes or was she healed by her faith in Jesus Christ? How can increasing your faith in Jesus Christ improve your life?

49 While he yet spake, there cometh one from the ruler of the synagogue's house, saying to him, Thy daughter is dead; trouble not the Master.

50 But when Jesus heard it, he answered him, saying, Fear not: believe only, and she shall be made whole.

51 And when he came into the house, he suffered no man to go in, save Peter, and James, and John, and the father and the mother of the maiden.

52 And all wept, and bewailed her: but he said, Weep not; she is not dead, but sleepeth.

53 And they laughed him to scorn, knowing that she was dead.

54 And he put them all out, and took her by the hand, and called, saying, Maid, arise.

55 And her spirit came again, and she arose straightway: and he commanded to give her meat.

56 And her parents were astonished: but he charged them that they should tell no man what was done.

# CHAPTER 9

*This chapter shows that Jesus Christ spent much time preparing and instructing his Apostles. Look for how Jesus prepared his Apostles to lead his church.*

## JESUS SENDS HIS APOSTLES ON MISSIONS

1 ¶ THEN he called his twelve disciples together, and gave them power and authority over all devils, and to cure diseases.

2 And he sent them to preach the kingdom of God, and to heal the sick.

3 And he said unto them, Take nothing for your journey, neither staves, nor scrip, neither bread, neither money; neither have two coats apiece.

4 And whatsoever house ye enter into, there abide, and thence depart.

5 And whosoever will not receive you, when ye go out of that city, shake off the very dust from your feet for a testimony against them.

6 And they departed, and went through the towns, preaching the gospel, and healing every where.

## HEROD AND THE PEOPLE WONDER WHO JESUS IS

7 Now Herod the tetrarch heard of all that was done by him: and he was perplexed, because that it was said of some, that John was risen from the dead;

8 And of some, that Elias had appeared; and of others, that one of the old prophets was risen again.

9 And Herod said, John have I beheaded: but who is this, of whom I hear such things? And he desired to see him.

## THE APOSTLES RETURN AND JESUS FEEDS THE FIVE THOUSAND

10 ¶ And the apostles, when they were returned, told him all that they had done. And he took them, and went aside privately into a desert place belonging to the city called Bethsaida.

11 And the people, when they knew it, followed him: and he received them, and spake unto them of the kingdom of God, and healed them that had need of healing.

12 And when the day began to wear away, then came the twelve, and said unto him, Send the multitude away, that they may go into the towns and country round about, and lodge, and get victuals: for we are here in a desert place.

13 But he said unto them, Give ye them to eat. And they said, We have no more but five loaves and two fishes; except we should go and buy meat for all this people.

14 For they were about five thousand men. And he said to his disciples, Make them sit down by fifties in a company.

---

8:51    **maiden**—young girl

8:52    **bewailed her**—cried out loud over her death and hit their chests because of sadness

8:53    **laughed him to scorn**—made fun of him

8:54    Why do you think Jesus would not let the people be in the room when he blessed the girl? (See Mormon 9:20.)

8:56    **astonished**—amazed

9:1    To learn who these twelve men were, see Luke 6:13-16.

9:3    **staves**—walking sticks
**scrip**—bag for food or clothing

9:7    Herod the tetrarch was the son of Herod the Great, who killed the children in Bethlehem (see Matthew 2:16-18). Herod the tetrarch had John the Baptist killed.

   **was perplexed**—could not understand, was confused

9:12    **victuals**—food

15 And they did so, and made them all sit down.

16 Then he took the five loaves and the two fishes, and looking up to heaven, he blessed them, and brake, and gave to the disciples to set before the multitude.

17 And they did eat, and were all filled: and there was taken up of fragments that remained to them twelve baskets.

## PETER TESTIFIES THAT JESUS IS THE CHRIST

18 ¶ And it came to pass, as he was alone praying, his disciples were with him: and he asked them, saying, Whom say the people that I am?

19 They answering said, John the Baptist; but some say, Elias; and others say, that one of the old prophets is risen again.

20 He said unto them, But whom say ye that I am? Peter answering said, The Christ of God.

21 And he straitly charged them, and commanded them to tell no man that thing;

22 Saying, The Son of man must suffer many things, and be rejected of the elders and chief priests and scribes, and be slain, and be raised the third day.

## JESUS EXPLAINS WHAT A PERSON MUST DO TO COME UNTO HIM

23 And he said to them all, If any man will come after me, let him deny himself, and take up his cross daily, and follow me.

24 For whosoever will save his life shall lose it: but whosoever will lose his life for my sake, the same shall save it.

25 For what is a man advantaged, if he gain the whole world, and lose himself, or be cast away?

26 For whosoever shall be ashamed of me and of my words, of him shall the Son of man be ashamed, when he shall come in his own glory, and in his Father's, and of the holy angels.

27 But I tell you of a truth, there be some standing here, which shall not taste of death, till they see the kingdom of God.

## JESUS TAKES PETER, JAMES, AND JOHN UP THE MOUNT OF TRANSFIGURATION

28 ¶ And it came to pass about an eight days after these sayings, he took Peter and John and James, and went up into a mountain to pray.

29 And as he prayed, the fashion of his countenance was altered, and his raiment was white and glistering.

30 And, behold, there talked with him two men, which were Moses and Elias:

31 Who appeared in glory, and spake of his decease which he should accomplish at Jerusalem.

32 But Peter and they that were with him were heavy

---

9:17   *fragments*—pieces of food

9:20   How would you answer the Savior's question?

9:23   The Joseph Smith Translation explains that to take up our "cross" means to keep the commandments and stay away from everything that is unholy or evil (see JST, Matthew 16:26).

9:24   The Joseph Smith Translation changes verse 24 to read, "For whosoever will save his life, must be willing to lose it for my sake; and whosoever will be willing to lose his life for my sake, the same shall save it" (JST, Luke 9:24).

9:25   *is a man advantaged*—does a man get

9:26   The Joseph Smith Translation changes the last part of this verse to read, "…when he shall come in his own kingdom, clothed in the glory of his Father, with the holy angels" (JST, Luke 9:26).

9:28-36   See the helps for Matthew 17:1-13.

9:29   *fashion of his countenance*—way his face looked
*glistering*—shining brightly

9:31   The Joseph Smith Translation changes the word *decease* to *death,* and immediately after adds "and also his resurrection" (JST, Luke 9:31).

*Some believe that this mountain, known as Mount Tabor, was the site of the Transfiguration described in Luke 9:28-36. In comparison with the tall Rocky Mountains in America or with the Himalayas in Asia, Mount Tabor may not seem to qualify as a "mountain." In comparison with the relatively flat terrain in the immediate surrounding area, however, this hill can indeed be called a "mountain" or "mount."*

*Christ with children and disciples*

with sleep: and when they were awake, they saw his glory, and the two men that stood with him.

33 And it came to pass, as they departed from him, Peter said unto Jesus, Master, it is good for us to be here: and let us make three tabernacles; one for thee, and one for Moses, and one for Elias: not knowing what he said.

34 While he thus spake, there came a cloud, and overshadowed them: and they feared as they entered into the cloud.

35 And there came a voice out of the cloud, saying, This is my beloved Son: hear him.

36 And when the voice was past, Jesus was found alone. And they kept it close, and told no man in those days any of those things which they had seen.

## JESUS CASTS OUT A DEVIL

37 ¶ And it came to pass, that on the next day, when they were come down from the hill, much people met him.

38 And, behold, a man of the company cried out, saying, Master, I beseech thee, look upon my son: for he is mine only child.

39 And, lo, a spirit taketh him, and he suddenly crieth out; and it teareth him that he foameth again, and bruising him hardly departeth from him.

40 And I besought thy disciples to cast him out; and they could not.

41 And Jesus answering said, O faithless and perverse generation, how long shall I be with you, and suffer you? Bring thy son hither.

---

9:35    When Heavenly Father speaks to man it is to introduce his Son (see JST, John 1:19). Can you think of other times when Heavenly Father has introduced his Son?

9:41    **perverse generation**—people who have turned against God

42 And as he was yet a coming, the devil threw him down, and tare him. And Jesus rebuked the unclean spirit, and healed the child, and delivered him again to his father.

## JESUS TEACHES ABOUT GREATNESS

43 ¶ And they were all amazed at the mighty power of God. But while they wondered every one at all things which Jesus did, he said unto his disciples,

44 Let these sayings sink down into your ears: for the Son of man shall be delivered into the hands of men.

45 But they understood not this saying, and it was hid from them, that they perceived it not: and they feared to ask him of that saying.

46 Then there arose a reasoning among them, which of them should be greatest.

47 And Jesus, perceiving the thought of their heart, took a child, and set him by him,

48 And said unto them, Whosoever shall receive this child in my name receiveth me: and whosoever shall receive me receiveth him that sent me: for he that is least among you all, the same shall be great.

49 And John answered and said, Master, we saw one casting out devils in thy name; and we forbade him, because he followeth not with us.

50 And Jesus said unto him, Forbid him not: for he that is not against us is for us.

51 ¶ And it came to pass, when the time was come that he should be received up, he stedfastly set his face to go to Jerusalem,

52 And sent messengers before his face: and they went, and entered into a village of the Samaritans, to make ready for him.

53 And they did not receive him, because his face was as though he would go to Jerusalem.

54 And when his disciples James and John saw this, they said, Lord, wilt thou that we command fire to come down from heaven, and consume them, even as Elias did?

55 But he turned, and rebuked them, and said, Ye know not what manner of spirit ye are of.

56 For the Son of man is not come to destroy men's lives, but to save them. And they went to another village.

## JESUS EXPLAINS WHAT A PERSON MUST DO TO FOLLOW HIM

57 ¶ And it came to pass, that, as they went in the way, a certain man said unto him, Lord, I will follow thee whithersoever thou goest.

58 And Jesus said unto him, Foxes have holes, and birds of the air have nests; but the Son of man hath not where to lay his head.

59 And he said unto another, Follow me. But he said, Lord, suffer me first to go and bury my father.

60 Jesus said unto him, Let the dead bury their dead: but go thou and preach the kingdom of God.

61 And another also said, Lord, I will follow thee; but let me first go bid them farewell, which are at home at my house.

62 And Jesus said unto him, No man, having put his hand to the plough, and looking back, is fit for the kingdom of God.

## CHAPTER 10

*Jesus chooses seventy others to help preach the gospel. See what they were able to do with the priesthood power Jesus gave them.*

## THE LORD SENDS THE SEVENTY ON MISSIONS

1 ¶ AFTER these things the Lord appointed other seventy also, and sent them two and two before his

---

9:44 The Joseph Smith Translation changes the word *ears* to *hearts* (JST, Luke 9:44).

9:54 *consume them*—burn them up

9:57 *whithersoever*—wherever

9:57-62 What must you do to follow Jesus? To be true disciples Jesus says we must be willing to give up houses, family, and friends when necessary. Read also Matthew 16:25-26 and 19:29 and ponder why a person would want to give up the things of this life to serve Jesus.

9:59 *suffer*—allow, let

9:59-60 Elder Bruce R. McConkie explained that these verses apply specifically to those called to serve full-time: "When men are called of God . . . , those calls take precedence over all conflicting interests. Missionaries so sent forth habitually forsake all personal and family obligations. Loved ones may pass away, but missionaries remain at their posts, preaching the kingdom of God." (*Doctrinal New Testament Commentary* 1:304.)

10:1 Why do you think the Lord sends out his missionaries "two by two"?

*appointed*—called and gave authority to

face into every city and place, whither he himself would come.

2 Therefore said he unto them, The harvest truly is great, but the labourers are few: pray ye therefore the Lord of the harvest, that he would send forth labourers into his harvest.

3 Go your ways: behold, I send you forth as lambs among wolves.

4 Carry neither purse, nor scrip, nor shoes: and salute no man by the way.

5 And into whatsoever house ye enter, first say, Peace be to this house.

6 And if the son of peace be there, your peace shall rest upon it: if not, it shall turn to you again.

7 And in the same house remain, eating and drinking such things as they give: for the labourer is worthy of his hire. Go not from house to house.

8 And into whatsoever city ye enter, and they receive you, eat such things as are set before you:

9 And heal the sick that are therein, and say unto them, The kingdom of God is come nigh unto you.

10 But into whatsoever city ye enter, and they receive you not, go your ways out into the streets of the same, and say,

11 Even the very dust of your city, which cleaveth on us, we do wipe off against you: notwithstanding be ye sure of this, that the kingdom of God is come nigh unto you.

12 But I say unto you, that it shall be more tolerable in that day for Sodom, than for that city.

13 Woe unto thee, Chorazin! woe unto thee, Bethsaida! for if the mighty works had been done in Tyre and Sidon, which have been done in you, they had a great while ago repented, sitting in sackcloth and ashes.

14 But it shall be more tolerable for Tyre and Sidon at the judgment, than for you.

15 And thou, Capernaum, which art exalted to heaven, shalt be thrust down to hell.

16 He that heareth you heareth me; and he that despiseth you despiseth me; and he that despiseth me despiseth him that sent me.

## THE SEVENTY REPORT THE SUCCESS OF THEIR MISSIONS

17 ¶ And the seventy returned again with joy, saying, Lord, even the devils are subject unto us through thy name.

18 And he said unto them, I beheld Satan as lightning fall from heaven.

19 Behold, I give unto you power to tread on serpents and scorpions, and over all the power of the enemy: and nothing shall by any means hurt you.

20 Notwithstanding in this rejoice not, that the spirits are subject unto you; but rather rejoice, because your names are written in heaven.

21 In that hour Jesus rejoiced in spirit, and said, I thank thee, O Father, Lord of heaven and earth, that thou hast hid these things from the wise and prudent, and hast revealed them unto babes: even so, Father; for so it seemed good in thy sight.

22 All things are delivered to me of my Father: and no man knoweth who the Son is, but the Father; and who the Father is, but the Son, and he to whom the Son will reveal him.

23 And he turned him unto his disciples, and said privately, Blessed are the eyes which see the things that ye see:

24 For I tell you, that many prophets and kings have desired to see those things which ye see, and have not seen them; and to hear those things which ye hear, and have not heard them.

---

10:2   The "labourers" are missionaries and the "harvest" is the people who accept their message (see D&C 4:4 and 31:4-5).

10:4   **Carry neither purse, nor scrip**—Do not take a money bag or a bag to carry food or your belongings in

10:7   **his hire**—what a laborer gets paid

10:10-14   See helps for Matthew 11:20-24.

10:11   **which cleaveth**—that sticks or stays

10:15   **exalted**—lifted up
**thrust**—pushed

10:16   **despiseth**—hates

10:17   **subject**—obedient

10:19   **tread**—walk

10:21   The Joseph Smith Translation explains that the Savior was grateful that Heavenly Father hid the gospel "from them *who think they are* wise and prudent" and instead revealed it to humble members of the Church (JST, Luke 10:22; emphasis added).

10:24   What had prophets and kings wanted to see that the Savior's disciples actually witnessed? What miraculous events have you seen that you think the prophets and kings would have wanted to see? How do you think the ancient prophets would have felt about the great missionary program and the remarkable growth of the Church in our day?

## JESUS TELLS THE PARABLE OF THE GOOD SAMARITAN

25 ¶ And, behold, a certain lawyer stood up, and tempted him, saying, Master, what shall I do to inherit eternal life?

26 He said unto him, What is written in the law? how readest thou?

27 And he answering said, Thou shalt love the Lord thy God with all thy heart, and with all thy soul, and with all thy strength, and with all thy mind; and thy neighbour as thyself.

28 And he said unto him, Thou hast answered right: this do, and thou shalt live.

29 But he, willing to justify himself, said unto Jesus, And who is my neighbour?

30 And Jesus answering said, A certain man went down from Jerusalem to Jericho, and fell among thieves, which stripped him of his raiment, and wounded him, and departed, leaving him half dead.

31 And by chance there came down a certain priest that way: and when he saw him, he passed by on the other side.

32 And likewise a Levite, when he was at the place, came and looked on him, and passed by on the other side.

33 But a certain Samaritan, as he journeyed, came where he was: and when he saw him, he had compassion on him,

34 And went to him, and bound up his wounds, pouring in oil and wine, and set him on his own beast, and brought him to an inn, and took care of him.

35 And on the morrow when he departed, he took out two pence, and gave them to the host, and said unto him, Take care of him; and whatsoever thou spendest more, when I come again, I will repay thee.

36 Which now of these three, thinkest thou, was neighbour unto him that fell among the thieves?

37 And he said, He that shewed mercy on him. Then said Jesus unto him, Go, and do thou likewise.

## JESUS VISITS MARY AND MARTHA

38 ¶ Now it came to pass, as they went, that he entered into a certain village: and a certain woman named Martha received him into her house.

39 And she had a sister called Mary, which also sat at Jesus' feet, and heard his word.

40 But Martha was cumbered about much serving, and came to him, and said, Lord, dost thou not care that my sister hath left me to serve alone? bid her therefore that she help me.

41 And Jesus answered and said unto her, Martha, Martha, thou art careful and troubled about many things:

42 But one thing is needful: and Mary hath chosen that good part, which shall not be taken away from her.

# CHAPTER 11

*In this chapter it is clear that Jesus knew his relationship to Heavenly Father. He was also very aware of Satan and his evil followers. As you read, look for what the Savior taught about Heavenly Father, Himself, and Satan and his followers.*

## JESUS TEACHES ABOUT PRAYER

1 ¶ AND it came to pass, that, as he was praying in a certain place, when he ceased, one of his disciples said unto him, Lord, teach us to pray, as John also taught his disciples.

2 And he said unto them, When ye pray, say, Our Father which art in heaven, Hallowed be thy name. Thy kingdom come. Thy will be done, as in heaven, so in earth.

3 Give us day by day our daily bread.

---

10:25-37   How is the good Samaritan like Jesus? How are you like the man who had fallen among thieves? Have you ever been a "good Samaritan" to someone?

10:27   Why do you think keeping these two commandments would make it possible for a person to get eternal life?

10:29   **willing to justify himself**—desiring to prove he was worthy

10:40   **cumbered about**—burdened down or distracted with

10:42   What do you think Jesus meant when he said that Mary had "chosen that good part"? What could you do about some of the things in your life that keep you from spending time with the Savior?

11:2   **Hallowed**—Holy

11:2-4   This passage is known as the Lord's Prayer. In it Jesus teaches us how to pray. What do you learn here that could make your prayers better?

*"Love thy neighbour as thyself."*

4 And forgive us our sins; for we also forgive every one that is indebted to us. And lead us not into temptation; but deliver us from evil.

5 And he said unto them, Which of you shall have a friend, and shall go unto him at midnight, and say unto him, Friend, lend me three loaves;

6 For a friend of mine in his journey is come to me, and I have nothing to set before him?

7 And he from within shall answer and say, Trouble me not: the door is now shut, and my children are with me in bed; I cannot rise and give thee.

8 I say unto you, Though he will not rise and give him, because he is his friend, yet because of his importunity he will rise and give him as many as he needeth.

9 And I say unto you, Ask, and it shall be given you; seek, and ye shall find; knock, and it shall be opened unto you.

10 For every one that asketh receiveth; and he that seeketh findeth; and to him that knocketh it shall be opened.

11 If a son shall ask bread of any of you that is a father, will he give him a stone? or if he ask a fish, will he for a fish give him a serpent?

12 Or if he shall ask an egg, will he offer him a scorpion?

13 If ye then, being evil, know how to give good gifts unto your children: how much more shall your heavenly Father give the Holy Spirit to them that ask him?

## JESUS TEACHES ABOUT SATAN AND HIS FOLLOWERS

14 ¶ And he was casting out a devil, and it was dumb. And it came to pass, when the devil was gone out, the dumb spake; and the people wondered.

15 But some of them said, He casteth out devils through Beelzebub the chief of the devils.

16 And others, tempting him, sought of him a sign from heaven.

17 But he, knowing their thoughts, said unto them, Every kingdom divided against itself is brought to desolation; and a house divided against a house falleth.

18 If Satan also be divided against himself, how shall his kingdom stand? because ye say that I cast out devils through Beelzebub.

19 And if I by Beelzebub cast out devils, by whom do your sons cast them out? therefore shall they be your judges.

20 But if I with the finger of God cast out devils, no doubt the kingdom of God is come upon you.

21 When a strong man armed keepeth his palace, his goods are in peace:

22 But when a stronger than he shall come upon him, and overcome him, he taketh from him all his armour wherein he trusted, and divideth his spoils.

23 He that is not with me is against me: and he that gathereth not with me scattereth.

24 When the unclean spirit is gone out of a man, he walketh through dry places, seeking rest; and finding none, he saith, I will return unto my house whence I came out.

25 And when he cometh, he findeth it swept and garnished.

26 Then goeth he, and taketh to him seven other spirits more wicked than himself; and they enter in, and dwell there: and the last state of that man is worse than the first.

---

11:4    Neither Heavenly Father nor Jesus Christ would lead us into temptation. The Joseph Smith Translation changes this verse to say, "And let us not be led unto temptation" (JST, Luke 11:4).

11:8    **importunity**—continuing to ask

11:9    How does this promise help you know that God will answer your prayers?

11:11    **serpent**—snake

11:13    The Joseph Smith Translation tells us that Heavenly Father gives us "good gifts, through the Holy Spirit" (JST, Luke 11:14).

11:14    The Joseph Smith Translation helps us understand that Jesus was casting "a devil out of a man, and he [the devil] was dumb" (JST, Luke 11:15).

   **was dumb**—could not speak

11:15    Beelzebub was another name for Satan (see LDS Bible Dictionary, s.v. "Beelzebub," p. 620).

11:16    **sought**—wanted

11:17    **desolation**—destruction

11:22    **divideth his spoils**—takes and gives away his belongings

## Jesus Is the Greatest Person Who Has Ever Lived on the Earth

27 ¶ And it came to pass, as he spake these things, a certain woman of the company lifted up her voice, and said unto him, Blessed is the womb that bare thee, and the paps which thou hast sucked.

28 But he said, Yea rather, blessed are they that hear the word of God, and keep it.

29 ¶ And when the people were gathered thick together, he began to say, This is an evil generation: they seek a sign; and there shall no sign be given it, but the sign of Jonas the prophet.

30 For as Jonas was a sign unto the Ninevites, so shall also the Son of man be to this generation.

31 The queen of the south shall rise up in the judgment with the men of this generation, and condemn them: for she came from the utmost parts of the earth to hear the wisdom of Solomon; and, behold, a greater than Solomon is here.

32 The men of Nineve shall rise up in the judgment with this generation, and shall condemn it: for they repented at the preaching of Jonas; and, behold, a greater than Jonas is here.

33 No man, when he hath lighted a candle, putteth it in a secret place, neither under a bushel, but on a candlestick, that they which come in may see the light.

34 The light of the body is the eye: therefore when thine eye is single, thy whole body also is full of light; but when thine eye is evil, thy body also is full of darkness.

35 Take heed therefore that the light which is in thee be not darkness.

36 If thy whole body therefore be full of light, having no part dark, the whole shall be full of light, as when the bright shining of a candle doth give thee light.

## Jesus Scolds the Leaders of the Jews

37 ¶ And as he spake, a certain Pharisee besought him to dine with him: and he went in, and sat down to meat.

38 And when the Pharisee saw it, he marvelled that he had not first washed before dinner.

39 And the Lord said unto him, Now do ye Pharisees make clean the outside of the cup and the platter; but your inward part is full of ravening and wickedness.

40 Ye fools, did not he that made that which is without make that which is within also?

41 But rather give alms of such things as ye have; and, behold, all things are clean unto you.

42 But woe unto you, Pharisees! for ye tithe mint and rue and all manner of herbs, and pass over judgment and the love of God: these ought ye to have done, and not to leave the other undone.

43 Woe unto you, Pharisees! for ye love the uppermost seats in the synagogues, and greetings in the markets.

44 Woe unto you, scribes and Pharisees, hypocrites! for ye are as graves which appear not, and the men that walk over them are not aware of them.

45 Then answered one of the lawyers, and said unto him, Master, thus saying thou reproachest us also.

46 And he said, Woe unto you also, ye lawyers! for ye lade men with burdens grievous to be borne, and ye yourselves touch not the burdens with one of your fingers.

---

11:27    After an angel told Mary that she would give birth to the Son of God, she knew that many people would bless her name (see Luke 1:48). This woman praised Mary, the mother who gave birth to Jesus and nursed him.

11:28    Millions of people have lived on the earth. Those who live the gospel will receive more blessings than those who don't. How does this help you want to live the gospel?

11:29    *generation*—people who are living now

11:29-30    Jonas, or Jonah, spent three days in the belly of a great fish (see Jonah 1:17). The sign of Jonah was that Jesus would spend three days in the belly of the earth after the Crucifixion.

11:32    *condemn it*—find it guilty

11:33-36    Jesus taught his disciples to not hide their light under a basket but to put it on a candlestick so that others could see it. Those whose "minds become single to God" will see him one day (see D&C 88:67-68).

11:39    Jesus accused the Pharisees of being hypocrites, comparing them to a cup and platter that are clean on the outside but are full of greed and wickedness on the inside. The Joseph Smith Translation tells us that Jesus said that those who would "do all things which I have commanded you" would be clean on the inside (see JST, Luke 11:42).

11:46    *burdens grievous to be borne*—loads too hard to carry

47 Woe unto you! for ye build the sepulchres of the prophets, and your fathers killed them.

48 Truly ye bear witness that ye allow the deeds of your fathers: for they indeed killed them, and ye build their sepulchres.

49 Therefore also said the wisdom of God, I will send them prophets and apostles, and some of them they shall slay and persecute:

50 That the blood of all the prophets, which was shed from the foundation of the world, may be required of this generation;

51 From the blood of Abel unto the blood of Zacharias, which perished between the altar and the temple: verily I say unto you, It shall be required of this generation.

52 Woe unto you, lawyers! for ye have taken away the key of knowledge: ye entered not in yourselves, and them that were entering in ye hindered.

53 And as he said these things unto them, the scribes and the Pharisees began to urge him vehemently, and to provoke him to speak of many things:

54 Laying wait for him, and seeking to catch something out of his mouth, that they might accuse him.

# CHAPTER 12

*Jesus gives his disciples warnings and hope. Watch for what he said we should do to prepare for his second coming.*

## REPENT OF YOUR SINS AND THE LORD WILL BLESS YOU AND PROTECT YOU

1 ¶ IN the mean time, when there were gathered together an innumerable multitude of people, insomuch that they trode one upon another, he began to say unto his disciples first of all, Beware ye of the leaven of the Pharisees, which is hypocrisy.

2 For there is nothing covered, that shall not be revealed; neither hid, that shall not be known.

3 Therefore whatsoever ye have spoken in darkness shall be heard in the light; and that which ye have spoken in the ear in closets shall be proclaimed upon the housetops.

4 And I say unto you my friends, Be not afraid of them that kill the body, and after that have no more that they can do.

5 But I will forewarn you whom ye shall fear: Fear him, which after he hath killed hath power to cast into hell; yea, I say unto you, Fear him.

6 Are not five sparrows sold for two farthings, and not one of them is forgotten before God?

7 But even the very hairs of your head are all numbered. Fear not therefore: ye are of more value than many sparrows.

8 Also I say unto you, Whosoever shall confess me before men, him shall the Son of man also confess before the angels of God:

9 But he that denieth me before men shall be denied before the angels of God.

10 And whosoever shall speak a word against the Son of man, it shall be forgiven him: but unto him that blasphemeth against the Holy Ghost it shall not be forgiven.

11 And when they bring you unto the synagogues, and unto magistrates, and powers, take ye no thought how or what thing ye shall answer, or what ye shall say:

---

11:47 **sepulchres**—graves or tombs

11:50 **required of**—held against

11:51 When Herod gave orders to kill all the children two years and younger, John the Baptist would have been included. Elisabeth took John to the mountains to hide. When Zacharias refused to tell the hiding place of his son he "was slain by Herod's order, between the porch and the altar." (*The Teachings of Joseph Smith*, p. 351.)

11:52 The Joseph Smith Translation explains that the lawyers had taken away the "fulness of the scriptures" (JST, Luke 11:53). This loss of true scripture knowledge had led the Jews into spiritual darkness.

11:53 **vehemently**—strongly

11:54 **Laying wait for him**—Trying to trap him

12:1 **trode**—walked

For help with the phrase "leaven of the Pharisees," see for Mark 8:15.

12:6 **farthings**—a unit of money worth very little

12:6-7 If your Heavenly Father loves even the littlest bird, how much more do you think he loves you? (See D&C 18:10-12.)

12:10 The Joseph Smith Translation makes it clear that "whosoever shall speak a word against the Son of man, and repenteth, it shall be forgiven him" (JST, Luke 12:12).

**blasphemeth against the Holy Ghost**—"willfully [denies] Christ after having received a perfect knowledge of him from the Holy Ghost" (LDS Bible Dictionary, s.v. "Blasphemy," p. 626).

12:11 **magistrates**—judges

12 For the Holy Ghost shall teach you in the same hour what ye ought to say.

## TREASURE THE THINGS OF GOD

13 ¶ And one of the company said unto him, Master, speak to my brother, that he divide the inheritance with me.

14 And he said unto him, Man, who made me a judge or a divider over you?

15 And he said unto them, Take heed, and beware of covetousness: for a man's life consisteth not in the abundance of the things which he possesseth.

16 And he spake a parable unto them, saying, The ground of a certain rich man brought forth plentifully:

17 And he thought within himself, saying, What shall I do, because I have no room where to bestow my fruits?

18 And he said, This will I do: I will pull down my barns, and build greater; and there will I bestow all my fruits and my goods.

19 And I will say to my soul, Soul, thou hast much goods laid up for many years; take thine ease, eat, drink, and be merry.

20 But God said unto him, Thou fool, this night thy soul shall be required of thee: then whose shall those things be, which thou hast provided?

21 So is he that layeth up treasure for himself, and is not rich toward God.

22 ¶ And he said unto his disciples, Therefore I say unto you, Take no thought for your life, what ye shall eat; neither for the body, what ye shall put on.

23 The life is more than meat, and the body is more than raiment.

24 Consider the ravens: for they neither sow nor reap; which neither have storehouse nor barn; and God feedeth them: how much more are ye better than the fowls?

25 And which of you with taking thought can add to his stature one cubit?

26 If ye then be not able to do that thing which is least, why take ye thought for the rest?

27 Consider the lilies how they grow: they toil not, they spin not; and yet I say unto you, that Solomon in all his glory was not arrayed like one of these.

28 If then God so clothe the grass, which is to day in the field, and to morrow is cast into the oven; how much more will he clothe you, O ye of little faith?

29 And seek not ye what ye shall eat, or what ye shall drink, neither be ye of doubtful mind.

30 For all these things do the nations of the world seek after: and your Father knoweth that ye have need of these things.

31 But rather seek ye the kingdom of God; and all these things shall be added unto you.

32 Fear not, little flock; for it is your Father's good pleasure to give you the kingdom.

33 Sell that ye have, and give alms; provide yourselves bags which wax not old, a treasure in the heavens that faileth not, where no thief approacheth, neither moth corrupteth.

34 For where your treasure is, there will your heart be also.

---

12:15 **abundance of the things which he possesseth**—large number of things he owns

12:16-21 What does it mean to be "rich toward God"? How can you become rich toward God?

"Consider the lilies . . . Solomon in all his glory was not arrayed like one of these."

12:17 **bestow**—store or keep

12:19 **take thine ease**—take life easy

12:24 **fowls**—birds

12:25 **stature one cubit**—height eighteen inches

12:27 Solomon was the most wealthy king of Israel. To find out how much wealth he had, see 1 Kings 10:14-29.

**arrayed**—dressed

12:33 **alms**—items such as food, clothes, or money given to those in need

12:33-34 What kind of treasure do you think the Lord is talking about? How does your heart decide what your "treasure" will be? What can you do now so that you will receive "a heavenly treasure"?

## GET READY AND WATCH FOR THE SECOND COMING OF CHRIST

35 Let your loins be girded about, and your lights burning;

36 And ye yourselves like unto men that wait for their lord, when he will return from the wedding; that when he cometh and knocketh, they may open unto him immediately.

37 Blessed are those servants, whom the lord when he cometh shall find watching: verily I say unto you, that he shall gird himself, and make them to sit down to meat, and will come forth and serve them.

38 And if he shall come in the second watch, or come in the third watch, and find them so, blessed are those servants.

39 And this know, that if the goodman of the house had known what hour the thief would come, he would have watched, and not have suffered his house to be broken through.

40 Be ye therefore ready also: for the Son of man cometh at an hour when ye think not.

41 ¶ Then Peter said unto him, Lord, speakest thou this parable unto us, or even to all?

42 And the Lord said, Who then is that faithful and wise steward, whom his lord shall make ruler over his household, to give them their portion of meat in due season?

43 Blessed is that servant, whom his lord when he cometh shall find so doing.

44 Of a truth I say unto you, that he will make him ruler over all that he hath.

45 But and if that servant say in his heart, My lord delayeth his coming; and shall begin to beat the menservants and maidens, and to eat and drink, and to be drunken;

46 The lord of that servant will come in a day when he looketh not for him, and at an hour when he is not aware, and will cut him in sunder, and will appoint him his portion with the unbelievers.

47 And that servant, which knew his lord's will, and prepared not himself, neither did according to his will, shall be beaten with many stripes.

48 But he that knew not, and did commit things worthy of stripes, shall be beaten with few stripes. For unto whomsoever much is given, of him shall be much required: and to whom men have committed much, of him they will ask the more.

49 I am come to send fire on the earth; and what will I, if it be already kindled?

50 But I have a baptism to be baptized with; and how am I straitened till it be accomplished!

51 Suppose ye that I am come to give peace on earth? I tell you, Nay; but rather division:

52 For from henceforth there shall be five in one house divided, three against two, and two against three.

53 The father shall be divided against the son, and the son against the father; the mother against the daughter, and the daughter against the mother; the mother in law against her daughter in law, and the daughter in law against her mother in law.

54 ¶ And he said also to the people, When ye see a cloud rise out of the west, straightway ye say, There cometh a shower; and so it is.

55 And when ye see the south wind blow, ye say, There will be heat; and it cometh to pass.

56 Ye hypocrites, ye can discern the face of the sky and of the earth; but how is it that ye do not discern this time?

57 Yea, and why even of yourselves judge ye not what is right?

---

12:38 The Jews divided the evening into three watches: the beginning watch (from sunset to 10 P.M.); the middle watch (from 10 P.M. to 2 A.M.); and the morning watch (from 2 A.M. to sunrise) (see LDS Bible Dictionary, s.v. "Watches," p. 788).

12:39 **suffered**—let

12:42 **steward**—person who takes care of the lord's property

12:45 **delayeth his coming**—is not going to come for a long time

12:46 **sunder**—pieces

12:48 The Lord revealed this same truth to Joseph Smith (see D&C 82:3). No one will be punished more than he or she deserves.

12:49 **kindled**—burning

12:50 **how am I straitened**—how distressed I am

12:51-53 The Apostle Paul taught that righteousness and wickedness always oppose each other (see 2 Corinthians 6:14-16). In this sense, the gospel of Jesus Christ causes divisions between believers and unbelievers, as well as between the faithful and the wicked.

58 When thou goest with thine adversary to the magistrate, as thou art in the way, give diligence that thou mayest be delivered from him; lest he hale thee to the judge, and the judge deliver thee to the officer, and the officer cast thee into prison.

59 I tell thee, thou shalt not depart thence, till thou hast paid the very last mite.

# CHAPTER 13

*What does it mean to be a follower of Christ? What must a person avoid to be a true Christian? Look for answers to these questions as you study this chapter.*

## Jesus Teaches: Repent or Perish

1 ¶ THERE were present at that season some that told him of the Galilaeans, whose blood Pilate had mingled with their sacrifices.

2 And Jesus answering said unto them, Suppose ye that these Galilaeans were sinners above all the Galilaeans, because they suffered such things?

3 I tell you, Nay: but, except ye repent, ye shall all likewise perish.

4 Or those eighteen, upon whom the tower in Siloam fell, and slew them, think ye that they were sinners above all men that dwelt in Jerusalem?

5 I tell you, Nay: but, except ye repent, ye shall all likewise perish.

## Jesus Gives the Parable of the Barren Fig Tree

6 ¶ He spake also this parable; A certain man had a fig tree planted in his vineyard; and he came and sought fruit thereon, and found none.

7 Then said he unto the dresser of his vineyard, Behold, these three years I come seeking fruit on this fig tree, and find none: cut it down; why cumbereth it the ground?

8 And he answering said unto him, Lord, let it alone this year also, till I shall dig about it, and dung it:

9 And if it bear fruit, well: and if not, then after that thou shalt cut it down.

## Jesus Heals a Woman

10 ¶ And he was teaching in one of the synagogues on the sabbath.

11 And, behold, there was a woman which had a spirit of infirmity eighteen years, and was bowed together, and could in no wise lift up herself.

12 And when Jesus saw her, he called her to him, and said unto her, Woman, thou art loosed from thine infirmity.

13 And he laid his hands on her: and immediately she was made straight, and glorified God.

14 And the ruler of the synagogue answered with indignation, because that Jesus had healed on the sabbath day, and said unto the people, There are six days in which men ought to work: in them therefore come and be healed, and not on the sabbath day.

15 The Lord then answered him, and said, Thou hypocrite, doth not each one of you on the sabbath loose his ox or his ass from the stall, and lead him away to watering?

16 And ought not this woman, being a daughter of Abraham, whom Satan hath bound, lo, these eighteen years, be loosed from this bond on the sabbath day?

17 And when he had said these things, all his adversaries were ashamed: and all the people rejoiced for all the glorious things that were done by him.

## Jesus Teaches in Parables

18 ¶ Then said he, Unto what is the kingdom of

---

12:58 **adversary**—enemy
**magistrate**—judge
**hale thee**—make you go

12:59 **mite**—unit of money worth very little

13:1 Pilate had ordered his soldiers to kill a group of Galileans who had probably rebelled against Rome. They were killed as they sacrificed lambs for the Passover, so their blood was "mingled with their sacrifices."

13:1-5 Some Jews believed that all hardship was a result of sin. Jesus explains that being spared a particular disaster doesn't mean you are righteous. "The real lesson to be learned from Jesus' conclusion, 'Except ye repent, ye shall all likewise perish,' is that there was no difference in righteousness between the slain and the living, and that unless the living repent they would perish with the dead" (Bruce R. McConkie, *Doctrinal New Testament Commentary* 1:476).

13:6-9 How are people much like the fig tree in this parable?

13:7 **dresser of his vineyard**—gardener

13:11 **infirmity**—sickness or disease

13:14 **indignation**—anger

13:16 "The devil uses and delights in diseases and afflictions, and in some cases he has power to impose them" (Bruce R. McConkie, *Doctrinal New Testament Commentary* 2:448).

God like? and whereunto shall I resemble it?

19 It is like a grain of mustard seed, which a man took, and cast into his garden; and it grew, and waxed a great tree; and the fowls of the air lodged in the branches of it.

20 And again he said, Whereunto shall I liken the kingdom of God?

21 It is like leaven, which a woman took and hid in three measures of meal, till the whole was leavened.

22 And he went through the cities and villages, teaching, and journeying toward Jerusalem.

23 ¶ Then said one unto him, Lord, are there few that be saved? And he said unto them,

24 Strive to enter in at the strait gate: for many, I say unto you, will seek to enter in, and shall not be able.

25 When once the master of the house is risen up, and hath shut to the door, and ye begin to stand without, and to knock at the door, saying, Lord, Lord, open unto us; and he shall answer and say unto you, I know you not whence ye are:

26 Then shall ye begin to say, We have eaten and drunk in thy presence, and thou hast taught in our streets.

27 But he shall say, I tell you, I know you not whence ye are; depart from me, all ye workers of iniquity.

28 There shall be weeping and gnashing of teeth, when ye shall see Abraham, and Isaac, and Jacob, and all the prophets, in the kingdom of God, and you yourselves thrust out.

29 And they shall come from the east, and from the west, and from the north, and from the south, and shall sit down in the kingdom of God.

30 And, behold, there are last which shall be first, and there are first which shall be last.

31 ¶ The same day there came certain of the Pharisees, saying unto him, Get thee out, and depart hence: for Herod will kill thee.

32 And he said unto them, Go ye, and tell that fox, Behold, I cast out devils, and I do cures to day and to morrow, and the third day I shall be perfected.

33 Nevertheless I must walk to day, and to morrow, and the day following: for it cannot be that a prophet perish out of Jerusalem.

### JESUS MOURNS OVER JERUSALEM

34 O Jerusalem, Jerusalem, which killest the prophets, and stonest them that are sent unto thee; how often would I have gathered thy children together, as a hen doth gather her brood under her wings, and ye would not!

35 Behold, your house is left unto you desolate: and verily I say unto you, Ye shall not see me, until the time come when ye shall say, Blessed is he that cometh in the name of the Lord.

## CHAPTER 14

*Jesus teaches about the Sabbath day and about his second coming. Note what Jesus expects from those who follow him.*

### JESUS HEALS ON THE SABBATH

1 ¶ AND it came to pass, as he went into the house of one of the chief Pharisees to eat bread on the sabbath day, that they watched him.

2 And, behold, there was a certain man before him which had the dropsy.

3 And Jesus answering spake unto the lawyers and Pharisees, saying, Is it lawful to heal on the sabbath day?

4 And they held their peace. And he took him, and healed him, and let him go;

5 And answered them, saying, Which of you shall

---

13:21 **leaven**—yeast
**three measures of meal**—almost fifty pounds of flour

13:24 **strait**—narrow

To enter in at the strait gate we must repent of our sins and be baptized by one holding the priesthood (see 2 Nephi 31:17).

Have you been baptized yet? Do you continue to repent of your sins and try to live the gospel? Why is it so important to learn and live the gospel when you are young?

13:28 **gnashing**—grinding; expressing pain and grief

13:32 In this verse "our Lord definitely predicted His resurrection from the dead on the third day" (James E. Talmage, *Jesus the Christ*, p. 697).

13:34 **brood**—nest of little chicks

13:34-35 Even though the people of Jerusalem had been so wicked, Jesus loved them and was sad because of the punishments they would bring upon themselves. Do you think Jesus Christ cares about the wicked in our day? Will Jesus Christ's love and concern prevent the wicked from being punished?

14:2 **the dropsy**—a disease that causes the body to swell

have an ass or an ox fallen into a pit, and will not straightway pull him out on the sabbath day?

6 And they could not answer him again to these things.

## Jesus Teaches About Humility

7 ¶ And he put forth a parable to those which were bidden, when he marked how they chose out the chief rooms; saying unto them,

8 When thou art bidden of any man to a wedding, sit not down in the highest room; lest a more honourable man than thou be bidden of him;

9 And he that bade thee and him come and say to thee, Give this man place; and thou begin with shame to take the lowest room.

10 But when thou art bidden, go and sit down in the lowest room; that when he that bade thee cometh, he may say unto thee, Friend, go up higher: then shalt thou have worship in the presence of them that sit at meat with thee.

11 For whosoever exalteth himself shall be abased; and he that humbleth himself shall be exalted.

12 Then said he also to him that bade him, When thou makest a dinner or a supper, call not thy friends, nor thy brethren, neither thy kinsmen, nor thy rich neighbours; lest they also bid thee again, and a recompence be made thee.

13 But when thou makest a feast, call the poor, the maimed, the lame, the blind:

14 And thou shalt be blessed; for they cannot recompense thee: for thou shalt be recompensed at the resurrection of the just.

## Jesus Gives the Parable of the Great Supper

15 ¶ And when one of them that sat at meat with him heard these things, he said unto him, Blessed is he that shall eat bread in the kingdom of God.

16 Then said he unto him, A certain man made a great supper, and bade many:

17 And sent his servant at supper time to say to them that were bidden, Come; for all things are now ready.

18 And they all with one consent began to make excuse. The first said unto him, I have bought a piece of ground, and I must needs go and see it: I pray thee have me excused.

19 And another said, I have bought five yoke of oxen, and I go to prove them: I pray thee have me excused.

20 And another said, I have married a wife, and therefore I cannot come.

21 So that servant came, and shewed his lord these things. Then the master of the house being angry said to his servant, Go out quickly into the streets and lanes of the city, and bring in hither the poor, and the maimed, and the halt, and the blind.

22 And the servant said, Lord, it is done as thou hast commanded, and yet there is room.

23 And the lord said unto the servant, Go out into the highways and hedges, and compel them to come in, that my house may be filled.

24 For I say unto you, That none of those men which were bidden shall taste of my supper.

## Jesus Explains What It Means to Be a Disciple

25 ¶ And there went great multitudes with him: and he turned, and said unto them,

---

14:7 **bidden**—invited
**marked**—noticed
**chief rooms**—highest seats for the most honored guests

14:10 **bade**—invited

14:11 **whosoever exalteth himself shall be abased**—whoever makes himself look important will be humbled

14:12 **kinsmen**—family, relatives
**a recompence be made thee**—you would thus be repaid

14:13 **maimed**—crippled or disabled

14:13-14 The "resurrection of the just" refers to the time when the spirits of the righteous are reunited with their bodies for eternity (see D&C 76:50-58). Is

that blessing worthwhile enough for you to share what you have with the poor and needy?

14:16 **bade**—invited

14:21 **halt**—lame or crippled

14:23 **hedges**—country roads lined with hedges or fences

14:24 This parable is about people who are invited but refuse to accept the gospel of Jesus Christ. The Jews were first invited, but most refused. Who are being invited in our time? Who are the "servants" carrying that invitation to the world? (See D&C 58:8-11.)

26 If any man come to me, and hate not his father, and mother, and wife, and children, and brethren, and sisters, yea, and his own life also, he cannot be my disciple.

27 And whosoever doth not bear his cross, and come after me, cannot be my disciple.

28 For which of you, intending to build a tower, sitteth not down first, and counteth the cost, whether he have sufficient to finish it?

29 Lest haply, after he hath laid the foundation, and is not able to finish it, all that behold it begin to mock him,

30 Saying, This man began to build, and was not able to finish.

31 Or what king, going to make war against another king, sitteth not down first, and consulteth whether he be able with ten thousand to meet him that cometh against him with twenty thousand?

32 Or else, while the other is yet a great way off, he sendeth an ambassage, and desireth conditions of peace.

33 So likewise, whosoever he be of you that forsaketh not all that he hath, he cannot be my disciple.

34 Salt is good: but if the salt have lost his savour, wherewith shall it be seasoned?

35 It is neither fit for the land, nor yet for the dunghill; but men cast it out. He that hath ears to hear, let him hear.

## CHAPTER 15

*Jesus often taught his followers by telling parables. A parable is an earthly story with a spiritual meaning. Look for the spiritual meanings taught by each of the parables in this chapter.*

### JESUS TEACHES THE PARABLE OF THE LOST SHEEP

1 ¶ THEN drew near unto him all the publicans and sinners for to hear him.

2 And the Pharisees and scribes murmured, saying, This man receiveth sinners, and eateth with them.

3 And he spake this parable unto them, saying,

4 What man of you, having an hundred sheep, if he lose one of them, doth not leave the ninety and nine in the wilderness, and go after that which is lost, until he find it?

5 And when he hath found it, he layeth it on his shoulders, rejoicing.

6 And when he cometh home, he calleth together his friends and neighbours, saying unto them, Rejoice with me; for I have found my sheep which was lost.

7 I say unto you, that likewise joy shall be in heaven over one sinner that repenteth, more than over ninety and nine just persons, which need no repentance.

### JESUS GIVES THE PARABLE OF THE LOST COIN

8 Either what woman having ten pieces of silver, if she lose one piece, doth not light a candle, and sweep the house, and seek diligently till she find it?

---

14:26 　In the Joseph Smith Translation, some additional words appear in this verse: "If any man come to me, and hate not his father, and mother, and wife, and children, and brethren, and sisters, *or husband,* yea and his own life also; *or in other words, is afraid to lay down his life for my sake,* he cannot be my disciple" (emphasis added). Elder Bruce R. McConkie explained that when we look at life eternally, "there is no such thing as sacrifice for the gospel cause. Men may forsake . . . friends, families, and possessions for the gospel's sake, but they gain these same things again in far greater measure in the mansions on high." (*Doctrinal New Testament Commentary* 1:557.)

14:32 　*sendeth an ambassage*—sends a servant who can speak for him

14:34 　*have lost his savour, wherewith shall it be seasoned*—becomes tasteless, how can it be given flavor again

14:35 　*dunghill*—manure pile

15:4 　The Joseph Smith Translation explains that the shepherd left the ninety and nine in safety and went "into the wilderness" after the lost sheep (see JST, Luke 15:4).

15:5 　When the shepherd found his lost sheep he carried it home on his shoulders and rejoiced. Jesus is our "Good Shepherd" (see John 10:14). In what ways can Jesus "carry" us when we become lost?

15:8 　One coin was worth a day's wages, and the woman looked very hard to find it. How much more important than a silver coin are your family and friends? If they become "lost," how hard should you try to help them?

9 And when she hath found it, she calleth her friends and her neighbours together, saying, Rejoice with me; for I have found the piece which I had lost.

10 Likewise, I say unto you, there is joy in the presence of the angels of God over one sinner that repenteth.

## JESUS TEACHES THE PARABLE OF THE PRODIGAL SON

11 ¶ And he said, A certain man had two sons:

12 And the younger of them said to his father, Father, give me the portion of goods that falleth to me. And he divided unto them his living.

13 And not many days after the younger son gathered all together, and took his journey into a far country, and there wasted his substance with riotous living.

14 And when he had spent all, there arose a mighty famine in that land; and he began to be in want.

15 And he went and joined himself to a citizen of that country; and he sent him into his fields to feed swine.

16 And he would fain have filled his belly with the husks that the swine did eat: and no man gave unto him.

17 And when he came to himself, he said, How many hired servants of my father's have bread enough and to spare, and I perish with hunger!

18 I will arise and go to my father, and will say unto him, Father, I have sinned against heaven, and before thee,

19 And am no more worthy to be called thy son: make me as one of thy hired servants.

20 And he arose, and came to his father. But when he was yet a great way off, his father saw him, and had compassion, and ran, and fell on his neck, and kissed him.

21 And the son said unto him, Father, I have sinned against heaven, and in thy sight, and am no more worthy to be called thy son.

22 But the father said to his servants, Bring forth the best robe, and put it on him; and put a ring on his hand, and shoes on his feet:

23 And bring hither the fatted calf, and kill it; and let us eat, and be merry:

24 For this my son was dead, and is alive again; he was lost, and is found. And they began to be merry.

25 Now his elder son was in the field: and as he came and drew nigh to the house, he heard musick and dancing.

26 And he called one of the servants, and asked what these things meant.

27 And he said unto him, Thy brother is come; and thy father hath killed the fatted calf, because he hath received him safe and sound.

28 And he was angry, and would not go in: therefore came his father out, and intreated him.

29 And he answering said to his father, Lo, these many years do I serve thee, neither transgressed I at any time thy commandment: and yet thou never gavest me a kid, that I might make merry with my friends:

30 But as soon as this thy son was come, which hath devoured thy living with harlots, thou hast killed for him the fatted calf.

31 And he said unto him, Son, thou art ever with me, and all that I have is thine.

32 It was meet that we should make merry, and be glad: for this thy brother was dead, and is alive again; and was lost, and is found.

---

15:10   We feel joy when we help someone come back to God. The Lord revealed to Joseph Smith, "If your joy will be great with one soul . . ., how great will be your joy if you should bring many souls unto me!" (D&C 18:16.)

15:12   **the portion of goods that falleth to me**—my share of the family belongings

15:13   **wasted his substance with riotous living**—wasted his wealth with wild living

15:15   **swine**—pigs

15:17   **when he came to himself**—when he realized that he had made mistakes

15:18, 21   An important part of repentance is to confess or admit when we have done wrong. Jesus said, "By this ye may know if a man repenteth of his sins—behold, he will confess them and forsake them" (D&C 58:43).

15:20   **fell on his neck**—hugged him

15:23   **hither**—here

15:27-31   What kind of person is jealous when someone else does well? What kind of person is genuinely happy when someone else succeeds?

15:28   **intreated**—begged

15:29   **neither transgressed I at any time**—nor have I ever disobeyed
**kid**—young goat

15:30   **devoured thy living with harlots**—wasted your wealth with wicked women

15:31   Like this father's promise to his faithful son, Jesus' promise to the faithful is: "All that my Father hath shall be given unto [them]" (D&C 84:38).

*If we return to the Lord, he will accept us.*

# CHAPTER 16

*Jesus taught that doing good and serving God is more important than gaining worldly power or riches. As you read this chapter, watch for these teachings and the blessings that come to those who follow them.*

## JESUS GIVES THE PARABLE OF THE UNJUST STEWARD

1 ¶ AND he said also unto his disciples, There was a certain rich man, which had a steward; and the same was accused unto him that he had wasted his goods.

2 And he called him, and said unto him, How is it that I hear this of thee? give an account of thy stewardship; for thou mayest be no longer steward.

3 Then the steward said within himself, What shall I do? for my lord taketh away from me the stewardship: I cannot dig; to beg I am ashamed.

4 I am resolved what to do, that, when I am put out of the stewardship, they may receive me into their houses.

5 So he called every one of his lord's debtors unto him, and said unto the first, How much owest thou unto my lord?

6 And he said, An hundred measures of oil. And he said unto him, Take thy bill, and sit down quickly, and write fifty.

7 Then said he to another, And how much owest thou? And he said, An hundred measures of wheat. And he said unto him, Take thy bill, and write fourscore.

8 And the lord commended the unjust steward, because he had done wisely: for the children of this world are in their generation wiser than the children of light.

9 And I say unto you, Make to yourselves friends of the mammon of unrighteousness; that, when ye fail, they may receive you into everlasting habitations.

10 He that is faithful in that which is least is faithful also in much: and he that is unjust in the least is unjust also in much.

11 If therefore ye have not been faithful in the unrighteous mammon, who will commit to your trust the true riches?

12 And if ye have not been faithful in that which is another man's, who shall give you that which is your own?

## JESUS TEACHES AGAINST DIVORCE

13 No servant can serve two masters: for either he will hate the one, and love the other; or else he will hold to the one, and despise the other. Ye cannot serve God and mammon.

14 And the Pharisees also, who were covetous, heard all these things: and they derided him.

15 And he said unto them, Ye are they which justify yourselves before men; but God knoweth your hearts: for that which is highly esteemed among men is abomination in the sight of God.

16 The law and the prophets were until John: since that time the kingdom of God is preached, and every man presseth into it.

---

16:1    *steward*—servant who has been given a responsibility

16:4-8    Jesus Christ teaches his followers that they need to put forth as much effort as the children of this world in doing and teaching what they believe in and represent, for, as Elder Neal A. Maxwell has said, "the children of light often are lax and slack" ("Some Thoughts on the Gospel and the Behavioral Sciences," p. 596).

16:5    *debtors*—people who owe others money

16:7    *fourscore*—eighty

16:8    *commended*—praised
         *children of light*—followers of Jesus Christ

16:9    *mammon*—riches

         The Lord was saying to his disciples that they should use worldly wealth to do good, so that when this life is over and material goods are useless they "would have friends to welcome them into 'the eternal tabernacles' or heavenly mansions" (James E. Talmage, *Jesus the Christ,* p. 483).

16:13    We have the choice between serving God or following evil. Which choice have you made?

         *mammon*—money or riches

16:14    *were covetous*—loved money

16:15    *abomination*—a wicked thing

16:16    The Joseph Smith Translation helps us know that the Pharisees claimed to follow the scriptures, or "the law," but they rejected Jesus Christ. Jesus declared that the scriptures teach that he is truly the Savior. The harsh words the Savior spoke in these verses and the parable which follow were meant for the Pharisees. (See JST, Luke 16:16-23.)

17 And it is easier for heaven and earth to pass, than one tittle of the law to fail.

18 Whosoever putteth away his wife, and marrieth another, committeth adultery: and whosoever marrieth her that is put away from her husband committeth adultery.

## JESUS GIVES THE PARABLE OF LAZARUS AND THE RICH MAN

19 ¶ There was a certain rich man, which was clothed in purple and fine linen, and fared sumptuously every day:

20 And there was a certain beggar named Lazarus, which was laid at his gate, full of sores,

21 And desiring to be fed with the crumbs which fell from the rich man's table: moreover the dogs came and licked his sores.

22 And it came to pass, that the beggar died, and was carried by the angels into Abraham's bosom: the rich man also died, and was buried;

23 And in hell he lift up his eyes, being in torments, and seeth Abraham afar off, and Lazarus in his bosom.

24 And he cried and said, Father Abraham, have mercy on me, and send Lazarus, that he may dip the tip of his finger in water, and cool my tongue; for I am tormented in this flame.

25 But Abraham said, Son, remember that thou in thy lifetime receivedst thy good things, and likewise Lazarus evil things: but now he is comforted, and thou art tormented.

26 And beside all this, between us and you there is a great gulf fixed: so that they which would pass from hence to you cannot; neither can they pass to us, that would come from thence.

27 Then he said, I pray thee therefore, father, that thou wouldest send him to my father's house:

28 For I have five brethren; that he may testify unto them, lest they also come into this place of torment.

29 Abraham saith unto him, They have Moses and the prophets; let them hear them.

30 And he said, Nay, father Abraham: but if one went unto them from the dead, they will repent.

31 And he said unto him, If they hear not Moses and the prophets, neither will they be persuaded, though one rose from the dead.

## CHAPTER 17

*Jesus served and sacrificed for others. As you read this chapter, look for ways to become more like the Savior.*

## JESUS SPEAKS OF OFFENCES

1 ¶ THEN said he unto the disciples, It is impossible but that offences will come: but woe unto him, through whom they come!

2 It were better for him that a millstone were hanged about his neck, and he cast into the sea, than that he should offend one of these little ones.

3 Take heed to yourselves: If thy brother trespass against thee, rebuke him; and if he repent, forgive him.

4 And if he trespass against thee seven times in a day, and seven times in a day turn again to thee, saying, I repent; thou shalt forgive him.

---

16:17 A "tittle" is a very small mark used in ancient writing. Every part, even the smallest, of Jesus' laws will be fulfilled and not fail (see D&C 1:37-38).

16:19 **fared sumptuously**—was well taken care of

16:22- "Our Lord, in the parable of Lazarus and the
23 rich man, uses the term *Abraham's bosom* to mean paradise. Abraham, the friend of God, not at that time having been resurrected, was continuing his life in the paradise of God, the same place to which the righteous beggar went." (Bruce R. McConkie, *Mormon Doctrine*, p. 15.)

16:24 **I am tormented in this flame**—I am miserable in spirit prison

16:26 Jesus Christ's atonement made it possible for the gospel to be preached to those who have died (see D&C 138:1-4, 29-32).

17:1 The word *offences* as used here means "stumbling blocks." A stumbling block is anyone or anything that blocks someone from doing what is right or causes them to sin.

17:3 **trespass**—sin

17:4 How often should we forgive one another?

## JESUS TEACHES OF FAITH

5 And the apostles said unto the Lord, Increase our faith.

6 And the Lord said, If ye had faith as a grain of mustard seed, ye might say unto this sycamine tree, Be thou plucked up by the root, and be thou planted in the sea; and it should obey you.

7 But which of you, having a servant plowing or feeding cattle, will say unto him by and by, when he is come from the field, Go and sit down to meat?

8 And will not rather say unto him, Make ready wherewith I may sup, and gird thyself, and serve me, till I have eaten and drunken; and afterward thou shalt eat and drink?

9 Doth he thank that servant because he did the things that were commanded him? I trow not.

10 So likewise ye, when ye shall have done all those things which are commanded you, say, We are unprofitable servants: we have done that which was our duty to do.

## TEN LEPERS ARE HEALED

11 ¶ And it came to pass, as he went to Jerusalem, that he passed through the midst of Samaria and Galilee.

12 And as he entered into a certain village, there met him ten men that were lepers, which stood afar off:

13 And they lifted up their voices, and said, Jesus, Master, have mercy on us.

14 And when he saw them, he said unto them, Go shew yourselves unto the priests. And it came to pass, that, as they went, they were cleansed.

15 And one of them, when he saw that he was healed, turned back, and with a loud voice glorified God,

16 And fell down on his face at his feet, giving him thanks: and he was a Samaritan.

17 And Jesus answering said, Were there not ten cleansed? but where are the nine?

18 There are not found that returned to give glory to God, save this stranger.

19 And he said unto him, Arise, go thy way: thy faith hath made thee whole.

## JESUS WARNS HIS FOLLOWERS TO BE PREPARED FOR THE SECOND COMING

20 ¶ And when he was demanded of the Pharisees, when the kingdom of God should come, he answered them and said, The kingdom of God cometh not with observation:

21 Neither shall they say, Lo here! or, lo there! for, behold, the kingdom of God is within you.

22 And he said unto the disciples, The days will come, when ye shall desire to see one of the days of the Son of man, and ye shall not see it.

23 And they shall say to you, See here; or, see there: go not after them, nor follow them.

24 For as the lightning, that lighteneth out of the one part under heaven, shineth unto the other part under heaven; so shall also the Son of man be in his day.

25 But first must he suffer many things, and be rejected of this generation.

26 And as it was in the days of Noe, so shall it be also in the days of the Son of man.

---

*A mustard seed will grow into a large tree.*

17:7    **sit down to meat**—sit down to eat

17:8    **sup**—eat

17:9    **trow**—think (the word *trow* is pronounced "TROH")

17:10    Even after we do all we can to obey the commandments, we are still saved because of Jesus' atonement. That is why we often are given the title of "unprofitable servants," or servants who depend on someone else to be saved (see Mosiah 2:20-24).

17:16-    How pleased was the Savior with the one
19    leper who thanked him? Why is it important for us to give thanks?

17:20    **observation**—outward show

17:21    Commenting on this verse, President Harold B. Lee said, "A more correct translation probably would have said, 'The kingdom of God is among you or in your midst' " (*Stand Ye in Holy Places*, p. 274).

17:26    **Noe**—Noah

27 They did eat, they drank, they married wives, they were given in marriage, until the day that Noe entered into the ark, and the flood came, and destroyed them all.

28 Likewise also as it was in the days of Lot; they did eat, they drank, they bought, they sold, they planted, they builded;

29 But the same day that Lot went out of Sodom it rained fire and brimstone from heaven, and destroyed them all.

30 Even thus shall it be in the day when the Son of man is revealed.

31 In that day, he which shall be upon the housetop, and his stuff in the house, let him not come down to take it away: and he that is in the field, let him likewise not return back.

32 Remember Lot's wife.

33 Whosoever shall seek to save his life shall lose it; and whosoever shall lose his life shall preserve it.

34 I tell you, in that night there shall be two men in one bed; the one shall be taken, and the other shall be left.

35 Two women shall be grinding together; the one shall be taken, and the other left.

36 Two men shall be in the field; the one shall be taken, and the other left.

37 And they answered and said unto him, Where, Lord? And he said unto them, Wheresoever the body is, thither will the eagles be gathered together.

# CHAPTER 18

*It is just a few days before Jesus will go to Jerusalem for the last time. Watch for what Jesus does in this chapter to teach us how to receive blessings from heaven.*

## JESUS TEACHES THE PARABLE OF THE UNJUST JUDGE

1 ¶ AND he spake a parable unto them to this end, that men ought always to pray, and not to faint;

2 Saying, There was in a city a judge, which feared not God, neither regarded man:

3 And there was a widow in that city; and she came unto him, saying, Avenge me of mine adversary.

4 And he would not for a while: but afterward he said within himself, Though I fear not God, nor regard man;

5 Yet because this widow troubleth me, I will avenge her, lest by her continual coming she weary me.

6 And the Lord said, Hear what the unjust judge saith.

7 And shall not God avenge his own elect, which cry day and night unto him, though he bear long with them?

8 I tell you that he will avenge them speedily. Nevertheless when the Son of man cometh, shall he find faith on the earth?

## JESUS TEACHES THE PARABLE OF THE PHARISEE AND THE PUBLICAN

9 ¶ And he spake this parable unto certain which trusted in themselves that they were righteous, and despised others:

10 Two men went up into the temple to pray; the one a Pharisee, and the other a publican.

11 The Pharisee stood and prayed thus with himself, God, I thank thee, that I am not as other men are, extortioners, unjust, adulterers, or even as this publican.

12 I fast twice in the week, I give tithes of all that I possess.

---

17:31-32 In Genesis 19:26 Lot's wife is described as looking back and then becoming a pillar of salt. In Luke 17:31 Jesus uses her as an example as he warns concerning his second coming, "He that is in the field, let him likewise not return."

18:1 **not to faint**—not give up

Like the widow in this parable, you should pray even when you do not feel like you are getting an answer. Why do you think Heavenly Father wants you to pray always and never give up? Why do you feel that answers to some prayers do not come immediately?

18:2 **regarded man**—cared about people

18:3 **Avenge me of mine adversary**—Give me justice against my enemy

18:7-8 The Joseph Smith Translation clarifies that the Lord has great patience. However, when Jesus Christ comes again "he will avenge his saints speedily." (JST, Luke 18:7-8.)

18:9 **despised**—hated, looked down on

18:11 **extortioners**—people who steal by violence or threats

18:11-13 What do you see as the difference between the prayer of the Pharisee and that of the publican? Who was more humble and ready to receive help? In your own prayers do you humbly seek help from God?

13 And the publican, standing afar off, would not lift up so much as his eyes unto heaven, but smote upon his breast, saying, God be merciful to me a sinner.

14 I tell you, this man went down to his house justified rather than the other: for every one that exalteth himself shall be abased; and he that humbleth himself shall be exalted.

## ONLY THE HUMBLE SHALL ENTER THE KINGDOM OF GOD

15 ¶ And they brought unto him also infants, that he would touch them: but when his disciples saw it, they rebuked them.

16 But Jesus called them unto him, and said, Suffer little children to come unto me, and forbid them not: for of such is the kingdom of God.

17 Verily I say unto you, Whosoever shall not receive the kingdom of God as a little child shall in no wise enter therein.

18 ¶ And a certain ruler asked him, saying, Good Master, what shall I do to inherit eternal life?

19 And Jesus said unto him, Why callest thou me good? none is good, save one, that is, God.

20 Thou knowest the commandments, Do not commit adultery, Do not kill, Do not steal, Do not bear false witness, Honour thy father and thy mother.

21 And he said, All these have I kept from my youth up.

22 Now when Jesus heard these things, he said unto him, Yet lackest thou one thing: sell all that thou hast, and distribute unto the poor, and thou shalt have treasure in heaven: and come, follow me.

23 And when he heard this, he was very sorrowful: for he was very rich.

24 And when Jesus saw that he was very sorrowful, he said, How hardly shall they that have riches enter into the kingdom of God!

25 For it is easier for a camel to go through a needle's eye, than for a rich man to enter into the kingdom of God.

26 And they that heard it said, Who then can be saved?

27 And he said, The things which are impossible with men are possible with God.

28 Then Peter said, Lo, we have left all, and followed thee.

29 And he said unto them, Verily I say unto you, There is no man that hath left house, or parents, or brethren, or wife, or children, for the kingdom of God's sake,

30 Who shall not receive manifold more in this present time, and in the world to come life everlasting.

## JESUS TELLS OF HIS DEATH AND RESURRECTION

31 ¶ Then he took unto him the twelve, and said unto them, Behold, we go up to Jerusalem, and all things that are written by the prophets concerning the Son of man shall be accomplished.

32 For he shall be delivered unto the Gentiles, and shall be mocked, and spitefully entreated, and spitted on:

33 And they shall scourge him, and put him to death: and the third day he shall rise again.

34 And they understood none of these things: and this saying was hid from them, neither knew they the things which were spoken.

## JESUS HEALS A BLIND BEGGAR

35 ¶ And it came to pass, that as he was come nigh unto Jericho, a certain blind man sat by the way side begging:

36 And hearing the multitude pass by, he asked what it meant.

37 And they told him, that Jesus of Nazareth passeth by.

38 And he cried, saying, Jesus, thou Son of David, have mercy on me.

39 And they which went before rebuked him, that he should hold his peace: but he cried so much the more, Thou Son of David, have mercy on me.

---

18:14 **justified**—approved of God
**exalteth himself shall be abased**—makes himself look important shall be humbled

18:16- Why does Jesus want us to be more like little
17 children? Is there a difference between being childish and being childlike? How are you childlike?

18:20 **adultery**—misuse of the sacred creative powers; that is, use of these powers with someone other than your husband or wife

18:25 See the helps for Matthew 19:23-28.

18:30 **manifold more**—many times more

18:31 **accomplished**—finished

18:32 **spitefully entreated**—treated badly

18:35- What did the blind man do that showed he
42 had faith in the power of Jesus Christ? Why wouldn't he stop calling for the Lord, even when others told him to be quiet? How persistent should you be in your faith and prayers?

40 And Jesus stood, and commanded him to be brought unto him: and when he was come near, he asked him,

41 Saying, What wilt thou that I shall do unto thee? And he said, Lord, that I may receive my sight.

42 And Jesus said unto him, Receive thy sight: thy faith hath saved thee.

43 And immediately he received his sight, and followed him, glorifying God: and all the people, when they saw it, gave praise unto God.

# CHAPTER 19

*Jesus was the promised Messiah, the Anointed One, who would come to save the children of Israel. As you read this chapter look for ways in which Jesus declared this message.*

## JESUS CAME TO SAVE THOSE WHO REPENT

1 ¶ AND Jesus entered and passed through Jericho.

2 And, behold, there was a man named Zacchaeus, which was the chief among the publicans, and he was rich.

3 And he sought to see Jesus who he was; and could not for the press, because he was little of stature.

4 And he ran before, and climbed up into a sycomore tree to see him: for he was to pass that way.

5 And when Jesus came to the place, he looked up, and saw him, and said unto him, Zacchaeus, make haste, and come down; for to day I must abide at thy house.

6 And he made haste, and came down, and received him joyfully.

7 And when they saw it, they all murmured, saying, That he was gone to be guest with a man that is a sinner.

8 And Zacchaeus stood, and said unto the Lord; Behold, Lord, the half of my goods I give to the poor; and if I have taken any thing from any man by false accusation, I restore him fourfold.

9 And Jesus said unto him, This day is salvation come to this house, forsomuch as he also is a son of Abraham.

10 For the Son of man is come to seek and to save that which was lost.

## JESUS TEACHES THE PARABLE OF THE POUNDS

11 ¶ And as they heard these things, he added and spake a parable, because he was nigh to Jerusalem, and because they thought that the kingdom of God should immediately appear.

12 He said therefore, A certain nobleman went into a far country to receive for himself a kingdom, and to return.

13 And he called his ten servants, and delivered them ten pounds, and said unto them, Occupy till I come.

14 But his citizens hated him, and sent a message after him, saying, We will not have this man to reign over us.

15 And it came to pass, that when he was returned, having received the kingdom, then he commanded these servants to be called unto him, to whom he had given the money, that he might know how much every man had gained by trading.

16 Then came the first, saying, Lord, thy pound hath gained ten pounds.

17 And he said unto him, Well, thou good servant: because thou hast been faithful in a very little, have thou authority over ten cities.

18 And the second came, saying, Lord, thy pound hath gained five pounds.

19 And he said likewise to him, Be thou also over five cities.

---

19:2   *chief among the publicans*—head tax collector

19:3   *press*—crowd

19:5-6   How would you feel if Jesus Christ called to you by your name and said he wanted to spend the day at your house? Would you need to make any changes at your home before you would welcome Jesus there?

19:7   *murmured*—complained

19:8   The Joseph Smith Translation makes this verse more clear by changing the last part to read: "and if I have taken anything from any man by unjust means, I restore fourfold" (JST, Luke 19:8).

19:9   The Jews treated publicans badly. What do you think Jesus was trying to teach the Jews by choosing to stay with Zacchaeus? What do you learn from the Lord's example about how you should treat others?

19:13   A pound was an amount of money equal to about three or four months' wages for the average worker.

*Occupy till I come*—Do business until I return

20 And another came, saying, Lord, behold, here is thy pound, which I have kept laid up in a napkin:

21 For I feared thee, because thou art an austere man: thou takest up that thou layedst not down, and reapest that thou didst not sow.

22 And he saith unto him, Out of thine own mouth will I judge thee, thou wicked servant. Thou knewest that I was an austere man, taking up that I laid not down, and reaping that I did not sow:

23 Wherefore then gavest not thou my money into the bank, that at my coming I might have required mine own with usury?

24 And he said unto them that stood by, Take from him the pound, and give it to him that hath ten pounds.

25 (And they said unto him, Lord, he hath ten pounds.)

26 For I say unto you, That unto every one which hath shall be given; and from him that hath not, even that he hath shall be taken away from him.

27 But those mine enemies, which would not that I should reign over them, bring hither, and slay them before me.

### Jesus Enters Jerusalem Triumphantly

28 ¶ And when he had thus spoken, he went before, ascending up to Jerusalem.

29 And it came to pass, when he was come nigh to Bethphage and Bethany, at the mount called the mount of Olives, he sent two of his disciples,

30 Saying, Go ye into the village over against you; in the which at your entering ye shall find a colt tied, whereon yet never man sat: loose him, and bring him hither.

31 And if any man ask you, Why do ye loose him? thus shall ye say unto him, Because the Lord hath need of him.

32 And they that were sent went their way, and found even as he had said unto them.

33 And as they were loosing the colt, the owners thereof said unto them, Why loose ye the colt?

34 And they said, The Lord hath need of him.

35 And they brought him to Jesus: and they cast their garments upon the colt, and they set Jesus thereon.

36 And as he went, they spread their clothes in the way.

37 And when he was come nigh, even now at the descent of the mount of Olives, the whole multitude of the disciples began to rejoice and praise God with a loud voice for all the mighty works that they had seen;

38 Saying, Blessed be the King that cometh in the name of the Lord: peace in heaven, and glory in the highest.

39 And some of the Pharisees from among the multitude said unto him, Master, rebuke thy disciples.

40 And he answered and said unto them, I tell you that, if these should hold their peace, the stones would immediately cry out.

### Jesus Weeps over Jerusalem

41 ¶ And when he was come near, he beheld the city, and wept over it,

42 Saying, If thou hadst known, even thou, at least in this thy day, the things which belong unto thy peace! but now they are hid from thine eyes.

43 For the days shall come upon thee, that thine enemies shall cast a trench about thee, and compass thee round, and keep thee in on every side,

44 And shall lay thee even with the ground, and thy children within thee; and they shall not leave in thee one stone upon another; because thou knewest not the time of thy visitation.

### Jesus Cleanses the Temple Again

45 And he went into the temple, and began to cast out them that sold therein, and them that bought;

46 Saying unto them, It is written, My house is the

---

19:21   austere—unkind, harsh

19:23   usury—interest

19:28-  See the helps for Matthew 21:1-11 and Mark
40      11:1-11.

19:30   hither—here

19:41-  Jesus said that Jerusalem would soon be
44      destroyed. This happened when it was surrounded by Roman legions and destroyed in A.D. 70. Moses prophesied about this same event (see Deuteronomy 28:52).

19:43   cast a trench . . . and compass thee round—build a dirt wall around the city

19:44   The "visitation" referred to here was Jesus' mortal ministry among them. Though he did many miracles and taught them true doctrine, yet they rejected him as the promised Messiah and crucified him.

19:45-  Jesus said that the temple "is the house of
46      prayer." What were these men doing that made it difficult to pray and worship in the temple?

*"Blessed be the King that cometh in the name of the Lord: peace in heaven."*

house of prayer: but ye have made it a den of thieves.

47 And he taught daily in the temple. But the chief priests and the scribes and the chief of the people sought to destroy him,

48 And could not find what they might do: for all the people were very attentive to hear him.

## CHAPTER 20

*In the last week of his mortal life, Jesus taught many important lessons. Many people who questioned his power and authority often tried to trick him into saying something that they could later use against him. See how Jesus handled their questions.*

### JESUS TEACHES OF HIS AUTHORITY BY TELLING A PARABLE

1 ¶ AND it came to pass, that on one of those days, as he taught the people in the temple, and preached the gospel, the chief priests and the scribes came upon him with the elders,

2 And spake unto him, saying, Tell us, by what authority doest thou these things? or who is he that gave thee this authority?

3 And he answered and said unto them, I will also ask you one thing; and answer me:

4 The baptism of John, was it from heaven, or of men?

5 And they reasoned with themselves, saying, If we shall say, From heaven; he will say, Why then believed ye him not?

6 But and if we say, Of men; all the people will stone us: for they be persuaded that John was a prophet.

7 And they answered, that they could not tell whence it was.

8 And Jesus said unto them, Neither tell I you by what authority I do these things.

9 ¶ Then began he to speak to the people this parable; A certain man planted a vineyard, and let it forth to husbandmen, and went into a far country for a long time.

10 And at the season he sent a servant to the husbandmen, that they should give him of the fruit of the vineyard: but the husbandmen beat him, and sent him away empty.

11 And again he sent another servant: and they beat him also, and entreated him shamefully, and sent him away empty.

12 And again he sent a third: and they wounded him also, and cast him out.

13 Then said the lord of the vineyard, What shall I do? I will send my beloved son: it may be they will reverence him when they see him.

14 But when the husbandmen saw him, they reasoned among themselves, saying, This is the heir: come, let us kill him, that the inheritance may be ours.

15 So they cast him out of the vineyard, and killed him. What therefore shall the lord of the vineyard do unto them?

16 He shall come and destroy these husbandmen, and shall give the vineyard to others. And when they heard it, they said, God forbid.

17 And he beheld them, and said, What is this then that is written, The stone which the builders rejected, the same is become the head of the corner?

18 Whosoever shall fall upon that stone shall be broken; but on whomsoever it shall fall, it will grind him to powder.

### JESUS IS QUESTIONED ABOUT PAYING TAXES TO CAESAR

19 And the chief priests and the scribes the same hour sought to lay hands on him; and they feared the people: for they perceived that he had spoken this parable against them.

---

20:2    *authority*—permission, right, or power

20:3-8    How sincere were those who asked about Jesus' authority? Why do you think he answered their question the way he did?

20:9-18    See the helps for Mark 12:1-12.

20:9    *let it forth to husbandmen*—rented the property to some men to care for it

20:10-12    The servants in this parable represent ancient prophets who were rejected. Prophets are often referred to as servants (see Amos 3:7).

20:13-16    An heir is a child who inherits a parent's possessions. In this parable the heir refers to Jesus

Christ, who should have been respected by the people but was rejected and killed like many other prophets.

20:17-18    Jesus Christ is sometimes called the "stone" or "rock" (see Helaman 5:12).

20:19-26    The question asked of Jesus was meant to trap him. If he said the Jews should pay taxes to Rome, the Jews would be angry because they hated the Romans. If he said they should not pay, the Romans could arrest him for rebelling against their authority. Jesus' answer was perfect, and he avoided the trap.

20 ¶ And they watched him, and sent forth spies, which should feign themselves just men, that they might take hold of his words, that so they might deliver him unto the power and authority of the governor.

21 And they asked him, saying, Master, we know that thou sayest and teachest rightly, neither acceptest thou the person of any, but teachest the way of God truly:

22 Is it lawful for us to give tribute unto Caesar, or no?

23 But he perceived their craftiness, and said unto them, Why tempt ye me?

24 Shew me a penny. Whose image and superscription hath it? They answered and said, Caesar's.

25 And he said unto them, Render therefore unto Caesar the things which be Caesar's, and unto God the things which be God's.

26 And they could not take hold of his words before the people: and they marvelled at his answer, and held their peace.

### JESUS IS QUESTIONED ABOUT MARRIAGE AFTER THE RESURRECTION

27 ¶ Then came to him certain of the Sadducees, which deny that there is any resurrection; and they asked him,

28 Saying, Master, Moses wrote unto us, If any man's brother die, having a wife, and he die without children, that his brother should take his wife, and raise up seed unto his brother.

29 There were therefore seven brethren: and the first took a wife, and died without children.

30 And the second took her to wife, and he died childless.

31 And the third took her; and in like manner the seven also: and they left no children, and died.

32 Last of all the woman died also.

33 Therefore in the resurrection whose wife of them is she? for seven had her to wife.

34 And Jesus answering said unto them, The children of this world marry, and are given in marriage:

35 But they which shall be accounted worthy to obtain that world, and the resurrection from the dead, neither marry, nor are given in marriage:

36 Neither can they die any more: for they are equal unto the angels; and are the children of God, being the children of the resurrection.

37 Now that the dead are raised, even Moses shewed at the bush, when he calleth the Lord the God of Abraham, and the God of Isaac, and the God of Jacob.

38 For he is not a God of the dead, but of the living: for all live unto him.

39 ¶ Then certain of the scribes answering said, Master, thou hast well said.

40 And after that they durst not ask him any question at all.

### JESUS WARNS OF THE ACTIONS OF THE SCRIBES

41 And he said unto them, How say they that Christ is David's son?

42 And David himself saith in the book of Psalms, The LORD said unto my Lord, Sit thou on my right hand,

43 Till I make thine enemies thy footstool.

44 David therefore calleth him Lord, how is he then his son?

45 Then in the audience of all the people he said unto his disciples,

46 Beware of the scribes, which desire to walk in long robes, and love greetings in the markets, and the highest seats in the synagogues, and the chief rooms at feasts;

47 Which devour widows' houses, and for a shew

---

20:20 *feign themselves just men*—pretend to be good men

20:24 *image and superscription*—picture and title

20:25 *Render*—Give

20:27 Sadducees were religious and political leaders of the Jews.

20:28 *raise up seed unto*—raise up children for

20:28-33 The Sadducees did not even believe in the resurrection (see verse 27). They made up this story to make fun of the doctrine of life after death.

20:34-36 Marriages and families can be eternal. Jesus

said that people do not get married in the next life because eternal marriage is an earthly ordinance that must be performed in holy temples by the priesthood (see D&C 132:15-19).

20:42-43 David, who was an ancestor of Jesus Christ and was king of Israel, made this statement in Psalm 110:1.

20:46-47 Jesus warned his disciples not to be like the scribes. The scribes (see Glossary), as described here by Jesus, were hypocrites (see Glossary). Do you ever find yourself doing good things but for the wrong reason?

20:47 *devour widows' houses*—take away the property of poor widows

make long prayers: the same shall receive greater damnation.

# CHAPTER 21

*In this chapter Jesus tells his followers about some troubles and some signs that are going to happen after his death. Look for which events have already occurred and which ones we are still waiting for.*

## A POOR WIDOW GIVES ALL SHE HAS TO THE LORD

1 ¶ AND he looked up, and saw the rich men casting their gifts into the treasury.

2 And he saw also a certain poor widow casting in thither two mites.

3 And he said, Of a truth I say unto you, that this poor widow hath cast in more than they all:

4 For all these have of their abundance cast in unto the offerings of God: but she of her penury hath cast in all the living that she had.

## JESUS PROPHESIES THE DESTRUCTION OF JERUSALEM AND HIS SECOND COMING

5 ¶ And as some spake of the temple, how it was adorned with goodly stones and gifts, he said,

6 As for these things which ye behold, the days will come, in the which there shall not be left one stone upon another, that shall not be thrown down.

7 And they asked him, saying, Master, but when shall these things be? and what sign will there be when these things shall come to pass?

8 And he said, Take heed that ye be not deceived: for many shall come in my name, saying, I am Christ; and the time draweth near: go ye not therefore after them.

9 But when ye shall hear of wars and commotions, be not terrified: for these things must first come to pass; but the end is not by and by.

10 Then said he unto them, Nation shall rise against nation, and kingdom against kingdom:

11 And great earthquakes shall be in divers places, and famines, and pestilences; and fearful sights and great signs shall there be from heaven.

12 But before all these, they shall lay their hands on you, and persecute you, delivering you up to the synagogues, and into prisons, being brought before kings and rulers for my name's sake.

13 And it shall turn to you for a testimony.

14 Settle it therefore in your hearts, not to meditate before what ye shall answer:

15 For I will give you a mouth and wisdom, which all your adversaries shall not be able to gainsay nor resist.

16 And ye shall be betrayed both by parents, and brethren, and kinsfolks, and friends; and some of you shall they cause to be put to death.

17 And ye shall be hated of all men for my name's sake.

18 But there shall not an hair of your head perish.

19 In your patience possess ye your souls.

20 ¶ And when ye shall see Jerusalem compassed with armies, then know that the desolation thereof is nigh.

21 Then let them which are in Judaea flee to the mountains; and let them which are in the midst of it depart out; and let not them that are in the countries enter thereinto.

22 For these be the days of vengeance, that all things which are written may be fulfilled.

---

21:2 **mites**—small thin coins made of copper that were the smallest coins in use at that time

21:4 **penury**—poverty

Why does the Lord want us to sacrifice? How do the blessings of God compare with anything we might be asked to give up?

21:5-33 The Joseph Smith Translation makes many changes in these verses. It might be helpful to see the notes that are included with Matthew 24 and Mark 13 as well as study Joseph Smith—Matthew in the Pearl of Great Price.

21:9 **commotions**—fighting and unrest

21:11 **divers**—different
**pestilences**—plagues

21:15 **gainsay**—speak against

21:18 "The disciples were to be tormented and slain in this life, but raised to peace and glorious immortality in the next. The literal nature of the promise is confirmed by Alma who expressed the same assurance" in Alma 40:23. (Bruce R. McConkie, *Doctrinal New Testament Commentary* 1:641).

21:19 This is a promise to the faithful Saints who patiently seek the Lord; they shall save their souls and "have eternal life" (D&C 101:38).

21:20 This was partly fulfilled by the destruction of Jerusalem by the Roman army in A.D. 70, and it will happen again before the second coming of Jesus Christ (see Bruce R. McConkie, *The Millennial Messiah*, pp. 473-74).

**desolation**—destruction

23 But woe unto them that are with child, and to them that give suck, in those days! for there shall be great distress in the land, and wrath upon this people.

24 And they shall fall by the edge of the sword, and shall be led away captive into all nations: and Jerusalem shall be trodden down of the Gentiles, until the times of the Gentiles be fulfilled.

25 And there shall be signs in the sun, and in the moon, and in the stars; and upon the earth distress of nations, with perplexity; the sea and the waves roaring;

26 Men's hearts failing them for fear, and for looking after those things which are coming on the earth: for the powers of heaven shall be shaken.

27 And then shall they see the Son of man coming in a cloud with power and great glory.

28 And when these things begin to come to pass, then look up, and lift up your heads; for your redemption draweth nigh.

29 ¶ And he spake to them a parable; Behold the fig tree, and all the trees;

30 When they now shoot forth, ye see and know of your own selves that summer is now nigh at hand.

31 So likewise ye, when ye see these things come to pass, know ye that the kingdom of God is nigh at hand.

32 Verily I say unto you, This generation shall not pass away, till all be fulfilled.

33 Heaven and earth shall pass away: but my words shall not pass away.

## THE LORD WARNS: WATCH AND BE READY

34 And take heed to yourselves, lest at any time your hearts be overcharged with surfeiting, and drunkenness, and cares of this life, and so that day come upon you unawares.

35 For as a snare shall it come on all them that dwell on the face of the whole earth.

36 Watch ye therefore, and pray always, that ye may be accounted worthy to escape all these things that shall come to pass, and to stand before the Son of man.

37 And in the day time he was teaching in the temple; and at night he went out, and abode in the mount that is called the mount of Olives.

38 And all the people came early in the morning to him in the temple, for to hear him.

## CHAPTER 22

*Jesus came into the world to atone for our sins. As you read this chapter, look for how terribly the Savior suffered that we might have eternal life.*

### JUDAS PLANS HIS BETRAYAL OF JESUS

1 ¶ NOW the feast of unleavened bread drew nigh, which is called the Passover.

2 And the chief priests and scribes sought how they might kill him; for they feared the people.

3 Then entered Satan into Judas surnamed Iscariot, being of the number of the twelve.

4 And he went his way, and communed with the chief priests and captains, how he might betray him unto them.

5 And they were glad, and covenanted to give him money.

6 And he promised, and sought opportunity to betray him unto them in the absence of the multitude.

### JESUS AND HIS APOSTLES PREPARE FOR THE LAST SUPPER

7 ¶ Then came the day of unleavened bread, when the passover must be killed.

8 And he sent Peter and John, saying, Go and prepare us the passover, that we may eat.

9 And they said unto him, Where wilt thou that we prepare?

---

21:25 *perplexity*—confusion

21:34 *overcharged with surfeiting*—made heavy and careless by heavy eating and drinking

21:35 *snare*—trap used to catch birds

21:36 What did Jesus say we should do to prepare for his second coming? What do you need to work on?

22:4 *communed*—spoke

22:5 *covenanted*—promised

22:7 The Feast of Unleavened Bread took place immediately after the Feast of the Passover, and the two feasts were often considered as one. The Feast of Unleavened Bread commemorated the exodus of Israel out of Egypt. (See Exodus 12; Leviticus 23:5-6.) The Feast of the Passover was held each year by the Jews to remember the night the destroying angel passed over the children of Israel and slew the firstborn of Egypt. It was a time to celebrate their release from Egyptian bondage. Every year at Passover a male lamb was killed to remind the people that a Savior would someday come to deliver them. (See Exodus 12.)

10 And he said unto them, Behold, when ye are entered into the city, there shall a man meet you, bearing a pitcher of water; follow him into the house where he entereth in.

11 And ye shall say unto the goodman of the house, The Master saith unto thee, Where is the guest-chamber, where I shall eat the passover with my disciples?

12 And he shall shew you a large upper room furnished: there make ready.

13 And they went, and found as he had said unto them: and they made ready the passover.

## JESUS BEGINS THE ORDINANCE OF THE SACRAMENT

14 And when the hour was come, he sat down, and the twelve apostles with him.

15 And he said unto them, With desire I have desired to eat this passover with you before I suffer:

16 For I say unto you, I will not any more eat thereof, until it be fulfilled in the kingdom of God.

17 And he took the cup, and gave thanks, and said, Take this, and divide it among yourselves:

18 For I say unto you, I will not drink of the fruit of the vine, until the kingdom of God shall come.

19 And he took bread, and gave thanks, and brake it, and gave unto them, saying, This is my body which is given for you: this do in remembrance of me.

20 Likewise also the cup after supper, saying, This cup is the new testament in my blood, which is shed for you.

## JESUS FORETELLS JUDAS'S BETRAYAL

21 ¶ But, behold, the hand of him that betrayeth me is with me on the table.

22 And truly the Son of man goeth, as it was determined: but woe unto that man by whom he is betrayed!

23 And they began to enquire among themselves, which of them it was that should do this thing.

## JESUS TEACHES HIS DISCIPLES TO LEAD BY SERVING

24 And there was also a strife among them, which of them should be accounted the greatest.

25 And he said unto them, The kings of the Gentiles exercise lordship over them; and they that exercise authority upon them are called benefactors.

26 But ye shall not be so: but he that is greatest among you, let him be as the younger; and he that is chief, as he that doth serve.

27 For whether is greater, he that sitteth at meat, or he that serveth? is not he that sitteth at meat? but I am among you as he that serveth.

28 Ye are they which have continued with me in my temptations.

29 And I appoint unto you a kingdom, as my Father hath appointed unto me;

30 That ye may eat and drink at my table in my kingdom, and sit on thrones judging the twelve tribes of Israel.

---

22:10-16  How did Jesus know Peter and John would meet a man carrying water? How did he know they would find a room to have the Passover in? How did he know this would be his last supper? What does this tell you about Jesus?

22:18  *fruit of the vine*—wine

22:20  *new testament*—new covenant or promise

22:24  *a strife*—an argument
*accounted*—looked upon as

22:25  *exercise lordship over them*—give the people orders and commands
*benefactors*—defenders or protectors

22:25-27  Jesus teaches that in this world, kings who give orders are looked upon as greater than the servants who take orders. In the Lord's eyes the greatest is the one who serves the most (see D&C 50:26).

An "upper room" in Jerusalem, much like the room in which the Last Supper was held

## THE SAVIOR ASSURES PETER THAT PETER'S FAITH WILL NOT FAIL

31 And the Lord said, Simon, Simon, behold, Satan hath desired to have you, that he may sift you as wheat:

32 But I have prayed for thee, that thy faith fail not: and when thou art converted, strengthen thy brethren.

33 And he said unto him, Lord, I am ready to go with thee, both into prison, and to death.

34 And he said, I tell thee, Peter, the cock shall not crow this day, before that thou shalt thrice deny that thou knowest me.

## JESUS WARNS THAT PROPHECIES ABOUT HIMSELF WILL SOON BE FULFILLED

35 And he said unto them, When I sent you without purse, and scrip, and shoes, lacked ye any thing? And they said, Nothing.

36 Then said he unto them, But now, he that hath a purse, let him take it, and likewise his scrip: and he that hath no sword, let him sell his garment, and buy one.

37 For I say unto you, that this that is written must yet be accomplished in me, And he was reckoned among the transgressors: for the things concerning me have an end.

38 And they said, Lord, behold, here are two swords. And he said unto them, It is enough.

## JESUS PRAYS AND SUFFERS IN GETHSEMANE

39 ¶ And he came out, and went, as he was wont, to the mount of Olives; and his disciples also followed him.

40 And when he was at the place, he said unto them, Pray that ye enter not into temptation.

41 And he was withdrawn from them about a stone's cast, and kneeled down, and prayed,

42 Saying, Father, if thou be willing, remove this cup from me: nevertheless not my will, but thine, be done.

43 And there appeared an angel unto him from heaven, strengthening him.

44 And being in an agony he prayed more earnestly: and his sweat was as it were great drops of blood falling down to the ground.

45 And when he rose up from prayer, and was come to his disciples, he found them sleeping for sorrow,

46 And said unto them, Why sleep ye? rise and pray, lest ye enter into temptation.

## JESUS IS BETRAYED AND ARRESTED

47 ¶ And while he yet spake, behold a multitude, and he that was called Judas, one of the twelve, went before them, and drew near unto Jesus to kiss him.

48 But Jesus said unto him, Judas, betrayest thou the Son of man with a kiss?

49 When they which were about him saw what would follow, they said unto him, Lord, shall we smite with the sword?

50 And one of them smote the servant of the high priest, and cut off his right ear.

51 And Jesus answered and said, Suffer ye thus far. And he touched his ear, and healed him.

52 Then Jesus said unto the chief priests, and captains of the temple, and the elders, which were come to him, Be ye come out, as against a thief, with swords and staves?

53 When I was daily with you in the temple, ye stretched forth no hands against me: but this is your hour, and the power of darkness.

---

22:31 To "sift you as wheat" means, in effect, "to give you trials in the hope of destroying your faith." The Joseph Smith Translation adds that Satan desired to destroy not just Peter but all of "the children of the kingdom" (JST, Luke 22:31).

22:32 We know Peter had a testimony (see Matthew 16:16-17). But there is a difference between having a testimony and being truly converted (see Mosiah 27:25; Alma 5:14).

22:34 *thrice*—three times

22:42-44 This cup, also called a "bitter cup," is a symbol that stands for the suffering Jesus went through. The Lord told Joseph Smith more about what His suffering was like (see D&C 19:18).

22:42 Why did Heavenly Father allow his Beloved Son to suffer so much? (See John 3:16.) Why was Jesus willing to go through so much suffering? (See D&C 19:16-19 and D&C 34:3.)

22:44 *an agony*—great pain

22:50 In John 18:10 we learn that it was Peter who cut off the man's ear.

22:51 These people had come to arrest Jesus and lead him to his death. Why do you think Jesus still took the time to heal one of them?

*Christ praying in the Garden of Gethsemane*

## PETER DENIES KNOWING JESUS

54 ¶ Then took they him, and led him, and brought him into the high priest's house. And Peter followed afar off.

55 And when they had kindled a fire in the midst of the hall, and were set down together, Peter sat down among them.

56 But a certain maid beheld him as he sat by the fire, and earnestly looked upon him, and said, This man was also with him.

57 And he denied him, saying, Woman, I know him not.

58 And after a little while another saw him, and said, Thou art also of them. And Peter said, Man, I am not.

59 And about the space of one hour after another confidently affirmed, saying, Of a truth this fellow also was with him: for he is a Galilaean.

60 And Peter said, Man, I know not what thou sayest. And immediately, while he yet spake, the cock crew.

61 And the Lord turned, and looked upon Peter. And Peter remembered the word of the Lord, how he had said unto him, Before the cock crow, thou shalt deny me thrice.

62 And Peter went out, and wept bitterly.

## JESUS IS MOCKED AND TAKEN BEFORE THE COUNCIL

63 ¶ And the men that held Jesus mocked him, and smote him.

64 And when they had blindfolded him, they struck him on the face, and asked him, saying, Prophesy, who is it that smote thee?

65 And many other things blasphemously spake they against him.

66 And as soon as it was day, the elders of the people and the chief priests and the scribes came together, and led him into their council, saying,

67 Art thou the Christ? tell us. And he said unto them, If I tell you, ye will not believe:

68 And if I also ask you, ye will not answer me, nor let me go.

69 Hereafter shall the Son of man sit on the right hand of the power of God.

70 Then said they all, Art thou then the Son of God? And he said unto them, Ye say that I am.

71 And they said, What need we any further witness? for we ourselves have heard of his own mouth.

## CHAPTER 23

*Jesus Christ lived a perfect life. Yet he was falsely accused of blasphemy for declaring that he was God's Son. As you read, watch for what Jesus did that shows that he was who he said he was.*

## JESUS CHRIST IS TAKEN BEFORE PILATE

1 ¶ AND the whole multitude of them arose, and led him unto Pilate.

2 And they began to accuse him, saying, We found this fellow perverting the nation, and forbidding to give tribute to Caesar, saying that he himself is Christ a King.

3 And Pilate asked him, saying, Art thou the King of the Jews? And he answered him and said, Thou sayest it.

4 Then said Pilate to the chief priests and to the people, I find no fault in this man.

5 And they were the more fierce, saying, He stirreth up the people, teaching throughout all Jewry, beginning from Galilee to this place.

6 When Pilate heard of Galilee, he asked whether the man were a Galilaean.

7 And as soon as he knew that he belonged unto Herod's jurisdiction, he sent him to Herod, who himself also was at Jerusalem at that time.

---

22:59 **confidently affirmed**—that is, was sure he had seen Peter with Jesus

22:61-62 Jesus knew Peter's strengths and his weaknesses and loved him anyway. He helped Peter become strong enough to lead the Church after Jesus was gone. Jesus also loves you. Can he also help you overcome your weaknesses and make you strong in keeping the commandments?

22:66 The Sanhedrin, often called "the council," was a group of seventy-one men who ruled the Jews. It was made up of Pharisees, Sadduccees, and scribes and was led by a high priest. (See LDS Bible Dictionary, s.v. "Sanhedrin," p. 769.)

23:1 Pilate was the Roman governor in Judea. He lived in another city named Caesarea but usually visited Jerusalem during the Passover feast. (See LDS Bible Dictionary, s.v. "Pilate," p. 751.)

23:2 **tribute**—tax

23:5 **Jewry**—Judea

23:7 This was Herod Antipas, the same one who had John the Baptist beheaded. He had rule over an area named Galilee. Pilate sent Jesus to Herod so that he wouldn't have to judge him (see Matthew 14:1-12).

## CHRIST IS TAKEN BEFORE HEROD

8 And when Herod saw Jesus, he was exceeding glad: for he was desirous to see him of a long season, because he had heard many things of him; and he hoped to have seen some miracle done by him.

9 Then he questioned with him in many words; but he answered him nothing.

10 And the chief priests and scribes stood and vehemently accused him.

11 And Herod with his men of war set him at nought, and mocked him, and arrayed him in a gorgeous robe, and sent him again to Pilate.

12 And the same day Pilate and Herod were made friends together: for before they were at enmity between themselves.

## CHRIST IS TAKEN TO PILATE AGAIN

13 ¶ And Pilate, when he had called together the chief priests and the rulers and the people,

14 Said unto them, Ye have brought this man unto me, as one that perverteth the people: and, behold, I, having examined him before you, have found no fault in this man touching those things whereof ye accuse him:

15 No, nor yet Herod: for I sent you to him; and, lo, nothing worthy of death is done unto him.

16 I will therefore chastise him, and release him.

## BARABBAS IS RELEASED

17 (For of necessity he must release one unto them at the feast.)

18 And they cried out all at once, saying, Away with this man, and release unto us Barabbas:

19 (Who for a certain sedition made in the city, and for murder, was cast into prison.)

20 Pilate therefore, willing to release Jesus, spake again to them.

21 But they cried, saying, Crucify him, crucify him.

22 And he said unto them the third time, Why, what evil hath he done? I have found no cause of death in him: I will therefore chastise him, and let him go.

23 And they were instant with loud voices, requiring that he might be crucified. And the voices of them and of the chief priests prevailed.

24 And Pilate gave sentence that it should be as they required.

25 And he released unto them him that for sedition and murder was cast into prison, whom they had desired; but he delivered Jesus to their will.

## CHRIST IS CRUCIFIED BETWEEN TWO THIEVES

26 ¶ And as they led him away, they laid hold upon one Simon, a Cyrenian, coming out of the country, and on him they laid the cross, that he might bear it after Jesus.

27 And there followed him a great company of people, and of women, which also bewailed and lamented him.

28 But Jesus turning unto them said, Daughters of Jerusalem, weep not for me, but weep for yourselves, and for your children.

29 For, behold, the days are coming, in the which they shall say, Blessed are the barren, and the wombs that never bare, and the paps which never gave suck.

30 Then shall they begin to say to the mountains, Fall on us; and to the hills, Cover us.

31 For if they do these things in a green tree, what shall be done in the dry?

---

23:8 *of a long season*—for a long time

23:10 *vehemently*—fiercely

23:11 *set him at nought, and mocked him*—made fun of him

23:12 *were at enmity*—were enemies

23:14-16 Only a Roman official could issue the death penalty. Pilate questioned Jesus and found nothing serious enough to put him to death. He offered instead to punish Jesus and release him. (See LDS Bible Dictionary, s.v. "Pilate," p. 751.)

23:17-23 It was a custom for a Roman official to release a prisoner during the Feast of the Passover. Pilate wanted to release Jesus, but the Jewish leaders cried to have Barabbas released. (See John 18:39-

40.) Barabbas, whose name means "son of the father," was a terrorist and murderer (see LDS Bible Dictionary, s.v. "Barabbas," p. 619).

23:27 *bewailed and lamented him*—mourned and cried over him

23:28-30 Jesus had no comfort for the women who wept. He told them not to weep for him but for themselves. He knew that one day Roman soldiers would destroy Jerusalem. It would be so terrible that mothers would wish they had no children. (See Luke 19:41-44.)

23:31 The "green tree" represents Jesus Christ and the "dry" tree represents apostate Judaism (see JST, Luke 23:31-32 and Bruce R. McConkie, *Doctrinal New Testament Commentary* 1:817).

32 ¶ And there were also two other, malefactors, led with him to be put to death.

33 And when they were come to the place, which is called Calvary, there they crucified him, and the malefactors, one on the right hand, and the other on the left.

## JESUS CHRIST IS MOCKED WHILE ON THE CROSS

34 Then said Jesus, Father, forgive them; for they know not what they do. And they parted his raiment, and cast lots.

35 And the people stood beholding. And the rulers also with them derided him, saying, He saved others; let him save himself, if he be Christ, the chosen of God.

36 And the soldiers also mocked him, coming to him, and offering him vinegar,

37 And saying, If thou be the king of the Jews, save thyself.

38 And a superscription also was written over him in letters of Greek, and Latin, and Hebrew, THIS IS THE KING OF THE JEWS.

39 And one of the malefactors which were hanged railed on him, saying, If thou be Christ, save thyself and us.

40 But the other answering rebuked him, saying, Dost not thou fear God, seeing thou art in the same condemnation?

41 And we indeed justly; for we receive the due reward of our deeds: but this man hath done nothing amiss.

42 And he said unto Jesus, Lord, remember me when thou comest into thy kingdom.

43 And Jesus said unto him, Verily I say unto thee, To day shalt thou be with me in paradise.

44 ¶ And it was about the sixth hour, and there was a darkness over all the earth until the ninth hour.

45 And the sun was darkened, and the veil of the temple was rent in the midst.

---

23:32 **malefactors**—criminals

23:33 Calvary is the same as Golgotha, and both mean "skull" (see LDS Bible Dictionary, s.v. "Calvary," p. 629).

"Few details of the actual crucifixion are given us. We know however that our Lord was nailed to the cross by spikes driven through the hands and feet, as was the Roman method, and not bound only by cords as was the custom in inflicting this form of punishment among some other nations. Death by crucifixion was at once the most lingering and most painful of all forms of execution." (James E. Talmage, *Jesus the Christ,* p. 655.)

*Where Jesus was crucified*

23:34 The Joseph Smith Translation indicates that when Jesus said, "Father, forgive them," he was referring to "the soldiers who crucified him" (JST, Luke 23:35).

**they parted his raiment, and cast lots**—they divided his clothes among them by gambling

23:35 **derided**—sneered at

Those who gathered around the cross challenged Jesus to prove that he was the Son of God. They asked Jesus, in a mocking way, "if he be Christ" to save himself. Satan asked similar questions of Jesus during the temptations (see Matthew 4:1-11). Why would Satan or others not want us to believe we are the children of God?

23:36 This vinegar, or sour wine, was a mercy drink given to help relieve pain (see James E. Talmage, *Jesus the Christ,* pp. 654-55). This act also fulfilled a prophecy given in Psalm 69:21.

23:38 **superscription**—notice or title

23:43 Jesus did not promise this criminal a place in heaven. "All the Lord's statement promised the thief was that both of them would soon be in the spirit world" (*The Teachings of Spencer W. Kimball,* p. 90).

23:44 The sixth hour was equal to twelve o'clock noon, while the ninth hour was three o'clock in the afternoon (see LDS Bible Dictionary, s.v. "Watches," p. 788).

23:45 **rent in the midst**—torn in two

## JESUS DIES UPON THE CROSS

46 And when Jesus had cried with a loud voice, he said, Father, into thy hands I commend my spirit: and having said thus, he gave up the ghost.

47 Now when the centurion saw what was done, he glorified God, saying, Certainly this was a righteous man.

48 And all the people that came together to that sight, beholding the things which were done, smote their breasts, and returned.

49 And all his acquaintance, and the women that followed him from Galilee, stood afar off, beholding these things.

## JESUS IS BURIED IN A TOMB

50 ¶ And, behold, there was a man named Joseph, a counsellor; and he was a good man, and a just:

51 (The same had not consented to the counsel and deed of them;) he was of Arimathaea, a city of the Jews: who also himself waited for the kingdom of God.

52 This man went unto Pilate, and begged the body of Jesus.

53 And he took it down, and wrapped it in linen, and laid it in a sepulchre that was hewn in stone, wherein never man before was laid.

54 And that day was the preparation, and the sabbath drew on.

55 And the women also, which came with him from Galilee, followed after, and beheld the sepulchre, and how his body was laid.

56 And they returned, and prepared spices and ointments; and rested the sabbath day according to the commandment.

## CHAPTER 24

*Angels made the glorious announcement that Jesus Christ was resurrected. As you read this wonderful message, look for whom Jesus appears to, as well as for what a resurrected being is like.*

## JESUS CHRIST IS RESURRECTED

1 ¶ NOW upon the first day of the week, very early in the morning, they came unto the sepulchre, bringing the spices which they had prepared, and certain others with them.

2 And they found the stone rolled away from the sepulchre.

3 And they entered in, and found not the body of the Lord Jesus.

4 And it came to pass, as they were much perplexed thereabout, behold, two men stood by them in shining garments:

5 And as they were afraid, and bowed down their faces to the earth, they said unto them, Why seek ye the living among the dead?

6 He is not here, but is risen: remember how he spake unto you when he was yet in Galilee,

7 Saying, The Son of man must be delivered into the hands of sinful men, and be crucified, and the third day rise again.

8 And they remembered his words,

9 And returned from the sepulchre, and told all these things unto the eleven, and to all the rest.

10 It was Mary Magdalene, and Joanna, and Mary the mother of James, and other women that were with them, which told these things unto the apostles.

---

23:46　Referring to Jesus' giving up the ghost, Elder James E. Talmage said, "He bowed His head, and voluntarily gave up His life" (*Jesus the Christ,* p. 662).

23:49　***all his acquaintance***—all those who knew him

23:50-54　Joseph was a member of the Sanhedrin, which was the ruling body of the Jews. He had not agreed to the killing of Jesus. Pilate granted his request to take the body of Jesus, and he buried it in a newly made tomb. It was the day before the Jewish Sabbath.

24:1　***sepulchre***—tomb or grave

24:4　***perplexed***—confused

*A garden tomb like that wherein it is said that the Lord's body was laid*

11 And their words seemed to them as idle tales, and they believed them not.

12 Then arose Peter, and ran unto the sepulchre; and stooping down, he beheld the linen clothes laid by themselves, and departed, wondering in himself at that which was come to pass.

### JESUS APPEARS TO TWO DISCIPLES ON THE ROAD TO EMMAUS

13 ¶ And, behold, two of them went that same day to a village called Emmaus, which was from Jerusalem about threescore furlongs.

14 And they talked together of all these things which had happened.

15 And it came to pass, that, while they communed together and reasoned, Jesus himself drew near, and went with them.

16 But their eyes were holden that they should not know him.

17 And he said unto them, What manner of communications are these that ye have one to another, as ye walk, and are sad?

18 And the one of them, whose name was Cleopas, answering said unto him, Art thou only a stranger in Jerusalem, and hast not known the things which are come to pass there in these days?

19 And he said unto them, What things? And they said unto him, Concerning Jesus of Nazareth, which was a prophet mighty in deed and word before God and all the people:

20 And how the chief priests and our rulers delivered him to be condemned to death, and have crucified him.

21 But we trusted that it had been he which should have redeemed Israel: and beside all this, to day is the third day since these things were done.

22 Yea, and certain women also of our company made us astonished, which were early at the sepulchre;

23 And when they found not his body, they came, saying, that they had also seen a vision of angels, which said that he was alive.

24 And certain of them which were with us went to the sepulchre, and found it even so as the women had said: but him they saw not.

25 Then he said unto them, O fools, and slow of heart to believe all that the prophets have spoken:

26 Ought not Christ to have suffered these things, and to enter into his glory?

27 And beginning at Moses and all the prophets, he expounded unto them in all the scriptures the things concerning himself.

28 And they drew nigh unto the village, whither they went: and he made as though he would have gone further.

29 But they constrained him, saying, Abide with us: for it is toward evening, and the day is far spent. And he went in to tarry with them.

30 And it came to pass, as he sat at meat with them, he took bread, and blessed it, and brake, and gave to them.

31 And their eyes were opened, and they knew him; and he vanished out of their sight.

32 And they said one to another, Did not our heart burn within us, while he talked with us by the way, and while he opened to us the scriptures?

33 And they rose up the same hour, and returned to Jerusalem, and found the eleven gathered together, and them that were with them,

34 Saying, The Lord is risen indeed, and hath appeared to Simon.

35 And they told what things were done in the way, and how he was known of them in breaking of bread.

### JESUS APPEARS TO THE APOSTLES

36 ¶ And as they thus spake, Jesus himself stood in the midst of them, and saith unto them, Peace be unto you.

37 But they were terrified and affrighted, and supposed that they had seen a spirit.

---

24:13 *threescore furlongs*—eight miles

24:15 *communed*—talked

24:16 *their eyes were holden*—they were not allowed to recognize Jesus

24:18- Why were Cleopas and his companion sad?
24 How do you imagine they felt about their Savior, Jesus Christ?

24:25 *O fools*—Oh, unwise ones

24:27 All of the scriptures bear testimony of Jesus Christ (see Moses 6:63; 2 Nephi 11:4).

24:29 *constrained*—strongly urged

24:32 One way the Holy Ghost talks to us is by feelings in our hearts (see D&C 8:2; 9:8).

24:32, How do you think Jesus opened the scriptures
45 to their understanding?

*Christ with two disciples at Emmaus*

38 And he said unto them, Why are ye troubled? and why do thoughts arise in your hearts?

39 Behold my hands and my feet, that it is I myself: handle me, and see; for a spirit hath not flesh and bones, as ye see me have.

40 And when he had thus spoken, he shewed them his hands and his feet.

41 And while they yet believed not for joy, and wondered, he said unto them, Have ye here any meat?

42 And they gave him a piece of a broiled fish, and of an honeycomb.

43 And he took it, and did eat before them.

44 And he said unto them, These are the words which I spake unto you, while I was yet with you, that all things must be fulfilled, which were written in the law of Moses, and in the prophets, and in the psalms, concerning me.

45 Then opened he their understanding, that they might understand the scriptures,

46 And said unto them, Thus it is written, and thus it behoved Christ to suffer, and to rise from the dead the third day:

47 And that repentance and remission of sins should be preached in his name among all nations, beginning at Jerusalem.

48 And ye are witnesses of these things.

---

24:39    A resurrected person has a glorified, perfected body of flesh and bones (see Alma 11:33–34).

24:39-    What do you learn about resurrected beings
43    from these verses?

24:48    The Apostles were witnesses of Jesus Christ's resurrection. Apostles in our day also are given the title of "special witnesses" (see D&C 107:23, 26).

*"Ye men of Galilee"*

## JESUS IS CARRIED INTO HEAVEN

49 And, behold, I send the promise of my Father upon you: but tarry ye in the city of Jerusalem, until ye be endued with power from on high.

50 ¶ And he led them out as far as to Bethany, and he lifted up his hands, and blessed them.

51 And it came to pass, while he blessed them, he was parted from them, and carried up into heaven.

52 And they worshipped him, and returned to Jerusalem with great joy:

53 And were continually in the temple, praising and blessing God. Amen.

24:49    *tarry*—stay and wait
    **endued with**—given or clothed with

# THE GOSPEL ACCORDING TO
# ST. JOHN*

*The Gospel of St. John is the Apostle John's testimony of the life and teachings of Jesus Christ written to members of the Church. John's Gospel has many of the Lord's teachings that are not in the other three Gospels.*

## CHAPTER 1

*John begins by bearing testimony that Jesus Christ was the premortal Son of God. He then includes the testimonies of many others. Look for the many testimonies that are borne about Jesus Christ in this chapter.*

### JESUS CHRIST IS THE WORD AND THE LIGHT AND LIFE OF THE WORLD

1 IN the beginning was the Word, and the Word was with God, and the Word was God.

2 The same was in the beginning with God.

3 All things were made by him; and without him was not any thing made that was made.

4 In him was life; and the life was the light of men.

5 ¶ And the light shineth in darkness; and the darkness comprehended it not.

6 There was a man sent from God, whose name was John.

7 The same came for a witness, to bear witness of the Light, that all men through him might believe.

8 He was not that Light, but was sent to bear witness of that Light.

9 That was the true Light, which lighteth every man that cometh into the world.

10 He was in the world, and the world was made by him, and the world knew him not.

11 He came unto his own, and his own received him not.

12 But as many as received him, to them gave he power to become the sons of God, even to them that believe on his name:

13 Which were born, not of blood, nor of the will of the flesh, nor of the will of man, but of God.

14 And the Word was made flesh, and dwelt among us, (and we beheld his glory, the glory as of the only begotten of the Father,) full of grace and truth.

15 ¶ John bare witness of him, and cried, saying, This was he of whom I spake, He that cometh after me is preferred before me: for he was before me.

16 And of his fulness have all we received, and grace for grace.

---

*    The Joseph Smith Translation changes the title of this book from "The Gospel According to St. John" to "The Testimony of St. John."

1:1    The Joseph Smith Translation changes verse 1 to read: "In the beginning was the gospel preached through the Son. And the gospel was the word, and the word was with the Son, and the Son was with God, and the Son was of God." (JST, John 1:1.)

1:4-5    The Joseph Smith Translation changes verses 4 and 5 to read: "In him was the gospel, and the gospel was the life, and the life was the light of men; and the light shineth in the world, and the world perceiveth [sees] it not" (JST, John 1:4-5).

1:6    The man named John mentioned in verse 6 is John the Baptist.

1:7-10    The Joseph Smith Translation changes verses 7-10 to make it clear that John the Baptist "came into the world for a witness, to bear witness of the light," and that that "true light, which lighteth every man who cometh into the world," is Jesus Christ (JST, John 1:7-10).

1:12    We are the children of God the Father because he is the Father of our spirits. This verse shows that we can also become children of Jesus Christ. He becomes the father of our spiritual rebirth. (See Mosiah 5:5-8.)

1:13    The Joseph Smith Translation changes the first part of verse 13 to read, "He was born, not of blood, . . ." (JST, John 1:13). Jesus' birth was like no other birth on this earth. He was not the son of a man but the Son of Heavenly Father.

1:16    The Joseph Smith Translation helps clarify this verse. It adds: "And as many as believe on his name shall receive of his fullness. And of his fullness have all we received, even immortality and eternal life, through his grace." (JST, John 1:16.)

---

   = Word Help      = A Closer Look

   = More Light      = Ponder This

Words in pink are explained in the Glossary.

*Christ is the Creator.*

17 For the law was given by Moses, but grace and truth came by Jesus Christ.

18 No man hath seen God at any time; the only begotten Son, which is in the bosom of the Father, he hath declared him.

## JOHN THE BAPTIST IDENTIFIES AND TESTIFIES OF JESUS CHRIST

19 ¶ And this is the record of John, when the Jews sent priests and Levites from Jerusalem to ask him, Who art thou?

20 And he confessed, and denied not; but confessed, I am not the Christ.

21 And they asked him, What then? Art thou Elias? And he saith, I am not. Art thou that prophet? And he answered, No.

22 Then said they unto him, Who art thou? that we may give an answer to them that sent us. What sayest thou of thyself?

23 He said, I am the voice of one crying in the wilderness, Make straight the way of the Lord, as said the prophet Esaias.

24 And they which were sent were of the Pharisees.

25 And they asked him, and said unto him, Why baptizest thou then, if thou be not that Christ, nor Elias, neither that prophet?

26 John answered them, saying, I baptize with water: but there standeth one among you, whom ye know not;

27 He it is, who coming after me is preferred before me, whose shoe's latchet I am not worthy to unloose.

28 These things were done in Bethabara beyond Jordan, where John was baptizing.

29 ¶ The next day John seeth Jesus coming unto him, and saith, Behold the Lamb of God, which taketh away the sin of the world.

30 This is he of whom I said, After me cometh a man which is preferred before me: for he was before me.

31 And I knew him not: but that he should be made manifest to Israel, therefore am I come baptizing with water.

---

1:19 In Bible times, a priest was a descendant of Aaron who served the people in religious matters, particularly at the temple (see Numbers 16:3-10, 40; 18:1). The priest officiated at the sacrifices and other temple ordinances (see Numbers 16:40; 18:2-3, 5, 7; Deuteronomy 33:10) and also taught the people the law of Moses (see Deuteronomy 33:10; Leviticus 10:10, 11; Malachi 2:7). (See LDS Bible Dictionary, s.v. "Priests," p. 753.) Levites were descendants of Levi who had the work of ministering in the temple. They did such jobs as "the housekeeping of the tabernacle, keeping oil in the lamps, transporting the Ark of the Covenant, taking down and setting up the tabernacle when moving, and related tasks in assisting the priests (Num. 3:5-10; 18:1-7; 1 Chr. 23:27-32)." (LDS Bible Dictionary, s.v. "Aaronic Priesthood," p. 600; see also "Levites," p. 724).

1:20 The Joseph Smith Translation changes this passage to say that John "confessed, and denied not that he was Elias; but confessed, saying; I am not the Christ" (JST, John 1:21).

1:21 *Elias* is the Greek word for *Elijah*. Elias is also a title for someone who goes first to prepare the way for another. John the Baptist prepared the way before Jesus Christ, and so he was an Elias. (See LDS Bible Dictionary, s.v. "Elias," p. 663.)

1:23 **Esaias**—Isaiah

1:24 Pharisees were religious and political leaders of the Jews.

1:27 The Joseph Smith Translation points out that one reason why Jesus Christ was greater than John is that Jesus "shall baptize, not only with water, but with fire, and with the Holy Ghost" (JST, John 1:28).

1:29 From the days of Adam to those of Jesus Christ, faithful people offered firstborn male lambs as sacrifices to God. This sacrifice was to remind them of the great and last sacrifice of the Savior. Why is "the Lamb of God" such a good title for Jesus?

*The Jordan River near Bethabara, where Jesus was baptized by John (see 1 Nephi 10:9).*

32 And John bare record, saying, I saw the Spirit descending from heaven like a dove, and it abode upon him.

33 And I knew him not: but he that sent me to baptize with water, the same said unto me, Upon whom thou shalt see the Spirit descending, and remaining on him, the same is he which baptizeth with the Holy Ghost.

34 And I saw, and bare record that this is the Son of God.

## JOHN'S DISCIPLES FOLLOW JESUS

35 Again the next day after John stood, and two of his disciples;

36 And looking upon Jesus as he walked, he saith, Behold the Lamb of God!

37 ¶ And the two disciples heard him speak, and they followed Jesus.

38 Then Jesus turned, and saw them following, and saith unto them, What seek ye? They said unto him, Rabbi, (which is to say, being interpreted, Master,) where dwellest thou?

39 He saith unto them, Come and see. They came and saw where he dwelt, and abode with him that day: for it was about the tenth hour.

40 One of the two which heard John speak, and followed him, was Andrew, Simon Peter's brother.

41 He first findeth his own brother Simon, and saith unto him, We have found the Messias, which is, being interpreted, the Christ.

42 And he brought him to Jesus. And when Jesus beheld him, he said, Thou art Simon the son of Jona: thou shalt be called Cephas, which is by interpretation, A stone.

## NATHANAEL IS CALLED TO FOLLOW THE SAVIOR

43 ¶ The day following Jesus would go forth into Galilee, and findeth Philip, and saith unto him, Follow me.

44 Now Philip was of Bethsaida, the city of Andrew and Peter.

45 Philip findeth Nathanael, and saith unto him, We have found him, of whom Moses in the law, and the prophets, did write, Jesus of Nazareth, the son of Joseph.

46 And Nathanael said unto him, Can there any good thing come out of Nazareth? Philip saith unto him, Come and see.

47 Jesus saw Nathanael coming to him, and saith of him, Behold an Israelite indeed, in whom is no guile!

48 Nathanael saith unto him, Whence knowest thou me? Jesus answered and said unto him, Before that Philip called thee, when thou wast under the fig tree, I saw thee.

49 Nathanael answered and saith unto him, Rabbi, thou art the Son of God; thou art the King of Israel.

50 Jesus answered and said unto him, Because I said unto thee, I saw thee under the fig tree, believest thou? thou shalt see greater things than these.

51 And he saith unto him, Verily, verily, I say unto you, Hereafter ye shall see heaven open, and the angels of God ascending and descending upon the Son of man.

# CHAPTER 2

*This chapter includes the first public miracle of Jesus Christ, as well as many other miracles. Look for what Jesus did for his mother on earth and his Father in Heaven.*

## JESUS TURNS WATER INTO WINE

1 ¶ AND the third day there was a marriage in Cana of Galilee; and the mother of Jesus was there:

2 And both Jesus was called, and his disciples, to the marriage.

---

1:32   **abode**—remained

1:33   The Joseph Smith Translation changes this passage to say "I knew him" rather than "I knew him not" (JST, John 1:32).

1:34   In his Gospel, John the Apostle includes the testimony of John the Baptist. If you could have your testimony written in the Gospel of John, what would you say?

1:35   **disciples**—followers

1:38   **interpreted**—explained or translated

1:39   **dwelt**—lived
**the tenth hour**—four o'clock in the afternoon

1:45   Every part of the law of Moses pointed to Jesus Christ (see Alma 34:14). Prophets of the Old Testament and the Book of Mormon testified that Jesus Christ would be the Savior (see 1 Nephi 10:5).

1:47   **guile**—dishonesty or deceit

1:47-51   Jesus knew all about Nathanael before he met him. Do you think that the Savior knows all about you too? How does this make you feel?

*Jesus turned water into wine.*

3 And when they wanted wine, the mother of Jesus saith unto him, They have no wine.

4 Jesus saith unto her, Woman, what have I to do with thee? mine hour is not yet come.

5 His mother saith unto the servants, Whatsoever he saith unto you, do it.

6 And there were set there six waterpots of stone, after the manner of the purifying of the Jews, containing two or three firkins apiece.

7 Jesus saith unto them, Fill the waterpots with water. And they filled them up to the brim.

8 And he saith unto them, Draw out now, and bear unto the governor of the feast. And they bare it.

9 When the ruler of the feast had tasted the water that was made wine, and knew not whence it was: (but the servants which drew the water knew;) the governor of the feast called the bridegroom,

10 And saith unto him, Every man at the beginning doth set forth good wine; and when men have well drunk, then that which is worse: but thou hast kept the good wine until now.

11 This beginning of miracles did Jesus in Cana of Galilee, and manifested forth his glory; and his disciples believed on him.

## JESUS CLEANSES THE TEMPLE

12 ¶ After this he went down to Capernaum, he, and his mother, and his brethren, and his disciples: and they continued there not many days.

13 And the Jews' passover was at hand, and Jesus went up to Jerusalem,

14 And found in the temple those that sold oxen and sheep and doves, and the changers of money sitting:

15 And when he had made a scourge of small cords, he drove them all out of the temple, and the sheep, and the oxen; and poured out the changers' money, and overthrew the tables;

16 And said unto them that sold doves, Take these things hence; make not my Father's house an house of merchandise.

17 And his disciples remembered that it was written, The zeal of thine house hath eaten me up.

## JESUS SPEAKS OF HIS DEATH AND RESURRECTION

18 Then answered the Jews and said unto him, What sign shewest thou unto us, seeing that thou doest these things?

19 Jesus answered and said unto them, Destroy this temple, and in three days I will raise it up.

20 Then said the Jews, Forty and six years was this temple in building, and wilt thou rear it up in three days?

21 But he spake of the temple of his body.

22 When therefore he was risen from the dead, his disciples remembered that he had said this unto them; and they believed the scripture, and the word which Jesus had said.

23 ¶ Now when he was in Jerusalem at the passover, in the feast day, many believed in his name, when they saw the miracles which he did.

24 But Jesus did not commit himself unto them, because he knew all men,

25 And needed not that any should testify of man: for he knew what was in man.

---

2:4    The Joseph Smith Translation changes verse 4 to read: "Jesus said unto her, Woman, what wilt thou have me to do for thee? that will I do; for mine hour is not yet come" (JST, John 2:4).

Using the term *woman* was a loving way to address a lady in Jesus' day (see Frederic W. Farrar, *The Life of Christ,* pp. 144-45).

2:6    A firkin is nearly nine gallons.

2:11    The Joseph Smith Translation changes "his disciples believed on him" to "the faith of his disciples was strengthened in him" (JST, John 2:11).

Jesus turned the water to wine in order to help his mother. Jesus always respected and honored his parents. How is his example helpful to you?

2:13    The Feast of the Passover was an important Jewish celebration and a reminder that the angel of death "passed over" the children of Israel when the firstborn children of Egypt all died (see LDS Bible Dictionary, s.v. "Feasts," pp. 672-74).

2:15    *scourge*—whip

2:16    *an house of merchandise*—a market

2:17    *zeal of*—love for
*eaten me up*—consumed me

2:18-25    Notice the reverence Jesus has for his "Father's house." He then compares his own body to the holy temple. How do feel about your own body? How can you treat your body reverently, as you would the holy temple?

2:20    *rear*—build

2:24    *commit*—entrust

# CHAPTER 3

*People often asked Jesus questions about the gospel. Watch for how Jesus answered these questions and also how his answers are important to us today.*

## WE MUST BE BORN AGAIN

1 ¶ THERE was a man of the Pharisees, named Nicodemus, a ruler of the Jews:

2 The same came to Jesus by night, and said unto him, Rabbi, we know that thou art a teacher come from God: for no man can do these miracles that thou doest, except God be with him.

3 Jesus answered and said unto him, Verily, verily, I say unto thee, Except a man be born again, he cannot see the kingdom of God.

4 Nicodemus saith unto him, How can a man be born when he is old? can he enter the second time into his mother's womb, and be born?

5 Jesus answered, Verily, verily, I say unto thee, Except a man be born of water and of the Spirit, he cannot enter into the kingdom of God.

6 That which is born of the flesh is flesh; and that which is born of the Spirit is spirit.

7 Marvel not that I said unto thee, Ye must be born again.

8 The wind bloweth where it listeth, and thou hearest the sound thereof, but canst not tell whence it cometh, and whither it goeth: so is every one that is born of the Spirit.

## GOD SENT HIS SON TO SAVE US

9 Nicodemus answered and said unto him, How can these things be?

10 Jesus answered and said unto him, Art thou a master of Israel, and knowest not these things?

11 Verily, verily, I say unto thee, We speak that we do know, and testify that we have seen; and ye receive not our witness.

12 If I have told you earthly things, and ye believe not, how shall ye believe, if I tell you of heavenly things?

13 And no man hath ascended up to heaven, but he that came down from heaven, even the Son of man which is in heaven.

14 And as Moses lifted up the serpent in the wilderness, even so must the Son of man be lifted up:

15 That whosoever believeth in him should not perish, but have eternal life.

---

3:2    *Rabbi* means "My master." It is a Jewish title for a teacher. (See LDS Bible Dictionary, s.v. "Rabbi," p. 759.)

3:3    **Except**—Unless

The kingdom of God, as used in the scriptures, is usually the Church. It is a preparation for the celestial kingdom or kingdom of heaven (see D&C 65). "In the eternal worlds, the celestial kingdom is the kingdom of God" (Bruce R. McConkie, *Mormon Doctrine*, p. 416).

3:3-7    "To gain salvation in the celestial kingdom men must be born again (Alma 7:14); born of water and of the Spirit (John 3:1-13); born of God, so that they are changed from their 'carnal and fallen state, to a state of righteousness,' becoming new creatures of the Holy Ghost. (Mosiah 27:24-29.) They must become newborn babes in Christ (1 Pet. 2:2); they must be 'spiritually begotten' of God, be born of Christ, thus becoming his sons and daughters. (Mosiah 5:7.)" (Bruce R. McConkie, *Mormon Doctrine*, p. 100.)

3:4    **womb**—belly

3:5    Being "born of water" refers to baptism by immersion by someone who has the priesthood authority (see Bruce R. McConkie, *Mormon Doctrine*, pp. 69-72). Being "born of the Spirit" refers to the actual reception of the Holy Ghost which is offered by the laying on of hands at the time of baptism (see Bruce R. McConkie, *Mormon Doctrine*, p. 73).

How do you feel about what Jesus told Nicodemus? Have you been baptized? How did it feel when you received this important ordinance?

3:10    **master**—teacher

3:11    **witness**—testimony

3:13    **ascended**—risen

"In the language of Adam, Man of Holiness is [Heavenly Father's] name, and the name of his Only Begotten is the Son of Man, even Jesus Christ" (Moses 6:57).

3:14    To learn more about the serpent Moses lifted up, read Numbers 21:4-9.

*"There was a man of the Pharisees, named Nicodemus, a ruler of the Jews:
the same came to Jesus by night" in order to question Jesus.*

16 For God so loved the world, that he gave his only begotten Son, that whosoever believeth in him should not perish, but have everlasting life.

17 For God sent not his Son into the world to condemn the world; but that the world through him might be saved.

18 He that believeth on him is not condemned: but he that believeth not is condemned already, because he hath not believed in the name of the only begotten Son of God.

19 And this is the condemnation, that light is come into the world, and men loved darkness rather than light, because their deeds were evil.

20 For every one that doeth evil hateth the light, neither cometh to the light, lest his deeds should be reproved.

21 But he that doeth truth cometh to the light, that his deeds may be made manifest, that they are wrought in God.

## JOHN THE BAPTIST TESTIFIES OF JESUS

22 ¶ After these things came Jesus and his disciples into the land of Judaea; and there he tarried with them, and baptized.

23 And John also was baptizing in Aenon near to Salim, because there was much water there: and they came, and were baptized.

24 For John was not yet cast into prison.

25 Then there arose a question between some of John's disciples and the Jews about purifying.

26 And they came unto John, and said unto him, Rabbi, he that was with thee beyond Jordan, to whom thou barest witness, behold, the same baptizeth, and all men come to him.

27 John answered and said, A man can receive nothing, except it be given him from heaven.

28 Ye yourselves bear me witness, that I said, I am not the Christ, but that I am sent before him.

29 He that hath the bride is the bridegroom: but the friend of the bridegroom, which standeth and heareth him, rejoiceth greatly because of the bridegroom's voice: this my joy therefore is fulfilled.

30 He must increase, but I must decrease.

31 He that cometh from above is above all: he that is of the earth is earthly, and speaketh of the earth: he that cometh from heaven is above all.

32 And what he hath seen and heard, that he testifieth; and no man receiveth his testimony.

33 He that hath received his testimony hath set to his seal that God is true.

34 For he whom God hath sent speaketh the words of God: for God giveth not the Spirit by measure unto him.

35 The Father loveth the Son, and hath given all things into his hand.

36 He that believeth on the Son hath everlasting life: and he that believeth not the Son shall not see life; but the wrath of God abideth on him.

## CHAPTER 4

*As you read this chapter, look for reasons why the Savior could be called "living water."*

## JESUS TEACHES A SAMARITAN WOMAN

1 ¶ WHEN therefore the Lord knew how the Pharisees had heard that Jesus made and baptized more disciples than John,

2 (Though Jesus himself baptized not, but his disciples,)

3 He left Judaea, and departed again into Galilee.

4 ¶ And he must needs go through Samaria.

---

3:16    *Only Begotten Son* is a name for Jesus, meaning that he is "literally the Son of God the Father," being the only one born of Heavenly Father in the flesh (see LDS Bible Dictionary, s.v. "Son of God," p. 776).

How much does your Heavenly Father love you? How does knowing this help you?

3:20    *reproved*—exposed or punished

3:21    *wrought*—done

3:22    *tarried*—stayed

3:25    *purifying*—being made clean from sin

3:29    Jesus is the "bridegroom" whom John the Baptist is speaking about. A bridegroom is a man who is about to get married. A bridegroom is usually filled with joy and love. (See LDS Bible Dictionary, s.v., "Marriage," pp. 728-29.)

3:33    *hath set to his seal*—has proven

4:1-3    The Joseph Smith Translation changes the first part of chapter 4 to read, "When therefore the Pharisees had heard that Jesus made and baptized more disciples than John, they sought more diligently some means that they might put him to death; for many received John as a prophet, but they believed not on Jesus. Now the Lord knew this, though he himself baptized not so many as his disciples." (JST, John 4:1-3.)

*The woman at the well*

5 Then cometh he to a city of Samaria, which is called Sychar, near to the parcel of ground that Jacob gave to his son Joseph.

6 Now Jacob's well was there. Jesus therefore, being wearied with his journey, sat thus on the well: and it was about the sixth hour.

7 There cometh a woman of Samaria to draw water: Jesus saith unto her, Give me to drink.

8 (For his disciples were gone away unto the city to buy meat.)

9 Then saith the woman of Samaria unto him, How is it that thou, being a Jew, askest drink of me, which am a woman of Samaria? for the Jews have no dealings with the Samaritans.

10 Jesus answered and said unto her, If thou knewest the gift of God, and who it is that saith to thee, Give me to drink; thou wouldest have asked of him, and he would have given thee living water.

11 The woman saith unto him, Sir, thou hast nothing to draw with, and the well is deep: from whence then hast thou that living water?

12 Art thou greater than our father Jacob, which gave us the well, and drank thereof himself, and his children, and his cattle?

13 Jesus answered and said unto her, Whosoever drinketh of this water shall thirst again:

---

4:5    *parcel*—piece

4:9    Samaritans were the people who lived in Samaria after the Assyrians conquered the northern kingdom of Israel. They were a mixed race: Israelite and Gentile. The religion of the Samaritans was a mixture of truth and error. They were greatly despised by the Jews.

4:10-15    When you drink water, how soon afterwards do you thirst again? Would you be interested in water that would cause you to never thirst again? How are Jesus' words and teachings like "living water"?

14 But whosoever drinketh of the water that I shall give him shall never thirst; but the water that I shall give him shall be in him a well of water springing up into everlasting life.

15 The woman saith unto him, Sir, give me this water, that I thirst not, neither come hither to draw.

16 Jesus saith unto her, Go, call thy husband, and come hither.

17 The woman answered and said, I have no husband. Jesus said unto her, Thou hast well said, I have no husband:

18 For thou hast had five husbands; and he whom thou now hast is not thy husband: in that saidst thou truly.

19 The woman saith unto him, Sir, I perceive that thou art a prophet.

20 Our fathers worshipped in this mountain; and ye say, that in Jerusalem is the place where men ought to worship.

21 Jesus saith unto her, Woman, believe me, the hour cometh, when ye shall neither in this mountain, nor yet at Jerusalem, worship the Father.

22 Ye worship ye know not what: we know what we worship: for salvation is of the Jews.

23 But the hour cometh, and now is, when the true worshippers shall worship the Father in spirit and in truth: for the Father seeketh such to worship him.

24 God is a Spirit: and they that worship him must worship him in spirit and in truth.

25 The woman saith unto him, I know that Messias cometh, which is called Christ: when he is come, he will tell us all things.

26 Jesus saith unto her, I that speak unto thee am he.

27 ¶ And upon this came his disciples, and marvelled that he talked with the woman: yet no man said, What seekest thou? or, Why talkest thou with her?

28 The woman then left her waterpot, and went her way into the city, and saith to the men,

29 Come, see a man, which told me all things that ever I did: is not this the Christ?

30 Then they went out of the city, and came unto him.

## JESUS INVITES HIS DISCIPLES TO BRING OTHERS TO HEAVENLY FATHER

31 In the mean while his disciples prayed him, saying, Master, eat.

32 But he said unto them, I have meat to eat that ye know not of.

33 Therefore said the disciples one to another, Hath any man brought him ought to eat?

34 Jesus saith unto them, My meat is to do the will of him that sent me, and to finish his work.

35 Say not ye, There are yet four months, and then cometh harvest? behold, I say unto you, Lift up your eyes, and look on the fields; for they are white already to harvest.

36 And he that reapeth receiveth wages, and gathereth fruit unto life eternal: that both he that soweth and he that reapeth may rejoice together.

37 And herein is that saying true, One soweth, and another reapeth.

---

4:15   The woman thought Jesus spoke of real water. However, the living water he spoke of is "the words of eternal life, . . . the truths about God . . . ; it is the doctrines of the gospel" (Bruce R. McConkie, *Doctrinal New Testament Commentary* 1:151).

4:19   Why might this woman think Jesus was a prophet?

4:20   "This mountain" was Mount Gerizim, which was a holy place for Samaritans.

4:24   The Joseph Smith Translation changes this passage to read, "For unto such hath God promised his Spirit. And they who worship him, must worship in spirit and in truth." (JST, John 4:26.)

4:26   The Joseph Smith Translation changes the word "he" to "the Messias"; that is, the Messiah (see JST, John 4:28).

4:29   What did the woman at the well call Jesus in the following verses: 9, 11, 19, 29? How do these names show that she was gaining a testimony of Jesus?

4:32   *meat*—food

4:32-38   Jesus is talking about spiritual food, but his disciples do not understand. Jesus' "food" is doing Heavenly Father's will. Do you feel "spiritually fed" when you keep the commandments?

4:33   *ought*—anything

4:35   These "fields" are the many people who are ready to hear and accept the gospel. To learn more about the field and the harvest, see D&C 4.

4:36   *wages*—rewards
**he that soweth**—the person who plants the seeds
**he that reapeth**—the person who harvests the crop

38 I sent you to reap that whereon ye bestowed no labour: other men laboured, and ye are entered into their labours.

## MANY SAMARITANS HEAR AND BELIEVE THE SAVIOR

39 And many of the Samaritans of that city believed on him for the saying of the woman, which testified, He told me all that ever I did.

40 So when the Samaritans were come unto him, they besought him that he would tarry with them: and he abode there two days.

41 And many more believed because of his own word;

42 And said unto the woman, Now we believe, not because of thy saying: for we have heard him ourselves, and know that this is indeed the Christ, the Saviour of the world.

## JESUS HEALS A NOBLEMAN'S SON

43 ¶ Now after two days he departed thence, and went into Galilee.

44 For Jesus himself testified, that a prophet hath no honour in his own country.

45 Then when he was come into Galilee, the Galilaeans received him, having seen all the things that he did at Jerusalem at the feast: for they also went unto the feast.

46 So Jesus came again into Cana of Galilee, where he made the water wine. And there was a certain nobleman, whose son was sick at Capernaum.

47 When he heard that Jesus was come out of Judaea into Galilee, he went unto him, and besought him that he would come down, and heal his son: for he was at the point of death.

48 Then said Jesus unto him, Except ye see signs and wonders, ye will not believe.

49 The nobleman saith unto him, Sir, come down ere my child die.

50 Jesus saith unto him, Go thy way; thy son liveth.

And the man believed the word that Jesus had spoken unto him, and he went his way.

51 And as he was now going down, his servants met him, and told him, saying, Thy son liveth.

52 Then enquired he of them the hour when he began to amend. And they said unto him, Yesterday at the seventh hour the fever left him.

53 So the father knew that it was at the same hour, in the which Jesus said unto him, Thy son liveth: and himself believed, and his whole house.

54 This is again the second miracle that Jesus did, when he was come out of Judaea into Galilee.

# CHAPTER 5

*In this chapter look for the many testimonies that Jesus Christ is the Savior.*

## JESUS HEALS A MAN AT THE POOL OF BETHESDA

1 ¶ AFTER this there was a feast of the Jews; and Jesus went up to Jerusalem.

2 Now there is at Jerusalem by the sheep market a pool, which is called in the Hebrew tongue Bethesda, having five porches.

3 In these lay a great multitude of impotent folk, of blind, halt, withered, waiting for the moving of the water.

4 For an angel went down at a certain season into the pool, and troubled the water: whosoever then first after the troubling of the water stepped in was made whole of whatsoever disease he had.

5 And a certain man was there, which had an infirmity thirty and eight years.

6 When Jesus saw him lie, and knew that he had been now a long time in that case, he saith unto him, Wilt thou be made whole?

7 The impotent man answered him, Sir, I have no man, when the water is troubled, to put me into the pool: but while I am coming, another steppeth down before me.

---

4:38    **bestowed**—gave
**labour**—work

4:40    **tarry**—stay

4:49    **ere**—before

What do you learn about this man from his answer to the Savior?

4:52    **enquired**—asked
**amend**—get better

5:3    **impotent**—disabled or handicapped

5:4    **troubled**—stirred

The idea "that an angel came down and troubled the waters, so that the first person thereafter entering them would be healed, was pure superstition" (Bruce R. McConkie, *Doctrinal New Testament Commentary* 1:188).

**whole of**—well from

5:5    **infirmity**—sickness

*Christ heals the man at Bethesda.*

8 Jesus saith unto him, Rise, take up thy bed, and walk.

9 And immediately the man was made whole, and took up his bed, and walked: and on the same day was the sabbath.

10 The Jews therefore said unto him that was cured, It is the sabbath day: it is not lawful for thee to carry thy bed.

11 He answered them, He that made me whole, the same said unto me, Take up thy bed, and walk.

12 Then asked they him, What man is that which said unto thee, Take up thy bed, and walk?

13 And he that was healed wist not who it was: for Jesus had conveyed himself away, a multitude being in that place.

14 Afterward Jesus findeth him in the temple, and said unto him, Behold, thou art made whole: sin no more, lest a worse thing come unto thee.

15 The man departed, and told the Jews that it was Jesus, which had made him whole.

## JESUS TESTIFIES THAT HE IS THE SON OF GOD

16 And therefore did the Jews persecute Jesus, and sought to slay him, because he had done these things on the sabbath day.

17 ¶ But Jesus answered them, My Father worketh hitherto, and I work.

18 Therefore the Jews sought the more to kill him, because he not only had broken the sabbath, but said also that God was his Father, making himself equal with God.

19 Then answered Jesus and said unto them, Verily, verily, I say unto you, The Son can do nothing of himself, but what he seeth the Father do: for what things soever he doeth, these also doeth the Son likewise.

20 For the Father loveth the Son, and sheweth him all things that himself doeth: and he will shew him greater works than these, that ye may marvel.

21 For as the Father raiseth up the dead, and quickeneth them; even so the Son quickeneth whom he will.

22 For the Father judgeth no man, but hath committed all judgment unto the Son:

23 That all men should honour the Son, even as they honour the Father. He that honoureth not the Son honoureth not the Father which hath sent him.

24 Verily, verily, I say unto you, He that heareth my word, and believeth on him that sent me, hath everlasting life, and shall not come into condemnation; but is passed from death unto life.

25 Verily, verily, I say unto you, The hour is coming, and now is, when the dead shall hear the voice of the Son of God: and they that hear shall live.

26 For as the Father hath life in himself; so hath he given to the Son to have life in himself;

27 And hath given him authority to execute judgment also, because he is the Son of man.

28 Marvel not at this: for the hour is coming, in the which all that are in the graves shall hear his voice,

29 And shall come forth; they that have done good, unto the resurrection of life; and they that have done evil, unto the resurrection of damnation.

30 I can of mine own self do nothing: as I hear, I judge: and my judgment is just; because I seek not mine own will, but the will of the Father which hath sent me.

## THERE ARE MANY WITNESSES OF JESUS CHRIST

31 ¶ If I bear witness of myself, my witness is not true.

32 There is another that beareth witness of me; and I

---

5:13 **wist**—knew
**conveyed**—moved

5:17 **hitherto**—at this moment (on the Sabbath day)

5:18 Even though Heavenly Father and Jesus Christ are separate beings (see Joseph Smith—History 1:17; D&C 130:22), they are perfectly unified in purpose, desire, and goodness. Jesus' life was in perfect harmony with Heavenly Father's will.

5:20 **shew**—This word is pronounced the same way as the word *show* and has the same meaning; *shew* is simply an old spelling of *show*.

5:21 **quickeneth them**—gives them life

5:22 After we die, Jesus Christ will judge us

according to our faith and works (see Revelation 20:12).

5:24 **condemnation**—damnation (not to be saved)

5:27 **to execute**—to make

5:29 The Joseph Smith Translation changes this verse to read: "they who have done good, in the resurrection of the just; and they who have done evil, in the resurrection of the unjust" (JST, John 5:29).

5:31 The Joseph Smith Translation changes this passage to read: "Therefore if I bear witness of myself, yet my witness is true" (JST, John 5:32).

know that the witness which he witnesseth of me is true.

33 Ye sent unto John, and he bare witness unto the truth.

34 But I receive not testimony from man: but these things I say, that ye might be saved.

35 He was a burning and a shining light: and ye were willing for a season to rejoice in his light.

36 But I have greater witness than that of John: for the works which the Father hath given me to finish, the same works that I do, bear witness of me, that the Father hath sent me.

37 And the Father himself, which hath sent me, hath borne witness of me. Ye have neither heard his voice at any time, nor seen his shape.

38 And ye have not his word abiding in you: for whom he hath sent, him ye believe not.

39 Search the scriptures; for in them ye think ye have eternal life: and they are they which testify of me.

40 And ye will not come to me, that ye might have life.

41 I receive not honour from men.

42 But I know you, that ye have not the love of God in you.

43 I am come in my Father's name, and ye receive me not: if another shall come in his own name, him ye will receive.

44 How can ye believe, which receive honour one of another, and seek not the honour that cometh from God only?

45 Do not think that I will accuse you to the Father: there is one that accuseth you, even Moses, in whom ye trust.

46 For had ye believed Moses, ye would have believed me: for he wrote of me.

47 But if ye believe not his writings, how shall ye believe my words?

## CHAPTER 6

*This chapter includes Jesus' miraculous feeding of the five thousand, his walking on the water to save his disciples, and his beautiful talk declaring that he is the "Bread of Life." Look for how Jesus Christ cares and provides for his followers.*

### JESUS FEEDS FIVE THOUSAND

1 ¶ AFTER these things Jesus went over the sea of Galilee, which is the sea of Tiberias.

2 And a great multitude followed him, because they saw his miracles which he did on them that were diseased.

3 And Jesus went up into a mountain, and there he sat with his disciples.

4 And the passover, a feast of the Jews, was nigh.

5 When Jesus then lifted up his eyes, and saw a great company come unto him, he saith unto Philip, Whence shall we buy bread, that these may eat?

6 And this he said to prove him: for he himself knew what he would do.

7 Philip answered him, Two hundred pennyworth of bread is not sufficient for them, that every one of them may take a little.

8 One of his disciples, Andrew, Simon Peter's brother, saith unto him,

9 There is a lad here, which hath five barley loaves, and two small fishes: but what are they among so many?

10 And Jesus said, Make the men sit down. Now there was much grass in the place. So the men sat down, in number about five thousand.

11 And Jesus took the loaves; and when he had given thanks, he distributed to the disciples, and the disciples to them that were set down; and likewise of the fishes as much as they would.

12 When they were filled, he said unto his disciples, Gather up the fragments that remain, that nothing be lost.

13 Therefore they gathered them together, and filled twelve baskets with the fragments of the five barley loaves, which remained over and above unto them that had eaten.

14 Then those men, when they had seen the miracle that Jesus did, said, This is of a truth that prophet that should come into the world.

---

5:36   What are some of the works or miracles Jesus did in his lifetime that bear witness to you that he is the Son of God and the Savior of the world?

5:38   *abiding*—living

5:39   What is your favorite scripture that testifies of Jesus Christ?

5:46   Every part of the law of Moses testified of Jesus Christ (see 2 Nephi 11:4; Alma 34:14-15).

6:5   *Whence*—Where

6:7   One penny was the average amount of money a person would earn in a day.

   *sufficient*—enough

6:11   *distributed*—gave

6:14   These men knew that Moses said God would send a great prophet (meaning the Savior) to the Jews (see Deuteronomy 18:15, 18).

## JESUS WALKS ON WATER

15 ¶ When Jesus therefore perceived that they would come and take him by force, to make him a king, he departed again into a mountain himself alone.

16 And when even was now come, his disciples went down unto the sea,

17 And entered into a ship, and went over the sea toward Capernaum. And it was now dark, and Jesus was not come to them.

18 And the sea arose by reason of a great wind that blew.

19 So when they had rowed about five and twenty or thirty furlongs, they see Jesus walking on the sea, and drawing nigh unto the ship: and they were afraid.

20 But he saith unto them, It is I; be not afraid.

21 Then they willingly received him into the ship: and immediately the ship was at the land whither they went.

## JESUS IS THE BREAD OF LIFE

22 ¶ The day following, when the people which stood on the other side of the sea saw that there was none other boat there, save that one whereinto his disciples were entered, and that Jesus went not with his disciples into the boat, but that his disciples were gone away alone;

23 (Howbeit there came other boats from Tiberias nigh unto the place where they did eat bread, after that the Lord had given thanks:)

24 When the people therefore saw that Jesus was not there, neither his disciples, they also took shipping, and came to Capernaum, seeking for Jesus.

25 And when they had found him on the other side of the sea, they said unto him, Rabbi, when camest thou hither?

26 Jesus answered them and said, Verily, verily, I say unto you, Ye seek me, not because ye saw the miracles, but because ye did eat of the loaves, and were filled.

27 Labour not for the meat which perisheth, but for that meat which endureth unto everlasting life, which the Son of man shall give unto you: for him hath God the Father sealed.

28 ¶ Then said they unto him, What shall we do, that we might work the works of God?

29 Jesus answered and said unto them, This is the work of God, that ye believe on him whom he hath sent.

30 They said therefore unto him, What sign shewest thou then, that we may see, and believe thee? what dost thou work?

31 Our fathers did eat manna in the desert; as it is written, He gave them bread from heaven to eat.

32 Then Jesus said unto them, Verily, verily, I say unto you, Moses gave you not that bread from heaven; but my Father giveth you the true bread from heaven.

33 For the bread of God is he which cometh down from heaven, and giveth life unto the world.

34 Then said they unto him, Lord, evermore give us this bread.

35 And Jesus said unto them, I am the bread of life: he that cometh to me shall never hunger; and he that believeth on me shall never thirst.

36 But I said unto you, That ye also have seen me, and believe not.

37 All that the Father giveth me shall come to me; and him that cometh to me I will in no wise cast out.

38 For I came down from heaven, not to do mine own will, but the will of him that sent me.

39 And this is the Father's will which hath sent me, that of all which he hath given me I should lose nothing, but should raise it up again at the last day.

---

6:15 **perceived**—saw

Why do you think Jesus refused to let the Jews make him the king of their country? What kind of a king did Jesus Christ come to earth to be? (See John 18:36.)

6:19 One furlong is about two hundred yards (see LDS Bible Dictionary, s.v., "Weights and Measures," p. 789).

6:25 *Rabbi* means "My master." It is a Jewish title for a teacher. (See LDS Bible Dictionary, s.v. "Rabbi," p. 759.)

6:26 The Joseph Smith Translation adds that the people followed after Jesus because they wanted bread, not because they saw the miracle or wanted to obey him (see JST, John 6:26).

6:27 **perisheth**—does not last very long
**endureth**—lasts forever
**sealed**—marked as his own

6:31 Manna was bread that God gave the children of Israel during the forty years they were in the wilderness (see Exodus 16:15).

6:35 Why is Jesus the "Bread of Life"? How are the blessings that Jesus Christ brings to your body and spirit like the benefits of eating bread?

*Jesus walked upon the stormy sea to save his disciples.*

40 And this is the will of him that sent me, that every one which seeth the Son, and believeth on him, may have everlasting life: and I will raise him up at the last day.

41 The Jews then murmured at him, because he said, I am the bread which came down from heaven.

42 And they said, Is not this Jesus, the son of Joseph, whose father and mother we know? how is it then that he saith, I came down from heaven?

43 Jesus therefore answered and said unto them, Murmur not among yourselves.

44 No man can come to me, except the Father which hath sent me draw him: and I will raise him up at the last day.

45 It is written in the prophets, And they shall be all taught of God. Every man therefore that hath heard, and hath learned of the Father, cometh unto me.

46 Not that any man hath seen the Father, save he which is of God, he hath seen the Father.

47 Verily, verily, I say unto you, He that believeth on me hath everlasting life.

48 I am that bread of life.

49 Your fathers did eat manna in the wilderness, and are dead.

50 This is the bread which cometh down from heaven, that a man may eat thereof, and not die.

51 I am the living bread which came down from heaven: if any man eat of this bread, he shall live for ever: and the bread that I will give is my flesh, which I will give for the life of the world.

52 The Jews therefore strove among themselves, saying, How can this man give us his flesh to eat?

53 Then Jesus said unto them, Verily, verily, I say unto you, Except ye eat the flesh of the Son of man, and drink his blood, ye have no life in you.

54 Whoso eateth my flesh, and drinketh my blood, hath eternal life; and I will raise him up at the last day.

55 For my flesh is meat indeed, and my blood is drink indeed.

56 He that eateth my flesh, and drinketh my blood, dwelleth in me, and I in him.

57 As the living Father hath sent me, and I live by the Father: so he that eateth me, even he shall live by me.

58 This is that bread which came down from heaven: not as your fathers did eat manna, and are dead: he that eateth of this bread shall live for ever.

59 These things said he in the synagogue, as he taught in Capernaum.

## MANY STOP FOLLOWING JESUS

60 ¶ Many therefore of his disciples, when they had heard this, said, This is an hard saying; who can hear it?

61 When Jesus knew in himself that his disciples murmured at it, he said unto them, Doth this offend you?

62 What and if ye shall see the Son of man ascend up where he was before?

63 It is the spirit that quickeneth; the flesh profiteth nothing: the words that I speak unto you, they are spirit, and they are life.

64 But there are some of you that believe not. For Jesus knew from the beginning who they were that believed not, and who should betray him.

65 And he said, Therefore said I unto you, that no man can come unto me, except it were given unto him of my Father.

66 From that time many of his disciples went back, and walked no more with him.

## PETER AND THE REST OF THE TWELVE STAY WITH JESUS

67 Then said Jesus unto the twelve, Will ye also go away?

68 Then Simon Peter answered him, Lord, to whom shall we go? thou hast the words of eternal life.

---

6:41 **murmured**—complained

6:44 The Joseph Smith Translation adds that to come to Jesus Christ we must keep Heavenly Father's commandments (see JST, John 6:44).

6:52 **strove**—argued

6:53 When we partake of the sacrament bread and water, we remember the body and blood of Jesus Christ. How do the things Jesus says in this chapter help you better understand the importance of the sacrament?

6:56 **dwelleth in**—is a part of

6:62 **ascend**—rise

6:63 **quickeneth**—gives life

6:65 The Joseph Smith Translation changes the end of verse 65 to read, "no man can come unto me, except he doeth the will of my Father who hath sent me" (JST, John 6:65).

6:68-
69 Peter's words are full of love for and testimony of the Savior. How do you feel about the Savior? What would you say if he asked if you were ever going to stop following him?

69 And we believe and are sure that thou art that Christ, the Son of the living God.

70 Jesus answered them, Have not I chosen you twelve, and one of you is a devil?

71 He spake of Judas Iscariot the son of Simon: for he it was that should betray him, being one of the twelve.

## CHAPTER 7

*As you read about Jesus at the Feast of Tabernacles, notice the way he testifies of himself and how the people react to his testimony.*

### Jesus' Brothers Do Not Believe in Him

1 ¶ AFTER these things Jesus walked in Galilee: for he would not walk in Jewry, because the Jews sought to kill him.

2 Now the Jews' feast of tabernacles was at hand.

3 His brethren therefore said unto him, Depart hence, and go into Judaea, that thy disciples also may see the works that thou doest.

4 For there is no man that doeth any thing in secret, and he himself seeketh to be known openly. If thou do these things, shew thyself to the world.

5 For neither did his brethren believe in him.

6 Then Jesus said unto them, My time is not yet come: but your time is alway ready.

7 The world cannot hate you; but me it hateth, because I testify of it, that the works thereof are evil.

8 Go ye up unto this feast: I go not up yet unto this feast; for my time is not yet full come.

9 When he had said these words unto them, he abode still in Galilee.

### Jesus Goes to the Feast of Tabernacles at Jerusalem

10 But when his brethren were gone up, then went he also up unto the feast, not openly, but as it were in secret.

11 Then the Jews sought him at the feast, and said, Where is he?

12 And there was much murmuring among the people concerning him: for some said, He is a good man: others said, Nay; but he deceiveth the people.

13 Howbeit no man spake openly of him for fear of the Jews.

14 ¶ Now about the midst of the feast Jesus went up into the temple, and taught.

15 And the Jews marvelled, saying, How knoweth this man letters, having never learned?

16 Jesus answered them, and said, My doctrine is not mine, but his that sent me.

17 If any man will do his will, he shall know of the doctrine, whether it be of God, or whether I speak of myself.

18 He that speaketh of himself seeketh his own glory: but he that seeketh his glory that sent him, the same is true, and no unrighteousness is in him.

19 Did not Moses give you the law, and yet none of you keepeth the law? Why go ye about to kill me?

20 The people answered and said, Thou hast a devil: who goeth about to kill thee?

21 Jesus answered and said unto them, I have done one work, and ye all marvel.

22 Moses therefore gave unto you circumcision; (not because it is of Moses, but of the fathers;) and ye on the sabbath day circumcise a man.

---

7:1    *in Jewry*—near Jerusalem (Judea)

7:2    The Jews celebrated five feasts each year. The Feast of Tabernacles was "the greatest and most joyful of all" (LDS Bible Dictionary, s.v. "Feasts," p. 673). In this feast the Jews remembered Israel's wanderings in the wilderness and the gathering in of the fruits of the harvest.

7:5    Jesus' brothers did not believe that he was the promised Messiah. How would you feel if your brothers or sisters didn't believe in you?

7:9    *abode*—stayed

7:12    *murmuring*—complaining or arguing

7:14    *midst*—middle

7:15    *knoweth this man letters*—can this man know so much

7:16    *doctrine*—teaching

7:17    Jesus teaches that if you want to have a testimony of the gospel you must live the gospel. Can you have a testimony of tithing if you do not pay tithing?

7:19    Jesus is talking about the law of Moses, which includes the commandment, "Thou shalt not kill" (Exodus 20:13).

7:22    Circumcision was first revealed to Abraham. It was an ordinance for boys who were eight days old to show they were God's covenant children. The Joseph Smith Translation indicates that it was also to remind the Lord's people that baptism was not necessary until the age of eight (see JST, Genesis 17:11-12).

23 If a man on the sabbath day receive circumcision, that the law of Moses should not be broken; are ye angry at me, because I have made a man every whit whole on the sabbath day?

24 Judge not according to the appearance, but judge righteous judgment.

25 Then said some of them of Jerusalem, Is not this he, whom they seek to kill?

26 But, lo, he speaketh boldly, and they say nothing unto him. Do the rulers know indeed that this is the very Christ?

27 Howbeit we know this man whence he is: but when Christ cometh, no man knoweth whence he is.

28 Then cried Jesus in the temple as he taught, saying, Ye both know me, and ye know whence I am: and I am not come of myself, but he that sent me is true, whom ye know not.

29 But I know him: for I am from him, and he hath sent me.

30 Then they sought to take him: but no man laid hands on him, because his hour was not yet come.

## THE PHARISEES SEND MEN TO ARREST JESUS

31 And many of the people believed on him, and said, When Christ cometh, will he do more miracles than these which this man hath done?

32 The Pharisees heard that the people murmured such things concerning him; and the Pharisees and the chief priests sent officers to take him.

33 Then said Jesus unto them, Yet a little while am I with you, and then I go unto him that sent me.

34 Ye shall seek me, and shall not find me: and where I am, thither ye cannot come.

35 Then said the Jews among themselves, Whither will he go, that we shall not find him? will he go unto the dispersed among the Gentiles, and teach the Gentiles?

36 What manner of saying is this that he said, Ye shall seek me, and shall not find me: and where I am, thither ye cannot come?

37 ¶ In the last day, that great day of the feast, Jesus stood and cried, saying, If any man thirst, let him come unto me, and drink.

38 He that believeth on me, as the scripture hath said, out of his belly shall flow rivers of living water.

39 (But this spake he of the Spirit, which they that believe on him should receive: for the Holy Ghost was not yet given; because that Jesus was not yet glorified.)

40 Many of the people therefore, when they heard this saying, said, Of a truth this is the Prophet.

41 Others said, This is the Christ. But some said, Shall Christ come out of Galilee?

42 Hath not the scripture said, That Christ cometh of the seed of David, and out of the town of Bethlehem, where David was?

43 So there was a division among the people because of him.

44 And some of them would have taken him; but no man laid hands on him.

## THE OFFICERS RETURN TO THE PHARISEES WITHOUT JESUS CHRIST

45 ¶ Then came the officers to the chief priests and Pharisees; and they said unto them, Why have ye not brought him?

46 The officers answered, Never man spake like this man.

47 Then answered them the Pharisees, Are ye also deceived?

48 Have any of the rulers or of the Pharisees believed on him?

49 But this people who knoweth not the law are cursed.

50 Nicodemus saith unto them, (he that came to Jesus by night, being one of them,)

51 Doth our law judge any man, before it hear him, and know what he doeth?

---

7:23 **whit**—part

7:31 The Book of Mormon says that the Messiah would come among men "working mighty miracles" (Mosiah 3:5), like healing the sick and raising the dead.

7:35 **dispersed**—scattered

*Gentiles* is a word that means "nations." It describes those not of the family of Israel or not believing in the God of Israel.

7:39 The Joseph Smith Translation explains that the Holy Ghost "was promised unto them who believe," after Jesus returned to Heavenly Father in glory (see JST, John 7:39).

7:42 **seed**—family

7:50 Nicodemus was the Pharisee who visited Jesus by night and may have been a secret believer (see John 3:1-21; see also LDS Bible Dictionary, s.v. "Nicodemus," p. 738).

52 They answered and said unto him, Art thou also of Galilee? Search, and look: for out of Galilee ariseth no prophet.

53 And every man went unto his own house.

## CHAPTER 8

*Jesus Christ was the Son of God, but many did not believe in him. As you read this chapter, see what Jesus testifies about himself and how people react to his testimony.*

### THE PHARISEES BRING TO JESUS A WOMAN TAKEN IN ADULTERY

1 ¶ JESUS went unto the mount of Olives.

2 And early in the morning he came again into the temple, and all the people came unto him; and he sat down, and taught them.

3 And the scribes and Pharisees brought unto him a woman taken in adultery; and when they had set her in the midst,

4 They say unto him, Master, this woman was taken in adultery, in the very act.

5 Now Moses in the law commanded us, that such should be stoned: but what sayest thou?

6 This they said, tempting him, that they might have to accuse him. But Jesus stooped down, and with his finger wrote on the ground, as though he heard them not.

7 So when they continued asking him, he lifted up himself, and said unto them, He that is without sin among you, let him first cast a stone at her.

8 And again he stooped down, and wrote on the ground.

9 And they which heard it, being convicted by their own conscience, went out one by one, beginning at the eldest, even unto the last: and Jesus was left alone, and the woman standing in the midst.

10 When Jesus had lifted up himself, and saw none but the woman, he said unto her, Woman, where are those thine accusers? hath no man condemned thee?

11 She said, No man, Lord. And Jesus said unto her, Neither do I condemn thee: go, and sin no more.

### JESUS CHRIST TESTIFIES THAT HE IS THE SAVIOR

12 ¶ Then spake Jesus again unto them, saying, I am the light of the world: he that followeth me shall not walk in darkness, but shall have the light of life.

13 The Pharisees therefore said unto him, Thou bearest record of thyself; thy record is not true.

---

7:52 One reason why Jewish leaders refused to believe that Jesus was the Messiah was that he was from Nazareth of Galilee. The scriptures prophesied of no prophets that would come from Galilee. But Jesus was born in Bethlehem of Judea, fulfilling a prophecy in Micah 5:2.

*The temple of Herod (as it has been reconstructed for the model city of ancient Jerusalem at the Holyland Hotel, Jerusalem)*

8:3 **adultery**—misuse of the sacred creative powers; that is, use of these powers with someone other than your husband or wife

8:5 The law of Moses required that those guilty of adultery "be put to death" (Leviticus 20:10).

8:6 **accuse**—blame

8:9 **convicted**—found guilty

The "conscience" is known as the Light of Christ and "is given to every man, that he may know good from evil" (Moroni 7:16). It is this spirit within us that causes us to feel guilty when we do something wrong.

8:10 **condemned thee**—found you guilty

8:11 Although the Savior did not condemn the woman, he did not forgive her either. Elder Spencer W. Kimball explained that Jesus could not forgive the woman until she had time to repent (see *The Miracle of Forgiveness*, p. 68).

What do you think the woman was thinking as she walked away from this experience? How do you think she felt about Christ?

14 Jesus answered and said unto them, Though I bear record of myself, yet my record is true: for I know whence I came, and whither I go; but ye cannot tell whence I come, and whither I go.

15 Ye judge after the flesh; I judge no man.

16 And yet if I judge, my judgment is true: for I am not alone, but I and the Father that sent me.

17 It is also written in your law, that the testimony of two men is true.

18 I am one that bear witness of myself, and the Father that sent me beareth witness of me.

19 Then said they unto him, Where is thy Father? Jesus answered, Ye neither know me, nor my Father: if ye had known me, ye should have known my Father also.

20 These words spake Jesus in the treasury, as he taught in the temple: and no man laid hands on him; for his hour was not yet come.

21 ¶ Then said Jesus again unto them, I go my way, and ye shall seek me, and shall die in your sins: whither I go, ye cannot come.

22 Then said the Jews, Will he kill himself? because he saith, Whither I go, ye cannot come.

23 And he said unto them, Ye are from beneath; I am from above: ye are of this world; I am not of this world.

24 I said therefore unto you, that ye shall die in your sins: for if ye believe not that I am he, ye shall die in your sins.

25 Then said they unto him, Who art thou? And Jesus saith unto them, Even the same that I said unto you from the beginning.

26 I have many things to say and to judge of you: but he that sent me is true; and I speak to the world those things which I have heard of him.

27 They understood not that he spake to them of the Father.

28 Then said Jesus unto them, When ye have lifted up the Son of man, then shall ye know that I am he, and that I do nothing of myself; but as my Father hath taught me, I speak these things.

29 And he that sent me is with me: the Father hath not left me alone; for I do always those things that please him.

30 As he spake these words, many believed on him.

31 ¶ Then said Jesus to those Jews which believed on him, If ye continue in my word, then are ye my disciples indeed;

32 And ye shall know the truth, and the truth shall make you free.

## SOME OF THE LEADERS OF THE JEWS ARE FOLLOWERS OF THE DEVIL

33 They answered him, We be Abraham's seed, and were never in bondage to any man: how sayest thou, Ye shall be made free?

34 Jesus answered them, Verily, verily, I say unto you, Whosoever committeth sin is the servant of sin.

35 And the servant abideth not in the house for ever: but the Son abideth ever.

36 If the Son therefore shall make you free, ye shall be free indeed.

37 I know that ye are Abraham's seed; but ye seek to kill me, because my word hath no place in you.

38 ¶ I speak that which I have seen with my Father: and ye do that which ye have seen with your father.

39 They answered and said unto him, Abraham is our father. Jesus saith unto them, If ye were Abraham's children, ye would do the works of Abraham.

40 But now ye seek to kill me, a man that hath told you the truth, which I have heard of God: this did not Abraham.

41 Ye do the deeds of your father. Then said they to him, We be not born of fornication; we have one Father, even God.

42 Jesus said unto them, If God were your Father, ye would love me: for I proceeded forth and came from God; neither came I of myself, but he sent me.

43 Why do ye not understand my speech? even because ye cannot hear my word.

44 Ye are of your father the devil, and the lusts of your father ye will do. He was a murderer from the beginning, and abode not in the truth, because there is no truth in him. When he speaketh a lie, he

---

8:14  Jesus said he knew where he came from and where he was going. What do you know about where you lived before coming to earth and where you will live after you leave this life?

8:15  **after the flesh**—as men judge

8:28  **lifted up**—hung on the cross

8:32-34  How does the truth about the gospel and the Savior make us free? (See verse 32.) How do sins put us in bondage? (See verses 33-34.)

8:33  **seed**—children
**bondage**—slavery

8:41  **born of fornication**—born of a man and a woman who were not married

8:44  **lusts**—evil thoughts or desires

speaketh of his own: for he is a liar, and the father of it.

45 And because I tell you the truth, ye believe me not.

46 ¶ Which of you convinceth me of sin? And if I say the truth, why do ye not believe me?

47 He that is of God heareth God's words: ye therefore hear them not, because ye are not of God.

## JESUS CHRIST AS GOD OF THE OLD TESTAMENT HAD APPEARED TO ABRAHAM

48 Then answered the Jews, and said unto him, Say we not well that thou art a Samaritan, and hast a devil?

49 Jesus answered, I have not a devil; but I honour my Father, and ye do dishonour me.

50 And I seek not mine own glory: there is one that seeketh and judgeth.

51 ¶ Verily, verily, I say unto you, If a man keep my saying, he shall never see death.

52 Then said the Jews unto him, Now we know that thou hast a devil. Abraham is dead, and the prophets; and thou sayest, If a man keep my saying, he shall never taste of death.

53 Art thou greater than our father Abraham, which is dead? and the prophets are dead: whom makest thou thyself?

54 Jesus answered, If I honour myself, my honour is nothing: it is my Father that honoureth me; of whom ye say, that he is your God:

55 Yet ye have not known him; but I know him: and if I should say, I know him not, I shall be a liar like unto you: but I know him, and keep his saying.

56 Your father Abraham rejoiced to see my day: and he saw it, and was glad.

57 Then said the Jews unto him, Thou art not yet fifty years old, and hast thou seen Abraham?

58 Jesus said unto them, Verily, verily, I say unto you, Before Abraham was, I am.

59 Then took they up stones to cast at him: but Jesus hid himself, and went out of the temple, going through the midst of them, and so passed by.

# CHAPTER 9

*Look for how the man born blind not only is healed of his physical blindness but also gains a testimony of Jesus Christ and sees the truthfulness of the gospel.*

## JESUS HEALS A MAN BORN BLIND

1 ¶ AND as Jesus passed by, he saw a man which was blind from his birth.

2 And his disciples asked him, saying, Master, who did sin, this man, or his parents, that he was born blind?

3 Jesus answered, Neither hath this man sinned, nor his parents: but that the works of God should be made manifest in him.

4 I must work the works of him that sent me, while it is day: the night cometh, when no man can work.

5 As long as I am in the world, I am the light of the world.

6 When he had thus spoken, he spat on the ground, and made clay of the spittle, and he anointed the eyes of the blind man with the clay,

7 And said unto him, Go, wash in the pool of Siloam, (which is by interpretation, Sent.) He went his way therefore, and washed, and came seeing.

## THE JEWISH LEADERS ACCUSE JESUS OF NOT KEEPING THE SABBATH HOLY

8 ¶ The neighbours therefore, and they which before had seen him that he was blind, said, Is not this he that sat and begged?

9 Some said, This is he: others said, He is like him: but he said, I am he.

---

8:58   The name *I Am* was the name used to identify Jehovah, the God of the Old Testament (see Exodus 3:14). When Jesus used this name he was saying that he is Jehovah.

8:58-
59   Why did the Jews react so angrily when Jesus said he was Jehovah? Could Jesus ever say anything that would upset you like this?

9:1   "Jesus' disciples—probably as a direct result of his teachings—knew and believed that men were the spirit children of God" in the premortal existence (Bruce R. McConkie, *Doctrinal New Testament Commentary* 1:480).

9:2-3   The doctrine of our premortal existence "reminds us mortals that we do not have all of the data. There are many times when we must withhold judgment and trust God lest we misread, as did Jesus' disciples when they inquired about the man blind from birth." (Neal A. Maxwell, *"But for a Small Moment,"* p. 94.)

9:5   How is Jesus a light to the world? In what ways is Jesus Christ a light in your life?

9:6   **spittle**—spit
**anointed the eyes of the blind man with the clay**—put the clay on the blind man's eyes

10 Therefore said they unto him, How were thine eyes opened?

11 He answered and said, A man that is called Jesus made clay, and anointed mine eyes, and said unto me, Go to the pool of Siloam, and wash: and I went and washed, and I received sight.

12 Then said they unto him, Where is he? He said, I know not.

13 ¶ They brought to the Pharisees him that aforetime was blind.

14 And it was the sabbath day when Jesus made the clay, and opened his eyes.

15 Then again the Pharisees also asked him how he had received his sight. He said unto them, He put clay upon mine eyes, and I washed, and do see.

16 Therefore said some of the Pharisees, This man is not of God, because he keepeth not the sabbath day. Others said, How can a man that is a sinner do such miracles? And there was a division among them.

17 They say unto the blind man again, What sayest thou of him, that he hath opened thine eyes? He said, He is a prophet.

18 But the Jews did not believe concerning him, that he had been blind, and received his sight, until they called the parents of him that had received his sight.

19 And they asked them, saying, Is this your son, who ye say was born blind? how then doth he now see?

20 His parents answered them and said, We know that this is our son, and that he was born blind:

21 But by what means he now seeth, we know not; or who hath opened his eyes, we know not: he is of age; ask him: he shall speak for himself.

22 These words spake his parents, because they feared the Jews: for the Jews had agreed already, that if any man did confess that he was Christ, he should be put out of the synagogue.

23 Therefore said his parents, He is of age; ask him.

24 Then again called they the man that was blind, and said unto him, Give God the praise: we know that this man is a sinner.

25 He answered and said, Whether he be a sinner or no, I know not: one thing I know, that, whereas I was blind, now I see.

26 Then said they to him again, What did he to thee? how opened he thine eyes?

27 He answered them, I have told you already, and ye did not hear: wherefore would ye hear it again? will ye also be his disciples?

28 Then they reviled him, and said, Thou art his disciple; but we are Moses' disciples.

29 We know that God spake unto Moses: as for this fellow, we know not from whence he is.

30 The man answered and said unto them, Why herein is a marvellous thing, that ye know not from whence he is, and yet he hath opened mine eyes.

31 Now we know that God heareth not sinners: but if any man be a worshipper of God, and doeth his will, him he heareth.

32 Since the world began was it not heard that any man opened the eyes of one that was born blind.

33 If this man were not of God, he could do nothing.

34 They answered and said unto him, Thou wast altogether born in sins, and dost thou teach us? And they cast him out.

### THE MAN BORN BLIND BELIEVES JESUS IS THE SAVIOR

35 ¶ Jesus heard that they had cast him out; and when he had found him, he said unto him, Dost thou believe on the Son of God?

36 He answered and said, Who is he, Lord, that I might believe on him?

37 And Jesus said unto him, Thou hast both seen him, and it is he that talketh with thee.

38 And he said, Lord, I believe. And he worshipped him.

39 ¶ And Jesus said, For judgment I am come into this world, that they which see not might see; and that they which see might be made blind.

40 And some of the Pharisees which were with him heard these words, and said unto him, Are we blind also?

41 Jesus said unto them, If ye were blind, ye should have no sin: but now ye say, We see; therefore your sin remaineth.

---

9:13　aforetime—before

9:16　The Jews thought Jesus worked on the Sabbath day when he made clay. This was not a violation of the law but of their man-made tradition.

9:28　reviled—scolded

9:32-33　Prophets before Christ's day prophesied that Jesus would do many miracles like giving sight to blind people (see Isaiah 29:18; 35:5).

9:39-41　Have you ever wondered why some people are able to see the truth and follow it, yet others seem blind to spiritual truth? What causes spiritual blindness? How can someone overcome spiritual blindness?

# CHAPTER 10

*Jesus testifies that he is the Good Shepherd. Watch for what a person must do to become one of the Savior's sheep.*

## JESUS IS THE GOOD SHEPHERD

1 ¶ VERILY, verily, I say unto you, He that entereth not by the door into the sheepfold, but climbeth up some other way, the same is a thief and a robber.

2 But he that entereth in by the door is the shepherd of the sheep.

3 To him the porter openeth; and the sheep hear his voice: and he calleth his own sheep by name, and leadeth them out.

4 And when he putteth forth his own sheep, he goeth before them, and the sheep follow him: for they know his voice.

5 And a stranger will they not follow, but will flee from him: for they know not the voice of strangers.

6 This parable spake Jesus unto them: but they understood not what things they were which he spake unto them.

7 Then said Jesus unto them again, Verily, verily, I say unto you, I am the door of the sheep.

8 All that ever came before me are thieves and robbers: but the sheep did not hear them.

9 I am the door: by me if any man enter in, he shall be saved, and shall go in and out, and find pasture.

10 The thief cometh not, but for to steal, and to kill, and to destroy: I am come that they might have life, and that they might have it more abundantly.

11 I am the good shepherd: the good shepherd giveth his life for the sheep.

12 But he that is an hireling, and not the shepherd, whose own the sheep are not, seeth the wolf coming, and leaveth the sheep, and fleeth: and the wolf catcheth them, and scattereth the sheep.

13 The hireling fleeth, because he is an hireling, and careth not for the sheep.

14 I am the good shepherd, and know my sheep, and am known of mine.

15 As the Father knoweth me, even so know I the Father: and I lay down my life for the sheep.

16 And other sheep I have, which are not of this fold: them also I must bring, and they shall hear my voice; and there shall be one fold, and one shepherd.

17 Therefore doth my Father love me, because I lay down my life, that I might take it again.

18 No man taketh it from me, but I lay it down of myself. I have power to lay it down, and I have power to take it again. This commandment have I received of my Father.

## MANY JEWS REFUSE TO BELIEVE

19 ¶ There was a division therefore again among the Jews for these sayings.

20 And many of them said, He hath a devil, and is mad; why hear ye him?

21 Others said, These are not the words of him that hath a devil. Can a devil open the eyes of the blind?

22 ¶ And it was at Jerusalem the feast of the dedication, and it was winter.

23 And Jesus walked in the temple in Solomon's porch.

24 Then came the Jews round about him, and said unto him, How long dost thou make us to doubt? If thou be the Christ, tell us plainly.

*Sheep following their shepherd*

10:1 **sheepfold**—fenced-in place where animals are kept safely together

10:3 **porter**—doorkeeper

10:6 **parable**—earthly story with heavenly or spiritual meaning

10:9 **pasture**—food (that is, for the person who hungers and thirsts for what is right)

10:10 **more abundantly**—in great amounts

10:12 **hireling**—person who works for money

10:16 To learn more about the sheep that are in another fold, see 3 Nephi 15:11-24.

10:17-18 "The Good Shepherd gave His life for the sheep—for you and me—for us all" (*The Teachings of Ezra Taft Benson*, p. 231).

25 Jesus answered them, I told you, and ye believed not: the works that I do in my Father's name, they bear witness of me.

26 But ye believe not, because ye are not of my sheep, as I said unto you.

27 My sheep hear my voice, and I know them, and they follow me:

28 And I give unto them eternal life; and they shall never perish, neither shall any man pluck them out of my hand.

29 My Father, which gave them me, is greater than all; and no man is able to pluck them out of my Father's hand.

30 I and my Father are one.

31 Then the Jews took up stones again to stone him.

32 Jesus answered them, Many good works have I shewed you from my Father; for which of those works do ye stone me?

33 The Jews answered him, saying, For a good work we stone thee not; but for blasphemy; and because that thou, being a man, makest thyself God.

34 Jesus answered them, Is it not written in your law, I said, Ye are gods?

35 If he called them gods, unto whom the word of God came, and the scripture cannot be broken;

36 Say ye of him, whom the Father hath sanctified, and sent into the world, Thou blasphemest; because I said, I am the Son of God?

37 If I do not the works of my Father, believe me not.

38 But if I do, though ye believe not me, believe the works: that ye may know, and believe, that the Father is in me, and I in him.

39 ¶ Therefore they sought again to take him: but he escaped out of their hand,

40 And went away again beyond Jordan into the place where John at first baptized; and there he abode.

41 And many resorted unto him, and said, John did no miracle: but all things that John spake of this man were true.

42 And many believed on him there.

# CHAPTER 11

*Raising Lazarus from the dead was one of Jesus' greatest miracles. Look for the different ways people felt about this event.*

## LAZARUS DIES

1 ¶ NOW a certain man was sick, named Lazarus, of Bethany, the town of Mary and her sister Martha.

2 (It was that Mary which anointed the Lord with ointment, and wiped his feet with her hair, whose brother Lazarus was sick.)

3 Therefore his sisters sent unto him, saying, Lord, behold, he whom thou lovest is sick.

4 When Jesus heard that, he said, This sickness is not unto death, but for the glory of God, that the Son of God might be glorified thereby.

5 Now Jesus loved Martha, and her sister, and Lazarus.

6 When he had heard therefore that he was sick, he abode two days still in the same place where he was.

7 Then after that saith he to his disciples, Let us go into Judaea again.

---

10:25  What did Jesus do that testifies to you that he is the Son of God?

10:27  What did Jesus say we must do to be one of his sheep? What can you do to hear his voice and follow him?

10:28  **perish**—die

10:32  **shewed**—This word is pronounced the same way as the word *showed* and has the same meaning; *shewed* is simply an old spelling of *showed*.

10:33  For an explanation of how Jesus and Heavenly Father are one, see  for John 17:11.

10:36  "To be *sanctified* is to become clean, pure, and spotless; to be free from the blood and sins of the world. . . . *Sanctification* is a state of saintliness."

(Bruce R. McConkie, *Mormon Doctrine*, p. 675.) It comes only by obedience to the commandments and through the power of the Holy Ghost.

10:41  **resorted**—came

11:4-6  Jesus purposely waited until Lazarus was dead before going to Bethany. Many Jews believed that a spirit stayed with its body three days before leaving it permanently. Jesus did this to help his followers believe in his power over death. (See John 11:14-15, 25, 38-42.)

8 His disciples say unto him, Master, the Jews of late sought to stone thee; and goest thou thither again?

9 Jesus answered, Are there not twelve hours in the day? If any man walk in the day, he stumbleth not, because he seeth the light of this world.

10 But if a man walk in the night, he stumbleth, because there is no light in him.

11 These things said he: and after that he saith unto them, Our friend Lazarus sleepeth; but I go, that I may awake him out of sleep.

12 Then said his disciples, Lord, if he sleep, he shall do well.

13 Howbeit Jesus spake of his death: but they thought that he had spoken of taking of rest in sleep.

14 Then said Jesus unto them plainly, Lazarus is dead.

15 And I am glad for your sakes that I was not there, to the intent ye may believe; nevertheless let us go unto him.

16 Then said Thomas, which is called Didymus, unto his fellowdisciples, Let us also go, that we may die with him.

## Jesus Comforts Lazarus's Sisters

17 ¶ Then when Jesus came, he found that he had lain in the grave four days already.

18 Now Bethany was nigh unto Jerusalem, about fifteen furlongs off:

19 And many of the Jews came to Martha and Mary, to comfort them concerning their brother.

20 Then Martha, as soon as she heard that Jesus was coming, went and met him: but Mary sat still in the house.

21 Then said Martha unto Jesus, Lord, if thou hadst been here, my brother had not died.

22 But I know, that even now, whatsoever thou wilt ask of God, God will give it thee.

23 Jesus saith unto her, Thy brother shall rise again.

24 Martha saith unto him, I know that he shall rise again in the resurrection at the last day.

25 Jesus said unto her, I am the resurrection, and the life: he that believeth in me, though he were dead, yet shall he live:

26 And whosoever liveth and believeth in me shall never die. Believest thou this?

27 She saith unto him, Yea, Lord: I believe that thou art the Christ, the Son of God, which should come into the world.

28 And when she had so said, she went her way, and called Mary her sister secretly, saying, The Master is come, and calleth for thee.

29 As soon as she heard that, she arose quickly, and came unto him.

30 Now Jesus was not yet come into the town, but was in that place where Martha met him.

31 The Jews then which were with her in the house, and comforted her, when they saw Mary, that she rose up hastily and went out, followed her, saying, She goeth unto the grave to weep there.

32 Then when Mary was come where Jesus was, and saw him, she fell down at his feet, saying unto him, Lord, if thou hadst been here, my brother had not died.

33 ¶ When Jesus therefore saw her weeping, and the Jews also weeping which came with her, he groaned in the spirit, and was troubled,

34 And said, Where have ye laid him? They said unto him, Lord, come and see.

35 Jesus wept.

36 Then said the Jews, Behold how he loved him!

37 And some of them said, Could not this man, which opened the eyes of the blind, have caused that even this man should not have died?

---

11:8   *thither*—there

11:8-10   To explain what Jesus meant, Elder Bruce R. McConkie rephrased the Savior's words: " 'This is the time given me to do my work. . . . He that shirks his responsibilities and puts off his labors until the night shall stumble in the darkness and fail in his work.' " (*Doctrinal New Testament Commentary* 1:531.)

11:16   The name Didymus means "twin."

  The Joseph Smith Translation adds that the Apostles wanted to go to Jerusalem with Jesus because "they feared lest the Jews should take Jesus and put him to death" (JST, John 11:16).

11:18   *fifteen furlongs*—less than two miles

11:21-27   Martha bore an important testimony. What did Martha know about Jesus? What more is Jesus trying to tell her about himself? (See also verses 39-45.)

11:33-37   "What a scene this is—the Son of God in tears! . . . He rejoiced with his friends, wept with the mourners, loved those who kept his commandments, satisfied his hunger with food, and in all things set a proper example for his fellow beings to follow." (Bruce R. McConkie, *Doctrinal New Testament Commentary* 1:533. See also Mosiah 3:7 and 3 Nephi 17:21.)

## JESUS RAISES LAZARUS FROM THE DEAD

38 Jesus therefore again groaning in himself cometh to the grave. It was a cave, and a stone lay upon it.

39 Jesus said, Take ye away the stone. Martha, the sister of him that was dead, saith unto him, Lord, by this time he stinketh: for he hath been dead four days.

40 Jesus saith unto her, Said I not unto thee, that, if thou wouldest believe, thou shouldest see the glory of God?

41 Then they took away the stone from the place where the dead was laid. And Jesus lifted up his eyes, and said, Father, I thank thee that thou hast heard me.

42 And I knew that thou hearest me always: but because of the people which stand by I said it, that they may believe that thou hast sent me.

43 And when he thus had spoken, he cried with a loud voice, Lazarus, come forth.

44 And he that was dead came forth, bound hand and foot with graveclothes: and his face was bound about with a napkin. Jesus saith unto them, Loose him, and let him go.

45 ¶ Then many of the Jews which came to Mary, and had seen the things which Jesus did, believed on him.

46 But some of them went their ways to the Pharisees, and told them what things Jesus had done.

## JEWISH LEADERS PLOT TO KILL JESUS

47 Then gathered the chief priests and the Pharisees a council, and said, What do we? for this man doeth many miracles.

48 If we let him thus alone, all men will believe on him: and the Romans shall come and take away both our place and nation.

49 And one of them, named Caiaphas, being the high priest that same year, said unto them, Ye know nothing at all,

50 Nor consider that it is expedient for us, that one man should die for the people, and that the whole nation perish not.

51 And this spake he not of himself: but being high priest that year, he prophesied that Jesus should die for that nation;

52 And not for that nation only, but that also he should gather together in one the children of God that were scattered abroad.

53 Then from that day forth they took counsel together for to put him to death.

54 Jesus therefore walked no more openly among the Jews; but went thence unto a country near to the wilderness, into a city called Ephraim, and there continued with his disciples.

55 And the Jews' passover was nigh at hand: and many went out of the country up to Jerusalem before the passover, to purify themselves.

56 Then sought they for Jesus, and spake among themselves, as they stood in the temple, What think ye, that he will not come to the feast?

57 Now both the chief priests and the Pharisees had given a commandment, that, if any man knew where he were, he should shew it, that they might take him.

---

*The traditional tomb of Lazarus in Bethany*

11:43-45   Jesus testified that he had the power to raise the dead (see John 11:25). Many believed only after they saw Lazarus come out of the tomb. Why is it important for us to increase in our faith without waiting for proof? (See John 20:29.)

11:44   **bound hand and foot with graveclothes—** wrapped tightly in long strips of linen
**napkin—**facecloth

11:48   When the chief priests asked themselves what they should do about Jesus' many miracles, why do you think they did not consider *believing him?* They were afraid that "all men [would] believe on him [Jesus]" instead of following them.

11:50   **expedient—**better, advisable

*"Lazarus, come forth."*

# CHAPTER 12

*Even though Jesus knew he would soon be crucified, he willingly traveled to Jerusalem and prepared to fulfill that part of Heavenly Father's plan. Note why Jesus said it was important that he die, and how he prepared for that event.*

## MARY ANOINTS JESUS' FEET

1 ¶ THEN Jesus six days before the passover came to Bethany, where Lazarus was which had been dead, whom he raised from the dead.

2 There they made him a supper; and Martha served: but Lazarus was one of them that sat at the table with him.

3 Then took Mary a pound of ointment of spikenard, very costly, and anointed the feet of Jesus, and wiped his feet with her hair: and the house was filled with the odour of the ointment.

4 Then saith one of his disciples, Judas Iscariot, Simon's son, which should betray him,

5 Why was not this ointment sold for three hundred pence, and given to the poor?

6 This he said, not that he cared for the poor; but because he was a thief, and had the bag, and bare what was put therein.

7 Then said Jesus, Let her alone: against the day of my burying hath she kept this.

8 For the poor always ye have with you; but me ye have not always.

9 Much people of the Jews therefore knew that he was there: and they came not for Jesus' sake only, but that they might see Lazarus also, whom he had raised from the dead.

10 But the chief priests consulted that they might put Lazarus also to death;

11 Because that by reason of him many of the Jews went away, and believed on Jesus.

## JESUS ENTERS JERUSALEM TRIUMPHANTLY

12 ¶ On the next day much people that were come to the feast, when they heard that Jesus was coming to Jerusalem,

13 Took branches of palm trees, and went forth to meet him, and cried, Hosanna: Blessed is the King of Israel that cometh in the name of the Lord.

14 And Jesus, when he had found a young ass, sat thereon; as it is written,

15 Fear not, daughter of Sion: behold, thy King cometh, sitting on an ass's colt.

16 These things understood not his disciples at the first: but when Jesus was glorified, then remembered they that these things were written of him, and that they had done these things unto him.

17 The people therefore that was with him when he called Lazarus out of his grave, and raised him from the dead, bare record.

18 For this cause the people also met him, for that they heard that he had done this miracle.

19 The Pharisees therefore said among themselves, Perceive ye how ye prevail nothing? behold, the world is gone after him.

## JESUS PREDICTS HIS DEATH

20 ¶ And there were certain Greeks among them that came up to worship at the feast:

21 The same came therefore to Philip, which was of

---

12:1    John 11:32-45 tells the story of Lazarus being raised from the dead.

12:3    ***ointment of spikenard***—very expensive oil and perfume

In Jesus' day, caring for someone's feet was a job for a servant and showed humility. What does this teach you about Mary and her love for Jesus?

12:5    A "pence" was a silver coin. Three hundred pence was a large sum of money, probably more than an average worker would make in an entire year (see Matthew 20:2).

12:7    In the Joseph Smith Translation, Jesus teaches that Mary had saved the ointment "until now, that she might anoint me in token of my burial" (JST, John 12:7).

12:10-11    The chief priests first wanted to kill only Jesus (see John 11:50), but now they also wanted to kill Lazarus. Why would they want to kill Lazarus?

12:15    Such displays of respect and honor were reserved only for kings and conquerors (see 2 Kings 9:13).

12:16    Old Testament prophets foretold of Jesus' entering Jerusalem on a colt (see Zechariah 9:9).

12:19    ***Perceive ye how ye prevail nothing?***—Can you see how you have not triumphed?

Why did so many people of the world praise Jesus at this time? Where do you think all of these people were when Jesus was betrayed, tried, and crucified?

*Mary anoints Jesus' feet in preparation for the day of his burial.*

Bethsaida of Galilee, and desired him, saying, Sir, we would see Jesus.

22 Philip cometh and telleth Andrew: and again Andrew and Philip tell Jesus.

23 And Jesus answered them, saying, The hour is come, that the Son of man should be glorified.

24 Verily, verily, I say unto you, Except a corn of wheat fall into the ground and die, it abideth alone: but if it die, it bringeth forth much fruit.

25 He that loveth his life shall lose it; and he that hateth his life in this world shall keep it unto life eternal.

26 If any man serve me, let him follow me; and where I am, there shall also my servant be: if any man serve me, him will my Father honour.

27 ¶ Now is my soul troubled; and what shall I say? Father, save me from this hour: but for this cause came I unto this hour.

28 Father, glorify thy name. Then came there a voice from heaven, saying, I have both glorified it, and will glorify it again.

29 The people therefore, that stood by, and heard it, said that it thundered: others said, An angel spake to him.

30 Jesus answered and said, This voice came not because of me, but for your sakes.

31 Now is the judgment of this world: now shall the prince of this world be cast out.

32 And I, if I be lifted up from the earth, will draw all men unto me.

33 This he said, signifying what death he should die.

34 The people answered him, We have heard out of the law that Christ abideth for ever: and how sayest thou, The Son of man must be lifted up? who is this Son of man?

35 Then Jesus said unto them, Yet a little while is the light with you. Walk while ye have the light, lest darkness come upon you: for he that walketh in darkness knoweth not whither he goeth.

36 While ye have light, believe in the light, that ye may be the children of light. These things spake Jesus, and departed, and did hide himself from them.

## THE JEWS CONTINUE IN THEIR UNBELIEF

37 ¶ But though he had done so many miracles before them, yet they believed not on him:

38 That the saying of Esaias the prophet might be fulfilled, which he spake, Lord, who hath believed our report? and to whom hath the arm of the Lord been revealed?

39 Therefore they could not believe, because that Esaias said again,

40 He hath blinded their eyes, and hardened their heart; that they should not see with their eyes, nor understand with their heart, and be converted, and I should heal them.

41 These things said Esaias, when he saw his glory, and spake of him.

42 ¶ Nevertheless among the chief rulers also many believed on him; but because of the Pharisees they did not confess him, lest they should be put out of the synagogue:

43 For they loved the praise of men more than the praise of God.

44 ¶ Jesus cried and said, He that believeth on me, believeth not on me, but on him that sent me.

45 And he that seeth me seeth him that sent me.

46 I am come a light into the world, that whosoever believeth on me should not abide in darkness.

47 And if any man hear my words, and believe not, I judge him not: for I came not to judge the world, but to save the world.

48 He that rejecteth me, and receiveth not my words, hath one that judgeth him: the word that I have spoken, the same shall judge him in the last day.

49 For I have not spoken of myself; but the Father

---

12:23-24 Jesus was teaching about his coming death, and how his death would bring life to others through the resurrection. The idea that death can bring life can be understood by looking at plants. Even though all plants die, new life comes through their seed.

12:25-26 What can you do to love, serve, and follow Jesus?

12:31 "The prince of this world" is a title for Satan. Jesus Christ conquered Satan by doing all that Heavenly Father wanted Him to do.

12:32 The Book of Mormon contains an example of the resurrected Lord drawing, or bringing, all people unto him (see 3 Nephi 11:8-15).

12:34 **abideth for ever**—lives forever

12:37-41 Esaias (the Greek name for Isaiah) prophesied that even though Christ would perform many miracles, many people would not believe in him (see Isaiah 53:1). President Spencer W. Kimball taught that miracles do not produce faith but that miracles come after we have faith (see *Faith Precedes the Miracle,* p. 4).

12:44 **cried**—spoke loudly

which sent me, he gave me a commandment, what I should say, and what I should speak.

50 And I know that his commandment is life everlasting: whatsoever I speak therefore, even as the Father said unto me, so I speak.

# CHAPTER 13

*This chapter begins the account of what Jesus did on the day before his crucifixion. He knew that his suffering would begin that night and that the next day he would be crucified. Look for what he chose to teach his disciples about love and humility.*

## JESUS WASHES THE FEET OF HIS DISCIPLES

1 ¶ NOW before the feast of the passover, when Jesus knew that his hour was come that he should depart out of this world unto the Father, having loved his own which were in the world, he loved them unto the end.

2 And supper being ended, the devil having now put into the heart of Judas Iscariot, Simon's son, to betray him;

3 Jesus knowing that the Father had given all things into his hands, and that he was come from God, and went to God;

4 He riseth from supper, and laid aside his garments; and took a towel, and girded himself.

5 After that he poureth water into a bason, and began to wash the disciples' feet, and to wipe them with the towel wherewith he was girded.

6 Then cometh he to Simon Peter: and Peter saith unto him, Lord, dost thou wash my feet?

7 Jesus answered and said unto him, What I do thou knowest not now; but thou shalt know hereafter.

8 Peter saith unto him, Thou shalt never wash my feet. Jesus answered him, If I wash thee not, thou hast no part with me.

9 Simon Peter saith unto him, Lord, not my feet only, but also my hands and my head.

10 Jesus saith to him, He that is washed needeth not save to wash his feet, but is clean every whit: and ye are clean, but not all.

11 For he knew who should betray him; therefore said he, Ye are not all clean.

12 So after he had washed their feet, and had taken his garments, and was set down again, he said unto them, Know ye what I have done to you?

13 Ye call me Master and Lord: and ye say well; for so I am.

14 If I then, your Lord and Master, have washed your feet; ye also ought to wash one another's feet.

15 For I have given you an example, that ye should do as I have done to you.

16 Verily, verily, I say unto you, The servant is not greater than his lord; neither he that is sent greater than he that sent him.

17 If ye know these things, happy are ye if ye do them.

## JESUS ANNOUNCES HIS BETRAYAL

18 ¶ I speak not of you all: I know whom I have chosen: but that the scripture may be fulfilled, He that eateth bread with me hath lifted up his heel against me.

19 Now I tell you before it come, that, when it is come to pass, ye may believe that I am he.

20 Verily, verily, I say unto you, He that receiveth whomsoever I send receiveth me; and he that receiveth me receiveth him that sent me.

21 When Jesus had thus said, he was troubled in spirit, and testified, and said, Verily, verily, I say unto you, that one of you shall betray me.

22 Then the disciples looked one on another, doubting of whom he spake.

---

13:1 **his own which were in the world**—his disciples, who would have to remain on earth

13:4 **girded himself**—wrapped the towel around his waist

13:8-16 Washing of the feet, like baptism, is a special ceremony called a gospel ordinance. By this ordinance Jesus taught his disciples that they should be humble and serve one another. The Joseph Smith Translation adds, "Now this was the custom of the Jews under their law; wherefore, Jesus did this that the law might be fulfilled" (JST, John 13:10).

13:17 What is Jesus telling us here about how to be happy? Are you happiest when you are helping and serving others or when you serve only yourself?

13:18-19 Jesus explained that he would be betrayed by a friend as was prophesied long before (see Psalm 41:9). He told his disciples about it before it happened so that they would know he is the Christ.

13:22 **doubting of whom he spake**—wondering whom he meant

23 Now there was leaning on Jesus' bosom one of his disciples, whom Jesus loved.

24 Simon Peter therefore beckoned to him, that he should ask who it should be of whom he spake.

25 He then lying on Jesus' breast saith unto him, Lord, who is it?

26 Jesus answered, He it is, to whom I shall give a sop, when I have dipped it. And when he had dipped the sop, he gave it to Judas Iscariot, the son of Simon.

27 And after the sop Satan entered into him. Then said Jesus unto him, That thou doest, do quickly.

28 Now no man at the table knew for what intent he spake this unto him.

29 For some of them thought, because Judas had the bag, that Jesus had said unto him, Buy those things that we have need of against the feast; or, that he should give something to the poor.

30 He then having received the sop went immediately out: and it was night.

## Jesus Gives a New Commandment

31 ¶ Therefore, when he was gone out, Jesus said, Now is the Son of man glorified, and God is glorified in him.

32 If God be glorified in him, God shall also glorify him in himself, and shall straightway glorify him.

33 Little children, yet a little while I am with you. Ye shall seek me: and as I said unto the Jews, Whither I go, ye cannot come; so now I say to you.

34 A new commandment I give unto you, That ye love one another; as I have loved you, that ye also love one another.

35 By this shall all men know that ye are my disciples, if ye have love one to another.

36 Simon Peter said unto him, Lord, whither goest thou? Jesus answered him, Whither I go, thou canst not follow me now; but thou shalt follow me afterwards.

37 Peter said unto him, Lord, why cannot I follow thee now? I will lay down my life for thy sake.

38 Jesus answered him, Wilt thou lay down thy life for my sake? Verily, verily, I say unto thee, The cock shall not crow, till thou hast denied me thrice.

## CHAPTER 14

*The Savior promised his followers peace in a troubled world. Look for what that peace is and how it is received.*

## Jesus Is the Way, the Truth, and the Life

1 ¶ LET not your heart be troubled: ye believe in God, believe also in me.

2 In my Father's house are many mansions: if it were not so, I would have told you. I go to prepare a place for you.

3 And if I go and prepare a place for you, I will come again, and receive you unto myself; that where I am, there ye may be also.

4 ¶ And whither I go ye know, and the way ye know.

*This drawing shows a typical evening meal or feast during New Testament times. As seen here, people did not sit down to a meal but rather reclined, which is what Jesus and his disciples would have done at the Last Supper.*

13:23 **bosom**—chest

13:26 **sop**—piece of bread

13:28 **for what intent**—why or for what purpose

13:31-32 Jesus brought glory to his Heavenly Father and himself. His atonement—meaning his suffering, death, and resurrection—made it possible for all Heavenly Father's children to have eternal life. Bringing eternal life to his children is God's "work" and his "glory" (see Moses 1:39).

13:34-35 How would the world be different if people loved one another as much as Jesus loves us?

13:36 **whither**—where

13:38 **cock**—rooster
**thrice**—three times

14:2 The Prophet Joseph Smith said this verse should read, "In my Father's kingdom are many kingdoms" (*The Teachings of Joseph Smith*, p.175). Jesus prepares a place for all the faithful sons and daughters of God.

5 Thomas saith unto him, Lord, we know not whither thou goest; and how can we know the way?

6 Jesus saith unto him, I am the way, the truth, and the life: no man cometh unto the Father, but by me.

## JESUS CHRIST EXPLAINS HIS RELATIONSHIP WITH THE FATHER

7 If ye had known me, ye should have known my Father also: and from henceforth ye know him, and have seen him.

8 Philip saith unto him, Lord, shew us the Father, and it sufficeth us.

9 Jesus saith unto him, Have I been so long time with you, and yet hast thou not known me, Philip? he that hath seen me hath seen the Father; and how sayest thou then, Shew us the Father?

10 Believest thou not that I am in the Father, and the Father in me? the words that I speak unto you I speak not of myself: but the Father that dwelleth in me, he doeth the works.

11 Believe me that I am in the Father, and the Father in me: or else believe me for the very works' sake.

12 ¶ Verily, verily, I say unto you, He that believeth on me, the works that I do shall he do also; and greater works than these shall he do; because I go unto my Father.

13 And whatsoever ye shall ask in my name, that will I do, that the Father may be glorified in the Son.

14 If ye shall ask any thing in my name, I will do it.

## JESUS PROMISES THE HOLY GHOST

15 ¶ If ye love me, keep my commandments.

16 And I will pray the Father, and he shall give you another Comforter, that he may abide with you for ever;

17 Even the Spirit of truth; whom the world cannot receive, because it seeth him not, neither knoweth him: but ye know him; for he dwelleth with you, and shall be in you.

18 ¶ I will not leave you comfortless: I will come to you.

19 Yet a little while, and the world seeth me no more; but ye see me: because I live, ye shall live also.

20 At that day ye shall know that I am in my Father, and ye in me, and I in you.

21 He that hath my commandments, and keepeth them, he it is that loveth me: and he that loveth me shall be loved of my Father, and I will love him, and will manifest myself to him.

22 Judas saith unto him, not Iscariot, Lord, how is it that thou wilt manifest thyself unto us, and not unto the world?

23 Jesus answered and said unto him, If a man love me, he will keep my words: and my Father will love him, and we will come unto him, and make our abode with him.

24 He that loveth me not keepeth not my sayings: and the word which ye hear is not mine, but the Father's which sent me.

## THE PEACE OF JESUS CHRIST IS PROMISED

25 ¶ These things have I spoken unto you, being yet present with you.

26 But the Comforter, which is the Holy Ghost, whom

---

14:5    What gift is given to each of us at baptism to help show us the way back to our Father in Heaven?

14:5-6    The Apostle Paul taught that "we shall be saved by his [Jesus'] life" (Romans 5:10). Jesus showed us the way back to our Father in Heaven by how he lived his life. Following his example is the way back to heaven.

14:6    Concerning this verse, Elder David O. McKay stated: "There is only *one way* in which entrance into the Church of Jesus Christ may be obtained, and that is the way marked out by Jesus Christ, the Lord" (*Gospel Ideals,* p. 117; italics in original).

14:10    Jesus looked as the Father looked; he said what the Father would have said and did what the Father would have done (see Hebrews 1:3).

14:11    Jesus said that he and the Father are one (see John 10:30; 17:22). To know one is to know the

other. This means that all members of the Godhead are united in purpose and mind and testify of one another.

14:15    How can we prove our love for our Father in Heaven and Jesus Christ?

14:16    Jesus taught his disciples about two Comforters. "The first is the Holy Ghost. . . . The Second Comforter is the Lord Jesus Christ himself." (LDS Bible Dictionary, s.v. "Comforter," p. 648.) The Comforter is a name used to describe the Holy Ghost.

14:18-25    Worthy individuals can have the privilege of seeing and knowing Jesus Christ (see D&C 93:1).

14:26    What did Jesus say the Holy Ghost would do for those who are striving to live a good life? Have you felt the power and help of the Holy Ghost in your own life?

the Father will send in my name, he shall teach you all things, and bring all things to your remembrance, whatsoever I have said unto you.

27 Peace I leave with you, my peace I give unto you: not as the world giveth, give I unto you. Let not your heart be troubled, neither let it be afraid.

28 ¶ Ye have heard how I said unto you, I go away, and come again unto you. If ye loved me, ye would rejoice, because I said, I go unto the Father: for my Father is greater than I.

29 And now I have told you before it come to pass, that, when it is come to pass, ye might believe.

30 Hereafter I will not talk much with you: for the prince of this world cometh, and hath nothing in me.

31 But that the world may know that I love the Father; and as the Father gave me commandment, even so I do. Arise, let us go hence.

# CHAPTER 15

*Jesus Christ loves us. We should love him too. Watch for how we can show our love to him and to others.*

## JESUS IS THE TRUE VINE

1 ¶ I am the true vine, and my Father is the husbandman.

2 Every branch in me that beareth not fruit he taketh away: and every branch that beareth fruit, he purgeth it, that it may bring forth more fruit.

3 Now ye are clean through the word which I have spoken unto you.

4 Abide in me, and I in you. As the branch cannot bear fruit of itself, except it abide in the vine; no more can ye, except ye abide in me.

5 I am the vine, ye are the branches: He that abideth in me, and I in him, the same bringeth forth much fruit: for without me ye can do nothing.

6 If a man abide not in me, he is cast forth as a branch, and is withered; and men gather them, and cast them into the fire, and they are burned.

7 If ye abide in me, and my words abide in you, ye shall ask what ye will, and it shall be done unto you.

8 Herein is my Father glorified, that ye bear much fruit; so shall ye be my disciples.

## JESUS TEACHES THE PERFECT LAW OF LOVE

9 ¶ As the Father hath loved me, so have I loved you: continue ye in my love.

10 If ye keep my commandments, ye shall abide in my love; even as I have kept my Father's commandments, and abide in his love.

11 These things have I spoken unto you, that my joy might remain in you, and that your joy might be full.

12 This is my commandment, That ye love one another, as I have loved you.

13 Greater love hath no man than this, that a man lay down his life for his friends.

---

14:30 **the prince of this world**—Satan, the devil

15:1 **husbandman**—gardener

15:1-4 In these verses Jesus compares himself to a vine, meaning a grapevine. The vine provided life and nourishment for the branches that they might produce fruit. Branches broken or cut off from the vine died.

15:2 Old and dying branches were cut off the vine to allow nourishment to flow freely to healthy branches that could then produce fruit.

15:4 **Abide**—Remain

15:6 **cast forth**—cut off and thrown away

15:6-8 Jesus, as the true vine (see verse 1), provided nourishment for his branches, or disciples (see verse 5). Good branches that have fruit represent disciples that do good deeds. Branches with no fruit represent disciples that are cut off and burned.

15:13 Jesus told his disciples that the one who loves the most gives his life for another. Years after Christ's death, John the Apostle wrote: "He laid down his life for us: and we ought to lay down our lives for the brethren" (1 John 3:16).

*Jesus is the true vine, the source of life.*

14 Ye are my friends, if ye do whatsoever I command you.

15 Henceforth I call you not servants; for the servant knoweth not what his lord doeth: but I have called you friends; for all things that I have heard of my Father I have made known unto you.

16 Ye have not chosen me, but I have chosen you, and ordained you, that ye should go and bring forth fruit, and that your fruit should remain: that whatsoever ye shall ask of the Father in my name, he may give it you.

17 These things I command you, that ye love one another.

## THE WICKED HATE AND FIGHT AGAINST TRUE RELIGION

18 ¶ If the world hate you, ye know that it hated me before it hated you.

19 If ye were of the world, the world would love his own: but because ye are not of the world, but I have chosen you out of the world, therefore the world hateth you.

20 Remember the word that I said unto you, The servant is not greater than his lord. If they have persecuted me, they will also persecute you; if they have kept my saying, they will keep yours also.

21 But all these things will they do unto you for my name's sake, because they know not him that sent me.

22 If I had not come and spoken unto them, they had not had sin: but now they have no cloke for their sin.

23 He that hateth me hateth my Father also.

24 If I had not done among them the works which none other man did, they had not had sin: but now have they both seen and hated both me and my Father.

25 But this cometh to pass, that the word might be fulfilled that is written in their law, They hated me without a cause.

## THE HOLY GHOST TESTIFIES OF CHRIST

26 ¶ But when the Comforter is come, whom I will send unto you from the Father, even the Spirit of truth, which proceedeth from the Father, he shall testify of me:

27 And ye also shall bear witness, because ye have been with me from the beginning.

## CHAPTER 16

*Jesus taught the Apostles that he would die soon but that the Holy Ghost would guide them when he was gone. Look for the blessings that come from having the gift of the Holy Ghost.*

## JESUS TELLS OF HIS DEATH AND OF THE HOLY GHOST

1 ¶ THESE things have I spoken unto you, that ye should not be offended.

2 They shall put you out of the synagogues: yea, the time cometh, that whosoever killeth you will think that he doeth God service.

3 And these things will they do unto you, because they have not known the Father, nor me.

4 But these things have I told you, that when the time shall come, ye may remember that I told you of them. And these things I said not unto you at the beginning, because I was with you.

5 But now I go my way to him that sent me; and none of you asketh me, Whither goest thou?

6 But because I have said these things unto you, sorrow hath filled your heart.

---

15:14   Would you want Jesus as a friend? What can you do to be friends with Jesus?

15:16   Joseph Smith wrote that the only way a man can receive the priesthood is to "be called of God, by prophecy, and by the laying on of hands by those who are in authority" (Articles of Faith 1:5).

15:20   *persecute you*—treat you badly

15:21   Sometimes we suffer hardships to follow Jesus. How does it make you feel to know that he also suffered similar hardships?

15:21-25   "Satan is waging war against the members of the Church who have testimonies and are trying to keep the commandments" (*The Teachings of Ezra Taft Benson*, p. 400).

15:22   *no cloke for their sin*—no way to cover their sin

15:26   *Comforter*—Holy Ghost

  What is the mission of the Holy Ghost? Why is this mission so important to you?

16:2   *synagogues*—Jewish places of worship

16:5   "I go my way to him that sent me" meant Jesus was going to die and return to Heavenly Father (see JST, John 9:4).

7 ¶ Nevertheless I tell you the truth; It is expedient for you that I go away: for if I go not away, the Comforter will not come unto you; but if I depart, I will send him unto you.

8 And when he is come, he will reprove the world of sin, and of righteousness, and of judgment:

9 Of sin, because they believe not on me;

10 Of righteousness, because I go to my Father, and ye see me no more;

11 Of judgment, because the prince of this world is judged.

12 I have yet many things to say unto you, but ye cannot bear them now.

13 Howbeit when he, the Spirit of truth, is come, he will guide you into all truth: for he shall not speak of himself; but whatsoever he shall hear, that shall he speak: and he will shew you things to come.

14 He shall glorify me: for he shall receive of mine, and shall shew it unto you.

15 All things that the Father hath are mine: therefore said I, that he shall take of mine, and shall shew it unto you.

16 ¶ A little while, and ye shall not see me: and again, a little while, and ye shall see me, because I go to the Father.

## JESUS COMFORTS HIS DISCIPLES

17 Then said some of his disciples among themselves, What is this that he saith unto us, A little while, and ye shall not see me: and again, a little while, and ye shall see me: and, Because I go to the Father?

18 They said therefore, What is this that he saith, A little while? we cannot tell what he saith.

19 Now Jesus knew that they were desirous to ask him, and said unto them, Do ye enquire among yourselves of that I said, A little while, and ye shall not see me: and again, a little while, and ye shall see me?

20 Verily, verily, I say unto you, That ye shall weep and lament, but the world shall rejoice: and ye shall be sorrowful, but your sorrow shall be turned into joy.

21 A woman when she is in travail hath sorrow, because her hour is come: but as soon as she is delivered of the child, she remembereth no more the anguish, for joy that a man is born into the world.

22 And ye now therefore have sorrow: but I will see you again, and your heart shall rejoice, and your joy no man taketh from you.

23 ¶ And in that day ye shall ask me nothing. Verily, verily, I say unto you, Whatsoever ye shall ask the Father in my name, he will give it you.

24 Hitherto have ye asked nothing in my name: ask, and ye shall receive, that your joy may be full.

25 These things have I spoken unto you in proverbs: but the time cometh, when I shall no more speak unto you in proverbs, but I shall shew you plainly of the Father.

26 At that day ye shall ask in my name: and I say not unto you, that I will pray the Father for you:

27 For the Father himself loveth you, because ye have loved me, and have believed that I came out from God.

28 ¶ I came forth from the Father, and am come into the world: again, I leave the world, and go to the Father.

29 His disciples said unto him, Lo, now speakest thou plainly, and speakest no proverb.

---

16:7 ☀ The Holy Ghost is called the Comforter. D&C 130:22 teaches that he can dwell in us because he "has not a body of flesh and bones, but is a personage of Spirit."

16:8 ☀ *Reprove* can mean to convict, convince, or expose. The Holy Ghost helps people to see and understand what they have done wrong (see Spencer W. Kimball, *The Miracle of Forgiveness*, p. 152).

16:11 📖 **prince of this world**—Satan

16:12 📖 **bear**—understand

16:13-14 🔄 The Holy Ghost is also called the "Spirit of truth." What truths has the Holy Ghost helped you to know?

16:19 📖 **enquire**—question

16:20 📖 **weep and lament**—cry and be sad

16:20-22 🔄 Jesus said his Apostles would "weep" but the world would "rejoice" when he was gone. Why do you think that was so? Why would the Apostles later "rejoice" when they saw him again?

16:21 📖 **in travail**—about to give birth **anguish**—pain and sorrow

16:23 ☀ The Joseph Smith Translation changes the first part of this verse to say: "And in that day ye shall ask me nothing but it shall be done unto you" (JST, John 16:23).

16:23-24 🔄 What do these verses teach you about your prayers? Why should we always ask Heavenly Father for the blessings we need? (See James 1:5.)

16:24 📖 **Hitherto**—Until now

30 Now are we sure that thou knowest all things, and needest not that any man should ask thee: by this we believe that thou camest forth from God.

31 Jesus answered them, Do ye now believe?

32 Behold, the hour cometh, yea, is now come, that ye shall be scattered, every man to his own, and shall leave me alone: and yet I am not alone, because the Father is with me.

33 These things I have spoken unto you, that in me ye might have peace. In the world ye shall have tribulation: but be of good cheer; I have overcome the world.

## CHAPTER 17

*This chapter records the beautiful prayer Jesus offered for all those who believe in him. Notice the blessings Jesus asked Heavenly Father to give us.*

### JESUS PRAYS TO HEAVENLY FATHER

1 ¶ THESE words spake Jesus, and lifted up his eyes to heaven, and said, Father, the hour is come; glorify thy Son, that thy Son also may glorify thee:

2 As thou hast given him power over all flesh, that he should give eternal life to as many as thou hast given him.

3 And this is life eternal, that they might know thee the only true God, and Jesus Christ, whom thou hast sent.

4 I have glorified thee on the earth: I have finished the work which thou gavest me to do.

5 And now, O Father, glorify thou me with thine own self with the glory which I had with thee before the world was.

### JESUS PRAYS FOR HIS DISCIPLES

6 ¶ I have manifested thy name unto the men which thou gavest me out of the world: thine they were, and thou gavest them me; and they have kept thy word.

7 Now they have known that all things whatsoever thou hast given me are of thee.

8 For I have given unto them the words which thou gavest me; and they have received them, and have known surely that I came out from thee, and they have believed that thou didst send me.

9 I pray for them: I pray not for the world, but for them which thou hast given me; for they are thine.

10 And all mine are thine, and thine are mine; and I am glorified in them.

11 ¶ And now I am no more in the world, but these are in the world, and I come to thee. Holy Father, keep through thine own name those whom thou hast given me, that they may be one, as we are.

12 While I was with them in the world, I kept them in thy name: those that thou gavest me I have kept, and none of them is lost, but the son of perdition; that the scripture might be fulfilled.

13 And now come I to thee; and these things I speak in the world, that they might have my joy fulfilled in themselves.

14 I have given them thy word; and the world hath hated them, because they are not of the world, even as I am not of the world.

15 I pray not that thou shouldest take them out of the world, but that thou shouldest keep them from the evil.

16 They are not of the world, even as I am not of the world.

---

16:33   In this verse the "world" refers not only to the earth but also to the conditions of wickedness or worldliness found on the earth. In the latter days Jesus again reminded his Saints that he had overcome or conquered the "world." He promised that those who overcome all things will obtain the celestial kingdom. (See D&C 50:41; 76:60-62.)

17:1-5   Jesus brought glory to Heavenly Father by completing the Atonement, which provided the way for Heavenly Father's children to return to him (see   for John 13:31-32). The Father glorified Jesus by anointing him to be the Savior (see Moses 4:2), testifying of him (see Matthew 3:17), and making him a God (see John 1:1-3).

17:3   The only way to *know* Heavenly Father and Jesus is to become like them. We do this as we keep the commandments (see 1 John 2:3). When we do become like them, we will have eternal life (see Moroni 7:48).

17:6   **manifested**—shown, revealed

17:11   To "be one" means to be united. In other words, it is to think, do, and want the same things. This is the kind of unity Heavenly Father and Jesus enjoy. God wants all his people to be "of one heart and one mind" (Moses 7:18).

17:12   *Perdition* is another name for Satan and means "destruction." A "son of perdition" is a follower of Satan. This verse refers to Judas, who betrayed Jesus.

17:14-17   What did Jesus ask Heavenly Father to do for his disciples so that they could stay righteous even in this wicked world? How will the scriptures also help keep us from evil?

*"This is life eternal, that they might know thee the only true God, and Jesus Christ."*

17 ¶ Sanctify them through thy truth: thy word is truth.

18 As thou hast sent me into the world, even so have I also sent them into the world.

19 And for their sakes I sanctify myself, that they also might be sanctified through the truth.

## JESUS PRAYS FOR ALL WHO BELIEVE IN HIM

20 ¶ Neither pray I for these alone, but for them also which shall believe on me through their word;

21 That they all may be one; as thou, Father, art in me, and I in thee, that they also may be one in us: that the world may believe that thou hast sent me.

22 And the glory which thou gavest me I have given them; that they may be one, even as we are one:

23 I in them, and thou in me, that they may be made perfect in one; and that the world may know that thou hast sent me, and hast loved them, as thou hast loved me.

24 ¶ Father, I will that they also, whom thou hast given me, be with me where I am; that they may behold my glory, which thou hast given me: for thou lovedst me before the foundation of the world.

25 O righteous Father, the world hath not known thee: but I have known thee, and these have known that thou hast sent me.

26 And I have declared unto them thy name, and will declare it: that the love wherewith thou hast loved me may be in them, and I in them.

## CHAPTER 18

*The last week of the Savior's life reveals much of his greatness. In this chapter look for the trials and sufferings Jesus endured prior to his crucifixion.*

## JESUS IS BETRAYED AND ARRESTED

1 ¶ WHEN Jesus had spoken these words, he went forth with his disciples over the brook Cedron, where was a garden, into the which he entered, and his disciples.

2 And Judas also, which betrayed him, knew the place: for Jesus ofttimes resorted thither with his disciples.

3 Judas then, having received a band of men and officers from the chief priests and Pharisees, cometh thither with lanterns and torches and weapons.

4 Jesus therefore, knowing all things that should come upon him, went forth, and said unto them, Whom seek ye?

5 They answered him, Jesus of Nazareth. Jesus saith unto them, I am he. And Judas also, which betrayed him, stood with them.

6 As soon then as he had said unto them, I am he, they went backward, and fell to the ground.

7 Then asked he them again, Whom seek ye? And they said, Jesus of Nazareth.

8 Jesus answered, I have told you that I am he: if therefore ye seek me, let these go their way:

9 That the saying might be fulfilled, which he spake, Of them which thou gavest me have I lost none.

10 Then Simon Peter having a sword drew it, and smote the high priest's servant, and cut off his right ear. The servant's name was Malchus.

11 Then said Jesus unto Peter, Put up thy sword into the sheath: the cup which my Father hath given me, shall I not drink it?

12 Then the band and the captain and officers of the Jews took Jesus, and bound him,

13 ¶ And led him away to Annas first; for he was father in law to Caiaphas, which was the high priest that same year.

---

17:17 **Sanctify them**—Make them righteous or holy

17:20-24 If you believe the words you are reading in the scriptures, then the prayer Jesus offered in these verses is also for you. Re-read verses 20-24, understanding that Jesus is praying for you. What does Jesus want you to be? Where does he want you to go? How does this make you feel?

18:2 **ofttimes resorted thither**—often met there

18:4-14 Knowing he was about to be arrested, Jesus could have escaped, but instead he voluntarily submitted to go through the pain and suffering that were ahead (see Matthew 26:53).

18:10 Luke 22:51 says that Jesus healed Malchus's ear after Peter cut it off.

18:11 The term *cup* here symbolizes the suffering and death Jesus Christ would undergo to atone for the sins of mankind (see D&C 19:13-20).

18:13 Annas was high priest from A.D. 7 to 15, and his son-in-law Joseph Caiaphas held the office from A.D. 18 to 36. Both Annas and Caiaphas were Sadducees and politically powerful men who led in the attack against Jesus Christ and his Apostles. (See LDS Bible Dictionary, s.v. "Annas," p. 609, and "Caiaphas," p. 628.)

14 Now Caiaphas was he, which gave counsel to the Jews, that it was expedient that one man should die for the people.

## PETER DENIES KNOWING JESUS

15 And Simon Peter followed Jesus, and so did another disciple: that disciple was known unto the high priest, and went in with Jesus into the palace of the high priest.

16 But Peter stood at the door without. Then went out that other disciple, which was known unto the high priest, and spake unto her that kept the door, and brought in Peter.

17 Then saith the damsel that kept the door unto Peter, Art not thou also one of this man's disciples? He saith, I am not.

18 And the servants and officers stood there, who had made a fire of coals; for it was cold: and they warmed themselves: and Peter stood with them, and warmed himself.

19 The high priest then asked Jesus of his disciples, and of his doctrine.

20 Jesus answered him, I spake openly to the world; I ever taught in the synagogue, and in the temple, whither the Jews always resort; and in secret have I said nothing.

21 Why askest thou me? ask them which heard me, what I have said unto them: behold, they know what I said.

22 And when he had thus spoken, one of the officers which stood by struck Jesus with the palm of his hand, saying, Answerest thou the high priest so?

23 Jesus answered him, If I have spoken evil, bear witness of the evil: but if well, why smitest thou me?

24 Now Annas had sent him bound unto Caiaphas the high priest.

25 And Simon Peter stood and warmed himself. They said therefore unto him, Art not thou also one of his disciples? He denied it, and said, I am not.

26 One of the servants of the high priest, being his kinsman whose ear Peter cut off, saith, Did not I see thee in the garden with him?

27 Peter then denied again: and immediately the cock crew.

## JESUS IS ACCUSED BEFORE PILATE

28 ¶ Then led they Jesus from Caiaphas unto the hall of judgment: and it was early; and they themselves went not into the judgment hall, lest they should be defiled; but that they might eat the passover.

29 Pilate then went out unto them, and said, What accusation bring ye against this man?

30 They answered and said unto him, If he were not a malefactor, we would not have delivered him up unto thee.

31 Then said Pilate unto them, Take ye him, and judge him according to your law. The Jews therefore said unto him, It is not lawful for us to put any man to death:

32 That the saying of Jesus might be fulfilled, which he spake, signifying what death he should die.

33 Then Pilate entered into the judgment hall again, and called Jesus, and said unto him, Art thou the King of the Jews?

34 Jesus answered him, Sayest thou this thing of thyself, or did others tell it thee of me?

35 Pilate answered, Am I a Jew? Thine own nation and the chief priests have delivered thee unto me: what hast thou done?

36 Jesus answered, My kingdom is not of this world: if my kingdom were of this world, then would my servants fight, that I should not be delivered to the Jews: but now is my kingdom not from hence.

37 Pilate therefore said unto him, Art thou a king then? Jesus answered, Thou sayest that I am a king. To this end was I born, and for this cause came I into the world, that I should bear witness unto the truth. Every one that is of the truth heareth my voice.

---

18:14    **expedient**—good, advisable

18:15    Many people, including Elder Bruce R. McConkie, feel that the other disciple who was familiar with the high priest was John the Apostle (see *Doctrinal New Testament Commentary* 1:825-27).

18:27    For the third time Peter denied knowing Jesus, just as the Savior prophesied (see John 13:38).

18:28    These Jewish leaders were more concerned about becoming "unclean" by entering a house of

a non-Jew than they were about the fact that they were plotting to have Jesus Christ unjustly judged and murdered.

18:29    **accusation**—charge

18:30    **a malefactor**—an evildoer

18:37    According to the Savior's own statement, why was he born? Who will believe his testimony?

38 Pilate saith unto him, What is truth? And when he had said this, he went out again unto the Jews, and saith unto them, I find in him no fault at all.

39 But ye have a custom, that I should release unto you one at the passover: will ye therefore that I release unto you the King of the Jews?

40 Then cried they all again, saying, Not this man, but Barabbas. Now Barabbas was a robber.

# CHAPTER 19

*Crucifixion, and the scourging that preceded it, was a terribly painful punishment. As you read this chapter, look for the concern that Jesus had for his mother and others even while he was undergoing great torment.*

## JESUS IS SENTENCED TO BE CRUCIFIED

1 ¶ THEN Pilate therefore took Jesus, and scourged him.

2 And the soldiers platted a crown of thorns, and put it on his head, and they put on him a purple robe,

3 And said, Hail, King of the Jews! and they smote him with their hands.

4 Pilate therefore went forth again, and saith unto them, Behold, I bring him forth to you, that ye may know that I find no fault in him.

5 Then came Jesus forth, wearing the crown of thorns, and the purple robe. And Pilate saith unto them, Behold the man!

6 When the chief priests therefore and officers saw him, they cried out, saying, Crucify him, crucify him. Pilate saith unto them, Take ye him, and crucify him: for I find no fault in him.

7 The Jews answered him, We have a law, and by our law he ought to die, because he made himself the Son of God.

8 When Pilate therefore heard that saying, he was the more afraid;

9 And went again into the judgment hall, and saith unto Jesus, Whence art thou? But Jesus gave him no answer.

10 Then saith Pilate unto him, Speakest thou not unto me? knowest thou not that I have power to crucify thee, and have power to release thee?

11 Jesus answered, Thou couldest have no power at all against me, except it were given thee from above: therefore he that delivered me unto thee hath the greater sin.

12 And from thenceforth Pilate sought to release him: but the Jews cried out, saying, If thou let this man go, thou art not Caesar's friend: whosoever maketh himself a king speaketh against Caesar.

13 When Pilate therefore heard that saying, he brought Jesus forth, and sat down in the judgment seat in a place that is called the Pavement, but in the Hebrew, Gabbatha.

14 And it was the preparation of the passover, and about the sixth hour: and he saith unto the Jews, Behold your King!

15 But they cried out, Away with him, away with him,

---

19:1 🔍 Pilate was the Roman governor assigned to rule Judea (see LDS Bible Dictionary, s.v. "Pilate," p. 751).

19:2-3 🔍 Purple was the color of royalty. The soldiers put this robe on Jesus and hailed, or praised, him as "King of the Jews" to make fun of him.

19:4 ☀ "Jesus is innocent. Pilate knew it; Herod knew it; Caiaphas knew it; the Sanhedrin knew it; the mob-multitude knew it—and Satan knew it. Yet he

is to be pronounced guilty and sentenced to death." (Bruce R. McConkie, *Doctrinal New Testament Commentary* 1:809.)

19:7 🔍 Jewish law declared, "He that blasphemeth [speaks disrespectfully of] the name of the Lord, he shall surely be put to death" (Leviticus 24:16). When Jesus said that he was the Son of God (see John 5:18), even though it was true, the Jews accused him of blasphemy and called for his death. (See Glossary, s.v. "blasphemy.")

19:9 🗒 **Whence art thou?**—Where are you from?

19:11 🔍 Pilate had power over Jesus only because God allowed it (see John 7:20). The greater sin was on the heads of the Jews who delivered Jesus to Pilate (see John 15:22).

19:14 🗒 **the sixth hour**—noon

19:14-
15 🔄 The Jewish leaders chose Caesar as their king instead of Jesus. How can you show Jesus that he is your king today?

The crown of thorns was forced onto Jesus' head.

crucify him. Pilate saith unto them, Shall I crucify your King? The chief priests answered, We have no king but Caesar.

16 ¶ Then delivered he him therefore unto them to be crucified. And they took Jesus, and led him away.

## ROMAN SOLDIERS CRUCIFY JESUS

17 And he bearing his cross went forth into a place called the place of a skull, which is called in the Hebrew Golgotha:

18 Where they crucified him, and two other with him, on either side one, and Jesus in the midst.

19 ¶ And Pilate wrote a title, and put it on the cross. And the writing was, JESUS OF NAZARETH THE KING OF THE JEWS.

20 This title then read many of the Jews: for the place where Jesus was crucified was nigh to the city: and it was written in Hebrew, and Greek, and Latin.

21 Then said the chief priests of the Jews to Pilate, Write not, The King of the Jews; but that he said, I am King of the Jews.

22 Pilate answered, What I have written I have written.

23 Then the soldiers, when they had crucified Jesus, took his garments, and made four parts, to every soldier a part; and also his coat: now the coat was without seam, woven from the top throughout.

24 They said therefore among themselves, Let us not rend it, but cast lots for it, whose it shall be: that the scripture might be fulfilled, which saith, They parted my raiment among them, and for my vesture they did cast lots. These things therefore the soldiers did.

25 Now there stood by the cross of Jesus his mother, and his mother's sister, Mary the wife of Cleophas, and Mary Magdalene.

26 When Jesus therefore saw his mother, and the disciple standing by, whom he loved, he saith unto his mother, Woman, behold thy son!

27 Then saith he to the disciple, Behold thy mother! And from that hour that disciple took her unto his own home.

## JESUS DIES ON THE CROSS

28 After this, Jesus knowing that all things were now accomplished, that the scripture might be fulfilled, saith, I thirst.

29 Now there was set a vessel full of vinegar: and they filled a spunge with vinegar, and put it upon hyssop, and put it to his mouth.

30 When Jesus therefore had received the vinegar, he said, It is finished: and he bowed his head, and gave up the ghost.

31 ¶ The Jews therefore, because it was the preparation, that the bodies should not remain upon the cross on the sabbath day, (for that sabbath day was an high day,) besought Pilate that their legs might be broken, and that they might be taken away.

32 Then came the soldiers, and brake the legs of the first, and of the other which was crucified with him.

33 But when they came to Jesus, and saw that he was dead already, they brake not his legs:

34 But one of the soldiers with a spear pierced his side, and forthwith came there out blood and water.

35 And he that saw it bare record, and his record is true: and he knoweth that he saith true, that ye might believe.

---

19:20 **nigh**—near

19:24 **rend**— tear

The soldiers "cast lots" (a form of gambling) for the coat, which fulfilled the prophecy in Psalm 22:18.

19:25-
27 Whom was Jesus so concerned about during this terrible time? What does this teach you about the kind of person he was? How can you follow his example?

19:29 For help understanding what the vinegar was, see for Luke 23:36.

**hyssop**—a branch from a hyssop plant

19:31-
37 Jewish law required that the dead be buried before the Sabbath began. Roman soldiers broke the legs of those on the crosses to bring death quicker. They didn't break Jesus' legs, because he

was already dead. This fulfilled scriptures that required that the lamb being sacrificed (Jesus being the Lamb of God) could have no broken legs (see Exodus 12:46).

*Hyssop was a plant used by the Jews for sprinkling in some sacrifices and purifications. A sponge moistened with vinegar was attached to a stock of hyssop and pressed to the Savior's mouth.*

*The Crucifixion*

36 For these things were done, that the scripture should be fulfilled, A bone of him shall not be broken.

37 And again another scripture saith, They shall look on him whom they pierced.

## Jesus Is Buried in a Tomb

38 ¶ And after this Joseph of Arimathaea, being a disciple of Jesus, but secretly for fear of the Jews, besought Pilate that he might take away the body of Jesus: and Pilate gave him leave. He came therefore, and took the body of Jesus.

39 And there came also Nicodemus, which at the first came to Jesus by night, and brought a mixture of myrrh and aloes, about an hundred pound weight.

40 Then took they the body of Jesus, and wound it in linen clothes with the spices, as the manner of the Jews is to bury.

41 Now in the place where he was crucified there was a garden; and in the garden a new sepulchre, wherein was never man yet laid.

42 There laid they Jesus therefore because of the Jews' preparation day; for the sepulchre was nigh at hand.

## CHAPTER 20

*The resurrection of Jesus Christ is one of the most important events in all eternity. Because of his resurrection, we will also be resurrected one day (see 1 Corinthians 15:22). Watch for the many witnesses of the resurrection of Jesus Christ.*

## Some Disciples Discover the Empty Tomb

1 ¶ THE first day of the week cometh Mary Magdalene early, when it was yet dark, unto the sepulchre, and seeth the stone taken away from the sepulchre.

2 Then she runneth, and cometh to Simon Peter, and to the other disciple, whom Jesus loved, and saith unto them, They have taken away the Lord out of the sepulchre, and we know not where they have laid him.

3 Peter therefore went forth, and that other disciple, and came to the sepulchre.

4 So they ran both together: and the other disciple did outrun Peter, and came first to the sepulchre.

5 And he stooping down, and looking in, saw the linen clothes lying; yet went he not in.

6 Then cometh Simon Peter following him, and went into the sepulchre, and seeth the linen clothes lie,

7 And the napkin, that was about his head, not lying with the linen clothes, but wrapped together in a place by itself.

8 Then went in also that other disciple, which came first to the sepulchre, and he saw, and believed.

9 For as yet they knew not the scripture, that he must rise again from the dead.

10 Then the disciples went away again unto their own home.

## The Resurrected Lord Appears to Mary

11 ¶ But Mary stood without at the sepulchre weeping: and as she wept, she stooped down, and looked into the sepulchre,

12 And seeth two angels in white sitting, the one at the head, and the other at the feet, where the body of Jesus had lain.

13 And they say unto her, Woman, why weepest thou? She saith unto them, Because they have taken away my Lord, and I know not where they have laid him.

14 And when she had thus said, she turned herself back, and saw Jesus standing, and knew not that it was Jesus.

15 Jesus saith unto her, Woman, why weepest thou? whom seekest thou? She, supposing him to be the

---

19:38-42   Joseph and Nicodemus carefully prepared Jesus' body for burial and laid it in a new garden tomb. How do you think they felt about Jesus?

19:39-40   Myrrh and aloes were expensive herbs used in preparing the dead for burial.

20:1   "There is evidence that the members of the Church following the resurrection of Jesus changed their Sabbath from the last to the first day of the week and that Christians have followed it ever since. . . . Our Savior was in the tomb during the Jewish Sabbath [Saturday], and . . . he came forth on the early morning of the first day of the week." (Joseph Fielding Smith, *Answers to Gospel Questions* 2:61.)

*sepulchre*—grave or tomb

20:3-10   Why did Peter and John run to the tomb? How do you think they felt when they discovered the empty tomb? How do you feel when you read about this sacred event?

20:5   *linen clothes*—strips of cloth used to wrap the dead

20:11   Why do you think Mary stayed by the tomb and wept when the others went home?

*Peter and John go to the tomb.*

*Christ appears to Mary.*

gardener, saith unto him, Sir, if thou have borne him hence, tell me where thou hast laid him, and I will take him away.

16 Jesus saith unto her, Mary. She turned herself, and saith unto him, Rabboni; which is to say, Master.

17 Jesus saith unto her, Touch me not; for I am not yet ascended to my Father: but go to my brethren, and say unto them, I ascend unto my Father, and your Father; and to my God, and your God.

18 Mary Magdalene came and told the disciples that she had seen the Lord, and that he had spoken these things unto her.

## JESUS APPEARS TO HIS DISCIPLES

19 ¶ Then the same day at evening, being the first day of the week, when the doors were shut where the disciples were assembled for fear of the Jews, came Jesus and stood in the midst, and saith unto them, Peace be unto you.

20 And when he had so said, he shewed unto them his hands and his side. Then were the disciples glad, when they saw the Lord.

21 Then said Jesus to them again, Peace be unto you: as my Father hath sent me, even so send I you.

22 And when he had said this, he breathed on them, and saith unto them, Receive ye the Holy Ghost:

23 Whose soever sins ye remit, they are remitted unto them; and whose soever sins ye retain, they are retained.

## THOMAS DOUBTS UNTIL HE SEES THE RESURRECTED LORD

24 But Thomas, one of the twelve, called Didymus, was not with them when Jesus came.

25 The other disciples therefore said unto him, We have seen the Lord. But he said unto them, Except I shall see in his hands the print of the nails, and put my finger into the print of the nails, and thrust my hand into his side, I will not believe.

26 ¶ And after eight days again his disciples were within, and Thomas with them: then came Jesus, the doors being shut, and stood in the midst, and said, Peace be unto you.

27 Then saith he to Thomas, Reach hither thy finger, and behold my hands; and reach hither thy hand, and thrust it into my side: and be not faithless, but believing.

28 And Thomas answered and said unto him, My Lord and my God.

29 Jesus saith unto him, Thomas, because thou hast seen me, thou hast believed: blessed are they that have not seen, and yet have believed.

30 And many other signs truly did Jesus in the presence of his disciples, which are not written in this book:

31 But these are written, that ye might believe that Jesus is the Christ, the Son of God; and that believing ye might have life through his name.

---

20:17   The Joseph Smith Translation changes the word *touch* to *hold* (JST, John 20:17). Mary was not allowed to "hold" Jesus, because he had not yet ascended, or returned, to heaven. During the three days Jesus Christ's physical body was in the tomb, his spirit went to the spirit world, where he preached the gospel to the dead (see D&C 138:18-19, 30-32).

20:19   **in the midst**—among them

Jesus appeared to his disciples and said, "Peace be unto you." How would seeing Jesus bring them joy and peace? How does Jesus bring peace into your life?

20:22   The Holy Ghost is a spirit (see D&C 130:22). When Jesus "breathed" on the Apostles it symbolized his giving them the Holy Ghost. The gift of the Holy Ghost is given by the laying on of hands (see Articles of Faith 1:4). Elder Bruce R. McConkie explained: "Jesus 'breathed on them,' which probably means that he laid his hands upon them as he uttered the decree: 'Receive the Holy

Ghost.' Thus they *received*, but did not at that moment actually *enjoy*, the gift of the Holy Ghost. . . . In the case of the apostles the actual enjoyment of the gift was delayed until the day of Pentecost. (Acts 2.)" (*Doctrinal New Testament Commentary* 1:857.)

20:23   **remit; remitted**—forgive; forgiven **retain; retained**— keep (that is, do not forgive); kept (that is, not forgiven)

20:25   **thrust**—put

20:29   Faith is believing in things that we can't see but that are true (see Alma 32:21). Jesus taught that those who have faith are very blessed.

Do you believe in the resurrection, even though you may not have seen Jesus Christ? How can you help your faith grow?

20:31   The "life" spoken of here is eternal life in the celestial kingdom. Eternal life comes through the power of Jesus Christ to those who believe (see Mosiah 3:17).

## CHAPTER 21

*In this chapter the resurrected Lord appears to his Apostles in Galilee. Look for the special work assigned to Peter, as well as the Savior's prophecy of Peter's death.*

### A MIRACULOUS CATCH OF FISH OCCURS

1 ¶ AFTER these things Jesus shewed himself again to the disciples at the sea of Tiberias; and on this wise shewed he himself.

2 There were together Simon Peter, and Thomas called Didymus, and Nathanael of Cana in Galilee, and the sons of Zebedee, and two other of his disciples.

3 Simon Peter saith unto them, I go a fishing. They say unto him, We also go with thee. They went forth, and entered into a ship immediately; and that night they caught nothing.

4 But when the morning was now come, Jesus stood on the shore: but the disciples knew not that it was Jesus.

5 Then Jesus saith unto them, Children, have ye any meat? They answered him, No.

6 And he said unto them, Cast the net on the right side of the ship, and ye shall find. They cast therefore, and now they were not able to draw it for the multitude of fishes.

7 Therefore that disciple whom Jesus loved saith unto Peter, It is the Lord. Now when Simon Peter heard that it was the Lord, he girt his fisher's coat unto him, (for he was naked,) and did cast himself into the sea.

8 And the other disciples came in a little ship; (for they were not far from land, but as it were two hundred cubits,) dragging the net with fishes.

9 As soon then as they were come to land, they saw a fire of coals there, and fish laid thereon, and bread.

10 Jesus saith unto them, Bring of the fish which ye have now caught.

11 Simon Peter went up, and drew the net to land full of great fishes, an hundred and fifty and three: and for all there were so many, yet was not the net broken.

12 Jesus saith unto them, Come and dine. And none of the disciples durst ask him, Who art thou? knowing that it was the Lord.

13 Jesus then cometh, and taketh bread, and giveth them, and fish likewise.

14 This is now the third time that Jesus shewed himself to his disciples, after that he was risen from the dead.

### PETER IS CALLED TO LEAD CHRIST'S CHURCH

15 ¶ So when they had dined, Jesus saith to Simon Peter, Simon, son of Jonas, lovest thou me more than these? He saith unto him, Yea, Lord; thou knowest that I love thee. He saith unto him, Feed my lambs.

16 He saith to him again the second time, Simon, son of Jonas, lovest thou me? He saith unto him, Yea, Lord; thou knowest that I love thee. He saith unto him, Feed my sheep.

17 He saith unto him the third time, Simon, son of Jonas, lovest thou me? Peter was grieved because he said unto him the third time, Lovest thou me? And he said unto him, Lord, thou knowest all things; thou knowest that I love thee. Jesus saith unto him, Feed my sheep.

18 Verily, verily, I say unto thee, When thou wast young, thou girdedst thyself, and walkedst whither thou wouldest: but when thou shalt be old, thou shalt stretch forth thy hands, and another shall gird thee, and carry thee whither thou wouldest not.

19 This spake he, signifying by what death he should

---

21:1 *Tiberias*—Galilee

21:2 *Didymus*—twin

21:6 Jesus performed a miracle just like this when he first called Peter, James, and John to be "fishers of men" (see Luke 5:5-10).

21:7 *girt*—tied
*for he was naked*—because he was wearing only underclothing

21:15 Peter had gone fishing instead of continuing to teach the gospel. "Our Lord now calls him back and asks: 'Lovest thou me more than these one hundred and fifty-three fish, more than the things of this world?'" (Bruce R. McConkie, *Doctrinal New Testament Commentary* 1:863.)

21:15-17 Do you remember when Peter denied knowing Jesus three times? (See Luke 22:56-62.) Do you think Peter thought of that when Jesus asked him three times if he loved Him? When Jesus called Peter three times to "feed my lambs . . . feed my sheep," he was calling him to spend the rest of his life leading the Church and teaching the gospel to all of Heavenly Father's children. Could you give up all you have, as Peter did, and spend the rest of your life in loving service to Jesus Christ?

21:18 *girdedst thyself*—dressed yourself

21:18-19 According to tradition Peter was crucified in Rome (see LDS Bible Dictionary, s.v. "Peter," p. 749).

glorify God. And when he had spoken this, he saith unto him, Follow me.

20 ¶ Then Peter, turning about, seeth the disciple whom Jesus loved following; which also leaned on his breast at supper, and said, Lord, which is he that betrayeth thee?

21 Peter seeing him saith to Jesus, Lord, and what shall this man do?

22 Jesus saith unto him, If I will that he tarry till I come, what is that to thee? follow thou me.

23 Then went this saying abroad among the brethren, that that disciple should not die: yet Jesus said not unto him, He shall not die; but, If I will that he tarry till I come, what is that to thee?

24 This is the disciple which testifieth of these things, and wrote these things: and we know that his testimony is true.

25 And there are also many other things which Jesus did, the which, if they should be written every one, I suppose that even the world itself could not contain the books that should be written. Amen.

---

21:20-
24    John the Apostle was translated, meaning that his body was changed in such a way that he would "not taste of death" until the second coming of Jesus Christ (see Matthew 16:28; Revelation 10; D&C 7; 77:14).

# THE ACTS
# OF THE APOSTLES

*Luke wrote the book of Acts to continue the story he began in the Gospel of Luke. Acts tells the story of some of the missionary journeys of the early Apostles, especially the travels of Paul.*

## CHAPTER 1

*The book of Acts tells the story of how the Apostles taught the gospel after Jesus was gone. Note how they chose a man to take Judas's place.*

### THE RESURRECTED SAVIOR TEACHES HIS APOSTLES FOR FORTY DAYS

1 THE former treatise have I made, O Theophilus, of all that Jesus began both to do and teach,

2 Until the day in which he was taken up, after that he through the Holy Ghost had given commandments unto the apostles whom he had chosen:

3 To whom also he shewed himself alive after his passion by many infallible proofs, being seen of them forty days, and speaking of the things pertaining to the kingdom of God:

4 And, being assembled together with them, commanded them that they should not depart from Jerusalem, but wait for the promise of the Father, which, saith he, ye have heard of me.

5 For John truly baptized with water; but ye shall be baptized with the Holy Ghost not many days hence.

6 ¶ When they therefore were come together, they asked of him, saying, Lord, wilt thou at this time restore again the kingdom to Israel?

7 And he said unto them, It is not for you to know the times or the seasons, which the Father hath put in his own power.

8 But ye shall receive power, after that the Holy Ghost is come upon you: and ye shall be witnesses unto me both in Jerusalem, and in all Judaea, and in Samaria, and unto the uttermost part of the earth.

### THE SAVIOR GOES UP INTO HEAVEN

9 And when he had spoken these things, while they beheld, he was taken up; and a cloud received him out of their sight.

10 And while they looked stedfastly toward heaven as he went up, behold, two men stood by them in white apparel;

11 Which also said, Ye men of Galilee, why stand ye gazing up into heaven? this same Jesus, which is taken up from you into heaven, shall so come in like manner as ye have seen him go into heaven.

---

1:1 The "former treatise" (meaning the earlier book) Luke wrote was the Gospel of Luke (see Luke 1:3).

1:2 After forty days of teaching the Apostles, the Lord was "taken up" to heaven to be with Heavenly Father.

1:3 **shewed**—This word is pronounced the same way as the word *showed* and has the same meaning; *shewed* is simply an old spelling of *showed*.
**passion**—sufferings and death
**infallible**—perfect, cannot be wrong
**pertaining to**—about

1:4 Elder Bruce R. McConkie said that the "promise of the Father" was that the Apostles would receive the blessings of the temple endowment and the gift of the Holy Ghost (see *Doctrinal New Testament Commentary* 2:22).

1:6 **restore**—give back

1:10 **looked stedfastly**—kept looking

1:11 At his second coming Jesus would come in "like manner," meaning in the same way that the Apostles now saw him go into heaven.

---

= Word Help    = A Closer Look

= More Light    = Ponder This

Words in pink are explained in the Glossary.

*The Ascension*

## MATTHIAS IS CHOSEN BY REVELATION TO REPLACE JUDAS

12 ¶ Then returned they unto Jerusalem from the mount called Olivet, which is from Jerusalem a sabbath day's journey.

13 And when they were come in, they went up into an upper room, where abode both Peter, and James, and John, and Andrew, Philip, and Thomas, Bartholomew, and Matthew, James the son of Alphaeus, and Simon Zelotes, and Judas the brother of James.

14 These all continued with one accord in prayer and supplication, with the women, and Mary the mother of Jesus, and with his brethren.

15 ¶ And in those days Peter stood up in the midst of the disciples, and said, (the number of names together were about an hundred and twenty,)

16 Men and brethren, this scripture must needs have been fulfilled, which the Holy Ghost by the mouth of David spake before concerning Judas, which was guide to them that took Jesus.

17 For he was numbered with us, and had obtained part of this ministry.

18 Now this man purchased a field with the reward of iniquity; and falling headlong, he burst asunder in the midst, and all his bowels gushed out.

19 And it was known unto all the dwellers at Jerusalem; insomuch as that field is called in their proper tongue, Aceldama, that is to say, The field of blood.

20 For it is written in the book of Psalms, Let his habitation be desolate, and let no man dwell therein: and his bishoprick let another take.

21 Wherefore of these men which have companied with us all the time that the Lord Jesus went in and out among us,

22 Beginning from the baptism of John, unto that same day that he was taken up from us, must one be ordained to be a witness with us of his resurrection.

23 And they appointed two, Joseph called Barsabas, who was surnamed Justus, and Matthias.

24 And they prayed, and said, Thou, Lord, which knowest the hearts of all men, shew whether of these two thou hast chosen,

25 That he may take part of this ministry and apostleship, from which Judas by transgression fell, that he might go to his own place.

26 And they gave forth their lots; and the lot fell upon Matthias; and he was numbered with the eleven apostles.

## CHAPTER 2

*Jesus' followers are all together for the feast of Pentecost. The Holy Ghost comes to them with great power just as Jesus promised. Look for the miracles and wonders the Apostles do and the gospel principles Peter teaches.*

## THE DISCIPLES ARE FILLED WITH THE HOLY GHOST

1 ¶ AND when the day of Pentecost was fully come, they were all with one accord in one place.

---

1:12 A Sabbath day's journey was about three-quarters of a mile (1.2 km) (see LDS Bible Dictionary, s.v. "Sabbath Day's Journey," p. 765).

1:14 **with one accord**—united, together
**supplication**—pleading or asking

1:19 The field mentioned here is the one the chief priests bought with the money Judas gave back to them after he betrayed the Lord. Matthew says that Judas hanged himself (see Matthew 27:3-8). Luke says in Acts 1:18 that Judas fell down and his body broke open. It may be that Luke is describing what happened after Judas hanged himself.

1:20 **habitation be desolate**—house be ruined or empty
**bishoprick**—calling in the Church

1:20-26 How did the eleven Apostles know they should choose a new Apostle? How was he chosen? What did the Lord do to help the Apostles make the correct choice? How are leaders and teachers in the Church chosen today? (See Articles of Faith 1:5.)

1:21 **companied**—been

1:24 **shew**—This word is pronounced the same way as the word *show* and has the same meaning; *shew* is simply an old spelling of *show*.

2:1 The Feast of Pentecost was celebrated fifty days after the Feast of the Passover. This feast celebrated the beginning of the harvest. (See LDS Bible Dictionary, s.v. "Feasts," p. 673.)

**with one accord**—together

2 And suddenly there came a sound from heaven as of a rushing mighty wind, and it filled all the house where they were sitting.

3 And there appeared unto them cloven tongues like as of fire, and it sat upon each of them.

4 And they were all filled with the Holy Ghost, and began to speak with other tongues, as the Spirit gave them utterance.

5 ¶ And there were dwelling at Jerusalem Jews, devout men, out of every nation under heaven.

6 Now when this was noised abroad, the multitude came together, and were confounded, because that every man heard them speak in his own language.

7 And they were all amazed and marvelled, saying one to another, Behold, are not all these which speak Galilaeans?

8 And how hear we every man in our own tongue, wherein we were born?

9 Parthians, and Medes, and Elamites, and the dwellers in Mesopotamia, and in Judaea, and Cappadocia, in Pontus, and Asia,

10 Phrygia, and Pamphylia, in Egypt, and in the parts of Libya about Cyrene, and strangers of Rome, Jews and proselytes,

11 Cretes and Arabians, we do hear them speak in our tongues the wonderful works of God.

12 And they were all amazed, and were in doubt, saying one to another, What meaneth this?

13 Others mocking said, These men are full of new wine.

## PETER TESTIFIES OF JESUS CHRIST

14 ¶ But Peter, standing up with the eleven, lifted up his voice, and said unto them, Ye men of Judaea, and all ye that dwell at Jerusalem, be this known unto you, and hearken to my words:

15 For these are not drunken, as ye suppose, seeing it is but the third hour of the day.

16 But this is that which was spoken by the prophet Joel;

17 And it shall come to pass in the last days, saith God, I will pour out of my Spirit upon all flesh: and your sons and your daughters shall prophesy, and your young men shall see visions, and your old men shall dream dreams:

18 And on my servants and on my handmaidens I will pour out in those days of my Spirit; and they shall prophesy:

19 And I will shew wonders in heaven above, and signs in the earth beneath; blood, and fire, and vapour of smoke:

20 The sun shall be turned into darkness, and the moon into blood, before that great and notable day of the Lord come:

21 And it shall come to pass, that whosoever shall call on the name of the Lord shall be saved.

22 Ye men of Israel, hear these words; Jesus of Nazareth, a man approved of God among you by miracles and wonders and signs, which God did by him in the midst of you, as ye yourselves also know:

23 Him, being delivered by the determinate counsel and foreknowledge of God, ye have taken, and by wicked hands have crucified and slain:

24 Whom God hath raised up, having loosed the pains of death: because it was not possible that he should be holden of it.

25 For David speaketh concerning him, I foresaw the Lord always before my face, for he is on my right hand, that I should not be moved:

26 Therefore did my heart rejoice, and my tongue was glad; moreover also my flesh shall rest in hope:

---

2:2 A powerful outpouring of the Spirit, similar to this event, happened at the Kirtland Temple in 1836 (see D&C 109:36-37).

2:3 **cloven**—separated or parted

2:4 **tongues**—languages
**utterance**—the ability to speak

2:4-8 The ability "to speak with tongues" and the "interpretation of tongues" are gifts of the Spirit of God (see D&C 46:24-25; Moroni 10:15-16). "An ideal and proper use of tongues was shown forth on the day of Pentecost. By using this gift the apostles were enabled to speak in their own tongue and be understood by persons of many different tongues." (Bruce R. McConkie, *Mormon Doctrine*, p. 800.)

2:5 **devout**—faithful

2:6 **confounded**—puzzled or confused

2:13 **mocking**—making fun of them

2:16 Joel was an Old Testament prophet. See Joel 2:28-32.

2:18 **handmaidens**—female servants

2:23 **the determinate counsel and foreknowledge of God**—that which had been determined and known before by God

2:24 **holden of**—held by or trapped by

27 Because thou wilt not leave my soul in hell, neither wilt thou suffer thine Holy One to see corruption.

28 Thou hast made known to me the ways of life; thou shalt make me full of joy with thy countenance.

29 Men and brethren, let me freely speak unto you of the patriarch David, that he is both dead and buried, and his sepulchre is with us unto this day.

30 Therefore being a prophet, and knowing that God had sworn with an oath to him, that of the fruit of his loins, according to the flesh, he would raise up Christ to sit on his throne;

31 He seeing this before spake of the resurrection of Christ, that his soul was not left in hell, neither his flesh did see corruption.

32 This Jesus hath God raised up, whereof we all are witnesses.

33 Therefore being by the right hand of God exalted, and having received of the Father the promise of the Holy Ghost, he hath shed forth this, which ye now see and hear.

34 For David is not ascended into the heavens: but he saith himself, The LORD said unto my Lord, Sit thou on my right hand,

35 Until I make thy foes thy footstool.

36 Therefore let all the house of Israel know assuredly, that God hath made that same Jesus, whom ye have crucified, both Lord and Christ.

37 ¶ Now when they heard this, they were pricked in their heart, and said unto Peter and to the rest of the apostles, Men and brethren, what shall we do?

38 Then Peter said unto them, Repent, and be baptized every one of you in the name of Jesus Christ for the remission of sins, and ye shall receive the gift of the Holy Ghost.

39 For the promise is unto you, and to your children, and to all that are afar off, even as many as the Lord our God shall call.

40 And with many other words did he testify and exhort, saying, Save yourselves from this untoward generation.

## MANY PEOPLE ARE BAPTIZED AND LIVE THE GOSPEL

41 Then they that gladly received his word were baptized: and the same day there were added unto them about three thousand souls.

42 ¶ And they continued stedfastly in the apostles' doctrine and fellowship, and in breaking of bread, and in prayers.

43 And fear came upon every soul: and many wonders and signs were done by the apostles.

44 And all that believed were together, and had all things common;

45 And sold their possessions and goods, and parted them to all men, as every man had need.

46 And they, continuing daily with one accord in the temple, and breaking bread from house to house, did eat their meat with gladness and singleness of heart,

47 Praising God, and having favour with all the people. And the Lord added to the church daily such as should be saved.

---

2:27    The Joseph Smith Translation changes "hell" to "prison," meaning that part of the spirit world where the wicked are placed (see JST, Acts 2:27; see also Alma 40:14).

   *corruption*—the decay of the body after death

2:28    *countenance*—appearance or presence

2:29    *sepulchre*—grave

2:30    *of the fruit of his loins*—through David's children

2:33    *exalted*—raised to the highest degree of the celestial kingdom

2:34    *ascended*—risen

2:35    *foes*—enemies

2:37    When these people heard Peter's testimony of Jesus, they felt inspired or prompted by the Holy Ghost. How does it feel when you are prompted by the Holy Ghost?

2:37-   Referring to these words of Peter, Elder David
2:38    O. McKay stated: "Thus are given the four requirements, the four essential principles and ordinances, obedience to which are essential to membership in Christ's Church: viz., faith, repentance, baptism, and the reception of the Holy Ghost" (*Gospel Ideals*, p. 118; see also Articles of Faith 1:4).

2:38    *remission*—washing away

2:40    *untoward*—crooked or wicked

2:42    *stedfastly*—without stopping or faithfully

2:45    *parted*—gave

*Gathering of New Testament Saints*

## CHAPTER 3

*Through the power of the holy priesthood, righteous followers of Jesus Christ can perform miracles. Watch for things Peter teaches about the power of Jesus Christ.*

### PETER AND JOHN HEAL A LAME MAN

1 ¶ NOW Peter and John went up together into the temple at the hour of prayer, being the ninth hour.

2 And a certain man lame from his mother's womb was carried, whom they laid daily at the gate of the temple which is called Beautiful, to ask alms of them that entered into the temple;

3 Who seeing Peter and John about to go into the temple asked an alms.

4 And Peter, fastening his eyes upon him with John, said, Look on us.

5 And he gave heed unto them, expecting to receive something of them.

6 Then Peter said, Silver and gold have I none; but such as I have give I thee: In the name of Jesus Christ of Nazareth rise up and walk.

7 And he took him by the right hand, and lifted him up: and immediately his feet and ankle bones received strength.

8 And he leaping up stood, and walked, and entered with them into the temple, walking, and leaping, and praising God.

---

3:1-11 Peter and the Apostles had no money, but healed this man by the power and authority of Jesus Christ. There are many around us needing help, encouragement, and service. What could you offer that is more valuable than "silver and gold" or money?

3:2 **mother's womb**—birth
**alms**—gifts or kind deeds

9 And all the people saw him walking and praising God:

10 And they knew that it was he which sat for alms at the Beautiful gate of the temple: and they were filled with wonder and amazement at that which had happened unto him.

11 And as the lame man which was healed held Peter and John, all the people ran together unto them in the porch that is called Solomon's, greatly wondering.

### Peter Teaches About the Power of Jesus Christ

12 ¶ And when Peter saw it, he answered unto the people, Ye men of Israel, why marvel ye at this? or why look ye so earnestly on us, as though by our own power or holiness we had made this man to walk?

13 The God of Abraham, and of Isaac, and of Jacob, the God of our fathers, hath glorified his Son Jesus; whom ye delivered up, and denied him in the presence of Pilate, when he was determined to let him go.

14 But ye denied the Holy One and the Just, and desired a murderer to be granted unto you;

15 And killed the Prince of life, whom God hath raised from the dead; whereof we are witnesses.

16 And his name through faith in his name hath made this man strong, whom ye see and know: yea, the faith which is by him hath given him this perfect soundness in the presence of you all.

17 And now, brethren, I wot that through ignorance ye did it, as did also your rulers.

18 But those things, which God before had shewed by the mouth of all his prophets, that Christ should suffer, he hath so fulfilled.

### Peter Teaches About the Restoration of the Gospel

19 Repent ye therefore, and be converted, that your sins may be blotted out, when the times of refreshing shall come from the presence of the Lord;

20 And he shall send Jesus Christ, which before was preached unto you:

21 Whom the heaven must receive until the times of restitution of all things, which God hath spoken by the mouth of all his holy prophets since the world began.

22 For Moses truly said unto the fathers, A prophet shall the Lord your God raise up unto you of your brethren, like unto me; him shall ye hear in all things whatsoever he shall say unto you.

23 And it shall come to pass, that every soul, which will not hear that prophet, shall be destroyed from among the people.

24 Yea, and all the prophets from Samuel and those that follow after, as many as have spoken, have likewise foretold of these days.

---

*A man born lame was healed on Solomon's Porch.*

today people turn from the Savior to things that can kill them spiritually. How do you decide what you will keep in your life and what you will push away?

3:16 **perfect soundness**—full health and strength

3:17 **I wot that through ignorance**—I know that because of lack of knowledge

3:19 **blotted out**—wiped away

3:21 **restitution**—restoration

Referring to the fulfillment of this verse, President Harold B. Lee said: "You and I have been privileged to be born in a dispensation [period of time] known in the scriptures as the fulness of times, which is to precede the second coming of Jesus Christ" (*Stand Ye in Holy Places*, p. 71).

3:14 The people had chosen the murderer Barabbas to be released rather than Jesus Christ, who was without sin (see Luke 23:18-19).

3:14-15 These people let a murderer go free and saw to it that the "Prince of life" was killed. Sometimes

3:22 Moses spoke about a prophet who would be raised up who would be like unto him (see Deuteronomy 18:15). Moroni told Joseph Smith that this prophet is Jesus Christ (see Joseph Smith—History 1:40).

25 Ye are the children of the prophets, and of the covenant which God made with our fathers, saying unto Abraham, And in thy seed shall all the kindreds of the earth be blessed.

26 Unto you first God, having raised up his Son Jesus, sent him to bless you, in turning away every one of you from his iniquities.

# CHAPTER 4

*The righteous must be bold in their testimony of Jesus, even when opposed by the wicked. Notice what Peter and John value more than anything else.*

## PETER AND JOHN ARE ARRESTED

1 ¶ AND as they spake unto the people, the priests, and the captain of the temple, and the Sadducees, came upon them,

2 Being grieved that they taught the people, and preached through Jesus the resurrection from the dead.

3 And they laid hands on them, and put them in hold unto the next day: for it was now eventide.

4 Howbeit many of them which heard the word believed; and the number of the men was about five thousand.

5 ¶ And it came to pass on the morrow, that their rulers, and elders, and scribes,

6 And Annas the high priest, and Caiaphas, and John, and Alexander, and as many as were of the kindred of the high priest, were gathered together at Jerusalem.

7 And when they had set them in the midst, they asked, By what power, or by what name, have ye done this?

8 Then Peter, filled with the Holy Ghost, said unto them, Ye rulers of the people, and elders of Israel,

9 If we this day be examined of the good deed done to the impotent man, by what means he is made whole;

10 Be it known unto you all, and to all the people of Israel, that by the name of Jesus Christ of Nazareth, whom ye crucified, whom God raised from the dead, even by him doth this man stand here before you whole.

11 This is the stone which was set at nought of you builders, which is become the head of the corner.

12 Neither is there salvation in any other: for there is none other name under heaven given among men, whereby we must be saved.

## PETER AND JOHN DEFEND THEMSELVES BEFORE THE JEWISH LEADERS

13 Now when they saw the boldness of Peter and John, and perceived that they were unlearned and ignorant men, they marvelled; and they took knowledge of them, that they had been with Jesus.

14 And beholding the man which was healed standing with them, they could say nothing against it.

15 ¶ But when they had commanded them to go aside out of the council, they conferred among themselves,

16 Saying, What shall we do to these men? for that

---

3:25 *kindreds*—families

Those who faithfully follow the teachings of the prophets are the children of the prophets (see D&C 84:33-34). As the children of Abraham, the righteous have the responsibility to bless the whole earth. What can you do to bless other people?

3:26 *iniquities*—sins

4:1 Sadducees were religious and political leaders of the Jews (see LDS Bible Dictionary, s.v. "Sadducees," p. 767).

4:2 Why would these Jewish leaders be so grieved or upset with Peter and the Apostles for preaching about Jesus Christ and the resurrection? Why do the wicked fight the truth? (See 1 Nephi 16:2.)

4:3 *hold*—prison
*eventide*—nighttime

4:6 *kindred*—family

4:9 The "impotent man" was the man lame from birth who was healed by Peter and John (see Acts 3:1-11).

*examined of*—questioned about

4:11 The "stone" which the builders (the leaders of the Jews) thought had no value is a symbol for Jesus Christ (see Ephesians 2:20).

4:12 An angel taught King Benjamin: "There shall be no other name given nor any other way nor means whereby salvation can come unto the children of men, only in and through the name of Christ, the Lord Omnipotent" (Mosiah 3:17).

4:13 *perceived*—could see
*unlearned and ignorant*—not educated

4:15 *conferred*—talked

indeed a notable miracle hath been done by them is manifest to all them that dwell in Jerusalem; and we cannot deny it.

17 But that it spread no further among the people, let us straitly threaten them, that they speak henceforth to no man in this name.

18 And they called them, and commanded them not to speak at all nor teach in the name of Jesus.

19 But Peter and John answered and said unto them, Whether it be right in the sight of God to hearken unto you more than unto God, judge ye.

20 For we cannot but speak the things which we have seen and heard.

21 So when they had further threatened them, they let them go, finding nothing how they might punish them, because of the people: for all men glorified God for that which was done.

22 For the man was above forty years old, on whom this miracle of healing was shewed.

## PETER AND JOHN MEET WITH MEMBERS OF THE CHURCH

23 ¶ And being let go, they went to their own company, and reported all that the chief priests and elders had said unto them.

24 And when they heard that, they lifted up their voice to God with one accord, and said, Lord, thou art God, which hast made heaven, and earth, and the sea, and all that in them is:

25 Who by the mouth of thy servant David hast said, Why did the heathen rage, and the people imagine vain things?

26 The kings of the earth stood up, and the rulers were gathered together against the Lord, and against his Christ.

27 For of a truth against thy holy child Jesus, whom thou hast anointed, both Herod, and Pontius Pilate, with the Gentiles, and the people of Israel, were gathered together,

28 For to do whatsoever thy hand and thy counsel determined before to be done.

29 And now, Lord, behold their threatenings: and grant unto thy servants, that with all boldness they may speak thy word,

30 By stretching forth thine hand to heal; and that signs and wonders may be done by the name of thy holy child Jesus.

31 And when they had prayed, the place was shaken where they were assembled together; and they were all filled with the Holy Ghost, and they spake the word of God with boldness.

32 ¶ And the multitude of them that believed were of one heart and of one soul: neither said any of them that ought of the things which he possessed was his own; but they had all things common.

33 And with great power gave the apostles witness of the resurrection of the Lord Jesus: and great grace was upon them all.

34 Neither was there any among them that lacked: for as many as were possessors of lands or houses sold them, and brought the prices of the things that were sold,

35 And laid them down at the apostles' feet: and distribution was made unto every man according as he had need.

36 And Joses, who by the apostles was surnamed Barnabas, (which is, being interpreted, The son of consolation,) a Levite, and of the country of Cyprus,

37 Having land, sold it, and brought the money, and laid it at the apostles' feet.

---

4:17   **henceforth**—from now on

4:19-
20   One of the earliest lessons learned by the young Prophet Joseph Smith was that he "should not have feared man more than God" (D&C 3:7; see also Proverbs 3:5). How can you develop more trust in the Lord?

4:23   **their own company**—the leaders and members of the Church

4:31   How did the Holy Ghost help these powerful leaders of the Church? How can the Holy Ghost help you teach others the gospel of Jesus Christ?

4:32   **ought**—any

4:32-
37   Faithful members of the Church in Peter's day helped take care of one another. They obeyed the law of consecration. (See 4 Nephi 1:1-11 and D&C 42:30-39.)

4:36   **consolation**—comfort

# CHAPTER 5

*The Lord watches over and guides the leaders of his church. As you read this chapter, look for how this is true.*

## ANANIAS AND SAPPHIRA LIE TO THE LORD AND DIE

1 ¶ BUT a certain man named Ananias, with Sapphira his wife, sold a possession,

2 And kept back part of the price, his wife also being privy to it, and brought a certain part, and laid it at the apostles' feet.

3 But Peter said, Ananias, why hath Satan filled thine heart to lie to the Holy Ghost, and to keep back part of the price of the land?

4 Whiles it remained, was it not thine own? and after it was sold, was it not in thine own power? why hast thou conceived this thing in thine heart? thou hast not lied unto men, but unto God.

5 And Ananias hearing these words fell down, and gave up the ghost: and great fear came on all them that heard these things.

6 And the young men arose, wound him up, and carried him out, and buried him.

7 And it was about the space of three hours after, when his wife, not knowing what was done, came in.

8 And Peter answered unto her, Tell me whether ye sold the land for so much? And she said, Yea, for so much.

9 Then Peter said unto her, How is it that ye have agreed together to tempt the Spirit of the Lord? behold, the feet of them which have buried thy husband are at the door, and shall carry thee out.

10 Then fell she down straightway at his feet, and yielded up the ghost: and the young men came in, and found her dead, and, carrying her forth, buried her by her husband.

11 And great fear came upon all the church, and upon as many as heard these things.

## THE APOSTLES HEAL MANY PEOPLE

12 ¶ And by the hands of the apostles were many signs and wonders wrought among the people; (and they were all with one accord in Solomon's porch.

13 And of the rest durst no man join himself to them: but the people magnified them.

14 And believers were the more added to the Lord, multitudes both of men and women.)

15 Insomuch that they brought forth the sick into the streets, and laid them on beds and couches, that at the least the shadow of Peter passing by might overshadow some of them.

16 There came also a multitude out of the cities round about unto Jerusalem, bringing sick folks, and them which were vexed with unclean spirits: and they were healed every one.

## PETER AND JOHN ARE FREED FROM PRISON BY AN ANGEL

17 ¶ Then the high priest rose up, and all they that were with him, (which is the sect of the Sadducees,) and were filled with indignation,

18 And laid their hands on the apostles, and put them in the common prison.

---

5:1-11   Can a person receive undeserved blessings by lying and deceit? Why is it so important to always tell the truth?

5:2   *being privy to it*—knowing about it

5:4   A lie to leaders of the Church is like a lie to the Lord (see Alma 12:3). "Since 'the Comforter knoweth all things' (D. & C. 42:17), it follows that it is not possible to lie to the Holy Ghost and thereby gain an unearned or undeserved blessing, as Ananias and Sapphira found out to their sorrow" (Bruce R. McConkie, *Doctrinal New Testament Commentary* 3:335).

5:5   *gave up the ghost*—died

5:6   *wound him up*—wrapped him in burial cloth

5:12   *with one accord*—united or in agreement with each other

5:13   The Joseph Smith Translation changes "rest" to "rulers" (JST, Acts 5:13).

*durst*—dared

5:15   *overshadow*—fall on

5:16   *vexed*—troubled or tormented

5:17   Under the law of Moses the leading officer of the Aaronic Priesthood was called the high priest. The office was passed down through the firstborn among the family of Aaron. During New Testament times, apostate high priests were appointed by King Herod and the Romans. (See LDS Bible Dictionary, s.v. "High Priests," p. 702.)

*sect*—group
*indignation*—jealousy, anger

19 But the angel of the Lord by night opened the prison doors, and brought them forth, and said,

20 Go, stand and speak in the temple to the people all the words of this life.

## PETER AND JOHN TESTIFY OF CHRIST

21 And when they heard that, they entered into the temple early in the morning, and taught. But the high priest came, and they that were with him, and called the council together, and all the senate of the children of Israel, and sent to the prison to have them brought.

22 But when the officers came, and found them not in the prison, they returned, and told,

23 Saying, The prison truly found we shut with all safety, and the keepers standing without before the doors: but when we had opened, we found no man within.

24 Now when the high priest and the captain of the temple and the chief priests heard these things, they doubted of them whereunto this would grow.

25 Then came one and told them, saying, Behold, the men whom ye put in prison are standing in the temple, and teaching the people.

26 ¶ Then went the captain with the officers, and brought them without violence: for they feared the people, lest they should have been stoned.

27 And when they had brought them, they set them before the council: and the high priest asked them,

28 Saying, Did not we straitly command you that ye should not teach in this name? and, behold, ye have filled Jerusalem with your doctrine, and intend to bring this man's blood upon us.

29 Then Peter and the other apostles answered and said, We ought to obey God rather than men.

30 The God of our fathers raised up Jesus, whom ye slew and hanged on a tree.

31 Him hath God exalted with his right hand to be a Prince and a Saviour, for to give repentance to Israel, and forgiveness of sins.

32 And we are his witnesses of these things; and so is also the Holy Ghost, whom God hath given to them that obey him.

## GAMALIEL COUNSELS THE LEADERS OF THE JEWS

33 When they heard that, they were cut to the heart, and took counsel to slay them.

34 Then stood there up one in the council, a Pharisee, named Gamaliel, a doctor of the law, had in reputation among all the people, and commanded to put the apostles forth a little space;

35 And said unto them, Ye men of Israel, take heed to yourselves what ye intend to do as touching these men.

36 For before these days rose up Theudas, boasting himself to be somebody; to whom a number of men, about four hundred, joined themselves: who was slain; and all, as many as obeyed him, were scattered, and brought to nought.

37 After this man rose up Judas of Galilee in the days of the taxing, and drew away much people after him: he also perished; and all, even as many as obeyed him, were dispersed.

38 And now I say unto you, Refrain from these men, and let them alone: for if this counsel or this work be of men, it will come to nought:

39 But if it be of God, ye cannot overthrow it; lest haply ye be found even to fight against God.

40 And to him they agreed: and when they had called the apostles, and beaten them, they commanded that they should not speak in the name of Jesus, and let them go.

"The angel of the Lord . . . opened the prison doors."

5:28  **bring this man's blood upon us**—say that Jesus' death was our fault

5:31  **exalted**—put in the highest degree of the celestial kingdom

5:33  **cut to the heart**—enraged or furious

5:34  Gamaliel was a well-known and highly respected Jewish teacher (see LDS Bible Dictionary, s.v. "Gamaliel," p. 677).

5:36  **nought**—nothing

5:37  **dispersed**—scattered

5:38  **Refrain**—Stay away

5:39  **lest haply ye**—or else you may

## PETER AND JOHN CONTINUE TO TEACH ABOUT JESUS CHRIST

41 And they departed from the presence of the council, rejoicing that they were counted worthy to suffer shame for his name.

42 And daily in the temple, and in every house, they ceased not to teach and preach Jesus Christ.

# CHAPTER 6

*As the Church grows, the Apostles need others to help them serve. Notice the kind of people the Lord looks for to serve in his church.*

## SEVEN MEN ARE CHOSEN TO HELP THE APOSTLES

1 ¶ AND in those days, when the number of the disciples was multiplied, there arose a murmuring of the Grecians against the Hebrews, because their widows were neglected in the daily ministration.

2 Then the twelve called the multitude of the disciples unto them, and said, It is not reason that we should leave the word of God, and serve tables.

3 Wherefore, brethren, look ye out among you seven men of honest report, full of the Holy Ghost and wisdom, whom we may appoint over this business.

4 But we will give ourselves continually to prayer, and to the ministry of the word.

5 And the saying pleased the whole multitude: and they chose Stephen, a man full of faith and of the Holy Ghost, and Philip, and Prochorus, and Nicanor, and Timon, and Parmenas, and Nicolas a proselyte of Antioch:

6 Whom they set before the apostles: and when they had prayed, they laid their hands on them.

## STEPHEN PREACHES WITH POWER AND PERFORMS GREAT MIRACLES

7 And the word of God increased; and the number of the disciples multiplied in Jerusalem greatly; and a great company of the priests were obedient to the faith.

8 ¶ And Stephen, full of faith and power, did great wonders and miracles among the people.

9 Then there arose certain of the synagogue, which is called the synagogue of the Libertines, and Cyrenians, and Alexandrians, and of them of Cilicia and of Asia, disputing with Stephen.

10 And they were not able to resist the wisdom and the spirit by which he spake.

11 Then they suborned men, which said, We have heard him speak blasphemous words against Moses, and against God.

12 And they stirred up the people, and the elders, and the scribes, and came upon him, and caught him, and brought him to the council,

13 And set up false witnesses, which said, This man ceaseth not to speak blasphemous words against this holy place, and the law:

14 For we have heard him say, that this Jesus of Nazareth shall destroy this place, and shall change the customs which Moses delivered us.

15 And all that sat in the council, looking stedfastly on him, saw his face as it had been the face of an angel.

---

6:1 **murmuring**—complaining
**daily ministration**—daily gifts of food to the needy

6:1-3 The Church was getting too large for the Apostles to not only preach the gospel but also take care of all the poor. Whose responsibility is it to help needy people in the Church today?

6:3-6 Today, people are chosen in the same way to serve in the Church (see Articles of Faith 1:5).

6:4 **ministry of the word**—preaching of the gospel

6:9 **disputing**—arguing

6:11 **suborned men**—paid men to lie
**speak blasphemous words**—say evil or untrue words

6:14-15 How could men who had seen Stephen's face, "as it had been the face of an angel," continue to hate him? Do miracles and signs convert people to the truth? If miracles don't convert people to the gospel, what does?

# CHAPTER 7

*Stephen defends himself before the Jewish leaders. Look for ways in which Stephen uses the Old Testament to testify of Jesus Christ.*

## STEPHEN TELLS THE STORY OF ABRAHAM

1 ¶ THEN said the high priest, Are these things so?

2 And he said, Men, brethren, and fathers, hearken; The God of glory appeared unto our father Abraham, when he was in Mesopotamia, before he dwelt in Charran,

3 And said unto him, Get thee out of thy country, and from thy kindred, and come into the land which I shall shew thee.

4 Then came he out of the land of the Chaldaeans, and dwelt in Charran: and from thence, when his father was dead, he removed him into this land, wherein ye now dwell.

5 And he gave him none inheritance in it, no, not so much as to set his foot on: yet he promised that he would give it to him for a possession, and to his seed after him, when as yet he had no child.

6 And God spake on this wise, That his seed should sojourn in a strange land; and that they should bring them into bondage, and entreat them evil four hundred years.

7 And the nation to whom they shall be in bondage will I judge, said God: and after that shall they come forth, and serve me in this place.

8 And he gave him the covenant of circumcision: and so Abraham begat Isaac, and circumcised him the eighth day; and Isaac begat Jacob; and Jacob begat the twelve patriarchs.

## STEPHEN TELLS THE STORY OF JOSEPH WHO WAS SOLD INTO EGYPT

9 And the patriarchs, moved with envy, sold Joseph into Egypt: but God was with him,

10 And delivered him out of all his afflictions, and gave him favour and wisdom in the sight of Pharaoh king of Egypt; and he made him governor over Egypt and all his house.

11 Now there came a dearth over all the land of Egypt and Chanaan, and great affliction: and our fathers found no sustenance.

12 But when Jacob heard that there was corn in Egypt, he sent out our fathers first.

13 And at the second time Joseph was made known to his brethren; and Joseph's kindred was made known unto Pharaoh.

14 Then sent Joseph, and called his father Jacob to him, and all his kindred, threescore and fifteen souls.

15 So Jacob went down into Egypt, and died, he, and our fathers,

16 And were carried over into Sychem, and laid in the sepulchre that Abraham bought for a sum of money of the sons of Emmor the father of Sychem.

## STEPHEN TELLS THE STORY OF MOSES

17 ¶ But when the time of the promise drew nigh, which God had sworn to Abraham, the people grew and multiplied in Egypt,

18 Till another king arose, which knew not Joseph.

19 The same dealt subtilly with our kindred, and evil entreated our fathers, so that they cast out their young children, to the end they might not live.

20 In which time Moses was born, and was exceeding fair, and nourished up in his father's house three months:

---

7:2-8 How does the story of Abraham show that God watches over his children?

7:3 **kindred**—family

7:5 **none inheritance**—no land

7:6 **on this wise**—with these words
**sojourn**—live

7:8 **begat**—was the father of
**the twelve patriarchs**—the twelve sons of Jacob (whose name was changed to Israel)

7:9-16 How does the story of Joseph show that Heavenly Father blesses those who keep his commandments?

7:11 **dearth**—famine

7:14 **threescore and fifteen**—seventy-five

7:16 **sepulchre**—burial place

7:17 **sworn**—promised

7:18 **arose**—came to power

7:19 **subtilly**—in a sneaky way

*God appeared to Abraham, a righteous patriarch, and promised a land of inheritance for him and his posterity.*

21 And when he was cast out, Pharaoh's daughter took him up, and nourished him for her own son.

22 And Moses was learned in all the wisdom of the Egyptians, and was mighty in words and in deeds.

23 And when he was full forty years old, it came into his heart to visit his brethren the children of Israel.

24 And seeing one of them suffer wrong, he defended him, and avenged him that was oppressed, and smote the Egyptian:

25 For he supposed his brethren would have understood how that God by his hand would deliver them: but they understood not.

26 And the next day he shewed himself unto them as they strove, and would have set them at one again, saying, Sirs, ye are brethren; why do ye wrong one to another?

27 But he that did his neighbour wrong thrust him away, saying, Who made thee a ruler and a judge over us?

28 Wilt thou kill me, as thou diddest the Egyptian yesterday?

29 Then fled Moses at this saying, and was a stranger in the land of Madian, where he begat two sons.

30 ¶ And when forty years were expired, there appeared to him in the wilderness of mount Sina an angel of the Lord in a flame of fire in a bush.

31 When Moses saw it, he wondered at the sight: and as he drew near to behold it, the voice of the Lord came unto him,

32 Saying, I am the God of thy fathers, the God of Abraham, and the God of Isaac, and the God of Jacob. Then Moses trembled, and durst not behold.

33 Then said the Lord to him, Put off thy shoes from thy feet: for the place where thou standest is holy ground.

34 I have seen, I have seen the affliction of my people which is in Egypt, and I have heard their groaning, and am come down to deliver them. And now come, I will send thee into Egypt.

35 This Moses whom they refused, saying, Who made thee a ruler and a judge? the same did God send to be a ruler and a deliverer by the hand of the angel which appeared to him in the bush.

36 He brought them out, after that he had shewed wonders and signs in the land of Egypt, and in the Red sea, and in the wilderness forty years.

## STEPHEN TELLS THE STORY OF ISRAEL'S WICKEDNESS

37 This is that Moses, which said unto the children of Israel, A prophet shall the Lord your God raise up unto you of your brethren, like unto me; him shall ye hear.

38 This is he, that was in the church in the wilderness with the angel which spake to him in the mount Sina, and with our fathers: who received the lively oracles to give unto us:

39 To whom our fathers would not obey, but thrust him from them, and in their hearts turned back again into Egypt,

40 Saying unto Aaron, Make us gods to go before us: for as for this Moses, which brought us out of the land of Egypt, we wot not what is become of him.

41 And they made a calf in those days, and offered sacrifice unto the idol, and rejoiced in the works of their own hands.

42 ¶ Then God turned, and gave them up to worship the host of heaven; as it is written in the book of the prophets, O ye house of Israel, have ye offered to me slain beasts and sacrifices by the space of forty years in the wilderness?

43 Yea, ye took up the tabernacle of Moloch, and the star of your god Remphan, figures which ye made to worship them: and I will carry you away beyond Babylon.

---

7:24 **smote**—killed

7:26 **strove**—fought

7:30 **were expired**—passed

7:32 **durst**—dared

7:37 Moroni told Joseph Smith that the prophet spoken of in this verse was Jesus Christ (see Joseph Smith—History 1:40).

7:38 **lively oracles**—true revelations of God

7:39-43 What are some false gods people worship today?

7:40 **wot**—know

7:41 **idol**—false god

7:43 Moloch and Remphan were false gods.

*Moses counsels with Aaron near Mount Sinai.*

## ISRAEL BUILT TABERNACLES AND TEMPLES TO WORSHIP GOD

44 Our fathers had the tabernacle of witness in the wilderness, as he had appointed, speaking unto Moses, that he should make it according to the fashion that he had seen.

45 Which also our fathers that came after brought in with Jesus into the possession of the Gentiles, whom God drave out before the face of our fathers, unto the days of David;

46 Who found favour before God, and desired to find a tabernacle for the God of Jacob.

47 But Solomon built him an house.

48 Howbeit the most High dwelleth not in temples made with hands; as saith the prophet,

49 Heaven is my throne, and earth is my footstool: what house will ye build me? saith the Lord: or what is the place of my rest?

50 Hath not my hand made all these things?

## STEPHEN CONDEMNS THE JEWS FOR KILLING JESUS

51 ¶ Ye stiffnecked and uncircumcised in heart and ears, ye do always resist the Holy Ghost: as your fathers did, so do ye.

---

7:44    The "tabernacle of witness" was a temple Moses was commanded to build that could be set up and taken down as the children of Israel carried it through the wilderness.

**according to the fashion**—in the way

7:45    The name *Jesus* here is the same as the Hebrew name *Joshua,* referring to the Old Testament prophet.

7:51    **stiffnecked**—stubborn
**uncircumcised in heart and ears**—not obedient

*Persecution scattered Church members abroad throughout the regions of Judea and Samaria.*

52 Which of the prophets have not your fathers persecuted? and they have slain them which shewed before of the coming of the Just One; of whom ye have been now the betrayers and murderers:

53 Who have received the law by the disposition of angels, and have not kept it.

### STEPHEN SEES THE FATHER AND THE SON AND IS STONED TO DEATH

54 ¶ When they heard these things, they were cut to the heart, and they gnashed on him with their teeth.

55 But he, being full of the Holy Ghost, looked up stedfastly into heaven, and saw the glory of God, and Jesus standing on the right hand of God,

56 And said, Behold, I see the heavens opened, and the Son of man standing on the right hand of God.

57 Then they cried out with a loud voice, and stopped their ears, and ran upon him with one accord,

58 And cast him out of the city, and stoned him: and the witnesses laid down their clothes at a young man's feet, whose name was Saul.

59 And they stoned Stephen, calling upon God, and saying, Lord Jesus, receive my spirit.

60 And he kneeled down, and cried with a loud voice, Lord, lay not this sin to their charge. And when he had said this, he fell asleep.

## CHAPTER 8

*Philip, as one of the seven called by the Apostles to help with the work of the Lord (see Acts 6:5), performs great missionary labors. See how missionaries such as Philip help the Church grow during times of much trouble and persecution.*

### SAUL PERSECUTES MEMBERS OF THE CHURCH

1 ¶ AND Saul was consenting unto his death. And at that time there was a great persecution against the church which was at Jerusalem; and they were all scattered abroad throughout the regions of Judaea and Samaria, except the apostles.

2 And devout men carried Stephen to his burial, and made great lamentation over him.

---

7:52   *Just One*—Jesus Christ

7:53   *disposition*—direction

7:54   *cut to the heart*—furious
*gnashed on him with their teeth*—ground their teeth at him

7:55   *stedfastly*—without turning away

7:55-56   Some other religions teach that Heavenly Father, Jesus Christ, and the Holy Ghost are all the same person. What do you see in these verses that shows that they are three separate beings? (See also D&C 130:22-23.)

7:60   When Stephen forgave those who stoned him, he was doing what Jesus had taught (see Matthew 5:44).

8:1   *was consenting unto his death*—allowed or approved Stephen's death

8:2   *made great lamentation over him*—showed much sadness at his death

3 As for Saul, he made havock of the church, entering into every house, and haling men and women committed them to prison.

4 ¶ Therefore they that were scattered abroad went every where preaching the word.

## Philip Preaches the Gospel of Jesus Christ in Samaria

5 Then Philip went down to the city of Samaria, and preached Christ unto them.

6 And the people with one accord gave heed unto those things which Philip spake, hearing and seeing the miracles which he did.

7 For unclean spirits, crying with loud voice, came out of many that were possessed with them: and many taken with palsies, and that were lame, were healed.

8 And there was great joy in that city.

9 But there was a certain man, called Simon, which beforetime in the same city used sorcery, and bewitched the people of Samaria, giving out that himself was some great one:

10 To whom they all gave heed, from the least to the greatest, saying, This man is the great power of God.

11 And to him they had regard, because that of long time he had bewitched them with sorceries.

12 But when they believed Philip preaching the things concerning the kingdom of God, and the name of Jesus Christ, they were baptized, both men and women.

13 Then Simon himself believed also: and when he was baptized, he continued with Philip, and wondered, beholding the miracles and signs which were done.

## The Converted Samaritans Are Given the Gift of the Holy Ghost

14 ¶ Now when the apostles which were at Jerusalem heard that Samaria had received the word of God, they sent unto them Peter and John:

15 Who, when they were come down, prayed for them, that they might receive the Holy Ghost:

16 (For as yet he was fallen upon none of them: only they were baptized in the name of the Lord Jesus.)

17 Then laid they their hands on them, and they received the Holy Ghost.

## Simon Tries to Buy the Priesthood

18 And when Simon saw that through laying on of the apostles' hands the Holy Ghost was given, he offered them money,

19 Saying, Give me also this power, that on whomsoever I lay hands, he may receive the Holy Ghost.

---

8:3 **havock**—ruin
**haling**—dragging, carrying

8:6 **gave heed unto**—listened to and believed

8:7 **taken with palsies**—that were physically disabled

*Samaria was the ancient capital of the northern kingdom of Israel. Philip taught the gospel of Jesus Christ in the city of Samaria.*

8:9 Sorcery and witchcraft come from Satan and are forbidden by the Lord (see Deuteronomy 18:10-12; Isaiah 8:19-20).

**bewitched**—tricked or deceived with evil powers

8:11 **regard**—respect

8:12 People can become converted and change their lives when they hear the word of God (see Alma 31:5). Have you shared the gospel with anyone lately?

8:14-17 In these verses it is recorded that the gospel of Jesus Christ was given to the Samaritans (see also verse 5). The Apostles were told to take the gospel first to the Jews, then to the Samaritans, and then to people in all the earth (see Acts 1:8).

8:17 Have you received the gift of the Holy Ghost? How has or can this wonderful gift help you?

8:18-24 Simon wanted to buy the power of the priesthood. Of course the power of God cannot be bought; it can be attained only through faith in Jesus Christ, repentance, and worthiness. Why do you feel the priesthood is given only to men who are faithful, worthy, and spiritually prepared?

20 But Peter said unto him, Thy money perish with thee, because thou hast thought that the gift of God may be purchased with money.

21 Thou hast neither part nor lot in this matter: for thy heart is not right in the sight of God.

22 Repent therefore of this thy wickedness, and pray God, if perhaps the thought of thine heart may be forgiven thee.

23 For I perceive that thou art in the gall of bitterness, and in the bond of iniquity.

24 Then answered Simon, and said, Pray ye to the Lord for me, that none of these things which ye have spoken come upon me.

25 And they, when they had testified and preached the word of the Lord, returned to Jerusalem, and preached the gospel in many villages of the Samaritans.

## PHILIP TEACHES AND BAPTIZES A MAN FROM ETHIOPIA

26 ¶ And the angel of the Lord spake unto Philip, saying, Arise, and go toward the south unto the way that goeth down from Jerusalem unto Gaza, which is desert.

27 And he arose and went: and, behold, a man of Ethiopia, an eunuch of great authority under Candace queen of the Ethiopians, who had the charge of all her treasure, and had come to Jerusalem for to worship,

28 Was returning, and sitting in his chariot read Esaias the prophet.

29 Then the Spirit said unto Philip, Go near, and join thyself to this chariot.

30 And Philip ran thither to him, and heard him read the prophet Esaias, and said, Understandest thou what thou readest?

31 And he said, How can I, except some man should guide me? And he desired Philip that he would come up and sit with him.

32 The place of the scripture which he read was this, He was led as a sheep to the slaughter; and like a lamb dumb before his shearer, so opened he not his mouth:

33 In his humiliation his judgment was taken away: and who shall declare his generation? for his life is taken from the earth.

34 And the eunuch answered Philip, and said, I pray thee, of whom speaketh the prophet this? of himself, or of some other man?

35 Then Philip opened his mouth, and began at the same scripture, and preached unto him Jesus.

36 And as they went on their way, they came unto a certain water: and the eunuch said, See, here is water; what doth hinder me to be baptized?

37 And Philip said, If thou believest with all thine heart, thou mayest. And he answered and said, I believe that Jesus Christ is the Son of God.

38 And he commanded the chariot to stand still: and they went down both into the water, both Philip and the eunuch; and he baptized him.

39 And when they were come up out of the water, the Spirit of the Lord caught away Philip, that the eunuch saw him no more: and he went on his way rejoicing.

40 But Philip was found at Azotus: and passing through he preached in all the cities, till he came to Caesarea.

## CHAPTER 9

*Saul sees a vision and is taught, converted, and baptized. Watch for how Saul changes after his conversion to the gospel of Jesus Christ.*

---

8:20 *perish*—die

8:23 *in the gall of bitterness*—feeling terrible misery for your sins
*the bond of iniquity*—spiritual captivity to sin

8:27 This faithful man was a high ranking officer of Queen Candace of the Nubians (Ethiopians). He is called a *eunuch,* which may have had reference to his being a servant to the queen.

8:28 *Esaias* is the Greek name for *Isaiah.*

8:30-31 Some scriptures are difficult to understand without an inspired teacher. Who has helped you understand the scriptures better?

8:32 The Ethiopian was reading a prophecy about Jesus from Isaiah 53.

*to the slaughter*—to be killed
*dumb*—silent

8:36 *hinder*—stop

8:37 When we are baptized we promise to follow Jesus Christ and to serve our fellowmen (see Mosiah 18:8-10).

*Philip teaches an Ethiopian official the gospel of Jesus Christ from the scriptures.*

## JESUS APPEARS TO SAUL

1 ¶ AND Saul, yet breathing out threatenings and slaughter against the disciples of the Lord, went unto the high priest,

2 And desired of him letters to Damascus to the synagogues, that if he found any of this way, whether they were men or women, he might bring them bound unto Jerusalem.

3 And as he journeyed, he came near Damascus: and suddenly there shined round about him a light from heaven:

4 And he fell to the earth, and heard a voice saying unto him, Saul, Saul, why persecutest thou me?

5 And he said, Who art thou, Lord? And the Lord said, I am Jesus whom thou persecutest: it is hard for thee to kick against the pricks.

6 And he trembling and astonished said, Lord, what

---

9:1-40 Consider the blessings that came to Saul, Aeneas, and Tabitha as they were helped by the Church and its leaders. How have you been blessed because of the Church and its leaders?

9:2 **bound**—tied up like prisoners

9:5 Pricks, or goads, were pointed sticks used to urge oxen forward when plowing fields. Sometimes the oxen would kick when they were jabbed. (See LDS Bible Dictionary, s.v. "Goads," p. 681.)

9:6 Of Saul's question, "What wilt thou have me to do?" President Ezra Taft Benson said, "There is no greater question that you can ask in this world" ("Think on Christ," p. 11).

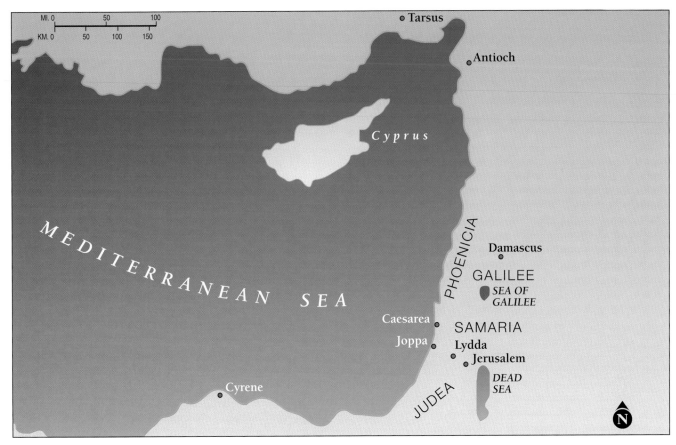

*Some important locations in the early Church*

wilt thou have me to do? And the Lord said unto him, Arise, and go into the city, and it shall be told thee what thou must do.

7 And the men which journeyed with him stood speechless, hearing a voice, but seeing no man.

8 And Saul arose from the earth; and when his eyes were opened, he saw no man: but they led him by the hand, and brought him into Damascus.

9 And he was three days without sight, and neither did eat nor drink.

### ANANIAS BLESSES AND BAPTIZES SAUL

10 ¶ And there was a certain disciple at Damascus, named Ananias; and to him said the Lord in a vision, Ananias. And he said, Behold, I am here, Lord.

11 And the Lord said unto him, Arise, and go into the street which is called Straight, and enquire in the house of Judas for one called Saul, of Tarsus: for, behold, he prayeth,

12 And hath seen in a vision a man named Ananias coming in, and putting his hand on him, that he might receive his sight.

13 Then Ananias answered, Lord, I have heard by many of this man, how much evil he hath done to thy saints at Jerusalem:

14 And here he hath authority from the chief priests to bind all that call on thy name.

15 But the Lord said unto him, Go thy way: for he is a chosen vessel unto me, to bear my name before the Gentiles, and kings, and the children of Israel:

---

9:7    The Joseph Smith Translation changes this verse to read, "And they who were journeying with him saw indeed the light, and were afraid; but they heard not the voice of him who spake to him" (JST, Acts 9:7).

9:10-18  Why do you think Saul was sent to Ananias? How did the Lord prepare Ananias to receive Saul? Why was it necessary for Saul to be baptized? (See John 3:3-5.)

9:11   *enquire*—ask

9:15   *chosen vessel unto me*—man chosen to be a servant of the Lord

*Gentiles* is a word that means "nations." It refers to those not of the family of Israel or who do not believe in the God of Israel. (See LDS Bible Dictionary, s.v. "Gentile," pp. 679-80.)

16 For I will shew him how great things he must suffer for my name's sake.

17 And Ananias went his way, and entered into the house; and putting his hands on him said, Brother Saul, the Lord, even Jesus, that appeared unto thee in the way as thou camest, hath sent me, that thou mightest receive thy sight, and be filled with the Holy Ghost.

18 And immediately there fell from his eyes as it had been scales: and he received sight forthwith, and arose, and was baptized.

## SAUL PREACHES ABOUT CHRIST

19 And when he had received meat, he was strengthened. Then was Saul certain days with the disciples which were at Damascus.

20 And straightway he preached Christ in the synagogues, that he is the Son of God.

21 But all that heard him were amazed, and said; Is not this he that destroyed them which called on this name in Jerusalem, and came hither for that intent, that he might bring them bound unto the chief priests?

22 But Saul increased the more in strength, and confounded the Jews which dwelt at Damascus, proving that this is very Christ.

## SAUL ESCAPES TO JERUSALEM

23 ¶ And after that many days were fulfilled, the Jews took counsel to kill him:

24 But their laying await was known of Saul. And they watched the gates day and night to kill him.

25 Then the disciples took him by night, and let him down by the wall in a basket.

26 And when Saul was come to Jerusalem, he assayed to join himself to the disciples: but they were all afraid of him, and believed not that he was a disciple.

27 But Barnabas took him, and brought him to the apostles, and declared unto them how he had seen the Lord in the way, and that he had spoken to him, and how he had preached boldly at Damascus in the name of Jesus.

28 And he was with them coming in and going out at Jerusalem.

29 And he spake boldly in the name of the Lord Jesus, and disputed against the Grecians: but they went about to slay him.

30 Which when the brethren knew, they brought him down to Caesarea, and sent him forth to Tarsus.

31 Then had the churches rest throughout all Judaea and Galilee and Samaria, and were edified; and walking in the fear of the Lord, and in the comfort of the Holy Ghost, were multiplied.

## PETER PERFORMS MIRACLES

32 ¶ And it came to pass, as Peter passed throughout all quarters, he came down also to the saints which dwelt at Lydda.

33 And there he found a certain man named AEneas,

---

9:18    *forthwith*—immediately

9:19-   Saul immediately began testifying of Jesus
22      Christ in the synagogues while he stayed at Damascus (see vv. 19-20). He grew stronger and was soon able to confound the Jews at Damascus (see v. 22). Saul later wrote that he also spent time in Arabia and returned to Damascus (see Galatians 1:16-17). This was before he went down to Jerusalem (see Acts 9:26).

9:20    *straightway*—immediately

9:21    *hither*—here

9:22    *confounded the Jews*—made it so they could not think of anything to say to stop him

9:26    *assayed*—tried

9:27    To learn more about Barnabas, see Acts 4:36-37.

9:29    *disputed*—argued

        People who practiced Greek customs and manners were called "Grecians" (see LDS Bible Dictionary, s.v. "Grecians," p. 697).

9:31    *edified*—made stronger spiritually

9:33    *kept his bed*—been in bed

*Many cities in Saul's day had walls built around them. The only way in and out of these cities was through the guarded gates.*

*Peter raises Dorcas from the dead and presents her to her friends.*

which had kept his bed eight years, and was sick of the palsy.

34 And Peter said unto him, AEneas, Jesus Christ maketh thee whole: arise, and make thy bed. And he arose immediately.

35 And all that dwelt at Lydda and Saron saw him, and turned to the Lord.

36 ¶ Now there was at Joppa a certain disciple named Tabitha, which by interpretation is called Dorcas: this woman was full of good works and almsdeeds which she did.

37 And it came to pass in those days, that she was sick, and died: whom when they had washed, they laid her in an upper chamber.

38 And forasmuch as Lydda was nigh to Joppa, and

the disciples had heard that Peter was there, they sent unto him two men, desiring him that he would not delay to come to them.

39 Then Peter arose and went with them. When he was come, they brought him into the upper chamber: and all the widows stood by him weeping, and shewing the coats and garments which Dorcas made, while she was with them.

40 But Peter put them all forth, and kneeled down, and prayed; and turning him to the body said, Tabitha, arise. And she opened her eyes: and when she saw Peter, she sat up.

41 And he gave her his hand, and lifted her up, and when he had called the saints and widows, presented her alive.

9:36   **almsdeeds**—charitable deeds                9:40   **forth**—out of the room

42 And it was known throughout all Joppa; and many believed in the Lord.

43 And it came to pass, that he tarried many days in Joppa with one Simon a tanner.

# CHAPTER 10

*During the time of Jesus Christ the gospel was taken only to the Jews. In Acts 10 the Lord reveals that it is time to take the gospel to all the people of the world. Look for how the Lord guides Peter, the leader of the Church.*

## CORNELIUS HAS A VISION

1 ¶ THERE was a certain man in Caesarea called Cornelius, a centurion of the band called the Italian band,

2 A devout man, and one that feared God with all his house, which gave much alms to the people, and prayed to God alway.

3 He saw in a vision evidently about the ninth hour of the day an angel of God coming in to him, and saying unto him, Cornelius.

4 And when he looked on him, he was afraid, and said, What is it, Lord? And he said unto him, Thy prayers and thine alms are come up for a memorial before God.

5 And now send men to Joppa, and call for one Simon, whose surname is Peter:

6 He lodgeth with one Simon a tanner, whose house is by the sea side: he shall tell thee what thou oughtest to do.

7 And when the angel which spake unto Cornelius was departed, he called two of his household servants, and a devout soldier of them that waited on him continually;

8 And when he had declared all these things unto them, he sent them to Joppa.

## PETER HAS A VISION

9 ¶ On the morrow, as they went on their journey, and drew nigh unto the city, Peter went up upon the housetop to pray about the sixth hour:

10 And he became very hungry, and would have eaten: but while they made ready, he fell into a trance,

11 And saw heaven opened, and a certain vessel descending unto him, as it had been a great sheet knit at the four corners, and let down to the earth:

12 Wherein were all manner of fourfooted beasts of the earth, and wild beasts, and creeping things, and fowls of the air.

13 And there came a voice to him, Rise, Peter; kill, and eat.

14 But Peter said, Not so, Lord; for I have never eaten any thing that is common or unclean.

15 And the voice spake unto him again the second time, What God hath cleansed, that call not thou common.

16 This was done thrice: and the vessel was received up again into heaven.

---

10:1 A "centurion" was a Roman military officer who commanded one hundred men (see LDS Bible Dictionary, s.v. "Centurion," p. 632).

10:2 *devout*—religious
*feared*—respected and loved
*alms*—gifts or service

Cornelius was a good, giving, and faithful man before his vision and his visit with Peter. Many good people today have not yet had the opportunity to hear and understand the gospel. How can you help find these good people and help prepare them to receive the gospel?

10:6 *lodgeth*—stays

10:10 *fell into a trance*—had a vision

10:14 The Lord revealed to Moses that some animals were "common" or "unclean" and should not be eaten (see Leviticus 11:4-8). Some of the animals Peter saw in the vision were unclean animals.

10:16 *thrice*—three times

*Modern-day Jaffa Harbor, the site of Joppa, an ancient seaport used by the prophet Jonah and also the place where Peter saw a vision commanding him to begin missionary work among the Gentiles*

17 Now while Peter doubted in himself what this vision which he had seen should mean, behold, the men which were sent from Cornelius had made enquiry for Simon's house, and stood before the gate,

18 And called, and asked whether Simon, which was surnamed Peter, were lodged there.

## PETER GOES TO CORNELIUS

19 ¶ While Peter thought on the vision, the Spirit said unto him, Behold, three men seek thee.

20 Arise therefore, and get thee down, and go with them, doubting nothing: for I have sent them.

21 Then Peter went down to the men which were sent unto him from Cornelius; and said, Behold, I am he whom ye seek: what is the cause wherefore ye are come?

22 And they said, Cornelius the centurion, a just man, and one that feareth God, and of good report among all the nation of the Jews, was warned from God by an holy angel to send for thee into his house, and to hear words of thee.

23 Then called he them in, and lodged them. And on the morrow Peter went away with them, and certain brethren from Joppa accompanied him.

24 And the morrow after they entered into Caesarea. And Cornelius waited for them, and had called together his kinsmen and near friends.

25 And as Peter was coming in, Cornelius met him, and fell down at his feet, and worshipped him.

26 But Peter took him up, saying, Stand up; I myself also am a man.

27 And as he talked with him, he went in, and found many that were come together.

28 And he said unto them, Ye know how that it is an unlawful thing for a man that is a Jew to keep company, or come unto one of another nation; but God hath shewed me that I should not call any man common or unclean.

29 Therefore came I unto you without gainsaying, as soon as I was sent for: I ask therefore for what intent ye have sent for me?

30 And Cornelius said, Four days ago I was fasting until this hour; and at the ninth hour I prayed in my house, and, behold, a man stood before me in bright clothing,

31 And said, Cornelius, thy prayer is heard, and thine alms are had in remembrance in the sight of God.

32 Send therefore to Joppa, and call hither Simon, whose surname is Peter; he is lodged in the house of one Simon a tanner by the sea side: who, when he cometh, shall speak unto thee.

33 Immediately therefore I sent to thee; and thou hast well done that thou art come. Now therefore are we all here present before God, to hear all things that are commanded thee of God.

## PETER PREACHES THE GOSPEL OF JESUS CHRIST TO CORNELIUS AND OTHER GENTILES

34 ¶ Then Peter opened his mouth, and said, Of a truth I perceive that God is no respecter of persons:

35 But in every nation he that feareth him, and worketh righteousness, is accepted with him.

36 The word which God sent unto the children of Israel, preaching peace by Jesus Christ: (he is Lord of all:)

37 That word, I say, ye know, which was published

10:17 *made enquiry for*—asked about

10:24 *kinsmen*—family

10:29 *gainsaying*—complaining
*intent*—purpose

10:34 God loves and accepts all people. But "he that is righteous is favored of God" (1 Nephi 17:35).

*Peter resided many days by the seaside at Joppa (Jaffa) in the house of Simon the tanner. Peter received his great vision of missionary work while "upon the housetop."*

throughout all Judaea, and began from Galilee, after the baptism which John preached;

38 How God anointed Jesus of Nazareth with the Holy Ghost and with power: who went about doing good, and healing all that were oppressed of the devil; for God was with him.

39 And we are witnesses of all things which he did both in the land of the Jews, and in Jerusalem; whom they slew and hanged on a tree:

40 Him God raised up the third day, and shewed him openly;

41 Not to all the people, but unto witnesses chosen before of God, even to us, who did eat and drink with him after he rose from the dead.

42 And he commanded us to preach unto the people, and to testify that it is he which was ordained of God to be the Judge of quick and dead.

43 To him give all the prophets witness, that through his name whosoever believeth in him shall receive remission of sins.

### THE GENTILES ARE BAPTIZED AND RECEIVE THE GIFT OF THE HOLY GHOST

44 ¶ While Peter yet spake these words, the Holy Ghost fell on all them which heard the word.

45 And they of the circumcision which believed were astonished, as many as came with Peter, because that on the Gentiles also was poured out the gift of the Holy Ghost.

46 For they heard them speak with tongues, and magnify God. Then answered Peter,

47 Can any man forbid water, that these should not be baptized, which have received the Holy Ghost as well as we?

48 And he commanded them to be baptized in the name of the Lord. Then prayed they him to tarry certain days.

## CHAPTER 11

*The Apostles help in taking the gospel of Jesus Christ to all people. Notice how the gospel continues to spread beyond the Jews of Judea and into the rest of the Roman world.*

### PETER TELLS THE APOSTLES HOW THE GENTILES RECEIVED THE HOLY GHOST

1 ¶ AND the apostles and brethren that were in Judaea heard that the Gentiles had also received the word of God.

2 And when Peter was come up to Jerusalem, they that were of the circumcision contended with him,

3 Saying, Thou wentest in to men uncircumcised, and didst eat with them.

4 But Peter rehearsed the matter from the beginning, and expounded it by order unto them, saying,

5 I was in the city of Joppa praying: and in a trance I saw a vision, A certain vessel descend, as it had been

---

10:39-43 Peter, as an Apostle, was a "special witness" of Jesus Christ (see D&C 107:23). What are some things Peter said that testify to you that Jesus is the Christ?

10:42 *quick*—living

10:43 *remission*—forgiveness

10:44-45 What did the Gentiles receive that let Peter know God also wanted them to have the gospel? How do you feel when the Holy Ghost is with you?

10:44-48 The Prophet Joseph Smith explained: "Cornelius received the Holy Ghost before he was baptized, which was the convincing power of God unto him of the truth of the Gospel, but he could not receive the gift of the Holy Ghost until after he was baptized. Had he not taken this sign or ordinance upon him, the Holy Ghost which convinced him of the truth of God, would have left him." (*The Teachings of Joseph Smith,* p. 286.)

10:45 Circumcision was first revealed to Abraham. It was an ordinance for boys who were eight days old to show they were God's covenant children. The Joseph Smith Translation indicates that it was also to remind the Lord's people that baptism was not necessary until the age of eight (see JST, Genesis 17:11-12). In Paul's writings circumcision came to represent the Jews and the law of Moses.

*they of the circumcision which believed*—the Jews who believed the gospel but also believed in the necessity of circumcision

10:48 *tarry*—stay

11:2-4 Circumcision became a part of the law of Moses (see John 7:22). When some Jews joined the Church of Jesus Christ they thought that circumcision should still be necessary for all males who joined the Church. The Gentiles were considered unclean because they were uncircumcised.

11:4 *rehearsed*—told
*expounded*—explained

a great sheet, let down from heaven by four corners; and it came even to me:

6 Upon the which when I had fastened mine eyes, I considered, and saw fourfooted beasts of the earth, and wild beasts, and creeping things, and fowls of the air.

7 And I heard a voice saying unto me, Arise, Peter; slay and eat.

8 But I said, Not so, Lord: for nothing common or unclean hath at any time entered into my mouth.

9 But the voice answered me again from heaven, What God hath cleansed, that call not thou common.

10 And this was done three times: and all were drawn up again into heaven.

11 And, behold, immediately there were three men already come unto the house where I was, sent from Caesarea unto me.

12 And the Spirit bade me go with them, nothing doubting. Moreover these six brethren accompanied me, and we entered into the man's house:

13 And he shewed us how he had seen an angel in his house, which stood and said unto him, Send men to Joppa, and call for Simon, whose surname is Peter;

14 Who shall tell thee words, whereby thou and all thy house shall be saved.

15 And as I began to speak, the Holy Ghost fell on them, as on us at the beginning.

16 Then remembered I the word of the Lord, how that he said, John indeed baptized with water; but ye shall be baptized with the Holy Ghost.

17 Forasmuch then as God gave them the like gift as he did unto us, who believed on the Lord Jesus Christ; what was I, that I could withstand God?

18 When they heard these things, they held their peace, and glorified God, saying, Then hath God also to the Gentiles granted repentance unto life.

## BARNABAS AND SAUL PREACH THE GOSPEL OF JESUS CHRIST IN ANTIOCH

19 ¶ Now they which were scattered abroad upon the persecution that arose about Stephen travelled as far as Phenice, and Cyprus, and Antioch, preaching the word to none but unto the Jews only.

20 And some of them were men of Cyprus and Cyrene, which, when they were come to Antioch, spake unto the Grecians, preaching the Lord Jesus.

21 And the hand of the Lord was with them: and a great number believed, and turned unto the Lord.

22 Then tidings of these things came unto the ears of the church which was in Jerusalem: and they sent forth Barnabas, that he should go as far as Antioch.

23 Who, when he came, and had seen the grace of God, was glad, and exhorted them all, that with purpose of heart they would cleave unto the Lord.

24 For he was a good man, and full of the Holy Ghost and of faith: and much people was added unto the Lord.

25 Then departed Barnabas to Tarsus, for to seek Saul:

26 And when he had found him, he brought him unto Antioch. And it came to pass, that a whole year they assembled themselves with the church, and taught much people. And the disciples were called Christians first in Antioch.

## FOOD IS SENT FROM THE ANTIOCH SAINTS TO THE JERUSALEM SAINTS

27 ¶ And in these days came prophets from Jerusalem unto Antioch.

28 And there stood up one of them named Agabus, and signified by the Spirit that there should be great dearth throughout all the world: which came to pass in the days of Claudius Caesar.

---

11:17　*withstand*—stand against or oppose

11:20　"Grecians" were Greek-speaking Jews from countries outside of the land of Israel. They were often called Hellenists. (See Acts 6:1; 9:29.) However, in this verse the word *Grecians* means something different: "Grecians in Acts 11:20 should be rendered Greeks to convey the proper thought, meaning persons of Greek lineage" (LDS Bible Dictionary, s.v. "Grecians," p. 697).

11:22　*tidings*—news

11:23　*cleave*—hold

11:26　In the Book of Mormon, we read that during the days of Captain Moroni, "all those who were true believers in Christ took upon them, gladly, the name of Christ, or Christians" (Alma 46:15).

11:28　*signified*—made known
*dearth*—famine

29 Then the disciples, every man according to his ability, determined to send relief unto the brethren which dwelt in Judaea:

30 Which also they did, and sent it to the elders by the hands of Barnabas and Saul.

# CHAPTER 12

*Herod tried to cause trouble for the Church, but it kept growing in spite of him. As you read this chapter, look for the sacrifices and suffering of the Saints during this time.*

## HEROD KILLS JAMES AND IMPRISONS PETER

1 ¶ NOW about that time Herod the king stretched forth his hands to vex certain of the church.

2 And he killed James the brother of John with the sword.

3 And because he saw it pleased the Jews, he proceeded further to take Peter also. (Then were the days of unleavened bread.)

4 And when he had apprehended him, he put him in prison, and delivered him to four quaternions of soldiers to keep him; intending after Easter to bring him forth to the people.

5 ¶ Peter therefore was kept in prison: but prayer was made without ceasing of the church unto God for him.

## PETER ESCAPES FROM PRISON

6 And when Herod would have brought him forth, the same night Peter was sleeping between two soldiers, bound with two chains: and the keepers before the door kept the prison.

7 And, behold, the angel of the Lord came upon him, and a light shined in the prison: and he smote Peter on the side, and raised him up, saying, Arise up quickly. And his chains fell off from his hands.

8 And the angel said unto him, Gird thyself, and bind on thy sandals. And so he did. And he saith unto him, Cast thy garment about thee, and follow me.

9 And he went out, and followed him; and wist not that it was true which was done by the angel; but thought he saw a vision.

10 When they were past the first and the second ward, they came unto the iron gate that leadeth unto the city; which opened to them of his own accord: and they went out, and passed on through one street; and forthwith the angel departed from him.

11 And when Peter was come to himself, he said, Now I know of a surety, that the Lord hath sent his angel, and hath delivered me out of the hand of Herod, and from all the expectation of the people of the Jews.

12 And when he had considered the thing, he came to the house of Mary the mother of John, whose surname was Mark; where many were gathered together praying.

13 And as Peter knocked at the door of the gate, a damsel came to hearken, named Rhoda.

14 And when she knew Peter's voice, she opened not the gate for gladness, but ran in, and told how Peter stood before the gate.

---

11:29 *relief*—help, food

11:29-30 What do you learn in these verses about how the Antioch Christians felt about the Jewish Christians? How do you feel about members of the Church who live in other parts of the world? Why?

12:1 Herod Agrippa I was the grandson of Herod the Great, who killed the babies at the time of Jesus' birth (see Matthew 2:16; see also LDS Bible Dictionary, s.v. "Herod," p. 701).

*vex*—trouble

12:2 This James is the brother of John (see Matthew 4:21-22).

12:2-12 James was killed by Herod, but Peter escaped. Why do you think the Lord allows the righteous to suffer? (See 2 Corinthians 4:17; Hebrews 12:6-7; Alma 14:10-13.)

12:3 The Feast of Unleavened Bread took place immediately after the Feast of the Passover, and the two feasts were often considered as one. The Feast of Unleavened Bread commemorated the exodus of Israel out of Egypt. (See Exodus 12 and Leviticus 23:5-6.)

12:4 *apprehended*—arrested
*four quaternions*—four squads (each squad consisting of four men for a total of sixteen soldiers)
*intending*—planning

12:6 *keepers*—guards

12:8 *Gird thyself*—Fasten your clothes with your belt
*Cast thy garment about thee*—Put on your cloak

12:9 *wist*—knew

12:10 *ward*—guard
*of his own accord*—by itself
*forthwith*—immediately

12:13 *damsel*—girl

15 And they said unto her, Thou art mad. But she constantly affirmed that it was even so. Then said they, It is his angel.

16 But Peter continued knocking: and when they had opened the door, and saw him, they were astonished.

17 But he, beckoning unto them with the hand to hold their peace, declared unto them how the Lord had brought him out of the prison. And he said, Go shew these things unto James, and to the brethren. And he departed, and went into another place.

18 Now as soon as it was day, there was no small stir among the soldiers, what was become of Peter.

19 And when Herod had sought for him, and found him not, he examined the keepers, and commanded that they should be put to death. And he went down from Judaea to Caesarea, and there abode.

## Wicked King Herod Dies

20 ¶ And Herod was highly displeased with them of Tyre and Sidon: but they came with one accord to him, and, having made Blastus the king's chamberlain their friend, desired peace; because their country was nourished by the king's country.

21 And upon a set day Herod, arrayed in royal apparel, sat upon his throne, and made an oration unto them.

22 And the people gave a shout, saying, It is the voice of a god, and not of a man.

23 And immediately the angel of the Lord smote him, because he gave not God the glory: and he was eaten of worms, and gave up the ghost.

24 But the word of God grew and multiplied.

25 And Barnabas and Saul returned from Jerusalem, when they had fulfilled their ministry, and took with them John, whose surname was Mark.

## CHAPTER 13

*Acts 13–14 is the account of the first of Paul's missionary journeys. Notice what Paul tells the Jews that should have convinced them that Jesus was their promised Messiah.*

### Saul and Barnabas Are Called and Set Apart as Missionaries

1 ¶ NOW there were in the church that was at Antioch certain prophets and teachers; as Barnabas, and Simeon that was called Niger, and Lucius of Cyrene, and Manaen, which had been brought up with Herod the tetrarch, and Saul.

2 As they ministered to the Lord, and fasted, the Holy Ghost said, Separate me Barnabas and Saul for the work whereunto I have called them.

3 And when they had fasted and prayed, and laid their hands on them, they sent them away.

4 ¶ So they, being sent forth by the Holy Ghost, departed unto Seleucia; and from thence they sailed to Cyprus.

5 And when they were at Salamis, they preached the word of God in the synagogues of the Jews: and they had also John to their minister.

---

12:15  *affirmed*—testified

12:17  *beckoning*—motioning
**hold their peace**—be quiet

This James is the brother of Jesus and the author of the book of James (see LDS Bible Dictionary, s.v. "James," p. 709).

12:19  *abode*—stayed

12:20  *with one accord*—all together
**chamberlain**—personal servant

12:20-23  Compare these verses with Acts 12:5-11. What do you learn from these two passages about the power of God? What does this teach you about trusting in and being faithful to the Lord?

12:21  *arrayed in royal apparel*—dressed in king's clothing
**oration**—speech

12:23  *smote*—struck

13:2-4  What happened to Saul and Barnabas that shows the hand of the Lord in their call to serve a mission? In what ways is this similar to how missionaries are sent out today?

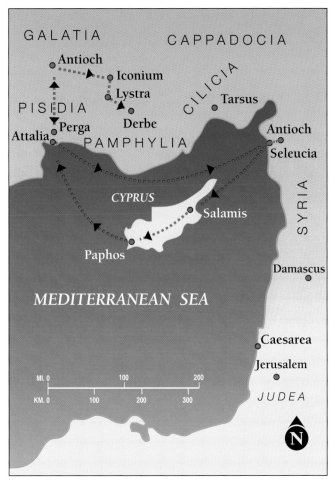

*Paul's first missionary journey*

## PAUL AND BARNABAS BLESS A GOVERNMENT LEADER AND CURSE A SORCERER

6 And when they had gone through the isle unto Paphos, they found a certain sorcerer, a false prophet, a Jew, whose name was Bar-jesus:

7 Which was with the deputy of the country, Sergius Paulus, a prudent man; who called for Barnabas and Saul, and desired to hear the word of God.

8 But Elymas the sorcerer (for so is his name by interpretation) withstood them, seeking to turn away the deputy from the faith.

9 Then Saul, (who also is called Paul,) filled with the Holy Ghost, set his eyes on him,

10 And said, O full of all subtilty and all mischief, thou child of the devil, thou enemy of all righteousness, wilt thou not cease to pervert the right ways of the Lord?

11 And now, behold, the hand of the Lord is upon thee, and thou shalt be blind, not seeing the sun for a season. And immediately there fell on him a mist and a darkness; and he went about seeking some to lead him by the hand.

12 Then the deputy, when he saw what was done, believed, being astonished at the doctrine of the Lord.

13 Now when Paul and his company loosed from Paphos, they came to Perga in Pamphylia: and John departing from them returned to Jerusalem.

## PAUL PREACHES THE GOSPEL OF CHRIST TO PEOPLE IN A JEWISH SYNAGOGUE

14 ¶ But when they departed from Perga, they came to Antioch in Pisidia, and went into the synagogue on the sabbath day, and sat down.

15 And after the reading of the law and the prophets the rulers of the synagogue sent unto them, saying, Ye men and brethren, if ye have any word of exhortation for the people, say on.

16 Then Paul stood up, and beckoning with his hand said, Men of Israel, and ye that fear God, give audience.

---

13:6 **sorcerer**—magician who claimed to foretell events

13:7 **deputy**—government leader
**prudent**—wise

13:9 Saul may have been named after Israel's first earthly king (see 1 Samuel 9:15-17). But Saul was also a Roman citizen, and like many Romans he had more than one name. Beginning with this verse, Luke (the author of the book of Acts) starts to refer to Saul as *Paul,* a Latin name that means "small one." The exact reason for the shift in use of names is not made clear, though it has been suggested that the change would have made it easier for Paul to teach the gospel in the Roman world.

13:9-11 How does knowing that Paul was "filled with the Holy Ghost" (verse 9) when he cursed the sorcerer help you to understand why he did it?

13:10 **subtilty**—deceit
**pervert**—turn people from

13:14- What truths do you find in Paul's sermon to
41 the Jews that help you believe more surely that Jesus Christ is the Savior?

13:15 **exhortation**—advice

13:16 **give audience**—listen

17 The God of this people of Israel chose our fathers, and exalted the people when they dwelt as strangers in the land of Egypt, and with an high arm brought he them out of it.

18 And about the time of forty years suffered he their manners in the wilderness.

19 And when he had destroyed seven nations in the land of Chanaan, he divided their land to them by lot.

20 And after that he gave unto them judges about the space of four hundred and fifty years, until Samuel the prophet.

21 And afterward they desired a king: and God gave unto them Saul the son of Cis, a man of the tribe of Benjamin, by the space of forty years.

22 And when he had removed him, he raised up unto them David to be their king; to whom also he gave testimony, and said, I have found David the son of Jesse, a man after mine own heart, which shall fulfil all my will.

23 Of this man's seed hath God according to his promise raised unto Israel a Saviour, Jesus:

24 When John had first preached before his coming the baptism of repentance to all the people of Israel.

25 And as John fulfilled his course, he said, Whom think ye that I am? I am not he. But, behold, there cometh one after me, whose shoes of his feet I am not worthy to loose.

26 Men and brethren, children of the stock of Abraham, and whosoever among you feareth God, to you is the word of this salvation sent.

27 For they that dwell at Jerusalem, and their rulers, because they knew him not, nor yet the voices of the prophets which are read every sabbath day, they have fulfilled them in condemning him.

28 And though they found no cause of death in him, yet desired they Pilate that he should be slain.

29 And when they had fulfilled all that was written of him, they took him down from the tree, and laid him in a sepulchre.

30 But God raised him from the dead:

31 And he was seen many days of them which came up with him from Galilee to Jerusalem, who are his witnesses unto the people.

32 And we declare unto you glad tidings, how that the promise which was made unto the fathers,

33 God hath fulfilled the same unto us their children, in that he hath raised up Jesus again; as it is also written in the second psalm, Thou art my Son, this day have I begotten thee.

34 And as concerning that he raised him up from the dead, now no more to return to corruption, he said on this wise, I will give you the sure mercies of David.

35 Wherefore he saith also in another psalm, Thou shalt not suffer thine Holy One to see corruption.

36 For David, after he had served his own generation by the will of God, fell on sleep, and was laid unto his fathers, and saw corruption:

37 But he, whom God raised again, saw no corruption.

38 Be it known unto you therefore, men and brethren, that through this man is preached unto you the forgiveness of sins:

39 And by him all that believe are justified from all things, from which ye could not be justified by the law of Moses.

40 Beware therefore, lest that come upon you, which is spoken of in the prophets;

41 Behold, ye despisers, and wonder, and perish: for I work a work in your days, a work which ye shall in no wise believe, though a man declare it unto you.

---

13:17-31  Much like Stephen's testimony in Acts 7, Paul taught the Jews in Antioch about their history as God's chosen people. From this chosen people God promised to raise up a Savior. Paul testified that Jesus, whom they had crucified, was that Savior.

13:25  *course*—mission or priesthood calling

13:26  *stock*—family

13:29  *sepulchre*—burial place, tomb

13:32  The message of "glad tidings" refers to the truth that God has kept his promise and sent his Son to save his children from sin and death through the atonement and resurrection of Jesus Christ (see Mosiah 3:1-12).

13:34  *corruption*—death and decay

13:39  *justified from all things*—freed from all sins

13:41  *despisers*—people who hate

## WICKED PEOPLE DRIVE PAUL AND BARNABAS OUT OF ANTIOCH

42 ¶ And when the Jews were gone out of the synagogue, the Gentiles besought that these words might be preached to them the next sabbath.

43 Now when the congregation was broken up, many of the Jews and religious proselytes followed Paul and Barnabas: who, speaking to them, persuaded them to continue in the grace of God.

44 And the next sabbath day came almost the whole city together to hear the word of God.

45 But when the Jews saw the multitudes, they were filled with envy, and spake against those things which were spoken by Paul, contradicting and blaspheming.

46 Then Paul and Barnabas waxed bold, and said, It was necessary that the word of God should first have been spoken to you: but seeing ye put it from you, and judge yourselves unworthy of everlasting life, lo, we turn to the Gentiles.

47 For so hath the Lord commanded us, saying, I have set thee to be a light of the Gentiles, that thou shouldest be for salvation unto the ends of the earth.

48 And when the Gentiles heard this, they were glad, and glorified the word of the Lord: and as many as were ordained to eternal life believed.

49 And the word of the Lord was published throughout all the region.

50 But the Jews stirred up the devout and honourable women, and the chief men of the city, and raised persecution against Paul and Barnabas, and expelled them out of their coasts.

51 But they shook off the dust of their feet against them, and came unto Iconium.

52 And the disciples were filled with joy, and with the Holy Ghost.

## CHAPTER 14

*Part of Heavenly Father's plan of happiness is enduring trials that come our way. Notice the trials Paul and Barnabas face as missionaries and how they overcome them.*

### PAUL AND BARNABAS ARE PERSECUTED AS THEY CONTINUE THEIR MISSION

1 ¶ AND it came to pass in Iconium, that they went both together into the synagogue of the Jews, and so spake, that a great multitude both of the Jews and also of the Greeks believed.

2 But the unbelieving Jews stirred up the Gentiles, and made their minds evil affected against the brethren.

3 Long time therefore abode they speaking boldly in the Lord, which gave testimony unto the word of his grace, and granted signs and wonders to be done by their hands.

4 But the multitude of the city was divided: and part held with the Jews, and part with the apostles.

5 And when there was an assault made both of the Gentiles, and also of the Jews with their rulers, to use them despitefully, and to stone them,

6 They were ware of it, and fled unto Lystra and Derbe, cities of Lycaonia, and unto the region that lieth round about:

7 And there they preached the gospel.

### PEOPLE TRY TO WORSHIP PAUL AND BARNABAS AS MERCURIUS AND JUPITER

8 ¶ And there sat a certain man at Lystra, impotent in his feet, being a cripple from his mother's womb, who never had walked:

---

13:43 "Religious proselytes" were Gentiles who had converted to Judaism (see LDS Bible Dictionary, s.v. "Proselytes," p. 754).

13:48 The Joseph Smith Translation changes this verse to say that we must believe first before we can have eternal life (see JST, Acts 13:48).

13:50 **devout**—faithful and obedient
**expelled**—forced

13:52 What made the disciples of Jesus Christ happy and joyful? If the Holy Ghost brings joy (see Galatians 5:22), what should we do to have the Holy Ghost with us each day?

14:2 **evil affected**—think evil thoughts

14:3 Grace is divine help given by God through the atonement of Jesus Christ. It provides us with the power needed to repent, keep the commandments, and become like God. (See LDS Bible Dictionary, s.v. "Grace," p. 697.)

14:5 **use them despitefully**—treat them shamefully

14:8 **impotent**—helpless

9 The same heard Paul speak: who stedfastly beholding him, and perceiving that he had faith to be healed,

10 Said with a loud voice, Stand upright on thy feet. And he leaped and walked.

11 And when the people saw what Paul had done, they lifted up their voices, saying in the speech of Lycaonia, The gods are come down to us in the likeness of men.

12 And they called Barnabas, Jupiter; and Paul, Mercurius, because he was the chief speaker.

13 Then the priest of Jupiter, which was before their city, brought oxen and garlands unto the gates, and would have done sacrifice with the people.

14 Which when the apostles, Barnabas and Paul, heard of, they rent their clothes, and ran in among the people, crying out,

15 And saying, Sirs, why do ye these things? We also are men of like passions with you, and preach unto you that ye should turn from these vanities unto the living God, which made heaven, and earth, and the sea, and all things that are therein:

16 Who in times past suffered all nations to walk in their own ways.

17 Nevertheless he left not himself without witness, in that he did good, and gave us rain from heaven, and fruitful seasons, filling our hearts with food and gladness.

18 And with these sayings scarce restrained they the people, that they had not done sacrifice unto them.

## PAUL IS STONED AND BROUGHT BACK TO LIFE

19 ¶ And there came thither certain Jews from Antioch and Iconium, who persuaded the people, and, having stoned Paul, drew him out of the city, supposing he had been dead.

20 Howbeit, as the disciples stood round about him, he rose up, and came into the city: and the next day he departed with Barnabas to Derbe.

## THE MISSIONARIES STRENGTHEN THE BRANCHES OF THE CHURCH AND REPORT THEIR MISSION

21 And when they had preached the gospel to that city, and had taught many, they returned again to Lystra, and to Iconium, and Antioch,

22 Confirming the souls of the disciples, and exhorting them to continue in the faith, and that we must through much tribulation enter into the kingdom of God.

23 And when they had ordained them elders in every church, and had prayed with fasting, they commended them to the Lord, on whom they believed.

24 And after they had passed throughout Pisidia, they came to Pamphylia.

25 And when they had preached the word in Perga, they went down into Attalia:

26 And thence sailed to Antioch, from whence they had been recommended to the grace of God for the work which they fulfilled.

27 And when they were come, and had gathered the church together, they rehearsed all that God had done with them, and how he had opened the door of faith unto the Gentiles.

28 And there they abode long time with the disciples.

## CHAPTER 15

*At Antioch the Jewish Christians argue that the Gentiles who believe in Jesus Christ must also live the*

---

14:9 **stedfastly beholding him**—looking only at him

14:12 Jupiter and Mercurius were false Roman gods (see LDS Bible Dictionary, s.v. "Jupiter," p. 720, and "Mercurius," p. 731).

14:13 **garlands**—wreaths made of flowers

14:14 **rent**—tore

14:15 **of like passions with**—with the same feelings as
**vanities**—useless beliefs

14:15-17 What do you find in these verses that helps you worship God?

14:16 **suffered**—allowed

14:18 **scarce restrained**—hardly stopped

14:19 Stoning was a legal method of execution during this time (see Deuteronomy 17:5; LDS Bible Dictionary, s.v. "Punishments," p. 756).

**drew**—dragged

14:22 **Confirming**—Strengthening
**exhorting**—urging, encouraging
**tribulation**—trials and hardships

14:22-23 What did these priesthood leaders do to strengthen people they had just baptized into the Church? How would you feel if you were one of these new believers?

14:27 **rehearsed**—went over or reviewed

*In approximately A.D. 49–50, a council of the Church leaders was held in Jerusalem to confer concerning the increased conversion of Gentiles.*

*law of Moses to be saved. Look for how this disagreement is settled.*

## THE QUESTION OF CIRCUMCISION IS TAKEN TO THE APOSTLES IN JERUSALEM

1 ¶ AND certain men which came down from Judaea taught the brethren, and said, Except ye be circumcised after the manner of Moses, ye cannot be saved.

2 When therefore Paul and Barnabas had no small dissension and disputation with them, they determined that Paul and Barnabas, and certain other of them, should go up to Jerusalem unto the apostles and elders about this question.

3 And being brought on their way by the church, they passed through Phenice and Samaria, declaring the conversion of the Gentiles: and they caused great joy unto all the brethren.

4 And when they were come to Jerusalem, they were received of the church, and of the apostles and elders, and they declared all things that God had done with them.

5 But there rose up certain of the sect of the Pharisees which believed, saying, That it was needful to circumcise them, and to command them to keep the law of Moses.

## APOSTLES DECIDE THE ISSUE AT THE JERUSALEM COUNCIL

6 ¶ And the apostles and elders came together for to consider of this matter.

7 And when there had been much disputing, Peter

---

15:1-5 Circumcision was a sign of the covenant the Lord made with Abraham and was continued as a part of the law of Moses (see Genesis 17:9-11 and Glossary, s.v. "circumcision"). Jesus told the Nephites, "The law in me is fulfilled, for I have come to fulfil the law; therefore it hath an end" (3 Nephi 15:5).

15:2 ***dissension and disputation***—disagreement and argument

rose up, and said unto them, Men and brethren, ye know how that a good while ago God made choice among us, that the Gentiles by my mouth should hear the word of the gospel, and believe.

8 And God, which knoweth the hearts, bare them witness, giving them the Holy Ghost, even as he did unto us;

9 And put no difference between us and them, purifying their hearts by faith.

10 Now therefore why tempt ye God, to put a yoke upon the neck of the disciples, which neither our fathers nor we were able to bear?

11 But we believe that through the grace of the Lord Jesus Christ we shall be saved, even as they.

12 Then all the multitude kept silence, and gave audience to Barnabas and Paul, declaring what miracles and wonders God had wrought among the Gentiles by them.

13 And after they had held their peace, James answered, saying, Men and brethren, hearken unto me:

14 Simeon hath declared how God at the first did visit the Gentiles, to take out of them a people for his name.

15 And to this agree the words of the prophets; as it is written,

16 After this I will return, and will build again the tabernacle of David, which is fallen down; and I will build again the ruins thereof, and I will set it up:

17 That the residue of men might seek after the Lord, and all the Gentiles, upon whom my name is called, saith the Lord, who doeth all these things.

18 Known unto God are all his works from the beginning of the world.

19 Wherefore my sentence is, that we trouble not them, which from among the Gentiles are turned to God:

20 But that we write unto them, that they abstain from pollutions of idols, and from fornication, and from things strangled, and from blood.

21 For Moses of old time hath in every city them that preach him, being read in the synagogues every sabbath day.

### A LETTER IS SENT TO CHURCH MEMBERS ANNOUNCING THE APOSTLES' DECISION

22 ¶ Then pleased it the apostles and elders, with the whole church, to send chosen men of their own company to Antioch with Paul and Barnabas; namely, Judas surnamed Barsabas, and Silas, chief men among the brethren:

23 And they wrote letters by them after this manner; The apostles and elders and brethren send greeting unto the brethren which are of the Gentiles in Antioch and Syria and Cilicia:

24 Forasmuch as we have heard, that certain which went out from us have troubled you with words, subverting your souls, saying, Ye must be circumcised, and keep the law: to whom we gave no such commandment:

25 It seemed good unto us, being assembled with one accord, to send chosen men unto you with our beloved Barnabas and Paul,

26 Men that have hazarded their lives for the name of our Lord Jesus Christ.

27 We have sent therefore Judas and Silas, who shall also tell you the same things by mouth.

---

15:8-10 Peter had received a revelation from God that opened the door to preaching the gospel to all people, not just the Jews (see Acts 10:34). He asked that the leaders not require Gentile converts to live the law of Moses, which the Jews themselves had a hard time living. He testified that it is Jesus Christ who saves us, not the law of Moses.

15:13 This James was the brother of Jesus Christ and the author of the book of James (see Galatians 1:19 and James 1:1).

15:14 *Simeon* was another name for *Peter.*

15:19 *sentence*—opinion

15:19-20 James suggested that Gentile converts not be required to live the law of Moses. They should "abstain from pollutions," meaning stay away from feasts of idol worshipers. "Things strangled, and from blood" refers to God's commandment, long before the law of Moses, not to eat the blood of animals (see Genesis 9:4).

15:24 *subverting*—troubling

15:25 The Apostles all agreed "with one accord" in their decision. Being united in this way is important, for, as President Gordon B. Hinckley said, "herein lies the great strength of this kingdom" (*Teachings of Gordon B. Hinckley*, p. 671).

15:26 *hazarded*—risked

28 For it seemed good to the Holy Ghost, and to us, to lay upon you no greater burden than these necessary things;

29 That ye abstain from meats offered to idols, and from blood, and from things strangled, and from fornication: from which if ye keep yourselves, ye shall do well. Fare ye well.

30 So when they were dismissed, they came to Antioch: and when they had gathered the multitude together, they delivered the epistle:

31 Which when they had read, they rejoiced for the consolation.

32 And Judas and Silas, being prophets also themselves, exhorted the brethren with many words, and confirmed them.

33 And after they had tarried there a space, they were let go in peace from the brethren unto the apostles.

34 Notwithstanding it pleased Silas to abide there still.

35 Paul also and Barnabas continued in Antioch, teaching and preaching the word of the Lord, with many others also.

## PAUL CHOOSES SILAS AS HIS MISSIONARY COMPANION

36 ¶ And some days after Paul said unto Barnabas, Let us go again and visit our brethren in every city where we have preached the word of the Lord, and see how they do.

37 And Barnabas determined to take with them John, whose surname was Mark.

38 But Paul thought not good to take him with them, who departed from them from Pamphylia, and went not with them to the work.

39 And the contention was so sharp between them, that they departed asunder one from the other: and so Barnabas took Mark, and sailed unto Cyprus;

40 And Paul chose Silas, and departed, being recommended by the brethren unto the grace of God.

41 And he went through Syria and Cilicia, confirming the churches.

## CHAPTER 16

*This chapter continues Paul's second missionary journey. Look for examples of Paul's love of God even when he is persecuted for it.*

### TIMOTHY JOINS PAUL AND SILAS IN PREACHING THE GOSPEL

1 ¶ THEN came he to Derbe and Lystra: and, behold, a certain disciple was there, named Timotheus, the son of a certain woman, which was a Jewess, and believed; but his father was a Greek:

2 Which was well reported of by the brethren that were at Lystra and Iconium.

3 Him would Paul have to go forth with him; and took and circumcised him because of the Jews which were in those quarters: for they knew all that his father was a Greek.

4 And as they went through the cities, they delivered them the decrees for to keep, that were ordained of the apostles and elders which were at Jerusalem.

5 And so were the churches established in the faith, and increased in number daily.

---

15:28 The decision the Apostles came to "seemed good to the Holy Ghost." In other words, this decision came by revelation. The Lord said, "I will tell you in your mind and in your heart, by the Holy Ghost. . . . This is the spirit of revelation." (D&C 8:2-3.)

What does it mean to you to know that our apostles and prophets receive the same spirit of revelation to lead the Church today? Have you ever felt the Spirit speak to your mind and heart to help you with your questions or problems?

15:30 **epistle**—letter

15:31 **consolation**—encouraging message

15:32 **exhorted**—encouraged
**confirmed**—strengthened

15:39 **contention**—disagreement
**departed asunder**—went separate ways

15:40 Paul and Silas were "recommended by the brethren," meaning the apostles and prophets, to go on a mission. Who calls missionaries to serve today? How would you feel if the Lord, through his prophet, recommended you to go on a mission?

16:1 **Timotheus**—Timothy

16:3 Why did Paul circumcise Timothy? Circumcision was no longer required for salvation (see for Acts 15:1-5, and Glossary, s.v. "Circumcision"). Timothy was circumcised because the Jews would not listen to someone who had not been circumcised (see Isaiah 52:1; Ezekiel 44:9).

16:4 In other words, the missionaries gave the Church members the decisions of the Church leaders in Jerusalem so that the people could obey them.

6 ¶ Now when they had gone throughout Phrygia and the region of Galatia, and were forbidden of the Holy Ghost to preach the word in Asia,

7 After they were come to Mysia, they assayed to go into Bithynia: but the Spirit suffered them not.

8 And they passing by Mysia came down to Troas.

## IN A VISION, PAUL IS CALLED TO MACEDONIA

9 And a vision appeared to Paul in the night; There stood a man of Macedonia, and prayed him, saying, Come over into Macedonia, and help us.

10 And after he had seen the vision, immediately we endeavoured to go into Macedonia, assuredly gathering that the Lord had called us for to preach the gospel unto them.

11 Therefore loosing from Troas, we came with a straight course to Samothracia, and the next day to Neapolis;

12 And from thence to Philippi, which is the chief city of that part of Macedonia, and a colony: and we were in that city abiding certain days.

13 And on the sabbath we went out of the city by a river side, where prayer was wont to be made; and we sat down, and spake unto the women which resorted thither.

14 And a certain woman named Lydia, a seller of purple, of the city of Thyatira, which worshipped God, heard us: whose heart the Lord opened, that she attended unto the things which were spoken of Paul.

15 And when she was baptized, and her household, she besought us, saying, If ye have judged me to be faithful to the Lord, come into my house, and abide there. And she constrained us.

## PAUL AND SILAS ARE THROWN INTO PRISON

16 ¶ And it came to pass, as we went to prayer, a certain damsel possessed with a spirit of divination met us, which brought her masters much gain by soothsaying:

17 The same followed Paul and us, and cried, saying, These men are the servants of the most high God, which shew unto us the way of salvation.

18 And this did she many days. But Paul, being grieved, turned and said to the spirit, I command thee in the name of Jesus Christ to come out of her. And he came out the same hour.

19 And when her masters saw that the hope of their gains was gone, they caught Paul and Silas, and drew them into the marketplace unto the rulers,

20 And brought them to the magistrates, saying, These men, being Jews, do exceedingly trouble our city,

21 And teach customs, which are not lawful for us to receive, neither to observe, being Romans.

22 And the multitude rose up together against them: and the magistrates rent off their clothes, and commanded to beat them.

23 And when they had laid many stripes upon them, they cast them into prison, charging the jailor to keep them safely:

24 Who, having received such a charge, thrust them into the inner prison, and made their feet fast in the stocks.

25 ¶ And at midnight Paul and Silas prayed, and sang praises unto God: and the prisoners heard them.

26 And suddenly there was a great earthquake, so that the foundations of the prison were shaken: and

---

16:7   *assayed*—tried
       ***suffered them not***—would not let them

16:10  *endeavored*—tried
       ***assuredly gathering***—knowing

16:11  *loosing*—sailing

16:13  *resorted thither*—gathered there

16:14  Purple dye and purple cloth were very valuable in the ancient world.

16:15  *she constrained us*—she made us

16:16  *soothsaying*—fortune-telling

16:17-  Paul stopped the evil spirit from telling the
18     truth about these missionaries. If Paul accepted the evil spirit's testimony the people would think that the girl's evil powers were just the same as Paul's God-given powers.

16:20  *magistrates*—judges

16:22  *rent*—tore

16:23  *laid many stripes upon them*—whipped them many times

*Wooden stocks held a prisoner's feet and/or hands.*

16:25  Why did Paul and Silas pray and sing "praises unto God" after being beaten and thrown into prison? How has saying your prayers and singing hymns helped you in the midst of trials?

immediately all the doors were opened, and every one's bands were loosed.

27 And the keeper of the prison awaking out of his sleep, and seeing the prison doors open, he drew out his sword, and would have killed himself, supposing that the prisoners had been fled.

28 But Paul cried with a loud voice, saying, Do thyself no harm: for we are all here.

29 Then he called for a light, and sprang in, and came trembling, and fell down before Paul and Silas,

30 And brought them out, and said, Sirs, what must I do to be saved?

31 And they said, Believe on the Lord Jesus Christ, and thou shalt be saved, and thy house.

32 And they spake unto him the word of the Lord, and to all that were in his house.

33 And he took them the same hour of the night, and washed their stripes; and was baptized, he and all his, straightway.

34 And when he had brought them into his house, he set meat before them, and rejoiced, believing in God with all his house.

35 ¶ And when it was day, the magistrates sent the serjeants, saying, Let those men go.

36 And the keeper of the prison told this saying to Paul, The magistrates have sent to let you go: now therefore depart, and go in peace.

37 But Paul said unto them, They have beaten us openly uncondemned, being Romans, and have cast us into prison; and now do they thrust us out privily? nay verily; but let them come themselves and fetch us out.

38 And the serjeants told these words unto the magistrates: and they feared, when they heard that they were Romans.

39 And they came and besought them, and brought them out, and desired them to depart out of the city.

40 And they went out of the prison, and entered into the house of Lydia: and when they had seen the brethren, they comforted them, and departed.

## CHAPTER 17

*Paul and Silas do missionary work in many cities. Many people listen and are converted to the gospel, but others reject their teachings. See how the people of Thessalonica, Berea, and Athens receive the message of the true and living God.*

### PAUL AND SILAS PREACH IN THESSALONICA

1 ¶ NOW when they had passed through Amphipolis and Apollonia, they came to Thessalonica, where was a synagogue of the Jews:

2 And Paul, as his manner was, went in unto them, and three sabbath days reasoned with them out of the scriptures,

3 Opening and alleging, that Christ must needs have suffered, and risen again from the dead; and that this Jesus, whom I preach unto you, is Christ.

4 And some of them believed, and consorted with Paul and Silas; and of the devout Greeks a great multitude, and of the chief women not a few.

5 But the Jews which believed not, moved with envy, took unto them certain lewd fellows of the baser sort, and gathered a company, and set all the city on an uproar, and assaulted the house of Jason, and sought to bring them out to the people.

6 And when they found them not, they drew Jason and certain brethren unto the rulers of the city, crying, These that have turned the world upside down are come hither also;

---

16:35 **serjeants**—officers

16:37 **uncondemned**—without a proper trial
**privily**—secretly

16:37-39 Paul insisted "not only that he and Silas be accorded their rights as Roman citizens, but also that hereafter missionaries and members of the Church be treated in a manner befitting their high station as ambassadors and representatives of Christ" (Sidney B. Sperry, *Paul's Life and Letters*, p. 79).

17:2 When missionaries use scriptures to teach others about God, it has a powerful spiritual effect (see Alma 31:5; D&C 42:12-14).

17:3 **alleging**—claiming

17:4 Those who believed "consorted," meaning joined or united, with Paul and Silas. Many were converted in Thessalonica and remained faithful (see 1 Thessalonians 1:1-7).

17:5 **lewd fellows of the baser sort**—wicked men

These converts were assaulted or persecuted. How hard is it to stay faithful to the Church when others hurt you or make fun of your beliefs?

17:6 **drew**—brought

17:6-9 The believers were brought to the leaders of the city and mistreated. Remember that Jesus promised great blessings to those who suffer persecution for his sake (see Matthew 5:10-12).

7 Whom Jason hath received: and these all do contrary to the decrees of Caesar, saying that there is another king, one Jesus.

8 And they troubled the people and the rulers of the city, when they heard these things.

9 And when they had taken security of Jason, and of the other, they let them go.

## PAUL AND SILAS GO TO BEREA

10 ¶ And the brethren immediately sent away Paul and Silas by night unto Berea: who coming thither went into the synagogue of the Jews.

11 These were more noble than those in Thessalonica, in that they received the word with all readiness of mind, and searched the scriptures daily, whether those things were so.

12 Therefore many of them believed; also of honourable women which were Greeks, and of men, not a few.

13 But when the Jews of Thessalonica had knowledge that the word of God was preached of Paul at Berea, they came thither also, and stirred up the people.

14 And then immediately the brethren sent away Paul to go as it were to the sea: but Silas and Timotheus abode there still.

15 And they that conducted Paul brought him unto Athens: and receiving a commandment unto Silas and Timotheus for to come to him with all speed, they departed.

## PAUL PREACHES ON MARS' HILL IN ATHENS

16 ¶ Now while Paul waited for them at Athens, his spirit was stirred in him, when he saw the city wholly given to idolatry.

17 Therefore disputed he in the synagogue with the Jews, and with the devout persons, and in the market daily with them that met with him.

18 Then certain philosophers of the Epicureans, and of the Stoicks, encountered him. And some said, What will this babbler say? other some, He seemeth to be a setter forth of strange gods: because he preached unto them Jesus, and the resurrection.

19 And they took him, and brought him unto Areopagus, saying, May we know what this new doctrine, whereof thou speakest, is?

20 For thou bringest certain strange things to our ears: we would know therefore what these things mean.

21 (For all the Athenians and strangers which were there spent their time in nothing else, but either to tell, or to hear some new thing.)

22 ¶ Then Paul stood in the midst of Mars' hill, and said, Ye men of Athens, I perceive that in all things ye are too superstitious.

---

17:10 **thither**—there

17:11-12 What blessings did daily scripture study bring to the people of Berea? What blessings come to you when you study each day?

17:14 **abode**—stayed

17:16 **wholly**—fully or completely

Idolatry is a worship of objects, often from nature but sometimes man-made (see LDS Bible Dictionary, s.v. "Idol," p. 706). "Idolatry is among the most serious of sins. There are unfortunately millions today who prostrate [bow] themselves before the images of gold and silver and wood and stone and clay." (Spencer W. Kimball, *Teachings of Spencer W. Kimball*, p. 243.)

17:17-21 Paul taught about Jesus daily. However, the people in Athens, who were very educated, had never heard of Jesus before, so Paul's teachings seemed strange to them. They finally took Paul to Areopagus, often called Mars' Hill, a rocky height in the city of Athens, where he taught the truth concerning the Godhead.

17:22 **too superstitious**—very religious

*Mars' Hill, where Paul testified of Heavenly Father*

23 For as I passed by, and beheld your devotions, I found an altar with this inscription, TO THE UNKNOWN GOD. Whom therefore ye ignorantly worship, him declare I unto you.

24 God that made the world and all things therein, seeing that he is Lord of heaven and earth, dwelleth not in temples made with hands;

25 Neither is worshipped with men's hands, as though he needed any thing, seeing he giveth to all life, and breath, and all things;

26 And hath made of one blood all nations of men for to dwell on all the face of the earth, and hath determined the times before appointed, and the bounds of their habitation;

27 That they should seek the Lord, if haply they might feel after him, and find him, though he be not far from every one of us:

28 For in him we live, and move, and have our being; as certain also of your own poets have said, For we are also his offspring.

29 Forasmuch then as we are the offspring of God, we ought not to think that the Godhead is like unto gold, or silver, or stone, graven by art and man's device.

30 And the times of this ignorance God winked at; but now commandeth all men every where to repent:

31 Because he hath appointed a day, in the which he will judge the world in righteousness by that man whom he hath ordained; whereof he hath given assurance unto all men, in that he hath raised him from the dead.

32 ¶ And when they heard of the resurrection of the dead, some mocked: and others said, We will hear thee again of this matter.

33 So Paul departed from among them.

34 Howbeit certain men clave unto him, and believed: among the which was Dionysius the Areopagite, and a woman named Damaris, and others with them.

## CHAPTER 18

*After being rejected by the Jews, Paul begins preaching to the Gentiles. Watch for reasons why Paul continues to serve so many missions in the midst of such great persecution.*

### PAUL PREACHES THE GOSPEL AT CORINTH

1 ¶ AFTER these things Paul departed from Athens, and came to Corinth;

2 And found a certain Jew named Aquila, born in Pontus, lately come from Italy, with his wife Priscilla; (because that Claudius had commanded all Jews to depart from Rome:) and came unto them.

---

17:23    Paul disagreed that God was "unknown." He knew that God has a body of flesh and bones and is our Heavenly Father (see D&C 130:22; Joseph Smith—History 1:17). He tried to help the people of Athens overcome their ignorance, or lack of understanding, by sharing his testimony with them (see verses 24-31).

17:24-31    What important and sacred messages do you learn about God from these verses? How is this message similar to the words in the hymn "I Am a Child of God"? (See *Hymns,* no. 301.)

17:26    When Paul said God "hath determined the times before appointed" he was speaking of the premortal life (see Abraham 3:22-23).

17:28    ***offspring***—children

17:30    ***winked at***—overlooked

17:32-34    How did the people of Athens feel about Paul's testimony? How do you feel about it?

18:1    Corinth was the capital of Achaia (Greece). It had a reputation as a city of great wickedness. (See LDS Bible Dictionary, s.v. "Corinth," p. 650.)

18:2    Aquila, a Jew, and his wife, Priscilla, moved from Rome to Corinth, where they met Paul. It appears that their home was the center of Church activity (1 Corinthians 16:19).

*While preaching on Mars' Hill, Paul told the people, "We ought not to think that the Godhead is like unto gold, or silver, or stone, graven by art and man's device." Within view of Mars' Hill was the Acropolis (shown here), a group of several temples built for the worship of different idols (false gods).*

3 And because he was of the same craft, he abode with them, and wrought: for by their occupation they were tentmakers.

4 And he reasoned in the synagogue every sabbath, and persuaded the Jews and the Greeks.

5 And when Silas and Timotheus were come from Macedonia, Paul was pressed in the spirit, and testified to the Jews that Jesus was Christ.

6 And when they opposed themselves, and blasphemed, he shook his raiment, and said unto them, Your blood be upon your own heads; I am clean: from henceforth I will go unto the Gentiles.

7 ¶ And he departed thence, and entered into a certain man's house, named Justus, one that worshipped God, whose house joined hard to the synagogue.

8 And Crispus, the chief ruler of the synagogue, believed on the Lord with all his house; and many of the Corinthians hearing believed, and were baptized.

9 Then spake the Lord to Paul in the night by a vision, Be not afraid, but speak, and hold not thy peace:

10 For I am with thee, and no man shall set on thee to hurt thee: for I have much people in this city.

11 And he continued there a year and six months, teaching the word of God among them.

12 ¶ And when Gallio was the deputy of Achaia, the Jews made insurrection with one accord against Paul, and brought him to the judgment seat,

13 Saying, This fellow persuadeth men to worship God contrary to the law.

14 And when Paul was now about to open his mouth, Gallio said unto the Jews, If it were a matter of wrong or wicked lewdness, O ye Jews, reason would that I should bear with you:

15 But if it be a question of words and names, and of your law, look ye to it; for I will be no judge of such matters.

16 And he drave them from the judgment seat.

17 Then all the Greeks took Sosthenes, the chief ruler of the synagogue, and beat him before the judgment seat. And Gallio cared for none of those things.

## PAUL TEACHES IN A SYNAGOGUE AT EPHESUS

18 ¶ And Paul after this tarried there yet a good while, and then took his leave of the brethren, and sailed thence into Syria, and with him Priscilla and Aquila; having shorn his head in Cenchrea: for he had a vow.

19 And he came to Ephesus, and left them there: but he himself entered into the synagogue, and reasoned with the Jews.

20 When they desired him to tarry longer time with them, he consented not;

21 But bade them farewell, saying, I must by all means keep this feast that cometh in Jerusalem: but I will return again unto you, if God will. And he sailed from Ephesus.

22 And when he had landed at Caesarea, and gone up, and saluted the church, he went down to Antioch.

23 And after he had spent some time there, he departed, and went over all the country of Galatia and Phrygia in order, strengthening all the disciples.

---

18:3 **craft**—trade or occupation

**tentmakers**—people who made small tents of leather, cloth, or linen for the use of travelers

18:6 Blasphemy is the sin of claiming to be like God or speaking evil of God.

Paul is saying that he is not responsible for the sins of these Jews who refused to listen (see Ezekiel 33:3-5; Jacob 1:18-19).

18:7 **joined hard to**—was next to or bordered

18:12 **insurrection**—riot or attack

18:14 **lewdness**—crime

18:16 **drave**—drove

18:18 It is unknown what Paul's vow or promise was, but it was common at the end of this set period to cut the hair and burn it as a symbol of offering oneself to God (see Numbers 6; Acts 21:23-26).

*Still visible today among the ancient ruins of Corinth is the BEMA, or platform, where Paul was brought before Gallio, deputy of Achaia.*

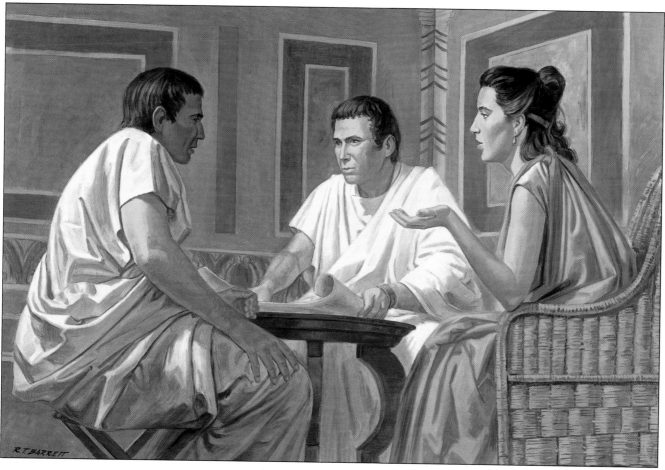

*Aquila and Priscilla teach Apollos.*

## APOLLOS BEARS TESTIMONY OF JESUS CHRIST

24 ¶ And a certain Jew named Apollos, born at Alexandria, an eloquent man, and mighty in the scriptures, came to Ephesus.

25 This man was instructed in the way of the Lord; and being fervent in the spirit, he spake and taught diligently the things of the Lord, knowing only the baptism of John.

26 And he began to speak boldly in the synagogue: whom when Aquila and Priscilla had heard, they took him unto them, and expounded unto him the way of God more perfectly.

27 And when he was disposed to pass into Achaia, the brethren wrote, exhorting the disciples to receive him: who, when he was come, helped them much which had believed through grace:

28 For he mightily convinced the Jews, and that publickly, shewing by the scriptures that Jesus was Christ.

## CHAPTER 19

*Paul preaches the gospel of Jesus Christ using his priesthood authority and the power of the Holy Ghost. Look for how Paul uses these powers in his ministry.*

18:24 **an eloquent man**—a good speaker

18:25- Apollos, a Jew, had great faith in Jesus Christ
28 just from hearing the teachings of John the Baptist. Aquila and Priscilla taught him more completely

of the gospel. One of the reasons we attend church is to continue to learn more about the Lord and his gospel. How does attending your Church meetings help you in your own gospel growth?

*Paul's third missionary journey*

## PAUL CONFERS THE GIFT OF THE HOLY GHOST

1 ¶ AND it came to pass, that, while Apollos was at Corinth, Paul having passed through the upper coasts came to Ephesus: and finding certain disciples,

2 He said unto them, Have ye received the Holy Ghost since ye believed? And they said unto him, We have not so much as heard whether there be any Holy Ghost.

3 And he said unto them, Unto what then were ye baptized? And they said, Unto John's baptism.

4 Then said Paul, John verily baptized with the baptism of repentance, saying unto the people, that they should believe on him which should come after him, that is, on Christ Jesus.

5 When they heard this, they were baptized in the name of the Lord Jesus.

6 And when Paul had laid his hands upon them, the Holy Ghost came on them; and they spake with tongues, and prophesied.

7 And all the men were about twelve.

## PAUL PREACHES THE GOSPEL AND PERFORMS MIRACLES

8 ¶ And he went into the synagogue, and spake boldly for the space of three months, disputing and persuading the things concerning the kingdom of God.

9 But when divers were hardened, and believed not,

---

19:2-4 Paul "found a number of men at Ephesus who claimed to have been baptized unto John's baptism, but when Paul questioned them as to the Holy Ghost, they had not heard even that there was such a Spirit. So doubting the validity of their baptism he re-baptized them; after which, 'when Paul had laid his hands upon them, the Holy Ghost came on them; and they spake with tongues, and prophesied [Acts 19:6].'" (B. H. Roberts, *The Seventy's Course in Theology* 5:92.)

19:6 Speaking in tongues is a gift of the Spirit that miraculously allows a person to speak another language. Prophecy is also a gift of the Spirit and, among other things, allows one to tell the future.

Soon after their baptism Joseph Smith and Oliver Cowdery had an experience similar to that of these Ephesian converts (see Joseph Smith—History 1:73).

19:8 *synagogue*—Jewish place of worship
*disputing and persuading*—arguing convincingly

19:9 *divers were hardened, and believed not*—some became stubborn and did not believe

Jesus said he is "the way, the truth, and the life" (John 14:6). The *Way* was a title given to the faith of those who were Christians and believers in Jesus Christ (see Acts 9:2; 16:17; 18:25-26; 19:23; 22:4; 24:14).

but spake evil of that way before the multitude, he departed from them, and separated the disciples, disputing daily in the school of one Tyrannus.

10 And this continued by the space of two years; so that all they which dwelt in Asia heard the word of the Lord Jesus, both Jews and Greeks.

11 And God wrought special miracles by the hands of Paul:

12 So that from his body were brought unto the sick handkerchiefs or aprons, and the diseases departed from them, and the evil spirits went out of them.

## THE SONS OF SCEVA TRY TO CAST OUT EVIL SPIRITS

13 ¶ Then certain of the vagabond Jews, exorcists, took upon them to call over them which had evil spirits the name of the Lord Jesus, saying, We adjure you by Jesus whom Paul preacheth.

14 And there were seven sons of one Sceva, a Jew, and chief of the priests, which did so.

15 And the evil spirit answered and said, Jesus I know, and Paul I know; but who are ye?

16 And the man in whom the evil spirit was leaped on them, and overcame them, and prevailed against them, so that they fled out of that house naked and wounded.

17 And this was known to all the Jews and Greeks also dwelling at Ephesus; and fear fell on them all, and the name of the Lord Jesus was magnified.

18 And many that believed came, and confessed, and shewed their deeds.

19 Many of them also which used curious arts brought their books together, and burned them before all men: and they counted the price of them, and found it fifty thousand pieces of silver.

20 So mightily grew the word of God and prevailed.

## EPHESIANS RIOT AGAINST PAUL

21 ¶ After these things were ended, Paul purposed in the spirit, when he had passed through Macedonia and Achaia, to go to Jerusalem, saying, After I have been there, I must also see Rome.

22 So he sent into Macedonia two of them that ministered unto him, Timotheus and Erastus; but he himself stayed in Asia for a season.

23 And the same time there arose no small stir about that way.

24 For a certain man named Demetrius, a silversmith, which made silver shrines for Diana, brought no small gain unto the craftsmen;

25 Whom he called together with the workmen of like occupation, and said, Sirs, ye know that by this craft we have our wealth.

26 Moreover ye see and hear, that not alone at

---

19:11 **wrought**—did or performed

19:12 Think of a time when you or a member of your family was blessed and made well through priesthood power. How do you feel knowing that God loves us enough to bless us?

19:13 **vagabond**—wandering
**exorcists**—those who pretend to cast out evil spirits
**adjure**—command

These Jews did not have the priesthood and could not command in Jesus' name. As Paul later taught, "No man taketh this honour [priesthood] unto himself, but he that is called of God" (Hebrews 5:4).

19:13-17 How does the power of evil spirits compare to the priesthood of God? Why is it so important to follow true and authorized priesthood power?

19:16 **prevailed against them**—overpowered them

19:19 **curious arts**—black magic and witchcraft

19:21 **purposed in the spirit**—was directed by the Holy Ghost

19:24-27 Diana was a false Greek goddess in whose honor a temple was built at Ephesus. The silversmiths there, including Demetrius, made and sold many silver images of Diana. (See LDS Bible Dictionary, s.v. "Diana," p. 657.)

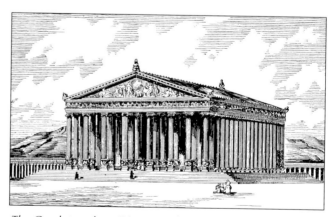

*The Greek temple to Diana at Ephesus*

Ephesus, but almost throughout all Asia, this Paul hath persuaded and turned away much people, saying that they be no gods, which are made with hands:

27 So that not only this our craft is in danger to be set at nought; but also that the temple of the great goddess Diana should be despised, and her magnificence should be destroyed, whom all Asia and the world worshippeth.

28 And when they heard these sayings, they were full of wrath, and cried out, saying, Great is Diana of the Ephesians.

29 And the whole city was filled with confusion: and having caught Gaius and Aristarchus, men of Macedonia, Paul's companions in travel, they rushed with one accord into the theatre.

30 And when Paul would have entered in unto the people, the disciples suffered him not.

31 And certain of the chief of Asia, which were his friends, sent unto him, desiring him that he would not adventure himself into the theatre.

32 Some therefore cried one thing, and some another: for the assembly was confused; and the more part knew not wherefore they were come together.

33 And they drew Alexander out of the multitude, the Jews putting him forward. And Alexander beckoned with the hand, and would have made his defence unto the people.

34 But when they knew that he was a Jew, all with one voice about the space of two hours cried out, Great is Diana of the Ephesians.

35 And when the townclerk had appeased the people, he said, Ye men of Ephesus, what man is there that knoweth not how that the city of the Ephesians is a worshipper of the great goddess Diana, and of the image which fell down from Jupiter?

36 Seeing then that these things cannot be spoken against, ye ought to be quiet, and to do nothing rashly.

37 For ye have brought hither these men, which are neither robbers of churches, nor yet blasphemers of your goddess.

38 Wherefore if Demetrius, and the craftsmen which are with him, have a matter against any man, the law is open, and there are deputies: let them implead one another.

39 But if ye enquire any thing concerning other matters, it shall be determined in a lawful assembly.

40 For we are in danger to be called in question for this day's uproar, there being no cause whereby we may give an account of this concourse.

41 And when he had thus spoken, he dismissed the assembly.

## CHAPTER 20

*Paul continues his third missionary journey. Note how Paul feels about those to whom he taught the gospel.*

### PAUL BRINGS EUTYCHUS BACK TO LIFE

1 ¶ AND after the uproar was ceased, Paul called unto him the disciples, and embraced them, and departed for to go into Macedonia.

2 And when he had gone over those parts, and had given them much exhortation, he came into Greece,

3 And there abode three months. And when the Jews laid wait for him, as he was about to sail into Syria, he purposed to return through Macedonia.

4 And there accompanied him into Asia Sopater of Berea; and of the Thessalonians, Aristarchus and Secundus; and Gaius of Derbe, and Timotheus; and of Asia, Tychicus and Trophimus.

5 These going before tarried for us at Troas.

6 And we sailed away from Philippi after the days of unleavened bread, and came unto them to Troas in five days; where we abode seven days.

---

19:30  **suffered him not**—would not allow it

19:31  **adventure himself**—dare go

19:32  **knew not wherefore they were come together**—did not know why they were there

19:38  **implead one another**—press charges or take them to court

19:40  **concourse**—commotion

20:2  **exhortation**—counsel and encouragement

20:3  **laid wait for him**—planned to kill him

20:5  **tarried**—waited

20:6  The Feast of Unleavened Bread took place immediately after the Feast of the Passover, and the two feasts were often considered as one. The Feast of Unleavened Bread commemorated the exodus of Israel out of Egypt. (See Exodus 12 and Leviticus 23:5-6.)

7 ¶ And upon the first day of the week, when the disciples came together to break bread, Paul preached unto them, ready to depart on the morrow; and continued his speech until midnight.

8 And there were many lights in the upper chamber, where they were gathered together.

9 And there sat in a window a certain young man named Eutychus, being fallen into a deep sleep: and as Paul was long preaching, he sunk down with sleep, and fell down from the third loft, and was taken up dead.

10 And Paul went down, and fell on him, and embracing him said, Trouble not yourselves; for his life is in him.

11 When he therefore was come up again, and had broken bread, and eaten, and talked a long while, even till break of day, so he departed.

12 And they brought the young man alive, and were not a little comforted.

## PAUL'S FAREWELL MESSAGE TO THE EPHESIANS

13 ¶ And we went before to ship, and sailed unto Assos, there intending to take in Paul: for so had he appointed, minding himself to go afoot.

14 And when he met with us at Assos, we took him in, and came to Mitylene.

15 And we sailed thence, and came the next day over against Chios; and the next day we arrived at Samos, and tarried at Trogyllium; and the next day we came to Miletus.

16 For Paul had determined to sail by Ephesus, because he would not spend the time in Asia: for he hasted, if it were possible for him, to be at Jerusalem the day of Pentecost.

17 ¶ And from Miletus he sent to Ephesus, and called the elders of the church.

18 And when they were come to him, he said unto them, Ye know, from the first day that I came into Asia, after what manner I have been with you at all seasons,

19 Serving the Lord with all humility of mind, and with many tears, and temptations, which befell me by the lying in wait of the Jews:

20 And how I kept back nothing that was profitable unto you, but have shewed you, and have taught you publickly, and from house to house,

21 Testifying both to the Jews, and also to the Greeks, repentance toward God, and faith toward our Lord Jesus Christ.

22 And now, behold, I go bound in the spirit unto Jerusalem, not knowing the things that shall befall me there:

23 Save that the Holy Ghost witnesseth in every city, saying that bonds and afflictions abide me.

24 But none of these things move me, neither count I my life dear unto myself, so that I might finish my course with joy, and the ministry, which I have received of the Lord Jesus, to testify the gospel of the grace of God.

25 And now, behold, I know that ye all, among whom I have gone preaching the kingdom of God, shall see my face no more.

26 Wherefore I take you to record this day, that I am pure from the blood of all men.

27 For I have not shunned to declare unto you all the counsel of God.

28 Take heed therefore unto yourselves, and to all the flock, over the which the Holy Ghost hath made you overseers, to feed the church of God, which he hath purchased with his own blood.

29 For I know this, that after my departing shall grievous wolves enter in among you, not sparing the flock.

---

20:7 Christians met together on Sunday to partake of the sacrament in memory of Jesus Christ's atonement and resurrection (see Luke 22:19-20 and 24:1-3).

20:16 *hasted*—hurried

The Feast of Pentecost was celebrated fifty days after the Feast of the Passover. This feast celebrated the beginning of the harvest. (See LDS Bible Dictionary, s.v. "Feasts," p. 673.)

20:20 *profitable*—helpful

20:22-24 The Spirit called Paul to Jerusalem, and he willingly obeyed, even though he knew by revelation that he would end up in prison. Why do you think Paul believed that the gospel was worth giving his life for? (See Romans 1:16.)

20:26-27 Missionaries must be faithful in teaching the people. If they are not, God will hold them responsible. (See Jacob 1:18-19.)

20:28-30 Paul knew that when the Apostles were gone, wicked men would try to destroy the Church of Jesus Christ. When Joseph Smith asked the Father and the Son which church he should join he was told to join none of them, "for they were all wrong" (Joseph Smith—History 1:19).

30 Also of your own selves shall men arise, speaking perverse things, to draw away disciples after them.

31 Therefore watch, and remember, that by the space of three years I ceased not to warn every one night and day with tears.

32 And now, brethren, I commend you to God, and to the word of his grace, which is able to build you up, and to give you an inheritance among all them which are sanctified.

33 I have coveted no man's silver, or gold, or apparel.

34 Yea, ye yourselves know, that these hands have ministered unto my necessities, and to them that were with me.

35 I have shewed you all things, how that so labouring ye ought to support the weak, and to remember the words of the Lord Jesus, how he said, It is more blessed to give than to receive.

36 ¶ And when he had thus spoken, he kneeled down, and prayed with them all.

37 And they all wept sore, and fell on Paul's neck, and kissed him,

38 Sorrowing most of all for the words which he spake, that they should see his face no more. And they accompanied him unto the ship.

## CHAPTER 21

*Trials, tribulations, and sufferings can give us experience and be for our good (see D&C 121:5–7).*

*Notice the sufferings Paul faces and why he willingly endures his trials.*

### PAUL TRAVELS TO JERUSALEM AND REPORTS ON HIS MISSION

1 ¶ AND it came to pass, that after we were gotten from them, and had launched, we came with a straight course unto Coos, and the day following unto Rhodes, and from thence unto Patara:

2 And finding a ship sailing over unto Phenicia, we went aboard, and set forth.

3 Now when we had discovered Cyprus, we left it on the left hand, and sailed into Syria, and landed at Tyre: for there the ship was to unlade her burden.

4 And finding disciples, we tarried there seven days: who said to Paul through the Spirit, that he should not go up to Jerusalem.

5 And when we had accomplished those days, we departed and went our way; and they all brought us on our way, with wives and children, till we were out of the city: and we kneeled down on the shore, and prayed.

6 And when we had taken our leave one of another, we took ship; and they returned home again.

7 And when we had finished our course from Tyre, we came to Ptolemais, and saluted the brethren, and abode with them one day.

8 ¶ And the next day we that were of Paul's company

*Paul traveled toward Jerusalem by ship.*

20:30 **perverse**—twisted, false

20:32 **commend you to God**—leave you in God's hands

20:33 **coveted**—desired

20:34 **ministered unto my necessities**—worked to earn what I needed

20:36- Why was everyone, including Paul, so tearful
38 at his leaving? Have you ever heard returned missionaries tell you of their love for the people to whom they were called to preach the gospel? Why do missionaries develop such love for those they teach?

20:37 **wept sore**—cried much

21:3 **her burden**—the ship's cargo

21:4 **tarried**—stayed

21:5 Do you pray before traveling? How does this help?

21:8 In the New Testament, an evangelist is one who proclaims the gospel. The Lord also revealed that an evangelist is another name for a patriarch (see D&C 107:39-53).

departed, and came unto Caesarea: and we entered into the house of Philip the evangelist, which was one of the seven; and abode with him.

9 And the same man had four daughters, virgins, which did prophesy.

10 And as we tarried there many days, there came down from Judaea a certain prophet, named Agabus.

11 And when he was come unto us, he took Paul's girdle, and bound his own hands and feet, and said, Thus saith the Holy Ghost, So shall the Jews at Jerusalem bind the man that owneth this girdle, and shall deliver him into the hands of the Gentiles.

12 And when we heard these things, both we, and they of that place, besought him not to go up to Jerusalem.

13 Then Paul answered, What mean ye to weep and to break mine heart? for I am ready not to be bound only, but also to die at Jerusalem for the name of the Lord Jesus.

14 And when he would not be persuaded, we ceased, saying, The will of the Lord be done.

15 ¶ And after those days we took up our carriages, and went up to Jerusalem.

16 There went with us also certain of the disciples of Caesarea, and brought with them one Mnason of Cyprus, an old disciple, with whom we should lodge.

17 And when we were come to Jerusalem, the brethren received us gladly.

18 And the day following Paul went in with us unto James; and all the elders were present.

19 And when he had saluted them, he declared particularly what things God had wrought among the Gentiles by his ministry.

## SOME JEWISH CONVERTS CONTINUE IN THE LAW OF MOSES

20 And when they heard it, they glorified the Lord, and said unto him, Thou seest, brother, how many thousands of Jews there are which believe; and they are all zealous of the law:

21 And they are informed of thee, that thou teachest all the Jews which are among the Gentiles to forsake Moses, saying that they ought not to circumcise their children, neither to walk after the customs.

22 What is it therefore? the multitude must needs come together: for they will hear that thou art come.

23 Do therefore this that we say to thee: We have four men which have a vow on them;

24 Them take, and purify thyself with them, and be at charges with them, that they may shave their heads: and all may know that those things, whereof they were informed concerning thee, are nothing; but that thou thyself also walkest orderly, and keepest the law.

25 As touching the Gentiles which believe, we have written and concluded that they observe no such thing, save only that they keep themselves from things offered to idols, and from blood, and from strangled, and from fornication.

26 Then Paul took the men, and the next day purifying himself with them entered into the temple, to signify the accomplishment of the days of purification, until that an offering should be offered for every one of them.

## PAUL IS PERSECUTED, ARRESTED, AND PUT IN PRISON

27 ¶ And when the seven days were almost ended, the Jews which were of Asia, when they saw him in the temple, stirred up all the people, and laid hands on him,

28 Crying out, Men of Israel, help: This is the man, that teacheth all men every where against the people, and the law, and this place: and further brought Greeks also into the temple, and hath polluted this holy place.

29 (For they had seen before with him in the city

---

21:9 **virgins**—unmarried women who live the law of chastity

21:11-12 Agabus tied his own hands and feet with Paul's girdle, or belt, to show that Paul would be put in prison at Jerusalem. Others also warned Paul not to go. Paul already knew he would face trials in Jerusalem (see Acts 20:22-24), but he still bravely followed the Lord.

21:13 How courageous was Paul? What are you willing to do for the Lord?

21:20-21 The Jews who were "zealous of the law" continued to follow the requirements of the law of Moses. This was wrong because Jesus fulfilled the law of Moses and wanted people to live the higher law of the gospel (see Matthew 5:17).

21:23 **have a vow on them**—made a promise

21:24 **be at charges with them**—pay their expenses for them

21:25 See the helps for Acts 15:19-35.

21:28-29 Only Jews were allowed in certain parts of the temple. Paul was falsely accused of bringing a gentile man into the temple.

Trophimus an Ephesian, whom they supposed that Paul had brought into the temple.)

30 And all the city was moved, and the people ran together: and they took Paul, and drew him out of the temple: and forthwith the doors were shut.

31 And as they went about to kill him, tidings came unto the chief captain of the band, that all Jerusalem was in an uproar.

32 Who immediately took soldiers and centurions, and ran down unto them: and when they saw the chief captain and the soldiers, they left beating of Paul.

33 Then the chief captain came near, and took him, and commanded him to be bound with two chains; and demanded who he was, and what he had done.

34 And some cried one thing, some another, among the multitude: and when he could not know the certainty for the tumult, he commanded him to be carried into the castle.

35 And when he came upon the stairs, so it was, that he was borne of the soldiers for the violence of the people.

36 For the multitude of the people followed after, crying, Away with him.

37 And as Paul was to be led into the castle, he said unto the chief captain, May I speak unto thee? Who said, Canst thou speak Greek?

38 Art not thou that Egyptian, which before these days madest an uproar, and leddest out into the wilderness four thousand men that were murderers?

39 But Paul said, I am a man which am a Jew of Tarsus, a city in Cilicia, a citizen of no mean city: and, I beseech thee, suffer me to speak unto the people.

40 And when he had given him licence, Paul stood on the stairs, and beckoned with the hand unto the people. And when there was made a great silence, he spake unto them in the Hebrew tongue, saying,

## CHAPTER 22

*This chapter records events that happened between the end of Paul's third mission and his trip to Rome. Look for Paul's ability to teach the gospel no matter how difficult the situation he is in.*

### PAUL SPEAKS TO A MOB IN JERUSALEM

1 ¶ MEN, brethren, and fathers, hear ye my defence which I make now unto you.

2 (And when they heard that he spake in the Hebrew tongue to them, they kept the more silence: and he saith,)

3 ¶ I am verily a man which am a Jew, born in Tarsus, a city in Cilicia, yet brought up in this city at the feet of Gamaliel, and taught according to the perfect manner of the law of the fathers, and was zealous toward God, as ye all are this day.

4 And I persecuted this way unto the death, binding and delivering into prisons both men and women.

5 As also the high priest doth bear me witness, and all the estate of the elders: from whom also I received letters unto the brethren, and went to Damascus, to bring them which were there bound unto Jerusalem, for to be punished.

6 And it came to pass, that, as I made my journey, and was come nigh unto Damascus about noon, suddenly there shone from heaven a great light round about me.

---

*Centurion*

21:32 *centurions*—Roman officers

21:34 *tumult*—confusion and arguments

21:38 The chief captain mistook Paul for an Egyptian man who had led some four thousand Jews in a revolt against Rome.

21:39 *beseech*—ask
*suffer*—allow

21:40 *beckoned*—motioned

22:2 Hebrew was the language of the learned Jews (see LDS Bible Dictionary, s.v. "Hebrew,"

p. 699). Many in the mob were Jewish scholars and were willing to listen when Paul spoke Hebrew.

22:3 Paul was born a Jew and was taught Jewish law by Gamaliel, a renowned "doctor of the law" (Acts 5:34).

*zealous toward God*—devoted to God

How do you act towards people who are mean to you? How would Jesus want you to act?

22:6-8 This light must have been great to be noticed at noon. When Joseph Smith saw Heavenly Father and Jesus Christ he also described the light that accompanied their appearance as "above the brightness of the sun" (Joseph Smith—History 1:16).

7 And I fell unto the ground, and heard a voice saying unto me, Saul, Saul, why persecutest thou me?

8 And I answered, Who art thou, Lord? And he said unto me, I am Jesus of Nazareth, whom thou persecutest.

9 And they that were with me saw indeed the light, and were afraid; but they heard not the voice of him that spake to me.

10 And I said, What shall I do, Lord? And the Lord said unto me, Arise, and go into Damascus; and there it shall be told thee of all things which are appointed for thee to do.

11 And when I could not see for the glory of that light, being led by the hand of them that were with me, I came into Damascus.

12 And one Ananias, a devout man according to the law, having a good report of all the Jews which dwelt there,

13 Came unto me, and stood, and said unto me, Brother Saul, receive thy sight. And the same hour I looked up upon him.

14 And he said, The God of our fathers hath chosen thee, that thou shouldest know his will, and see that Just One, and shouldest hear the voice of his mouth.

15 For thou shalt be his witness unto all men of what thou hast seen and heard.

16 And now why tarriest thou? arise, and be baptized, and wash away thy sins, calling on the name of the Lord.

17 And it came to pass, that, when I was come again to Jerusalem, even while I prayed in the temple, I was in a trance;

18 And saw him saying unto me, Make haste, and get thee quickly out of Jerusalem: for they will not receive thy testimony concerning me.

19 And I said, Lord, they know that I imprisoned and beat in every synagogue them that believed on thee:

20 And when the blood of thy martyr Stephen was shed, I also was standing by, and consenting unto his death, and kept the raiment of them that slew him.

21 And he said unto me, Depart: for I will send thee far hence unto the Gentiles.

## PAUL DECLARES HIS ROMAN CITIZENSHIP

22 ¶ And they gave him audience unto this word, and then lifted up their voices, and said, Away with such a fellow from the earth: for it is not fit that he should live.

23 And as they cried out, and cast off their clothes, and threw dust into the air,

24 The chief captain commanded him to be brought into the castle, and bade that he should be examined by scourging; that he might know wherefore they cried so against him.

25 And as they bound him with thongs, Paul said unto the centurion that stood by, Is it lawful for you to scourge a man that is a Roman, and uncondemned?

26 When the centurion heard that, he went and told the chief captain, saying, Take heed what thou doest: for this man is a Roman.

27 Then the chief captain came, and said unto him, Tell me, art thou a Roman? He said, Yea.

28 And the chief captain answered, With a great sum obtained I this freedom. And Paul said, But I was free born.

29 Then straightway they departed from him which should have examined him: and the chief captain also was afraid, after he knew that he was a Roman, and because he had bound him.

---

22:7-8   How was Saul (Paul) persecuting Jesus Christ? (See Matthew 25:40.)

22:9   Why do you think Paul was able to hear the voice of God and the others were not?

22:14   **see that Just One**—see Jesus Christ

22:16   **why tarriest thou?**—why do you wait?

Elder Bruce R. McConkie taught, "Sins are remitted [erased] not in the waters of baptism, . . . but when we receive the Holy Ghost" (*A New Witness for the Articles of Faith*, p. 290).

22:17   **was in a trance**—saw a vision

22:19-20   Paul confessed his part in persecuting the Christians, including approving the stoning of Stephen to death (see Acts 7:58).

22:24   **examined by scourging**—questioned by torture with the whip

22:24-25   When a person was scourged he was usually tied to a pillar (pole) with leather straps. He was then whipped with a leather strap that had pieces of bone or metal fastened to it. This punishment was used to cripple or kill the victim.

22:25   **thongs**—straps of leather used for tying

22:25-29   It was a crime to whip a Roman citizen. Paul was a Roman citizen by birth.

30 On the morrow, because he would have known the certainty wherefore he was accused of the Jews, he loosed him from his bands, and commanded the chief priests and all their council to appear, and brought Paul down, and set him before them.

## CHAPTER 23

*Paul narrowly escapes a plan by many Jews to kill him. Notice how the Lord kept his promise to watch over Paul.*

### PAUL IS JUDGED BY THE JEWISH SANHEDRIN

1 ¶ AND Paul, earnestly beholding the council, said, Men and brethren, I have lived in all good conscience before God until this day.

2 And the high priest Ananias commanded them that stood by him to smite him on the mouth.

3 Then said Paul unto him, God shall smite thee, thou whited wall: for sittest thou to judge me after the law, and commandest me to be smitten contrary to the law?

4 And they that stood by said, Revilest thou God's high priest?

5 Then said Paul, I wist not, brethren, that he was the high priest: for it is written, Thou shalt not speak evil of the ruler of thy people.

6 ¶ But when Paul perceived that the one part were Sadducees, and the other Pharisees, he cried out in the council, Men and brethren, I am a Pharisee, the son of a Pharisee: of the hope and resurrection of the dead I am called in question.

7 And when he had so said, there arose a dissension between the Pharisees and the Sadducees: and the multitude was divided.

8 For the Sadducees say that there is no resurrection, neither angel, nor spirit: but the Pharisees confess both.

9 And there arose a great cry: and the scribes that were of the Pharisees' part arose, and strove, saying, We find no evil in this man: but if a spirit or an angel hath spoken to him, let us not fight against God.

10 And when there arose a great dissension, the chief captain, fearing lest Paul should have been pulled in pieces of them, commanded the soldiers to go down, and to take him by force from among them, and to bring him into the castle.

11 And the night following the Lord stood by him, and said, Be of good cheer, Paul: for as thou hast testified of me in Jerusalem, so must thou bear witness also at Rome.

### MORE THAN FORTY JEWS PLOT TO KILL PAUL

12 ¶ And when it was day, certain of the Jews banded together, and bound themselves under a curse, saying that they would neither eat nor drink till they had killed Paul.

13 And they were more than forty which had made this conspiracy.

14 And they came to the chief priests and elders, and said, We have bound ourselves under a great curse, that we will eat nothing until we have slain Paul.

---

23:1 The Sanhedrin, often called "the council," was a group of seventy-one men who ruled the Jews. It was made up of Pharisees, Sadducees, and scribes and was led by a high priest. (See LDS Bible Dictionary, s.v. "Sanhedrin," p. 769.)

Paul lived his life "in all good conscience," or in other words, he had nothing to be ashamed of and was not afraid to meet God face to face. Why is it so wonderful to have a good and clear conscience?

23:2 **smite**—strike

23:2-3 Paul calls the high priest a "whited wall," one that only looks white and clean but is not. Years earlier, Jesus accused Jewish leaders of being like "whited sepulchres." They looked clean on the outside but were wicked inside. (See Matthew 23:27.)

23:4 **Revilest thou**—Do you insult

23:5 **wist not**—did not know

23:7 **a dissension**—an argument

23:9 **strove**—argued strongly

23:11 How do you think Paul felt knowing that the Lord "stood by him"? What would it mean to you? Could you be of "good cheer" having this promise?

23:12-14 These evil men, filled with hatred, plotted with an oath to kill Paul. Cain made this kind of promise with Satan when he planned to kill his brother, Abel (see Moses 5:29).

23:13 **conspiracy**—secret plot

23:14 The chief priests and scribes were Jewish religious leaders and teachers.

15 Now therefore ye with the council signify to the chief captain that he bring him down unto you to morrow, as though ye would enquire something more perfectly concerning him: and we, or ever he come near, are ready to kill him.

16 And when Paul's sister's son heard of their lying in wait, he went and entered into the castle, and told Paul.

17 Then Paul called one of the centurions unto him, and said, Bring this young man unto the chief captain: for he hath a certain thing to tell him.

18 So he took him, and brought him to the chief captain, and said, Paul the prisoner called me unto him, and prayed me to bring this young man unto thee, who hath something to say unto thee.

19 Then the chief captain took him by the hand, and went with him aside privately, and asked him, What is that thou hast to tell me?

20 And he said, The Jews have agreed to desire thee that thou wouldest bring down Paul to morrow into the council, as though they would enquire somewhat of him more perfectly.

21 But do not thou yield unto them: for there lie in wait for him of them more than forty men, which have bound themselves with an oath, that they will neither eat nor drink till they have killed him: and now are they ready, looking for a promise from thee.

22 So the chief captain then let the young man depart, and charged him, See thou tell no man that thou hast shewed these things to me.

23 And he called unto him two centurions, saying, Make ready two hundred soldiers to go to Caesarea, and horsemen threescore and ten, and spearmen two hundred, at the third hour of the night;

24 And provide them beasts, that they may set Paul on, and bring him safe unto Felix the governor.

## PAUL IS RESCUED AND DELIVERED TO FELIX

25 And he wrote a letter after this manner:

26 Claudius Lysias unto the most excellent governor Felix sendeth greeting.

27 This man was taken of the Jews, and should have been killed of them: then came I with an army, and rescued him, having understood that he was a Roman.

28 And when I would have known the cause wherefore they accused him, I brought him forth into their council:

29 Whom I perceived to be accused of questions of their law, but to have nothing laid to his charge worthy of death or of bonds.

30 And when it was told me how that the Jews laid wait for the man, I sent straightway to thee, and gave commandment to his accusers also to say before thee what they had against him. Farewell.

31 Then the soldiers, as it was commanded them, took Paul, and brought him by night to Antipatris.

32 On the morrow they left the horsemen to go with him, and returned to the castle:

33 Who, when they came to Caesarea, and delivered the epistle to the governor, presented Paul also before him.

34 And when the governor had read the letter, he asked of what province he was. And when he understood that he was of Cilicia;

35 I will hear thee, said he, when thine accusers are also come. And he commanded him to be kept in Herod's judgment hall.

---

23:15   *or ever he come near*—before he gets here

23:21   *a promise from thee*—your approval

23:23   *threescore and ten*—seventy

The nighttime hours began at six o'clock in the evening. The third hour was about nine o'clock.

23:26-27   Jesus promised to stand by Paul. How was this Roman captain a tool in Jesus' hands to help Paul? Whom has the Lord sent to help you in your life?

23:30   *straightway*—immediately

# CHAPTER 24

*Paul is tried before the Roman governor, Felix. Look for how Paul showed courage even though Felix could condemn him to death.*

## THE JEWS FALSELY ACCUSE PAUL

1 ¶ AND after five days Ananias the high priest descended with the elders, and with a certain orator named Tertullus, who informed the governor against Paul.

2 And when he was called forth, Tertullus began to accuse him, saying, Seeing that by thee we enjoy great quietness, and that very worthy deeds are done unto this nation by thy providence,

3 We accept it always, and in all places, most noble Felix, with all thankfulness.

4 Notwithstanding, that I be not further tedious unto thee, I pray thee that thou wouldest hear us of thy clemency a few words.

5 For we have found this man a pestilent fellow, and a mover of sedition among all the Jews throughout the world, and a ringleader of the sect of the Nazarenes:

6 Who also hath gone about to profane the temple: whom we took, and would have judged according to our law.

7 But the chief captain Lysias came upon us, and with great violence took him away out of our hands,

8 Commanding his accusers to come unto thee: by examining of whom thyself mayest take knowledge of all these things, whereof we accuse him.

9 And the Jews also assented, saying that these things were so.

## PAUL DEFENDS HIS LIFE AND HIS DOCTRINE

10 ¶ Then Paul, after that the governor had beckoned unto him to speak, answered, Forasmuch as I know that thou hast been of many years a judge unto this nation, I do the more cheerfully answer for myself:

11 Because that thou mayest understand, that there are yet but twelve days since I went up to Jerusalem for to worship.

12 And they neither found me in the temple disputing with any man, neither raising up the people, neither in the synagogues, nor in the city:

13 Neither can they prove the things whereof they now accuse me.

14 But this I confess unto thee, that after the way which they call heresy, so worship I the God of my fathers, believing all things which are written in the law and in the prophets:

15 And have hope toward God, which they themselves also allow, that there shall be a resurrection of the dead, both of the just and unjust.

16 And herein do I exercise myself, to have always a conscience void of offence toward God, and toward men.

---

24:1    *descended*—went down (to Caesarea)
       *orator*—good speaker

*An ancient Roman aqueduct can still be seen at Caesarea today. Paul was tried before Felix at Caesarea.*

24:5    *a pestilent fellow, and a mover of sedition*—a troublemaker and a creator of rebellion

Tertullus wanted Felix to believe that Paul was the leader of a rebellious group that wanted to overthrow the Romans. Notice how often in the book of Acts the enemies of the Church misrepresent the truth in order to hurt the growth of the Church (see Acts 6:13; 16:20-21; 17:6-7; and 21:28).

24:6    *profane the temple*—make the temple unclean or unholy

24:8    *by examining of whom thyself mayest take knowledge of*—by questioning Paul yourself, you (Felix) can understand

24:12   *disputing*—arguing
        *raising up the people*—stirring up rebellion

24:14   Paul boldly admits that he believes and lives what these Jews call "heresy," or false doctrine (see also Acts 22:6-21).

24:16   *And herein do I exercise myself*—This is what I try to do

*Paul speaks to Felix about Jesus Christ.*

17 Now after many years I came to bring alms to my nation, and offerings.

18 Whereupon certain Jews from Asia found me purified in the temple, neither with multitude, nor with tumult.

19 Who ought to have been here before thee, and object, if they had ought against me.

20 Or else let these same here say, if they have found any evil doing in me, while I stood before the council,

21 Except it be for this one voice, that I cried standing among them, Touching the resurrection of the dead I am called in question by you this day.

22 ¶ And when Felix heard these things, having more perfect knowledge of that way, he deferred them, and said, When Lysias the chief captain shall come down, I will know the uttermost of your matter.

23 And he commanded a centurion to keep Paul, and to let him have liberty, and that he should forbid none of his acquaintance to minister or come unto him.

---

24:17 **alms**—gifts or service for the poor

24:18 **purified**—clean or worthy
**neither with multitude, nor with tumult**—without any crowd and with no trouble

24:19-  Paul testifies that he did nothing wrong in the
21      temple or before the Jewish council (the

Sanhedrin). He explains that what they really hate is Paul's testimony that there is a resurrection (see Acts 23:6).

24:22 **he deferred them**—he told the Jews to wait

24:23  Paul is placed under guard but allowed to have visitors.

24 And after certain days, when Felix came with his wife Drusilla, which was a Jewess, he sent for Paul, and heard him concerning the faith in Christ.

25 And as he reasoned of righteousness, temperance, and judgment to come, Felix trembled, and answered, Go thy way for this time; when I have a convenient season, I will call for thee.

26 He hoped also that money should have been given him of Paul, that he might loose him: wherefore he sent for him the oftener, and communed with him.

27 But after two years Porcius Festus came into Felix' room: and Felix, willing to shew the Jews a pleasure, left Paul bound.

## CHAPTER 25

*Paul knows that God wants him to go to Rome and preach the gospel. Look for what Paul does to be sure he fulfills the Lord's desire.*

### PAUL IS TRIED BEFORE FESTUS

1 ¶ NOW when Festus was come into the province, after three days he ascended from Caesarea to Jerusalem.

2 Then the high priest and the chief of the Jews informed him against Paul, and besought him,

3 And desired favour against him, that he would send for him to Jerusalem, laying wait in the way to kill him.

4 But Festus answered, that Paul should be kept at Caesarea, and that he himself would depart shortly thither.

5 Let them therefore, said he, which among you are able, go down with me, and accuse this man, if there be any wickedness in him.

6 And when he had tarried among them more than ten days, he went down unto Caesarea; and the next day sitting on the judgment seat commanded Paul to be brought.

7 And when he was come, the Jews which came down from Jerusalem stood round about, and laid many and grievous complaints against Paul, which they could not prove.

8 While he answered for himself, Neither against the law of the Jews, neither against the temple, nor yet against Caesar, have I offended any thing at all.

9 But Festus, willing to do the Jews a pleasure, answered Paul, and said, Wilt thou go up to Jerusalem, and there be judged of these things before me?

10 Then said Paul, I stand at Caesar's judgment seat, where I ought to be judged: to the Jews have I done no wrong, as thou very well knowest.

11 For if I be an offender, or have committed any thing worthy of death, I refuse not to die: but if there be none of these things whereof these accuse me, no man may deliver me unto them. I appeal unto Caesar.

12 Then Festus, when he had conferred with the council, answered, Hast thou appealed unto Caesar? unto Caesar shalt thou go.

### KING AGRIPPA COMES TO CAESAREA

13 ¶ And after certain days king Agrippa and Bernice came unto Caesarea to salute Festus.

14 And when they had been there many days, Festus declared Paul's cause unto the king, saying, There is a certain man left in bonds by Felix:

---

24:24-25 When Felix heard Paul teach of Christ, righteousness, self-control, and the judgment to come, he became frightened. Felix was famous for his wickedness and cruelty (see Bruce R. McConkie, *Doctrinal New Testament Commentary* 2:196).

24:27 Would it be discouraging to be in prison for two years without even being convicted of a crime? Why do you think Paul was not discouraged? (See Acts 23:11.) How could knowing Heavenly Father's will for you help you to overcome discouragement?

25:1 province—part of the country that Festus ruled over

Caesarea was a city on the coast of the Mediterranean Sea about fifty miles northwest of Jerusalem (see map on p. 266). Festus "ascended" to Jerusalem because it was situated in mountains 2,600 feet above sea level (see LDS Bible Dictionary, s.v. "Jerusalem," p. 712).

25:2-4 The Jewish leaders wanted Festus to send Paul to Jerusalem. They planned to kill Paul while he was on the way. This was another of several conspiracies to kill Paul (see Acts 9:23-25; 23:12-13).

25:4 depart shortly thither—leave soon for there

25:5 accuse this man—say this man did wrong

25:10-11 Paul knew he was not guilty of any crime. It could be said he had a clear conscience. How can you keep your conscience free from guilt?

25:14 bonds—jail

15 About whom, when I was at Jerusalem, the chief priests and the elders of the Jews informed me, desiring to have judgment against him.

16 To whom I answered, It is not the manner of the Romans to deliver any man to die, before that he which is accused have the accusers face to face, and have licence to answer for himself concerning the crime laid against him.

17 Therefore, when they were come hither, without any delay on the morrow I sat on the judgment seat, and commanded the man to be brought forth.

18 Against whom when the accusers stood up, they brought none accusation of such things as I supposed:

19 But had certain questions against him of their own superstition, and of one Jesus, which was dead, whom Paul affirmed to be alive.

20 And because I doubted of such manner of questions, I asked him whether he would go to Jerusalem, and there be judged of these matters.

21 But when Paul had appealed to be reserved unto the hearing of Augustus, I commanded him to be kept till I might send him to Caesar.

22 Then Agrippa said unto Festus, I would also hear the man myself. To morrow, said he, thou shalt hear him.

## PAUL IS CALLED TO APPEAR BEFORE KING AGRIPPA

23 And on the morrow, when Agrippa was come, and Bernice, with great pomp, and was entered into the place of hearing, with the chief captains, and principal men of the city, at Festus' commandment Paul was brought forth.

24 And Festus said, King Agrippa, and all men which are here present with us, ye see this man, about whom all the multitude of the Jews have dealt with me, both at Jerusalem, and also here, crying that he ought not to live any longer.

25 But when I found that he had committed nothing worthy of death, and that he himself hath appealed to Augustus, I have determined to send him.

26 Of whom I have no certain thing to write unto my lord. Wherefore I have brought him forth before you, and specially before thee, O king Agrippa, that, after examination had, I might have somewhat to write.

27 For it seemeth to me unreasonable to send a prisoner, and not withal to signify the crimes laid against him.

## CHAPTER 26

*In the book of Acts, Paul is often asked to tell of his conversion to Christ. In this chapter notice what he says caused him to change his earlier lifestyle and become a Christian.*

## PAUL TELLS OF HIS EARLY LIFE

1 ¶ THEN Agrippa said unto Paul, Thou art permitted to speak for thyself. Then Paul stretched forth the hand, and answered for himself:

2 I think myself happy, king Agrippa, because I shall answer for myself this day before thee touching all the things whereof I am accused of the Jews:

3 Especially because I know thee to be expert in all customs and questions which are among the Jews: wherefore I beseech thee to hear me patiently.

4 My manner of life from my youth, which was at the first among mine own nation at Jerusalem, know all the Jews;

5 Which knew me from the beginning, if they would testify, that after the most straitest sect of our religion I lived a Pharisee.

6 And now I stand and am judged for the hope of the promise made of God unto our fathers:

7 Unto which promise our twelve tribes, instantly serving God day and night, hope to come. For which

---

25:19 **superstition**—religious beliefs

Paul "affirmed," or testified, that Jesus Christ was truly resurrected. How much courage do you think it would take to share your feelings about Jesus with evil people?

25:23 **on the morrow**—the next day

25:25-27 Festus brought Paul before King Agrippa because he did not want to send Paul to Rome without something to accuse him of (see Acts 23:29). He wanted the king to help record the crimes to accuse Paul of as they sent him to face Caesar.

26:4-5 In his earlier life Paul was trained to be a Pharisee. The Pharisees were a religious party of the Jews who strictly lived the law of Moses (see LDS Bible Dictionary, s.v. "Pharisees," p. 750).

26:6-8 God had promised that one day all would rise from the dead. Paul believed in this resurrection and taught others to hope for it. He was like the many faithful Saints who had "departed the mortal life, firm in the hope of a glorious resurrection" (D&C 138:14).

hope's sake, king Agrippa, I am accused of the Jews.

8 Why should it be thought a thing incredible with you, that God should raise the dead?

9 I verily thought with myself, that I ought to do many things contrary to the name of Jesus of Nazareth.

10 Which thing I also did in Jerusalem: and many of the saints did I shut up in prison, having received authority from the chief priests; and when they were put to death, I gave my voice against them.

11 And I punished them oft in every synagogue, and compelled them to blaspheme; and being exceedingly mad against them, I persecuted them even unto strange cities.

## PAUL RETELLS HIS CONVERSION

12 ¶ Whereupon as I went to Damascus with authority and commission from the chief priests,

13 At midday, O king, I saw in the way a light from heaven, above the brightness of the sun, shining round about me and them which journeyed with me.

14 And when we were all fallen to the earth, I heard a voice speaking unto me, and saying in the Hebrew tongue, Saul, Saul, why persecutest thou me? it is hard for thee to kick against the pricks.

15 And I said, Who art thou, Lord? And he said, I am Jesus whom thou persecutest.

16 But rise, and stand upon thy feet: for I have appeared unto thee for this purpose, to make thee a minister and a witness both of these things which thou hast seen, and of those things in the which I will appear unto thee;

17 Delivering thee from the people, and from the Gentiles, unto whom now I send thee,

18 To open their eyes, and to turn them from darkness to light, and from the power of Satan unto God, that they may receive forgiveness of sins, and inheritance among them which are sanctified by faith that is in me.

## PAUL TELLS HOW HIS CONVERSION CHANGED HIS LIFE

19 Whereupon, O king Agrippa, I was not disobedient unto the heavenly vision:

20 But shewed first unto them of Damascus, and at Jerusalem, and throughout all the coasts of Judaea, and then to the Gentiles, that they should repent and turn to God, and do works meet for repentance.

21 For these causes the Jews caught me in the temple, and went about to kill me.

22 Having therefore obtained help of God, I continue unto this day, witnessing both to small and great, saying none other things than those which the prophets and Moses did say should come:

23 That Christ should suffer, and that he should be the first that should rise from the dead, and should shew light unto the people, and to the Gentiles.

## AGRIPPA AVOIDS PAUL'S CHALLENGE

24 ¶ And as he thus spake for himself, Festus said with a loud voice, Paul, thou art beside thyself; much learning doth make thee mad.

25 But he said, I am not mad, most noble Festus; but speak forth the words of truth and soberness.

26 For the king knoweth of these things, before whom also I speak freely: for I am persuaded that none of these things are hidden from him; for this thing was not done in a corner.

27 King Agrippa, believest thou the prophets? I know that thou believest.

---

26:9 As a Pharisee, Paul had been against all who followed Jesus of Nazareth. He had searched for and imprisoned Christians wherever he could find them. (See Acts 8:1-4.)

26:10 **voice**—vote

26:11 **compelled**—forced
**strange cities**—foreign cities (like Damascus)

26:14 **why persecutest thou me**—why do you make trouble or cause problems for me

A prick was a "pole or stick with a sharp metal point, used to prick oxen while plowing" (see LDS Bible Dictionary, s.v. "Goads," p. 681). The Lord was warning Paul about how difficult it is to fight against Him.

26:15- Jesus appeared to Paul to call him on a mission
18 to lead people out of darkness into the light of the gospel. How would it feel to be like Paul and serve a mission where you helped people see the light of the gospel?

26:20 When a person realizes he is doing something wrong, then turns away from his wrong actions and starts doing what is right, he is doing "works meet for repentance."

26:23 **shew**—show

26:26 **in a corner**—in secret

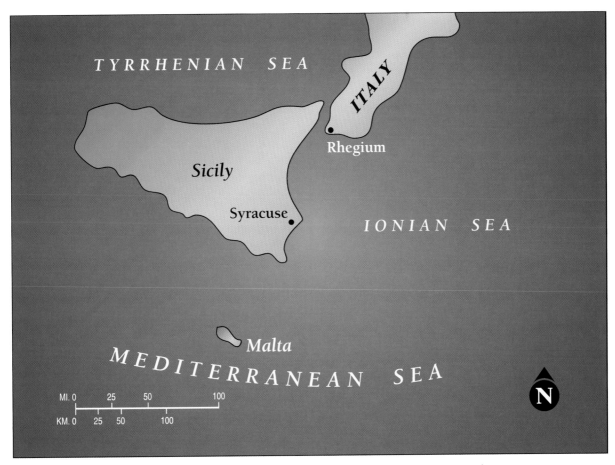

*Paul was shipwrecked on Melita, an island known today as Malta.*

28 Then Agrippa said unto Paul, Almost thou persuadest me to be a Christian.

29 And Paul said, I would to God, that not only thou, but also all that hear me this day, were both almost, and altogether such as I am, except these bonds.

30 And when he had thus spoken, the king rose up, and the governor, and Bernice, and they that sat with them:

31 And when they were gone aside, they talked between themselves, saying, This man doeth nothing worthy of death or of bonds.

32 Then said Agrippa unto Festus, This man might have been set at liberty, if he had not appealed unto Caesar.

## CHAPTER 27

*Paul and every person on board his ship miraculously survive a shipwreck. Look for why they are saved.*

### PAUL HAS A DANGEROUS VOYAGE TO ROME

1 ¶ AND when it was determined that we should sail into Italy, they delivered Paul and certain other prisoners unto one named Julius, a centurion of Augustus' band.

2 And entering into a ship of Adramyttium, we launched, meaning to sail by the coasts of Asia; one

---

26:28-
30 Paul's testimony nearly convinced Agrippa to become a covenant follower of Jesus Christ. But the only way to become a covenant child of God is to "repent and believe in his Son, who is the Holy One of Israel" (2 Nephi 30:2).

26:32 A lower judge could not release Paul from charges once Paul had appealed to Caesar. This

appeal would take Paul to Rome, where he would fulfill prophecy by bearing his testimony of Christ there (see Acts 23:11).

27:1 **centurion**—Roman officer

Aristarchus, a Macedonian of Thessalonica, being with us.

3 And the next day we touched at Sidon. And Julius courteously entreated Paul, and gave him liberty to go unto his friends to refresh himself.

4 And when we had launched from thence, we sailed under Cyprus, because the winds were contrary.

5 And when we had sailed over the sea of Cilicia and Pamphylia, we came to Myra, a city of Lycia.

6 And there the centurion found a ship of Alexandria sailing into Italy; and he put us therein.

7 And when we had sailed slowly many days, and scarce were come over against Cnidus, the wind not suffering us, we sailed under Crete, over against Salmone;

8 And, hardly passing it, came unto a place which is called The fair havens; nigh whereunto was the city of Lasea.

9 Now when much time was spent, and when sailing was now dangerous, because the fast was now already past, Paul admonished them,

10 And said unto them, Sirs, I perceive that this voyage will be with hurt and much damage, not only of the lading and ship, but also of our lives.

11 Nevertheless the centurion believed the master and the owner of the ship, more than those things which were spoken by Paul.

12 ¶ And because the haven was not commodious to winter in, the more part advised to depart thence also, if by any means they might attain to Phenice, and there to winter; which is an haven of Crete, and lieth toward the south west and north west.

13 And when the south wind blew softly, supposing that they had obtained their purpose, loosing thence, they sailed close by Crete.

14 But not long after there arose against it a tempestuous wind, called Euroclydon.

15 And when the ship was caught, and could not bear up into the wind, we let her drive.

16 And running under a certain island which is called Clauda, we had much work to come by the boat:

17 Which when they had taken up, they used helps, undergirding the ship; and, fearing lest they should fall into the quicksands, strake sail, and so were driven.

18 And we being exceedingly tossed with a tempest, the next day they lightened the ship;

19 And the third day we cast out with our own hands the tackling of the ship.

20 And when neither sun nor stars in many days appeared, and no small tempest lay on us, all hope that we should be saved was then taken away.

## GOD SENDS AN ANGEL TO COMFORT PAUL

21 ¶ But after long abstinence Paul stood forth in the midst of them, and said, Sirs, ye should have hearkened unto me, and not have loosed from Crete, and to have gained this harm and loss.

22 And now I exhort you to be of good cheer: for there shall be no loss of any man's life among you, but of the ship.

23 For there stood by me this night the angel of God, whose I am, and whom I serve,

24 Saying, Fear not, Paul; thou must be brought before Caesar: and, lo, God hath given thee all them that sail with thee.

25 Wherefore, sirs, be of good cheer: for I believe God, that it shall be even as it was told me.

26 Howbeit we must be cast upon a certain island.

---

27:4 **contrary**—against us

27:7 **scarce were come over against Cnidus**—had difficulty arriving at Cnidus
**suffering**—allowing

27:8 **nigh**—close

27:9 The fast mentioned here refers to the Day of Atonement, which occurred in the fall of the year (see Leviticus 23:27, 29). Because of poor weather, sailing during this time of year was dangerous.

27:10 **lading**—cargo

27:12 **haven**—harbor
**not commodious**—not comfortable

27:14 Euroclydon was a violent windstorm that came from the northeast (see LDS Bible Dictionary, s.v. "Euroclydon," p. 668).

27:16 **much work to come by the boat**—difficulty securing the lifeboat

27:17 **helps**— ropes
**strake sail**—let down the sail

27:21 **long abstinence**—long time without food

27:25 Paul knew they would all be safe because an angel told him so. You may never see an angel, but have you ever been comforted by an answer you have received to your prayers?

## PAUL IS SHIPWRECKED

27 But when the fourteenth night was come, as we were driven up and down in Adria, about midnight the shipmen deemed that they drew near to some country;

28 And sounded, and found it twenty fathoms: and when they had gone a little further, they sounded again, and found it fifteen fathoms.

29 Then fearing lest we should have fallen upon rocks, they cast four anchors out of the stern, and wished for the day.

30 And as the shipmen were about to flee out of the ship, when they had let down the boat into the sea, under colour as though they would have cast anchors out of the foreship,

31 Paul said to the centurion and to the soldiers, Except these abide in the ship, ye cannot be saved.

32 Then the soldiers cut off the ropes of the boat, and let her fall off.

33 And while the day was coming on, Paul besought them all to take meat, saying, This day is the fourteenth day that ye have tarried and continued fasting, having taken nothing.

34 Wherefore I pray you to take some meat: for this is for your health: for there shall not an hair fall from the head of any of you.

35 And when he had thus spoken, he took bread, and gave thanks to God in presence of them all:

and when he had broken it, he began to eat.

36 Then were they all of good cheer, and they also took some meat.

37 And we were in all in the ship two hundred threescore and sixteen souls.

38 And when they had eaten enough, they lightened the ship, and cast out the wheat into the sea.

39 And when it was day, they knew not the land: but they discovered a certain creek with a shore, into the which they were minded, if it were possible, to thrust in the ship.

40 And when they had taken up the anchors, they committed themselves unto the sea, and loosed the rudder bands, and hoised up the mainsail to the wind, and made toward shore.

41 And falling into a place where two seas met, they ran the ship aground; and the forepart stuck fast, and remained unmoveable, but the hinder part was broken with the violence of the waves.

42 And the soldiers' counsel was to kill the prisoners, lest any of them should swim out, and escape.

43 But the centurion, willing to save Paul, kept them from their purpose; and commanded that they which could swim should cast themselves first into the sea, and get to land:

44 And the rest, some on boards, and some on broken pieces of the ship. And so it came to pass, that they escaped all safe to land.

---

27:27 **Adria**—the Adriatic Sea
**deemed**—determined

27:28 The phrase "they sounded" means they checked how deep the water was. A fathom is about 6 feet, and 20 fathoms is a depth of about 120 feet (37 meters).

27:30 **under colour**—pretending

27:33 **besought them all to take meat**—urged them all to eat

27:35-36 How did Paul show his faith in God at this dangerous moment? How did it help the sailors who were with him?

27:37 **two hundred threescore and sixteen souls**—276 people

27:39 **creek**—bay
**were minded**—decided

27:40 **loosed the rudder bands**—untied the ropes that held the rudder

# CHAPTER 28

*Good can come from the troubles that beset us. Notice how the troubles in Paul's life—such as his shipwreck, his snakebite, and even his being under guard in Rome—are used by the Lord to spread the gospel.*

## PAUL PERFORMS MIRACLES ON MALTA

1 ¶ AND when they were escaped, then they knew that the island was called Melita.

2 And the barbarous people shewed us no little kindness: for they kindled a fire, and received us every one, because of the present rain, and because of the cold.

3 And when Paul had gathered a bundle of sticks, and laid them on the fire, there came a viper out of the heat, and fastened on his hand.

4 And when the barbarians saw the venomous beast hang on his hand, they said among themselves, No doubt this man is a murderer, whom, though he hath escaped the sea, yet vengeance suffereth not to live.

5 And he shook off the beast into the fire, and felt no harm.

6 Howbeit they looked when he should have swollen, or fallen down dead suddenly: but after they had looked a great while, and saw no harm come to him, they changed their minds, and said that he was a god.

7 In the same quarters were possessions of the chief man of the island, whose name was Publius; who received us, and lodged us three days courteously.

8 And it came to pass, that the father of Publius lay sick of a fever and of a bloody flux: to whom Paul entered in, and prayed, and laid his hands on him, and healed him.

9 So when this was done, others also, which had diseases in the island, came, and were healed:

10 Who also honoured us with many honours; and when we departed, they laded us with such things as were necessary.

## PAUL IS TAKEN TO ROME

11 ¶ And after three months we departed in a ship of Alexandria, which had wintered in the isle, whose sign was Castor and Pollux.

12 And landing at Syracuse, we tarried there three days.

13 And from thence we fetched a compass, and came to Rhegium: and after one day the south wind blew, and we came the next day to Puteoli:

14 Where we found brethren, and were desired to tarry with them seven days: and so we went toward Rome.

15 And from thence, when the brethren heard of us, they came to meet us as far as Appii forum, and The three taverns: whom when Paul saw, he thanked God, and took courage.

16 And when we came to Rome, the centurion delivered the prisoners to the captain of the guard: but Paul was suffered to dwell by himself with a soldier that kept him.

*Melita (modern Malta) is an island in the Mediterranean sixty miles south of Sicily and approximately twelve hundred miles from Jerusalem. It is seventeen miles long by nine miles wide. The shipwreck involving Paul likely occurred at the place traditionally known as Paul's Bay, an inlet with a creek two miles deep and one mile broad.*

28:2 **the barbarous people**—the natives of the island (Greeks usually referred to those who did not speak Greek as "barbarians")

28:3 **viper**—poisonous snake

28:4 Why do you think the snake did not kill Paul? (See Mark 16:17-18.)

28:7 **In the same quarters were possessions**—In the neighborhood was the home

28:8-9 Why do you think Heavenly Father let Paul be shipwrecked here and be bitten by a snake? What was Paul able to do on this island?

28:8 **bloody flux**—bowel ailment

28:10 **laded us with**—gave us for our journey

28:13 **fetched a compass**—sailed around

## Paul Teaches the Gospel in Rome

17 ¶ And it came to pass, that after three days Paul called the chief of the Jews together: and when they were come together, he said unto them, Men and brethren, though I have committed nothing against the people, or customs of our fathers, yet was I delivered prisoner from Jerusalem into the hands of the Romans.

18 Who, when they had examined me, would have let me go, because there was no cause of death in me.

19 But when the Jews spake against it, I was constrained to appeal unto Caesar; not that I had ought to accuse my nation of.

20 For this cause therefore have I called for you, to see you, and to speak with you: because that for the hope of Israel I am bound with this chain.

21 And they said unto him, We neither received letters out of Judaea concerning thee, neither any of the brethren that came shewed or spake any harm of thee.

22 But we desire to hear of thee what thou thinkest: for as concerning this sect, we know that every where it is spoken against.

23 ¶ And when they had appointed him a day, there came many to him into his lodging; to whom he expounded and testified the kingdom of God, persuading them concerning Jesus, both out of the law of Moses, and out of the prophets, from morning till evening.

24 And some believed the things which were spoken, and some believed not.

25 And when they agreed not among themselves, they departed, after that Paul had spoken one word, Well spake the Holy Ghost by Esaias the prophet unto our fathers,

26 Saying, Go unto this people, and say, Hearing ye shall hear, and shall not understand; and seeing ye shall see, and not perceive:

27 For the heart of this people is waxed gross, and their ears are dull of hearing, and their eyes have they closed; lest they should see with their eyes, and hear with their ears, and understand with their heart, and should be converted, and I should heal them.

28 Be it known therefore unto you, that the salvation of God is sent unto the Gentiles, and that they will hear it.

29 And when he had said these words, the Jews departed, and had great reasoning among themselves.

30 ¶ And Paul dwelt two whole years in his own hired house, and received all that came in unto him,

31 Preaching the kingdom of God, and teaching those things which concern the Lord Jesus Christ, with all confidence, no man forbidding him.

---

28:19 **ought**—anything

28:22 **this sect**—the Christians

28:23 **expounded**—explained

"The law of Moses" and "the prophets" are two parts of the Old Testament (see LDS Bible Dictionary, s.v. "Bible, Structure of the Bible," p. 622). Paul spent the whole day showing the Jews that the scriptures testify of Jesus Christ.

28:25-27 Paul quoted to the Jews a prophecy from Isaiah (see Isaiah 6:9-10). The prophecy means that the truth would be shown plainly to the Jews but they would refuse to see and be saved.

28:29 **great reasoning**—much discussion

28:30-31 Even though Paul had a lot of troubles getting to Rome and he was still a prisoner there, do you think he was sad about being there?

Tradition and suggestions from Paul's letters indicate that he "remained in Rome two years (Acts 28:30) and was then released. He then appears to have visited Asia, Macedonia, Crete, and perhaps Spain. At the end of about four years he was again taken a prisoner to Rome, and suffered martyrdom, probably in the spring of A.D. 65." (LDS Bible Dictionary, s.v. "Paul," p. 743.)

Paul's fourteen letters, or "epistles," found in the New Testament were written to Church members who lived in different parts of the world. They are not found in our current version of the New Testament in their proper chronological order. Rather, "those that were written to churches are followed by those written to individuals, and within each group the order is that of decreasing length, except that Galatians is (slightly) shorter than Ephesians, which follows it" (Bruce M. Metzger, THE CANON OF THE NEW TESTAMENT, p. 297). Hebrews was placed last because its authorship was contested.

The following is a list of Paul's epistles arranged in order according to the date each one was probably written (see also LDS Bible Dictionary, s.v. "Pauline Epistles," p. 743):

1 Thessalonians (A.D. 50–51)    Romans (A.D. 55–58)    Hebrews (A.D. 64–65)
2 Thessalonians (A.D. 50–51)    Philippians (A.D. 60–62)    1 Timothy (A.D. 64–65)
1 Corinthians (A.D. 55–57)    Colossians (A.D. 60–62)    Titus (A.D. 64–65)
2 Corinthians (A.D. 55–57)    Ephesians (A.D. 60–62)    2 Timothy (A.D. 64–66)
Galatians (A.D. 55–58)    Philemon (A.D. 60–62)

# THE EPISTLE OF PAUL THE APOSTLE TO THE
# ROMANS

*The book of Romans is a letter written by the Apostle Paul to the Saints living in Rome to prepare them for his visit to them. He wrote the letter about A.D. 57 while staying in Corinth (see Acts 20:2-3).*

## CHAPTER 1

*Paul was a fearless missionary. Notice what he says that shows his courage.*

### PAUL LONGS TO PREACH THE GOSPEL TO THE SAINTS IN ROME

1 PAUL, a servant of Jesus Christ, called to be an apostle, separated unto the gospel of God,

2 (Which he had promised afore by his prophets in the holy scriptures,)

3 Concerning his Son Jesus Christ our Lord, which was made of the seed of David according to the flesh;

4 And declared to be the Son of God with power, according to the spirit of holiness, by the resurrection from the dead:

5 By whom we have received grace and apostleship, for obedience to the faith among all nations, for his name:

6 Among whom are ye also the called of Jesus Christ:

7 To all that be in Rome, beloved of God, called to be saints: Grace to you and peace from God our Father, and the Lord Jesus Christ.

8 ¶ First, I thank my God through Jesus Christ for you all, that your faith is spoken of throughout the whole world.

9 For God is my witness, whom I serve with my spirit in the gospel of his Son, that without ceasing I make mention of you always in my prayers;

10 Making request, if by any means now at length I might have a prosperous journey by the will of God to come unto you.

11 For I long to see you, that I may impart unto you some spiritual gift, to the end ye may be established;

12 That is, that I may be comforted together with you by the mutual faith both of you and me.

13 Now I would not have you ignorant, brethren, that oftentimes I purposed to come unto you, (but was let hitherto,) that I might have some fruit among you also, even as among other Gentiles.

14 I am debtor both to the Greeks, and to the Barbarians; both to the wise, and to the unwise.

15 So, as much as in me is, I am ready to preach the gospel to you that are at Rome also.

16 ¶ For I am not ashamed of the gospel of Christ: for it is the power of God unto salvation to every one that believeth; to the Jew first, and also to the Greek.

---

1:1    Apostles are "special witnesses of the name of Christ in all the world" (D&C 107:23).

     **separated**—set apart

1:2    **afore**—before

1:2-4   The prophets taught that Jesus would be born of the seed or lineage of King David (see Matthew 22:42) and also be the Son of God (see Luke 1:35).

1:5    The Joseph Smith Translation tells us that Paul became an Apostle of Jesus Christ "through obedience, and faith in his name" (JST, Romans 1:5).

1:9    Paul prayed "without ceasing" for the Saints. How does it make you feel to know that the leaders of the Church pray for you?

1:11   **impart**—give
     **established**—strengthened

1:13   **let hitherto**—prevented until now
     **some fruit**—converts

1:14   **debtor**—one who owes

     Greeks were civilized people known for their wisdom. To them, everyone else was barbaric, or uncivilized. Paul had been blessed by both the civilized and the uncivilized (see Acts 28:2).

1:16   Paul was not ashamed to share his testimony of Jesus Christ. How do you feel about sharing your testimony?

---

| | |
|---|---|
| = Word Help | = A Closer Look |
| = More Light | = Ponder This |

Words in pink are explained in the Glossary.

17 For therein is the righteousness of God revealed from faith to faith: as it is written, The just shall live by faith.

## PAUL TEACHES ABOUT WICKEDNESS AND GOD'S PUNISHMENT

18 For the wrath of God is revealed from heaven against all ungodliness and unrighteousness of men, who hold the truth in unrighteousness;

19 ¶ Because that which may be known of God is manifest in them; for God hath shewed it unto them.

20 For the invisible things of him from the creation of the world are clearly seen, being understood by the things that are made, even his eternal power and Godhead; so that they are without excuse:

21 Because that, when they knew God, they glorified him not as God, neither were thankful; but became vain in their imaginations, and their foolish heart was darkened.

22 Professing themselves to be wise, they became fools,

23 And changed the glory of the uncorruptible God into an image made like to corruptible man, and to birds, and fourfooted beasts, and creeping things.

24 Wherefore God also gave them up to uncleanness through the lusts of their own hearts, to dishonour their own bodies between themselves:

25 Who changed the truth of God into a lie, and worshipped and served the creature more than the Creator, who is blessed for ever. Amen.

26 For this cause God gave them up unto vile affections: for even their women did change the natural use into that which is against nature:

27 And likewise also the men, leaving the natural use of the woman, burned in their lust one toward another; men with men working that which is unseemly, and receiving in themselves that recompence of their error which was meet.

28 And even as they did not like to retain God in their knowledge, God gave them over to a reprobate mind, to do those things which are not convenient;

29 Being filled with all unrighteousness, fornication, wickedness, covetousness, maliciousness; full of envy, murder, debate, deceit, malignity; whisperers,

30 Backbiters, haters of God, despiteful, proud, boasters, inventors of evil things, disobedient to parents,

31 Without understanding, covenantbreakers, without natural affection, implacable, unmerciful:

32 Who knowing the judgment of God, that they which commit such things are worthy of death, not only do the same, but have pleasure in them that do them.

---

1:17    The Joseph Smith Translation changes this verse to say that God's righteousness is revealed "through faith on his name" (JST, Romans 1:17).

1:18    **the wrath of God**—God's punishment

   The Joseph Smith Translation tells us that God punishes those "who love not the truth, but remain in unrighteousness" (JST, Romans 1:18).

1:20    The Joseph Smith Translation clarifies this verse to show that since the Creation, God has revealed his eternal power and nature to mankind by the things he has made. He has done this "so that they [men] are without excuse." (JST, Romans 1:20.)

1:21    "Gratitude is of the very essence of worship— thanksgiving to the God of Heaven, who has given us all that we have that is good" (Gordon B. Hinckley, *Teachings of Gordon B. Hinckley*, p. 250). When we fail to thank God, we fail to worship him and we become vain (meaning empty or shallow) and foolish.

1:22-23    When men no longer worship God the way they are supposed to, they create for themselves idols. Sometimes they make images of birds or beasts; sometimes they worship men, money, or power (see Exodus 32:4).

1:23    **corruptible**—perishable

1:24    **to dishonour their own bodies**—to misuse the sacred creative power

1:25    **worshipped . . . the creature more than the Creator**—worshipped men instead of God

1:26-27    "The Spirit of the Lord will not argue with men" (Joseph Fielding Smith, *Answers to Gospel Questions* 3:29). When we refuse to listen to the Spirit we eventually fall into doing evil activities.

1:28    **did not like to retain God in their knowledge**—did not think it necessary to acknowledge God
**reprobate**—base, worthless

1:29    **maliciousness**—desire to hurt

1:30    **backbiters**—gossipers

1:31    **implacable**—unforgiving

1:32    Some people know that God will punish the wicked but they continue to do evil things anyway. Why do they choose not to change?

# CHAPTER 2

*Paul explains that God judges righteously. Look for what Paul says about those who have been taught the truth but do not live it.*

## GOD JUDGES ALL ACCORDING TO THE TRUTH THEY HAVE BEEN GIVEN

1 ¶ THEREFORE thou art inexcusable, O man, whosoever thou art that judgest: for wherein thou judgest another, thou condemnest thyself; for thou that judgest doest the same things.

2 But we are sure that the judgment of God is according to truth against them which commit such things.

3 And thinkest thou this, O man, that judgest them which do such things, and doest the same, that thou shalt escape the judgment of God?

4 Or despisest thou the riches of his goodness and forbearance and longsuffering; not knowing that the goodness of God leadeth thee to repentance?

5 But after thy hardness and impenitent heart treasurest up unto thyself wrath against the day of wrath and revelation of the righteous judgment of God;

6 Who will render to every man according to his deeds:

7 To them who by patient continuance in well doing seek for glory and honour and immortality, eternal life:

8 But unto them that are contentious, and do not obey the truth, but obey unrighteousness, indignation and wrath,

9 Tribulation and anguish, upon every soul of man that doeth evil, of the Jew first, and also of the Gentile;

10 But glory, honour, and peace, to every man that worketh good, to the Jew first, and also to the Gentile:

11 For there is no respect of persons with God.

12 For as many as have sinned without law shall also perish without law: and as many as have sinned in the law shall be judged by the law;

13 (For not the hearers of the law are just before God, but the doers of the law shall be justified.

14 For when the Gentiles, which have not the law, do by nature the things contained in the law, these, having not the law, are a law unto themselves:

15 Which shew the work of the law written in their hearts, their conscience also bearing witness, and their thoughts the mean while accusing or else excusing one another;)

16 In the day when God shall judge the secrets of men by Jesus Christ according to my gospel.

---

2:1    **thou art inexcusable**—you cannot be excused or pardoned
**thou condemnest thyself**—you make yourself guilty

2:4    **despisest**—treat as unimportant or undesirable
**forbearance and longsuffering**—patience

Paul says that the "goodness of God leadeth thee to repentance." What spirit leads us away from repentance? (See Moroni 7:17; also read verses 15 and 16.)

2:5    **after thy hardness and impenitent heart**—because of your stubborn and unrepentant heart
**treasurest up unto thyself wrath**—you store up for yourself anger
**the day of wrath**—the day of God's judgment

2:6    **render**—give back

2:6-11    This principle is sometimes called "the law of the harvest." We receive the judgment that we have brought upon ourselves. (See Galatians 6:7-8.)

2:8    **contentious**—unfriendly, prone to argue

2:9    **Tribulation and anguish**—Trouble and suffering

2:11-13    The Prophet Joseph Smith said that God will judge people, " 'not according to what they have not, but according to what they have,' those who have lived without law, will be judged without law, and those who have a law, will be judged by that law" (*The Teachings of Joseph Smith*, p. 16).

2:12-13    Hearing and knowing the law is not sufficient; we must live God's law to be considered righteous. How are you doing at living the laws of God that you know are true?

2:13    **justified**—judged to be righteous, not guilty of sin

2:14-15    The Gentiles who believe and are baptized may not understand the law of Moses, but "their conscience," or the Light of Christ, teaches them what they should do (see 2 Nephi 32:5 and Moroni 7:15-16).

## JEWS WHO KNOW THE LAW BUT DO NOT LIVE IT ARE WORSE THAN THOSE WHO DO NOT KNOW THE LAW

17 ¶ Behold, thou art called a Jew, and restest in the law, and makest thy boast of God,

18 And knowest his will, and approvest the things that are more excellent, being instructed out of the law;

19 And art confident that thou thyself art a guide of the blind, a light of them which are in darkness,

20 An instructor of the foolish, a teacher of babes, which hast the form of knowledge and of the truth in the law.

21 Thou therefore which teachest another, teachest thou not thyself? thou that preachest a man should not steal, dost thou steal?

22 Thou that sayest a man should not commit adultery, dost thou commit adultery? thou that abhorrest idols, dost thou commit sacrilege?

23 Thou that makest thy boast of the law, through breaking the law dishonourest thou God?

24 For the name of God is blasphemed among the Gentiles through you, as it is written.

25 For circumcision verily profiteth, if thou keep the law: but if thou be a breaker of the law, thy circumcision is made uncircumcision.

26 Therefore if the uncircumcision keep the righteousness of the law, shall not his uncircumcision be counted for circumcision?

27 And shall not uncircumcision which is by nature, if it fulfil the law, judge thee, who by the letter and circumcision dost transgress the law?

28 For he is not a Jew, which is one outwardly; neither is that circumcision, which is outward in the flesh:

29 But he is a Jew, which is one inwardly; and circumcision is that of the heart, in the spirit, and not in the letter; whose praise is not of men, but of God.

## CHAPTER 3

*Paul explains that both Jews and Gentiles are guilty of sin and are cut off from God. Watch for what Paul teaches is their only hope for salvation.*

## GOD IS FAITHFUL AND TRUE TO ALL HE HAS SAID

1 ¶ WHAT advantage then hath the Jew? or what profit is there of circumcision?

2 Much every way: chiefly, because that unto them were committed the oracles of God.

3 For what if some did not believe? shall their unbelief make the faith of God without effect?

4 God forbid: yea, let God be true, but every man a liar; as it is written, That thou mightest be justified in thy sayings, and mightest overcome when thou art judged.

5 But if our unrighteousness commend the righteousness of God, what shall we say? Is God unrighteous who taketh vengeance? (I speak as a man)

6 God forbid: for then how shall God judge the world?

7 For if the truth of God hath more abounded through my lie unto his glory; why yet am I also judged as a sinner?

---

2:17   *restest in the law*—rely on the law to save you

2:19-20   The Jews, even some who were converted to Jesus Christ, felt that they were wiser and more righteous just because they knew the law of Moses.

2:22   *thou that abhorrest idols, dost thou commit sacrilege?*—you who hate idols, do you rob the shrines or temples of idols?

2:23   *dishonourest thou God?*—do you bring shame to God?

2:25-29   *Circumcision* and *uncircumcision* are used in these verses as another way of saying *Jew* and *Gentile* (see Ephesians 2:11). For more information, see the Glossary, s.v. "Circumcision," "Jew" and "Gentile."

2:28-29   God's covenant people are those who keep their covenants, not just outwardly but also in their hearts. What do you think Paul would say to a member of the Church today who believes that all it takes to be saved is to be baptized?

3:1-2   The Joseph Smith Translation of these verses indicates that there is no advantage to being a Jew "who is not a Jew from the heart." Jews who were sincere in their religion were blessed by having the oracles, or words of God, revealed to them.

3:5-8   Some argued in Paul's day that their own evil acts actually made God's righteousness more obvious. They claimed that they should not be punished as sinners because their sins actually glorified God. The Joseph Smith Translation simply says: "But this is false" (JST, Romans 3:8).

8 And not rather, (as we be slanderously reported, and as some affirm that we say,) Let us do evil, that good may come? whose damnation is just.

## ALL HAVE SINNED

9 What then? are we better than they? No, in no wise: for we have before proved both Jews and Gentiles, that they are all under sin;

10 As it is written, There is none righteous, no, not one:

11 There is none that understandeth, there is none that seeketh after God.

12 They are all gone out of the way, they are together become unprofitable; there is none that doeth good, no, not one.

13 Their throat is an open sepulchre; with their tongues they have used deceit; the poison of asps is under their lips:

14 Whose mouth is full of cursing and bitterness:

15 Their feet are swift to shed blood:

16 Destruction and misery are in their ways:

17 And the way of peace have they not known:

18 There is no fear of God before their eyes.

19 ¶ Now we know that what things soever the law saith, it saith to them who are under the law: that every mouth may be stopped, and all the world may become guilty before God.

20 Therefore by the deeds of the law there shall no flesh be justified in his sight: for by the law is the knowledge of sin.

## WE BECOME RIGHTEOUS THROUGH FAITH IN JESUS CHRIST

21 But now the righteousness of God without the law is manifested, being witnessed by the law and the prophets;

22 Even the righteousness of God which is by faith of Jesus Christ unto all and upon all them that believe: for there is no difference:

23 For all have sinned, and come short of the glory of God;

24 Being justified freely by his grace through the redemption that is in Christ Jesus:

25 Whom God hath set forth to be a propitiation through faith in his blood, to declare his righteousness for the remission of sins that are past, through the forbearance of God;

26 To declare, I say, at this time his righteousness: that he might be just, and the justifier of him which believeth in Jesus.

27 Where is boasting then? It is excluded. By what law? of works? Nay: but by the law of faith.

28 Therefore we conclude that a man is justified by faith without the deeds of the law.

29 Is he the God of the Jews only? is he not also of the Gentiles? Yes, of the Gentiles also:

30 Seeing it is one God, which shall justify the circumcision by faith, and uncircumcision through faith.

31 Do we then make void the law through faith? God forbid: yea, we establish the law.

---

3:9-12 Paul explains that no one is perfect; everyone has sinned (see Psalms 14:1-3; 53:1-3). John the Beloved also taught, "If we say that we have no sin, we deceive ourselves, and the truth is not in us" (1 John 1:8).

3:10-12 Why do you think Paul wants us to realize that no mortal has lived a perfect life? What or who is our only hope if we cannot be perfect on our own? (See Romans 3:24-25.)

3:13 sepulchre—tomb or grave
asps—snakes

3:20 Paul explains again that because all people break God's laws, the law cannot declare us clean and innocent (or justified). The law only teaches us where we are wrong.

3:21-26 Since all are sinners and "come short of the glory of God," it would seem we have no hope. But God, in his mercy, gave his Son as a sacrifice to take our sins away. Jesus is our only hope. The

prophet Lehi said, "There is no flesh that can dwell in the presence of God, save it be through the merits, and mercy, and grace of the Holy Messiah" (2 Nephi 2:8).

3:23-24 How do you feel about Jesus, who freely gave his life so you can become clean again? What would happen to you if Jesus had not come?

3:25 a propitiation—a sacrifice or payment for our sins
forbearance—patience

3:27-28 In these verses the "law" is the law of Moses. Many Jews believed that living this law would save them. Paul taught that "the deeds of the law" would not save them. Salvation comes by living the "law of faith," or the gospel of Jesus Christ (see 2 Nephi 25:24-25).

3:30 circumcision . . . uncircumcision—Jews . . . Gentiles

*Abraham and Sarah: because of their faith and righteousness (Romans 4:3), "in the world and out of the world should they continue as innumerable as the stars" (D&C 132:30).*

## CHAPTER 4

*Paul shows in the previous chapters that there is no righteousness before God by the works of the law, because no one can live the law perfectly. In this chapter look for examples he uses to support that statement.*

### GOD CALLED ABRAHAM RIGHTEOUS BECAUSE OF HIS FAITH, NOT BECAUSE HE WAS PERFECT

1 ¶ WHAT shall we say then that Abraham our father, as pertaining to the flesh, hath found?

2 For if Abraham were justified by works, he hath whereof to glory; but not before God.

3 For what saith the scripture? Abraham believed God, and it was counted unto him for righteousness.

### BY FAITH IN JESUS CHRIST WE CAN BECOME RIGHTEOUS

4 Now to him that worketh is the reward not reckoned of grace, but of debt.

5 But to him that worketh not, but believeth on him that justifieth the ungodly, his faith is counted for righteousness.

6 Even as David also describeth the blessedness of the man, unto whom God imputeth righteousness without works,

7 Saying, Blessed are they whose iniquities are forgiven, and whose sins are covered.

8 Blessed is the man to whom the Lord will not impute sin.

---

4:2    **whereof to glory**—reason for boasting or bragging

4:3    The scripture Paul was referring to is Genesis 15:6.

4:4    Grace is divine help given by God through the atonement of Jesus Christ. It provides us with the power needed to repent, keep the commandments, and become like God. (See LDS Bible Dictionary, s.v. "Grace," p. 697.)

4:4-8    The Joseph Smith Translation helps us understand that if we depend upon our obedience to the law to save us, then we will get just what we earn and no more. But if we have faith in God and try to be obedient, our faith will be counted as righteousness and our sins forgiven. (See JST, Romans 4:2-7.)

4:6    **imputeth**—counts

## BY FAITH, GENTILES AND JEWS CAN BECOME RIGHTEOUS, EVEN IF THEY DON'T LIVE THE LAW OF MOSES

9 ¶ Cometh this blessedness then upon the circumcision only, or upon the uncircumcision also? for we say that faith was reckoned to Abraham for righteousness.

10 How was it then reckoned? when he was in circumcision, or in uncircumcision? Not in circumcision, but in uncircumcision.

11 And he received the sign of circumcision, a seal of the righteousness of the faith which he had yet being uncircumcised: that he might be the father of all them that believe, though they be not circumcised; that righteousness might be imputed unto them also:

12 And the father of circumcision to them who are not of the circumcision only, but who also walk in the steps of that faith of our father Abraham, which he had being yet uncircumcised.

13 For the promise, that he should be the heir of the world, was not to Abraham, or to his seed, through the law, but through the righteousness of faith.

14 For if they which are of the law be heirs, faith is made void, and the promise made of none effect:

15 Because the law worketh wrath: for where no law is, there is no transgression.

16 Therefore it is of faith, that it might be by grace; to the end the promise might be sure to all the seed; not to that only which is of the law, but to that also which is of the faith of Abraham; who is the father of us all,

17 ¶ (As it is written, I have made thee a father of many nations,) before him whom he believed, even God, who quickeneth the dead, and calleth those things which be not as though they were.

18 Who against hope believed in hope, that he might become the father of many nations, according to that which was spoken, So shall thy seed be.

19 And being not weak in faith, he considered not his own body now dead, when he was about an hundred years old, neither yet the deadness of Sara's womb:

20 He staggered not at the promise of God through unbelief; but was strong in faith, giving glory to God;

21 And being fully persuaded that, what he had promised, he was able also to perform.

22 And therefore it was imputed to him for righteousness.

23 ¶ Now it was not written for his sake alone, that it was imputed to him;

24 But for us also, to whom it shall be imputed, if we believe on him that raised up Jesus our Lord from the dead;

25 Who was delivered for our offences, and was raised again for our justification.

## CHAPTER 5

*Adam's fall brought death into the world. Look for what Paul explains is the only way that we can be saved.*

## OUR FAITH WILL CARRY US THROUGH OUR TRIALS

1 ¶ THEREFORE being justified by faith, we have peace with God through our Lord Jesus Christ:

2 By whom also we have access by faith into this grace wherein we stand, and rejoice in hope of the glory of God.

3 And not only so, but we glory in tribulations also: knowing that tribulation worketh patience;

---

4:9-12 The word *circumcision* is used here as a symbol of the law of Moses (see Glossary, s.v. "Circumcision"). Many Jews felt they were the only ones that could be called righteous, since only they observed the law of Moses. Paul reminds them that God called Abraham righteous because of his faith long before the law was given to Moses.

4:12 **walk in the steps of**—have the same faith as

4:13 **he should be the heir of the world**—all nations would be blessed through him and his seed

4:14-16 The Joseph Smith Translation explains that we are justified, or declared righteous, by our faith, our righteous works, and by God's grace. This same promise applies to both the Jews and the Gentiles. (See JST, Romans 4:16.)

4:17-22 Abraham had faith that he and his wife Sarah would have a child even though they were very old. What does this story teach us about God's power to keep his promises?

4:22 **imputed**—counted

4:23-25 God called Abraham righteous because he had faith in His promises. What promise does Paul say we need to believe in to be called righteous?

5:1 **justified**—declared righteous

4 And patience, experience; and experience, hope:

5 And hope maketh not ashamed; because the love of God is shed abroad in our hearts by the Holy Ghost which is given unto us.

## WE ARE SAVED THROUGH THE ATONEMENT OF JESUS CHRIST

6 ¶ For when we were yet without strength, in due time Christ died for the ungodly.

7 For scarcely for a righteous man will one die: yet peradventure for a good man some would even dare to die.

8 But God commendeth his love toward us, in that, while we were yet sinners, Christ died for us.

9 Much more then, being now justified by his blood, we shall be saved from wrath through him.

10 For if, when we were enemies, we were reconciled to God by the death of his Son, much more, being reconciled, we shall be saved by his life.

11 And not only so, but we also joy in God through our Lord Jesus Christ, by whom we have now received the atonement.

## DEATH CAME THROUGH ADAM AND LIFE THROUGH JESUS CHRIST

12 Wherefore, as by one man sin entered into the world, and death by sin; and so death passed upon all men, for that all have sinned:

13 (For until the law sin was in the world: but sin is not imputed when there is no law.

14 Nevertheless death reigned from Adam to Moses, even over them that had not sinned after the similitude of Adam's transgression, who is the figure of him that was to come.

15 But not as the offence, so also is the free gift. For if through the offence of one many be dead, much more the grace of God, and the gift by grace, which is by one man, Jesus Christ, hath abounded unto many.

16 And not as it was by one that sinned, so is the gift: for the judgment was by one to condemnation, but the free gift is of many offences unto justification.

17 For if by one man's offence death reigned by one; much more they which receive abundance of grace and of the gift of righteousness shall reign in life by one, Jesus Christ.)

18 Therefore as by the offence of one judgment came upon all men to condemnation; even so by the righteousness of one the free gift came upon all men unto justification of life.

19 For as by one man's disobedience many were made sinners, so by the obedience of one shall many be made righteous.

20 Moreover the law entered, that the offence might abound. But where sin abounded, grace did much more abound:

21 That as sin hath reigned unto death, even so might grace reign through righteousness unto eternal life by Jesus Christ our Lord.

---

5:5    *maketh not ashamed*—does not disappoint us

We receive God's love in our hearts through the Holy Ghost. What can you do to have the Holy Ghost as your constant companion?

5:7    *peradventure*—perhaps

5:9    *wrath*—punishment

5:10   *reconciled to God*—returned to God's favor

5:11   "*Atonement* is really three words: *At-one-ment*, meaning to set at one, one with God" (Boyd K. Packer, in Conference Report, April 1988, p. 81). The Atonement refers to the sacrifice that Jesus made both in Gethsemane and on the cross. Jesus' atonement allows us to be forgiven of sins when we repent, be resurrected, and return to God's presence.

5:13   *sin is not imputed*—people are not charged with sin

5:14   *similitude*—likeness

5:14-  Through the transgression of one, Adam, sin
21     and death entered the world. By the mission of another, Jesus Christ, we receive the gift of God and are saved from sin and death. (See 1 Corinthians 15:21-22.)

5:15   *abounded*—overflowed

5:18   *came upon all men to condemnation*—left all men subject to death and sin

5:20-  Sin and death are a part of mortal life. Because
21     of the atonement of Jesus Christ, Heavenly Father promises eternal life to those who live righteously. How do you feel about God's promise? What can you do to be worthy of this great gift?

# CHAPTER 6

*Paul teaches the importance of controlling our bodies as we try to become righteous. Watch for what Paul teaches about the symbolism of baptism and how we can get God's help in keeping the commandments.*

## BAPTISM IS A SYMBOL OF JESUS' RESURRECTION AND OF OUR NEW LIFE

1 ¶ WHAT shall we say then? Shall we continue in sin, that grace may abound?

2 God forbid. How shall we, that are dead to sin, live any longer therein?

3 Know ye not, that so many of us as were baptized into Jesus Christ were baptized into his death?

4 Therefore we are buried with him by baptism into death: that like as Christ was raised up from the dead by the glory of the Father, even so we also should walk in newness of life.

5 For if we have been planted together in the likeness of his death, we shall be also in the likeness of his resurrection:

6 Knowing this, that our old man is crucified with him, that the body of sin might be destroyed, that henceforth we should not serve sin.

7 For he that is dead is freed from sin.

8 Now if we be dead with Christ, we believe that we shall also live with him:

9 Knowing that Christ being raised from the dead dieth no more; death hath no more dominion over him.

10 For in that he died, he died unto sin once: but in that he liveth, he liveth unto God.

11 Likewise reckon ye also yourselves to be dead indeed unto sin, but alive unto God through Jesus Christ our Lord.

## THE REWARD OF SIN IS DEATH; THE REWARD OF RIGHTEOUSNESS IS ETERNAL LIFE

12 Let not sin therefore reign in your mortal body, that ye should obey it in the lusts thereof.

13 Neither yield ye your members as instruments of unrighteousness unto sin: but yield yourselves unto God, as those that are alive from the dead, and your members as instruments of righteousness unto God.

14 For sin shall not have dominion over you: for ye are not under the law, but under grace.

15 What then? shall we sin, because we are not under the law, but under grace? God forbid.

16 Know ye not, that to whom ye yield yourselves servants to obey, his servants ye are to whom ye obey; whether of sin unto death, or of obedience unto righteousness?

17 But God be thanked, that ye were the servants of sin, but ye have obeyed from the heart that form of doctrine which was delivered you.

18 Being then made free from sin, ye became the servants of righteousness.

---

6:1    *abound*—increase

6:3-6    Some churches teach that baptism can be done by sprinkling water on a person's head. Elder Bruce R. McConkie said that these verses from Paul help explain that "baptism is performed by immersion to typify [represent] the death, burial, and resurrection of our Redeemer" (*Mormon Doctrine*, p. 773). Baptism by immersion is also a symbol for burying our sins and rising again to live a new life.

6:6    *our old man*—our old sinful self

6:7    The Joseph Smith Translation changes this verse to read, "For he that is dead *to sin* is freed from sin" (JST, Romans 6:7; emphasis added). Being "dead to sin" means that we no longer desire to commit sin.

6:9    *dominion*—power

6:11    *reckon ye also yourselves*—count yourselves also

Have you been baptized? How did that day help you feel "alive unto God"?

6:12    *reign in*—have power over, control
*lusts*—unrighteous desires

6:13-18    Paul tells us not to let our bodies serve sin but instead turn to God and live righteously. To be "under the law" means that we know God's commandments and will be judged by them. To be "under grace" means to have God's help to live those commandments. In the Book of Mormon, King Benjamin teaches that it is through the atonement of Jesus Christ that we are given the grace or spiritual power to live righteously (see Mosiah 3:19; 4:1-3).

19 I speak after the manner of men because of the infirmity of your flesh: for as ye have yielded your members servants to uncleanness and to iniquity unto iniquity; even so now yield your members servants to righteousness unto holiness.

20 For when ye were the servants of sin, ye were free from righteousness.

21 What fruit had ye then in those things whereof ye are now ashamed? for the end of those things is death.

22 But now being made free from sin, and become servants to God, ye have your fruit unto holiness, and the end everlasting life.

23 For the wages of sin is death; but the gift of God is eternal life through Jesus Christ our Lord.

## CHAPTER 7

*In this chapter Paul teaches that the law of Moses was fulfilled by the atonement of Jesus Christ. Look for how and why this is so.*

### THE LAW OF MOSES IS FULFILLED IN JESUS CHRIST

1 ¶ KNOW ye not, brethren, (for I speak to them that know the law,) how that the law hath dominion over a man as long as he liveth?

2 For the woman which hath an husband is bound by the law to her husband so long as he liveth; but if the husband be dead, she is loosed from the law of her husband.

3 So then if, while her husband liveth, she be married to another man, she shall be called an adulteress: but if her husband be dead, she is free from that law; so that she is no adulteress, though she be married to another man.

4 Wherefore, my brethren, ye also are become dead to the law by the body of Christ; that ye should be married to another, even to him who is raised from the dead, that we should bring forth fruit unto God.

5 For when we were in the flesh, the motions of sins, which were by the law, did work in our members to bring forth fruit unto death.

6 But now we are delivered from the law, that being dead wherein we were held; that we should serve in newness of spirit, and not in the oldness of the letter.

### THE LAW OF CHRIST REPLACES THE LAW OF MOSES

7 ¶ What shall we say then? Is the law sin? God forbid. Nay, I had not known sin, but by the law: for I had not known lust, except the law had said, Thou shalt not covet.

8 But sin, taking occasion by the commandment, wrought in me all manner of concupiscence. For without the law sin was dead.

---

6:19 **the infirmity of your flesh**—your mortal weakness
**iniquity**—sin, wickedness

6:21 **fruit**—blessing or reward

6:23 What difference do you think it would make if all people in the world really understood that if they serve Satan they will be paid by Satan, and if they serve God they will be rewarded by God? How can reading the scriptures and praying daily help you remember to serve God? (See 2 Nephi 32:3.)

7:1 **the law**—the law of Moses
**dominion**—power or authority

7:2-4 Paul compares the fulfillment of the law of Moses to marriage. Once a person's spouse dies, that person is free to marry another. Similarly, once the law of Moses was done away with, the people were free to accept a higher law, meaning the gospel of Jesus Christ.

7:4 **fruit unto God**—righteousness

7:5 **motions of sins**—evil desires and afflictions

In verse 5, the Joseph Smith Translation changes the phrase "which were by the law" to "which were not according to the law."

7:6 Paul taught that when someone chooses to follow Jesus Christ, the person becomes "a new creature" (2 Corinthians 5:17), one who is led by the Spirit and not by the written code of the old Jewish law.

7:7-8 Paul explains that the law didn't lead people to sin but helped them recognize when they were guilty of sin. The Book of Mormon teaches that it is necessary to have law, for without it there would be no sin or righteousness (see 2 Nephi 2:13).

7:8 Paul explains that when he knew that a thing was forbidden by the law, it raised in him "concupiscence," meaning a desire for the forbidden thing.

9 For I was alive without the law once: but when the commandment came, sin revived, and I died.

10 And the commandment, which was ordained to life, I found to be unto death.

11 For sin, taking occasion by the commandment, deceived me, and by it slew me.

12 Wherefore the law is holy, and the commandment holy, and just, and good.

13 Was then that which is good made death unto me? God forbid. But sin, that it might appear sin, working death in me by that which is good; that sin by the commandment might become exceeding sinful.

14 ¶ For we know that the law is spiritual: but I am carnal, sold under sin.

15 For that which I do I allow not: for what I would, that do I not; but what I hate, that do I.

16 If then I do that which I would not, I consent unto the law that it is good.

17 Now then it is no more I that do it, but sin that dwelleth in me.

18 For I know that in me (that is, in my flesh,) dwelleth no good thing: for to will is present with me; but how to perform that which is good I find not.

19 For the good that I would I do not: but the evil which I would not, that I do.

20 Now if I do that I would not, it is no more I that do it, but sin that dwelleth in me.

21 I find then a law, that, when I would do good, evil is present with me.

22 For I delight in the law of God after the inward man:

23 But I see another law in my members, warring against the law of my mind, and bringing me into captivity to the law of sin which is in my members.

24 O wretched man that I am! who shall deliver me from the body of this death?

25 I thank God through Jesus Christ our Lord. So then with the mind I myself serve the law of God; but with the flesh the law of sin.

## CHAPTER 8

*We are forgiven when we truly repent because of the atonement of Jesus Christ. Look for how living the gospel of Christ brings forgiveness and peace.*

### THE LAW OF CHRIST FREES US FROM SIN

1 ¶ There is therefore now no condemnation to them which are in Christ Jesus, who walk not after the flesh, but after the Spirit.

2 For the law of the Spirit of life in Christ Jesus hath made me free from the law of sin and death.

3 For what the law could not do, in that it was weak through the flesh, God sending his own Son in the likeness of sinful flesh, and for sin, condemned sin in the flesh:

---

7:9-13   The Joseph Smith Translation helps explain that before Paul knew about Christ, he thought he was "alive" and sinless. But when he first learned of Christ and "believed not the commandment of Christ . . . it condemned [him] unto death." (JST, Romans 7:9-10.) In other words, when we are taught the commandments (the law), it shows us right from wrong. If we then disobey we are "slain," meaning killed spiritually.

7:14   *carnal*—physical or worldly

7:14-16   The Joseph Smith Translation changes the entire meaning of these verses to show that Paul grew in spirituality and in his ability to do what he was "commanded to do." It also adds the important phrase, "And that which I am commanded not to allow, I allow not." (See JST, Romans 7:14-17.)

7:17-20   Life is a constant struggle between good and evil. Moroni taught that if we will come unto Christ, He will help us overcome our weaknesses that lead us to sin (see Ether 12:27).

7:21-25   Even though Paul said, "I delight in the law of God after the inward man," meaning his spiritual side, he also saw that his natural, or physical, side struggled with the desire to sin. What are some things the Lord has told us to do to help our spiritual side overcome the weaknesses of our physical side? (See 1 Nephi 15:24; Mosiah 3:19; Ether 12:27.)

7:24   The Joseph Smith Translation makes it clear that Paul is saying that he is a "wretched man" if he cannot overcome the sin which is in him (see JST, Romans 7:26).

8:1   *condemnation*—punishment

8:2   *law of sin and death*—law of Moses

8:3   People cannot atone for their own sins. Such an atonement came about only because Heavenly Father sent his Son, Jesus Christ (see John 3:16).

4 That the righteousness of the law might be fulfilled in us, who walk not after the flesh, but after the Spirit.

5 For they that are after the flesh do mind the things of the flesh; but they that are after the Spirit the things of the Spirit.

6 For to be carnally minded is death; but to be spiritually minded is life and peace.

7 Because the carnal mind is enmity against God: for it is not subject to the law of God, neither indeed can be.

8 So then they that are in the flesh cannot please God.

9 But ye are not in the flesh, but in the Spirit, if so be that the Spirit of God dwell in you. Now if any man have not the Spirit of Christ, he is none of his.

10 ¶ And if Christ be in you, the body is dead because of sin; but the Spirit is life because of righteousness.

11 But if the Spirit of him that raised up Jesus from the dead dwell in you, he that raised up Christ from the dead shall also quicken your mortal bodies by his Spirit that dwelleth in you.

## WE BECOME THE SONS OF GOD AND JOINT-HEIRS WITH CHRIST

12 Therefore, brethren, we are debtors, not to the flesh, to live after the flesh.

13 For if ye live after the flesh, ye shall die: but if ye through the Spirit do mortify the deeds of the body, ye shall live.

14 For as many as are led by the Spirit of God, they are the sons of God.

15 For ye have not received the spirit of bondage again to fear; but ye have received the Spirit of adop-

tion, whereby we cry, Abba, Father.

16 The Spirit itself beareth witness with our spirit, that we are the children of God:

17 ¶ And if children, then heirs; heirs of God, and joint-heirs with Christ; if so be that we suffer with him, that we may be also glorified together.

## OUR SUFFERINGS BRING US GLORY

18 For I reckon that the sufferings of this present time are not worthy to be compared with the glory which shall be revealed in us.

19 For the earnest expectation of the creature waiteth for the manifestation of the sons of God.

20 For the creature was made subject to vanity, not willingly, but by reason of him who hath subjected the same in hope,

21 Because the creature itself also shall be delivered from the bondage of corruption into the glorious liberty of the children of God.

22 For we know that the whole creation groaneth and travaileth in pain together until now.

23 And not only they, but ourselves also, which have the firstfruits of the Spirit, even we ourselves groan within ourselves, waiting for the adoption, to wit, the redemption of our body.

24 For we are saved by hope: but hope that is seen is not hope: for what a man seeth, why doth he yet hope for?

25 But if we hope for that we see not, then do we with patience wait for it.

26 ¶ Likewise the Spirit also helpeth our infirmities: for we know not what we should pray for as we ought: but the Spirit itself maketh intercession for us with groanings which cannot be uttered.

---

8:4-7   Paul uses the word *flesh* to mean the natural, or fallen, man, who does not rely on the Spirit of God (see Mosiah 3:19). Great blessings come to those who follow the Spirit of God instead of the desires of the flesh.

8:7   **the carnal mind**—the human nature of man to sin

8:8   The Joseph Smith Translation changes the phrase "in the flesh" to "after the flesh." The natural man is an enemy to God and cannot please God (see Mosiah 3:18-19).

8:9   **none of his**—not of Christ

8:10   The Joseph Smith Translation renders this verse, "And if Christ be in you, though the body shall die because of sin, yet the Spirit is life, because of righteousness."

8:13   **mortify**—put to death

8:15   **received the Spirit of adoption**—become children of God

  "Abba" is a loving and personal way to say "Father."

8:17   **heirs**—children who inherit their parent's possessions

8:22   **and travaileth in pain**—as in the pain from childbirth

8:24   Hope is focusing on the realities of the resurrection, eternal life, a better world, and Christ's second coming.

8:26   **infirmities**—weakness
**maketh intercession for**—pleads in behalf of

27 And he that searcheth the hearts knoweth what is the mind of the Spirit, because he maketh intercession for the saints according to the will of God.

28 And we know that all things work together for good to them that love God, to them who are the called according to his purpose.

29 ¶ For whom he did foreknow, he also did predestinate to be conformed to the image of his Son, that he might be the firstborn among many brethren.

30 Moreover whom he did predestinate, them he also called: and whom he called, them he also justified: and whom he justified, them he also glorified.

## *GOD'S EVERLASTING LOVE IS SHOWN*

31 ¶ What shall we then say to these things? If God be for us, who can be against us?

32 He that spared not his own Son, but delivered him up for us all, how shall he not with him also freely give us all things?

33 Who shall lay any thing to the charge of God's elect? It is God that justifieth.

34 Who is he that condemneth? It is Christ that died, yea rather, that is risen again, who is even at the right hand of God, who also maketh intercession for us.

35 Who shall separate us from the love of Christ? shall tribulation, or distress, or persecution, or famine, or nakedness, or peril, or sword?

36 As it is written, For thy sake we are killed all the day long; we are accounted as sheep for the slaughter.

37 Nay, in all these things we are more than conquerors through him that loved us.

38 For I am persuaded, that neither death, nor life, nor angels, nor principalities, nor powers, nor things present, nor things to come,

39 Nor height, nor depth, nor any other creature, shall be able to separate us from the love of God, which is in Christ Jesus our Lord.

## CHAPTER 9

*The house of Israel was chosen in the premortal life to be the covenant people so that they might become a means of blessing the whole world. Notice what God expects of those who want to receive his full blessings.*

## *ISRAEL WAS FOREORDAINED TO RECEIVE THE BLESSINGS OF THE GOSPEL*

1 ¶ I say the truth in Christ, I lie not, my conscience also bearing me witness in the Holy Ghost,

2 That I have great heaviness and continual sorrow in my heart.

3 For I could wish that myself were accursed from Christ for my brethren, my kinsmen according to the flesh:

4 Who are Israelites; to whom pertaineth the adoption, and the glory, and the covenants, and the giving of the law, and the service of God, and the promises;

5 Whose are the fathers, and of whom as concerning the flesh Christ came, who is over all, God blessed for ever. Amen.

---

8:28    How does this promise made to those who love God make you feel? How important is it to you to love God?

8:29    ***predestinate***—decide before

8:31    God is all-powerful. With him nothing shall be impossible (see Luke 1:37).

8:33    ***lay anything to the charge of***—bring a charge against

8:33-39    Paul testifies that God's love is more powerful than anything else. Think about times when you have felt Heavenly Father's love and times when you have not felt it. What can you do to always feel the great love Heavenly Father has for you?

8:36-37    "In Paul's day the threat of persecution and death was greater than before or since. . . . Those who are persecuted for righteousness' sake . . . go on to eternal glory." (Bruce R. McConkie, *Doctrinal New Testament Commentary* 2:271.)

9:3    Elder Bruce R. McConkie stated: "Before his conversion Paul chose to be accursed [destroyed], meaning that by failing to accept Christ he was choosing to be accursed, and this was so despite the fact he was born in the house of Israel" (*Doctrinal New Testament Commentary* 2:275). This explanation helps us understand why Joseph Smith added the word *once* to Paul's statement, so that it reads, "For once I could have wished that myself were accursed from Christ" (JST, Romans 9:3).

9:4-5    Israel was "adopted," or chosen, by God to be his covenant people. They would have the blessings of the gospel. How do you feel to have been chosen to enjoy the blessings of the gospel in your life? What do you think Heavenly Father would like you to do for him in return?

*"Who shall separate us from the love of Christ?"*

6 ¶ Not as though the word of God hath taken none effect. For they are not all Israel, which are of Israel:

7 Neither, because they are the seed of Abraham, are they all children: but, In Isaac shall thy seed be called.

8 That is, They which are the children of the flesh, these are not the children of God: but the children of the promise are counted for the seed.

9 For this is the word of promise, At this time will I come, and Sara shall have a son.

## God's Will Is Done on the Earth

10 And not only this; but when Rebecca also had conceived by one, even by our father Isaac;

11 (For the children being not yet born, neither having done any good or evil, that the purpose of God according to election might stand, not of works, but of him that calleth;)

12 It was said unto her, The elder shall serve the younger.

13 As it is written, Jacob have I loved, but Esau have I hated.

14 ¶ What shall we say then? Is there unrighteousness with God? God forbid.

15 For he saith to Moses, I will have mercy on whom I will have mercy, and I will have compassion on whom I will have compassion.

16 So then it is not of him that willeth, nor of him that runneth, but of God that sheweth mercy.

17 For the scripture saith unto Pharaoh, Even for this same purpose have I raised thee up, that I might shew my power in thee, and that my name might be declared throughout all the earth.

18 Therefore hath he mercy on whom he will have mercy, and whom he will he hardeneth.

## The Gentiles, Like the House of Israel, Are Saved by Faith in Jesus Christ

19 Thou wilt say then unto me, Why doth he yet find fault? For who hath resisted his will?

20 Nay but, O man, who art thou that repliest against God? Shall the thing formed say to him that formed it, Why hast thou made me thus?

21 Hath not the potter power over the clay, of the same lump to make one vessel unto honour, and another unto dishonour?

22 What if God, willing to shew his wrath, and to make his power known, endured with much longsuffering the vessels of wrath fitted to destruction:

23 And that he might make known the riches of his glory on the vessels of mercy, which he had afore prepared unto glory,

24 Even us, whom he hath called, not of the Jews only, but also of the Gentiles?

25 ¶ As he saith also in Osee, I will call them my people, which were not my people; and her beloved, which was not beloved.

26 And it shall come to pass, that in the place where it was said unto them, Ye are not my people; there shall they be called the children of the living God.

27 Esaias also crieth concerning Israel, Though the number of the children of Israel be as the sand of the sea, a remnant shall be saved:

28 For he will finish the work, and cut it short in righteousness: because a short work will the Lord make upon the earth.

---

9:6    **hath taken none effect**—has failed

9:6-8    Not all who are born into the house of Israel will be the covenant children of God. Only those who are "willing and obedient shall eat the good of the land of Zion. . . . And the rebellious shall be cut off." (D&C 64:34-35.)

9:10-13    God elected (chose or foreordained) his children to do certain things on the earth. For example, God chose Jacob to rule over Esau. Similarly, Joseph Smith said he was ordained to be a prophet before the world was (see *The Teachings of Joseph Smith*, p. 270).

9:14-16    When God chooses some over others to be his covenant children, is he unfair? No. Nephi explains that "the Lord esteemeth [prizes] all flesh in one; he that is righteous is favored of God" (1 Nephi 17:35).

9:18    **hardeneth**—allows to be stubborn

9:19-21    God chooses those who rule and those who serve according to his own will. Some of his children "repliest," or complain, against him and challenge his choices. God answers, "As clay is in the potters hand, so are ye in mine" (Jeremiah 18:6).

9:21    **unto honour . . . unto dishonour**—for noble uses . . . for ordinary uses

9:22    "Vessels of wrath" refers to those who refuse to repent of their sins even though God gave them chances to. If they die in their sins their "destruction is made sure" (Helaman 13:38).

9:25-28    Osee (Hosea) and Esaias (Isaiah), both prophets of the Old Testament, prophesied that some people not born into the family of Israel would also be called the children of God (see Hosea 2:23; Isaiah 10:22).

29 And as Esaias said before, Except the Lord of Sabaoth had left us a seed, we had been as Sodoma, and been made like unto Gomorrha.

30 ¶ What shall we say then? That the Gentiles, which followed not after righteousness, have attained to righteousness, even the righteousness which is of faith.

### ISRAEL LOST THE BLESSINGS OF THE GOSPEL THROUGH A LACK OF FAITH

31 But Israel, which followed after the law of righteousness, hath not attained to the law of righteousness.

32 Wherefore? Because they sought it not by faith, but as it were by the works of the law. For they stumbled at that stumblingstone;

33 As it is written, Behold, I lay in Sion a stumblingstone and rock of offence: and whosoever believeth on him shall not be ashamed.

# CHAPTER 10

*Paul testifies that all those who have faith will be saved. Watch for how we can gain the kind of faith that saves.*

### WE ARE SAVED BY FAITH IN JESUS CHRIST

1 ¶ BRETHREN, my heart's desire and prayer to God for Israel is, that they might be saved.

2 For I bear them record that they have a zeal of God, but not according to knowledge.

3 For they being ignorant of God's righteousness, and going about to establish their own righteousness, have not submitted themselves unto the righteousness of God.

4 For Christ is the end of the law for righteousness to every one that believeth.

5 For Moses describeth the righteousness which is of the law, That the man which doeth those things shall live by them.

6 But the righteousness which is of faith speaketh on this wise, Say not in thine heart, Who shall ascend into heaven? (that is, to bring Christ down from above:)

7 Or, Who shall descend into the deep? (that is, to bring up Christ again from the dead.)

8 But what saith it? The word is nigh thee, even in thy mouth, and in thy heart: that is, the word of faith, which we preach;

9 That if thou shalt confess with thy mouth the Lord Jesus, and shalt believe in thine heart that God hath raised him from the dead, thou shalt be saved.

10 For with the heart man believeth unto righteousness; and with the mouth confession is made unto salvation.

11 For the scripture saith, Whosoever believeth on him shall not be ashamed.

12 ¶ For there is no difference between the Jew and the Greek: for the same Lord over all is rich unto all that call upon him.

13 For whosoever shall call upon the name of the Lord shall be saved.

---

9:29 **Lord of Sabaoth**—Lord of Hosts

Sodom and Gomorrah were cities destroyed by God for their wickedness during the time of Abraham and Lot (see Genesis 19:23-25).

9:30 Though the Gentiles are not of the house of Israel, through faith and righteousness they too can receive the blessings of the gospel. Nephi taught that "as many of the Gentiles as will repent are the covenant people of the Lord" (2 Nephi 30:2).

9:31-32 When the children of Israel failed to seek the gospel by faith, they lost "the law of righteousness," or, in other words, the blessings of the gospel. What can you do to have more faith in the gospel of Jesus Christ?

9:32 **Wherefore?**—Why?

9:32-33 Jesus Christ is the "stumblingstone and rock of offence." Though some would believe in him, others would "stumble at the word, being disobe-

dient" (1 Peter 2:7-8). In other words, many children of Israel would not recognize Jesus as the Son of God.

9:33 **Sion**—Zion

10:2-4 The Jews in Paul's day were devoted to God without really knowing God. They wanted God to accept their idea of righteousness. They did not want to learn to be righteous in God's way, which is to follow Jesus Christ. Are there people today who want to be called good for living by their own rules?

10:6 **ascend**—go up

10:7 **descend**—go down

10:9-10 Paul explains that to be saved we must have faith that Jesus is the Christ and truly believe in his resurrection. The Prophet Joseph Smith learned that this kind of faith is a gift from God (see D&C 46:13-14).

## FAITH COMES FROM HEARING THE TRUE GOSPEL TAUGHT BY GOD'S TRUE MESSENGERS

14 How then shall they call on him in whom they have not believed? and how shall they believe in him of whom they have not heard? and how shall they hear without a preacher?

15 And how shall they preach, except they be sent? as it is written, How beautiful are the feet of them that preach the gospel of peace, and bring glad tidings of good things!

16 But they have not all obeyed the gospel. For Esaias saith, Lord, who hath believed our report?

17 So then faith cometh by hearing, and hearing by the word of God.

18 But I say, Have they not heard? Yes verily, their sound went into all the earth, and their words unto the ends of the world.

19 But I say, Did not Israel know? First Moses saith, I will provoke you to jealousy by them that are no people, and by a foolish nation I will anger you.

20 But Esaias is very bold, and saith, I was found of them that sought me not; I was made manifest unto them that asked not after me.

21 But to Israel he saith, All day long I have stretched forth my hands unto a disobedient and gainsaying people.

## CHAPTER 11

*The gospel of Jesus Christ was first taught to the house of Israel. Believing Gentiles are brought into the house of Israel. Look for evidence showing that God wants all of his children to have the blessings of the gospel of Jesus Christ.*

## SOME OF THE CHILDREN OF ISRAEL BELIEVE THE GOSPEL OF JESUS CHRIST, BUT MANY DO NOT

1 ¶ I say then, Hath God cast away his people? God forbid. For I also am an Israelite, of the seed of Abraham, of the tribe of Benjamin.

2 God hath not cast away his people which he foreknew. Wot ye not what the scripture saith of Elias? how he maketh intercession to God against Israel, saying,

3 Lord, they have killed thy prophets, and digged down thine altars; and I am left alone, and they seek my life.

4 But what saith the answer of God unto him? I have reserved to myself seven thousand men, who have not bowed the knee to the image of Baal.

5 Even so then at this present time also there is a remnant according to the election of grace.

6 And if by grace, then is it no more of works: otherwise grace is no more grace. But if it be of works, then is it no more grace: otherwise work is no more work.

---

10:15 This prophecy comes from Isaiah 52:7. The Book of Mormon prophet Abinadi explained that these messengers are all who preach the gospel of peace (see Mosiah 15:13-19).

10:17 The Prophet Joseph Smith taught, "Faith comes by hearing the word of God, through the testimony of the servants of God; that testimony is always attended by the Spirit of prophecy and revelation" (*The Teachings of Joseph Smith*, p. 236).

10:19-
21 Does the Lord love Israel? Why would God try to make Israel angry? Do your parents love you? What do your parents do to cause you to listen and obey them? How can this be compared to how the Lord works with his people?

10:21 *gainsaying*—contrary, opposing

11:1 *seed*—family

11:2 *foreknew*—knew before they were born
**Wot**—Know
*maketh intercession*—speaks

*Elias* is the Greek word for *Elijah* (see LDS Bible Dictionary, s.v. "Elias," p. 663).

11:4 *reserved*—saved

The "image of Baal" was an idol, or false god (see LDS Bible Dictionary, s.v. "Baal," pp. 617-18).

11:5 *remnant*—group that is left

Many people, because of their faithfulness in the premortal existence, are born in a place where they can learn the gospel. This blessing is called "the election of grace." (See Bruce R. McConkie, *Mormon Doctrine*, p. 216.)

7 What then? Israel hath not obtained that which he seeketh for; but the election hath obtained it, and the rest were blinded

8 (According as it is written, God hath given them the spirit of slumber, eyes that they should not see, and ears that they should not hear;) unto this day.

9 And David saith, Let their table be made a snare, and a trap, and a stumblingblock, and a recompence unto them:

10 Let their eyes be darkened, that they may not see, and bow down their back alway.

## TAKING THE GOSPEL TO THE GENTILES MAY CAUSE ISRAEL TO BE SAVED

11 I say then, Have they stumbled that they should fall? God forbid: but rather through their fall salvation is come unto the Gentiles, for to provoke them to jealousy.

12 Now if the fall of them be the riches of the world, and the diminishing of them the riches of the Gentiles; how much more their fulness?

13 For I speak to you Gentiles, inasmuch as I am the apostle of the Gentiles, I magnify mine office:

14 If by any means I may provoke to emulation them which are my flesh, and might save some of them.

15 For if the casting away of them be the reconciling of the world, what shall the receiving of them be, but life from the dead?

## GENTILES WHO BELIEVE THE GOSPEL OF JESUS CHRIST ARE INCLUDED IN THE FAMILY OF ISRAEL

16 For if the firstfruit be holy, the lump is also holy: and if the root be holy, so are the branches.

17 And if some of the branches be broken off, and thou, being a wild olive tree, wert graffed in among them, and with them partakest of the root and fatness of the olive tree;

18 Boast not against the branches. But if thou boast, thou bearest not the root, but the root thee.

19 Thou wilt say then, The branches were broken off, that I might be graffed in.

20 Well; because of unbelief they were broken off, and thou standest by faith. Be not highminded, but fear:

21 For if God spared not the natural branches, take heed lest he also spare not thee.

22 Behold therefore the goodness and severity of God: on them which fell, severity; but toward thee, goodness, if thou continue in his goodness: otherwise thou also shalt be cut off.

23 And they also, if they abide not still in unbelief, shall be graffed in: for God is able to graff them in again.

24 For if thou wert cut out of the olive tree which is wild by nature, and wert graffed contrary to nature into a good olive tree: how much more shall these, which be the natural branches, be graffed into their own olive tree?

---

11:7 **the election**—God's chosen ones

11:7-10 Those who know that the gospel of Jesus Christ is true but are not living it "sleep and slumber spiritually, with that which should have been for their welfare becoming a trap unto them" (Bruce R. McConkie, *Doctrinal New Testament Commentary* 2:285).

11:8 **slumber**—sleep, stupor

*The image of the olive tree is often used in the scriptures to symbolize God's relationship with and work on behalf of his children.*

11:9 **recompence**—payback, retribution

11:11 **provoke**—stir

11:12 **the diminishing of them**—their failure

11:14 **emulation**—imitation

11:15 **reconciling**—saving

11:17 **graffed [grafted] in among**—united with or put in among

The natural olive tree is a symbol for the children of Israel. The wild olive branches are a symbol for the Gentiles. (See Jacob 5.)

11:18 **Boast**—Brag

11:20 **highminded**—proud

11:22 **severity**—strictness, sternness

11:23 **abide**—stay

## THE CHILDREN OF ISRAEL WILL AGAIN BELIEVE THE GOSPEL OF JESUS CHRIST

25 For I would not, brethren, that ye should be ignorant of this mystery, lest ye should be wise in your own conceits; that blindness in part is happened to Israel, until the fulness of the Gentiles be come in.

26 And so all Israel shall be saved: as it is written, There shall come out of Sion the Deliverer, and shall turn away ungodliness from Jacob:

27 For this is my covenant unto them, when I shall take away their sins.

28 As concerning the gospel, they are enemies for your sakes: but as touching the election, they are beloved for the fathers' sakes.

29 For the gifts and calling of God are without repentance.

30 For as ye in times past have not believed God, yet have now obtained mercy through their unbelief:

31 Even so have these also now not believed, that through your mercy they also may obtain mercy.

32 For God hath concluded them all in unbelief, that he might have mercy upon all.

33 ¶ O the depth of the riches both of the wisdom and knowledge of God! how unsearchable are his judgments, and his ways past finding out!

34 For who hath known the mind of the Lord? or who hath been his counsellor?

35 Or who hath first given to him, and it shall be recompensed unto him again?

36 For of him, and through him, and to him, are all things: to whom be glory for ever. Amen.

# CHAPTER 12

*Paul teaches us how to be better followers of the Savior and members of his church. As you read, look for changes you could make that would help you be more like Jesus Christ and a better member of his church.*

## GIVE YOURSELF AS A LIVING SACRIFICE TO GOD

1 ¶ I beseech you therefore, brethren, by the mercies of God, that ye present your bodies a living sacrifice, holy, acceptable unto God, which is your reasonable service.

2 And be not conformed to this world: but be ye transformed by the renewing of your mind, that ye may prove what is that good, and acceptable, and perfect, will of God.

3 For I say, through the grace given unto me, to every man that is among you, not to think of himself more highly than he ought to think; but to think soberly, according as God hath dealt to every man the measure of faith.

## CHURCH MEMBERS SHOULD USE THEIR GIFTS TO BLESS OTHER MEMBERS OF THE CHURCH

4 For as we have many members in one body, and all members have not the same office:

5 So we, being many, are one body in Christ, and every one members one of another.

---

11:25 **be ignorant**—not know
**be wise in your own conceits**—think that you are better than other people

The "fulness of the Gentiles" means the time when the Gentiles have had their full chance to hear and believe the gospel of Jesus Christ and they, on the whole, reject it (see Bruce R. McConkie, *Doctrinal New Testament Commentary* 2:290).

11:26 **Sion**—Zion

11:28-32 "Because the Jews (as a nation) rejected the gospel in Paul's day, it was taken to the Gentiles; because the Gentiles (as a whole) shall reject the gospel in this day, it shall be taken again to the Jews, when the fulness of the Gentiles comes in" (Bruce R. McConkie, *Doctrinal New Testament Commentary* 2:291).

11:33-36 Paul's words of praise testify of the greatness of God. Have you ever felt to praise Heavenly Father or Jesus in this way? How do these words remind you of some of the hymns?

12:1 **beseech**—beg

We can give God a "living sacrifice" by offering to him "a broken heart and a contrite spirit" (D&C 59:8; see also Omni 1:26). This means being humble and teachable.

12:2-3 Instead of conforming to the world, which is following the world's fads and fashions, Paul says we should be "transformed," or changed, through the renewal of our minds. Elder Bruce R. McConkie said that we renew our minds "by thinking pure and wholesome thoughts" (*Doctrinal New Testament Commentary* 2:292).

12:4 **members**—body parts (legs, arms, ears)
**office**—function, assignment

6 Having then gifts differing according to the grace that is given to us, whether prophecy, let us prophesy according to the proportion of faith;

7 Or ministry, let us wait on our ministering: or he that teacheth, on teaching;

8 Or he that exhorteth, on exhortation: he that giveth, let him do it with simplicity; he that ruleth, with diligence; he that sheweth mercy, with cheerfulness.

## BE A RIGHTEOUS MEMBER OF THE CHURCH

9 Let love be without dissimulation. Abhor that which is evil; cleave to that which is good.

10 Be kindly affectioned one to another with brotherly love; in honour preferring one another;

11 Not slothful in business; fervent in spirit; serving the Lord;

12 Rejoicing in hope; patient in tribulation; continuing instant in prayer;

13 Distributing to the necessity of saints; given to hospitality.

14 Bless them which persecute you: bless, and curse not.

15 Rejoice with them that do rejoice, and weep with them that weep.

16 Be of the same mind one toward another. Mind not high things, but condescend to men of low estate. Be not wise in your own conceits.

17 Recompense to no man evil for evil. Provide things honest in the sight of all men.

18 If it be possible, as much as lieth in you, live peaceably with all men.

19 Dearly beloved, avenge not yourselves, but rather give place unto wrath: for it is written, Vengeance is mine; I will repay, saith the Lord.

20 Therefore if thine enemy hunger, feed him; if he thirst, give him drink: for in so doing thou shalt heap coals of fire on his head.

21 Be not overcome of evil, but overcome evil with good.

## CHAPTER 13

*Paul encourages the Saints to obey their leaders and to keep the commandments. Watch for reasons why we should follow Paul's counsel.*

## MEMBERS OF THE CHURCH SHOULD OBEY THEIR PRIESTHOOD LEADERS

1 ¶ LET every soul be subject unto the higher powers. For there is no power but of God: the powers that be are ordained of God.

2 Whosoever therefore resisteth the power, resisteth the ordinance of God: and they that resist shall receive to themselves damnation.

3 For rulers are not a terror to good works, but to the evil. Wilt thou then not be afraid of the power? do that which is good, and thou shalt have praise of the same:

---

12:6-8 Paul taught that God gives each of us different gifts to share with others. There are gifts to prophesy, minister (serve), teach, exhort (encourage), give, lead, and show mercy. All these gifts work according to our faith. What gift has God given you to bless others?

12:9-21 In these verses Paul teaches what you can do to be a better member of the Church. Mark those things you would like to do.

12:9 *without dissimulation*—sincere, real
*Abhor*—Hate
*cleave*—hold

12:11 *slothful in business*—slow or lazy in getting things done
*fervent*—eager

12:12 *continuing instant in prayer*—praying always

12:16 Paul said we should be friends with those "of low estate," or the humble. He warned against conceit, which is thinking too much of ourselves. The Lord taught that his people should be "of one heart and one mind" and that they can do this only if they live righteously (see Moses 7:18).

12:17 *Recompense*—Pay back

12:19 *avenge not yourselves*—do not get back at those who hurt you
*wrath*—God's anger

12:20 To "heap coals of fire" on the head of an enemy means that our kindness can make the person feel bad for his or her unkindness. How do you think people who have hurt you might change if you treated them in a kindly manner?

13:1 *subject unto the higher powers*—obedient to the authorities

The Joseph Smith Translation tells us that the power and authority mentioned here are "in the church" (see JST, Romans 13:1).

13:2 A person who is damned (stopped) cannot progress to become like God (see D&C 76:112).

13:3-4 How have your priesthood leaders helped you to do good?

4 For he is the minister of God to thee for good. But if thou do that which is evil, be afraid; for he beareth not the sword in vain: for he is the minister of God, a revenger to execute wrath upon him that doeth evil.

5 Wherefore ye must needs be subject, not only for wrath, but also for conscience sake.

6 For for this cause pay ye tribute also: for they are God's ministers, attending continually upon this very thing.

7 ¶ Render therefore to all their dues: tribute to whom tribute is due; custom to whom custom; fear to whom fear; honour to whom honour.

## MEMBERS OF THE CHURCH SHOULD OBEY ALL OF GOD'S COMMANDMENTS

8 Owe no man any thing, but to love one another: for he that loveth another hath fulfilled the law.

9 For this, Thou shalt not commit adultery, Thou shalt not kill, Thou shalt not steal, Thou shalt not bear false witness, Thou shalt not covet; and if there be any other commandment, it is briefly comprehended in this saying, namely, Thou shalt love thy neighbour as thyself.

10 Love worketh no ill to his neighbour: therefore love is the fulfilling of the law.

11 ¶ And that, knowing the time, that now it is high time to awake out of sleep: for now is our salvation nearer than when we believed.

12 The night is far spent, the day is at hand: let us therefore cast off the works of darkness, and let us put on the armour of light.

13 Let us walk honestly, as in the day; not in rioting and drunkenness, not in chambering and wantonness, not in strife and envying.

14 But put ye on the Lord Jesus Christ, and make not provision for the flesh, to fulfil the lusts thereof.

## CHAPTER 14

*Paul wants members of the Church to know that their actions can strengthen or weaken other members of the Church. Look for what you can do to strengthen other members of the Church.*

---

13:4 Priesthood leaders are responsible to make sure there is no iniquity, or wickedness, among the members of the Church (see Moroni 6:7). As servants of God they have a "sword," or the power to judge. Sometimes when members disobey the commandments, priesthood leaders must "execute wrath," or, in other words, place punishment on them.

13:5 Our conscience helps us feel bad when we do things that are wrong (see LDS Bible Dictionary, s.v. "Conscience," p. 649).

13:6-7 The Joseph Smith Translation explains that we should give our "consecrations," meaning our tithing and fast offerings, to our Church leaders (see JST, Romans 13:6-7).

13:7-10 Paul counseled the Saints to live the Ten Commandments. These were not to be disobeyed, although the law of Moses was fulfilled by Jesus Christ. According to President Joseph Fielding Smith: "Some people have the idea that the Ten Commandments were first given by Moses when he directed the children of Israel and formulated their code of laws. This is not the case. These great commandments are from the beginning and were understood in righteous communities in the days of Adam. They are, in fact, fundamental parts of the gospel of Jesus Christ, and the gospel in its fulness was first given to Adam." (*Doctrines of Salvation* 1:96.)

13:9 Paul lists four of the Ten Commandments here and says that all four are "comprehended," or included, in one commandment that Jesus gave. He said, "Thou shalt love thy neighbour as thyself" (Matthew 22:39).

13:10 **worketh no ill**—causes no bad things to happen

13:11-12 Like Paul, Amulek taught that "this life is the time for men to prepare to meet God" (Alma 34:32). If we choose not to prepare, Amulek says, we will become "subjected to the spirit of the devil" (Alma 34:35).

13:12 What Paul calls the "armour of light" here he calls "the whole armour of God" in a letter to the Ephesians (see Ephesians 6:11-17). In a revelation to Joseph Smith, the Lord said it was His armor (see D&C 27:15-18).

13:14 **make not provision for**—do not give chances to

"The flesh" refers to the body and is sometimes called "the natural man" (Mosiah 3:19). Satan tempts us to "lust," or to have evil desires, through our bodies.

What do you think it means to "put . . . on the Lord Jesus Christ"? How does knowing about Jesus Christ and trying to be like him help you do this?

*Moses and the Ten Commandments*

## PAUL TEACHES SAINTS NOT TO ARGUE OVER THINGS THAT DO NOT REALLY MATTER

1 ¶ HIM that is weak in the faith receive ye, but not to doubtful disputations.

2 For one believeth that he may eat all things: another, who is weak, eateth herbs.

3 Let not him that eateth despise him that eateth not; and let not him which eateth not judge him that eateth: for God hath received him.

4 Who art thou that judgest another man's servant? to his own master he standeth or falleth. Yea, he shall be holden up: for God is able to make him stand.

5 One man esteemeth one day above another: another esteemeth every day alike. Let every man be fully persuaded in his own mind.

6 He that regardeth the day, regardeth it unto the Lord; and he that regardeth not the day, to the Lord he doth not regard it. He that eateth, eateth to the Lord, for he giveth God thanks; and he that eateth not, to the Lord he eateth not, and giveth God thanks.

## JESUS CHRIST DIED TO SAVE ALL MEN, JEW AND GENTILE

7 For none of us liveth to himself, and no man dieth to himself.

8 For whether we live, we live unto the Lord; and whether we die, we die unto the Lord: whether we live therefore, or die, we are the Lord's.

9 For to this end Christ both died, and rose, and revived, that he might be Lord both of the dead and living.

10 But why dost thou judge thy brother? or why dost thou set at nought thy brother? for we shall all stand before the judgment seat of Christ.

11 For it is written, As I live, saith the Lord, every knee shall bow to me, and every tongue shall confess to God.

12 So then every one of us shall give account of himself to God.

13 Let us not therefore judge one another any more: but judge this rather, that no man put a stumblingblock or an occasion to fall in his brother's way.

14 I know, and am persuaded by the Lord Jesus, that there is nothing unclean of itself: but to him that esteemeth any thing to be unclean, to him it is unclean.

15 But if thy brother be grieved with thy meat, now walkest thou not charitably. Destroy not him with thy meat, for whom Christ died.

16 Let not then your good be evil spoken of:

17 For the kingdom of God is not meat and drink; but righteousness, and peace, and joy in the Holy Ghost.

18 For he that in these things serveth Christ is acceptable to God, and approved of men.

19 Let us therefore follow after the things which make for peace, and things wherewith one may edify another.

---

14:1-6 Have you known anyone who argues a lot over issues that do not matter? What are some ways you can end contention and quarreling?

14:1 **to doubtful disputations**—for arguments over personal opinions

14:3 **despise**—dislike, look down on

14:4 **holden**—held

14:5 **esteemeth**—honors

14:6 **regardeth**—prefers, likes

14:9 **revived**—lived again

14:10 **set at nought**—treat as not worth anything

14:12 **give account of**—explain

14:13 **a stumblingblock or an occasion to fall**—an obstacle that causes another to sin

What kinds of things happen today that might cause those who are weak in the faith to sin? How can you avoid hurting someone else's faith?

14:14 **esteemeth**—believes

14:15 **grieved**—troubled

The Joseph Smith Translation makes it clear that if we eat what we know will offend another, we are not charitable or loving. We should not let what we choose to eat cause another to lose faith. (See JST, Romans 14:15.)

14:17-21 In these verses, Paul tells us that the peace and joy of the gospel are more important than any food or drink. He counsels us to avoid doing anything that might offend another Church member or cause him or her to lose faith. Would you be willing to give up something that is not exactly forbidden just so you wouldn't cause another member to sin?

14:19 **edify**—spiritually lift up

20 For meat destroy not the work of God. All things indeed are pure; but it is evil for that man who eateth with offence.

21 It is good neither to eat flesh, nor to drink wine, nor any thing whereby thy brother stumbleth, or is offended, or is made weak.

22 Hast thou faith? have it to thyself before God. Happy is he that condemneth not himself in that thing which he alloweth.

23 And he that doubteth is damned if he eat, because he eateth not of faith: for whatsoever is not of faith is sin.

## CHAPTER 15

*True followers of Jesus Christ serve and love each other. Look for what Paul teaches you should do for other people.*

### PAUL TEACHES THAT MEMBERS OF THE CHURCH SHOULD HELP ONE ANOTHER

1 ¶ WE then that are strong ought to bear the infirmities of the weak, and not to please ourselves.

2 Let every one of us please his neighbour for his good to edification.

3 For even Christ pleased not himself; but, as it is written, The reproaches of them that reproached thee fell on me.

4 For whatsoever things were written aforetime were written for our learning, that we through patience and comfort of the scriptures might have hope.

5 ¶ Now the God of patience and consolation grant you to be likeminded one toward another according to Christ Jesus:

6 That ye may with one mind and one mouth glorify God, even the Father of our Lord Jesus Christ.

7 ¶ Wherefore receive ye one another, as Christ also received us to the glory of God.

### GENTILES SHOULD PRAISE THE LORD FOR SAVING THEM

8 Now I say that Jesus Christ was a minister of the circumcision for the truth of God, to confirm the promises made unto the fathers:

9 And that the Gentiles might glorify God for his mercy; as it is written, For this cause I will confess to thee among the Gentiles, and sing unto thy name.

10 And again he saith, Rejoice, ye Gentiles, with his people.

11 And again, Praise the Lord, all ye Gentiles; and laud him, all ye people.

12 And again, Esaias saith, There shall be a root of Jesse, and he that shall rise to reign over the Gentiles; in him shall the Gentiles trust.

13 ¶ Now the God of hope fill you with all joy and peace in believing, that ye may abound in hope, through the power of the Holy Ghost.

### PAUL TAUGHT GENTILES ABOUT JESUS CHRIST

14 ¶ And I myself also am persuaded of you, my brethren, that ye also are full of goodness, filled with all knowledge, able also to admonish one another.

15 Nevertheless, brethren, I have written the more boldly unto you in some sort, as putting you in mind, because of the grace that is given to me of God,

16 That I should be the minister of Jesus Christ to the Gentiles, ministering the gospel of God, that the offering up of the Gentiles might be acceptable, being sanctified by the Holy Ghost.

---

15:1 To "bear the infirmities" of others is to help them in any way they may need. We covenant to do this when we are baptized (see Mosiah 18:8-10).

15:2 **edification**—lift him up

15:3 **reproaches**—scoldings, insults

15:4-6 Have there been times in your life when you have received comfort from the scriptures and that comfort has given you hope? How does that help you be more kind and loving to others?

15:5 **consolation**—comfort

15:8 **a minister of the circumcision**—a servant of the Jews
**confirm**—prove

15:11 **laud**—honor

15:12 Elder Bruce R. McConkie explained that Paul used this quote from Isaiah 11:10 to show "that the gospel was to go to the Gentiles, and that it was an ensign [flag or banner] to which 'the nations,' who are the Gentiles, should look" (*The Promised Messiah*, p. 503).

15:14 **admonish**—teach and encourage

15:15 **grace**—special gift or assignment

15:16 **sanctified**—purified, made holy

One of the purposes of the Holy Ghost is to cleanse us of our sins (see 2 Nephi 31:17).

17 ¶ I have therefore whereof I may glory through Jesus Christ in those things which pertain to God.

18 For I will not dare to speak of any of those things which Christ hath not wrought by me, to make the Gentiles obedient, by word and deed,

19 Through mighty signs and wonders, by the power of the Spirit of God; so that from Jerusalem, and round about unto Illyricum, I have fully preached the gospel of Christ.

20 Yea, so have I strived to preach the gospel, not where Christ was named, lest I should build upon another man's foundation:

21 But as it is written, To whom he was not spoken of, they shall see: and they that have not heard shall understand.

### PAUL DESIRES TO VISIT THE SAINTS IN ROME

22 ¶ For which cause also I have been much hindered from coming to you.

23 But now having no more place in these parts, and having a great desire these many years to come unto you;

24 Whensoever I take my journey into Spain, I will come to you: for I trust to see you in my journey, and to be brought on my way thitherward by you, if first I be somewhat filled with your company.

25 But now I go unto Jerusalem to minister unto the saints.

26 For it hath pleased them of Macedonia and Achaia to make a certain contribution for the poor saints which are at Jerusalem.

27 It hath pleased them verily; and their debtors they are. For if the Gentiles have been made partakers of their spiritual things, their duty is also to minister unto them in carnal things.

28 When therefore I have performed this, and have

sealed to them this fruit, I will come by you into Spain.

29 And I am sure that, when I come unto you, I shall come in the fulness of the blessing of the gospel of Christ.

30 ¶ Now I beseech you, brethren, for the Lord Jesus Christ's sake, and for the love of the Spirit, that ye strive together with me in your prayers to God for me;

31 That I may be delivered from them that do not believe in Judaea; and that my service which I have for Jerusalem may be accepted of the saints;

32 That I may come unto you with joy by the will of God, and may with you be refreshed.

33 Now the God of peace be with you all. Amen.

## CHAPTER 16

*Paul gives greetings, encouragement, and counsel to various members of the Church. As you read, think about how Paul's counsel can help you.*

### PAUL SENDS GREETINGS AND THANKS TO VARIOUS MEMBERS OF THE CHURCH

1 ¶ I commend unto you Phebe our sister, which is a servant of the church which is at Cenchrea:

2 That ye receive her in the Lord, as becometh saints, and that ye assist her in whatsoever business she hath need of you: for she hath been a succourer of many, and of myself also.

3 Greet Priscilla and Aquila my helpers in Christ Jesus:

4 Who have for my life laid down their own necks: unto whom not only I give thanks, but also all the churches of the Gentiles.

5 Likewise greet the church that is in their house. Salute my wellbeloved Epaenetus, who is the firstfruits of Achaia unto Christ.

---

15:18  **wrought**—done

15:20-21  Paul desired to take the gospel of Jesus Christ to people who had not heard of it. How can you prepare yourself to share the gospel with people who have not heard it?

15:22  **hindered**—slowed down

15:26-28  The Saints in Macedonia gave Paul some money to take to the poor Saints in Jerusalem. This is a great example of what Paul had requested of the members (see Romans 15:1-2).

15:27  **carnal**—physical

15:30  **beseech**—beg

16:1-16  Did you notice how many friends Paul greets? President Gordon B. Hinckley said every convert to the Church needs a friend (see Conference Report, October 1997, p. 71). What can you do to welcome and greet other members of the Church?

16:2  **a succourer of many**—one who has helped many others

16:4  "Laid down their own necks" is a way of saying they were willing to die for Paul.

16:5  **Salute**—Greet
**the firstfruits of Achaia unto Christ**—the first to join the Church in Achaia (Asia Minor)

6 Greet Mary, who bestowed much labour on us.

7 Salute Andronicus and Junia, my kinsmen, and my fellowprisoners, who are of note among the apostles, who also were in Christ before me.

8 Greet Amplias my beloved in the Lord.

9 Salute Urbane, our helper in Christ, and Stachys my beloved.

10 Salute Apelles approved in Christ. Salute them which are of Aristobulus' household.

11 Salute Herodion my kinsman. Greet them that be of the household of Narcissus, which are in the Lord.

12 Salute Tryphena and Tryphosa, who labour in the Lord. Salute the beloved Persis, which laboured much in the Lord.

13 Salute Rufus chosen in the Lord, and his mother and mine.

14 Salute Asyncritus, Phlegon, Hermas, Patrobas, Hermes, and the brethren which are with them.

15 Salute Philologus, and Julia, Nereus, and his sister, and Olympas, and all the saints which are with them.

16 Salute one another with an holy kiss. The churches of Christ salute you.

## BEWARE OF AND STAY AWAY FROM PEOPLE WHO CAUSE TROUBLE FOR THE CHURCH

17 ¶ Now I beseech you, brethren, mark them which cause divisions and offences contrary to the doctrine which ye have learned; and avoid them.

18 For they that are such serve not our Lord Jesus Christ, but their own belly; and by good words and fair speeches deceive the hearts of the simple.

19 For your obedience is come abroad unto all men. I am glad therefore on your behalf: but yet I would have you wise unto that which is good, and simple concerning evil.

20 And the God of peace shall bruise Satan under your feet shortly. The grace of our Lord Jesus Christ be with you. Amen.

## PAUL SENDS GREETINGS FROM HIS FELLOW MISSIONARIES AND MEMBERS

21 ¶ Timotheus my workfellow, and Lucius, and Jason, and Sosipater, my kinsmen, salute you.

22 I Tertius, who wrote this epistle, salute you in the Lord.

23 Gaius mine host, and of the whole church, saluteth you. Erastus the chamberlain of the city saluteth you, and Quartus a brother.

24 The grace of our Lord Jesus Christ be with you all. Amen.

25 ¶ Now to him that is of power to stablish you according to my gospel, and the preaching of Jesus Christ, according to the revelation of the mystery, which was kept secret since the world began,

26 But now is made manifest, and by the scriptures of the prophets, according to the commandment of the everlasting God, made known to all nations for the obedience of faith:

27 To God only wise, be glory through Jesus Christ for ever. Amen.

---

16:10-11 The Joseph Smith Translation changes the word *household* in these two verses to the word *church*.

16:16 The Joseph Smith Translation changes the first phrase of this verse to say: "Salute one another with a holy salutation" (JST, Romans 16:16). *Salutation* means "greeting."

16:17 *beseech*—beg
*mark*—watch out for
*contrary to the doctrine*—against the teachings of the Church

16:17-18 According to Paul, why should we avoid those who try to hurt the Church?

16:18 *deceive*—trick

16:22 *epistle*—letter

16:25 *stablish*—strengthen

The "mystery, which was kept secret since the world began" is the eternal plan of God, centered in Jesus Christ's atonement (see 1 Corinthians 2:6-16 and Colossians 1:27-28).

16:26 *is made manifest*—can be seen

# THE FIRST EPISTLE OF PAUL THE APOSTLE TO THE
# CORINTHIANS

*Paul had taught the Corinthian Saints during his second mission. After he left, many false teachings were introduced into the Church. While in Ephesus, Paul wrote to encourage them to return to gospel truths and live close to the Holy Ghost.*

## CHAPTER 1

*The people of Corinth were surrounded by many of the same temptations we face today. Look for things Paul says that can help you stay strong and faithful.*

### PAUL IS GRATEFUL FOR THE BLESSINGS THE CORINTHIAN SAINTS HAVE RECEIVED

1 PAUL, called to be an apostle of Jesus Christ through the will of God, and Sosthenes our brother,

2 Unto the church of God which is at Corinth, to them that are sanctified in Christ Jesus, called to be saints, with all that in every place call upon the name of Jesus Christ our Lord, both theirs and ours:

3 Grace be unto you, and peace, from God our Father, and from the Lord Jesus Christ.

4 I thank my God always on your behalf, for the grace of God which is given you by Jesus Christ;

5 That in every thing ye are enriched by him, in all utterance, and in all knowledge;

6 Even as the testimony of Christ was confirmed in you:

7 So that ye come behind in no gift; waiting for the coming of our Lord Jesus Christ:

8 Who shall also confirm you unto the end, that ye may be blameless in the day of our Lord Jesus Christ.

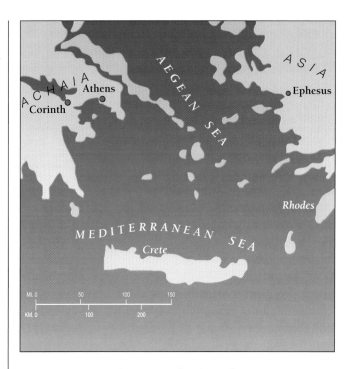

*Paul wrote to the Corinthians while staying in Ephesus.*

9 God is faithful, by whom ye were called unto the fellowship of his Son Jesus Christ our Lord.

---

1:2   "Paul is writing to . . . faithful saints, not to the world. He is giving counsel to those who have the gift of the Holy Ghost." (Bruce R. McConkie, *Doctrinal New Testament Commentary* 2:312.) "To be *sanctified* is to become clean, pure, and spotless" (Bruce R. McConkie, *Mormon Doctrine*, p. 675; see also Glossary, s.v. "Sanctified").

1:3   Given by and through the mercy and love of Jesus Christ, grace is the divine help, power, and strength to repent, keep the commandments, and become like God (see LDS Bible Dictionary, s.v. "Grace," p. 697; see also Glossary, s.v. "Grace").

1:5   **utterance**—speaking

1:6   **confirmed**—strengthened

1:9   **fellowship**—brotherhood, union

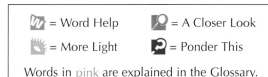

= Word Help    = A Closer Look

= More Light    = Ponder This

Words in pink are explained in the Glossary.

## CHURCH MEMBERS SHOULD BE UNITED

10 ¶ Now I beseech you, brethren, by the name of our Lord Jesus Christ, that ye all speak the same thing, and that there be no divisions among you; but that ye be perfectly joined together in the same mind and in the same judgment.

11 For it hath been declared unto me of you, my brethren, by them which are of the house of Chloe, that there are contentions among you.

12 Now this I say, that every one of you saith, I am of Paul; and I of Apollos; and I of Cephas; and I of Christ.

13 Is Christ divided? was Paul crucified for you? or were ye baptized in the name of Paul?

14 ¶ I thank God that I baptized none of you, but Crispus and Gaius;

15 Lest any should say that I had baptized in mine own name.

16 And I baptized also the household of Stephanas: besides, I know not whether I baptized any other.

## GOD USES WEAK AND SIMPLE PEOPLE TO TEACH HIS GOSPEL

17 ¶ For Christ sent me not to baptize, but to preach the gospel: not with wisdom of words, lest the cross of Christ should be made of none effect.

18 For the preaching of the cross is to them that perish foolishness; but unto us which are saved it is the power of God.

19 For it is written, I will destroy the wisdom of the wise, and will bring to nothing the understanding of the prudent.

20 Where is the wise? where is the scribe? where is the disputer of this world? hath not God made foolish the wisdom of this world?

21 For after that in the wisdom of God the world by wisdom knew not God, it pleased God by the foolishness of preaching to save them that believe.

22 For the Jews require a sign, and the Greeks seek after wisdom:

23 But we preach Christ crucified, unto the Jews a stumblingblock, and unto the Greeks foolishness;

24 But unto them which are called, both Jews and Greeks, Christ the power of God, and the wisdom of God.

25 Because the foolishness of God is wiser than men; and the weakness of God is stronger than men.

26 For ye see your calling, brethren, how that not many wise men after the flesh, not many mighty, not many noble, are called:

27 But God hath chosen the foolish things of the world to confound the wise; and God hath chosen the weak things of the world to confound the things which are mighty;

28 And base things of the world, and things which are despised, hath God chosen, yea, and things which are not, to bring to nought things that are:

29 That no flesh should glory in his presence.

30 But of him are ye in Christ Jesus, who of God is made unto us wisdom, and righteousness, and sanctification, and redemption:

---

1:11   **contentions**—arguments

1:13   Paul wanted the Saints in Corinth to be united. Doctrine and Covenants 1:30 and Joseph Smith—History 1:19 show how Jesus feels about the hundreds of different churches today.

1:17-18   When you read or hear about what Jesus did for you in Gethsemane and on the cross, what feelings come into your heart? How does remembering Jesus Christ's sacrifice give you the power to be a better member of the Church?

1:19   **prudent**—intelligent

1:19-24   The message of the Atonement sounds foolish to people who do not have the Holy Ghost. Faithful members of the Church who teach with the Spirit please God and help other people "who believe" come to know him (see JST, 1 Corinthians 1:24; see also D&C 42:16-17).

1:20   **disputer**—debater, arguer

1:25   How do the things you learn about God in verse 25 help you love and understand him more?

1:27-28   The missionaries the Lord sends are generally young—"weak" and even "foolish" in the eyes of the world. In latter-day revelation the Lord says that "the weak things of the world shall come forth and break down the mighty and strong ones" (D&C 1:19).

1:27   **confound**—put to shame

1:28   **base**—humble
**nought**—nothing

1:29-31   Even those who become righteous and do great things cannot "glory," or brag, about themselves. The Book of Mormon prophet Ammon said, "We will glory in the Lord. . . . for he has all power, all wisdom, and all understanding; . . . he is a merciful Being, even unto salvation, to those who will repent and believe on his name." (Alma 26:16, 35.)

31 That, according as it is written, He that glorieth, let him glory in the Lord.

## CHAPTER 2

*Those who value the world's wisdom often do not know the things of God. Note what Paul teaches about how we can learn the things of God.*

### PAUL TEACHES WITH THE POWER OF THE SPIRIT, NOT BY THE WISDOM OF MEN

1 ¶ AND I, brethren, when I came to you, came not with excellency of speech or of wisdom, declaring unto you the testimony of God.

2 For I determined not to know any thing among you, save Jesus Christ, and him crucified.

3 And I was with you in weakness, and in fear, and in much trembling.

4 And my speech and my preaching was not with enticing words of man's wisdom, but in demonstration of the Spirit and of power:

5 That your faith should not stand in the wisdom of men, but in the power of God.

### THE THINGS OF GOD ARE LEARNED ONLY WITH THE HELP OF THE SPIRIT OF GOD

6 ¶ Howbeit we speak wisdom among them that are perfect: yet not the wisdom of this world, nor of the princes of this world, that come to nought:

7 But we speak the wisdom of God in a mystery, even the hidden wisdom, which God ordained before the world unto our glory:

8 Which none of the princes of this world knew: for had they known it, they would not have crucified the Lord of glory.

9 But as it is written, Eye hath not seen, nor ear heard, neither have entered into the heart of man, the things which God hath prepared for them that love him.

10 But God hath revealed them unto us by his Spirit: for the Spirit searcheth all things, yea, the deep things of God.

11 For what man knoweth the things of a man, save the spirit of man which is in him? even so the things of God knoweth no man, but the Spirit of God.

12 Now we have received, not the spirit of the world, but the spirit which is of God; that we might know the things that are freely given to us of God.

13 Which things also we speak, not in the words which man's wisdom teacheth, but which the Holy Ghost teacheth; comparing spiritual things with spiritual.

14 But the natural man receiveth not the things of the Spirit of God: for they are foolishness unto him: neither can he know them, because they are spiritually discerned.

15 But he that is spiritual judgeth all things, yet he himself is judged of no man.

16 For who hath known the mind of the Lord, that he may instruct him? But we have the mind of Christ.

## CHAPTER 3

*Each member of the Church can help do Heavenly Father's work. Watch for what Paul says you can do to serve the Lord.*

### MILK IS GIVEN BEFORE MEAT

1 ¶ AND I, brethren, could not speak unto you as unto spiritual, but as unto carnal, even as unto babes in Christ.

---

2:4-5 Paul did not teach using "enticing," or persuasive, words the way wise men of the world did. Instead, he taught by the power of the Spirit the things of God. Why would it be better for you to have faith in God's wisdom than in the wisdom of men?

2:7 An example of the wisdom "which God ordained before the world" was created is the plan of salvation (see Moses 1:39; 4:1-2).

2:11 The Joseph Smith Translation reveals that no man can know the things of God "except he has the Spirit of God" (JST, 1 Corinthians 2:11).

2:11-14 Paul explains that we must have the Spirit to understand spiritual things. To those who rely on man's wisdom, spiritual things seem foolish. What are some things about the gospel that would be hard to explain to someone who doesn't believe in God? How can such a person come to know the things of God?

2:14 *discerned*—understood

The "natural man" is a person in this world who has not listened to and obeyed the inspiration of the Holy Ghost (see Mosiah 3:19).

2:16 Without the Holy Ghost we cannot know "the mind of the Lord" (see Isaiah 55:8-9). With the Holy Ghost we can "have the mind of Christ" (see 2 Nephi 32:2-3).

3:1 *carnal*—worldly

*"Who hath known the mind of the Lord, that he may instruct him? But we have the mind of Christ."*

2 I have fed you with milk, and not with meat: for hitherto ye were not able to bear it, neither yet now are ye able.

3 For ye are yet carnal: for whereas there is among you envying, and strife, and divisions, are ye not carnal, and walk as men?

## ALL PEOPLE WHO HELP IN THE CHURCH DO A GOOD WORK

4 For while one saith, I am of Paul; and another, I am of Apollos; are ye not carnal?

5 ¶ Who then is Paul, and who is Apollos, but ministers by whom ye believed, even as the Lord gave to every man?

6 I have planted, Apollos watered; but God gave the increase.

7 So then neither is he that planteth any thing, neither he that watereth; but God that giveth the increase.

8 Now he that planteth and he that watereth are one: and every man shall receive his own reward according to his own labour.

9 For we are labourers together with God: ye are God's husbandry, ye are God's building.

## OUR WORKS SHALL BE JUDGED BY FIRE

10 According to the grace of God which is given unto me, as a wise masterbuilder, I have laid the foundation, and another buildeth thereon. But let every man take heed how he buildeth thereupon.

11 ¶ For other foundation can no man lay than that is laid, which is Jesus Christ.

12 Now if any man build upon this foundation gold, silver, precious stones, wood, hay, stubble;

13 Every man's work shall be made manifest: for the day shall declare it, because it shall be revealed by fire; and the fire shall try every man's work of what sort it is.

14 If any man's work abide which he hath built thereupon, he shall receive a reward.

15 If any man's work shall be burned, he shall suffer loss: but he himself shall be saved; yet so as by fire.

16 ¶ Know ye not that ye are the temple of God, and that the Spirit of God dwelleth in you?

17 If any man defile the temple of God, him shall God destroy; for the temple of God is holy, which temple ye are.

## THOSE WHO FOLLOW THE WISDOM OF THE WORLD ARE FOOLISH

18 ¶ Let no man deceive himself. If any man among you seemeth to be wise in this world, let him become a fool, that he may be wise.

19 For the wisdom of this world is foolishness with God. For it is written, He taketh the wise in their own craftiness.

20 And again, The Lord knoweth the thoughts of the wise, that they are vain.

---

3:2   "God's earthly kingdom [his church] is a school in which his saints learn the doctrines of salvation. Some members of the Church are being taught elementary courses [milk]; others are approaching graduation [meat]." (Bruce R. McConkie, *Doctrinal New Testament Commentary* 2:324.)

3:3   **envying, and strife, and divisions**—jealousy, and arguing, and disagreements

3:5   **ministers**—servants, teachers

3:5-8   Planting and watering can be compared to the service rendered by different members of the Church; "one makes friends for the Church, another teaches the deep doctrines. . . . All are needful." (Bruce R. McConkie, *Doctrinal New Testament Commentary* 2:324.) But only through the Spirit of God can testimonies grow.

3:6   Apollos was a mighty missionary like Paul (see Acts 18:24-28).

**gave the increase**—caused the production or growth of fruit

3:9   **husbandry**—field, garden

3:10-11   The foundation is the starting place upon which a building is constructed. Jesus is the foundation, or "cornerstone," upon which every gospel truth is built and taught (see Ephesians 2:20).

3:11   The surest foundation that any one can build on is Jesus Christ (see Helaman 5:12). What can you do to build your life upon the foundation of Jesus Christ? How will it help you?

3:13   **made manifest**—uncovered for all to see

3:14   **abide which he hath built thereupon**—shall not be burned

3:17   **defile**—make unholy, destroy

3:19   **craftiness**—sneaky ways

3:20   **vain**—useless

21 ¶ Therefore let no man glory in men. For all things are yours;

22 Whether Paul, or Apollos, or Cephas, or the world, or life, or death, or things present, or things to come; all are yours;

23 And ye are Christ's; and Christ is God's.

## CHAPTER 4

*Faithful servants of the Lord do the right things for the right reasons. Look for what things Paul would have us do and why he wants us to do them.*

### PEOPLE WHO SERVE THE LORD MUST BE FAITHFUL

1 ¶ LET a man so account of us, as of the ministers of Christ, and stewards of the mysteries of God.

2 Moreover it is required in stewards, that a man be found faithful.

3 But with me it is a very small thing that I should be judged of you, or of man's judgment: yea, I judge not mine own self.

4 For I know nothing by myself; yet am I not hereby justified: but he that judgeth me is the Lord.

5 Therefore judge nothing before the time, until the Lord come, who both will bring to light the hidden things of darkness, and will make manifest the counsels of the hearts: and then shall every man have praise of God.

6 And these things, brethren, I have in a figure transferred to myself and to Apollos for your sakes; that ye

might learn in us not to think of men above that which is written, that no one of you be puffed up for one against another.

7 ¶ For who maketh thee to differ from another? and what hast thou that thou didst not receive? now if thou didst receive it, why dost thou glory, as if thou hadst not received it?

8 Now ye are full, now ye are rich, ye have reigned as kings without us: and I would to God ye did reign, that we also might reign with you.

### THE APOSTLES SUFFER BUT STAY FAITHFUL

9 For I think that God hath set forth us the apostles last, as it were appointed to death: for we are made a spectacle unto the world, and to angels, and to men.

10 We are fools for Christ's sake, but ye are wise in Christ; we are weak, but ye are strong; ye are honourable, but we are despised.

11 Even unto this present hour we both hunger, and thirst, and are naked, and are buffeted, and have no certain dwellingplace;

12 And labour, working with our own hands: being reviled, we bless; being persecuted, we suffer it:

13 Being defamed, we intreat: we are made as the filth of the world, and are the offscouring of all things unto this day.

14 ¶ I write not these things to shame you, but as my beloved sons I warn you.

15 For though ye have ten thousand instructors in Christ, yet have ye not many fathers: for in Christ Jesus I have begotten you through the gospel.

---

3:22    *Cephas* is the name the Lord gave to Simon Peter (see John 1:42).

4:1    *account of*—regard
*stewards*—caretakers

4:4    The Joseph Smith Translation changes the phrase "I know nothing by myself" to "I know nothing against myself."

     *justified*—found to have no sin

4:5    Rephrasing Paul's words, Elder Bruce R. McConkie wrote that when the Savior comes again "he shall reveal your hidden acts and make manifest what is in your hearts; then shall those who are saints be rewarded" (*Doctrinal New Testament Commentary* 2:330).

4:6    *in a figure*—as an example
*puffed up*—proud

4:7    *to differ*—to be different

We receive many talents and blessings from the Lord. What are some talents and blessings that you have received?

4:8    *reigned . . . reign*—led . . . lead

4:9    *a spectacle*—someone who is seen and made fun of

4:10    *despised*—hated

4:11    *buffeted*—beaten

4:12    *being reviled*—having bad things said about us

Do you know anyone who has suffered a lot for the sake of the gospel? How do you feel about them?

4:13    *Being defamed, we intreat*—Though we are seen as nothing, we encourage
*offscouring*—waste

## THE GOSPEL IS MORE THAN WORDS

16 Wherefore I beseech you, be ye followers of me.

17 ¶ For this cause have I sent unto you Timotheus, who is my beloved son, and faithful in the Lord, who shall bring you into remembrance of my ways which be in Christ, as I teach every where in every church.

18 Now some are puffed up, as though I would not come to you.

19 But I will come to you shortly, if the Lord will, and will know, not the speech of them which are puffed up, but the power.

20 For the kingdom of God is not in word, but in power.

21 What will ye? shall I come unto you with a rod, or in love, and in the spirit of meekness?

## CHAPTER 5

*Sometimes our friends can be our worst enemies. Watch for Paul's warning not to be friends with members of the Church who tempt us to sin.*

### BEWARE OF THOSE WHO TEMPT YOU TO SIN

1 ¶ IT is reported commonly that there is fornication among you, and such fornication as is not so much as named among the Gentiles, that one should have his father's wife.

2 And ye are puffed up, and have not rather mourned, that he that hath done this deed might be taken away from among you.

3 For I verily, as absent in body, but present in spirit, have judged already, as though I were present, concerning him that hath so done this deed,

4 In the name of our Lord Jesus Christ, when ye are gathered together, and my spirit, with the power of our Lord Jesus Christ,

5 To deliver such an one unto Satan for the destruction of the flesh, that the spirit may be saved in the day of the Lord Jesus.

6 Your glorying is not good. Know ye not that a little leaven leaveneth the whole lump?

7 ¶ Purge out therefore the old leaven, that ye may be a new lump, as ye are unleavened. For even Christ our passover is sacrificed for us:

8 Therefore let us keep the feast, not with old leaven, neither with the leaven of malice and wickedness; but with the unleavened bread of sincerity and truth.

9 ¶ I wrote unto you in an epistle not to company with fornicators:

10 Yet not altogether with the fornicators of this world, or with the covetous, or extortioners, or with idolaters; for then must ye needs go out of the world.

11 But now I have written unto you not to keep company, if any man that is called a brother be a fornicator, or covetous, or an idolater, or a railer, or a

---

4:16  Paul was a follower of Jesus Christ. If we follow his example, it will be like following the Savior (see 2 Nephi 31:10; 3 Nephi 27:27).

4:17  *Timotheus* is Greek for the name *Timothy.* Timothy was a faithful convert and companion of the Apostle Paul (see Acts 16:1-3; 1 Timothy 1:1-2).

4:20  The power of the gospel of Jesus Christ may be seen in the "priesthood, the gift of the Holy Ghost, revelation, visions, miracles, [and] glorious manifestations of God's power" (Bruce R. McConkie, *Doctrinal New Testament Commentary* 2:333).

5:1  **fornication**—misuse of the sacred creative powers; that is, use of these powers between people who are not married

5:2  **puffed up**—proud

5:6  **glorying**—boasting, bragging

5:6-8  Leaven is yeast and allows bread dough to rise and become fluffy. But in time the yeast also allows the bread to become old, moldy, and useless. Paul compared leaven to the effects of sin and wickedness in our lives. (See LDS Bible Dictionary, s.v. "Leaven," p. 723.)

5:7  The Passover lamb that was sacrificed reminded the children of Israel how the Lord saved the firstborn children of Israel when the firstborn of the Egyptians were killed (see Exodus 12:3-30). The Savior's sacrifice and atonement saves repentant people from their sins.

5:8  **malice**—hate

5:9  **company**—be friends

5:9-13  Elder Spencer W. Kimball taught, "Oh, if our young people could learn . . . to always keep good company, never to be found with those who tend to lower their standards!" (*The Teachings of Spencer W. Kimball*, p. 287.)

5:10  **the covetous**—people who have evil desires for those things that belong to other people
**extortioners**—robbers
**idolaters**—people who worship false gods

5:11  **railer**—person who speaks angrily against others

drunkard, or an extortioner; with such an one no not to eat.

12 For what have I to do to judge them also that are without? do not ye judge them that are within?

13 But them that are without God judgeth. Therefore put away from among yourselves that wicked person.

## CHAPTER 6

*Paul continues to warn the Saints of Corinth about being hurt spiritually. Note what Paul says we must not do if we want to be saved.*

### SAINTS SHOULD NOT TAKE ONE ANOTHER TO COURT

1 ¶ DARE any of you, having a matter against another, go to law before the unjust, and not before the saints?

2 Do ye not know that the saints shall judge the world? and if the world shall be judged by you, are ye unworthy to judge the smallest matters?

3 Know ye not that we shall judge angels? how much more things that pertain to this life?

4 If then ye have judgments of things pertaining to this life, set them to judge who are least esteemed in the church.

5 I speak to your shame. Is it so, that there is not a wise man among you? no, not one that shall be able to judge between his brethren?

6 But brother goeth to law with brother, and that before the unbelievers.

7 Now therefore there is utterly a fault among you, because ye go to law one with another. Why do ye not rather take wrong? why do ye not rather suffer yourselves to be defrauded?

8 Nay, ye do wrong, and defraud, and that your brethren.

### UNRIGHTEOUS PEOPLE WILL NOT BE SAVED IN THE KINGDOM OF HEAVEN

9 ¶ Know ye not that the unrighteous shall not inherit the kingdom of God? Be not deceived: neither fornicators, nor idolaters, nor adulterers, nor effeminate, nor abusers of themselves with mankind,

10 Nor thieves, nor covetous, nor drunkards, nor revilers, nor extortioners, shall inherit the kingdom of God.

11 And such were some of you: but ye are washed, but ye are sanctified, but ye are justified in the name of the Lord Jesus, and by the Spirit of our God.

12 ¶ All things are lawful unto me, but all things are not expedient: all things are lawful for me, but I will not be brought under the power of any.

13 Meats for the belly, and the belly for meats: but God shall destroy both it and them. Now the body is not for fornication, but for the Lord; and the Lord for the body.

---

5:13 How hard would it be to keep from joining your friends if they do bad things? Could you find new friends if the Lord wanted you to?

6:1-7 Paul counseled the Saints not to take one another to court. Modern revelation teaches that we should first try to handle our differences with each other ourselves. If that fails, then we should take the matter to the leaders of the Church and "not before the world." (D&C 42:88-89.)

6:6 *to law*—to court

6:7 *utterly*—completely
*defrauded*—stolen from or cheated

6:9-11 Some of the Corinthian Saints were guilty of the wicked things listed in verses 9-10. But the good news of the gospel is that we can "repent . . . and be baptized . . . [and] be sanctified by the reception of the Holy Ghost" (3 Nephi 27:20).

6:9 *deceived*—tricked
*idolaters*—those who worship things other than God

*adulterers*—those who misuse the sacred creative powers; that is, people who use these powers with someone other than their spouses
*effeminate . . . abusers of themselves with mankind*—homosexuals

6:10 *revilers*—those who say evil things against others
*extortioners*—robbers

6:11 "To be *sanctified* is to become clean, pure, and spotless; to be free from the blood and sins of the world. . . . *Sanctification* is a state of saintliness." (Bruce R. McConkie, *Mormon Doctrine*, p. 675.) It comes only by obedience to the commandments and through the power of the Holy Ghost.

*justified*—found to have no sin

6:12 The Joseph Smith Translation changes the beginning of this verse to say that "all these things [those things mentioned in verses 9 and 10] are not lawful unto me."

14 And God hath both raised up the Lord, and will also raise up us by his own power.

### A Saint's Body Is the Temple of the Holy Ghost

15 Know ye not that your bodies are the members of Christ? shall I then take the members of Christ, and make them the members of an harlot? God forbid.

16 What? know ye not that he which is joined to an harlot is one body? for two, saith he, shall be one flesh.

17 But he that is joined unto the Lord is one spirit.

18 Flee fornication. Every sin that a man doeth is without the body; but he that committeth fornication sinneth against his own body.

19 What? know ye not that your body is the temple of the Holy Ghost which is in you, which ye have of God, and ye are not your own?

20 For ye are bought with a price: therefore glorify God in your body, and in your spirit, which are God's.

### CHAPTER 7

*Paul answers questions about marriage for those who are called on missions. Look for counsel that can help you be a better missionary.*

### Paul Speaks About Missionaries and Marriage

1 ¶ NOW concerning the things whereof ye wrote unto me: It is good for a man not to touch a woman.

2 Nevertheless, to avoid fornication, let every man have his own wife, and let every woman have her own husband.

3 Let the husband render unto the wife due benevolence: and likewise also the wife unto the husband.

4 The wife hath not power of her own body, but the husband: and likewise also the husband hath not power of his own body, but the wife.

5 Defraud ye not one the other, except it be with consent for a time, that ye may give yourselves to fasting and prayer; and come together again, that Satan tempt you not for your incontinency.

6 But I speak this by permission, and not of commandment.

7 For I would that all men were even as I myself. But every man hath his proper gift of God, one after this manner, and another after that.

8 I say therefore to the unmarried and widows, It is good for them if they abide even as I.

9 But if they cannot contain, let them marry: for it is better to marry than to burn.

10 ¶ And unto the married I command, yet not I, but the Lord, Let not the wife depart from her husband:

11 But and if she depart, let her remain unmarried, or be reconciled to her husband: and let not the husband put away his wife.

12 But to the rest speak I, not the Lord: If any brother hath a wife that believeth not, and she be pleased to dwell with him, let him not put her away.

13 And the woman which hath an husband that believeth not, and if he be pleased to dwell with her, let her not leave him.

14 For the unbelieving husband is sanctified by the wife, and the unbelieving wife is sanctified by the husband: else were your children unclean; but now are they holy.

15 But if the unbelieving depart, let him depart. A brother or a sister is not under bondage in such cases: but God hath called us to peace.

16 For what knowest thou, O wife, whether thou shalt save thy husband? or how knowest thou, O man, whether thou shalt save thy wife?

17 ¶ But as God hath distributed to every man, as the Lord hath called every one, so let him walk. And so ordain I in all churches.

---

6:19-20　Paul says our bodies are temples. What can you do to always keep your body as a place where the Holy Ghost can dwell?

7:3　*render*—give
*benevolence*—kindness

7:5　The Joseph Smith Translation changes the first part of this verse to say, "Depart ye not one from the other." In other words, married couples should stay together.

*incontinency*—lack of self-control

7:9　*contain*—have self-control

7:11　*reconciled to*—reunited with
*put away*—divorce

7:13-14　Doctrine and Covenants 74 explains these verses by saying that a believer and a nonbeliever should not marry without their agreeing that their children should be raised as members of the Church.

7:14　*sanctified*—made pure

18 Is any man called being circumcised? let him not become uncircumcised. Is any called in uncircumcision? let him not be circumcised.

19 Circumcision is nothing, and uncircumcision is nothing, but the keeping of the commandments of God.

20 Let every man abide in the same calling wherein he was called.

21 Art thou called being a servant? care not for it: but if thou mayest be made free, use it rather.

22 For he that is called in the Lord, being a servant, is the Lord's freeman: likewise also he that is called, being free, is Christ's servant.

23 Ye are bought with a price; be not ye the servants of men.

24 Brethren, let every man, wherein he is called, therein abide with God.

## Paul Counsels Missionaries Who Are Not Married

25 ¶ Now concerning virgins I have no commandment of the Lord: yet I give my judgment, as one that hath obtained mercy of the Lord to be faithful.

26 I suppose therefore that this is good for the present distress, I say, that it is good for a man so to be.

27 Art thou bound unto a wife? seek not to be loosed. Art thou loosed from a wife? seek not a wife.

28 But and if thou marry, thou hast not sinned; and if a virgin marry, she hath not sinned. Nevertheless such shall have trouble in the flesh: but I spare you.

29 But this I say, brethren, the time is short: it remaineth, that both they that have wives be as though they had none;

30 And they that weep, as though they wept not; and they that rejoice, as though they rejoiced not; and they that buy, as though they possessed not;

31 And they that use this world, as not abusing it: for the fashion of this world passeth away.

32 But I would have you without carefulness. He that is unmarried careth for the things that belong to the Lord, how he may please the Lord:

33 But he that is married careth for the things that are of the world, how he may please his wife.

34 There is difference also between a wife and a virgin. The unmarried woman careth for the things of the Lord, that she may be holy both in body and in spirit: but she that is married careth for the things of the world, how she may please her husband.

35 And this I speak for your own profit; not that I may cast a snare upon you, but for that which is comely, and that ye may attend upon the Lord without distraction.

36 ¶ But if any man think that he behaveth himself uncomely toward his virgin, if she pass the flower of her age, and need so require, let him do what he will, he sinneth not: let them marry.

37 Nevertheless, he that standeth stedfast in his heart, having no necessity, but hath power over his own will, and hath so decreed in his heart that he will keep his virgin, doeth well.

38 So then he that giveth her in marriage doeth well; but he that giveth her not in marriage doeth better.

39 ¶ The wife is bound by the law as long as her husband liveth; but if her husband be dead, she is at liberty to be married to whom she will; only in the Lord.

40 But she is happier if she so abide, after my judgment: and I think also that I have the Spirit of God.

## CHAPTER 8

*Paul warns against eating foods that are sacrificed to false gods. Watch for what members of the Church should do to help strengthen weaker members.*

---

7:18-19 Circumcision was first revealed to Abraham. It was an ordinance for boys who were eight days old to show they were God's covenant children. The Joseph Smith Translation indicates that it was also to remind the Lord's people that baptism was not necessary until the age of eight (see JST, Genesis 17:11-12). In Paul's writings circumcision came to represent the Jews and the law of Moses.

7:26 *distress*—hard times

7:29-34 The Joseph Smith Translation makes it clear that Paul was speaking to missionaries in these verses (see JST, 1 Corinthians 7:29-33).

7:32 What do married people have to worry about that might make it difficult to serve a full-time mission? Why are single people usually better able to focus on the Lord's work as missionaries?

7:35 *comely*—pretty
*distraction*—thinking about other things

7:37 *stedfast*—firm
*decreed*—determined

## SAINTS SHOULD SET AN APPROPRIATE EXAMPLE FOR WEAKER MEMBERS OF THE CHURCH

1 ¶ NOW as touching things offered unto idols, we know that we all have knowledge. Knowledge puffeth up, but charity edifieth.

2 And if any man think that he knoweth any thing, he knoweth nothing yet as he ought to know.

3 But if any man love God, the same is known of him.

4 ¶ As concerning therefore the eating of those things that are offered in sacrifice unto idols, we know that an idol is nothing in the world, and that there is none other God but one.

5 For though there be that are called gods, whether in heaven or in earth, (as there be gods many, and lords many,)

6 But to us there is but one God, the Father, of whom are all things, and we in him; and one Lord Jesus Christ, by whom are all things, and we by him.

7 ¶ Howbeit there is not in every man that knowledge: for some with conscience of the idol unto this hour eat it as a thing offered unto an idol; and their conscience being weak is defiled.

8 But meat commendeth us not to God: for neither, if we eat, are we the better; neither, if we eat not, are we the worse.

9 But take heed lest by any means this liberty of yours become a stumblingblock to them that are weak.

10 For if any man see thee which hast knowledge sit at meat in the idol's temple, shall not the conscience of him which is weak be emboldened to eat those things which are offered to idols;

11 And through thy knowledge shall the weak brother perish, for whom Christ died?

12 But when ye sin so against the brethren, and wound their weak conscience, ye sin against Christ.

13 Wherefore, if meat make my brother to offend, I will eat no flesh while the world standeth, lest I make my brother to offend.

## CHAPTER 9

*Paul served the Lord as an Apostle out of love, not for money or for glory. Paul wanted all people to be saved through the gospel of Jesus Christ. Look for what you can do to help other people be saved.*

### APOSTLES SERVE THE LORD

1 ¶ AM I not an apostle? am I not free? have I not seen Jesus Christ our Lord? are not ye my work in the Lord?

2 If I be not an apostle unto others, yet doubtless I am to you: for the seal of mine apostleship are ye in the Lord.

3 ¶ Mine answer to them that do examine me is this,

4 Have we not power to eat and to drink?

5 Have we not power to lead about a sister, a wife,

---

8:1    **idols**—false gods
       **puffeth up**—causes pride
       **charity edifieth**—the pure love of Christ builds us spiritually

8:5-6  Joseph Smith said, "I have a witness of the Holy Ghost, and a testimony that Paul had no allusion to the heathen [that is, false] gods" (*The Teachings of Joseph Smith*, p. 212). Though there be many true gods, we worship only God the Father and his Son, Jesus Christ.

8:7    **with conscience of the idol**—who are comfortable with idols
       **defiled**—made weak or unclean

8:8    **commendeth us not**—does not place us closer

8:9    **liberty**—freedom
       **a stumblingblock to them that are weak**—something that causes the weak to trip

8:9-13 Paul teaches that we should not do things that might cause weaker members of the Church to fall

away from the Church. How can you be a better example to those around you? How could you make them stronger?

8:10   **emboldened**—encouraged

8:11   **perish**—die spiritually

8:13   **offend**—sin

9:1    Apostles are "special witnesses of the name of Christ in all the world" (D&C 107:23). Paul declares this special witness to the Corinthians and declares that he has seen the Savior.

       God's work is to "bring to pass the immortality and eternal life of man" (Moses 1:39). Paul participated in God's work by teaching the gospel to the Corinthians.

9:2    **seal**—proof

9:3    **examine**—question

9:5    *Cephas* is another name for Peter (see LDS Bible Dictionary, s.v. "Peter," p. 749).

as well as other apostles, and as the brethren of the Lord, and Cephas?

6 Or I only and Barnabas, have not we power to forbear working?

7 Who goeth a warfare any time at his own charges? who planteth a vineyard, and eateth not of the fruit thereof? or who feedeth a flock, and eateth not of the milk of the flock?

8 Say I these things as a man? or saith not the law the same also?

9 For it is written in the law of Moses, Thou shalt not muzzle the mouth of the ox that treadeth out the corn. Doth God take care for oxen?

10 Or saith he it altogether for our sakes? For our sakes, no doubt, this is written: that he that ploweth should plow in hope; and that he that thresheth in hope should be partaker of his hope.

11 If we have sown unto you spiritual things, is it a great thing if we shall reap your carnal things?

12 If others be partakers of this power over you, are not we rather? Nevertheless we have not used this power; but suffer all things, lest we should hinder the gospel of Christ.

13 Do ye not know that they which minister about holy things live of the things of the temple? and they which wait at the altar are partakers with the altar?

14 Even so hath the Lord ordained that they which preach the gospel should live of the gospel.

15 ¶ But I have used none of these things: neither have I written these things, that it should be so done unto me: for it were better for me to die, than that any man should make my glorying void.

16 For though I preach the gospel, I have nothing to glory of: for necessity is laid upon me; yea, woe is unto me, if I preach not the gospel!

17 For if I do this thing willingly, I have a reward: but if against my will, a dispensation of the gospel is committed unto me.

18 What is my reward then? Verily that, when I preach the gospel, I may make the gospel of Christ without charge, that I abuse not my power in the gospel.

19 ¶ For though I be free from all men, yet have I made myself servant unto all, that I might gain the more.

20 And unto the Jews I became as a Jew, that I might gain the Jews; to them that are under the law, as under the law, that I might gain them that are under the law;

21 To them that are without law, as without law, (being not without law to God, but under the law to Christ,) that I might gain them that are without law.

22 To the weak became I as weak, that I might gain the weak: I am made all things to all men, that I might by all means save some.

23 And this I do for the gospel's sake, that I might be partaker thereof with you.

---

9:6 *forbear working*—not work

9:7 *goeth a warfare . . . at his own charges*—pays his own way to be a soldier

*An ox treading out, or threshing, grain*

9:9-10 The law of Moses did not allow people to "muzzle," or cover, the mouth of an ox while it walked on grain (see Deuteronomy 25:4). When an ox walked on grain, the wheat seed separated from its shell. Muzzling the ox would not allow the animal to eat the fruit of its labors. Paul explains here that those who are called to preach the gospel have the right to be treated as well as the ox and be supported by the Saints in return for their spiritual service.

9:11 *carnal*—physical

9:16-17 Paul realizes that he will be held accountable for his calling to preach the gospel. The Lord has said that where much is given much is required (see D&C 82:3). Paul's glory comes from preaching the gospel without cost, just like King Benjamin in the Book of Mormon (see Mosiah 2:12).

9:18 *abuse*—misuse

9:21 *them that are without the law*—the Gentiles who do not know the law of Moses

## PAUL COMPARES GAINING SALVATION TO WINNING A RACE

24 ¶ Know ye not that they which run in a race run all, but one receiveth the prize? So run, that ye may obtain.

25 And every man that striveth for the mastery is temperate in all things. Now they do it to obtain a corruptible crown; but we an incorruptible.

26 I therefore so run, not as uncertainly; so fight I, not as one that beateth the air:

27 But I keep under my body, and bring it into subjection: lest that by any means, when I have preached to others, I myself should be a castaway.

## CHAPTER 10

*Paul reminds the Corinthians that Jesus Christ was the power that brought ancient Israel out of Egypt. All those who rebelled against God died in the wilderness. Look for the reason Paul gives for telling this story. What does Paul say that can help you follow the Savior better?*

## THE CHILDREN OF ISRAEL SAW GREAT MIRACLES BUT STILL REBELLED AGAINST GOD

1 ¶ MOREOVER, brethren, I would not that ye should be ignorant, how that all our fathers were under the cloud, and all passed through the sea;

2 And were all baptized unto Moses in the cloud and in the sea;

3 And did all eat the same spiritual meat;

4 And did all drink the same spiritual drink: for they drank of that spiritual Rock that followed them: and that Rock was Christ.

5 But with many of them God was not well pleased: for they were overthrown in the wilderness.

6 ¶ Now these things were our examples, to the intent we should not lust after evil things, as they also lusted.

7 Neither be ye idolaters, as were some of them; as it is written, The people sat down to eat and drink, and rose up to play.

8 Neither let us commit fornication, as some of them committed, and fell in one day three and twenty thousand.

9 Neither let us tempt Christ, as some of them also tempted, and were destroyed of serpents.

10 Neither murmur ye, as some of them also murmured, and were destroyed of the destroyer.

11 Now all these things happened unto them for ensamples: and they are written for our admonition, upon whom the ends of the world are come.

## GOD WILL HELP US ESCAPE ALL TEMPTATIONS

12 Wherefore let him that thinketh he standeth take heed lest he fall.

13 There hath no temptation taken you but such as is common to man: but God is faithful, who will not suffer you to be tempted above that ye are able; but will with the temptation also make a way to escape, that ye may be able to bear it.

---

9:24 **obtain**—get the prize

Paul reminds us that in an earthly race only one can win. Is that also true in our "race" to gain salvation in heaven? (See Galatians 3:28–29; 2 Nephi 26:33.) What do you think Paul meant when he said, "So run, that ye may obtain"?

9:25 **striveth for the mastery**—tries to win
**temperate**—self-disciplined
**corruptible**—perishable

9:27 **subjection**—control
**be a castaway**—not be saved

10:1 **ignorant**—uneducated

10:3-4 The children of Israel were given manna from heaven and water out of rocks by the blessings of the Savior, and yet they were not thankful. What are some blessings you have received that you could be more thankful for?

10:5 **overthrown**—killed

10:6 **intent**—purpose
**lust after**—desire or want

10:7 The children of Israel became idolaters when they worshiped a golden calf (see Exodus 32).

10:9 The story of the children of Israel being bitten by serpents (snakes) is found in Numbers 21:1-9.

10:10 **murmur**—complain

10:11 Paul explains that the stories of ancient Israel and their mistakes were written down as examples to teach us and encourage us not to make those same mistakes. Nephi did the same thing for his brothers by recounting to them some of these stories (see 1 Nephi 17:23-35).

10:12 **take heed**—be careful

10:13 **suffer**—allow
**bear**—overcome or resist

Alma taught that as we humble ourselves and pray continually we will not "be tempted above that which [we] can bear" (Alma 13:28).

*The children of Israel "passed through the sea."*

14 Wherefore, my dearly beloved, flee from idolatry.

15 ¶ I speak as to wise men; judge ye what I say.

## ONLY DO THAT WHICH STRENGTHENS OTHER PEOPLE

16 The cup of blessing which we bless, is it not the communion of the blood of Christ? The bread which we break, is it not the communion of the body of Christ?

17 For we being many are one bread, and one body: for we are all partakers of that one bread.

18 Behold Israel after the flesh: are not they which eat of the sacrifices partakers of the altar?

19 What say I then? that the idol is any thing, or that which is offered in sacrifice to idols is any thing?

20 But I say, that the things which the Gentiles sacrifice, they sacrifice to devils, and not to God: and I would not that ye should have fellowship with devils.

21 Ye cannot drink the cup of the Lord, and the cup of devils: ye cannot be partakers of the Lord's table, and of the table of devils.

22 Do we provoke the Lord to jealousy? are we stronger than he?

---

10:16 **communion**—sacrament

10:18- Paul tells the Corinthians that to join in feasts
21 offered to idols is to be friendly with devils and that a person cannot serve the Lord and the devil. What has Heavenly Father asked us to do that will keep us from serving the devil?

10:20 **have fellowship**—be friends

10:22 **provoke the Lord to jealousy**—make the Lord angry

23 ¶ All things are lawful for me, but all things are not expedient: all things are lawful for me, but all things edify not.

24 Let no man seek his own, but every man another's wealth.

25 Whatsoever is sold in the shambles, that eat, asking no question for conscience sake:

26 For the earth is the Lord's, and the fulness thereof.

27 If any of them that believe not bid you to a feast, and ye be disposed to go; whatsoever is set before you, eat, asking no question for conscience sake.

28 But if any man say unto you, This is offered in sacrifice unto idols, eat not for his sake that shewed it, and for conscience sake: for the earth is the Lord's, and the fulness thereof:

29 Conscience, I say, not thine own, but of the other: for why is my liberty judged of another man's conscience?

30 For if I by grace be a partaker, why am I evil spoken of for that for which I give thanks?

31 Whether therefore ye eat, or drink, or whatsoever ye do, do all to the glory of God.

32 Give none offence, neither to the Jews, nor to the Gentiles, nor to the church of God:

33 Even as I please all men in all things, not seeking mine own profit, but the profit of many, that they may be saved.

## CHAPTER 11

*We must make and keep sacred covenants in order to be saved in the kingdom of heaven. Eternal marriage and the sacrament are examples of these covenants. Watch for reasons why marriage and the sacrament are so important.*

### BOTH MEN AND WOMEN ARE IMPORTANT TO THE LORD

1 ¶ BE ye followers of me, even as I also am of Christ.

2 Now I praise you, brethren, that ye remember me in all things, and keep the ordinances, as I delivered them to you.

3 But I would have you know, that the head of every man is Christ; and the head of the woman is the man; and the head of Christ is God.

4 Every man praying or prophesying, having his head covered, dishonoureth his head.

5 But every woman that prayeth or prophesieth with her head uncovered dishonoureth her head: for that is even all one as if she were shaven.

6 For if the woman be not covered, let her also be shorn: but if it be a shame for a woman to be shorn or shaven, let her be covered.

7 For a man indeed ought not to cover his head, forasmuch as he is the image and glory of God: but the woman is the glory of the man.

8 For the man is not of the woman; but the woman of the man.

9 Neither was the man created for the woman; but the woman for the man.

10 For this cause ought the woman to have power on her head because of the angels.

11 Nevertheless neither is the man without the woman, neither the woman without the man, in the Lord.

12 For as the woman is of the man, even so is the man also by the woman; but all things of God.

---

10:23-24 Paul asks all members of the Church only to do things that will help other people want to come unto the Savior. What can you do to help other people come unto Christ?

10:23-33 Paul explains that we must be careful not to hurt another person's faith by the things we do. The Joseph Smith Translation changes verse 23 to say that anything that is not helpful or not uplifting is against the laws of God (see JST, 1 Corinthians 10:23).

10:25 **shambles**—market

10:28 **shewed**—This word is pronounced the same way as the word *showed* and has the same meaning; *shewed* is simply an old spelling of *showed*.

11:1-8 In Paul's day it was customary for women to wear their hair long and to cover their heads when praying. Paul referred to this custom in order to teach the importance of humbly following those who lead (see 2 Thessalonians 3:7).

11:3 *Head*, as it is used in this verse, means "leader" and refers to spiritually presiding. To learn more about the man's responsibility to his wife, see Ephesians 5:22-33.

11:11 We must be married eternally to enter into the highest degree of the celestial kingdom (see D&C 131:1-4).

11:12 Even though men and women have different roles and responsibilities, they are, as the First Presidency declared, "equally important before the Lord" (quoted in *Encyclopedia of Mormonism*, s.v. "Politics").

13 Judge in yourselves: is it comely that a woman pray unto God uncovered?

14 Doth not even nature itself teach you, that, if a man have long hair, it is a shame unto him?

15 But if a woman have long hair, it is a glory to her: for her hair is given her for a covering.

16 But if any man seem to be contentious, we have no such custom, neither the churches of God.

## PAUL WARNS AGAINST FALSE BELIEFS AND PRACTICES IN THE CHURCH

17 ¶ Now in this that I declare unto you I praise you not, that ye come together not for the better, but for the worse.

18 For first of all, when ye come together in the church, I hear that there be divisions among you; and I partly believe it.

19 For there must be also heresies among you, that they which are approved may be made manifest among you.

20 When ye come together therefore into one place, this is not to eat the Lord's supper.

21 For in eating every one taketh before other his own supper: and one is hungry, and another is drunken.

22 What? have ye not houses to eat and to drink in? or despise ye the church of God, and shame them that have not? What shall I say to you? shall I praise you in this? I praise you not.

## PAUL TEACHES THE SACREDNESS OF THE SACRAMENT

23 ¶ For I have received of the Lord that which also I delivered unto you, That the Lord Jesus the same night in which he was betrayed took bread:

24 And when he had given thanks, he brake it, and said, Take, eat: this is my body, which is broken for you: this do in remembrance of me.

25 After the same manner also he took the cup, when he had supped, saying, This cup is the new testament in my blood: this do ye, as oft as ye drink it, in remembrance of me.

26 For as often as ye eat this bread, and drink this cup, ye do shew the Lord's death till he come.

27 Wherefore whosoever shall eat this bread, and drink this cup of the Lord, unworthily, shall be guilty of the body and blood of the Lord.

28 But let a man examine himself, and so let him eat of that bread, and drink of that cup.

29 For he that eateth and drinketh unworthily, eateth and drinketh damnation to himself, not discerning the Lord's body.

30 For this cause many are weak and sickly among you, and many sleep.

31 For if we would judge ourselves, we should not be judged.

32 But when we are judged, we are chastened of the Lord, that we should not be condemned with the world.

---

11:13 *comely*—proper

11:16 *be contentious*—want to argue or fight

11:19 *heresies*—false beliefs and practices

11:20 *Lord's supper*—sacrament

11:23-25 This first sacrament service is recorded in Matthew 26:26-30.

11:25 *supped*—eaten

11:26 *shew*—This word is pronounced the same way as the word *show* and has the same meaning; *shew* is simply an old spelling of *show*.

11:26-27 "The partaking of these emblems constitutes one of the most holy and sacred ordinances in the Church" (Joseph Fielding Smith, *Doctrines of Salvation* 2:339). Why do you think it is so important to be worthy when you take the sacrament? (See 3 Nephi 18:28-33.)

11:28-29 Elder John H. Groberg taught: "What does it mean to partake of the sacrament worthily? . . . If we desire to improve (which is to repent) and are not under priesthood restriction, then, in my opinion, we are worthy. . . . If, however, we refuse to repent and improve, if we do not remember him and keep his commandments, then we have stopped our growth, and that is damnation to our souls." ("The Beauty and Importance of the Sacrament," p. 38.)

11:29 *damnation*—punishment
*discerning*—seeing clearly

11:30 *sleep*—are dead

11:31 As you examine or judge yourself, what are some things you could change so that God would find you worthy?

11:32 *chastened*—disciplined

*"Take, eat: this is my body, which is broken for you: this do in remembrance of me."*

33 Wherefore, my brethren, when ye come together to eat, tarry one for another.

34 And if any man hunger, let him eat at home; that ye come not together unto condemnation. And the rest will I set in order when I come.

## CHAPTER 12

*Members of the Church are given spiritual gifts so that they can bless the Church. Note some of the spiritual gifts Paul mentions and how they might be a blessing to the Church.*

### PAUL TEACHES MEMBERS OF THE CHURCH ABOUT SPIRITUAL GIFTS

1 ¶ NOW concerning spiritual gifts, brethren, I would not have you ignorant.

2 Ye know that ye were Gentiles, carried away unto these dumb idols, even as ye were led.

3 Wherefore I give you to understand, that no man speaking by the Spirit of God calleth Jesus accursed: and that no man can say that Jesus is the Lord, but by the Holy Ghost.

4 Now there are diversities of gifts, but the same Spirit.

5 And there are differences of administrations, but the same Lord.

6 And there are diversities of operations, but it is the same God which worketh all in all.

7 But the manifestation of the Spirit is given to every man to profit withal.

8 For to one is given by the Spirit the word of wisdom; to another the word of knowledge by the same Spirit;

9 To another faith by the same Spirit; to another the gifts of healing by the same Spirit;

10 To another the working of miracles; to another prophecy; to another discerning of spirits; to another divers kinds of tongues; to another the interpretation of tongues:

11 But all these worketh that one and the selfsame Spirit, dividing to every man severally as he will.

### CHURCH MEMBERS RECEIVE SPIRITUAL GIFTS IN ORDER TO BLESS OTHERS

12 ¶ For as the body is one, and hath many members, and all the members of that one body, being many, are one body: so also is Christ.

13 For by one Spirit are we all baptized into one body, whether we be Jews or Gentiles, whether we be bond or free; and have been all made to drink into one Spirit.

14 For the body is not one member, but many.

15 If the foot shall say, Because I am not the hand, I am not of the body; is it therefore not of the body?

16 And if the ear shall say, Because I am not the eye, I am not of the body; is it therefore not of the body?

17 If the whole body were an eye, where were the hearing? If the whole were hearing, where were the smelling?

18 But now hath God set the members every one of them in the body, as it hath pleased him.

19 And if they were all one member, where were the body?

20 But now are they many members, yet but one body.

21 And the eye cannot say unto the hand, I have no need of thee: nor again the head to the feet, I have no need of you.

22 Nay, much more those members of the body, which seem to be more feeble, are necessary:

---

12:1 *ignorant*—uneducated

12:2 *dumb idols*—false gods

12:3 *accursed*—condemned

One of the missions of the Holy Ghost is to bear witness of Jesus Christ (see 2 Nephi 31:18).

12:4 *diversities*—different kinds

12:7 *withal*—everyone

12:10 *discerning of spirits*—being able to tell the difference between different kinds of spirits
*divers*—many
*interpretation of tongues*—ability to understand different languages

12:11 Satan and his followers try to lead God's children away from the truth through false miracles and teachings. God gives his children the gifts of the Spirit, "that ye may not be deceived" (D&C 46:8).

12:12 *members*—different parts

12:13-24 Paul compares the Church to a body. How can individual members of the Church bless the entire Church just as arms, legs, ears, and fingers help the human body?

12:22 *Nay*—No
*feeble*—weak

23 And those members of the body, which we think to be less honourable, upon these we bestow more abundant honour; and our uncomely parts have more abundant comeliness.

24 For our comely parts have no need: but God hath tempered the body together, having given more abundant honour to that part which lacked:

25 That there should be no schism in the body; but that the members should have the same care one for another.

26 And whether one member suffer, all the members suffer with it; or one member be honoured, all the members rejoice with it.

27 ¶ Now ye are the body of Christ, and members in particular.

28 And God hath set some in the church, first apostles, secondarily prophets, thirdly teachers, after that miracles, then gifts of healings, helps, governments, diversities of tongues.

29 Are all apostles? are all prophets? are all teachers? are all workers of miracles?

30 Have all the gifts of healing? do all speak with tongues? do all interpret?

31 But covet earnestly the best gifts: and yet shew I unto you a more excellent way.

## CHAPTER 13

*Of all the spiritual gifts of God, charity is the greatest. Look for reasons why charity is the greatest of all gifts of the Spirit.*

## PAUL SAYS THAT CHARITY IS THE GREATEST GIFT OF THE SPIRIT

1 ¶ THOUGH I speak with the tongues of men and of angels, and have not charity, I am become as sounding brass, or a tinkling cymbal.

2 And though I have the gift of prophecy, and understand all mysteries, and all knowledge; and though I have all faith, so that I could remove mountains, and have not charity, I am nothing.

3 And though I bestow all my goods to feed the poor, and though I give my body to be burned, and have not charity, it profiteth me nothing.

4 ¶ Charity suffereth long, and is kind; charity envieth not; charity vaunteth not itself, is not puffed up,

5 Doth not behave itself unseemly, seeketh not her own, is not easily provoked, thinketh no evil;

6 Rejoiceth not in iniquity, but rejoiceth in the truth;

7 Beareth all things, believeth all things, hopeth all things, endureth all things.

8 ¶ Charity never faileth: but whether there be prophecies, they shall fail; whether there be tongues, they shall cease; whether there be knowledge, it shall vanish away.

## WE NOW SEE ONLY A PART OF THE TRUTH

9 For we know in part, and we prophesy in part.

10 But when that which is perfect is come, then that which is in part shall be done away.

11 When I was a child, I spake as a child, I understood as a child, I thought as a child: but when I

---

12:23 **honourable**—important, deserving
**uncomely**—unattractive, unlovely

12:24 **tempered**—combined

12:25 **schism**—division

12:31 **covet**—desire to have

What spiritual gifts or strengths have you received from God? What are you doing to use them to bless others?

13:1 **as sounding brass, or a tinkling cymbal**—just meaningless noise

13:1-3 Mormon explains that charity is "the pure love of Christ" and that we can only get it if we "pray unto the Father with all the energy of heart" (Moroni 7:47-48). How can you pray with more "energy of heart"?

13:3 **bestow**—give
**profiteth**—gains

13:4 **envieth not**—wants not things that belong to others
**vaunteth not itself**—does not brag
**puffed up**—proud

13:5 **unseemly**—improperly
**provoked**—angered

13:6 **iniquity**—unrighteousness

13:8 The time will come when there will no longer be a need for prophecy and speaking in tongues. Looking at Paul's description of charity in verses 4-7, why do you think charity will never fail?

13:9-12 While here on earth we know only part of the truth. Paul says it is like seeing "through a glass darkly," which is like looking into a mirror that has a poor reflection (see James 1:23). When Jesus ("that which is perfect") comes again, "he shall reveal all things" (D&C 101:32). Then we shall know all truth and see more clearly.

became a man, I put away childish things.

12 For now we see through a glass, darkly; but then face to face: now I know in part; but then shall I know even as also I am known.

13 And now abideth faith, hope, charity, these three; but the greatest of these is charity.

## CHAPTER 14

*Paul describes the value of the gift of prophecy. Watch for reasons why the gift of prophecy blesses so many people.*

### THE GIFT OF PROPHECY IS MORE IMPORTANT IN THE CHURCH THAN THE GIFT OF TONGUES

1 ¶ FOLLOW after charity, and desire spiritual gifts, but rather that ye may prophesy.

2 For he that speaketh in an unknown tongue speaketh not unto men, but unto God: for no man understandeth him; howbeit in the spirit he speaketh mysteries.

3 But he that prophesieth speaketh unto men to edification, and exhortation, and comfort.

4 He that speaketh in an unknown tongue edifieth himself; but he that prophesieth edifieth the church.

5 I would that ye all spake with tongues, but rather that ye prophesied: for greater is he that prophesieth than he that speaketh with tongues, except he interpret, that the church may receive edifying.

6 ¶ Now, brethren, if I come unto you speaking with tongues, what shall I profit you, except I shall speak to you either by revelation, or by knowledge, or by prophesying, or by doctrine?

7 And even things without life giving sound, whether pipe or harp, except they give a distinction in the sounds, how shall it be known what is piped or harped?

8 For if the trumpet give an uncertain sound, who shall prepare himself to the battle?

9 So likewise ye, except ye utter by the tongue words easy to be understood, how shall it be known what is spoken? for ye shall speak into the air.

10 There are, it may be, so many kinds of voices in the world, and none of them is without signification.

11 Therefore if I know not the meaning of the voice, I shall be unto him that speaketh a barbarian, and he that speaketh shall be a barbarian unto me.

12 Even so ye, forasmuch as ye are zealous of spiritual gifts, seek that ye may excel to the edifying of the church.

13 Wherefore let him that speaketh in an unknown tongue pray that he may interpret.

14 For if I pray in an unknown tongue, my spirit prayeth, but my understanding is unfruitful.

15 ¶ What is it then? I will pray with the spirit, and I will pray with the understanding also: I will sing with the spirit, and I will sing with the understanding also.

16 Else when thou shalt bless with the spirit, how shall he that occupieth the room of the unlearned say Amen at thy giving of thanks, seeing he understandeth not what thou sayest?

17 For thou verily givest thanks well, but the other is not edified.

18 I thank my God, I speak with tongues more than ye all:

19 Yet in the church I had rather speak five words with my understanding, that by my voice I might teach others also, than ten thousand words in an unknown tongue.

---

13:13 *abideth*—continues

14:1 People who have a testimony of Jesus Christ have the gift of prophecy (see Revelation 19:10).

14:2 *tongue*—language
*howbeit*—however

14:3 *edification*—uplift
*exhortation*—encouragement to do better

14:3-5 Why do you think it is better to prophesy than to speak in tongues?

14:5 *interpret*—speak the same things in a language that can be understood

14:7 *pipe*—a musical instrument like a flute
*distinction*—difference

14:8 Paul uses the trumpet call for battle as an example of the weakness in speaking with tongues. If no one recognizes the battle call, who shall gather to fight? How could you teach the gospel if you spoke only your own language in a foreign land?

14:10 *signification*—meaning

14:11 *barbarian*—person who speaks a foreign language

14:12 *zealous of*—very desirous to have
*excel*—do well

14:14 *unfruitful*—not understood by others

14:16 *occupieth*—is in

14:19 President Joseph F. Smith said, "I believe in the gifts of the Holy Spirit unto men, but I do not want the gift of tongues, except when I need it" (*Gospel Doctrine*, p. 201).

20 Brethren, be not children in understanding: howbeit in malice be ye children, but in understanding be men.

21 ¶ In the law it is written, With men of other tongues and other lips will I speak unto this people; and yet for all that will they not hear me, saith the Lord.

22 Wherefore tongues are for a sign, not to them that believe, but to them that believe not: but prophesying serveth not for them that believe not, but for them which believe.

23 If therefore the whole church be come together into one place, and all speak with tongues, and there come in those that are unlearned, or unbelievers, will they not say that ye are mad?

24 But if all prophesy, and there come in one that believeth not, or one unlearned, he is convinced of all, he is judged of all:

25 And thus are the secrets of his heart made manifest; and so falling down on his face he will worship God, and report that God is in you of a truth.

26 ¶ How is it then, brethren? when ye come together, every one of you hath a psalm, hath a doctrine, hath a tongue, hath a revelation, hath an interpretation. Let all things be done unto edifying.

27 If any man speak in an unknown tongue, let it be by two, or at the most by three, and that by course; and let one interpret.

28 But if there be no interpreter, let him keep silence in the church; and let him speak to himself, and to God.

29 Let the prophets speak two or three, and let the other judge.

30 If any thing be revealed to another that sitteth by, let the first hold his peace.

31 For ye may all prophesy one by one, that all may learn, and all may be comforted.

32 And the spirits of the prophets are subject to the prophets.

## THERE SHOULD ALWAYS BE ORDER IN CHURCH MEETINGS

33 For God is not the author of confusion, but of peace, as in all churches of the saints.

34 ¶ Let your women keep silence in the churches: for it is not permitted unto them to speak; but they are commanded to be under obedience, as also saith the law.

35 And if they will learn any thing, let them ask their husbands at home: for it is a shame for women to speak in the church.

36 ¶ What? came the word of God out from you? or came it unto you only?

37 If any man think himself to be a prophet, or spiritual, let him acknowledge that the things that I write unto you are the commandments of the Lord.

38 But if any man be ignorant, let him be ignorant.

39 Wherefore, brethren, covet to prophesy, and forbid not to speak with tongues.

40 Let all things be done decently and in order.

# CHAPTER 15

*Paul proves there is a resurrection. See what Paul says that proves you will be resurrected.*

## MANY WITNESSES SAW THE RESURRECTED SAVIOR

1 ¶ MOREOVER, brethren, I declare unto you the gospel which I preached unto you, which also ye have received, and wherein ye stand;

2 By which also ye are saved, if ye keep in memory what I preached unto you, unless ye have believed in vain.

3 For I delivered unto you first of all that which I also received, how that Christ died for our sins according to the scriptures;

4 And that he was buried, and that he rose again the third day according to the scriptures:

---

14:20　*malice*—the desire to hurt others

14:23　*mad*—crazy

14:25　*manifest*—understandable

14:27　*that by course*—each in turn

14:33-35　God's house "is a house of order" (D&C 132:8). For his own purposes he has given the responsibility to preside in the Church to men and not to women. The Joseph Smith Translation clarifies this by changing the word *speak* to the word *rule* (see JST, 1 Corinthians 14:34).

14:38　*be ignorant*—does not know or understand this

14:39　*covet*—desire

14:40　*decently*—properly

15:2　*in vain*—for no purpose

5 And that he was seen of Cephas, then of the twelve:

6 After that, he was seen of above five hundred brethren at once; of whom the greater part remain unto this present, but some are fallen asleep.

7 After that, he was seen of James; then of all the apostles.

8 And last of all he was seen of me also, as of one born out of due time.

9 For I am the least of the apostles, that am not meet to be called an apostle, because I persecuted the church of God.

10 But by the grace of God I am what I am: and his grace which was bestowed upon me was not in vain; but I laboured more abundantly than they all: yet not I, but the grace of God which was with me.

11 Therefore whether it were I or they, so we preach, and so ye believed.

## CHRIST'S RESURRECTION MADE IT POSSIBLE FOR US TO BE RESURRECTED

12 ¶ Now if Christ be preached that he rose from the dead, how say some among you that there is no resurrection of the dead?

13 But if there be no resurrection of the dead, then is Christ not risen:

14 And if Christ be not risen, then is our preaching vain, and your faith is also vain.

15 Yea, and we are found false witnesses of God; because we have testified of God that he raised up Christ: whom he raised not up, if so be that the dead rise not.

16 For if the dead rise not, then is not Christ raised:

17 And if Christ be not raised, your faith is vain; ye are yet in your sins.

18 Then they also which are fallen asleep in Christ are perished.

19 If in this life only we have hope in Christ, we are of all men most miserable.

20 ¶ But now is Christ risen from the dead, and become the firstfruits of them that slept.

21 For since by man came death, by man came also the resurrection of the dead.

22 For as in Adam all die, even so in Christ shall all be made alive.

23 But every man in his own order: Christ the firstfruits; afterward they that are Christ's at his coming.

24 Then cometh the end, when he shall have delivered up the kingdom to God, even the Father; when he shall have put down all rule and all authority and power.

25 For he must reign, till he hath put all enemies under his feet.

26 The last enemy that shall be destroyed is death.

27 For he hath put all things under his feet. But when he saith all things are put under him, it is manifest that he is excepted, which did put all things under him.

28 And when all things shall be subdued unto him, then shall the Son also himself be subject unto him that put all things under him, that God may be all in all.

29 Else what shall they do which are baptized for the dead, if the dead rise not at all? why are they then baptized for the dead?

30 And why stand we in jeopardy every hour?

31 I protest by your rejoicing which I have in Christ Jesus our Lord, I die daily.

32 If after the manner of men I have fought with beasts at Ephesus, what advantageth it me, if the dead rise not? let us eat and drink; for to morrow we die.

33 Be not deceived: evil communications corrupt good manners.

---

15:5 *Cephas* is the Greek name for the Apostle Simon Peter (see Luke 24:34).

15:5-10 Apostles are called to be "special witnesses" of Jesus Christ (see D&C 107:23).

15:6 *fallen asleep*—dead

15:10 *bestowed upon*—given

15:18 *perished*—lost

15:19 *miserable*—unhappy

15:21-22 When Adam and Eve ate the forbidden fruit, they became mortal and eventually died (see Genesis 2:17; 3:17-19). This event is known as the Fall and opened the door for God's children to come to earth and experience mortality and death—an important part of God's plan.

15:28 *subdued unto*—ruled by
*subject unto*—presided (ruled) over by

15:30 *jeopardy*—danger

15:31 *protest*—declare, say

15:33 *corrupt*—spoil

*"For as in Adam all die, even so in Christ shall all be made alive."*

34 Awake to righteousness, and sin not; for some have not the knowledge of God: I speak this to your shame.

## RESURRECTED BODIES WILL DIFFER IN GLORY

35 ¶ But some man will say, How are the dead raised up? and with what body do they come?

36 Thou fool, that which thou sowest is not quickened, except it die:

37 And that which thou sowest, thou sowest not that body that shall be, but bare grain, it may chance of wheat, or of some other grain:

38 But God giveth it a body as it hath pleased him, and to every seed his own body.

39 All flesh is not the same flesh: but there is one kind of flesh of men, another flesh of beasts, another of fishes, and another of birds.

40 There are also celestial bodies, and bodies terrestrial: but the glory of the celestial is one, and the glory of the terrestrial is another.

41 There is one glory of the sun, and another glory of the moon, and another glory of the stars: for one star differeth from another star in glory.

42 So also is the resurrection of the dead. It is sown in corruption; it is raised in incorruption:

43 It is sown in dishonour; it is raised in glory: it is sown in weakness; it is raised in power:

44 It is sown a natural body; it is raised a spiritual body. There is a natural body, and there is a spiritual body.

45 And so it is written, The first man Adam was made a living soul; the last Adam was made a quickening spirit.

46 Howbeit that was not first which is spiritual, but that which is natural; and afterward that which is spiritual.

47 The first man is of the earth, earthy: the second man is the Lord from heaven.

48 As is the earthy, such are they also that are earthy: and as is the heavenly, such are they also that are heavenly.

49 And as we have borne the image of the earthy, we shall also bear the image of the heavenly.

## AT THE RESURRECTION OUR MORTAL BODIES WILL BECOME IMMORTAL BODIES

50 Now this I say, brethren, that flesh and blood cannot inherit the kingdom of God; neither doth corruption inherit incorruption.

51 ¶ Behold, I shew you a mystery; We shall not all sleep, but we shall all be changed,

52 In a moment, in the twinkling of an eye, at the last trump: for the trumpet shall sound, and the dead shall be raised incorruptible, and we shall be changed.

53 For this corruptible must put on incorruption, and this mortal must put on immortality.

54 So when this corruptible shall have put on incorruption, and this mortal shall have put on immortality, then shall be brought to pass the saying that is written, Death is swallowed up in victory.

55 O death, where is thy sting? O grave, where is thy victory?

56 The sting of death is sin; and the strength of sin is the law.

57 But thanks be to God, which giveth us the victory through our Lord Jesus Christ.

58 ¶ Therefore, my beloved brethren, be ye stedfast, unmoveable, always abounding in the work of the Lord, forasmuch as ye know that your labour is not in vain in the Lord.

---

15:36 The seed that is planted dies so that the plant can grow and produce new seeds.

15:40 The Joseph Smith Translation adds the fact that there are also "bodies telestial" (JST, 1 Corinthians 15:40).

15:40-42 How do these verses teach that we will be resurrected to different degrees of glory? To learn more about the three degrees of glory, see Doctrine and Covenants 76.

15:42 *corruption*—decay, destruction

15:46 *Howbeit*—However

15:49 *borne*—carried
*image*—appearance

15:50 Our bodies of mortal flesh and blood are corruptible, or subject to disease and death. The Prophet Joseph Smith taught that "all will be raised by the power of God, having spirit in their bodies, and not blood" (*The Teachings of Joseph Smith*, p. 559).

15:56 Paul describes death as our "last enemy." But death is only a lasting enemy to those who have sinned. This is why the Nephites regretted going to war with the Lamanites, killing those who were "unprepared to meet their God" (Alma 48:23).

15:58 *stedfast*—firm
*abounding*—overflowing

# CHAPTER 16

*Paul finishes his letter to the Corinthian Saints. Look for words or phrases that show how Paul feels about these Church members.*

## PAUL MAKES PLANS TO VISIT THE CORINTHIAN SAINTS

1 ¶ NOW concerning the collection for the saints, as I have given order to the churches of Galatia, even so do ye.

2 Upon the first day of the week let every one of you lay by him in store, as God hath prospered him, that there be no gatherings when I come.

3 And when I come, whomsoever ye shall approve by your letters, them will I send to bring your liberality unto Jerusalem.

4 And if it be meet that I go also, they shall go with me.

5 ¶ Now I will come unto you, when I shall pass through Macedonia: for I do pass through Macedonia.

6 And it may be that I will abide, yea, and winter with you, that ye may bring me on my journey whithersoever I go.

7 For I will not see you now by the way; but I trust to tarry a while with you, if the Lord permit.

8 But I will tarry at Ephesus until Pentecost.

9 For a great door and effectual is opened unto me, and there are many adversaries.

10 ¶ Now if Timotheus come, see that he may be with you without fear: for he worketh the work of the Lord, as I also do.

11 Let no man therefore despise him: but conduct him forth in peace, that he may come unto me: for I look for him with the brethren.

12 As touching our brother Apollos, I greatly desired him to come unto you with the brethren: but his will was not at all to come at this time; but he will come when he shall have convenient time.

## PAUL GIVES FINAL COUNSEL AND PRAISE TO THE CORINTHIAN SAINTS

13 ¶ Watch ye, stand fast in the faith, quit you like men, be strong.

14 Let all your things be done with charity.

15 I beseech you, brethren, (ye know the house of Stephanas, that it is the firstfruits of Achaia, and that they have addicted themselves to the ministry of the saints,)

16 That ye submit yourselves unto such, and to every one that helpeth with us, and laboureth.

17 I am glad of the coming of Stephanas and Fortunatus and Achaicus: for that which was lacking on your part they have supplied.

18 For they have refreshed my spirit and yours: therefore acknowledge ye them that are such.

19 ¶ The churches of Asia salute you. Aquila and Priscilla salute you much in the Lord, with the church that is in their house.

20 All the brethren greet you. Greet ye one another with an holy kiss.

21 The salutation of me Paul with mine own hand.

22 If any man love not the Lord Jesus Christ, let him be Anathema Maran-atha.

23 The grace of our Lord Jesus Christ be with you.

24 My love be with you all in Christ Jesus. Amen.

---

16:1 The Church in Jerusalem had many who were poor and needy (see Acts 6:1). Paul had "given order" or arranged to collect donations throughout the churches in Asia to help provide for the Saints in Jerusalem (see Acts 24:17, 26).

16:3 **liberality**—gift

16:4 **meet**—proper

16:9 **effectual**—one that will produce desired results
**adversaries**—things that oppose

16:13 **quit you**—behave

16:14 Charity is the pure love of Christ (see Moroni 7:46-48; 1 Corinthians 13).

How can you show your family and friends that you love them?

16:15 **beseech**—beg
**addicted**—devoted

16:16 **submit yourselves unto**—obey

16:19 In Paul's day the Saints often held church services in members' homes. What would it be like to have church in your house?

16:20-21 The Joseph Smith Translation changes the word "kiss" to "salutation" (JST, 1 Corinthians 16:20). A salutation was a greeting common to the Saints in Paul's day.

16:22 **Anathema**—cursed
**Maran-atha**—Our Lord, come! or, Our Lord will come!

# THE SECOND EPISTLE OF PAUL THE APOSTLE TO THE
# CORINTHIANS

*Paul the Apostle wrote this letter to the same Church members he addressed in his first letter to the Corinthians. False teachers had made their way into the Church, causing arguments and leading some members away from the truth. Paul wrote to answer questions and encourage the Saints in their faith.*

## CHAPTER 1

*Often our lives can be difficult and we may feel great pain or sadness. Look for how God promises to comfort his faithful Saints during their times of trouble.*

### PAUL SPEAKS OF GOD'S COMFORT

1 PAUL, an apostle of Jesus Christ by the will of God, and Timothy our brother, unto the church of God which is at Corinth, with all the saints which are in all Achaia:

2 Grace be to you and peace from God our Father, and from the Lord Jesus Christ.

3 ¶ Blessed be God, even the Father of our Lord Jesus Christ, the Father of mercies, and the God of all comfort;

4 Who comforteth us in all our tribulation, that we may be able to comfort them which are in any trouble, by the comfort wherewith we ourselves are comforted of God.

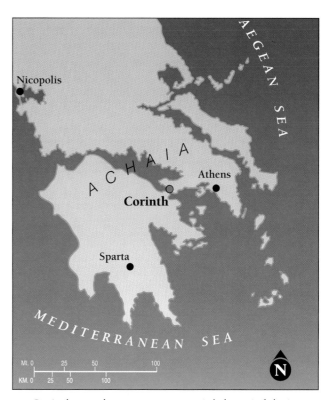

Corinth was known as a very rich but sinful city.

In this view of the ruins of Corinth can be seen, among other things, the Lechaion Road, which led to the port of Lechaion less than two miles north of Corinth. The rocky hill in the background is the Acrocorinth, on which false worship was practiced anciently.

1:3   Jesus can comfort us in all things because he has suffered all things (see Alma 7:11-13).

1:4   **tribulation**—sufferings

| | | | |
|---|---|---|---|
| = Word Help | | = A Closer Look | |
| = More Light | | = Ponder This | |

Words in pink are explained in the Glossary.

5 For as the sufferings of Christ abound in us, so our consolation also aboundeth by Christ.

6 And whether we be afflicted, it is for your consolation and salvation, which is effectual in the enduring of the same sufferings which we also suffer: or whether we be comforted, it is for your consolation and salvation.

7 ¶ And our hope of you is stedfast, knowing, that as ye are partakers of the sufferings, so shall ye be also of the consolation.

8 For we would not, brethren, have you ignorant of our trouble which came to us in Asia, that we were pressed out of measure, above strength, insomuch that we despaired even of life:

9 But we had the sentence of death in ourselves, that we should not trust in ourselves, but in God which raiseth the dead:

10 Who delivered us from so great a death, and doth deliver: in whom we trust that he will yet deliver us;

11 Ye also helping together by prayer for us, that for the gift bestowed upon us by the means of many persons thanks may be given by many on our behalf.

## PAUL CHANGES HIS PLANS

12 ¶ For our rejoicing is this, the testimony of our conscience, that in simplicity and godly sincerity, not with fleshly wisdom, but by the grace of God, we have had our conversation in the world, and more abundantly to you-ward.

13 For we write none other things unto you, than what ye read or acknowledge; and I trust ye shall acknowledge even to the end;

14 As also ye have acknowledged us in part, that we are your rejoicing, even as ye also are ours in the day of the Lord Jesus.

15 ¶ And in this confidence I was minded to come unto you before, that ye might have a second benefit;

16 And to pass by you into Macedonia, and to come again out of Macedonia unto you, and of you to be brought on my way toward Judaea.

17 When I therefore was thus minded, did I use lightness? or the things that I purpose, do I purpose according to the flesh, that with me there should be yea yea, and nay nay?

18 But as God is true, our word toward you was not yea and nay.

19 For the Son of God, Jesus Christ, who was preached among you by us, even by me and Silvanus and Timotheus, was not yea and nay, but in him was yea.

20 For all the promises of God in him are yea, and in him Amen, unto the glory of God by us.

21 Now he which stablisheth us with you in Christ, and hath anointed us, is God;

22 Who hath also sealed us, and given the earnest of the Spirit in our hearts.

23 Moreover I call God for a record upon my soul, that to spare you I came not as yet unto Corinth.

24 Not for that we have dominion over your faith, but are helpers of your joy: for by faith ye stand.

## CHAPTER 2

*Paul explains his reasons for delaying his visit to Corinth. He also shares some of his recent missionary successes. Look for reasons why Paul could not visit the Corinthian members at that time.*

## FORGIVENESS IS GIVEN THROUGH CHRIST

1 ¶ BUT I determined this with myself, that I would not come again to you in heaviness.

---

1:5  **abound**—are found in abundance
**our consolation . . . aboundeth by**—much comfort comes to us through

1:6  *Effectual* means "possible" or "effective." Just as coal is transformed into a diamond by heat, pressure, and time, we can learn to become like God through sufferings and afflictions.

1:7  **stedfast**—strong, immovable

1:8  Paul's sufferings in Asia were so great he almost died.

1:9  Paul found that sadness and pain led him to depend more on God. How do you handle pressures that seem too difficult to deal with?

1:11  How did the prayers of others help Paul? Whom do you pray for regularly?

1:12  Paul knew in his heart that he followed God. He followed God's ways and wisdom because God's ways are greater than man's ways (see Isaiah 55:8-9).

1:14  **acknowledged**—understood

1:20-22  What blessings come to us through the power of God?

1:21  **stablisheth**—establishes

1:24  **dominion**—rule or power

2:1  **heaviness**—sorrow

2 For if I make you sorry, who is he then that maketh me glad, but the same which is made sorry by me?

3 And I wrote this same unto you, lest, when I came, I should have sorrow from them of whom I ought to rejoice; having confidence in you all, that my joy is the joy of you all.

4 For out of much affliction and anguish of heart I wrote unto you with many tears; not that ye should be grieved, but that ye might know the love which I have more abundantly unto you.

5 ¶ But if any have caused grief, he hath not grieved me, but in part: that I may not overcharge you all.

6 Sufficient to such a man is this punishment, which was inflicted of many.

7 So that contrariwise ye ought rather to forgive him, and comfort him, lest perhaps such a one should be swallowed up with overmuch sorrow.

8 Wherefore I beseech you that ye would confirm your love toward him.

9 For to this end also did I write, that I might know the proof of you, whether ye be obedient in all things.

10 To whom ye forgive any thing, I forgive also: for if I forgave any thing, to whom I forgave it, for your sakes forgave I it in the person of Christ;

11 Lest Satan should get an advantage of us: for we are not ignorant of his devices.

## THE SAINTS LOVE AND FORGIVE ONE ANOTHER

12 ¶ Furthermore, when I came to Troas to preach Christ's gospel, and a door was opened unto me of the Lord,

13 I had no rest in my spirit, because I found not Titus my brother: but taking my leave of them, I went from thence into Macedonia.

14 Now thanks be unto God, which always causeth us to triumph in Christ, and maketh manifest the savour of his knowledge by us in every place.

15 For we are unto God a sweet savour of Christ, in them that are saved, and in them that perish:

16 To the one we are the savour of death unto death; and to the other the savour of life unto life. And who is sufficient for these things?

17 For we are not as many, which corrupt the word of God: but as of sincerity, but as of God, in the sight of God speak we in Christ.

## CHAPTER 3

*Paul compares the gospel with the law of Moses. Watch for what Paul says about how the gospel is greater than the law of Moses.*

### PAUL'S POWER AS A MISSIONARY COMES FROM GOD

1 ¶ DO we begin again to commend ourselves? or need we, as some others, epistles of commendation to you, or letters of commendation from you?

2 Ye are our epistle written in our hearts, known and read of all men:

3 Forasmuch as ye are manifestly declared to be the epistle of Christ ministered by us, written not with ink,

---

2:2-4   Paul expresses his deep love for the Saints and notes his concern that his earlier letter has caused the members grief. How does it make you feel to realize that the leaders of the Church care so much for the members?

2:4   **affliction**—hardship and sorrow
**grieved**—sad

  In a previous letter to the Corinthians, Paul detailed their sins and weaknesses. In this letter Paul lets the Saints in Corinth know that he loves them. This is following the pattern that the Lord revealed in latter-day revelation (see D&C 121:41-43).

2:5   **overcharge**—burden

2:6   **inflicted of**—given or delivered by

2:7   **contrariwise**—just the opposite

2:10   The Lord revealed to the Prophet Joseph Smith that we are required to forgive all people (see D&C 64:9-10).

2:10-11   How does forgiving others help you feel better?

2:14   **savour**—smell or fragrance

2:14-17   How would someone feel about Jesus Christ if you were the only Christian that person knew?

3:1   **epistles of commendation**—letters of recommendation, letters that say good things

but with the Spirit of the living God; not in tables of stone, but in fleshy tables of the heart.

4 And such trust have we through Christ to Godward:

5 Not that we are sufficient of ourselves to think any thing as of ourselves; but our sufficiency is of God;

6 ¶ Who also hath made us able ministers of the new testament; not of the letter, but of the spirit: for the letter killeth, but the spirit giveth life.

## THE GOSPEL IS MORE GLORIOUS THAN THE LAW OF MOSES

7 But if the ministration of death, written and engraven in stones, was glorious, so that the children of Israel could not stedfastly behold the face of Moses for the glory of his countenance; which glory was to be done away:

8 How shall not the ministration of the spirit be rather glorious?

9 For if the ministration of condemnation be glory, much more doth the ministration of righteousness exceed in glory.

10 For even that which was made glorious had no glory in this respect, by reason of the glory that excelleth.

11 For if that which is done away was glorious, much more that which remaineth is glorious.

12 ¶ Seeing then that we have such hope, we use great plainness of speech:

13 And not as Moses, which put a vail over his face, that the children of Israel could not stedfastly look to the end of that which is abolished:

14 But their minds were blinded: for until this day remaineth the same vail untaken away in the reading of the old testament; which vail is done away in Christ.

15 But even unto this day, when Moses is read, the vail is upon their heart.

16 Nevertheless when it shall turn to the Lord, the vail shall be taken away.

17 Now the Lord is that Spirit: and where the Spirit of the Lord is, there is liberty.

18 But we all, with open face beholding as in a glass the glory of the Lord, are changed into the same image from glory to glory, even as by the Spirit of the Lord.

---

*A depiction of the "tables of stone" received by Moses*

3:4 **such trust have we through Christ to God-ward**—we trust in God's power because of our faith in Christ

3:5 Paul was a humble follower of Christ. He said that he was "sufficient," or capable, not because of his own strength but because he received strength from God. Similarly, Ammon, one of the sons of Mosiah, said, "I will not boast of myself, but I will boast of my God, for in his strength I can do all things" (Alma 26:12).

3:6 Some Jews, such as the Pharisees, were so concerned about living every little point of the law of Moses that they no longer listened to the very God who gave the law to them. Paul taught that living only the letter of the law (every little point) "killeth" but that listening to the spirit "giveth life."

3:7 Paul calls the law of Moses "the ministration of death" because even though the law was good, no one could live it perfectly. Breaking the law meant being cut off from God. That is why Heavenly Father sent Jesus to save us from our sins (see John 3:16-17).

3:13-16 After seeing God, Moses' face shone. Since this frightened his people, Moses wore a veil. The veil also symbolized that the children of Israel were not ready for the light and knowledge that Moses received. (See Exodus 34:29-35 and D&C 84:19-25.) Paul taught that a veil was still over the minds of the Jews and that when they read the Old Testament they did not understand it. The gospel of Jesus Christ takes away that veil so that those who are willing to receive it can understand.

3:17 *Liberty* means "freedom." How can having the Spirit of the Lord bring you freedom? (See Romans 6:22-23; 2 Nephi 2:26-27.)

3:18 **open face beholding as in a glass**—unveiled faces reflecting as in a mirror

## CHAPTER 4

*Paul suffered many trials as a missionary for the Lord. Notice his attitude as he faces them.*

### THE GOSPEL LIGHT SHINES ON THE SAINTS

1 ¶ THEREFORE seeing we have this ministry, as we have received mercy, we faint not;

2 But have renounced the hidden things of dishonesty, not walking in craftiness, nor handling the word of God deceitfully; but by manifestation of the truth commending ourselves to every man's conscience in the sight of God.

3 But if our gospel be hid, it is hid to them that are lost:

4 In whom the god of this world hath blinded the minds of them which believe not, lest the light of the glorious gospel of Christ, who is the image of God, should shine unto them.

5 For we preach not ourselves, but Christ Jesus the Lord; and ourselves your servants for Jesus' sake.

6 For God, who commanded the light to shine out of darkness, hath shined in our hearts, to give the light of the knowledge of the glory of God in the face of Jesus Christ.

7 But we have this treasure in earthen vessels, that the excellency of the power may be of God, and not of us.

### MORTAL TRIALS ARE NOTHING COMPARED TO ETERNAL GLORY

8 ¶ We are troubled on every side, yet not distressed; we are perplexed, but not in despair;

9 Persecuted, but not forsaken; cast down, but not destroyed;

10 Always bearing about in the body the dying of the Lord Jesus, that the life also of Jesus might be made manifest in our body.

11 For we which live are alway delivered unto death for Jesus' sake, that the life also of Jesus might be made manifest in our mortal flesh.

12 So then death worketh in us, but life in you.

13 We having the same spirit of faith, according as it is written, I believed, and therefore have I spoken; we also believe, and therefore speak;

14 Knowing that he which raised up the Lord Jesus shall raise up us also by Jesus, and shall present us with you.

15 For all things are for your sakes, that the abundant grace might through the thanksgiving of many redound to the glory of God.

16 For which cause we faint not; but though our

---

4:1-2 Paul "renounced" (refused or turned away from) dishonesty and deception and manifested (taught) the truth. He was "not ashamed of the gospel of Jesus Christ" (Romans 1:16).

4:3-4 Not everyone knows about the gospel of Jesus Christ, because Satan, "the god of this world," works to keep people in the dark. In addition to Satan's tactics, other forces are at work. As the Prophet Joseph Smith indicated, "There are many yet on the earth . . . who are blinded by the subtle craftiness [clever lies] of men" (D&C 123:12).

4:7 **earthen vessels**—clay jars (a way of referring to imperfect human beings)

*When Paul wrote of "earthen vessels," he was referring to the common pottery of his time as a symbol for people. Though breakable and plain-looking, ancient clay jars and pots served many useful purposes, such as the storing of valuable items. Similarly, human beings, despite their weaknesses, can do much good as God's power works through them.*

4:8-9 Paul kept a positive attitude, even though he faced many trials. He was willing to suffer all of these things for "the knowledge of Christ Jesus my Lord" (Philippians 3:8).

4:11-14 Many would die for the gospel of Jesus Christ, but their dying would be only temporary. Jesus said, "I am the resurrection, and the life: he that believeth in me, though he were dead, yet shall he live" (John 11:25).

4:15 Grace is divine help given by God through the atonement of Jesus Christ. It provides us with the power needed to repent, keep the commandments, and become like God. (See LDS Bible Dictionary, s.v. "Grace," p. 697.)

**redound**—overflow

4:16 Paul said that though the "outward man" (the body) ages and dies, "the inward man" (the spirit) grows daily. What can you do to keep your spirit growing daily?

outward man perish, yet the inward man is renewed day by day.

17 For our light affliction, which is but for a moment, worketh for us a far more exceeding and eternal weight of glory;

18 While we look not at the things which are seen, but at the things which are not seen: for the things which are seen are temporal; but the things which are not seen are eternal.

## CHAPTER 5

*Paul compares our mortal bodies to earthly tabernacles or buildings. He testifies that in the resurrection we will receive, or be clothed with, heavenly bodies. Look for how that blessing comes to us because of Jesus Christ.*

### PAUL TESTIFIES OF THE RESURRECTION

1 ¶ FOR we know that if our earthly house of this tabernacle were dissolved, we have a building of God, an house not made with hands, eternal in the heavens.

2 For in this we groan, earnestly desiring to be clothed upon with our house which is from heaven:

3 If so be that being clothed we shall not be found naked.

4 For we that are in this tabernacle do groan, being burdened: not for that we would be unclothed, but clothed upon, that mortality might be swallowed up of life.

5 Now he that hath wrought us for the selfsame thing

is God, who also hath given unto us the earnest of the Spirit.

6 Therefore we are always confident, knowing that, whilst we are at home in the body, we are absent from the Lord:

7 (For we walk by faith, not by sight:)

8 We are confident, I say, and willing rather to be absent from the body, and to be present with the Lord.

### JESUS CHRIST WILL JUDGE US

9 Wherefore we labour, that, whether present or absent, we may be accepted of him.

10 For we must all appear before the judgment seat of Christ; that every one may receive the things done in his body, according to that he hath done, whether it be good or bad.

11 Knowing therefore the terror of the Lord, we persuade men; but we are made manifest unto God; and I trust also are made manifest in your consciences.

### WE CAN BE ONE WITH GOD

12 ¶ For we commend not ourselves again unto you, but give you occasion to glory on our behalf, that ye may have somewhat to answer them which glory in appearance, and not in heart.

13 For whether we be beside ourselves, it is to God: or whether we be sober, it is for your cause.

14 For the love of Christ constraineth us; because we thus judge, that if one died for all, then were all dead:

15 And that he died for all, that they which live should not henceforth live unto themselves, but unto him which died for them, and rose again.

---

4:17-18   Our trials in life are "temporal," or temporary. They will seem like "a moment" compared to eternity. The Lord said to Joseph Smith (and by extension to us), "If thou endure it well, God shall exalt thee on high" (D&C 121:8).

5:1   **if our earthly house of this tabernacle were dissolved**—if we died

Resurrected bodies can be called "building[s] of God" because they are "quickened" (given life), glorified, and perfected by the power of God (see D&C 88:27-31).

5:2-4   Paul taught that some groan, or are sad, because they desire to have a perfected resurrected body (verse 2), even though they do not look forward to being "unclothed," or dead (verse 4). What are some reasons you have for looking forward to the resurrection?

5:5   **wrought us for the selfsame thing**—made us for this very purpose
**earnest**—guarantee or security

5:6-8   Because we cannot remember the premortal life, we walk by faith in this life. Faith is a belief in things we cannot see that are true (see Alma 32:21).

5:9   What labor or work do you do in order to please Jesus? How does doing that work make you feel?

5:11   Everyone has a conscience. We know good from evil because of the Light of Christ that is in each of us. (See Moroni 7:16-17.)

5:14   **constraineth**—invites, encourages, compels

16 ¶ Wherefore henceforth know we no man after the flesh: yea, though we have known Christ after the flesh, yet now henceforth know we him no more.

17 Therefore if any man be in Christ, he is a new creature: old things are passed away; behold, all things are become new.

18 And all things are of God, who hath reconciled us to himself by Jesus Christ, and hath given to us the ministry of reconciliation;

19 To wit, that God was in Christ, reconciling the world unto himself, not imputing their trespasses unto them; and hath committed unto us the word of reconciliation.

20 Now then we are ambassadors for Christ, as though God did beseech you by us: we pray you in Christ's stead, be ye reconciled to God.

21 For he hath made him to be sin for us, who knew no sin; that we might be made the righteousness of God in him.

## CHAPTER 6

*Paul urges the Saints at Corinth to return to God and stay away from unbelievers. In this chapter watch for counsel Paul gives to aid them in accomplishing these two purposes.*

### DO SAINTS HAVE A SECOND CHANCE FOR SALVATION?

1 ¶ WE then, as workers together with him, beseech you also that ye receive not the grace of God in vain.

2 (For he saith, I have heard thee in a time accepted, and in the day of salvation have I succoured thee: behold, now is the accepted time; behold, now is the day of salvation.)

3 Giving no offence in any thing, that the ministry be not blamed:

4 But in all things approving ourselves as the ministers of God, in much patience, in afflictions, in necessities, in distresses,

5 In stripes, in imprisonments, in tumults, in labours, in watchings, in fastings;

6 By pureness, by knowledge, by longsuffering, by kindness, by the Holy Ghost, by love unfeigned,

7 By the word of truth, by the power of God, by the armour of righteousness on the right hand and on the left,

8 By honour and dishonour, by evil report and good report: as deceivers, and yet true;

9 As unknown, and yet well known; as dying, and, behold, we live; as chastened, and not killed;

10 As sorrowful, yet alway rejoicing; as poor, yet making many rich; as having nothing, and yet possessing all things.

11 ¶ O ye Corinthians, our mouth is open unto you, our heart is enlarged.

12 Ye are not straitened in us, but ye are straitened in your own bowels.

13 Now for a recompence in the same, (I speak as unto my children,) be ye also enlarged.

---

5:17    Paul taught that true followers of Jesus put away their old habits and become "new creature[s]," not wanting to do evil but only good (see Mosiah 5:2). The prophet Alma described this as being "born of God" (Alma 5:14).

5:17-21    Why do you think Paul pleads so strongly with the Saints to live according to the will of God? Why is it important to be reconciled with God, or to have him be pleased with your life?

5:18    *reconciled us to*—made us one or unified with *reconciliation*—being brought into harmony or unity with God

5:19    *To wit*—That is

5:20    *ambassadors*—representatives *beseech you*—ask you strongly

6:1    *in vain*—with no results, for nothing

6:2    *succoured*—helped

   Paul speaks about the day of salvation being now. Compare this with Amulek's teaching about procrastinating (putting off until later) the day of our repentance (see Alma 34:32-35).

6:4    *necessities*—food, drink, and clothing

6:5    The word *stripes* had particular meaning to Paul as he had been beaten with rods three times and scourged (whipped) five different times (see 2 Corinthians 11:24-25).

6:7    *the word of truth*—preaching the gospel

6:11    Paul had a great love for the Corinthian Saints. The apostles and prophets love the Saints today. What does it mean to you that prophets love and pray for you?

6:12    *straitened*—limited or restrained *bowels*—affections

6:13    *recompence*—fair exchange, reward given for some act

## WE SHOULD NOT BE MARRIED TO UNBELIEVERS

14 Be ye not unequally yoked together with unbelievers: for what fellowship hath righteousness with unrighteousness? and what communion hath light with darkness?

15 And what concord hath Christ with Belial? or what part hath he that believeth with an infidel?

16 And what agreement hath the temple of God with idols? for ye are the temple of the living God; as God hath said, I will dwell in them, and walk in them; and I will be their God, and they shall be my people.

17 Wherefore come out from among them, and be ye separate, saith the Lord, and touch not the unclean thing; and I will receive you,

18 And will be a Father unto you, and ye shall be my sons and daughters, saith the Lord Almighty.

## CHAPTER 7

*Paul worried that the Corinthian Saints were angry with him. In an earlier letter he told them they needed to repent. Look for what they did about that letter and what Paul teaches us about sorrow and repentance.*

## PAUL REJOICES THAT THE CORINTHIAN SAINTS REPENTED

1 ¶ HAVING therefore these promises, dearly beloved, let us cleanse ourselves from all filthiness of the flesh and spirit, perfecting holiness in the fear of God.

2 Receive us; we have wronged no man, we have corrupted no man, we have defrauded no man.

3 I speak not this to condemn you: for I have said before, that ye are in our hearts to die and live with you.

4 Great is my boldness of speech toward you, great is my glorying of you: I am filled with comfort, I am exceeding joyful in all our tribulation.

5 ¶ For, when we were come into Macedonia, our flesh had no rest, but we were troubled on every side; without were fightings, within were fears.

6 Nevertheless God, that comforteth those that are cast down, comforted us by the coming of Titus;

Today, Latter-day Saint couples can be married for time and eternity in a temple like this one in Logan, Utah.

become worthy to go to the temple . . . or will leave . . . because neither of you should want to be unequally yoked." (Ezra Taft Benson, *The Teachings of Ezra Taft Benson*, p. 351.)

6:15 **concord**—agreement

In this verse the name *Belial* is generally thought to refer to Satan. In other passages, phrases such as "son of Belial" and "children of Belial" are used to refer to those who are wicked. (See LDS Bible Dictionary, s.v. "Belial," p. 620.)

6:17 **unclean thing**—that which must be avoided according to Jewish law

6:18 How does it make you feel to know that our Father in Heaven loves you as his son or daughter?

7:1 The promises referred to here are that God will be our Father and we will be his children (see 2 Corinthians 6:16-18). Paul taught that these blessings are worth repenting for.

6:14 **yoked**—joined
**communion**—fellowship

"If someone wants to marry you outside the temple, whom will you strive to please—God or a mortal? If you insist on a temple marriage, you will be pleasing the Lord and blessing the other party. Why? Because that person will either

7:2 **defrauded**—cheated, tricked

7:4 **tribulation**—trouble, suffering

7:6-8 Why do you think our Church leaders find joy when we "mourn" for our sins and repent?

7 And not by his coming only, but by the consolation wherewith he was comforted in you, when he told us your earnest desire, your mourning, your fervent mind toward me; so that I rejoiced the more.

## GODLY SORROW FOR SIN LEADS TO REPENTANCE AND SALVATION

8 For though I made you sorry with a letter, I do not repent, though I did repent: for I perceive that the same epistle hath made you sorry, though it were but for a season.

9 Now I rejoice, not that ye were made sorry, but that ye sorrowed to repentance: for ye were made sorry after a godly manner, that ye might receive damage by us in nothing.

10 For godly sorrow worketh repentance to salvation not to be repented of: but the sorrow of the world worketh death.

11 For behold this selfsame thing, that ye sorrowed after a godly sort, what carefulness it wrought in you, yea, what clearing of yourselves, yea, what indignation, yea, what fear, yea, what vehement desire, yea, what zeal, yea, what revenge! In all things ye have approved yourselves to be clear in this matter.

12 ¶ Wherefore, though I wrote unto you, I did it not for his cause that had done the wrong, nor for his cause that suffered wrong, but that our care for you in the sight of God might appear unto you.

13 Therefore we were comforted in your comfort: yea, and exceedingly the more joyed we for the joy of Titus, because his spirit was refreshed by you all.

14 For if I have boasted any thing to him of you, I am not ashamed; but as we spake all things to you in truth, even so our boasting, which I made before Titus, is found a truth.

15 And his inward affection is more abundant toward you, whilst he remembereth the obedience of you all, how with fear and trembling ye received him.

16 I rejoice therefore that I have confidence in you in all things.

# CHAPTER 8

*The Saints in Jerusalem were poor and hungry. Paul collected offerings from the Saints in Asia to help them. Note how Paul encourages the Corinthians to share.*

## THE SAINTS IN MACEDONIA GIVE TO THE POOR AND NEEDY

1 ¶ MOREOVER, brethren, we do you to wit of the grace of God bestowed on the churches of Macedonia;

2 How that in a great trial of affliction the abundance of their joy and their deep poverty abounded unto the riches of their liberality.

3 For to their power, I bear record, yea, and beyond their power they were willing of themselves;

4 Praying us with much intreaty that we would receive the gift, and take upon us the fellowship of the ministering to the saints.

5 And this they did, not as we hoped, but first gave their own selves to the Lord, and unto us by the will of God.

6 Insomuch that we desired Titus, that as he had begun, so he would also finish in you the same grace also.

7 ¶ Therefore, as ye abound in every thing, in faith, and utterance, and knowledge, and in all diligence, and in your love to us, see that ye abound in this grace also.

---

7:7  *consolation*—comfort, support

7:9-10  The Corinthian Saints were "sorry after a godly manner" for their sins, which led them to repent. The "sorrow of the world" does not lead to repentance. It is what the Book of Mormon describes as "the sorrowing of the damned, because the Lord would not always suffer [allow] them to take happiness in sin" (Mormon 2:13).

7:11  *indignation*—disapproval of sin

7:15  *inward affection*—love, compassion

8:1  *we do you to wit of*—we make known to you

8:1-5  Paul wrote to the Corinthian Saints about the kindness of the Saints in Macedonia, who gave much to help the poor even though they were poor themselves. They believed what Jesus taught: "It is more blessed to give than to receive" (Acts 20:35).

8:2  *liberality*—sincerity, generosity

8:4  *intreaty*—pleading

8:5  The Macedonian Saints gave to the poor because they put God first in their lives. How can you more fully show your love and put God first in your life?

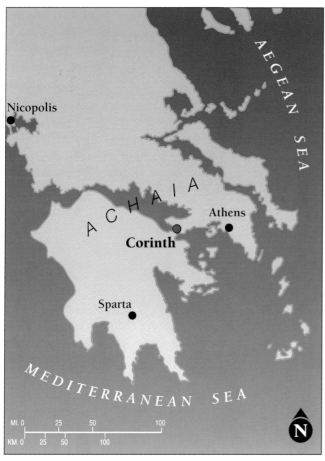

*The lands of Paul's travels*

8 I speak not by commandment, but by occasion of the forwardness of others, and to prove the sincerity of your love.

## Jesus Showed Us How to Care for the Poor

9 For ye know the grace of our Lord Jesus Christ, that, though he was rich, yet for your sakes he became poor, that ye through his poverty might be rich.

10 And herein I give my advice: for this is expedient for you, who have begun before, not only to do, but also to be forward a year ago.

11 Now therefore perform the doing of it; that as there was a readiness to will, so there may be a performance also out of that which ye have.

12 For if there be first a willing mind, it is accepted according to that a man hath, and not according to that he hath not.

13 For I mean not that other men be eased, and ye burdened:

14 But by an equality, that now at this time your abundance may be a supply for their want, that their abundance also may be a supply for your want: that there may be equality:

15 As it is written, He that had gathered much had nothing over; and he that had gathered little had no lack.

## Titus Is Sent to Collect the Offerings of the Corinthian Saints

16 ¶ But thanks be to God, which put the same earnest care into the heart of Titus for you.

17 For indeed he accepted the exhortation; but being more forward, of his own accord he went unto you.

18 And we have sent with him the brother, whose praise is in the gospel throughout all the churches;

19 And not that only, but who was also chosen of the churches to travel with us with this grace, which is administered by us to the glory of the same Lord, and declaration of your ready mind:

20 Avoiding this, that no man should blame us in this abundance which is administered by us:

21 Providing for honest things, not only in the sight of the Lord, but also in the sight of men.

22 And we have sent with them our brother, whom we have oftentimes proved diligent in many things, but now much more diligent, upon the great confidence which I have in you.

23 Whether any do enquire of Titus, he is my partner and fellowhelper concerning you: or our brethren be enquired of, they are the messengers of the churches, and the glory of Christ.

---

8:9 Jesus, the creator of this earth, "became poor" by humbling himself and becoming "obedient unto death, even the death of the cross" (Philippians 2:8). Because of his death we are richly blessed through the resurrection.

8:10-12 A year earlier the Corinthians had gathered offerings for the poor. Now Paul asked them to willingly finish what they had begun. Mormon, a prophet in the Book of Mormon, taught that if your gift is given grudgingly the Lord will not bless you (see Moroni 7:8).

8:15 Paul told about how Jehovah rained manna from heaven and everyone gathered enough to provide for their families. This is described in Exodus 16:14-18.

8:17 **exhortation**—request

8:19 **with this grace**—to carry the offering

8:21 **Providing for honest things**—Doing the right thing

24 Wherefore shew ye to them, and before the churches, the proof of your love, and of our boasting on your behalf.

## CHAPTER 9

*When we serve our fellowman, we are serving God at the same time (see Mosiah 2:17). Look for what Paul teaches about God's feelings toward those who cheerfully serve.*

### GOD LOVES AND REWARDS A CHEERFUL GIVER

1 ¶ FOR as touching the ministering to the saints, it is superfluous for me to write to you:

2 For I know the forwardness of your mind, for which I boast of you to them of Macedonia, that Achaia was ready a year ago; and your zeal hath provoked very many.

3 Yet have I sent the brethren, lest our boasting of you should be in vain in this behalf; that, as I said, ye may be ready:

4 Lest haply if they of Macedonia come with me, and find you unprepared, we (that we say not, ye) should be ashamed in this same confident boasting.

5 Therefore I thought it necessary to exhort the brethren, that they would go before unto you, and make up beforehand your bounty, whereof ye had notice before, that the same might be ready, as a matter of bounty, and not as of covetousness.

6 ¶ But this I say, He which soweth sparingly shall reap also sparingly; and he which soweth bountifully shall reap also bountifully.

7 Every man according as he purposeth in his heart, so let him give; not grudgingly, or of necessity: for God loveth a cheerful giver.

8 And God is able to make all grace abound toward you; that ye, always having all sufficiency in all things, may abound to every good work:

9 (As it is written, He hath dispersed abroad; he hath given to the poor: his righteousness remaineth for ever.

10 Now he that ministereth seed to the sower both minister bread for your food, and multiply your seed sown, and increase the fruits of your righteousness;)

11 Being enriched in every thing to all bountifulness, which causeth through us thanksgiving to God.

12 For the administration of this service not only supplieth the want of the saints, but is abundant also by many thanksgivings unto God;

13 Whiles by the experiment of this ministration they glorify God for your professed subjection unto the gospel of Christ, and for your liberal distribution unto them, and unto all men;

---

8:24 **shew**—This word is pronounced the same way as the word *show* and has the same meaning; *shew* is simply an old spelling of *show*.
**boasting on your behalf**—praise for you

Paul loved the Corinthian Saints and had spoken highly of them to Titus and others. He asked them to prove their love. How can you prove your love for your leaders?

9:1 **For as touching**—About
**superfluous**—unnecessary

9:2 **boast of**—praise

9:5 "Bounty" has to do with blessings and service. Paul strongly encouraged the Corinthian Saints to prepare themselves so that they could serve others cheerfully instead of with "covetousness," or grudgingly (see also Moroni 7:5-8).

9:6 Bounteous or great blessings from the Lord come by obedience to his laws (see D&C 130:20-21). This is sometimes called "the law of the harvest."

9:7 What do you think it means to be a cheerful giver?

*In ancient times, seeds were "sown," or planted, by casting them on the ground by hand, as shown here. Then, when the fruit became ripe, it was "reaped," or picked.*

9:8-10 God gives us every blessing we need so that we can prosper and serve others (see Mosiah 2:22-24).

9:11 **enriched**—blessed
**bountifulness**—readiness to give generously

9:12 **administration**—giving

9:13 **Whiles by the experiment of this ministration**—By proving yourselves through service
**professed subjection**—testimony and obedience
**liberal distribution**—willingness to give

14 And by their prayer for you, which long after you for the exceeding grace of God in you.

15 Thanks be unto God for his unspeakable gift.

## CHAPTER 10

*Things have improved in Corinth since Paul wrote his last letter, but some members are criticizing Paul while he is not there to defend himself. Watch for what Paul says in defense of his work as an Apostle.*

### PAUL DEFENDS HIS MINISTRY AGAINST SOME CRITICS

1 ¶ NOW I Paul myself beseech you by the meekness and gentleness of Christ, who in presence am base among you, but being absent am bold toward you:

2 But I beseech you, that I may not be bold when I am present with that confidence, wherewith I think to be bold against some, which think of us as if we walked according to the flesh.

3 For though we walk in the flesh, we do not war after the flesh:

4 (For the weapons of our warfare are not carnal, but mighty through God to the pulling down of strong holds;)

5 Casting down imaginations, and every high thing that exalteth itself against the knowledge of God, and bringing into captivity every thought to the obedience of Christ;

6 And having in a readiness to revenge all disobedience, when your obedience is fulfilled.

7 ¶ Do ye look on things after the outward appearance? If any man trust to himself that he is Christ's, let

him of himself think this again, that, as he is Christ's, even so are we Christ's.

8 For though I should boast somewhat more of our authority, which the Lord hath given us for edification, and not for your destruction, I should not be ashamed:

9 That I may not seem as if I would terrify you by letters.

10 For his letters, say they, are weighty and powerful; but his bodily presence is weak, and his speech contemptible.

11 Let such an one think this, that, such as we are in word by letters when we are absent, such will we be also in deed when we are present.

12 ¶ For we dare not make ourselves of the number, or compare ourselves with some that commend themselves: but they measuring themselves by themselves, and comparing themselves among themselves, are not wise.

13 But we will not boast of things without our measure, but according to the measure of the rule which God hath distributed to us, a measure to reach even unto you.

14 For we stretch not ourselves beyond our measure, as though we reached not unto you: for we are come as far as to you also in preaching the gospel of Christ:

15 Not boasting of things without our measure, that is, of other men's labours; but having hope, when your faith is increased, that we shall be enlarged by you according to our rule abundantly,

16 To preach the gospel in the regions beyond you, and not to boast in another man's line of things made ready to our hand.

17 But he that glorieth, let him glory in the Lord.

---

10:1-6 Paul's enemies criticized him for being tough in his letters but weak in person (see verse 10). He explains that true disciples behave differently from those of the world. Elder Neal A. Maxwell said, "Being *in* the world but not being *of* the world sets apart the serious, meek disciple not only in viewpoint but also in lifestyle" (*Meek and Lowly*, p. 85).

10:1 **base**—mild, timid

10:4 **carnal**—of this world

10:5 "To be saved men must repent of their evil thoughts" (Bruce R. McConkie, *Mormon Doctrine*, p. 792). This is why King Benjamin counseled his people, "Watch yourselves, and your thoughts, and your words, and your deeds, and observe the commandments of God" (Mosiah 4:30).

10:8 **edification**—building up

10:10 **contemptible**—despised, not worth listening to

10:12 Paul criticizes his enemies, who praised their own greatness when all they had done was compare themselves to themselves. They had forgotten the proverb: "Let another man praise thee, and not thine own mouth" (Proverbs 27:2).

10:13 **without our measure**—beyond the limits of what God has assigned us

10:15 **we shall be enlarged by you according to our rule abundantly**—our field of labor will expand greatly among you

10:15-16 Paul explains that he does not want to take credit for the work done by anyone else. This appears to be a criticism of Paul's enemies in Corinth, who were trying to take some credit for Paul's work (see verses 10-14).

18 For not he that commendeth himself is approved, but whom the Lord commendeth.

## CHAPTER 11

*Paul continues to defend himself against false apostles in Corinth. Look for what Paul says about his sufferings in Christ's service.*

### PAUL WANTS THE SAINTS TO BE FAITHFUL TO JESUS CHRIST AND NOT BE DECEIVED BY FALSE APOSTLES

1 ¶ WOULD to God ye could bear with me a little in my folly: and indeed bear with me.

2 For I am jealous over you with godly jealousy: for I have espoused you to one husband, that I may present you as a chaste virgin to Christ.

3 But I fear, lest by any means, as the serpent beguiled Eve through his subtilty, so your minds should be corrupted from the simplicity that is in Christ.

4 For if he that cometh preacheth another Jesus, whom we have not preached, or if ye receive another spirit, which ye have not received, or another gospel, which ye have not accepted, ye might well bear with him.

5 ¶ For I suppose I was not a whit behind the very chiefest apostles.

6 But though I be rude in speech, yet not in knowledge; but we have been throughly made manifest among you in all things.

7 Have I committed an offence in abasing myself that ye might be exalted, because I have preached to you the gospel of God freely?

8 I robbed other churches, taking wages of them, to do you service.

9 And when I was present with you, and wanted, I was chargeable to no man: for that which was lacking to me the brethren which came from Macedonia supplied: and in all things I have kept myself from being burdensome unto you, and so will I keep myself.

10 As the truth of Christ is in me, no man shall stop me of this boasting in the regions of Achaia.

11 Wherefore? because I love you not? God knoweth.

12 But what I do, that I will do, that I may cut off occasion from them which desire occasion; that wherein they glory, they may be found even as we.

13 For such are false apostles, deceitful workers, transforming themselves into the apostles of Christ.

14 And no marvel; for Satan himself is transformed into an angel of light.

15 Therefore it is no great thing if his ministers also be transformed as the ministers of righteousness; whose end shall be according to their works.

### PAUL GLORIES IN HIS SUFFERINGS FOR JESUS CHRIST

16 ¶ I say again, Let no man think me a fool; if otherwise, yet as a fool receive me, that I may boast myself a little.

17 That which I speak, I speak it not after the Lord, but as it were foolishly, in this confidence of boasting.

18 Seeing that many glory after the flesh, I will glory also.

---

10:18   What could you do that shows your desire to serve others and lift their spirits?

11:2   When we are baptized, we covenant (or promise) to take upon us the name of Jesus Christ (see D&C 20:77). Paul describes this covenant relationship between the Church and Jesus Christ as being "espoused" (or married). By keeping our covenants, the Church can be a "chaste virgin" (or pure and holy bride) to Christ.

11:3   **corrupted**—polluted and turned away

11:4-5   Paul scolds the Corinthians for being so easily led away by false teachers who claimed to be the "chiefest apostles" and superior to Paul.

11:6   **rude in speech**—unskilled in speaking
**throughly made manifest**—made perfectly clear

11:7   **an offence in abasing myself**—a sin in lowering myself

11:7-9   When Paul was in Corinth he received no support from the members there but was supported instead by the congregations of the Church in Macedonia.

11:10-12   Paul defends his service in order to keep the false apostles from claiming to have the same power he has.

11:13   **transforming**—changing

11:14   **no marvel**—do not be surprised

11:16   **yet as a fool receive me**—be patient with me as you would a fool

11:18   **glory after the flesh**—boast or brag about worldly things

19 For ye suffer fools gladly, seeing ye yourselves are wise.

20 For ye suffer, if a man bring you into bondage, if a man devour you, if a man take of you, if a man exalt himself, if a man smite you on the face.

21 I speak as concerning reproach, as though we had been weak. Howbeit whereinsoever any is bold, (I speak foolishly,) I am bold also.

22 ¶ Are they Hebrews? so am I. Are they Israelites? so am I. Are they the seed of Abraham? so am I.

23 Are they ministers of Christ? (I speak as a fool) I am more; in labours more abundant, in stripes above measure, in prisons more frequent, in deaths oft.

24 Of the Jews five times received I forty stripes save one.

25 Thrice was I beaten with rods, once was I stoned, thrice I suffered shipwreck, a night and a day I have been in the deep;

26 In journeyings often, in perils of waters, in perils of robbers, in perils by mine own countrymen, in perils by the heathen, in perils in the city, in perils in the wilderness, in perils in the sea, in perils among false brethren;

27 In weariness and painfulness, in watchings often, in hunger and thirst, in fastings often, in cold and nakedness.

28 Beside those things that are without, that which cometh upon me daily, the care of all the churches.

29 Who is weak, and I am not weak? who is offended, and I burn not?

30 If I must needs glory, I will glory of the things which concern mine infirmities.

31 The God and Father of our Lord Jesus Christ, which is blessed for evermore, knoweth that I lie not.

32 In Damascus the governor under Aretas the king kept the city of the Damascenes with a garrison, desirous to apprehend me:

33 And through a window in a basket was I let down by the wall, and escaped his hands.

## CHAPTER 12

*Paul wants to prove to the Corinthians that he is an Apostle, without sounding prideful. Watch for how Paul testifies of his calling and what keeps him humble.*

### PAUL IS TAKEN UP TO THE CELESTIAL WORLD

1 ¶ IT is not expedient for me doubtless to glory. I will come to visions and revelations of the Lord.

2 I knew a man in Christ above fourteen years ago, (whether in the body, I cannot tell; or whether out of the body, I cannot tell: God knoweth;) such an one caught up to the third heaven.

3 And I knew such a man, (whether in the body, or out of the body, I cannot tell: God knoweth;)

4 How that he was caught up into paradise, and heard unspeakable words, which it is not lawful for a man to utter.

### OUR WEAKNESSES CAN BECOME OUR STRENGTHS

5 Of such an one will I glory: yet of myself I will not glory, but in mine infirmities.

---

11:20 📖 Paul scolds the Corinthian Saints for being so tolerant that they allowed false teachers to take advantage of them and even slap them in the face.

11:23 📖 **stripes**—whippings

11:23-27 🔄 How do your trials compare to Paul's sufferings?

11:26 📖 **in perils**—in danger

11:28-29 🔄 Not only did Paul suffer physically, but he suffered with those who were weak and those who sinned. Do your parents or Church leaders ever feel sad because those they love make bad choices?

11:30 📖 **infirmities**—weaknesses

11:32 📖 **kept the city . . . with a garrison**—guarded the city . . . with soldiers
**apprehend**—catch, arrest

12:1 📖 **not expedient for me doubtless to glory**—not useful for me to boast

12:2 📖 **above**—about

12:2-4 🌟 "Speaking of himself, Paul says he was 'caught up to the third heaven,' which is the celestial kingdom" (Bruce R. McConkie, *Mortal Messiah* 4:394). Paul also saw "paradise," or the spirit world, and heard things he was not allowed to repeat.

12:5 📖 **glory**—boast
**infirmities**—weaknesses

6 For though I would desire to glory, I shall not be a fool; for I will say the truth: but now I forbear, lest any man should think of me above that which he seeth me to be, or that he heareth of me.

7 And lest I should be exalted above measure through the abundance of the revelations, there was given to me a thorn in the flesh, the messenger of Satan to buffet me, lest I should be exalted above measure.

8 For this thing I besought the Lord thrice, that it might depart from me.

9 And he said unto me, My grace is sufficient for thee: for my strength is made perfect in weakness. Most gladly therefore will I rather glory in my infirmities, that the power of Christ may rest upon me.

10 Therefore I take pleasure in infirmities, in reproaches, in necessities, in persecutions, in distresses for Christ's sake: for when I am weak, then am I strong.

## PAUL EXPRESSES CONCERNS FOR THE CORINTHIANS

11 ¶ I am become a fool in glorying; ye have compelled me: for I ought to have been commended of you: for in nothing am I behind the very chiefest apostles, though I be nothing.

12 Truly the signs of an apostle were wrought among you in all patience, in signs, and wonders, and mighty deeds.

13 For what is it wherein ye were inferior to other churches, except it be that I myself was not burdensome to you? forgive me this wrong.

14 Behold, the third time I am ready to come to you; and I will not be burdensome to you: for I seek not yours, but you: for the children ought not to lay up for the parents, but the parents for the children.

15 And I will very gladly spend and be spent for you; though the more abundantly I love you, the less I be loved.

16 But be it so, I did not burden you: nevertheless, being crafty, I caught you with guile.

17 Did I make a gain of you by any of them whom I sent unto you?

18 I desired Titus, and with him I sent a brother. Did Titus make a gain of you? walked we not in the same spirit? walked we not in the same steps?

19 Again, think ye that we excuse ourselves unto you? we speak before God in Christ: but we do all things, dearly beloved, for your edifying.

20 For I fear, lest, when I come, I shall not find you such as I would, and that I shall be found unto you such as ye would not: lest there be debates, envyings, wraths, strifes, backbitings, whisperings, swellings, tumults:

21 And lest, when I come again, my God will humble me among you, and that I shall bewail many which have sinned already, and have not repented of the uncleanness and fornication and lasciviousness which they have committed.

---

12:6 *I forbear*—I will avoid it (that is, glorying or boasting)

Why is it important to be humble even when we have accomplished great things?

12:7 *a thorn in the flesh*—a weakness in the body

12:8-10 Paul asked the Lord three times to take away his weakness. The Lord gave a similar answer to Moroni: "I give unto men weakness that they may be humble; . . . for if they humble themselves before me, and have faith in me, then will I make weak things become strong unto them" (Ether 12:27).

12:11-12 Paul was an Apostle of the Lord Jesus Christ (see 1 Corinthians 9:1). He performed miracles among the Corinthians by the power of the priesthood as a witness of his calling.

12:13-15 "In The Church of Jesus Christ of Latter-day Saints there is no paid ministry, no professional clergy, as is common in other churches" (Boyd K. Packer, *"That All May Be Edified,"* p. 237). This is one of the signs of the true Church (see Ephesians 4:11-14).

12:15 Like Paul, who was willing to be "spent" for the Saints, President Spencer W. Kimball once said, "My life is like my shoes—to be worn out in service" (quoted in Gordon B. Hinckley, "He Is at Peace," p. 41).

12:19 *excuse*—defend

12:20-21 Paul feared that when he visited the Corinthians again he would find them guilty of "uncleanness," or wickedness, and that would cause him to "bewail," or grieve, over them. Why are Church leaders so concerned about us when we sin and don't repent?

12:21 *fornication and lasciviousness*—uncontrolled unrighteous use of the sacred creative powers

# CHAPTER 13

*This is Paul's last known written message to the Corinthians. Look for the important instruction he gave them.*

## PAUL WARNS OF HIS FINAL VISIT TO THE CORINTHIANS

1 ¶ THIS is the third time I am coming to you. In the mouth of two or three witnesses shall every word be established.

2 I told you before, and foretell you, as if I were present, the second time; and being absent now I write to them which heretofore have sinned, and to all other, that, if I come again, I will not spare:

3 Since ye seek a proof of Christ speaking in me, which to you-ward is not weak, but is mighty in you.

4 For though he was crucified through weakness, yet he liveth by the power of God. For we also are weak in him, but we shall live with him by the power of God toward you.

5 Examine yourselves, whether ye be in the faith; prove your own selves. Know ye not your own selves, how that Jesus Christ is in you, except ye be reprobates?

6 But I trust that ye shall know that we are not reprobates.

7 ¶ Now I pray to God that ye do no evil; not that we should appear approved, but that ye should do that which is honest, though we be as reprobates.

8 For we can do nothing against the truth, but for the truth.

9 For we are glad, when we are weak, and ye are strong: and this also we wish, even your perfection.

10 Therefore I write these things being absent, lest being present I should use sharpness, according to the power which the Lord hath given me to edification, and not to destruction.

## PAUL GIVES CORINTH HIS FINAL FAREWELL

11 ¶ Finally, brethren, farewell. Be perfect, be of good comfort, be of one mind, live in peace; and the God of love and peace shall be with you.

12 Greet one another with an holy kiss.

13 All the saints salute you.

14 The grace of the Lord Jesus Christ, and the love of God, and the communion of the Holy Ghost, be with you all. Amen.

---

13:1 — Anciently it was necessary to have two or three witnesses to establish a person's guilt for sin (see Deuteronomy 19:15). Paul warned the Corinthians that his upcoming visit would be his third witness against them and that those who would not listen would be disciplined.

13:1-2 — God always provides more than one witness to support his words. This is called the law of witnesses (see 2 Nephi 11:3-4; D&C 6:28). Even today priesthood ordinances must be performed with more than one witness present.

13:4 — Paul testifies that everyone is "weak" and will die because of the mortal body. But everyone will be resurrected because of Jesus Christ (see 1 Corinthians 15:22).

13:5 — Paul asked the Corinthians to examine or look at their own faith. How strong is your faith? What are you doing to strengthen your faith?

**reprobates**—those who are unworthy or who fail the test

13:9 — Paul hoped that the Corinthians would become perfect. Jesus also commanded us to work toward perfection (see Matthew 5:48; 3 Nephi 12:48). We can be "perfected in him [Christ]" by being clean and loving God "with all [our] might" (Moroni 10:32).

13:10 — **sharpness**—strictness, harshness
**to edification, and not to destruction**—to build you up, not tear you down

13:11 — Paul promised that the faithful Saints would receive God's love and peace. Have you felt God's love and peace before?

13:12 — The Joseph Smith Translation changes the word "kiss" to "salutation," which is a warm greeting (JST, 2 Corinthians 13:12).

# THE EPISTLE OF PAUL THE APOSTLE TO THE
# GALATIANS

*The Apostle Paul wrote this letter to the Church members in Galatia. The Church converts were being led astray by false teachers and false doctrines. Paul wrote to encourage them not to lose their faith in Jesus Christ.*

## CHAPTER 1

*Truth from Heavenly Father can make us better people. Look for how Paul changed when he learned the gospel was true.*

### THERE IS ONLY ONE TRUE GOSPEL

1 PAUL, an apostle, (not of men, neither by man, but by Jesus Christ, and God the Father, who raised him from the dead;)

2 And all the brethren which are with me, unto the churches of Galatia:

3 Grace be to you and peace from God the Father, and from our Lord Jesus Christ,

4 Who gave himself for our sins, that he might deliver us from this present evil world, according to the will of God and our Father:

5 To whom be glory for ever and ever. Amen.

6 ¶ I marvel that ye are so soon removed from him that called you into the grace of Christ unto another gospel:

7 Which is not another; but there be some that trouble you, and would pervert the gospel of Christ.

8 But though we, or an angel from heaven, preach any other gospel unto you than that which we have preached unto you, let him be accursed.

9 As we said before, so say I now again, If any man preach any other gospel unto you than that ye have received, let him be accursed.

### PAUL TELLS ABOUT HIS CONVERSION

10 ¶ For do I now persuade men, or God? or do I seek to please men? for if I yet pleased men, I should not be the servant of Christ.

11 But I certify you, brethren, that the gospel which was preached of me is not after man.

12 For I neither received it of man, neither was I taught it, but by the revelation of Jesus Christ.

13 For ye have heard of my conversation in time past

---

1:1-3   Notice that Paul speaks of Jesus Christ and God the Father as two different beings. Who else taught that the Father and the Son are separate individuals?

1:3   Grace is divine help given by God through the atonement of Jesus Christ. It provides us with the power needed to repent, keep the commandments, and become like God. (See LDS Bible Dictionary, s.v. "Grace," p. 697).

1:6   *soon removed from him*—quickly turning away from God

1:6-7   "There is and can be only one gospel—one Church, one plan of salvation, one true religion" (Bruce R. McConkie, *Doctrinal New Testament Commentary* 2:457).

1:7   *pervert*—twist or change

1:8-9   People who purposely teach false doctrine can get into serious trouble. Nephi warned those who preach false teachings, saying, "They shall be thrust down to hell" (2 Nephi 28:15). Elder Harold

B. Lee taught, "If you want to be guided in truth, you follow the light the Lord has given us in the leaders He has set to preside" (*The Teachings of Harold B. Lee*, p. 516).

1:10   How can we show that we love God more than man?

1:11   *certify*—make known to

1:13   *conversation*—conduct; actions
*wasted*—was destroying

1:13-16   Paul's background as a zealous Jewish leader who tried to destroy the Church was well known (see Acts 22:3-4; 26:4-5, 9-11). Yet God knew Paul would change and sent Jesus to tell Paul to repent and teach the Gentiles (see Acts 22:6-10, 17-21).

---

| = Word Help | = A Closer Look |
|---|---|
| = More Light | = Ponder This |

Words in pink are explained in the Glossary.

*The area surrounding the Mediterranean Sea in New Testament times*

in the Jews' religion, how that beyond measure I persecuted the church of God, and wasted it:

14 And profited in the Jews' religion above many my equals in mine own nation, being more exceedingly zealous of the traditions of my fathers.

15 But when it pleased God, who separated me from my mother's womb, and called me by his grace,

16 To reveal his Son in me, that I might preach him among the heathen; immediately I conferred not with flesh and blood:

17 Neither went I up to Jerusalem to them which were apostles before me; but I went into Arabia, and returned again unto Damascus.

## Paul Meets with Peter, Then Starts His Mission

18 Then after three years I went up to Jerusalem to see Peter, and abode with him fifteen days.

19 But other of the apostles saw I none, save James the Lord's brother.

20 Now the things which I write unto you, behold, before God, I lie not.

21 Afterwards I came into the regions of Syria and Cilicia;

22 And was unknown by face unto the churches of Judaea which were in Christ:

23 But they had heard only, That he which persecuted us in times past now preacheth the faith which once he destroyed.

24 And they glorified God in me.

---

1:22    **unknown by face unto**—never seen before by

1:23    Paul had previously been cruel to Church members. Now he was a great missionary. Do you

know someone who changed his or her life for good after receiving a testimony?

# CHAPTER 2

*Some Church members thought the law of Moses should still be lived. Even some Church leaders had questions about it. Watch for how Paul reminds us that Jesus must be the center of our faith.*

## PAUL BOLDLY TEACHES IN JERUSALEM

1 ¶ THEN fourteen years after I went up again to Jerusalem with Barnabas, and took Titus with me also.

2 And I went up by revelation, and communicated unto them that gospel which I preach among the Gentiles, but privately to them which were of reputation, lest by any means I should run, or had run, in vain.

3 But neither Titus, who was with me, being a Greek, was compelled to be circumcised:

4 And that because of false brethren unawares brought in, who came in privily to spy out our liberty which we have in Christ Jesus, that they might bring us into bondage:

5 To whom we gave place by subjection, no, not for an hour; that the truth of the gospel might continue with you.

6 But of these who seemed to be somewhat, (whatsoever they were, it maketh no matter to me: God accepteth no man's person:) for they who seemed to be somewhat in conference added nothing to me:

7 But contrariwise, when they saw that the gospel of the uncircumcision was committed unto me, as the gospel of the circumcision was unto Peter;

8 (For he that wrought effectually in Peter to the apostleship of the circumcision, the same was mighty in me toward the Gentiles:)

9 And when James, Cephas, and John, who seemed to be pillars, perceived the grace that was given unto me, they gave to me and Barnabas the right hands of fellowship; that we should go unto the heathen, and they unto the circumcision.

10 Only they would that we should remember the poor; the same which I also was forward to do.

## DIFFERENCES ARISE BETWEEN PETER AND PAUL

11 ¶ But when Peter was come to Antioch, I withstood him to the face, because he was to be blamed.

12 For before that certain came from James, he did eat with the Gentiles: but when they were come, he withdrew and separated himself, fearing them which were of the circumcision.

13 And the other Jews dissembled likewise with him; insomuch that Barnabas also was carried away with their dissimulation.

14 But when I saw that they walked not uprightly according to the truth of the gospel, I said unto Peter before them all, If thou, being a Jew, livest after the manner of Gentiles, and not as do the Jews, why compellest thou the Gentiles to live as do the Jews?

---

2:2 — *Gentiles* is a word that means "nations." It refers to those not of the family of Israel or who do not believe in the God of Israel. (See LDS Bible Dictionary, s.v. "Gentile," pp. 679–80.)

Paul gave to the Church leaders in Jerusalem a report of the things he taught on his mission. Why do you think it is important to report to our Church leaders?

2:2–5 — Paul retells the story of the Church conference at Jerusalem that decided by revelation that Gentiles, like Titus, did not need to live the law of Moses in order to join the Church (see Acts 15:1–20). Paul explains here that false brethren at that conference tried to bring the members "into bondage" by making them all live the law of Moses (see JST, Galatians 2:4).

2:7–9 — Usually "Peter taught the gospel . . . to the Jews. . . . Paul, on the other hand, went primarily to the . . . Gentiles. . . . Both presented the same saving truth." (Bruce R. McConkie, *Doctrinal New Testament Commentary* 2:462.)

2:9 — Jesus gave Peter the name *Cephas,* which means "a seer, or a stone" (JST, John 1:42).

**right hands of fellowship**—authority and support from the Apostles

2:11–14 — When members who still obeyed the law of Moses came to Antioch, Peter started eating with them instead of with the Gentiles. Peter then appeared to favor the law of Moses. The way the Bible reads, Paul corrected Peter. But "if we had the full account, we would find Peter reversing [correcting] himself and doing all in his power to get the Jewish saints to believe that the law of Moses was fulfilled in Christ and no longer applied" (Bruce R. McConkie, *Doctrinal New Testament Commentary* 2:464).

2:13 — **dissimulation**—hypocrisy

### JESUS CHRIST CAN REMOVE SIN AND MAKE US CLEAN

15 We who are Jews by nature, and not sinners of the Gentiles,

16 Knowing that a man is not justified by the works of the law, but by the faith of Jesus Christ, even we have believed in Jesus Christ, that we might be justified by the faith of Christ, and not by the works of the law: for by the works of the law shall no flesh be justified.

17 But if, while we seek to be justified by Christ, we ourselves also are found sinners, is therefore Christ the minister of sin? God forbid.

18 For if I build again the things which I destroyed, I make myself a transgressor.

19 For I through the law am dead to the law, that I might live unto God.

20 I am crucified with Christ: nevertheless I live; yet not I, but Christ liveth in me: and the life which I now live in the flesh I live by the faith of the Son of God, who loved me, and gave himself for me.

21 I do not frustrate the grace of God: for if righteousness come by the law, then Christ is dead in vain.

### CHAPTER 3

*Much in the way that training wheels can prepare us to ride a bicycle, the law of Moses was given to prepare Israel to live the higher law of the gospel.*

*Look for how faith in Jesus Christ and keeping our covenants lead us to the greater blessings promised to Abraham's family.*

### ABRAHAM HAD THE GOSPEL OF JESUS CHRIST

1 ¶ O foolish Galatians, who hath bewitched you, that ye should not obey the truth, before whose eyes Jesus Christ hath been evidently set forth, crucified among you?

2 This only would I learn of you, Received ye the Spirit by the works of the law, or by the hearing of faith?

3 Are ye so foolish? having begun in the Spirit, are ye now made perfect by the flesh?

4 Have ye suffered so many things in vain? if it be yet in vain.

5 He therefore that ministereth to you the Spirit, and worketh miracles among you, doeth he it by the works of the law, or by the hearing of faith?

6 ¶ Even as Abraham believed God, and it was accounted to him for righteousness.

### THE HIGHER LAW REQUIRES FAITH IN JESUS CHRIST

7 Know ye therefore that they which are of faith, the same are the children of Abraham.

8 And the scripture, foreseeing that God would justify the heathen through faith, preached before the gospel unto Abraham, saying, In thee shall all nations be blessed.

---

2:16    "The law" is the law of Moses, which the children of Israel were commanded to follow from the days of Moses until the time of Jesus.

2:16-17   A person who is justified has had his sins forgiven. Our sins are forgiven when we exercise faith in the Savior's atonement, repent of our sins, and obey the commandments and ordinances of the gospel (see James 2:14-26).

2:20    *I am crucified with Christ*—a way of saying, Jesus Christ helps me destroy my sins

     "Christ liveth in me" means " 'I possess the Spirit of Christ and am like him' " (Bruce R. McConkie, *Doctrinal New Testament Commentary* 2:464; see also Alma 5:14).

2:21    Some people wrongly think we can become righteous by ourselves, without Christ. If this were true, we wouldn't need Jesus. How do you think life would be different without him?

3:1-6    Paul scolds the Galatians for being "bewitched," or tricked, into leaving the gospel. They had received the Holy Ghost and been made clean from their sins, just like Abraham. So Paul asks them what blessings will come to them by leaving their faith in Christ and returning to the rules of the law of Moses, which is now dead?

3:5    *ministereth*—serves, gives, provides, or brings

3:7    We become the children of Abraham when we enter into and keep the covenants of the gospel. As Abraham's children we can inherit all the blessings of Abraham. (See D&C 84:33-38.)

3:8    Paul explains that the "heathen," meaning Gentiles, would have to be saved by their faith because they did not know the law of Moses (see also Abraham 2:10).

9 So then they which be of faith are blessed with faithful Abraham.

10 For as many as are of the works of the law are under the curse: for it is written, Cursed is every one that continueth not in all things which are written in the book of the law to do them.

11 But that no man is justified by the law in the sight of God, it is evident: for, The just shall live by faith.

12 And the law is not of faith: but, The man that doeth them shall live in them.

13 Christ hath redeemed us from the curse of the law, being made a curse for us: for it is written, Cursed is every one that hangeth on a tree:

14 That the blessing of Abraham might come on the Gentiles through Jesus Christ; that we might receive the promise of the Spirit through faith.

## THE LAW OF MOSES DOES NOT CANCEL THE PROMISE THAT CHRIST CAME TO SAVE US

15 Brethren, I speak after the manner of men; Though it be but a man's covenant, yet if it be confirmed, no man disannulleth, or addeth thereto.

16 Now to Abraham and his seed were the promises made. He saith not, And to seeds, as of many; but as of one, And to thy seed, which is Christ.

17 And this I say, that the covenant, that was confirmed before of God in Christ, the law, which was four hundred and thirty years after, cannot disannul, that it should make the promise of none effect.

18 For if the inheritance be of the law, it is no more of promise: but God gave it to Abraham by promise.

## THE LAW OF MOSES WAS TO LEAD ISRAEL TO CHRIST

19 ¶ Wherefore then serveth the law? It was added because of transgressions, till the seed should come to whom the promise was made; and it was ordained by angels in the hand of a mediator

20 Now a mediator is not a mediator of one, but God is one.

21 Is the law then against the promises of God? God forbid: for if there had been a law given which could have given life, verily righteousness should have been by the law.

22 But the scripture hath concluded all under sin, that the promise by faith of Jesus Christ might be given to them that believe.

23 But before faith came, we were kept under the law, shut up unto the faith which should afterwards be revealed.

24 Wherefore the law was our schoolmaster to bring us unto Christ, that we might be justified by faith.

25 But after that faith is come, we are no longer under a schoolmaster.

## THE BAPTIZED FAITHFUL ARE A PART OF ABRAHAM'S FAMILY

26 For ye are all the children of God by faith in Christ Jesus.

27 For as many of you as have been baptized into Christ have put on Christ.

28 There is neither Jew nor Greek, there is neither bond nor free, there is neither male nor female: for ye are all one in Christ Jesus.

29 And if ye be Christ's, then are ye Abraham's seed, and heirs according to the promise.

---

3:10-14   The law of Moses requires that we live it perfectly or we cannot be saved (see Deuteronomy 27:26). That is the "curse" of the law. As Elder Bruce R. McConkie explained, "those who have faith in Christ are spiritually alive," and because "Christ hath fulfilled the law of Moses . . . we are no longer cursed for failure to obey all of its performances [requirements]" (*Doctrinal New Testament Commentary* 2:468).

3:15   *covenant*—serious promise between two people or between God and man
*confirmed*—made certain to be true
*disannulleth*—makes it not true or not legal

3:16   *seed*—children, family, or descendants

3:19   *a mediator*—one who helps solve problems between others

3:19-20   The Joseph Smith Translation explains that because of Israel's sins, a lesser law was given and Moses was its mediator. Christ helps us live the new law as "the mediator of life." (JST, Galatians 3:19-20.)

3:24   A schoolmaster watches over and teaches children until they are ready to care for themselves.

3:26-28   Baptized members start a new life. We all become "children of Christ, his sons, and his daughters," and our "hearts are changed through faith on his name" (Mosiah 5:7). If we keep our covenants, like father Abraham we "have the sure promise of exaltation in the kingdom of God" (Bruce R. McConkie, *Doctrinal New Testament Commentary* 2:473).

# CHAPTER 4

*When we are spiritually born again, we become the children of Christ and the covenant people of the Lord. Note what Paul suggests we do to become the covenant people.*

## THE SAINTS ARE CHILDREN OF GOD AND RECEIVE HIS BLESSINGS

1 ¶ NOW I say, That the heir, as long as he is a child, differeth nothing from a servant, though he be lord of all;

2 But is under tutors and governors until the time appointed of the father.

3 Even so we, when we were children, were in bondage under the elements of the world:

4 But when the fulness of the time was come, God sent forth his Son, made of a woman, made under the law,

5 To redeem them that were under the law, that we might receive the adoption of sons.

6 And because ye are sons, God hath sent forth the Spirit of his Son into your hearts, crying, Abba, Father.

7 Wherefore thou art no more a servant, but a son; and if a son, then an heir of God through Christ.

## PAUL WARNS THE CHURCH OF SPIRITUAL DANGERS

8 ¶ Howbeit then, when ye knew not God, ye did service unto them which by nature are no gods.

9 But now, after that ye have known God, or rather are known of God, how turn ye again to the weak and beggarly elements, whereunto ye desire again to be in bondage?

10 Ye observe days, and months, and times, and years.

11 I am afraid of you, lest I have bestowed upon you labour in vain.

12 ¶ Brethren, I beseech you, be as I am; for I am as ye are: ye have not injured me at all.

13 Ye know how through infirmity of the flesh I preached the gospel unto you at the first.

14 And my temptation which was in my flesh ye despised not, nor rejected; but received me as an angel of God, even as Christ Jesus.

15 Where is then the blessedness ye spake of? for I bear you record, that, if it had been possible, ye would have plucked out your own eyes, and have given them to me.

16 Am I therefore become your enemy, because I tell you the truth?

17 ¶ They zealously affect you, but not well; yea, they would exclude you, that ye might affect them.

18 But it is good to be zealously affected always in a good thing, and not only when I am present with you.

19 ¶ My little children, of whom I travail in birth again until Christ be formed in you,

20 I desire to be present with you now, and to change my voice; for I stand in doubt of you.

## PAUL COMPARES THE LAW OF MOSES WITH THE GOSPEL OF CHRIST

21 ¶ Tell me, ye that desire to be under the law, do ye not hear the law?

22 For it is written, that Abraham had two sons, the one by a bondmaid, the other by a freewoman.

23 But he who was of the bondwoman was born after the flesh; but he of the freewoman was by promise.

---

4:1 **heir**—one who receives all the blessings of his parents

4:2 **tutors**—teachers

4:6 Every mortal is born with the Spirit or Light of Christ, which helps him or her know right from wrong (see Moroni 7:16; John 1:9).

4:7 Only those who apply the atonement of Christ in their lives become the children of God (see John 1:12; D&C 35:2).

If a child, as an heir, receives all the blessings of his parents, what can the children of God expect to receive? (See D&C 84:33-38.)

4:9 Serving worldly things instead of God leads to spiritual slavery (see Matthew 6:24).

4:11 **labour in vain**—work without results

4:13 **infirmity**—illness or weakness

4:15-17 Wicked people often react negatively when they hear the truth because it condemns their wickedness (see 1 Nephi 16:1-3).

4:19 We work toward being spiritually born again, changed in our hearts from people who desire wickedness to people who desire righteousness (see Mosiah 5:2; Alma 5:14).

4:22-28 The two sons of Abraham were Ishmael, who was born to the "bondmaid" Hagar (Agar), and Isaac, who was born to the "freewoman" Sarah. Isaac was the promised, or covenant, son through whom the blessings of the priesthood would come.

24 Which things are an allegory: for these are the two covenants; the one from the mount Sinai, which gendereth to bondage, which is Agar.

25 For this Agar is mount Sinai in Arabia, and answereth to Jerusalem which now is, and is in bondage with her children.

26 But Jerusalem which is above is free, which is the mother of us all.

27 For it is written, Rejoice, thou barren that bearest not; break forth and cry, thou that travailest not: for the desolate hath many more children than she which hath an husband.

28 Now we, brethren, as Isaac was, are the children of promise.

29 But as then he that was born after the flesh persecuted him that was born after the Spirit, even so it is now.

30 Nevertheless what saith the scripture? Cast out the bondwoman and her son: for the son of the bondwoman shall not be heir with the son of the freewoman.

31 So then, brethren, we are not children of the bondwoman, but of the free.

# CHAPTER 5

*Paul warns us of some of the temptations of mortality. Look for ways that Paul suggests we can overcome these temptations.*

## PAUL ENCOURAGES US TO HOLD ON TO LIBERTIES FOUND IN THE GOSPEL

1 ¶ STAND fast therefore in the liberty wherewith Christ hath made us free, and be not entangled again with the yoke of bondage.

2 Behold, I Paul say unto you, that if ye be circumcised, Christ shall profit you nothing.

3 For I testify again to every man that is circumcised, that he is a debtor to do the whole law.

4 Christ is become of no effect unto you, whosoever of you are justified by the law; ye are fallen from grace.

5 For we through the Spirit wait for the hope of righteousness by faith.

## LOVE FULFILLS ALL THE LAW

6 For in Jesus Christ neither circumcision availeth any thing, nor uncircumcision; but faith which worketh by love.

7 Ye did run well; who did hinder you that ye should not obey the truth?

8 This persuasion cometh not of him that calleth you.

9 A little leaven leaveneth the whole lump.

10 I have confidence in you through the Lord, that ye will be none otherwise minded: but he that troubleth you shall bear his judgment, whosoever he be.

11 And I, brethren, if I yet preach circumcision, why do I yet suffer persecution? then is the offence of the cross ceased.

---

4:24 **are an allegory**—are symbolic of, or stand for, something else

4:24-26 Paul uses the life of Abraham as an allegory (a story whose elements represent or stand for other things) to teach that the gospel of Jesus Christ is greater than the law of Moses. In his allegory, Hagar represents the law of Moses, and Sarah represents the gospel. Mount Sinai and Jerusalem also represent the law of Moses, while Sarah symbolizes the future heavenly city, called spiritual Jerusalem, wherein all are free. (See Bruce R. McConkie, *Doctrinal New Testament Commentary* 2:478.)

4:27 **thou barren that bearest not**—you who are unable to have children

5:1 Christ frees us from sin's restrictions when we repent (see 2 Nephi 9:7-8, 10).

**be not entangled again with the yoke of bondage**—do not get involved with sin anymore

5:3 **is a debtor to do**—has to, or is bound to, obey

5:4 If the law of Moses saves us, then there is no need for Christ and the Atonement. However, the truth is that salvation is only in and through Jesus Christ's atonement. (See 2 Nephi 25:24-25.)

5:7 **did hinder**—tried to stop

5:8 **persuasion**—trick or deception

5:9 Leaven is yeast and is what makes bread rise.

5:11 Paul was persecuted for teaching about Jesus. What trials might you experience because you believe in Christ?

12 I would they were even cut off which trouble you.

13 ¶ For, brethren, ye have been called unto liberty; only use not liberty for an occasion to the flesh, but by love serve one another.

14 For all the law is fulfilled in one word, even in this; Thou shalt love thy neighbour as thyself.

15 But if ye bite and devour one another, take heed that ye be not consumed one of another.

## The Works of the Flesh and the Fruits of the Spirit Are Described

16 This I say then, Walk in the Spirit, and ye shall not fulfil the lust of the flesh.

17 For the flesh lusteth against the Spirit, and the Spirit against the flesh: and these are contrary the one to the other: so that ye cannot do the things that ye would.

18 But if ye be led of the Spirit, ye are not under the law.

19 Now the works of the flesh are manifest, which are these; Adultery, fornication, uncleanness, lasciviousness,

20 Idolatry, witchcraft, hatred, variance, emulations, wrath, strife, seditions, heresies,

21 Envyings, murders, drunkenness, revellings, and such like: of the which I tell you before, as I have also told you in time past, that they which do such things shall not inherit the kingdom of God.

22 But the fruit of the Spirit is love, joy, peace, longsuffering, gentleness, goodness, faith,

23 Meekness, temperance: against such there is no law.

24 And they that are Christ's have crucified the flesh with the affections and lusts.

25 If we live in the Spirit, let us also walk in the Spirit.

26 Let us not be desirous of vain glory, provoking one another, envying one another.

## CHAPTER 6

*Paul explains that the things we do matter to the Lord. Note what we should do for others and for ourselves.*

### Paul Teaches Us to Help Others and Ourselves

1 ¶ BRETHREN, if a man be overtaken in a fault, ye which are spiritual, restore such an one in the spirit of meekness; considering thyself, lest thou also be tempted.

---

5:13 **only use not liberty for an occasion to the flesh**—but do not use freedom to do what is wrong

5:14 Not only is loving our neighbor the second great commandment (see Matthew 22:39), but by serving our neighbor we serve our God, which is the first great commandment (see Mosiah 2:17; Matthew 22:36-37).

5:17-24 What does the Lord suggest we do to the desires of the "flesh"? (See verse 24.) How can we overcome these desires and concentrate more on spiritual concerns?

5:19 **manifest**—seen
**lasciviousness**—lustful or immoral desires and activities

5:20 **variance**—disagreement, quarreling
**emulations**—envy, jealousy
**wrath**—anger
**strife**—contention
**heresies**—false beliefs

5:21 **revellings**—partying in a drunken, out-of-control way

5:22 **longsuffering**—great patience

*Paul describes the blessings of the Spirit as fruit.*

How can you tell if you are enjoying the blessings of the Spirit?

5:23 **temperance**—self-control

5:26 **provoking**—causing contention with

6:1 **restore**—make right again

2 Bear ye one another's burdens, and so fulfil the law of Christ.

3 For if a man think himself to be something, when he is nothing, he deceiveth himself.

4 But let every man prove his own work, and then shall he have rejoicing in himself alone, and not in another.

5 For every man shall bear his own burden.

6 Let him that is taught in the word communicate unto him that teacheth in all good things.

## BE GOOD AND GOOD THINGS WILL COME BACK TO YOU

7 Be not deceived; God is not mocked: for whatsoever a man soweth, that shall he also reap.

8 For he that soweth to his flesh shall of the flesh reap corruption; but he that soweth to the Spirit shall of the Spirit reap life everlasting.

9 And let us not be weary in well doing: for in due season we shall reap, if we faint not.

10 As we have therefore opportunity, let us do good unto all men, especially unto them who are of the household of faith.

## LET US NOT GET TIRED OF DOING GOOD

11 ¶ Ye see how large a letter I have written unto you with mine own hand.

12 As many as desire to make a fair shew in the flesh, they constrain you to be circumcised; only lest they should suffer persecution for the cross of Christ.

13 For neither they themselves who are circumcised keep the law; but desire to have you circumcised, that they may glory in your flesh.

14 But God forbid that I should glory, save in the cross of our Lord Jesus Christ, by whom the world is crucified unto me, and I unto the world.

15 For in Christ Jesus neither circumcision availeth any thing, nor uncircumcision, but a new creature.

16 And as many as walk according to this rule, peace be on them, and mercy, and upon the Israel of God.

17 From henceforth let no man trouble me: for I bear in my body the marks of the Lord Jesus.

18 Brethren, the grace of our Lord Jesus Christ be with your spirit. Amen.

---

6:2    To bear one another's burdens (help others) we should "mourn with those that mourn; . . . and comfort those that stand in need of comfort." This responsibility is part of our baptismal covenants. (See Mosiah 18:8-10.)

6:3    **deceiveth**—tricks

6:5    What are some challenges in your life? How have you felt the Lord's help in overcoming hard experiences?

6:7    **mocked**—fooled, cheated

This verse describes the law of the harvest. A farmer sows (plants) seed of the kinds of crops he wants to reap (harvest). In our lives, we will reap (receive) the rewards of what we do. If we do good we will receive good rewards; if we do bad things we receive sadness.

6:8    **soweth to his flesh**—behaves according to the unrighteous desires of the natural man
**corruption**—destruction

6:12    **make a fair shew**—be pleasing
**constrain**—try to force or make

6:14    Paul explains that because of his devotion to Christ, the things of the world are no longer important to him, and neither is the world interested in him.

6:15-17    It doesn't matter what our physical bodies look like. If we put off our natural desires and replace them with the Lord's desires, we can become a "new creature," or be born again. Then we bear the "marks of the Lord," or receive "his image in [our] countenances," which means our faces and our manner reflect his love and his Spirit is in us. (See Mosiah 3:19; 5:2; Alma 5:14.)

# THE EPISTLE OF PAUL THE APOSTLE TO THE
# EPHESIANS

*This letter was written by the Apostle Paul to the members of the Church living in Ephesus. Paul wrote to clarify several important teachings of the gospel of Jesus Christ.*

## CHAPTER 1

*Paul teaches the Ephesians about foreordination and redemption through Jesus Christ. Look for what Paul asks the Lord to bless them with.*

### SALVATION COMES THROUGH JESUS CHRIST

1 PAUL, an apostle of Jesus Christ by the will of God, to the saints which are at Ephesus, and to the faithful in Christ Jesus:

2 Grace be to you, and peace, from God our Father, and from the Lord Jesus Christ.

3 ¶ Blessed be the God and Father of our Lord Jesus Christ, who hath blessed us with all spiritual blessings in heavenly places in Christ:

4 According as he hath chosen us in him before the foundation of the world, that we should be holy and without blame before him in love:

5 Having predestinated us unto the adoption of children by Jesus Christ to himself, according to the good pleasure of his will,

6 To the praise of the glory of his grace, wherein he hath made us accepted in the beloved.

7 In whom we have redemption through his blood, the forgiveness of sins, according to the riches of his grace;

8 Wherein he hath abounded toward us in all wisdom and prudence;

9 Having made known unto us the mystery of his will, according to his good pleasure which he hath purposed in himself:

10 That in the dispensation of the fulness of times he might gather together in one all things in Christ, both which are in heaven, and which are on earth; even in him:

11 In whom also we have obtained an inheritance, being predestinated according to the purpose of him who worketh all things after the counsel of his own will:

12 That we should be to the praise of his glory, who first trusted in Christ.

---

1:2    Grace is divine help given by God through the atonement of Jesus Christ. It provides us with the power needed to repent, keep the commandments, and become like God. (See LDS Bible Dictionary, s.v. "Grace," p. 697.)

1:3    All blessings come from God. In your prayers how can you show your Heavenly Father how grateful you are for these blessings? How about in the way you live your life?

1:3-5    "Before the foundation of the world," or in our premortal life, many were "predestinated," or foreordained, to receive the blessings of the gospel here on earth (see John 10:14, 27; D&C 29:1-2, 7; Alma 13:3; Abraham 3:22-23).

1:7    *Redemption* is the act of buying back, ransoming, or restoring. Jesus Christ paid the penalty for our sins and is our Redeemer. In this sense we have been "bought with a price" (1 Corinthians 6:20). That price was "the precious blood of Christ" (1 Peter 1:19).

1:8    *prudence*—understanding

1:10    The "dispensation of the fulness of times" refers to the last days when The Church of Jesus Christ of Latter-day Saints is on the earth, never to be removed again (see D&C 112:30-32). This dispensation will last until the Second Coming.

Why is it such a great blessing to live in the last days when the gospel is on the earth?

| | |
|---|---|
| 🖋 = Word Help | 🔍 = A Closer Look |
| 🌄 = More Light | 🔁 = Ponder This |

Words in pink are explained in the Glossary.

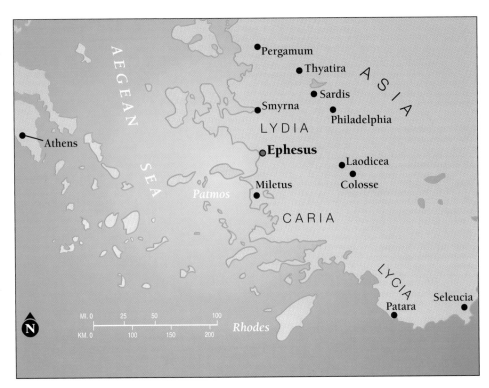

*Ephesus, considered in New Testament times to be "the first and greatest metropolis of Asia" (its official Roman title)*

13 In whom ye also trusted, after that ye heard the word of truth, the gospel of your salvation: in whom also after that ye believed, ye were sealed with that holy Spirit of promise,

14 Which is the earnest of our inheritance until the redemption of the purchased possession, unto the praise of his glory.

## PAUL PRAYS FOR AND THANKS THE EPHESIANS

15 ¶ Wherefore I also, after I heard of your faith in the Lord Jesus, and love unto all the saints,

16 Cease not to give thanks for you, making mention of you in my prayers;

17 That the God of our Lord Jesus Christ, the Father of glory, may give unto you the spirit of wisdom and revelation in the knowledge of him:

18 The eyes of your understanding being enlightened; that ye may know what is the hope of his calling, and what the riches of the glory of his inheritance in the saints,

19 And what is the exceeding greatness of his power to us-ward who believe, according to the working of his mighty power,

20 Which he wrought in Christ, when he raised him from the dead, and set him at his own right hand in the heavenly places,

21 Far above all principality, and power, and might, and dominion, and every name that is named, not only in this world, but also in that which is to come:

22 And hath put all things under his feet, and gave him to be the head over all things to the church,

23 Which is his body, the fulness of him that filleth all in all.

---

1:13-14 The Holy Spirit of Promise is another name for the Holy Ghost. He can seal the promise of eternal life upon us through our obedience. Paul called this guarantee of obtaining the celestial kingdom "the earnest of our inheritance" (see 2 Corinthians 1:22).

1:15-18 Heavenly Father has prepared eternal riches or treasures for his children. Paul prayed that the Ephesians would come to know of these great riches through "the spirit of wisdom and revela-

tion," which is the Holy Ghost (see 1 Corinthians 2:9-10).

1:20-22 Jesus was resurrected. He now rules above all things, including all earthly powers and glory, and is at the head of our church. How do these things help you to trust Jesus? How does having an understanding of his great power help you?

# CHAPTER 2

*The gospel of Jesus Christ has the power to save everyone who lives it. Watch for all those Paul welcomes into the Church as "fellowcitizens with the saints."*

## WE ARE SAVED BY GRACE THROUGH FAITH

1 ¶ AND you hath he quickened, who were dead in trespasses and sins;

2 Wherein in time past ye walked according to the course of this world, according to the prince of the power of the air, the spirit that now worketh in the children of disobedience:

3 Among whom also we all had our conversation in times past in the lusts of our flesh, fulfilling the desires of the flesh and of the mind; and were by nature the children of wrath, even as others.

4 ¶ But God, who is rich in mercy, for his great love wherewith he loved us,

5 Even when we were dead in sins, hath quickened us together with Christ, (by grace ye are saved;)

6 And hath raised us up together, and made us sit together in heavenly places in Christ Jesus:

7 That in the ages to come he might shew the exceeding riches of his grace in his kindness toward us through Christ Jesus.

8 For by grace are ye saved through faith; and that not of yourselves: it is the gift of God:

9 Not of works, lest any man should boast.

10 For we are his workmanship, created in Christ Jesus unto good works, which God hath before ordained that we should walk in them.

## ALL PEOPLE CAN BE SAVED BY THE ATONEMENT OF JESUS CHRIST

11 ¶ Wherefore remember, that ye being in time past Gentiles in the flesh, who are called Uncircumcision by that which is called the Circumcision in the flesh made by hands;

12 That at that time ye were without Christ, being aliens from the commonwealth of Israel, and strangers from the covenants of promise, having no hope, and without God in the world:

13 But now in Christ Jesus ye who sometimes were far off are made nigh by the blood of Christ.

14 ¶ For he is our peace, who hath made both one, and hath broken down the middle wall of partition between us;

15 Having abolished in his flesh the enmity, even the law of commandments contained in ordinances; for to make in himself of twain one new man, so making peace;

16 And that he might reconcile both unto God in one body by the cross, having slain the enmity thereby:

17 And came and preached peace to you which were afar off, and to them that were nigh.

18 For through him we both have access by one Spirit unto the Father.

---

2:1 **quickened**—made alive spiritually

2:2 **course**—ways

Referring to the phrase "prince of the power of the air," Elder Bruce R. McConkie wrote: "Paul applies this name to Satan, having apparent reference to his position as the god of this world" (*Mormon Doctrine*, p. 600).

2:3 **had our conversation**—lived

2:6 Because of the atonement of Jesus Christ all of us can repent and "sit together in heavenly places." Whom would you like to have with you in heaven?

2:7 **shew**—This word is pronounced the same way as the word *show* and has the same meaning; *shew* is simply an old spelling of *show*.

2:8-10 Paul was teaching Jewish Christians who believed they would be saved simply by living the law of Moses. Paul explains that it is by our faith

in Jesus Christ that God gives us his grace (help or strength) to be saved. The prophet Nephi adds that "it is by grace that we are saved, after all we can do" (2 Nephi 25:23).

2:11 Gentiles were called the "uncircumcised" by the Jews, who were the "circumcised" (see for Romans 2:25-29).

2:12 **aliens from the commonwealth of Israel**—foreign to the family of Israel

2:14-15 The wall that separated the Jews and the Gentiles was the ordinances of the law of Moses. Jesus Christ fulfilled the law through his sacrifice in Gethsemane and on the cross (see Matthew 5:17-18; Colossians 2:14). The law of Moses was no longer necessary.

2:16 **reconcile both unto**—bring both back to

### THE CHURCH IS BUILT ON THE FOUNDATION OF APOSTLES AND PROPHETS

19 Now therefore ye are no more strangers and foreigners, but fellowcitizens with the saints, and of the household of God;

20 And are built upon the foundation of the apostles and prophets, Jesus Christ himself being the chief corner stone;

21 In whom all the building fitly framed together groweth unto an holy temple in the Lord:

22 In whom ye also are builded together for an habitation of God through the Spirit.

## CHAPTER 3

*For hundreds of years the children of Israel were God's chosen people and were commanded to separate themselves from the other nations of the world. Look for how that changed after the death and resurrection of Jesus Christ.*

### GOD REVEALS THAT THE GOSPEL SHOULD NOW BE TAKEN TO THE GENTILES

1 ¶ FOR this cause I Paul, the prisoner of Jesus Christ for you Gentiles,

2 If ye have heard of the dispensation of the grace of God which is given me to you-ward:

3 How that by revelation he made known unto me the mystery; (as I wrote afore in few words,

4 Whereby, when ye read, ye may understand my knowledge in the mystery of Christ)

5 Which in other ages was not made known unto the sons of men, as it is now revealed unto his holy apostles and prophets by the Spirit;

6 That the Gentiles should be fellowheirs, and of the same body, and partakers of his promise in Christ by the gospel:

### PAUL'S SPECIAL CALLING IS TO TAKE THE GOSPEL TO THE GENTILES

7 Whereof I was made a minister, according to the gift of the grace of God given unto me by the effectual working of his power.

8 Unto me, who am less than the least of all saints, is this grace given, that I should preach among the Gentiles the unsearchable riches of Christ;

9 And to make all men see what is the fellowship of the mystery, which from the beginning of the world hath been hid in God, who created all things by Jesus Christ:

10 To the intent that now unto the principalities and powers in heavenly places might be known by the church the manifold wisdom of God,

11 According to the eternal purpose which he purposed in Christ Jesus our Lord:

12 In whom we have boldness and access with confidence by the faith of him.

13 Wherefore I desire that ye faint not at my tribulations for you, which is your glory.

---

2:19 By accepting the gospel of Jesus Christ, the Gentiles became Saints. President Gordon B. Hinckley has taught, "We are citizens in the greatest kingdom on earth—a kingdom not directed by the wisdom of men but led by the Lord Jesus Christ" (*Teachings of Gordon B. Hinckley*, p. 292).

People from all nations are invited to join the Lord's church. How would you feel about teaching the gospel to people from other countries?

3:1 Paul calls himself a "prisoner of Jesus Christ" because his only desire is to do what the Lord wants him to do. Jesus set the perfect example of this by obeying Heavenly Father's will and giving his life for us (see Matthew 26:39; Mosiah 15:7).

3:2 **dispensation**—administration

3:3-6 The Jews had difficulty believing that Gentiles could receive the same blessings that they could.

The "mystery" was that all of God's children, including the Gentiles, could obtain the promise of eternal life in the presence of the Father through the atonement of Jesus Christ (see Colossians 1:25-29).

3:8 The Gentiles were not offered the blessings of the gospel early in Christ's ministry. However, following his resurrection Christ taught that the gospel should be taught to all people (see Matthew 28:19-20). Paul was called as a missionary to the Gentiles.

Today the gospel is being preached throughout the world by missionaries of The Church of Jesus Christ of Latter-day Saints. Do you know any missionaries who have traveled to distant lands to proclaim the gospel?

3:9 **the fellowship of the mystery**—Heavenly Father's plan of salvation

3:10 **manifold**—many kinds of

## Paul Prays That the Saints May Know the Limitless Love of Christ

14 ¶ For this cause I bow my knees unto the Father of our Lord Jesus Christ,

15 Of whom the whole family in heaven and earth is named,

16 That he would grant you, according to the riches of his glory, to be strengthened with might by his Spirit in the inner man;

17 That Christ may dwell in your hearts by faith; that ye, being rooted and grounded in love,

18 May be able to comprehend with all saints what is the breadth, and length, and depth, and height;

19 And to know the love of Christ, which passeth knowledge, that ye might be filled with all the fulness of God.

20 Now unto him that is able to do exceeding abundantly above all that we ask or think, according to the power that worketh in us,

21 Unto him be glory in the church by Christ Jesus throughout all ages, world without end. Amen.

## CHAPTER 4

*Paul teaches about the importance of becoming united and Christlike. Notice why apostles, prophets, and other Church leaders are necessary for Church unity and growth.*

## The Church Is Organized to Help Us Become United in One Faith

1 ¶ I therefore, the prisoner of the Lord, beseech you that ye walk worthy of the vocation wherewith ye are called,

2 ¶ With all lowliness and meekness, with longsuffering, forbearing one another in love;

3 Endeavouring to keep the unity of the Spirit in the bond of peace.

4 There is one body, and one Spirit, even as ye are called in one hope of your calling;

5 One Lord, one faith, one baptism,

6 One God and Father of all, who is above all, and through all, and in you all.

7 But unto every one of us is given grace according to the measure of the gift of Christ.

8 Wherefore he saith, When he ascended up on high, he led captivity captive, and gave gifts unto men.

9 (Now that he ascended, what is it but that he also descended first into the lower parts of the earth?

10 He that descended is the same also that ascended up far above all heavens, that he might fill all things.)

11 And he gave some, apostles; and some, prophets; and some, evangelists; and some, pastors and teachers;

12 For the perfecting of the saints, for the work of the ministry, for the edifying of the body of Christ:

13 Till we all come in the unity of the faith, and of the knowledge of the Son of God, unto a perfect man, unto the measure of the stature of the fulness of Christ:

---

3:14-21 Have you ever felt amazed at how much Jesus loves you?

3:17 Jesus has a body of flesh and bones. He is able to "dwell in [our] hearts" through the Holy Ghost, who is "a personage of Spirit" (D&C 130:22).

4:1 *vocation*—calling

4:2 *forbearing*—accepting, bearing with

4:3 *Endeavouring*—Trying

4:4-6 There is only one true Church on the earth (see D&C 1:30). Heavenly Father wants his children who are members of his church to be one. This means they are to share the same desires and love one another. If we are not one we cannot belong to Heavenly Father and Jesus. (See John 17:21-22; D&C 38:27.)

4:8 Elder Bruce R. McConkie explained what the phrase "led captivity captive" means: "The captivity of the grave was swallowed up; it was

overcome; it became the captive of Him who had power over death" (*The Promised Messiah*, p. 266).

4:9-10 Before Jesus ascended (went up) to heaven, he first descended (went down) into the grave (see Matthew 27:57-60).

4:11-14 "Apostles and prophets have been set in the Church for the purpose of teaching and identifying true doctrine. . . . If a church has no prophets and apostles, then it has no way of knowing whether its doctrines are true or false." (Bruce R. McConkie, *Mormon Doctrine*, p. 205.)

4:12 *for the edifying of the body of Christ*—to teach and inspire the members of the Church

4:13 *unto the measure of the stature of the fulness of Christ*—until we all know and become like Christ

14 That we henceforth be no more children, tossed to and fro, and carried about with every wind of doctrine, by the sleight of men, and cunning craftiness, whereby they lie in wait to deceive;

15 But speaking the truth in love, may grow up into him in all things, which is the head, even Christ:

16 From whom the whole body fitly joined together and compacted by that which every joint supplieth, according to the effectual working in the measure of every part, maketh increase of the body unto the edifying of itself in love.

## SAINTS ARE TO WALK IN THE LIGHT AND FORGIVE ONE ANOTHER

17 ¶ This I say therefore, and testify in the Lord, that ye henceforth walk not as other Gentiles walk, in the vanity of their mind,

18 Having the understanding darkened, being alienated from the life of God through the ignorance that is in them, because of the blindness of their heart:

19 Who being past feeling have given themselves over unto lasciviousness, to work all uncleanness with greediness.

20 But ye have not so learned Christ;

21 If so be that ye have heard him, and have been taught by him, as the truth is in Jesus:

22 That ye put off concerning the former conversation the old man, which is corrupt according to the deceitful lusts;

23 And be renewed in the spirit of your mind;

24 And that ye put on the new man, which after God is created in righteousness and true holiness.

25 Wherefore putting away lying, speak every man truth with his neighbour: for we are members one of another.

26 Be ye angry, and sin not: let not the sun go down upon your wrath:

27 Neither give place to the devil.

28 Let him that stole steal no more: but rather let him labour, working with his hands the thing which is good, that he may have to give to him that needeth.

29 Let no corrupt communication proceed out of your mouth, but that which is good to the use of edifying, that it may minister grace unto the hearers.

30 And grieve not the holy Spirit of God, whereby ye are sealed unto the day of redemption.

31 Let all bitterness, and wrath, and anger, and clamour, and evil speaking, be put away from you, with all malice:

32 And be ye kind one to another, tenderhearted, forgiving one another, even as God for Christ's sake hath forgiven you.

# CHAPTER 5

*As disciples of Jesus we should live clean, pure, and holy lives. We should be loving towards our family members. Look for how Paul's teachings can help us follow these standards.*

## SAINTS SHOULD AVOID ALL WICKEDNESS

1 ¶ BE ye therefore followers of God, as dear children;

2 And walk in love, as Christ also hath loved us, and hath given himself for us an offering and a sacrifice to God for a sweetsmelling savour.

---

4:14  **sleight**—deception, dishonesty

4:15-16  Paul compares the Church to the physical body (see 1 Corinthians 12:12-18). With Jesus Christ at the head, the whole Church grows up in love to be like him.

4:17  **the vanity of their mind**—useless thinking

4:18  **alienated**—separated

4:19  **lasciviousness**—evil desires

4:22-24  Paul taught the Ephesians to leave their old way of life, which was controlled by the wicked desires of the body, and become new men of righteousness. Reporting the words of an angel, King Benjamin described this as changing from a "natural man," which is an "enemy to God," into a "saint" by following the guidance of the Holy Spirit (Mosiah 3:19).

4:26  The Joseph Smith Translation changes the first part of this verse to read, "Can ye be angry, and not sin?"

4:26-27  Do you ever get angry? Has your anger ever caused you to do things that you regretted afterwards? What would Paul have you do about it? (See also verse 32.)

4:29  **corrupt communication**—evil talk
**minister grace unto**—bless with inspired help

4:30  **grieve**—make sorrowful, offend

4:31  **malice**—hate, bad feelings

5:1  Children as well as adults can set good examples for others to follow (see Matthew 18:1-4). What are you doing to be a good example to others?

3 ¶ But fornication, and all uncleanness, or covetousness, let it not be once named among you, as becometh saints;

4 Neither filthiness, nor foolish talking, nor jesting, which are not convenient: but rather giving of thanks.

5 For this ye know, that no whoremonger, nor unclean person, nor covetous man, who is an idolater, hath any inheritance in the kingdom of Christ and of God.

6 Let no man deceive you with vain words: for because of these things cometh the wrath of God upon the children of disobedience.

7 Be not ye therefore partakers with them.

8 For ye were sometimes darkness, but now are ye light in the Lord: walk as children of light:

9 (For the fruit of the Spirit is in all goodness and righteousness and truth;)

10 Proving what is acceptable unto the Lord.

11 And have no fellowship with the unfruitful works of darkness, but rather reprove them.

12 For it is a shame even to speak of those things which are done of them in secret.

13 But all things that are reproved are made manifest by the light: for whatsoever doth make manifest is light.

14 Wherefore he saith, Awake thou that sleepest, and arise from the dead, and Christ shall give thee light.

15 See then that ye walk circumspectly, not as fools, but as wise,

16 Redeeming the time, because the days are evil.

17 Wherefore be ye not unwise, but understanding what the will of the Lord is.

18 And be not drunk with wine, wherein is excess; but be filled with the Spirit;

19 Speaking to yourselves in psalms and hymns and spiritual songs, singing and making melody in your heart to the Lord;

20 Giving thanks always for all things unto God and the Father in the name of our Lord Jesus Christ;

21 ¶ Submitting yourselves one to another in the fear of God.

## HUSBANDS AND WIVES ARE TO LOVE ONE ANOTHER

22 Wives, submit yourselves unto your own husbands, as unto the Lord.

23 For the husband is the head of the wife, even as Christ is the head of the church: and he is the saviour of the body.

24 Therefore as the church is subject unto Christ, so let the wives be to their own husbands in every thing.

25 Husbands, love your wives, even as Christ also loved the church, and gave himself for it;

26 That he might sanctify and cleanse it with the washing of water by the word,

27 That he might present it to himself a glorious church, not having spot, or wrinkle, or any such thing; but that it should be holy and without blemish.

28 So ought men to love their wives as their own bodies. He that loveth his wife loveth himself.

---

5:3-9   The scriptures use the word *darkness* to describe the wickedness of people (see John 3:19). When the light of the gospel comes into their lives, they may repent and "walk as children of light." This was what had happened to the Ephesian Saints. (Compare Galatians 5:22-26.)

5:11    **have no fellowship with**—do not participate in
        **reprove**—correct

5:14    Paul uses the example of waking up from sleep or rising from the grave to teach us to wake up from or rise out of sin and become righteous (see also Romans 6:1-6). The prophet Lehi used the same idea when he counseled Laman and Lemuel, "Awake, my sons; put on the armor of righteousness" (2 Nephi 1:23).

5:15    **circumspectly**—with care

5:18    Our bodies are temples (see 1 Corinthians 6:19). As we care for our bodies properly, we can have the Lord's Spirit (see D&C 89:5-21).

5:19    We can worship God through good, uplifting music. "The song of the righteous is a prayer" unto the Lord (D&C 25:12).

        What music do you listen to that helps you feel the Lord's Spirit? What is your favorite Primary song or hymn?

5:23-25   "Brethren, your first and most responsible role in life and in the eternities is to be a righteous husband. Second only to the title of husband is that of father." (L. Tom Perry, "Father—Your Role, Your Responsibility," p. 63.)

5:26    **sanctify**—make clean or holy

5:28-33   Jesus set the example by showing us how to love others. How much do you think Jesus loves the Church? What can you do to show greater love to your family?

29 For no man ever yet hated his own flesh; but nourisheth and cherisheth it, even as the Lord the church:

30 For we are members of his body, of his flesh, and of his bones.

31 For this cause shall a man leave his father and mother, and shall be joined unto his wife, and they two shall be one flesh.

32 This is a great mystery: but I speak concerning Christ and the church.

33 Nevertheless let every one of you in particular so love his wife even as himself; and the wife see that she reverence her husband.

# CHAPTER 6

*Even though Paul was in prison, the Lord blessed him and he continued to preach the gospel. Watch for how we can have the Lord's strength even during the most difficult times.*

## CHILDREN SHOULD HONOR THEIR PARENTS

1 ¶ CHILDREN, obey your parents in the Lord: for this is right.

2 Honour thy father and mother; (which is the first commandment with promise;)

3 That it may be well with thee, and thou mayest live long on the earth.

4 And, ye fathers, provoke not your children to wrath: but bring them up in the nurture and admonition of the Lord.

## SERVANTS AND THEIR MASTERS WILL ALL BE JUDGED BY GOD

5 Servants, be obedient to them that are your masters according to the flesh, with fear and trembling, in singleness of your heart, as unto Christ;

6 Not with eyeservice, as menpleasers; but as the servants of Christ, doing the will of God from the heart;

7 With good will doing service, as to the Lord, and not to men:

8 Knowing that whatsoever good thing any man doeth, the same shall he receive of the Lord, whether he be bond or free.

9 And, ye masters, do the same things unto them, forbearing threatening: knowing that your Master also is in heaven; neither is there respect of persons with him.

## SAINTS SHOULD PUT ON THE WHOLE ARMOR OF GOD

10 ¶ Finally, my brethren, be strong in the Lord, and in the power of his might.

11 Put on the whole armour of God, that ye may be able to stand against the wiles of the devil.

---

6:2-3 🔍 This commandment that includes a promise was given by the Lord to Moses as part of the Ten Commandments (see Exodus 20:12).

6:4 📖 **provoke not your children to wrath**—don't make your children angry
**nurture and admonition**—care and teachings

6:5 🔍 Paul taught servants to obey their earthly masters as they would obey Christ. Peter added that servants should be obedient even if their masters were not "good and gentle" (1 Peter 2:18).

6:6 📖 **Not with eyeservice**—Don't obey only when being watched
**as menpleasers**—to find favor with men

6:6-7 ❓ How would you do things differently if you did them first and foremost to please God?

6:8-9 🔍 The Lord will judge us in the way we have judged other people (see Matthew 7:1-2). In other words, "with that same judgment which ye judge ye shall also be judged" (Moroni 7:18).

6:9 📖 **forbearing threatening**—do not threaten them

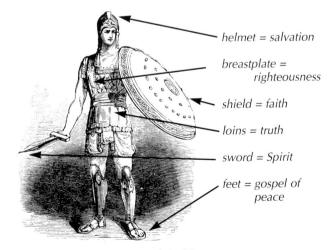

*helmet = salvation*

*breastplate = righteousness*

*shield = faith*

*loins = truth*

*sword = Spirit*

*feet = gospel of peace*

*"Put on the whole armour of God."*

6:10 ❓ Where should we get our strength? How can you have the strength of the Lord in your life?

6:11 📖 **wiles**—tricks

12 For we wrestle not against flesh and blood, but against principalities, against powers, against the rulers of the darkness of this world, against spiritual wickedness in high places.

13 Wherefore take unto you the whole armour of God, that ye may be able to withstand in the evil day, and having done all, to stand.

14 Stand therefore, having your loins girt about with truth, and having on the breastplate of righteousness;

15 And your feet shod with the preparation of the gospel of peace;

16 Above all, taking the shield of faith, wherewith ye shall be able to quench all the fiery darts of the wicked.

17 And take the helmet of salvation, and the sword of the Spirit, which is the word of God:

18 Praying always with all prayer and supplication in the Spirit, and watching thereunto with all perseverance and supplication for all saints;

19 ¶ And for me, that utterance may be given unto me, that I may open my mouth boldly, to make known the mystery of the gospel,

20 For which I am an ambassador in bonds: that therein I may speak boldly, as I ought to speak.

21 But that ye also may know my affairs, and how I do, Tychicus, a beloved brother and faithful minister in the Lord, shall make known to you all things:

22 Whom I have sent unto you for the same purpose, that ye might know our affairs, and that he might comfort your hearts.

23 Peace be to the brethren, and love with faith, from God the Father and the Lord Jesus Christ.

24 Grace be with all them that love our Lord Jesus Christ in sincerity. Amen.

---

6:12    We need the Lord's strength and protection because our fight is against an unseen enemy (Satan). Joseph Smith fought with this unseen enemy when he prayed to know which church to join. When this happened, Joseph pleaded for the Lord's help. Joseph was protected by the power of God. (See Joseph Smith—History 1:15-17.)

6:16    **quench**—put out, stop

   The "fiery darts of the wicked" are the temptations of Satan (see 1 Nephi 15:24).

6:18    **perseverance**—endurance and determination
**supplication**—prayer

6:19    **utterance**—speech

6:20    Paul was "an ambassador in bonds," or a minister of the Lord who, when he wrote this letter to the Ephesians, was a prisoner in Rome (see LDS Bible Dictionary, s.v. "Pauline Epistles," p. 746).

*Ruins of an ancient building in Ephesus*

# THE EPISTLE OF PAUL THE APOSTLE TO THE
# PHILIPPIANS

*Although some had joined the Church, most of the people of Philippi had rejected Paul's teachings. During his first visit there he had been beaten and put in prison. (See Acts 16:12–40.) Yet over the years, the Philippian Saints gave support to Paul by sending him food and other things he needed. Paul wrote this letter while he was a prisoner in Rome.*

## CHAPTER 1

*Paul loves, respects, and is grateful for the members of the Church in Philippi, and he desires that they remain righteous. Look for what Paul teaches that can help you stay righteous.*

### PAUL LOVES THE CHURCH MEMBERS IN PHILIPPI

1 PAUL and Timotheus, the servants of Jesus Christ, to all the saints in Christ Jesus which are at Philippi, with the bishops and deacons:

2 Grace be unto you, and peace, from God our Father, and from the Lord Jesus Christ.

3 ¶ I thank my God upon every remembrance of you,

4 Always in every prayer of mine for you all making request with joy,

5 For your fellowship in the gospel from the first day until now;

6 Being confident of this very thing, that he which hath begun a good work in you will perform it until the day of Jesus Christ:

7 ¶ Even as it is meet for me to think this of you all, because I have you in my heart; inasmuch as both in my bonds, and in the defence and confirmation of the gospel, ye all are partakers of my grace.

8 For God is my record, how greatly I long after you all in the bowels of Jesus Christ.

### PAUL INVITES THE PHILIPPIAN SAINTS TO LIVE THE GOSPEL MORE FULLY

9 ¶ And this I pray, that your love may abound yet more and more in knowledge and in all judgment;

10 That ye may approve things that are excellent; that ye may be sincere and without offence till the day of Christ;

11 Being filled with the fruits of righteousness, which are by Jesus Christ, unto the glory and praise of God.

### PAUL PREACHES THE GOSPEL AS A PRISONER IN ROME

12 ¶ But I would ye should understand, brethren, that the things which happened unto me have fallen out rather unto the furtherance of the gospel;

13 So that my bonds in Christ are manifest in all the palace, and in all other places;

14 And many of the brethren in the Lord, waxing confident by my bonds, are much more bold to speak the word without fear.

Paul spent years in a Roman prison.

1:9   **abound**—increase

1:10   **offence**—sin

1:11   Paul compares blessings we get from being righteous to fruits. What are some of the blessings you have received for being righteous?

1:13   **bonds**—chains

1:14   **waxing confident**—becoming more sure of themselves

| | | | |
|---|---|---|---|
| = Word Help | | = A Closer Look | |
| = More Light | | = Ponder This | |

Words in pink are explained in the Glossary.

1:8   **bowels**—feelings

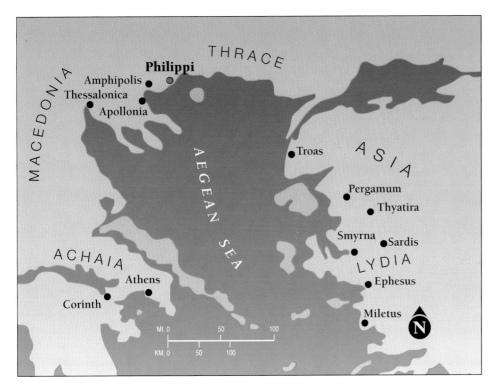

*Philippi, formerly Cremides but renamed after Philip of Macedon in 359 B.C., was in Paul's day a Roman military settlement.*

15 Some indeed preach Christ even of envy and strife; and some also of good will:

16 The one preach Christ of contention, not sincerely, supposing to add affliction to my bonds:

17 But the other of love, knowing that I am set for the defence of the gospel.

18 What then? notwithstanding, every way, whether in pretence, or in truth, Christ is preached; and I therein do rejoice, yea, and will rejoice.

## PAUL DESIRES TO REMAIN TRUE AND FAITHFUL

19 For I know that this shall turn to my salvation through your prayer, and the supply of the Spirit of Jesus Christ,

20 According to my earnest expectation and my hope, that in nothing I shall be ashamed, but that with all boldness, as always, so now also Christ shall be magnified in my body, whether it be by life, or by death.

21 ¶ For to me to live is Christ, and to die is gain.

22 But if I live in the flesh, this is the fruit of my labour: yet what I shall choose I wot not.

23 For I am in a strait betwixt two, having a desire to depart, and to be with Christ; which is far better:

24 Nevertheless to abide in the flesh is more needful for you.

25 And having this confidence, I know that I shall abide and continue with you all for your furtherance and joy of faith;

26 That your rejoicing may be more abundant in Jesus Christ for me by my coming to you again.

## PAUL URGES THE SAINTS TO STAY STRONG IN THE GOSPEL

27 ¶ Only let your conversation be as it becometh the gospel of Christ: that whether I come and see you, or else be absent, I may hear of your affairs, that ye stand fast in one spirit, with one mind striving together for the faith of the gospel;

---

1:20 **my earnest expectation and my hope**—my deeply felt trust and my heart's desire

Paul hopes and expects that he will remain a true Apostle of the Savior no matter what happens to him. How might our good examples, even when we are suffering, help others?

1:22 **wot**—know

1:23 **in a strait betwixt**—squeezed between

1:24 **abide**—live

28 And in nothing terrified by your adversaries: which is to them an evident token of perdition, but to you of salvation, and that of God.

29 For unto you it is given in the behalf of Christ, not only to believe on him, but also to suffer for his sake;

30 Having the same conflict which ye saw in me, and now hear to be in me.

## CHAPTER 2

*Paul urges the Philippian Saints to rely on the Savior's atonement in order to work out their own salvation. Watch for how this is accomplished.*

### PAUL ENCOURAGES MEMBERS OF THE CHURCH TO DO GOOD TO OTHERS

1 ¶ IF there be therefore any consolation in Christ, if any comfort of love, if any fellowship of the Spirit, if any bowels and mercies,

2 Fulfil ye my joy, that ye be likeminded, having the same love, being of one accord, of one mind.

3 Let nothing be done through strife or vainglory; but in lowliness of mind let each esteem other better than themselves.

4 Look not every man on his own things, but every man also on the things of others.

### JESUS CHRIST CAME TO EARTH TO OBEY HIS HEAVENLY FATHER

5 Let this mind be in you, which was also in Christ Jesus:

6 Who, being in the form of God, thought it not robbery to be equal with God:

7 But made himself of no reputation, and took upon him the form of a servant, and was made in the likeness of men:

8 And being found in fashion as a man, he humbled himself, and became obedient unto death, even the death of the cross.

9 Wherefore God also hath highly exalted him, and given him a name which is above every name:

10 That at the name of Jesus every knee should bow, of things in heaven, and things in earth, and things under the earth;

11 And that every tongue should confess that Jesus Christ is Lord, to the glory of God the Father.

### GOD MAKES IT POSSIBLE FOR US TO WORK OUT OUR OWN SALVATION

12 ¶ Wherefore, my beloved, as ye have always obeyed, not as in my presence only, but now much more in my absence, work out your own salvation with fear and trembling.

13 For it is God which worketh in you both to will and to do of his good pleasure.

14 ¶ Do all things without murmurings and disputings:

15 That ye may be blameless and harmless, the sons of God, without rebuke, in the midst of a crooked and perverse nation, among whom ye shine as lights in the world;

16 Holding forth the word of life; that I may rejoice in the day of Christ, that I have not run in vain, neither laboured in vain.

17 Yea, and if I be offered upon the sacrifice and service of your faith, I joy, and rejoice with you all.

18 For the same cause also do ye joy, and rejoice with me.

---

1:28  The Joseph Smith Translation explains that the "adversaries" mentioned here "reject the gospel, which bringeth on them destruction" (JST, Philippians 1:28).

**evident token of perdition**—obvious sign of their wickedness

1:29  When Paul first preached the gospel in Philippi, he was beaten and cast into prison (see Acts 16:22-24).

2:1  **consolation**—relief

2:2  **be likeminded**—think the same thoughts
**of one accord**—in agreement

2:3  **vainglory**—self-love
**esteem other**—consider or think of others as

2:4  Everyone who has been baptized and made a covenant to serve God should care for others (see Mosiah 18:9-10).

2:7  **reputation**—fame

2:9  **exalted**—glorified

2:10  Why will you bow your knees when Jesus comes to earth again?

2:13  God's work and glory is that we receive "immortality and eternal life" (see Moses 1:39).

2:14  **murmurings and disputings**—complaining and arguing

2:15  **crooked and perverse**—disobedient and wicked

Jesus taught his disciples that their lives should be examples for others to see and follow (see Matthew 5:16).

## PAUL WILL SEND MISSIONARIES TO PHILIPPI

19 But I trust in the Lord Jesus to send Timotheus shortly unto you, that I also may be of good comfort, when I know your state.

20 For I have no man likeminded, who will naturally care for your state.

21 For all seek their own, not the things which are Jesus Christ's.

22 But ye know the proof of him, that, as a son with the father, he hath served with me in the gospel.

23 Him therefore I hope to send presently, so soon as I shall see how it will go with me.

24 But I trust in the Lord that I also myself shall come shortly.

25 Yet I supposed it necessary to send to you Epaphroditus, my brother, and companion in labour, and fellowsoldier, but your messenger, and he that ministered to my wants.

26 For he longed after you all, and was full of heaviness, because that ye had heard that he had been sick.

27 For indeed he was sick nigh unto death: but God had mercy on him; and not on him only, but on me also, lest I should have sorrow upon sorrow.

28 I sent him therefore the more carefully, that, when ye see him again, ye may rejoice, and that I may be the less sorrowful.

29 Receive him therefore in the Lord with all gladness; and hold such in reputation:

30 Because for the work of Christ he was nigh unto death, not regarding his life, to supply your lack of service toward me.

# CHAPTER 3

*Paul speaks about his faith and commitment to the Lord Jesus Christ. Look for the way he describes his conversion story and what he counsels the Philippians to do.*

## PAUL GIVES UP ALL FOR JESUS CHRIST

1 ¶ FINALLY, my brethren, rejoice in the Lord. To write the same things to you, to me indeed is not grievous, but for you it is safe.

2 Beware of dogs, beware of evil workers, beware of the concision.

3 For we are the circumcision, which worship God in the spirit, and rejoice in Christ Jesus, and have no confidence in the flesh.

4 ¶ Though I might also have confidence in the flesh. If any other man thinketh that he hath whereof he might trust in the flesh, I more:

5 Circumcised the eighth day, of the stock of Israel, of the tribe of Benjamin, an Hebrew of the Hebrews; as touching the law, a Pharisee;

6 Concerning zeal, persecuting the church; touching the righteousness which is in the law, blameless.

7 But what things were gain to me, those I counted loss for Christ.

8 Yea doubtless, and I count all things but loss for the excellency of the knowledge of Christ Jesus my Lord: for whom I have suffered the loss of all things, and do count them but dung, that I may win Christ,

9 ¶ And be found in him, not having mine own righteousness, which is of the law, but that which is through the faith of Christ, the righteousness which is of God by faith:

---

2:20-22   Why was Timotheus someone Paul felt good about sending to the Philippians?

2:27   **nigh**—almost

2:29   **reputation**—honor

3:1   **not grievous**—not a problem

3:2   **the concision**—the cutting of the flesh by circumcision (see Glossary, s.v. "Circumcision").

3:3   **in the flesh**—in mortality

3:3-5   Circumcision was first revealed to Abraham. It was an ordinance for boys who were eight days old to show that they were God's covenant children. The Joseph Smith Translation indicates that it was also to remind the Lord's people that baptism was not necessary until the age of eight (see JST, Genesis 17:11-12). In Paul's writings circumcision came to represent the Jews and the law of Moses.

3:5   Pharisees were religious and political leaders of the Jews.

3:8   **dung**—waste or manure

10 That I may know him, and the power of his resurrection, and the fellowship of his sufferings, being made conformable unto his death;

11 If by any means I might attain unto the resurrection of the dead.

12 Not as though I had already attained, either were already perfect: but I follow after, if that I may apprehend that for which also I am apprehended of Christ Jesus.

13 Brethren, I count not myself to have apprehended: but this one thing I do, forgetting those things which are behind, and reaching forth unto those things which are before,

14 I press toward the mark for the prize of the high calling of God in Christ Jesus.

## PAUL ENCOURAGES THE SAINTS TO BE PERFECT

15 ¶ Let us therefore, as many as be perfect, be thus minded: and if in any thing ye be otherwise minded, God shall reveal even this unto you.

16 Nevertheless, whereto we have already attained, let us walk by the same rule, let us mind the same thing.

17 ¶ Brethren, be followers together of me, and mark them which walk so as ye have us for an ensample.

18 (For many walk, of whom I have told you often, and now tell you even weeping, that they are the enemies of the cross of Christ:

19 Whose end is destruction, whose God is their belly, and whose glory is in their shame, who mind earthly things.)

20 For our conversation is in heaven; from whence also we look for the Saviour, the Lord Jesus Christ:

21 Who shall change our vile body, that it may be fashioned like unto his glorious body, according to the working whereby he is able even to subdue all things unto himself.

## CHAPTER 4

*This chapter shows Paul's feelings for his friends. Notice what he says to them in the spirit of thanksgiving.*

## PAUL REJOICES IN THE LORD

1 ¶ THEREFORE, my brethren dearly beloved and longed for, my joy and crown, so stand fast in the Lord, my dearly beloved.

2 I beseech Euodias, and beseech Syntyche, that they be of the same mind in the Lord.

3 And I intreat thee also, true yokefellow, help those women which laboured with me in the gospel, with Clement also, and with other my fellowlabourers, whose names are in the book of life.

4 Rejoice in the Lord alway: and again I say, Rejoice.

5 Let your moderation be known unto all men. The Lord is at hand.

6 Be careful for nothing; but in every thing by prayer and supplication with thanksgiving let your requests be made known unto God.

7 And the peace of God, which passeth all understanding, shall keep your hearts and minds through Christ Jesus.

---

3:10 **being made conformable**—becoming like him

3:12 **apprehend**—take hold of

3:14 Paul says he is pressing forward to achieve the prize, or blessings, of Jesus Christ. This is like those in Lehi's vision who also pressed forward to partake of the fruit of the tree (see 1 Nephi 8:21, 24, 30).

3:15 To be perfect and have the mind of Christ, we need the help of the Atonement. If we come unto Christ, he will help us become perfect (see Moroni 10:32).

3:15- What can you do to become more like Jesus
21 Christ?

3:17 **ensample**—example

3:20 **conversation**—citizenship

3:21 **vile**—lowly or mortal

All mortals will be resurrected with perfect bodies (see 1 Corinthians 15:42-44, 50-53).

4:3 **intreat**—ask
**yokefellow**—friend, associate, or possibly wife

Paul's fellow workers had helped him in his ministry, and their names were recorded in the book of life. Joseph Smith taught that some of what the book of life contains is a record of those things we do on earth (see D&C 128:7).

4:4 Joseph Smith said, "Happiness is the object and design of our existence; and will be the end thereof, if we pursue the path that leads to it; and this path is virtue, uprightness, faithfulness, holiness, and keeping all the commandments of God" (*The Teachings of Joseph Smith,* pp. 310-11).

4:5 **moderation**—gentleness

4:6 **Be careful for nothing**—Do not be too concerned about anything
**supplication**—asking humbly

8 Finally, brethren, whatsoever things are true, whatsoever things are honest, whatsoever things are just, whatsoever things are pure, whatsoever things are lovely, whatsoever things are of good report; if there be any virtue, and if there be any praise, think on these things.

## PAUL THANKS THE SAINTS

9 Those things, which ye have both learned, and received, and heard, and seen in me, do: and the God of peace shall be with you.

10 ¶ But I rejoiced in the Lord greatly, that now at the last your care of me hath flourished again; wherein ye were also careful, but ye lacked opportunity.

11 Not that I speak in respect of want: for I have learned, in whatsoever state I am, therewith to be content.

12 I know both how to be abased, and I know how to abound: every where and in all things I am instructed both to be full and to be hungry, both to abound and to suffer need.

13 I can do all things through Christ which strengtheneth me.

14 Notwithstanding ye have well done, that ye did communicate with my affliction.

15 Now ye Philippians know also, that in the beginning of the gospel, when I departed from Macedonia, no church communicated with me as concerning giving and receiving, but ye only.

16 For even in Thessalonica ye sent once and again unto my necessity.

17 Not because I desire a gift: but I desire fruit that may abound to your account.

18 But I have all, and abound: I am full, having received of Epaphroditus the things which were sent from you, an odour of a sweet smell, a sacrifice acceptable, wellpleasing to God.

19 But my God shall supply all your need according to his riches in glory by Christ Jesus.

20 ¶ Now unto God and our Father be glory for ever and ever. Amen.

21 Salute every saint in Christ Jesus. The brethren which are with me greet you.

22 All the saints salute you, chiefly they that are of Caesar's household.

23 The grace of our Lord Jesus Christ be with you all. Amen.

---

4:8 Joseph Smith referred to this verse when he wrote as part of the thirteenth article of faith, "We may say that we follow the admonition of Paul" (Articles of Faith 1:13).

4:10 *flourished*—blossomed, grown
*lacked opportunity*—couldn't show it

4:12 *abased*—humble

4:13 Paul says that he can do all things through Christ, who will strengthen him. If you have enough faith in Christ, he will help you with all of your righteous desires (see Matthew 21:21-22).

4:21 *Salute*—Greet

4:22 *they that are of Caesar's household*—those who work and live in the emperor's palace

# THE EPISTLE OF PAUL THE APOSTLE TO THE
# COLOSSIANS

*Paul probably wrote Colossians while imprisoned in Rome. Epaphras, a fellow missionary, visited Paul and reported that the Saints in Colosse were falling into serious error. Many of them were believing false teachings. Paul wrote to encourage them to be faithful to Christ and His teachings.*

## CHAPTER 1

*Paul teaches that Jesus is the Savior and the only mediator between man and our Heavenly Father. Look for words or phrases that show the relationship between God and man.*

### PAUL OFFERS A PRAYER OF THANKS FOR THE COLOSSIAN SAINTS

1 PAUL, an apostle of Jesus Christ by the will of God, and Timotheus our brother,

2 To the saints and faithful brethren in Christ which are at Colosse: Grace be unto you, and peace, from God our Father and the Lord Jesus Christ.

3 ¶ We give thanks to God and the Father of our Lord Jesus Christ, praying always for you,

4 Since we heard of your faith in Christ Jesus, and of the love which ye have to all the saints,

5 For the hope which is laid up for you in heaven, whereof ye heard before in the word of the truth of the gospel;

6 Which is come unto you, as it is in all the world; and bringeth forth fruit, as it doth also in you, since the day ye heard of it, and knew the grace of God in truth:

7 As ye also learned of Epaphras our dear fellowservant, who is for you a faithful minister of Christ;

8 Who also declared unto us your love in the Spirit.

9 ¶ For this cause we also, since the day we heard it, do not cease to pray for you, and to desire that ye might be filled with the knowledge of his will in all wisdom and spiritual understanding;

10 That ye might walk worthy of the Lord unto all pleasing, being fruitful in every good work, and increasing in the knowledge of God;

11 Strengthened with all might, according to his glorious power, unto all patience and longsuffering with joyfulness;

12 ¶ Giving thanks unto the Father, which hath made us meet to be partakers of the inheritance of the saints in light:

### ALL THINGS WERE CREATED BY JESUS CHRIST

13 Who hath delivered us from the power of darkness, and hath translated us into the kingdom of his dear Son:

14 In whom we have redemption through his blood, even the forgiveness of sins:

15 Who is the image of the invisible God, the firstborn of every creature:

---

1:1    🔎 The word *apostle* means "one sent forth." It was the title Jesus gave to the twelve whom he chose and ordained. Paul was also an Apostle. (See LDS Bible Dictionary, s.v. "Apostle," p. 612.)

   📖 **Timotheus**—Timothy (see LDS Bible Dictionary, s.v. "Timothy," p. 785)

1:5-7    🔎 Christ told his Apostles that the gospel was to be preached in all the world and unto every creature (see Matthew 28:19-20). Paul and others like Epaphras were faithful servants of the Lord in fulfilling this commandment.

1:6    📖 **fruit**—good works

1:9-12    ☀ Paul's prayer was for the Colossians to be filled with "spiritual understanding" and to dwell with the "saints in light," or heavenly light.

Rephrasing Paul's counsel, Elder Bruce R. McConkie wrote: " 'Remember who you are. Honor the name of Christ. . . . Keep the commandments.' " (*Doctrinal New Testament Commentary* 3:24.)

1:15    ☀ Jesus looks like his Father—"the invisible God." "While God is invisible to men generally, he is not invisible to the prophets" (LeGrand Richards, *A Marvelous Work and a Wonder*, p. 21).

| | |
|---|---|
| 📖 = Word Help | 🔎 = A Closer Look |
| ☀ = More Light | 🔁 = Ponder This |

Words in pink are explained in the Glossary.

*Colosse, a small town in Phrygia near Laodicea and Hierapolis*

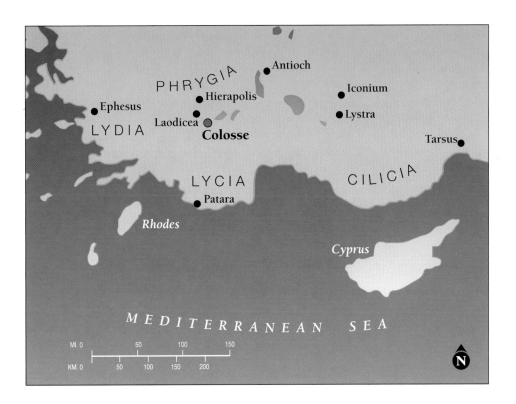

16 For by him were all things created, that are in heaven, and that are in earth, visible and invisible, whether they be thrones, or dominions, or principalities, or powers: all things were created by him, and for him:

17 And he is before all things, and by him all things consist.

18 And he is the head of the body, the church: who is the beginning, the firstborn from the dead; that in all things he might have the preeminence.

### THE ATONEMENT MAKES IT POSSIBLE FOR US TO RETURN TO OUR HEAVENLY FATHER

19 For it pleased the Father that in him should all fulness dwell;

20 And, having made peace through the blood of his cross, by him to reconcile all things unto himself; by him, I say, whether they be things in earth, or things in heaven.

21 And you, that were sometime alienated and enemies in your mind by wicked works, yet now hath he reconciled

22 In the body of his flesh through death, to present you holy and unblameable and unreproveable in his sight:

23 If ye continue in the faith grounded and settled, and be not moved away from the hope of the gospel, which ye have heard, and which was preached to every creature which is under heaven; whereof I Paul am made a minister;

24 Who now rejoice in my sufferings for you, and fill up that which is behind of the afflictions of Christ in my flesh for his body's sake, which is the church:

25 Whereof I am made a minister, according to the dispensation of God which is given to me for you, to fulfil the word of God;

26 Even the mystery which hath been hid from ages and from generations, but now is made manifest to his saints:

---

1:16    Jesus Christ created all things under the direction of our Heavenly Father (see Moses 1:33).

1:18    **have the preeminence**—have first place

1:20    **reconcile all things unto**—bring all things back into peace and harmony with

1:20-23    "Through the atonement of Christ, coupled with obedience to the laws and ordinances of the gospel, men are reconciled to God and to Christ"

(Bruce R. McConkie, *Doctrinal New Testament Commentary* 3:27; see also Articles of Faith 1:3).

1:21    **alienated**—distanced from God

1:24    **behind**—lacking

1:25    **dispensation**—mission

1:26-27 See   for Ephesians 3:3-6.

27 To whom God would make known what is the riches of the glory of this mystery among the Gentiles; which is Christ in you, the hope of glory:

28 Whom we preach, warning every man, and teaching every man in all wisdom; that we may present every man perfect in Christ Jesus:

29 Whereunto I also labour, striving according to his working, which worketh in me mightily.

## CHAPTER 2

*False teachers were trying to get the Saints in Colosse to follow them instead of Christ. Watch for what Paul says is wrong with their teachings.*

### Jesus Christ Paid for Our Sins to Free Us from the Demands of the Law

1 ¶ FOR I would that ye knew what great conflict I have for you, and for them at Laodicea, and for as many as have not seen my face in the flesh;

2 That their hearts might be comforted, being knit together in love, and unto all riches of the full assurance of understanding, to the acknowledgement of the mystery of God, and of the Father, and of Christ;

3 In whom are hid all the treasures of wisdom and knowledge.

4 ¶ And this I say, lest any man should beguile you with enticing words.

5 For though I be absent in the flesh, yet am I with you in the spirit, joying and beholding your order, and the stedfastness of your faith in Christ.

6 As ye have therefore received Christ Jesus the Lord, so walk ye in him:

7 Rooted and built up in him, and stablished in the faith, as ye have been taught, abounding therein with thanksgiving.

8 Beware lest any man spoil you through philosophy and vain deceit, after the tradition of men, after the rudiments of the world, and not after Christ.

9 For in him dwelleth all the fulness of the Godhead bodily.

10 And ye are complete in him, which is the head of all principality and power:

11 In whom also ye are circumcised with the circumcision made without hands, in putting off the body of the sins of the flesh by the circumcision of Christ:

12 Buried with him in baptism, wherein also ye are risen with him through the faith of the operation of God, who hath raised him from the dead.

13 ¶ And you, being dead in your sins and the uncircumcision of your flesh, hath he quickened together with him, having forgiven you all trespasses;

14 Blotting out the handwriting of ordinances that was against us, which was contrary to us, and took it out of the way, nailing it to his cross;

15 And having spoiled principalities and powers, he made a shew of them openly, triumphing over them in it.

---

1:28 Paul warned people of sin and invited them to come to the safety of the gospel. How do missionaries raise a warning voice today? (See D&C 42:12.)

2:1 *conflict*—worry

2:2 *unto all riches . . . the mystery of God*—that they might have the blessing of a full understanding of the things of God

2:4 *beguile you with enticing words*—deceive or trick you with flattering words

2:5 *stedfastness*—firmness

2:7 *stablished*—established, settled and growing

2:8 Paul warns the Saints against false teachers who would rob them of the truth by teaching ideas based on the traditions of men rather than Christ.

2:10 *principality*—authority

2:11-13 Circumcision in the Old Testament was a sign of the covenant between God and the children of Israel (see Genesis 17:9-12). Now that Christ has come, Paul calls the covenants we make at baptism a "circumcision made without hands" (verse 11). In baptism we promise to bury our sins and rise up with Christ to live a more righteous life by faith.

2:14-15 The "handwriting of ordinances" is the law of Moses. It "was against us" because we have all broken the law. Christ fulfilled the law of Moses and "blott[ed] out," or took away, our guilt through his atonement (see Matthew 5:17).

Now that you know that Jesus paid for your sins so you can be forgiven, what would you like to say to him when you see him again?

2:15 *shew*—This word is pronounced the same way as the word *show* and has the same meaning; *shew* is simply an old spelling of *show*.

## CHRIST FULFILLED THE LAW OF MOSES

16 ¶ Let no man therefore judge you in meat, or in drink, or in respect of an holyday, or of the new moon, or of the sabbath days:

17 Which are a shadow of things to come; but the body is of Christ.

18 Let no man beguile you of your reward in a voluntary humility and worshipping of angels, intruding into those things which he hath not seen, vainly puffed up by his fleshly mind,

19 And not holding the Head, from which all the body by joints and bands having nourishment ministered, and knit together, increaseth with the increase of God.

20 Wherefore if ye be dead with Christ from the rudiments of the world, why, as though living in the world, are ye subject to ordinances,

21 (Touch not; taste not; handle not;

22 Which all are to perish with the using;) after the commandments and doctrines of men?

23 Which things have indeed a shew of wisdom in will worship, and humility, and neglecting of the body; not in any honour to the satisfying of the flesh.

## CHAPTER 3

*Paul pleads with the Saints in Colosse to be holy and to serve the Lord. Look for guidelines that disciples of Jesus can follow to find happiness and peace.*

## MEMBERS OF THE CHURCH SHOULD TRY TO BECOME MORE LIKE JESUS CHRIST

1 ¶ IF ye then be risen with Christ, seek those things which are above, where Christ sitteth on the right hand of God.

2 Set your affection on things above, not on things on the earth.

3 For ye are dead, and your life is hid with Christ in God.

4 When Christ, who is our life, shall appear, then shall ye also appear with him in glory.

5 ¶ Mortify therefore your members which are upon the earth; fornication, uncleanness, inordinate affection, evil concupiscence, and covetousness, which is idolatry:

6 For which things' sake the wrath of God cometh on the children of disobedience:

7 In the which ye also walked some time, when ye lived in them.

8 ¶ But now ye also put off all these; anger, wrath, malice, blasphemy, filthy communication out of your mouth.

9 Lie not one to another, seeing that ye have put off the old man with his deeds;

10 And have put on the new man, which is renewed in knowledge after the image of him that created him:

11 Where there is neither Greek nor Jew, circumcision nor uncircumcision, Barbarian, Scythian, bond nor free: but Christ is all, and in all.

---

2:16-17 The "meat" and "drink" and "sabbath days" Paul mentions here are all parts of the law of Moses. They were to point the people to Jesus Christ and were ended after he fulfilled the law (see Alma 34:13-14).

2:18 **beguile**—rob
**voluntary humility**—false humility
**intruding into**—telling in great detail about

2:19 Jesus Christ is the head of the body (see Ephesians 4:15-16). When the body is "not holding," or is separated from the head, the body is no longer nourished or supported.

2:20 **rudiments of the world**—worldly teachings or ideas

2:20-23 The Joseph Smith Translation helps us understand that the rules of the law of Moses which forbid us to "touch" so many things are no longer necessary. Those who say we must still live them are following the laws of men. Those commandments of men may seem wise at first, but they do nothing to honor God. (See JST, Colossians 2:21-22.)

3:2 **affection**—feelings and thoughts

3:4 When Christ comes again, the Saints who are living on the earth and those who are dead will be "caught up to meet him" (D&C 88:96-98). Christ and the Saints shall "appear" together in the glory of the Lord.

3:5 Paul teaches members of the Church to mortify, meaning to put to death or do away with, the worldly and evil things in themselves.

3:6 **wrath**—punishment

3:8-10 Paul asked the Saints to rid themselves of certain sins. How do you feel when you overcome sin or bad behavior and become more like the Savior?

3:11 **bond**—slave

## PAUL NOTES SOME CHARACTERISTICS THAT FOLLOWERS OF CHRIST SHOULD HAVE

12 ¶ Put on therefore, as the elect of God, holy and beloved, bowels of mercies, kindness, humbleness of mind, meekness, longsuffering;

13 Forbearing one another, and forgiving one another, if any man have a quarrel against any: even as Christ forgave you, so also do ye.

14 And above all these things put on charity, which is the bond of perfectness.

15 And let the peace of God rule in your hearts, to the which also ye are called in one body; and be ye thankful.

16 Let the word of Christ dwell in you richly in all wisdom; teaching and admonishing one another in psalms and hymns and spiritual songs, singing with grace in your hearts to the Lord.

17 And whatsoever ye do in word or deed, do all in the name of the Lord Jesus, giving thanks to God and the Father by him.

## FAMILY MEMBERS SHOULD LOVE ONE ANOTHER AND BE HAPPY

18 ¶ Wives, submit yourselves unto your own husbands, as it is fit in the Lord.

19 Husbands, love your wives, and be not bitter against them.

20 Children, obey your parents in all things: for this is well pleasing unto the Lord.

21 Fathers, provoke not your children to anger, lest they be discouraged.

22 Servants, obey in all things your masters according to the flesh; not with eyeservice, as menpleasers; but in singleness of heart, fearing God:

23 And whatsoever ye do, do it heartily, as to the Lord, and not unto men;

24 Knowing that of the Lord ye shall receive the reward of the inheritance: for ye serve the Lord Christ.

25 But he that doeth wrong shall receive for the wrong which he hath done: and there is no respect of persons.

## CHAPTER 4

*Paul served with other faithful messengers of Jesus Christ. Watch for these fellow workers and what made them so faithful.*

## PAUL ENCOURAGES THE COLOSSIANS TO LIVE WISELY

1 ¶ MASTERS, give unto your servants that which is just and equal; knowing that ye also have a Master in heaven.

2 ¶ Continue in prayer, and watch in the same with thanksgiving;

3 Withal praying also for us, that God would open unto us a door of utterance, to speak the mystery of Christ, for which I am also in bonds:

4 That I may make it manifest, as I ought to speak.

---

3:12 **elect**—chosen
**bowels**—inner feelings

3:12-17 What teaching in Colossians 3:12-17 most touched your heart? How can these teachings help you be a better follower of Jesus Christ?

3:13 **Forbearing**—Being patient with

3:14 Charity is the pure love of Christ. It is the greatest gift of the Spirit we can have. (See Moroni 7:45-48.)

3:16 The "song of the righteous is a prayer unto [the Lord]" (D&C 25:12). Good music helps us have his Spirit in our lives.

3:18 **submit yourselves**—be obedient

3:18-21 In a document called "The Family: A Proclamation to the World," the leaders of the Church have said: "Happiness in family life is most likely to be achieved when founded [established] upon the teachings of the Lord Jesus Christ" (quoted in

Gordon B. Hinckley, "Stand Strong Against the Wiles of the World," p. 101).

3:20 The Lord commands children to honor their parents (see Exodus 20:12). What can you do to better honor and obey your parents?

3:21 **provoke not**—do not stir up

3:22 **not with eyeservice, as menpleasers**—not only when they are watching, to win their favor

3:23 **heartily**—with all your heart

4:1 We all have a master, who is Jesus Christ (see Matthew 23:8).

4:3 **of utterance**—for our message

Paul was "in bonds," or a prisoner in Rome, when he wrote this letter (see LDS Bible Dictionary, s.v. "Pauline Epistles," p. 745).

*"Children, obey your parents in all things: for this is well pleasing unto the Lord."*

5 ¶ Walk in wisdom toward them that are without, redeeming the time.

6 Let your speech be alway with grace, seasoned with salt, that ye may know how ye ought to answer every man.

## PAUL AND HIS COMPANIONS SEND THEIR GREETINGS

7 ¶ All my state shall Tychicus declare unto you, who is a beloved brother, and a faithful minister and fellowservant in the Lord:

---

4:5    **them that are without**—nonmembers of the Church
**redeeming the time**—making good use of your time

4:5-6    Salt seasoned foods and gave them a good flavor. It also preserved meats and kept them from becoming corrupt. Paul wanted the Saints to speak "that which is good" and to "let no corrupt communication proceed out of" their mouths (Ephesians 4:29) as they taught those "without," or who were not members of the Church.

8 Whom I have sent unto you for the same purpose, that he might know your estate, and comfort your hearts;

9 With Onesimus, a faithful and beloved brother, who is one of you. They shall make known unto you all things which are done here.

10 Aristarchus my fellowprisoner saluteth you, and Marcus, sister's son to Barnabas, (touching whom ye received commandments: if he come unto you, receive him;)

11 And Jesus, which is called Justus, who are of the circumcision. These only are my fellowworkers unto the kingdom of God, which have been a comfort unto me.

12 Epaphras, who is one of you, a servant of Christ, saluteth you, always labouring fervently for you in prayers, that ye may stand perfect and complete in all the will of God.

13 For I bear him record, that he hath a great zeal for you, and them that are in Laodicea, and them in Hierapolis.

14 Luke, the beloved physician, and Demas, greet you.

15 Salute the brethren which are in Laodicea, and Nymphas, and the church which is in his house.

16 And when this epistle is read among you, cause that it be read also in the church of the Laodiceans; and that ye likewise read the epistle from Laodicea.

17 And say to Archippus, Take heed to the ministry which thou hast received in the Lord, that thou fulfil it.

18 The salutation by the hand of me Paul. Remember my bonds. Grace be with you. Amen.

---

4:8 *estate*—situation

4:9-14 Paul sends greetings from those who ministered to him while he was a prisoner in Rome. One could describe Onesimus, Aristarchus, Marcus, Justus, Epaphras, Luke, and Demas "as witnesses of God at all times and in all things, and in all places" (Mosiah 18:9).

4:10 Marcus is another name for Mark. Mark was a companion of Paul's (see Acts 12:25) and was the author of the Gospel of Mark (see LDS Bible Dictionary, s.v. "Mark," p. 728).

4:11 *of the circumcision*—Jewish Christians (see also Glossary, s.v. "Circumcision")

4:11-13 Paul's fellow workers were faithful and loved the Saints. How would it have felt to be one of them? What can you do to help our Church leaders today?

4:13 *hath a great zeal*—is working very hard

4:14 Luke traveled with Paul and wrote the Gospel of Luke and the book of Acts (see LDS Bible Dictionary, s.v. "Luke," p. 726).

4:16 *epistle*—letter

4:17 Archippus listened to Paul's counsel. In a later letter Paul refers to Archippus as "our fellowsoldier" (Philemon 1:2).

# THE FIRST EPISTLE OF PAUL THE APOSTLE TO THE
# THESSALONIANS

*Shortly after the Church was established in Thessalonica, Paul sent Timothy there to find out how the Saints were doing. Timothy returned with many of their questions. In reply to those questions, Paul instructed the members to continue to live a good life and wait with patience for the second coming of Jesus Christ.*

## CHAPTER 1

*In this chapter Paul tells of his joy at the progress the new converts are making in the Church. Look for the encouragement and praise Paul gives these new members.*

### PAUL EXPRESSES THANKS FOR THE THESSALONIANS' FAITH

1 PAUL, and Silvanus, and Timotheus, unto the church of the Thessalonians which is in God the Father and in the Lord Jesus Christ: Grace be unto you, and peace, from God our Father, and the Lord Jesus Christ.

2 ¶ We give thanks to God always for you all, making mention of you in our prayers;

3 Remembering without ceasing your work of faith, and labour of love, and patience of hope in our Lord Jesus Christ, in the sight of God and our Father;

4 Knowing, brethren beloved, your election of God.

5 For our gospel came not unto you in word only, but also in power, and in the Holy Ghost, and in much assurance; as ye know what manner of men we were among you for your sake.

6 ¶ And ye became followers of us, and of the Lord, having received the word in much affliction, with joy of the Holy Ghost:

7 So that ye were ensamples to all that believe in Macedonia and Achaia.

8 For from you sounded out the word of the Lord not only in Macedonia and Achaia, but also in every place your faith to God-ward is spread abroad; so that we need not to speak any thing.

9 For they themselves shew of us what manner of entering in we had unto you, and how ye turned to God from idols to serve the living and true God;

10 And to wait for his Son from heaven, whom he raised from the dead, even Jesus, which delivered us from the wrath to come.

---

1:1 🔍 *Silvanus* is another name for *Silas*. He was one of the "chief men" among the early Christians at Jerusalem and was also called a prophet (see Acts 15:22, 32).

1:3 ✎ How could you improve your life with the qualities mentioned in verse 3?

1:4 📖 *your election of God*—you are chosen of God

1:5 📖 *assurance*—confidence

1:6 📖 *affliction*—difficulty

1:7 📖 *ensamples*—examples

1:8 ☀ The Joseph Smith Translation changes "faith to God-ward" to "faith toward God" (JST, 1 Thessalonians 1:8).

1:8-10 ✎ The First Presidency has declared: "All members are responsible to fellowship those who are new and to help them feel the strength of the gospel. Each new member should feel the influence of loving and caring friends within the Church." (Letter to Members of the Church, 15 May 1997.) How can we help keep new converts active in the faith?

1:9 📖 *shew*—This word is pronounced the same way as the word *show* and has the same meaning; *shew* is simply an old spelling of *show*.

1:10 ☀ The "wrath to come" is God's judgment of the earth (see D&C 88:85).

---

📖 = Word Help   🔍 = A Closer Look

☀ = More Light   ✎ = Ponder This

Words in pink are explained in the Glossary.

*Achaia and Macedonia were Roman provinces at the time of Paul.*

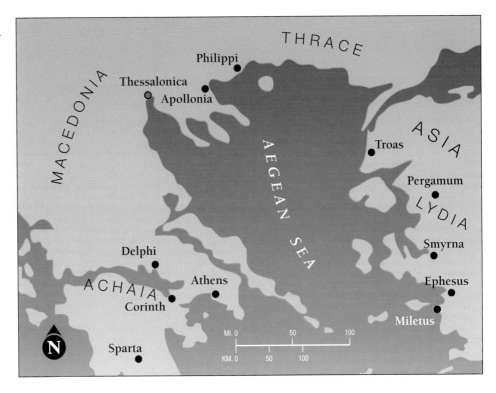

## CHAPTER 2

*Paul tells more about his ministry among the Thessalonians. Watch for the joy missionaries receive because of those who remain faithful in the gospel.*

### MISSIONARIES SHOULD PREACH THE GOSPEL IN A GODLY WAY

1 ¶ FOR yourselves, brethren, know our entrance in unto you, that it was not in vain:

2 But even after that we had suffered before, and were shamefully entreated, as ye know, at Philippi, we were bold in our God to speak unto you the gospel of God with much contention.

3 For our exhortation was not of deceit, nor of uncleanness, nor in guile:

4 But as we were allowed of God to be put in trust with the gospel, even so we speak; not as pleasing men, but God, which trieth our hearts.

5 For neither at any time used we flattering words, as ye know, nor a cloke of covetousness; God is witness:

6 Nor of men sought we glory, neither of you, nor yet of others, when we might have been burdensome, as the apostles of Christ.

7 ¶ But we were gentle among you, even as a nurse cherisheth her children:

8 So being affectionately desirous of you, we were willing to have imparted unto you, not the gospel of God only, but also our own souls, because ye were dear unto us.

9 For ye remember, brethren, our labour and travail: for labouring night and day, because we would not be chargeable unto any of you, we preached unto you the gospel of God.

10 Ye are witnesses, and God also, how holily and justly and unblameably we behaved ourselves among you that believe:

11 As ye know how we exhorted and comforted and charged every one of you, as a father doth his children,

12 That ye would walk worthy of God, who hath called you unto his kingdom and glory.

---

2:1    *in vain*—without any results

2:2    Paul had taught the gospel in the face of opposition, including being beaten and put in stocks at Philippi (see Acts 16:22-24).

2:3    *guile*—untrue words

2:5    People who preach the gospel for money and popularity are guilty of priestcraft (see 2 Nephi 26:29). Paul referred to this as "a cloke of covetousness."

2:9    *travail*—suffering

### FAITHFUL CONVERTS ARE THE GLORY AND JOY OF MISSIONARIES

13 ¶ For this cause also thank we God without ceasing, because, when ye received the word of God which ye heard of us, ye received it not as the word of men, but as it is in truth, the word of God, which effectually worketh also in you that believe.

14 For ye, brethren, became followers of the churches of God which in Judaea are in Christ Jesus: for ye also have suffered like things of your own countrymen, even as they have of the Jews:

15 Who both killed the Lord Jesus, and their own prophets, and have persecuted us; and they please not God, and are contrary to all men:

16 Forbidding us to speak to the Gentiles that they might be saved, to fill up their sins alway: for the wrath is come upon them to the uttermost.

17 ¶ But we, brethren, being taken from you for a short time in presence, not in heart, endeavoured the more abundantly to see your face with great desire.

18 Wherefore we would have come unto you, even I Paul, once and again; but Satan hindered us.

19 For what is our hope, or joy, or crown of rejoicing? Are not even ye in the presence of our Lord Jesus Christ at his coming?

20 For ye are our glory and joy.

### CHAPTER 3

*After we choose to follow Jesus and start on the path that leads back to Heavenly Father, we must move forward until we become perfect. Notice how Paul counsels the Thessalonian Saints to continue following a righteous course.*

### PAUL WORRIES ABOUT THE SUFFERINGS OF THE SAINTS

1 ¶ WHEREFORE when we could no longer forbear, we thought it good to be left at Athens alone;

2 And sent Timotheus, our brother, and minister of God, and our fellowlabourer in the gospel of Christ, to establish you, and to comfort you concerning your faith:

3 That no man should be moved by these afflictions: for yourselves know that we are appointed thereunto.

4 For verily, when we were with you, we told you before that we should suffer tribulation; even as it came to pass, and ye know.

5 For this cause, when I could no longer forbear, I sent to know your faith, lest by some means the tempter have tempted you, and our labour be in vain.

### THE THESSALONIANS STAND FAST IN THE LORD AND ARE ENCOURAGED TO PERFECT THEIR FAITH

6 ¶ But now when Timotheus came from you unto us, and brought us good tidings of your faith and charity, and that ye have good remembrance of us always, desiring greatly to see us, as we also to see you:

7 Therefore, brethren, we were comforted over you in all our affliction and distress by your faith:

8 For now we live, if ye stand fast in the Lord.

9 For what thanks can we render to God again for you, for all the joy wherewith we joy for your sakes before our God;

10 Night and day praying exceedingly that we might see your face, and might perfect that which is lacking in your faith?

---

2:16   *Gentiles* is a word that means "nations." It describes those not of the family of Israel or not believing in the God of Israel.

2:18   Paul wanted to visit the Saints in Thessalonica again. What would it be like to not be able to be with those you love?

2:18-19   The Doctrine and Covenants teaches that if you bring one soul unto Christ, "how great shall be your joy" (D&C 18:15). Imagine the happiness you would have if you had a close friend who became a member of the Church through your example and effort.

3:1   *forbear*—wait

3:2   *establish you*—strengthen and encourage you

3:3-5   Paul wants to make sure these new converts

are not troubled over the trials that sometimes come from being a member of the Church. Do you know any new Church members? What can you do to help them stay strong in the Church?

3:7   Afflictions, stress, and opposition are a natural part of earth life and living the gospel (see 2 Nephi 2:11-12). Elder Orson F. Whitney taught: "It is through sorrow and suffering, toil and tribulation, that we gain the education that we come here to acquire and which will make us more like our Father and Mother in heaven" (quoted in Spencer W. Kimball, *Faith Precedes the Miracle,* p. 98).

3:10-13   Paul prayed for these people to be strengthened. Did you know that your Church leaders also pray for you? Whom might you pray for?

11 ¶ Now God himself and our Father, and our Lord Jesus Christ, direct our way unto you.

12 And the Lord make you to increase and abound in love one toward another, and toward all men, even as we do toward you:

13 To the end he may stablish your hearts unblameable in holiness before God, even our Father, at the coming of our Lord Jesus Christ with all his saints.

## CHAPTER 4

*We can strengthen other members of the Church by loving them and by setting a good example for them. Look for what Paul teaches we can do to be good examples (holy).*

### LIVE IN SUCH A WAY THAT YOU PLEASE GOD

1 ¶ FURTHERMORE then we beseech you, brethren, and exhort you by the Lord Jesus, that as ye have received of us how ye ought to walk and to please God, so ye would abound more and more.

2 For ye know what commandments we gave you by the Lord Jesus.

3 For this is the will of God, even your sanctification, that ye should abstain from fornication:

4 That every one of you should know how to possess his vessel in sanctification and honour;

5 Not in the lust of concupiscence, even as the Gentiles which know not God:

6 That no man go beyond and defraud his brother in any matter: because that the Lord is the avenger of all such, as we also have forewarned you and testified.

7 For God hath not called us unto uncleanness, but unto holiness.

8 He therefore that despiseth, despiseth not man, but God, who hath also given unto us his holy Spirit.

9 ¶ But as touching brotherly love ye need not that I write unto you: for ye yourselves are taught of God to love one another.

10 And indeed ye do it toward all the brethren which are in all Macedonia: but we beseech you, brethren, that ye increase more and more;

11 And that ye study to be quiet, and to do your own business, and to work with your own hands, as we commanded you;

12 That ye may walk honestly toward them that are without, and that ye may have lack of nothing.

### THE RIGHTEOUS ARE RESURRECTED AT THE SECOND COMING OF JESUS CHRIST

13 ¶ But I would not have you to be ignorant, brethren, concerning them which are asleep, that ye sorrow not, even as others which have no hope.

14 For if we believe that Jesus died and rose again, even so them also which sleep in Jesus will God bring with him.

15 For this we say unto you by the word of the Lord, that we which are alive and remain unto the coming of the Lord shall not prevent them which are asleep.

---

3:13   *stablish your hearts unblameable in holiness*—strengthen your hearts so you will be blameless and holy

4:3   "To be *sanctified* is to become clean, pure, and spotless; to be free from the blood and sins of the world. . . . *Sanctification* is a state of saintliness." (Bruce R. McConkie, *Mormon Doctrine*, p. 675.) It comes only by obedience to the commandments and through the power of the Holy Ghost.

  *fornication*—misuse of the sacred creative powers; that is, use of these powers between people who are not married

4:4   Paul uses the word *vessel* to refer to the body. Each of us should know how to control our bodies, because they are the temples of God (see 1 Corinthians 6:19).

4:5   *concupiscence*—evil desires

4:6   *defraud*—cheat

4:7   God wants us to be clean and holy (see Psalm 24:3-4; see also D&C 88:74). What can you do to become clean from sin?

4:8   *despiseth*—rejects

4:9-12   Paul taught us to "increase more and more" in righteous actions. All prophets "beseech" us, or plead with us, to become better people (see Moroni 10:32). President Spencer W. Kimball did this when he encouraged us to "lengthen our stride" (*The Teachings of Spencer W. Kimball*, p. 174).

4:13   *them which are asleep*—those who have died

4:15-17   At the Second Coming, the righteous who have died will be resurrected and caught up into the air, along with the righteous who are alive, to meet Jesus (see D&C 88:96-98). The archangel, who is Adam, will announce this glorious reunion (see LDS Bible Dictionary, s.v. "Adam," p. 604).

16 For the Lord himself shall descend from heaven with a shout, with the voice of the archangel, and with the trump of God: and the dead in Christ shall rise first:

17 Then we which are alive and remain shall be caught up together with them in the clouds, to meet the Lord in the air: and so shall we ever be with the Lord.

18 Wherefore comfort one another with these words.

# CHAPTER 5

*The second coming of Jesus Christ will be glorious. Prophets have told us of many signs that will be given before that day. Watch for Paul's counsel on how we can prepare to meet the Savior when He comes again.*

## SAINTS CAN KNOW THE SEASON OF JESUS CHRIST'S SECOND COMING

1 ¶ BUT of the times and the seasons, brethren, ye have no need that I write unto you.

2 For yourselves know perfectly that the day of the Lord so cometh as a thief in the night.

3 For when they shall say, Peace and safety; then sudden destruction cometh upon them, as travail upon a woman with child; and they shall not escape.

4 But ye, brethren, are not in darkness, that that day should overtake you as a thief.

5 Ye are all the children of light, and the children of the day: we are not of the night, nor of darkness.

6 ¶ Therefore let us not sleep, as do others; but let us watch and be sober.

7 For they that sleep sleep in the night; and they that be drunken are drunken in the night.

8 But let us, who are of the day, be sober, putting on the breastplate of faith and love; and for an helmet, the hope of salvation.

9 For God hath not appointed us to wrath, but to obtain salvation by our Lord Jesus Christ,

10 Who died for us, that, whether we wake or sleep, we should live together with him.

11 ¶ Wherefore comfort yourselves together, and edify one another, even as also ye do.

## SAINTS ARE TO BE EXAMPLES OF RIGHTEOUSNESS

12 And we beseech you, brethren, to know them which labour among you, and are over you in the Lord, and admonish you;

13 And to esteem them very highly in love for their work's sake. And be at peace among yourselves.

14 Now we exhort you, brethren, warn them that are unruly, comfort the feebleminded, support the weak, be patient toward all men.

15 See that none render evil for evil unto any man; but ever follow that which is good, both among yourselves, and to all men.

16 ¶ Rejoice evermore.

17 Pray without ceasing.

---

4:18    Many people have lost loved ones to death. What comfort might come to those who know that all will rise from the dead and live again?

5:1    Elder Bruce R. McConkie taught that "the times and the seasons" refers to the "age or era or generation in which Christ shall come" (*Doctrinal New Testament Commentary* 3:57).

5:2    The Lord will come "as a thief in the night," which means suddenly, unexpectedly, or without warning. Jesus said that he would come "in such an hour as ye think not" (Matthew 24:44).

5:3    Paul compares the timing of Christ's coming to a woman in travail, meaning a woman who is about to give birth to a baby. "She does not know the hour or the minute of the child's arrival, but she does know the approximate time" (Bruce R. McConkie, *Doctrinal New Testament Commentary* 3:54).

5:4-6    Children of light, meaning the faithful members of the Church, will be ready at the time of the second coming of Jesus Christ because they will "cast off the works of darkness" (Romans 13:12) and watch for the signs of his coming.

5:7-11    How can faith, love, and the hope of being saved make you less afraid of the Second Coming? Are you looking forward to seeing Jesus again? What are you doing to get ready to meet him?

5:9    *wrath*—punishment

5:12-14    When the Lord's servants who preside over us warn and encourage us as directed by the Spirit, what they say is "the voice of the Lord, and the power of God unto salvation" (D&C 68:4; see also D&C 1:14).

5:13    *esteem*—respect and honor

5:14    *unruly. . . feebleminded . . . weak*—disobedient . . . afraid . . . timid

5:17-18    How often do you pray? How often do you give Heavenly Father thanks for all of your blessings?

18 In every thing give thanks: for this is the will of God in Christ Jesus concerning you.

19 Quench not the Spirit.

20 Despise not prophesyings.

21 Prove all things; hold fast that which is good.

22 Abstain from all appearance of evil.

23 ¶ And the very God of peace sanctify you wholly; and I pray God your whole spirit and soul and body be preserved blameless unto the coming of our Lord Jesus Christ.

24 Faithful is he that calleth you, who also will do it.

25 Brethren, pray for us.

26 Greet all the brethren with an holy kiss.

27 I charge you by the Lord that this epistle be read unto all the holy brethren.

28 The grace of our Lord Jesus Christ be with you. Amen.

---

5:19 🔲 **Quench not**—Do not hinder or stop

5:21 🔆 There are many good things we can "hold fast" to in order to receive protection and happiness. If we hold fast to the iron rod, which is the word of God, we shall "never perish" or be destroyed (see 1 Nephi 15:23-24).

5:22 🔄 Why do you think it would be important to stay away from those things which just appear evil? What blessings might come to you if you followed Paul's counsel?

5:23 🔲 **sanctify you wholly**—purify you completely

5:26 🔆 The Joseph Smith Translation changes the word "kiss" to "salutation," which means "greeting."

# THE SECOND EPISTLE OF PAUL THE APOSTLE TO THE
# THESSALONIANS

*In an earlier letter, Paul had taught the Saints in Thessalonica about the second coming of Jesus Christ. They believed Christ would come very soon. Paul wrote this letter to help them better understand when Jesus Christ would come again.*

## CHAPTER 1

*Paul loved the Saints in Thessalonica. He thanked God for them and always prayed for them. Look for the blessings Paul said they would receive for their faithfulness.*

### PAUL PRAISES THE FAITHFUL SAINTS IN THESSALONICA

1 PAUL, and Silvanus, and Timotheus, unto the church of the Thessalonians in God our Father and the Lord Jesus Christ:

2 Grace unto you, and peace, from God our Father and the Lord Jesus Christ.

3 We are bound to thank God always for you, brethren, as it is meet, because that your faith groweth exceedingly, and the charity of every one of you all toward each other aboundeth;

4 So that we ourselves glory in you in the churches of God for your patience and faith in all your persecutions and tribulations that ye endure:

5 ¶ Which is a manifest token of the righteous judgment of God, that ye may be counted worthy of the kingdom of God, for which ye also suffer:

6 Seeing it is a righteous thing with God to recompense tribulation to them that trouble you;

### THE WICKED WILL BE PUNISHED AT THE SECOND COMING OF JESUS CHRIST

7 And to you who are troubled rest with us, when the Lord Jesus shall be revealed from heaven with his mighty angels,

8 In flaming fire taking vengeance on them that know not God, and that obey not the gospel of our Lord Jesus Christ:

9 Who shall be punished with everlasting destruction from the presence of the Lord, and from the glory of his power;

10 When he shall come to be glorified in his saints, and to be admired in all them that believe (because our testimony among you was believed) in that day.

11 ¶ Wherefore also we pray always for you, that our God would count you worthy of this calling, and fulfil all the good pleasure of his goodness, and the work of faith with power:

12 That the name of our Lord Jesus Christ may be glorified in you, and ye in him, according to the grace of our God and the Lord Jesus Christ.

---

1.1 🔎 *Timotheus* is "the Greek form of the name Timothy" (LDS Bible Dictionary, s.v. "Timotheus," p. 785).

1:3-4 🔁 Paul praises these Saints for their faith, charity (godly love), and patience in their trials. Why does this make him happy? What can you do to make your leaders happy?

1:5 📖 *a manifest token*—evidence, proof

1:6 📖 *recompense*—pay back

1:7 ☀ The Lord promises those Saints who are faithful to the end that they shall enter "a state of rest, a state of peace, where they shall rest from all their troubles and from all care, and sorrow" (Alma 40:12).

1:7-9 🔎 At the Second Coming, Jesus will come "in flaming fire" and will punish those who did not obey the gospel (see Malachi 4:1). The wicked will have an "everlasting destruction," or a separation from their Father in Heaven forever.

| | |
|---|---|
| 📖 = Word Help | 🔎 = A Closer Look |
| ☀ = More Light | 🔁 = Ponder This |

Words in pink are explained in the Glossary.

## CHAPTER 2

*Paul taught that eventually the Church members of that time would fall away from the truth. Note Satan's actions in causing the Church to be taken from the earth.*

### THE CHURCH WOULD BE TAKEN FROM THE EARTH BEFORE THE SECOND COMING

1 ¶ NOW we beseech you, brethren, by the coming of our Lord Jesus Christ, and by our gathering together unto him,

2 That ye be not soon shaken in mind, or be troubled, neither by spirit, nor by word, nor by letter as from us, as that the day of Christ is at hand.

3 ¶ Let no man deceive you by any means: for that day shall not come, except there come a falling away first, and that man of sin be revealed, the son of perdition;

4 Who opposeth and exalteth himself above all that is called God, or that is worshipped; so that he as God sitteth in the temple of God, shewing himself that he is God.

5 Remember ye not, that, when I was yet with you, I told you these things?

6 And now ye know what withholdeth that he might be revealed in his time.

7 For the mystery of iniquity doth already work: only he who now letteth will let, until he be taken out of the way.

8 And then shall that Wicked be revealed, whom the Lord shall consume with the spirit of his mouth, and shall destroy with the brightness of his coming:

9 Even him, whose coming is after the working of Satan with all power and signs and lying wonders,

10 And with all deceivableness of unrighteousness in them that perish; because they received not the love of the truth, that they might be saved.

11 And for this cause God shall send them strong delusion, that they should believe a lie:

12 That they all might be damned who believed not the truth, but had pleasure in unrighteousness.

### THE GOSPEL PREPARES US FOR ETERNAL GLORY

13 ¶ But we are bound to give thanks alway to God for you, brethren beloved of the Lord, because God hath from the beginning chosen you to salvation through sanctification of the Spirit and belief of the truth:

14 Whereunto he called you by our gospel, to the obtaining of the glory of our Lord Jesus Christ.

15 Therefore, brethren, stand fast, and hold the traditions which ye have been taught, whether by word, or our epistle.

16 ¶ Now our Lord Jesus Christ himself, and God, even our Father, which hath loved us, and hath given us everlasting consolation and good hope through grace,

---

2:1-2 The Thessalonians worried because some people said that the Second Coming would come soon. The Joseph Smith Translation says that Paul told them not to worry about the Second Coming "except ye receive [hear about] it from us" (JST, 2 Thessalonians 2:2).

2:3 Paul prophesied that the second coming of Christ would not come until after "a falling away." This falling away is known as the Great Apostasy, a time when members of the Church would turn away from the gospel of Jesus Christ (see 2 Timothy 4:3-4).

2:3-4 "Lucifer [the devil] is the *man of sin* spoken of by Paul who was to be revealed in the last days before the Second Coming of our Lord" (Bruce R. McConkie, *Mormon Doctrine,* p. 467).

2:6 *what withholdeth*—who holds him back

2:7-9 Satan is "the mystery of iniquity" and "that Wicked" one. Jesus Christ "letteth," or allows, Satan to do his evil work for now. (See JST, 2 Thessalonians 2:7-9.)

2:10 *deceivableness of unrighteousness*—the evils that mislead

Wickedness leads people away from the truth. Paul taught that if we love the truth we can be saved. What can you do to always love the truth?

2:13 Paul tells these Saints that God chose them in the premortal existence to be saved in his kingdom if they would believe and live the truth (see Ephesians 1:4).

*sanctification*—being made holy

2:15 *traditions*—teachings

How do the teachings of Church leaders and the scriptures help you to stay strong in the Church?

2:16 *consolation*—encouragement

Grace is divine help given by God through the atonement of Jesus Christ. It provides us with the power needed to repent, keep the commandments, and become like God. (See LDS Bible Dictionary, s.v. "Grace," p. 697.)

17 Comfort your hearts, and stablish you in every good word and work.

# CHAPTER 3

*Paul gives some final counsel to the Thessalonian Saints. Look for what Paul says that can also help you be saved.*

## THE LORD WILL STRENGTHEN FAITHFUL MEMBERS OF THE CHURCH

1 ¶ FINALLY, brethren, pray for us, that the word of the Lord may have free course, and be glorified, even as it is with you:

2 And that we may be delivered from unreasonable and wicked men: for all men have not faith.

3 But the Lord is faithful, who shall stablish you, and keep you from evil.

4 And we have confidence in the Lord touching you, that ye both do and will do the things which we command you.

5 And the Lord direct your hearts into the love of God, and into the patient waiting for Christ.

## PAUL TEACHES THE IMPORTANCE OF WORK

6 ¶ Now we command you, brethren, in the name of our Lord Jesus Christ, that ye withdraw yourselves from every brother that walketh disorderly, and not after the tradition which he received of us.

7 For yourselves know how ye ought to follow us: for we behaved not ourselves disorderly among you;

8 Neither did we eat any man's bread for nought; but wrought with labour and travail night and day, that we might not be chargeable to any of you:

9 Not because we have not power, but to make ourselves an ensample unto you to follow us.

10 For even when we were with you, this we commanded you, that if any would not work, neither should he eat.

11 For we hear that there are some which walk among you disorderly, working not at all, but are busybodies.

12 Now them that are such we command and exhort by our Lord Jesus Christ, that with quietness they work, and eat their own bread.

13 But ye, brethren, be not weary in well doing.

14 And if any man obey not our word by this epistle, note that man, and have no company with him, that he may be ashamed.

15 Yet count him not as an enemy, but admonish him as a brother.

16 ¶ Now the Lord of peace himself give you peace always by all means. The Lord be with you all.

17 The salutation of Paul with mine own hand, which is the token in every epistle: so I write.

18 The grace of our Lord Jesus Christ be with you all. Amen.

---

2:17 **stablish**—strengthen

3:1 **have free course**—spread quickly

3:3 Paul taught that the Lord will "stablish," or strengthen, us and keep us from evil. How does knowing this help you?

3:6 **tradition**—teachings

3:8 **for nought**—without earning it

It was common in Paul's day for missionaries not only to teach the gospel but also to work for their own food and a place to stay. They did this to keep from burdening the people they taught. (See Acts 20:33–35.)

3:9 **ensample**—example

3:11 **busybodies**—busy doing useless things

3:12 **exhort**—encourage

3:13 Paul counsels the Saints not to grow tired of doing good. The promise is that if we continue in doing good, the time will come when we shall "reap" a reward "if we faint not" (Galatians 6:9; see also D&C 64:33–34).

3:14-15 Paul warns against being friends with people who don't live the gospel. We shouldn't see them as our enemies but should try to encourage them to live the gospel. How can you encourage your friends to better live the gospel?

3:17 **salutation**—greeting
**token**—sign, mark

# THE FIRST EPISTLE OF PAUL THE APOSTLE TO
# TIMOTHY

*In the course of Paul's travels, he came to Ephesus, where he left his missionary companion Timothy to check on the growth of any false teachings in the Church. Not being able to return to Ephesus as he wanted, Paul writes to Timothy, giving him counsel and encouragement in his ministry.*

## CHAPTER 1

*Timothy was a young missionary appointed to lead the Church at Ephesus. He had learned the doctrines of the gospel and was now ready to learn how to be a leader. In this chapter look for the advice and wisdom Paul shares with Timothy.*

### THE SAINTS ARE EXHORTED TO TEACH TRUE DOCTRINE

1 PAUL, an apostle of Jesus Christ by the commandment of God our Saviour, and Lord Jesus Christ, which is our hope;

2 Unto Timothy, my own son in the faith: Grace, mercy, and peace, from God our Father and Jesus Christ our Lord.

3 As I besought thee to abide still at Ephesus, when I went into Macedonia, that thou mightest charge some that they teach no other doctrine,

4 Neither give heed to fables and endless genealogies, which minister questions, rather than godly edifying which is in faith: so do.

### PAUL HELPS US UNDERSTAND THE LAW OF LOVE

5 ¶ Now the end of the commandment is charity out of a pure heart, and of a good conscience, and of faith unfeigned:

6 From which some having swerved have turned aside unto vain jangling;

7 Desiring to be teachers of the law; understanding neither what they say, nor whereof they affirm.

8 But we know that the law is good, if a man use it lawfully;

9 Knowing this, that the law is not made for a righteous man, but for the lawless and disobedient, for the ungodly and for sinners, for unholy and profane, for murderers of fathers and murderers of mothers, for manslayers,

10 For whoremongers, for them that defile themselves with mankind, for menstealers, for liars, for perjured persons, and if there be any other thing that is contrary to sound doctrine;

11 According to the glorious gospel of the blessed God, which was committed to my trust.

---

1:3    Church members are responsible to teach the principles and covenants of the gospel of Jesus Christ. They should teach by the power of the Holy Ghost, and their teaching should be uplifting and edifying. (See D&C 42:13-17; 50:14-23.)

1:4    **fables**—false doctrines or teachings
**edifying**—encouragement of spiritual improvement

   President Joseph Fielding Smith suggested that "fables and endless genealogies" refers to "a practice among the Jews in which the preparing of genealogies was fraudulently done" (*Answers to Gospel Questions* 1:214).

1:5    **charity**—Christlike love
**unfeigned**—sincere

1:7    **affirm**—strongly believe

1:10    **menstealers**—kidnappers or those who steal the slaves of others and sell them

---

| | |
|---|---|
| = Word Help | = A Closer Look |
| = More Light | = Ponder This |

Words in pink are explained in the Glossary.

*False teachers who tried to deceive and lead the Saints astray were a common problem for the Church in Paul's day. In his first letter to Timothy, Paul described the preaching of some of these teachers as "vain jangling."*

## JESUS CAME TO SAVE SINNERS

12 ¶ And I thank Christ Jesus our Lord, who hath enabled me, for that he counted me faithful, putting me into the ministry;

13 Who was before a blasphemer, and a persecutor, and injurious: but I obtained mercy, because I did it ignorantly in unbelief.

14 And the grace of our Lord was exceeding abundant with faith and love which is in Christ Jesus.

15 This is a faithful saying, and worthy of all acceptation, that Christ Jesus came into the world to save sinners; of whom I am chief.

16 Howbeit for this cause I obtained mercy, that in me first Jesus Christ might shew forth all longsuffering, for a pattern to them which should hereafter believe on him to life everlasting.

17 Now unto the King eternal, immortal, invisible, the only wise God, be honour and glory for ever and ever. Amen.

18 ¶ This charge I commit unto thee, son Timothy, according to the prophecies which went before on thee, that thou by them mightest war a good warfare;

19 Holding faith, and a good conscience; which some having put away concerning faith have made shipwreck:

---

1:13 **a blasphemer**—one who speaks evil of God

1:15 **acceptation**—acceptance, belief

1:16 **shew**—This word is pronounced the same way as the word *show* and has the same meaning; *shew* is simply an old spelling of *show*.

1:18 **charge**—message

1:19-20 "The highest punishment which the Church can impose upon its members is *excommunication*. This consists in cutting the person off from the Church so that he is no longer a member. Every blessing of the gospel is thereby lost, and unless the excommunicated person repents and gains his church status again, he cannot be saved in the celestial kingdom." (Bruce R. McConkie, *Mormon Doctrine,* p. 258.)

20 Of whom is Hymenaeus and Alexander; whom I have delivered unto Satan, that they may learn not to blaspheme.

## CHAPTER 2

*Paul writes about prayer and gives guidelines on how women should dress. Watch for the standards of modesty taught by Paul.*

### WE SHOULD PRAY FOR EVERYONE

1 ¶ I exhort therefore, that, first of all, supplications, prayers, intercessions, and giving of thanks, be made for all men;

2 For kings, and for all that are in authority; that we may lead a quiet and peaceable life in all godliness and honesty.

3 For this is good and acceptable in the sight of God our Saviour;

4 Who will have all men to be saved, and to come unto the knowledge of the truth.

5 For there is one God, and one mediator between God and men, the man Christ Jesus;

6 Who gave himself a ransom for all, to be testified in due time.

7 Whereunto I am ordained a preacher, and an apostle, (I speak the truth in Christ, and lie not;) a teacher of the Gentiles in faith and verity.

8 I will therefore that men pray every where, lifting up holy hands, without wrath and doubting.

### WOMEN SHOULD DRESS MODESTLY

9 ¶ In like manner also, that women adorn themselves in modest apparel, with shamefacedness and sobriety; not with broided hair, or gold, or pearls, or costly array;

10 But (which becometh women professing godliness) with good works.

11 Let the woman learn in silence with all subjection.

12 But I suffer not a woman to teach, nor to usurp authority over the man, but to be in silence.

13 For Adam was first formed, then Eve.

14 And Adam was not deceived, but the woman being deceived was in the transgression.

15 Notwithstanding she shall be saved in childbearing, if they continue in faith and charity and holiness with sobriety.

## CHAPTER 3

*Paul taught Timothy some of the requirements for bishops and deacons. Look for the qualities that bishops are expected to have.*

### PAUL SPEAKS OF THE QUALIFICATIONS TO BE A BISHOP

1 ¶ THIS is a true saying, If a man desire the office of a bishop, he desireth a good work.

2 A bishop then must be blameless, the husband of one wife, vigilant, sober, of good behaviour, given to hospitality, apt to teach;

---

1:20 **Hymenaeus and Alexander**—two men who were not enduring in faith to the end

2:1 **supplications**—requests
**intercessions**—prayers offered in behalf of others

2:1-3 Who are some people you pray for regularly? How does this help them?

2:4 The Joseph Smith Translation adds to this verse that the truth is in Jesus Christ, who is the Only Begotten Son of the Father (see JST, 1 Timothy 2:4).

2:5 "The way in which the Godhead is one is illustrated by Jesus' prayer that his disciples would be one, even as he and the Father are one (John 17:21-22; cf. 3 Ne. 11:27, 32-36; 28:10-11). Here he was praying for his disciples' unity of mind, purpose, and testimony, not for the merger of their identities into a single being." (*Encyclopedia of Mormonism*, s.v. "God.")

**mediator**—person who helps two people feel good toward each other

2:6 **ransom**—payment

2:7 **verity**—truth

2:9 **adorn**—dress
**shamefacedness and sobriety**—reverence or respect
**broided**—fancy

"Servants of God have always counseled his children to dress modestly to show respect for him and for themselves. . . . You should dress in such a way as to bring out the best in yourself and those around you." (*For the Strength of Youth*, p. 8.)

2:11 **subjection**—obedience

2:12 **usurp**—take

3:2-7 Why do you think these are important qualifications for bishops?

3:2 **vigilant, sober**—watchful, serious
**apt**—able

3 Not given to wine, no striker, not greedy of filthy lucre; but patient, not a brawler, not covetous;

4 One that ruleth well his own house, having his children in subjection with all gravity;

5 (For if a man know not how to rule his own house, how shall he take care of the church of God?)

6 Not a novice, lest being lifted up with pride he fall into the condemnation of the devil.

7 Moreover he must have a good report of them which are without; lest he fall into reproach and the snare of the devil.

## PAUL SPEAKS OF THE QUALIFICATIONS TO BE A DEACON

8 ¶ Likewise must the deacons be grave, not double-tongued, not given to much wine, not greedy of filthy lucre;

9 Holding the mystery of the faith in a pure conscience.

10 And let these also first be proved; then let them use the office of a deacon, being found blameless.

11 Even so must their wives be grave, not slanderers, sober, faithful in all things.

12 Let the deacons be the husbands of one wife, ruling their children and their own houses well.

13 For they that have used the office of a deacon well purchase to themselves a good degree, and great boldness in the faith which is in Christ Jesus.

14 ¶ These things write I unto thee, hoping to come unto thee shortly:

15 But if I tarry long, that thou mayest know how thou oughtest to behave thyself in the house of God, which is the church of the living God, the pillar and ground of the truth.

16 And without controversy great is the mystery of godliness: God was manifest in the flesh, justified in the Spirit, seen of angels, preached unto the Gentiles, believed on in the world, received up into glory.

## CHAPTER 4

*Timothy was one of Paul's most faithful companions in the work of the Church. Notice the warnings and counsel Paul gives him as Timothy fulfills his calling in Ephesus.*

### MANY WILL FALL AWAY FROM THE TRUTH IN THE LATTER DAYS

1 ¶ NOW the Spirit speaketh expressly, that in the latter times some shall depart from the faith, giving heed to seducing spirits, and doctrines of devils;

2 Speaking lies in hypocrisy; having their conscience seared with a hot iron;

3 Forbidding to marry, and commanding to abstain from meats, which God hath created to be received

---

3:3    **no striker**—not violent
       **lucre**—money
       **covetous**—wanting things that belong to other people

3:4-5  A bishop is to help care for every member of the ward, as a father cares for his family. A bishop is sometimes called "the father of the ward."

3:6    **novice**—beginner

3:7    **them which are without**—nonmembers of the Church

3:8    **doubletongued**—saying one thing to one person and something different to another person

3:8-13 How does the Lord expect deacons to act? What can young men do to prepare themselves to become faithful deacons?

3:11   In Paul's day, the needs of the Church were such that adults were ordained deacons. Today "it is the practice of the Church . . . to confer the Aaronic Priesthood upon worthy young men who are 12 years of age" (Bruce R. McConkie, *Mormon Doctrine*, p. 183).

grave—serious
slanderers—liars

4:1    **expressly**—clearly
       **seducing**—deceiving

       Elder Bruce R. McConkie indicated that "in the latter times" means "in later times, in a day then future, in the whole era of spiritual darkness which covered the earth from the loss of primitive Christianity to the restoration of the gospel, and also in the period of restoration itself, as far as most of the inhabitants of the earth are concerned" (*Doctrinal New Testament Commentary* 3:85).

4:2    Our conscience helps us know the difference between right and wrong. Elder James E. Faust taught, "Those who have not exercised their conscience have 'their conscience seared with a hot iron' (1 Timothy 4:2)" ("A Crown of Thorns, a Crown of Glory," p. 68).

4:3    The Lord told the Prophet Joseph Smith that those who teach that we cannot marry nor eat meat are "not ordained of God" (D&C 49:15, 18).

with thanksgiving of them which believe and know the truth.

4 For every creature of God is good, and nothing to be refused, if it be received with thanksgiving:

5 For it is sanctified by the word of God and prayer.

6 ¶ If thou put the brethren in remembrance of these things, thou shalt be a good minister of Jesus Christ, nourished up in the words of faith and of good doctrine, whereunto thou hast attained.

7 But refuse profane and old wives' fables, and exercise thyself rather unto godliness.

8 For bodily exercise profiteth little: but godliness is profitable unto all things, having promise of the life that now is, and of that which is to come.

9 This is a faithful saying and worthy of all acceptation.

## Jesus Christ Is the Savior of All

10 For therefore we both labour and suffer reproach, because we trust in the living God, who is the Saviour of all men, specially of those that believe.

11 These things command and teach.

12 Let no man despise thy youth; but be thou an example of the believers, in word, in conversation, in charity, in spirit, in faith, in purity.

13 Till I come, give attendance to reading, to exhortation, to doctrine.

14 Neglect not the gift that is in thee, which was given thee by prophecy, with the laying on of the hands of the presbytery.

15 Meditate upon these things; give thyself wholly to them; that thy profiting may appear to all.

16 Take heed unto thyself, and unto the doctrine; continue in them: for in doing this thou shalt both save thyself, and them that hear thee.

## CHAPTER 5

*Paul tells Timothy how to work with Church members. Notice how Church members are to help each other.*

### Paul Gives Advice on Caring for Widows and the Worthy Poor

1 ¶ REBUKE not an elder, but intreat him as a father; and the younger men as brethren;

2 The elder women as mothers; the younger as sisters, with all purity.

3 ¶ Honour widows that are widows indeed.

4 But if any widow have children or nephews, let them learn first to shew piety at home, and to requite their parents: for that is good and acceptable before God.

5 Now she that is a widow indeed, and desolate, trusteth in God, and continueth in supplications and prayers night and day.

6 But she that liveth in pleasure is dead while she liveth.

---

4:5 "To be *sanctified* is to become clean, pure, and spotless; to be free from the blood and sins of the world. . . . *Sanctification* is a state of saintliness." (Bruce R. McConkie, *Mormon Doctrine*, p. 675.) It comes only by obedience to the commandments and through the power of the Holy Ghost.

4:6 *put the brethren in remembrance*—remind the brethren
*whereunto thou hast attained*—which you have followed

4:7 *profane and old wives' fables*—godless and silly stories

4:8-9 Paul taught that exercising the body benefits us for a little while, but godliness, or spiritual exercise, benefits us forever. We exercise spiritually by putting God's commandments first in our lives (see Luke 12:31).

4:10 *reproach*—opposition

How can you show your belief in Jesus as your Savior?

4:12 Paul had left Timothy to watch over the Church in Ephesus (see LDS Bible Dictionary, s.v. "Pauline Epistles," p. 747). Timothy was a young man, and Paul encouraged him to not let his young age keep him from doing his duty.

4:14 According to Bruce R. McConkie, "the gift that is in thee" refers to "the gift of the Holy Ghost, which is the right to the constant companionship of that member of the Godhead based on faithfulness. The actual enjoyment of this gift is the greatest gift man can possess in mortality." (*Doctrinal New Testament Commentary* 3:87.)

5:3-5 "Widows that are widows indeed" were "widows who had no means of support except from the Church" (Bruce R. McConkie, *Doctrinal New Testament Commentary* 3:90).

5:4 *nephews*—that is, grandchildren

Heavenly Father expects children to show "piety," or be Christlike, at home and "requite," or repay, their parents by caring for them as they grow old (see Exodus 20:12).

7 And these things give in charge, that they may be blameless.

8 But if any provide not for his own, and specially for those of his own house, he hath denied the faith, and is worse than an infidel.

9 Let not a widow be taken into the number under threescore years old, having been the wife of one man,

10 Well reported of for good works; if she have brought up children, if she have lodged strangers, if she have washed the saints' feet, if she have relieved the afflicted, if she have diligently followed every good work.

11 But the younger widows refuse: for when they have begun to wax wanton against Christ, they will marry;

12 Having damnation, because they have cast off their first faith.

13 And withal they learn to be idle, wandering about from house to house; and not only idle, but tattlers also and busybodies, speaking things which they ought not.

14 I will therefore that the younger women marry, bear children, guide the house, give none occasion to the adversary to speak reproachfully.

15 For some are already turned aside after Satan.

16 If any man or woman that believeth have widows, let them relieve them, and let not the church be charged; that it may relieve them that are widows indeed.

17 ¶ Let the elders that rule well be counted worthy of double honour, especially they who labour in the word and doctrine.

18 For the scripture saith, Thou shalt not muzzle the ox that treadeth out the corn. And, The labourer is worthy of his reward.

## PAUL EXPLAINS HOW TO DEAL WITH SERIOUS SINS AND OTHER CHURCH BUSINESS

19 Against an elder receive not an accusation, but before two or three witnesses.

20 Them that sin rebuke before all, that others also may fear.

21 I charge thee before God, and the Lord Jesus Christ, and the elect angels, that thou observe these things without preferring one before another, doing nothing by partiality.

22 Lay hands suddenly on no man, neither be partaker of other men's sins: keep thyself pure.

23 Drink no longer water, but use a little wine for thy stomach's sake and thine often infirmities.

24 Some men's sins are open beforehand, going before to judgment; and some men they follow after.

25 Likewise also the good works of some are manifest beforehand; and they that are otherwise cannot be hid.

---

5:8 If a parent is able to work, he is to provide for his children (see D&C 42:42; 83:4). Why does Heavenly Father expect us to first try to care for ourselves before asking for help?

5:9-14 Widows in Paul's day who were over sixty years of age and had faithfully lived the gospel were cared for by the Church. "Young widows were counseled to marry again and raise families" (Bruce R. McConkie, *Doctrinal New Testament Commentary* 3:91).

5:13 **tattlers . . . and busybodies**—people who gossip and who pry into other people's lives

5:17-18 Paul explains a principle here that is also taught in modern revelation—that if it is necessary, the Church can help "support the families of those who are called and . . . sent unto the world to proclaim the gospel unto the world" (D&C 75:24). Did you know that most members serve without any pay?

5:21 **partiality**—showing favoritism

5:23 "Having knowledge of Timothy's physical infirmities, Paul is probably here counseling him that fruit juices will be more healthful than water" (Bruce R. McConkie, *Doctrinal New Testament Commentary* 3:92).

## CHAPTER 6

*Paul counsels Timothy to trust in faith, not riches. Look for how putting trust in God carries greater blessings than trusting in riches.*

### BEWARE OF THOSE WHO TEACH FALSE DOCTRINES

1 ¶ LET as many servants as are under the yoke count their own masters worthy of all honour, that the name of God and his doctrine be not blasphemed.

2 And they that have believing masters, let them not despise them, because they are brethren; but rather do them service, because they are faithful and beloved, partakers of the benefit. These things teach and exhort.

3 If any man teach otherwise, and consent not to wholesome words, even the words of our Lord Jesus Christ, and to the doctrine which is according to godliness;

4 He is proud, knowing nothing, but doting about questions and strifes of words, whereof cometh envy, strife, railings, evil surmisings,

5 Perverse disputings of men of corrupt minds, and destitute of the truth, supposing that gain is godliness: from such withdraw thyself.

6 ¶ But godliness with contentment is great gain.

### THE LOVE OF MONEY IS THE CAUSE OF ALL EVIL

7 For we brought nothing into this world, and it is certain we can carry nothing out.

8 And having food and raiment let us be therewith content.

9 But they that will be rich fall into temptation and a snare, and into many foolish and hurtful lusts, which drown men in destruction and perdition.

10 For the love of money is the root of all evil: which while some coveted after, they have erred from the faith, and pierced themselves through with many sorrows.

11 But thou, O man of God, flee these things; and follow after righteousness, godliness, faith, love, patience, meekness.

12 Fight the good fight of faith, lay hold on eternal life, whereunto thou art also called, and hast professed a good profession before many witnesses.

*A yoke helped unite the efforts of oxen.*

and evil thoughts. He counseled the Saints not to associate with them (see 2 Timothy 3:1-5).

6:5   *destitute of the truth*—without the truth

6:7   We cannot take physical things with us into the next life. What can we take with us when we die? (See D&C 130:18-19.) Since we can take only the knowledge gained in this life, what can you do to learn more at school? What about at church?

6:9-10   Those who desire to be rich can be drawn more easily into temptation and harmful lusts or evil desires. That may be why Jesus himself taught that it is easier for a camel to get through the eye of a needle than it is for a rich man to get into the kingdom of heaven (see Matthew 19:23-24).

6:10   *coveted after*—wanted in a greedy way

6:11-12   If we are rich but still want to go to heaven, what should we do with our money? How can you use money to help build the kingdom of God? (See Jacob 2:18-19.)

6:12   *professed a good profession*—promised to choose the good way

6:1   A yoke was frequently used as a symbol of any heavy burden people carry. In this case it has to do with the burden of slavery.

6:2   *exhort*—encourage

6:3-5   Paul warns against those who teach false doctrine and who do not agree with "wholesome words," or the true teachings of the gospel of Christ. In their pride they are obsessed with controversial questions and promote argument

## PAUL CHALLENGES TIMOTHY TO FOLLOW JESUS

13 ¶ I give thee charge in the sight of God, who quickeneth all things, and before Christ Jesus, who before Pontius Pilate witnessed a good confession;

14 That thou keep this commandment without spot, unrebukeable, until the appearing of our Lord Jesus Christ:

15 Which in his times he shall shew, who is the blessed and only Potentate, the King of kings, and Lord of lords;

16 Who only hath immortality, dwelling in the light which no man can approach unto; whom no man hath seen, nor can see: to whom be honour and power everlasting. Amen.

## PAUL COUNSELS TIMOTHY TO TRUST IN THE LORD, NOT RICHES

17 Charge them that are rich in this world, that they be not highminded, nor trust in uncertain riches, but in the living God, who giveth us richly all things to enjoy;

18 That they do good, that they be rich in good works, ready to distribute, willing to communicate;

19 Laying up in store for themselves a good foundation against the time to come, that they may lay hold on eternal life.

20 O Timothy, keep that which is committed to thy trust, avoiding profane and vain babblings, and oppositions of science falsely so called:

21 Which some professing have erred concerning the faith. Grace be with thee. Amen.

---

6:13  Pontius Pilate was the man who judged Jesus. Though he knew Jesus was innocent he still sent Him to be crucified. (See Matthew 27:19-26.)

6:14  **keep this commandment without spot, unrebukeable**—keep the commandments so well that you are beyond blame

6:15  **Potentate**—Royal Prince

6:17  Paul reminds Timothy that it is God who gives us "all things." Why does He bless us so richly? (See 2 Nephi 2:25.) If God wants us to have joy in life, what should be our attitude when we wake up each morning?

6:18  **distribute**—share

6:20  **vain babblings**—useless and meaningless talk
**oppositions of science falsely so called**—the opposing ideas which are called knowledge but which are false

6:20-21  The scriptures contain many warnings about allowing the false teachings of the world to lead us away from the gospel of Jesus Christ (see 2 Nephi 9:28-29; 28:15).

*The first archaeological evidence of Pontius Pilate's existence—a stone with an inscription that includes the ruler's name—was found at Caesarea.*

# THE SECOND EPISTLE OF PAUL THE APOSTLE TO
# TIMOTHY

*This letter was written while Paul was in prison for the second time, not long before he was killed. These are the Apostle Paul's last words, and they demonstrate his great courage and strong trust in the Lord as he faced death. (See LDS Bible Dictionary, s.v. "Pauline Epistles," p. 748.)*

## CHAPTER 1

*Paul encourages Timothy to serve faithfully in his calling as a bishop. Look for suggestions that could help any member of the Church better serve others.*

### PAUL LOVES TIMOTHY

1 PAUL, an apostle of Jesus Christ by the will of God, according to the promise of life which is in Christ Jesus,

2 To Timothy, my dearly beloved son: Grace, mercy, and peace, from God the Father and Christ Jesus our Lord.

3 I thank God, whom I serve from my forefathers with pure conscience, that without ceasing I have remembrance of thee in my prayers night and day;

4 Greatly desiring to see thee, being mindful of thy tears, that I may be filled with joy;

5 When I call to remembrance the unfeigned faith that is in thee, which dwelt first in thy grandmother Lois, and thy mother Eunice; and I am persuaded that in thee also.

### PAUL TELLS TIMOTHY TO BE FAITHFUL AND NOT BE ASHAMED OF HIS TESTIMONY

6 ¶ Wherefore I put thee in remembrance that thou stir up the gift of God, which is in thee by the putting on of my hands.

7 For God hath not given us the spirit of fear; but of power, and of love, and of a sound mind.

8 Be not thou therefore ashamed of the testimony of our Lord, nor of me his prisoner: but be thou partaker of the afflictions of the gospel according to the power of God;

9 Who hath saved us, and called us with an holy calling, not according to our works, but according to his own purpose and grace, which was given us in Christ Jesus before the world began,

---

1:2    Timothy [Timotheus] was not Paul's son, but they had served as missionary companions and Paul loved Timothy like a son (see Acts 16:1-5).

1:5    **unfeigned**—genuine, real

1:6    Timothy had been called to be a bishop (see note at the end of 2 Timothy).

1:7-8    Referring to verse 7 and the first part of verse 8, President Gordon B. Hinckley has written: "I wish that every member of this church would put those words where he might see them every morning as he begins his day. They would give us the courage to speak up, they would give us the faith to try, they would strengthen our conviction of the Lord Jesus Christ." ("'Be Not Afraid, Only Believe,'" p. 5.)

| | |
|---|---|
| = Word Help | = A Closer Look |
| = More Light | = Ponder This |

Words in pink are explained in the Glossary.

10 But is now made manifest by the appearing of our Saviour Jesus Christ, who hath abolished death, and hath brought life and immortality to light through the gospel:

11 Whereunto I am appointed a preacher, and an apostle, and a teacher of the Gentiles.

12 For the which cause I also suffer these things: nevertheless I am not ashamed: for I know whom I have believed, and am persuaded that he is able to keep that which I have committed unto him against that day.

13 Hold fast the form of sound words, which thou hast heard of me, in faith and love which is in Christ Jesus.

14 That good thing which was committed unto thee keep by the Holy Ghost which dwelleth in us.

### SOME MEMBERS DESERT PAUL WHILE OTHERS REMAIN FAITHFUL

15 ¶ This thou knowest, that all they which are in Asia be turned away from me; of whom are Phygellus and Hermogenes.

16 The Lord give mercy unto the house of Onesiphorus; for he oft refreshed me, and was not ashamed of my chain:

17 But, when he was in Rome, he sought me out very diligently, and found me.

18 The Lord grant unto him that he may find mercy of the Lord in that day: and in how many things he ministered unto me at Ephesus, thou knowest very well.

## CHAPTER 2

*After being put in prison a second time, Paul writes to Timothy and counsels him. Paul endures suffering for Christ's sake and will eventually die in his service. Watch for how Paul tells Timothy to live.*

### PAUL TELLS TIMOTHY TO ENDURE SUFFERING AS CHRIST DID

1 ¶ THOU therefore, my son, be strong in the grace that is in Christ Jesus.

2 And the things that thou hast heard of me among many witnesses, the same commit thou to faithful men, who shall be able to teach others also.

3 Thou therefore endure hardness, as a good soldier of Jesus Christ.

4 No man that warreth entangleth himself with the affairs of this life; that he may please him who hath chosen him to be a soldier.

5 And if a man also strive for masteries, yet is he not crowned, except he strive lawfully.

6 The husbandman that laboureth must be first partaker of the fruits.

7 Consider what I say; and the Lord give thee understanding in all things.

---

*The grave, or death, will not have the final victory. Because of Jesus Christ, everyone will be resurrected.*

To have immortality means that we will be resurrected and never die again (see *Mormon Doctrine*, pp. 376-77; see also Moses 1:39).

1:13 What are some sound, or true, words you have heard from your Church leaders that you keep in your mind and heart?

1:15 How might Paul feel about seeing those he had taught fall away from the Church? What can we do to make sure we never fall away?

2:3 Just as Paul counseled Timothy to endure hardships for Christ, the Lord also told Joseph Smith to remember that all things will be revealed to those "who have endured valiantly for the gospel of Jesus Christ" (D&C 121:29).

2:4 **entangleth himself with**—gets involved in

2:5 **strive for masteries**—compete in an athletic event
**strive lawfully**—live by the rules

2:6 **husbandman**—farmer

1:10 **manifest**—known
**abolished**—done away with

8 ¶ Remember that Jesus Christ of the seed of David was raised from the dead according to my gospel:

9 Wherein I suffer trouble, as an evil doer, even unto bonds; but the word of God is not bound.

10 Therefore I endure all things for the elect's sakes, that they may also obtain the salvation which is in Christ Jesus with eternal glory.

11 It is a faithful saying: For if we be dead with him, we shall also live with him:

12 If we suffer, we shall also reign with him: if we deny him, he also will deny us:

13 If we believe not, yet he abideth faithful: he cannot deny himself.

### PAUL TEACHES TIMOTHY ABOUT THE WORD OF GOD

14 ¶ Of these things put them in remembrance, charging them before the Lord that they strive not about words to no profit, but to the subverting of the hearers.

15 Study to shew thyself approved unto God, a workman that needeth not to be ashamed, rightly dividing the word of truth.

16 But shun profane and vain babblings: for they will increase unto more ungodliness.

17 And their word will eat as doth a canker: of whom is Hymenaeus and Philetus;

18 Who concerning the truth have erred, saying that the resurrection is past already; and overthrow the faith of some.

19 ¶ Nevertheless the foundation of God standeth sure, having this seal, The Lord knoweth them that are his. And, Let every one that nameth the name of Christ depart from iniquity.

20 But in a great house there are not only vessels of gold and of silver, but also of wood and of earth; and some to honour, and some to dishonour.

21 If a man therefore purge himself from these, he shall be a vessel unto honour, sanctified, and meet for the master's use, and prepared unto every good work.

22 ¶ Flee also youthful lusts: but follow righteousness, faith, charity, peace, with them that call on the Lord out of a pure heart.

23 But foolish and unlearned questions avoid, knowing that they do gender strifes.

24 And the servant of the Lord must not strive; but be gentle unto all men, apt to teach, patient,

25 In meekness instructing those that oppose themselves; if God peradventure will give them repentance to the acknowledging of the truth;

26 And that they may recover themselves out of the snare of the devil, who are taken captive by him at his will.

## CHAPTER 3

*Paul prophesies of the evils of the last days. Note the counsel Paul gives to help us avoid these evils.*

### PAUL PROPHESIES ABOUT THE DANGERS IN THE LAST DAYS

1 ¶ THIS know also, that in the last days perilous times shall come.

2 For men shall be lovers of their own selves, covetous, boasters, proud, blasphemers, disobedient to parents, unthankful, unholy,

---

2:8    Jesus' genealogy can be traced back to David (see Matthew 1:1-17).

2:9    **bonds**—chains

2:10-13    We are counseled by the Lord that we need to endure our trials. Those who deny the Lord cannot be made holy. (See D&C 101:1-5.)

2:15    **shew**—This word is pronounced the same way as the word *show* and has the same meaning; *shew* is simply an old spelling of *show*.
**rightly dividing**—correctly interpreting

2:16    **shun profane and vain babblings**—stay away from irreverent and meaningless talk

2:18    **erred**—made a mistake

2:20    **vessels**—articles

2:23    **gender strifes**—cause divisions

When teaching the gospel to others, what should we avoid? (See 3 Nephi 11:29.)

2:25    **peradventure**—possibly

3:1    **perilous**—dangerous

Most dangers we face can hurt our physical bodies. How can the dangers described in the next few verses hurt us?

3:2    **lovers of their own selves**—selfish
**covetous**—wanting things belonging to others

Blasphemy is the sin of claiming to be like God or speaking evil of God (see LDS Bible Dictionary, s.v. "Blasphemy," pp. 625-26).

3 Without natural affection, trucebreakers, false accusers, incontinent, fierce, despisers of those that are good,

4 Traitors, heady, highminded, lovers of pleasures more than lovers of God;

5 Having a form of godliness, but denying the power thereof: from such turn away.

6 For of this sort are they which creep into houses, and lead captive silly women laden with sins, led away with divers lusts,

7 Ever learning, and never able to come to the knowledge of the truth.

8 Now as Jannes and Jambres withstood Moses, so do these also resist the truth: men of corrupt minds, reprobate concerning the faith.

9 But they shall proceed no further: for their folly shall be manifest unto all men, as theirs also was.

### PAUL TELLS HOW MEMBERS OF THE CHURCH CAN AVOID THE EVILS OF THE LAST DAYS

10 ¶ But thou hast fully known my doctrine, manner of life, purpose, faith, longsuffering, charity, patience,

11 Persecutions, afflictions, which came unto me at Antioch, at Iconium, at Lystra; what persecutions I endured: but out of them all the Lord delivered me.

12 Yea, and all that will live godly in Christ Jesus shall suffer persecution.

13 But evil men and seducers shall wax worse and worse, deceiving, and being deceived.

14 But continue thou in the things which thou hast learned and hast been assured of, knowing of whom thou hast learned them;

15 And that from a child thou hast known the holy scriptures, which are able to make thee wise unto salvation through faith which is in Christ Jesus.

16 All scripture is given by inspiration of God, and is profitable for doctrine, for reproof, for correction, for instruction in righteousness:

17 That the man of God may be perfect, throughly furnished unto all good works.

## CHAPTER 4

*Paul set an example of keeping the faith and enduring to the end. Look for the rewards Paul promises to members of the Church who remain faithful to the end.*

### PAUL COMMANDS TIMOTHY TO PREACH THE GOSPEL

1 ¶ I charge thee therefore before God, and the Lord Jesus Christ, who shall judge the quick and the dead at his appearing and his kingdom;

2 Preach the word; be instant in season, out of season; reprove, rebuke, exhort with all longsuffering and doctrine.

3 For the time will come when they will not endure sound doctrine; but after their own lusts shall they heap to themselves teachers, having itching ears;

4 And they shall turn away their ears from the truth, and shall be turned unto fables.

---

3:3 **trucebreakers**—breakers of promises
**incontinent**—lacking self-control

3:6 **laden**—loaded down
**divers**—a variety of

3:7 In the Book of Mormon, Jacob teaches that to be learned is good only if we obey Heavenly Father (see 2 Nephi 9:28-29).

3:8 Jannes and Jambres, though not actually named in the Old Testament, were magicians who opposed Moses during the time of the plagues upon Egypt (see Exodus 7-9 and LDS Bible Dictionary, s.v. "Jannes and Jambres," p. 710).

3:9 **folly**—mistakes

3:15-16 Elder Boyd K. Packer said that after Paul prophesied of the evils of the last days (see 2 Timothy 3:1-7) he also explained how the scriptures can protect us from those evils (see "Teach the Scriptures," address to religious educators, 14 October 1977). How can the scriptures help you avoid the temptations and the dangers of the last days?

3:16 **reproof**—showing people their wrongdoing

4:1 **charge**—command

4:1-2 Paul reminds Timothy that Jesus Christ will return to earth a second time and will judge us (see John 5:22). Timothy is told that he must preach, teach, and correct those who are "out of season," or who are not living the gospel (see JST, 2 Timothy 4:2).

4:3 **heap to themselves teachers, having itching ears**—gather teachers who will teach them what they want to hear, instead of the truth

4:3-4 Paul explained that an apostasy would occur and that the gospel would be taken from the earth (see 2 Thessalonians 2:1-3). This falling away would happen because the people would turn the truth into "fables" or would not listen to the true doctrine or teachings of Jesus Christ.

4:4 **fables**—make-believe stories

*The scriptures with which Timothy might have been familiar were handwritten, often on scrolls, by scribes who produced copies for the people's use.*

5 But watch thou in all things, endure afflictions, do the work of an evangelist, make full proof of thy ministry.

## PAUL ENDURED IN FAITH TO THE END

6 For I am now ready to be offered, and the time of my departure is at hand.

7 I have fought a good fight, I have finished my course, I have kept the faith:

8 Henceforth there is laid up for me a crown of righteousness, which the Lord, the righteous judge, shall give me at that day: and not to me only, but unto all them also that love his appearing.

9 ¶ Do thy diligence to come shortly unto me:

## SOME PEOPLE REJECTED PAUL, BUT THE LORD ALWAYS STOOD WITH HIM

10 For Demas hath forsaken me, having loved this present world, and is departed unto Thessalonica; Crescens to Galatia, Titus unto Dalmatia.

11 Only Luke is with me. Take Mark, and bring him with thee: for he is profitable to me for the ministry.

12 And Tychicus have I sent to Ephesus.

13 The cloke that I left at Troas with Carpus, when thou comest, bring with thee, and the books, but especially the parchments.

14 Alexander the coppersmith did me much evil: the Lord reward him according to his works:

15 Of whom be thou ware also; for he hath greatly withstood our words.

16 ¶ At my first answer no man stood with me, but all men forsook me: I pray God that it may not be laid to their charge.

17 Notwithstanding the Lord stood with me, and strengthened me; that by me the preaching might be fully known, and that all the Gentiles might hear: and I was delivered out of the mouth of the lion.

18 And the Lord shall deliver me from every evil work, and will preserve me unto his heavenly kingdom: to whom be glory for ever and ever. Amen.

19 Salute Prisca and Aquila, and the household of Onesiphorus.

20 Erastus abode at Corinth: but Trophimus have I left at Miletum sick.

21 Do thy diligence to come before winter. Eubulus greeteth thee, and Pudens, and Linus, and Claudia, and all the brethren.

22 The Lord Jesus Christ be with thy spirit. Grace be with you. Amen.

---

4:5   In the New Testament, an evangelist is one who proclaims the gospel. The Lord also revealed that an evangelist is another name for a patriarch (see D&C 107:39-53).

*make full proof of thy ministry*—fulfill your calling

4:6-8   Paul sensed he would soon be killed, but he knew he had lived a faithful life and would be saved. How does Paul's example of faith and endurance help you?

4:8   "A crown of righteousness" is a way of describing the eternal blessings that come to those who love and serve God (see D&C 76:50-70).

4:10   *forsaken*—left

4:11   The Luke and Mark mentioned in this verse are the same men who wrote the Gospels of Luke and Mark. They were faithful servants of the Lord.

4:16-17   Even though many of his friends left him, Paul was always supported by the Lord. Even though people may fail us, the Lord will never leave us (see John 14:18; Luke 22:32; Hebrews 7:25).

4:18   When has the Lord protected, blessed, or comforted you?

# THE EPISTLE OF PAUL TO
# TITUS

*Titus was a faithful companion to Paul during his ministry. Paul called Titus to lead the Church on the island of Crete. Paul wrote this letter to encourage and counsel Titus in his calling.*

## CHAPTER 1

*God wants all his children to return to him one day. Look for how Paul counsels Titus to help God's children on Crete live the gospel.*

### ETERNAL LIFE WAS PROMISED TO THE FAITHFUL BEFORE THE WORLD BEGAN

1 PAUL, a servant of God, and an apostle of Jesus Christ, according to the faith of God's elect, and the acknowledging of the truth which is after godliness;

2 In hope of eternal life, which God, that cannot lie, promised before the world began;

3 But hath in due times manifested his word through preaching, which is committed unto me according to the commandment of God our Saviour;

4 To Titus, mine own son after the common faith: Grace, mercy, and peace, from God the Father and the Lord Jesus Christ our Saviour.

5 ¶ For this cause left I thee in Crete, that thou shouldest set in order the things that are wanting, and ordain elders in every city, as I had appointed thee:

### PAUL GIVES QUALIFICATIONS FOR THOSE WHO SERVE AS BISHOP

6 ¶ If any be blameless, the husband of one wife, having faithful children not accused of riot or unruly.

7 For a bishop must be blameless, as the steward of God; not selfwilled, not soon angry, not given to wine, no striker, not given to filthy lucre;

8 But a lover of hospitality, a lover of good men, sober, just, holy, temperate;

9 Holding fast the faithful word as he hath been taught, that he may be able by sound doctrine both to exhort and to convince the gainsayers.

### PAUL WARNS TITUS TO GUARD AGAINST FALSE TEACHERS

10 For there are many unruly and vain talkers and deceivers, specially they of the circumcision:

11 Whose mouths must be stopped, who subvert whole houses, teaching things which they ought not, for filthy lucre's sake.

---

1:1 ⚡ Paul was one of the Twelve Apostles in his day. They are "special witnesses of the name of Christ in all the world" (D&C 107:23).

1:2 ⚡ God's "work and . . . glory" are to provide a way for his children to obtain "immortality and eternal life" (Moses 1:39). This plan, sometimes called the plan of happiness, was given before we came to earth. It offers God's children hope for eternal life through the gospel and the atonement of Jesus Christ.

1:4-5 🔍 Titus was Paul's son "after the common faith," which means that he was likely converted by Paul. Paul also said that Timothy was "my own son in the faith" (1 Timothy 1:2).

1:6-9 📖 Titus was to "set in order" (verse 5), or organize, the Church on Crete. This included the calling of a bishop. Paul instructs Titus on what to look for in a man to serve as a bishop. These are excellent qualities for everyone to try to develop. What can you do to grow in these qualities?

1:7 📝 **no striker**—not violent
**filthy lucre**—making dishonest money

1:8 📝 **temperate**—self-controlled

1:9 📝 **the gainsayers**—those who deny the faith

1:10-11 🔍 "They of the circumcision" were Jewish Christians who believed it was necessary for Gentile converts to be circumcised to be saved (see Acts 15:1; see also Glossary, s.v. "Circumcision").

---

📝 = Word Help    🔍 = A Closer Look

⚡ = More Light    📖 = Ponder This

Words in pink are explained in the Glossary.

12 One of themselves, even a prophet of their own, said, The Cretians are alway liars, evil beasts, slow bellies.

13 This witness is true. Wherefore rebuke them sharply, that they may be sound in the faith;

- 14 Not giving heed to Jewish fables, and commandments of men, that turn from the truth.

15 Unto the pure all things are pure: but unto them that are defiled and unbelieving is nothing pure; but even their mind and conscience is defiled.

16 They profess that they know God; but in works they deny him, being abominable, and disobedient, and unto every good work reprobate.

# CHAPTER 2

*Paul speaks to many groups of people, teaching them to be righteous. Watch for teachings that apply to youth.*

## YOUNGER PEOPLE CAN LEARN FROM OLDER PEOPLE

1 ¶ BUT speak thou the things which become sound doctrine:

2 That the aged men be sober, grave, temperate, sound in faith, in charity, in patience.

3 The aged women likewise, that they be in behaviour as becometh holiness, not false accusers, not given to much wine, teachers of good things;

4 That they may teach the young women to be sober, to love their husbands, to love their children,

5 To be discreet, chaste, keepers at home, good, obedient to their own husbands, that the word of God be not blasphemed.

## WE CAN SHARE THE GOSPEL BY OUR GOOD EXAMPLE

6 Young men likewise exhort to be sober minded.

7 In all things shewing thyself a pattern of good works: in doctrine shewing uncorruptness, gravity, sincerity,

8 Sound speech, that cannot be condemned; that he that is of the contrary part may be ashamed, having no evil thing to say of you.

9 Exhort servants to be obedient unto their own masters, and to please them well in all things; not answering again;

10 Not purloining, but shewing all good fidelity; that they may adorn the doctrine of God our Saviour in all things.

## PREPARE FOR CHRIST'S COMING BY LIVING FAITHFULLY

11 ¶ For the grace of God that bringeth salvation hath appeared to all men,

12 Teaching us that, denying ungodliness and worldly lusts, we should live soberly, righteously, and godly, in this present world;

13 Looking for that blessed hope, and the glorious appearing of the great God and our Saviour Jesus Christ;

---

1:12 **slow bellies**—lazy people who eat too much

1:13-14 False teachers used fables, or untrue stories, to teach their doctrine. Paul counseled Titus to "rebuke them sharply" so that they might leave their errors and be firm in the faith. The Lord revealed that we should rebuke or correct others only "when moved upon by the Holy Ghost" (D&C 121:43).

1:16 **abominable**—very wicked
**reprobate**—unfit, worthless

2:1 **sound doctrine**—correct teachings

2:2 **sober, grave, temperate**—calm, reverent, self-controlled

2:3-5 Paul wanted older women to teach younger women how to be better wives and mothers. What can you learn from people who are older than you?

2:4-5 President Spencer W. Kimball counseled women, "You are to become a career woman in the greatest career on earth—that of homemaker, wife, and mother" (*Faith Precedes the Miracle*, p. 128).

2:6-8 Young men should use self-control and be honest, respectful, and sincere.

2:8 **Sound speech**—Good and wholesome words

2:9-10 By living as good Christians, slaves could set a positive example for their masters (see 1 Timothy 6:1-2).

2:10 **purloining**—stealing

14 Who gave himself for us, that he might redeem us from all iniquity, and purify unto himself a peculiar people, zealous of good works.

15 ¶ These things speak, and exhort, and rebuke with all authority. Let no man despise thee.

## CHAPTER 3

*After baptism the Lord expects us to live righteously. Look for what the Lord requires of us as we allow his grace to be effective in our lives.*

### WE ARE TO BE GOOD, BE OBEDIENT, AND AVOID HATRED

1 ¶ PUT them in mind to be subject to principalities and powers, to obey magistrates, to be ready to every good work,

2 To speak evil of no man, to be no brawlers, but gentle, shewing all meekness unto all men.

3 For we ourselves also were sometimes foolish, disobedient, deceived, serving divers lusts and pleasures, living in malice and envy, hateful, and hating one another.

4 But after that the kindness and love of God our Saviour toward man appeared,

### JESUS SAVES US BECAUSE OF HIS MERCY

5 Not by works of righteousness which we have done, but according to his mercy he saved us, by the washing of regeneration, and renewing of the Holy Ghost;

6 Which he shed on us abundantly through Jesus Christ our Saviour;

7 That being justified by his grace, we should be made heirs according to the hope of eternal life.

8 This is a faithful saying, and these things I will that thou affirm constantly, that they which have believed in God might be careful to maintain good works. These things are good and profitable unto men.

9 ¶ But avoid foolish questions, and genealogies, and contentions, and strivings about the law; for they are unprofitable and vain.

10 A man that is an heretick after the first and second admonition reject;

11 Knowing that he that is such is subverted, and sinneth, being condemned of himself.

12 When I shall send Artemas unto thee, or Tychicus, be diligent to come unto me to Nicopolis: for I have determined there to winter.

13 Bring Zenas the lawyer and Apollos on their journey diligently, that nothing be wanting unto them.

14 And let ours also learn to maintain good works for necessary uses, that they be not unfruitful.

15 All that are with me salute thee. Greet them that love us in the faith. Grace be with you all. Amen.

---

2:14 *redeem*—purchase or ransom
*zealous of*—eager to do good

In this verse *peculiar* means "purchased, preserved, treasured" (see LDS Edition of the Bible, 1 Peter 2:9, footnote f; LDS Bible Dictionary, s.v. "Peculiar," p. 748). Those Saints who are redeemed through Jesus' atonement become his treasure (see Malachi 3:16-18).

We are of value because Jesus paid for our sins with his blood (see 1 Corinthians 6:19-20). What can you do to show your thanks to the Savior for all he has done for you?

3:1 The Lord wants us to keep the laws of the land and be responsible citizens (see Articles of Faith 1:12).

3:3 *divers*—different
*lusts*—evil desires
*malice and envy*—hatred of others because of what they have or who they are

3:5 We are saved by Christ's grace, "after all we can do" (2 Nephi 25:23). The "washing of regeneration, and renewing of the Holy Ghost" is "baptism by immersion" and "the gift of the Holy Ghost" (Articles of Faith 1:4).

What are some of the acts of righteousness we must do to receive the blessings of Jesus Christ?

3:7 A person who is justified has had his sins forgiven. Our sins are forgiven when we exercise faith in the Savior's atonement, repent of our sins, and obey the commandments and ordinances of the gospel (see James 2:14-26).

3:8 *affirm*—declare, proclaim

3:9 *strivings*—arguments
*vain*—useless

3:10 *an heretick*—a follower of false doctrines or teachings

3:11 *subverted*—changed and lives against the commandments

3:14 All through this letter Paul counsels Saints on how important it is to "maintain good works" (see 2:7, 14; 3:1, 8, 14). Why do you think living a good life is so important to Paul? How can it help others?

# THE EPISTLE OF PAUL TO
# PHILEMON

*This letter was written by Paul to Philemon asking him to treat a runaway slave like a brother in the gospel of Jesus Christ. Philemon was a member of the Church in Colosse. Paul commended him for his faith, love, hospitality, and forgiving spirit.*

## CHAPTER 1

*Paul wanted Philemon to be kind to a runaway slave who had served Paul and joined the Church. Look for what Paul writes to Philemon that might help you better care for others.*

### PAUL PRAISES PHILEMON

1 PAUL, a prisoner of Jesus Christ, and Timothy our brother, unto Philemon our dearly beloved, and fellowlabourer,

2 And to our beloved Apphia, and Archippus our fellowsoldier, and to the church in thy house:

3 Grace to you, and peace, from God our Father and the Lord Jesus Christ.

4 I thank my God, making mention of thee always in my prayers,

5 Hearing of thy love and faith, which thou hast toward the Lord Jesus, and toward all saints;

6 That the communication of thy faith may become effectual by the acknowledging of every good thing which is in you in Christ Jesus.

7 For we have great joy and consolation in thy love, because the bowels of the saints are refreshed by thee, brother.

### PAUL ASKS PHILEMON TO BE KIND TO THE RUNAWAY SLAVE

8 ¶ Wherefore, though I might be much bold in Christ to enjoin thee that which is convenient,

9 Yet for love's sake I rather beseech thee, being such an one as Paul the aged, and now also a prisoner of Jesus Christ.

10 I beseech thee for my son Onesimus, whom I have begotten in my bonds:

11 Which in time past was to thee unprofitable, but now profitable to thee and to me:

12 Whom I have sent again: thou therefore receive him, that is, mine own bowels:

13 Whom I would have retained with me, that in thy stead he might have ministered unto me in the bonds of the gospel:

14 But without thy mind would I do nothing; that thy benefit should not be as it were of necessity, but willingly.

15 For perhaps he therefore departed for a season, that thou shouldest receive him for ever;

---

1:6  *communication*—sharing
*effectual*—active, alive

1:7  *consolation*—comfort
*bowels*—inner feelings

1:8  *enjoin*—direct
*convenient*—possible or fitting for you

1:8-10  Onesimus was a runaway slave who belonged to Philemon. In those days slavery was legal. Onesimus had been converted to the gospel of Jesus Christ and was going back to his master to try to make up for his running away. (See LDS Bible Dictionary, s.v. "Onesimus," p. 740.)

1:9  *beseech*—ask, beg

1:10-25  Though Onesimus was a slave, he was as important to God as a freeman. Divine revelation has repeatedly affirmed that God is "no respecter of persons" (Acts 10:34; D&C 38:16) and that "all are alike unto [him]" (2 Nephi 26:33).

1:13  *retained*—kept

1:14  *benefit*—kindness

---

| | | | |
|---|---|---|---|
| = Word Help | | = A Closer Look | |
| = More Light | | = Ponder This | |

Words in pink are explained in the Glossary.

16 Not now as a servant, but above a servant, a brother beloved, specially to me, but how much more unto thee, both in the flesh, and in the Lord?

17 If thou count me therefore a partner, receive him as myself.

18 If he hath wronged thee, or oweth thee ought, put that on mine account;

19 I Paul have written it with mine own hand, I will repay it: albeit I do not say to thee how thou owest unto me even thine own self besides.

20 Yea, brother, let me have joy of thee in the Lord: refresh my bowels in the Lord.

21 Having confidence in thy obedience I wrote unto thee, knowing that thou wilt also do more than I say.

22 But withal prepare me also a lodging: for I trust that through your prayers I shall be given unto you.

23 There salute thee Epaphras, my fellowprisoner in Christ Jesus;

24 Marcus, Aristarchus, Demas, Lucas, my fellow-labourers.

25 The grace of our Lord Jesus Christ be with your spirit. Amen.

---

1:16   Even though Onesimus was a slave, Paul cared about him and treated him as a brother. Whom do you know that could benefit from a little extra kindness and love from you?

1:18   *ought*—anything

1:19   *albeit*—although

# THE EPISTLE OF PAUL THE APOSTLE TO THE
# HEBREWS

*According to the Prophet Joseph Smith, this epistle was written "by Paul . . . to the Hebrew brethren" (THE TEACHINGS OF JOSEPH SMITH, p. 2). Many Hebrews, or Jews, who had joined the Church still felt it was necessary to observe the law of Moses. Paul wrote to convince them that Jesus Christ had fulfilled that law and that they no longer needed to follow it. They were to now live the law of the gospel.*

## CHAPTER 1

*Paul explains that Jesus Christ is greater than the law of Moses. Look for the evidence Paul gives to prove this doctrine.*

### CHRIST IS IN THE IMAGE OF HEAVENLY FATHER

1 GOD, who at sundry times and in divers manners spake in time past unto the fathers by the prophets,

2 Hath in these last days spoken unto us by his Son, whom he hath appointed heir of all things, by whom also he made the worlds;

3 Who being the brightness of his glory, and the express image of his person, and upholding all things by the word of his power, when he had by himself purged our sins, sat down on the right hand of the Majesty on high;

### CHRIST IS ABOVE THE ANGELS

4 ¶ Being made so much better than the angels, as he hath by inheritance obtained a more excellent name than they.

5 For unto which of the angels said he at any time, Thou art my Son, this day have I begotten thee? And again, I will be to him a Father, and he shall be to me a Son?

6 And again, when he bringeth in the firstbegotten into the world, he saith, And let all the angels of God worship him.

7 And of the angels he saith, Who maketh his angels spirits, and his ministers a flame of fire.

8 But unto the Son he saith, Thy throne, O God, is for ever and ever: a sceptre of righteousness is the sceptre of thy kingdom.

9 Thou hast loved righteousness, and hated iniquity; therefore God, even thy God, hath anointed thee with the oil of gladness above thy fellows.

10 And, Thou, Lord, in the beginning hast laid the foundation of the earth; and the heavens are the works of thine hands:

11 They shall perish; but thou remainest; and they all shall wax old as doth a garment;

12 And as a vesture shalt thou fold them up, and they shall be changed: but thou art the same, and thy years shall not fail.

---

1:1 **sundry times and in divers manners**—different times and in various ways

1:2 **heir**—one who receives all the blessings of his parents

Heavenly Father created worlds without number by Jesus Christ (see Moses 1:33).

1:3 **purged**—cleansed

Jesus Christ paid the price so that we can become clean from our sins. He did this work alone. How does knowing that help you have more love and gratitude for him?

1:5 **begotten thee**—fathered you

1:6 Christ was the firstborn spirit of Heavenly Father (see Colossians 1:15).

1:11 **wax old**—become worn out

A sceptre is a sign of a king's power (see Hebrews 1:8).

1:12 **vesture**—piece of clothing

13 But to which of the angels said he at any time, Sit on my right hand, until I make thine enemies thy footstool?

14 Are they not all ministering spirits, sent forth to minister for them who shall be heirs of salvation?

# CHAPTER 2

*Perfection is the goal of every true follower of Jesus Christ. We seek excellence in all we say and do. Watch for how Paul teaches us to progress towards perfection.*

## JESUS CAME TO SUFFER DEATH AND SAVE MEN

1 ¶ THEREFORE we ought to give the more earnest heed to the things which we have heard, lest at any time we should let them slip.

2 For if the word spoken by angels was stedfast, and every transgression and disobedience received a just recompence of reward;

3 How shall we escape, if we neglect so great salvation; which at the first began to be spoken by the Lord, and was confirmed unto us by them that heard him;

4 God also bearing them witness, both with signs and wonders, and with divers miracles, and gifts of the Holy Ghost, according to his own will?

5 ¶ For unto the angels hath he not put in subjection the world to come, whereof we speak.

## MAN IS A LITTLE LOWER THAN THE ANGELS

6 But one in a certain place testified, saying, What is man, that thou art mindful of him? or the son of man, that thou visitest him?

7 Thou madest him a little lower than the angels; thou crownedst him with glory and honour, and didst set him over the works of thy hands:

8 Thou hast put all things in subjection under his feet. For in that he put all in subjection under him, he left nothing that is not put under him. But now we see not yet all things put under him.

9 But we see Jesus, who was made a little lower than the angels for the suffering of death, crowned with glory and honour; that he by the grace of God should taste death for every man.

## JESUS IS THE CAPTAIN OF OUR SALVATION

10 ¶ For it became him, for whom are all things, and by whom are all things, in bringing many sons unto glory, to make the captain of their salvation perfect through sufferings.

11 For both he that sanctifieth and they who are sanctified are all of one: for which cause he is not ashamed to call them brethren,

12 Saying, I will declare thy name unto my brethren, in the midst of the church will I sing praise unto thee.

13 And again, I will put my trust in him. And again, Behold I and the children which God hath given me.

14 ¶ Forasmuch then as the children are partakers of flesh and blood, he also himself likewise took part of the same; that through death he might destroy him that had the power of death, that is, the devil;

15 And deliver them who through fear of death were all their lifetime subject to bondage.

16 For verily he took not on him the nature of angels; but he took on him the seed of Abraham.

17 Wherefore in all things it behoved him to be made like unto his brethren, that he might be a merciful and faithful high priest in things pertaining to God, to make reconciliation for the sins of the people.

---

2:1 To give "earnest heed" means to show serious interest—the kind of interest that causes us to live gospel principles better. How much "earnest heed" have you given the scriptures? How often do you read and study them?

2:2 *recompence*—payment

2:4 *divers*—various

2:5 *subjection*—a position to be ruled over

2:6-9 Paul quotes from Psalm 8:4-6 about the importance of each person. A clearer translation of verse 5 of this psalm teaches that the word *gods* could be substituted for the word *angels*. So, in truth, we are a little lower than the gods. We are the children of God and can become like him.

2:10 One reason for Christ's suffering was that through it "learned he obedience" (see Hebrews 5:8-9).

2:12-13 Why do you think Paul praised and trusted in the Lord? What words describe your feelings toward the Lord?

2:14-15 The plan of salvation teaches that everyone will die sometime. Jesus chose to die so that everyone could overcome death and be resurrected. The Book of Mormon teaches that no one could live with Heavenly Father again without the "merits, and mercy, and grace" of Jesus Christ (2 Nephi 2:8).

2:17 *make reconciliation*—bring about forgiveness

18 For in that he himself hath suffered being tempted, he is able to succour them that are tempted.

# CHAPTER 3

*Paul wants members of the Church to avoid the sins of the children of Israel in the days of Moses. Look for what we can do to avoid the errors of the ancient children of Israel.*

## JESUS CHRIST IS GREATER THAN ALL OF GOD'S CHILDREN

1 ¶ WHEREFORE, holy brethren, partakers of the heavenly calling, consider the Apostle and High Priest of our profession, Christ Jesus;

2 Who was faithful to him that appointed him, as also Moses was faithful in all his house.

3 For this man was counted worthy of more glory than Moses, inasmuch as he who hath builded the house hath more honour than the house.

4 For every house is builded by some man; but he that built all things is God.

5 And Moses verily was faithful in all his house, as a servant, for a testimony of those things which were to be spoken after;

6 But Christ as a son over his own house; whose house are we, if we hold fast the confidence and the rejoicing of the hope firm unto the end.

## PAUL URGES THE SAINTS NOT TO BE DISOBEDIENT LIKE THE ANCIENT ISRAELITES

7 ¶ Wherefore (as the Holy Ghost saith, To day if ye will hear his voice,

8 Harden not your hearts, as in the provocation, in the day of temptation in the wilderness:

9 When your fathers tempted me, proved me, and saw my works forty years.

10 Wherefore I was grieved with that generation, and said, They do alway err in their heart; and they have not known my ways.

11 So I sware in my wrath, They shall not enter into my rest.)

12 Take heed, brethren, lest there be in any of you an evil heart of unbelief, in departing from the living God.

13 But exhort one another daily, while it is called To day; lest any of you be hardened through the deceitfulness of sin.

14 For we are made partakers of Christ, if we hold the beginning of our confidence stedfast unto the end;

15 While it is said, To day if ye will hear his voice, harden not your hearts, as in the provocation.

16 For some, when they had heard, did provoke: howbeit not all that came out of Egypt by Moses.

17 But with whom was he grieved forty years? was it not with them that had sinned, whose carcases fell in the wilderness?

18 And to whom sware he that they should not enter into his rest, but to them that believed not?

19 So we see that they could not enter in because of unbelief.

---

2:18  succour—aid or care for

Christ can help us with our temptations because he faced the same temptations. He never gave into temptation or sinned (see Hebrews 4:15). Christ also suffered for our pains, afflictions, and sicknesses (see Alma 7:11-12).

3:1  profession—faith

3:3  this man—Jesus

3:5-6  Paul explains that Moses was God's faithful servant but that Jesus Christ was God's faithful Son. We belong to Christ (we are his house) if we remain faithful to the end.

3:7-11  The Israelites in Moses' day made God angry when, having seen God's miracles in Egypt and in the wilderness, they still disobeyed him. This is called "the provocation." As punishment they could not go into the promised land. (See

Numbers 14:22-23.) Paul warns the Saints not to do the same things the Israelites did.

3:13  exhort—encourage
deceitfulness—lying, trickery

How can sin cause members of the Church to forget the truth? (See Alma 12:9-11.)

3:14  confidence—testimony

3:15-19  Paul warns the Saints of his day not to disobey God as the Israelites of Moses' day did; even after seeing great miracles the children of Israel failed to obey. What miracles has Heavenly Father done in our day? What "promised land" will we lose if we forget those blessings and reject him?

3:16  provoke—cause God to be angry

3:17  carcases—bodies

3:18  enter into his rest—go into their promised land

# CHAPTER 4

*Jesus set a perfect example for us to follow. Watch for what we must do if we are to enter into God's kingdom.*

## THE GOSPEL WAS OFFERED TO ANCIENT ISRAEL

1 ¶ LET us therefore fear, lest, a promise being left us of entering into his rest, any of you should seem to come short of it.

2 For unto us was the gospel preached, as well as unto them: but the word preached did not profit them, not being mixed with faith in them that heard it.

3 For we which have believed do enter into rest, as he said, As I have sworn in my wrath, if they shall enter into my rest: although the works were finished from the foundation of the world.

4 For he spake in a certain place of the seventh day on this wise, And God did rest the seventh day from all his works.

5 And in this place again, If they shall enter into my rest.

6 Seeing therefore it remaineth that some must enter therein, and they to whom it was first preached entered not in because of unbelief:

7 Again, he limiteth a certain day, saying in David, To day, after so long a time; as it is said, To day if ye will hear his voice, harden not your hearts.

8 For if Jesus had given them rest, then would he not afterward have spoken of another day.

9 There remaineth therefore a rest to the people of God.

10 For he that is entered into his rest, he also hath ceased from his own works, as God did from his.

## WE CAN ENTER INTO THE LORD'S REST

11 ¶ Let us labour therefore to enter into that rest, lest any man fall after the same example of unbelief.

12 For the word of God is quick, and powerful, and sharper than any two-edged sword, piercing even to the dividing asunder of soul and spirit, and of the joints and marrow, and is a discerner of the thoughts and intents of the heart.

13 Neither is there any creature that is not manifest in his sight: but all things are naked and opened unto the eyes of him with whom we have to do.

## JESUS WAS TEMPTED IN ALL WAYS, BUT HE NEVER SINNED

14 Seeing then that we have a great high priest, that is passed into the heavens, Jesus the Son of God, let us hold fast our profession.

15 For we have not an high priest which cannot be touched with the feeling of our infirmities; but was in all points tempted like as we are, yet without sin.

16 Let us therefore come boldly unto the throne of grace, that we may obtain mercy, and find grace to help in time of need.

---

4:1   The Lord's "rest" is "the fulness of his glory" (D&C 84:24). The children of Israel in Moses' day could have seen God, but they hardened their hearts (became full of pride) and became frightened (see Exodus 19:10-11, 14-16; D&C 84:19-25).

4:3, 5   The Joseph Smith Translation makes it clear that if we who believe harden our hearts, we will not enter into the Lord's rest. But if we are humble we will return to Heavenly Father. (See JST, Hebrews 4:3, 5.)

4:4   This verse refers to the time when the Lord rested on the Sabbath day after he finished creating the earth (see Genesis 2:1-3).

4:6   *they to whom it was first preached*—ancient Israel, who were taught the gospel

4:7   *limiteth*—appoints

4:11   We ought to "labour," or work hard, to receive eternal life instead of falling short of that blessing

as did ancient Israel. What are you doing each day to get this great blessing?

4:12-13   All things being "naked and opened" to his eyes means God is able to know our thoughts and the desires of our hearts (see D&C 6:16; 2 Nephi 9:20).

4:13   How could remembering that God knows all things about your thoughts and actions change some of the things you do?

4:14   *hold fast our profession*—stay true to the gospel of Jesus Christ

4:15   How can knowing that Jesus was tempted in every way and did not sin help you not to sin?

4:15-16   Jesus was tempted and suffered in all the ways we suffer so that he could know better how to help us when we are tempted and suffer (see Alma 7:11-13).

# CHAPTER 5

*Those who are called by God to hold his priesthood must follow the example of Christ. Note what Jesus did to become perfect.*

## THOSE CALLED TO HOLD THE PRIESTHOOD MUST BE CALLED BY GOD

1 ¶ FOR every high priest taken from among men is ordained for men in things pertaining to God, that he may offer both gifts and sacrifices for sins:

2 Who can have compassion on the ignorant, and on them that are out of the way; for that he himself also is compassed with infirmity.

3 And by reason hereof he ought, as for the people, so also for himself, to offer for sins.

4 And no man taketh this honour unto himself, but he that is called of God, as was Aaron.

5 So also Christ glorified not himself to be made an high priest; but he that said unto him, Thou art my Son, to day have I begotten thee.

6 As he saith also in another place, Thou art a priest for ever after the order of Melchisedec.

## JESUS CHRIST LEARNED OBEDIENCE AND GREW IN PERFECTION

7 Who in the days of his flesh, when he had offered up prayers and supplications with strong crying and tears unto him that was able to save him from death, and was heard in that he feared;

8 Though he were a Son, yet learned he obedience by the things which he suffered;

9 And being made perfect, he became the author of eternal salvation unto all them that obey him;

10 ¶ Called of God an high priest after the order of Melchisedec.

## OBEYING THE GOSPEL HELPS US LEARN THE GOSPEL

11 Of whom we have many things to say, and hard to be uttered, seeing ye are dull of hearing.

12 For when for the time ye ought to be teachers, ye have need that one teach you again which be the first principles of the oracles of God; and are become such as have need of milk, and not of strong meat.

13 For every one that useth milk is unskilful in the word of righteousness: for he is a babe.

14 But strong meat belongeth to them that are of full age, even those who by reason of use have their senses exercised to discern both good and evil.

# CHAPTER 6

*Paul speaks of two very different groups of people. Look for the happiness promised to those who do their best to stay faithful.*

## SAINTS ARE TO LIVE THE DOCTRINES OF PERFECTION

1 ¶ THEREFORE leaving the principles of the

---

5:1    **ordained**—given the priesthood by the laying on of hands by one who has authority

5:1-3   Under the law of Moses, priests offered sacrifices as a symbol for when "Christ sacrificed himself for the sins of the people" (Bruce R. McConkie, *Doctrinal New Testament Commentary* 3:154).

5:4    Aaron was called by God to serve as a priest (see Exodus 28:1-4). He was anointed by the prophet Moses to this office (see Leviticus 8:12).

5:5-6   Jesus also held the Melchizedek Priesthood. In fact, the name of this higher priesthood is actually "the Holy Priesthood, after the Order of the Son of God." It is called "the Melchizedek Priesthood" out of reverence for the name of God. (See D&C 107:3-4.)

5:8    Though he was God's Son, Jesus needed to experience the pains of earth life. How does knowing that Jesus suffered the same things we suffer make it easier to obey his teachings?

5:8-9   Though Jesus never sinned, "he received not of the fulness [of perfection] at the first, but received grace for grace . . . until he received a fulness" (D&C 93:12-13).

5:11    **hard to be uttered**—difficult to be explained **dull of hearing**—slow to listen, or unwilling to learn

5:12-14  Milk represents the simple teachings of the "oracles," or word, of God. Meat represents more difficult teachings. Those who are young in the faith should begin with the simple teachings before trying to understand the more difficult ones. (See 1 Corinthians 3:2-3.)

5:14    How are you preparing now to be able to understand and teach others the "meat" of the gospel when you are of "full age"?

6:1    The Joseph Smith Translation changes the first words of this verse to "not leaving the principles."

6:1-2   Which article of faith do these verses remind you of?

doctrine of Christ, let us go on unto perfection; not laying again the foundation of repentance from dead works, and of faith toward God,

2 Of the doctrine of baptisms, and of laying on of hands, and of resurrection of the dead, and of eternal judgment.

3 And this will we do, if God permit.

## Sons of Perdition Would Crucify Jesus Again If They Could

4 For it is impossible for those who were once enlightened, and have tasted of the heavenly gift, and were made partakers of the Holy Ghost,

5 And have tasted the good word of God, and the powers of the world to come,

6 If they shall fall away, to renew them again unto repentance; seeing they crucify to themselves the Son of God afresh, and put him to an open shame.

7 For the earth which drinketh in the rain that cometh oft upon it, and bringeth forth herbs meet for them by whom it is dressed, receiveth blessing from God:

8 But that which beareth thorns and briers is rejected, and is nigh unto cursing; whose end is to be burned.

## God Promises the Faithful Saints Eternal Life

9 ¶ But, beloved, we are persuaded better things of you, and things that accompany salvation, though we thus speak.

10 For God is not unrighteous to forget your work and labour of love, which ye have shewed toward his name, in that ye have ministered to the saints, and do minister.

11 And we desire that every one of you do shew the same diligence to the full assurance of hope unto the end:

12 That ye be not slothful, but followers of them who through faith and patience inherit the promises.

13 For when God made promise to Abraham, because he could swear by no greater, he sware by himself,

14 Saying, Surely blessing I will bless thee, and multiplying I will multiply thee.

15 And so, after he had patiently endured, he obtained the promise.

16 For men verily swear by the greater: and an oath for confirmation is to them an end of all strife.

17 Wherein God, willing more abundantly to shew unto the heirs of promise the immutability of his counsel, confirmed it by an oath:

18 That by two immutable things, in which it was impossible for God to lie, we might have a strong consolation, who have fled for refuge to lay hold upon the hope set before us:

19 Which hope we have as an anchor of the soul, both sure and stedfast, and which entereth into that within the veil;

20 Whither the forerunner is for us entered, even Jesus, made an high priest for ever after the order of Melchisedec.

---

6:4-6　Those who have certain sacred experiences and then turn against Jesus, his gospel, and his servants may become sons of perdition. This sin cannot be forgiven. (See Joseph Fielding Smith, *Doctrines of Salvation* 1:47-49.)

6:7　**meet**—proper, useful
**dressed**—planted and cared for

6:10　**shewed**—This word is pronounced the same way as the word *showed* and has the same meaning; *shewed* is simply an old spelling of *showed*.

Because God is righteous "he will not forget your work and labor of love" for him (JST, Hebrews 6:10).

6:11　**shew**—This word is pronounced the same way as the word *show* and has the same meaning; *shew* is simply an old spelling of *show*.

6:13　**swear**—make a serious promise

6:13-15　Abraham was so faithful that God promised him eternal life (see Genesis 22:15-18; D&C 132:29-30).

6:17　**heirs of promise**—children who receive the blessings of their fathers
**immutability**—unchanging nature

6:18　Those who keep the commandments have comfort in the same promise Abraham received—that they will have eternal life (see 2 Nephi 31:20; D&C 14:7).

6:20　As the forerunner (one who goes first), Jesus has entered into heaven to prepare the way for those who obey his laws. How thankful will you feel when you see him again?

# CHAPTER 7

*Paul explains that in addition to the Aaronic Priesthood there is a need for the Melchizedek Priesthood. Watch for the blessings of having the Melchizedek Priesthood.*

## MELCHIZEDEK, THE GREAT HIGH PRIEST, HELD GREATER PRIESTHOOD THAN ABRAHAM

1 ¶ FOR this Melchisedec, king of Salem, priest of the most high God, who met Abraham returning from the slaughter of the kings, and blessed him;

2 To whom also Abraham gave a tenth part of all; first being by interpretation King of righteousness, and after that also King of Salem, which is, King of peace;

3 Without father, without mother, without descent, having neither beginning of days, nor end of life; but made like unto the Son of God; abideth a priest continually.

4 Now consider how great this man was, unto whom even the patriarch Abraham gave the tenth of the spoils.

5 And verily they that are of the sons of Levi, who receive the office of the priesthood, have a commandment to take tithes of the people according to the law, that is, of their brethren, though they come out of the loins of Abraham:

6 But he whose descent is not counted from them received tithes of Abraham, and blessed him that had the promises.

7 And without all contradiction the less is blessed of the better.

8 And here men that die receive tithes; but there he receiveth them, of whom it is witnessed that he liveth.

9 And as I may so say, Levi also, who receiveth tithes, payed tithes in Abraham.

10 For he was yet in the loins of his father, when Melchisedec met him.

## ONLY THE MELCHIZEDEK PRIESTHOOD, THROUGH JESUS CHRIST, HAS POWER TO SAVE US

11 ¶ If therefore perfection were by the Levitical priesthood, (for under it the people received the law,) what further need was there that another priest should rise after the order of Melchisedec, and not be called after the order of Aaron?

12 For the priesthood being changed, there is made of necessity a change also of the law.

13 For he of whom these things are spoken pertaineth to another tribe, of which no man gave attendance at the altar.

14 For it is evident that our Lord sprang out of Juda; of which tribe Moses spake nothing concerning priesthood.

15 And it is yet far more evident: for that after the similitude of Melchisedec there ariseth another priest,

16 Who is made, not after the law of a carnal commandment, but after the power of an endless life.

17 For he testifieth, Thou art a priest for ever after the order of Melchisedec.

---

7:1-4   Melchizedek was such a great high priest that the Lord named the priesthood after him (see D&C 107:2-4).

7:2   Years later the city of Salem was called Jerusalem.

7:2-10   Paul used the fact that Abraham was blessed by Melchizedek and paid tithing to him to show that the priesthood held by Melchizedek is greater than the Aaronic Priesthood.

7:3   The Joseph Smith Translation explains that it is the Melchizedek Priesthood, not the man Melchizedek, that is without father or mother (see JST, Hebrews 7:3).

7:4   **spoils**—wealth taken in battle

7:5   **they come out of the loins of Abraham**—they are descendants (children, grandchildren, etc.) of Abraham

7:7   **without all contradiction**—without any doubt

7:11   The law of Moses operated under the Aaronic Priesthood. The purpose of this law was to prepare the people for a higher law (see 2 Nephi 25:24-27). The Melchizedek Priesthood is necessary to administer in the higher ordinances of salvation (see D&C 107:18-19).

7:12   Just as the law of Moses was "changed" to the gospel of Christ, the Aaronic Priesthood had to give way to the Melchizedek Priesthood.

7:13   **pertaineth to**—has to do with

7:15   Paul says it is "evident," or understood, that after Melchizedek another priest would come who has the power to give us eternal life. Whom do you think this sounds like? (See John 17:3.)

7:15   **similitude**—likeness

7:16   **carnal**—physical

18 For there is verily a disannulling of the commandment going before for the weakness and unprofitableness thereof.

19 For the law made nothing perfect, but the bringing in of a better hope did; by the which we draw nigh unto God.

20 And inasmuch as not without an oath he was made priest:

## SALVATION COMES THROUGH THE INTERCESSION OF JESUS CHRIST

21 (For those priests were made without an oath; but this with an oath by him that said unto him, The Lord sware and will not repent, Thou art a priest for ever after the order of Melchisedec:)

22 By so much was Jesus made a surety of a better testament.

23 And they truly were many priests, because they were not suffered to continue by reason of death:

24 But this man, because he continueth ever, hath an unchangeable priesthood.

25 Wherefore he is able also to save them to the uttermost that come unto God by him, seeing he ever liveth to make intercession for them.

26 For such an high priest became us, who is holy, harmless, undefiled, separate from sinners, and made higher than the heavens;

27 Who needeth not daily, as those high priests, to offer up sacrifice, first for his own sins, and then for the people's: for this he did once, when he offered up himself.

28 For the law maketh men high priests which have infirmity; but the word of the oath, which was since the law, maketh the Son, who is consecrated for evermore.

## CHAPTER 8

*Paul explains the blessings of the Savior's sacrifice and the gospel of Jesus Christ. Look for what the Savior has done for all people.*

## JESUS CHRIST GAVE HIMSELF AS A SACRIFICE FOR SIN

1 ¶ NOW of the things which we have spoken this is the sum: We have such an high priest, who is set on the right hand of the throne of the Majesty in the heavens;

2 A minister of the sanctuary, and of the true tabernacle, which the Lord pitched, and not man.

3 For every high priest is ordained to offer gifts and sacrifices: wherefore it is of necessity that this man have somewhat also to offer.

4 For if he were on earth, he should not be a priest, seeing that there are priests that offer gifts according to the law:

5 Who serve unto the example and shadow of heavenly things, as Moses was admonished of God when he was about to make the tabernacle: for, See, saith he, that thou make all things according to the pattern shewed to thee in the mount.

---

7:18   The old law of Moses and the Aaronic order were fulfilled and replaced by the gospel of Christ and the Melchizedek Priesthood (see 2 Nephi 25:24-27).

7:19   One purpose of the law of Moses was to point the people to Christ, who is the "better hope" of bringing us back into God's presence (see JST, Hebrews 7:19).

7:20   Part of the responsibilities of the Melchizedek Priesthood include the "oath" and covenant of the priesthood (see D&C 84:33-39).

7:21   **sware and will not repent**—made promises he will not break

7:22   **testament**—covenant or promise between God and man

7:25   **make intercession for them**—plead with God on their behalf

7:27   Jesus is the Lamb of God, and he was the last sacrifice to end all sacrifices (see Alma 34:10).

7:28   **consecrated**—chosen and prepared for a special purpose

8:1   **sum**—whole meaning

  Under the law of Moses, the high priest of the Aaronic Priesthood went into the most sacred part of the tabernacle or temple once each year to offer sacrifice for the people (see Exodus 30:10). Under the gospel of Jesus Christ, the Savior, as a high priest in the Melchizedek Priesthood, offered himself once as a sacrifice for the sins of all people.

8:2   **pitched**—put up

8:4   The Joseph Smith Translation explains that Jesus Christ (our High Priest) offered "his own life" as a sacrifice for the sins of all people (JST, Hebrews 8:4).

8:5   **admonished**—warned

### THE NEW COVENANT (THE GOSPEL OF JESUS CHRIST) IS BETTER THAN THE OLD COVENANT (THE LAW OF MOSES)

6 ¶ But now hath he obtained a more excellent ministry, by how much also he is the mediator of a better covenant, which was established upon better promises.

7 For if that first covenant had been faultless, then should no place have been sought for the second.

8 For finding fault with them, he saith, Behold, the days come, saith the Lord, when I will make a new covenant with the house of Israel and with the house of Judah:

9 Not according to the covenant that I made with their fathers in the day when I took them by the hand to lead them out of the land of Egypt; because they continued not in my covenant, and I regarded them not, saith the Lord.

10 For this is the covenant that I will make with the house of Israel after those days, saith the Lord; I will put my laws into their mind, and write them in their hearts: and I will be to them a God, and they shall be to me a people:

11 And they shall not teach every man his neighbour, and every man his brother, saying, Know the Lord: for all shall know me, from the least to the greatest.

12 For I will be merciful to their unrighteousness, and their sins and their iniquities will I remember no more.

13 In that he saith, A new covenant, he hath made the first old. Now that which decayeth and waxeth old is ready to vanish away.

## CHAPTER 9

*The high priest represented all of Israel during his service in the tabernacle. He was also a symbol of Jesus Christ, who goes before Heavenly Father for all of us. Notice the ways the high priest is like Jesus.*

### THE TABERNACLE IN MOSES' DAY WAS A REMINDER OF THE COMING OF CHRIST

1 ¶ THEN verily the first covenant had also ordinances of divine service, and a worldly sanctuary.

2 For there was a tabernacle made; the first, wherein was the candlestick, and the table, and the shewbread; which is called the sanctuary.

3 And after the second veil, the tabernacle which is called the Holiest of all;

---

8:6-8    The "first covenant" was the law revealed to Moses. Jesus Christ was the mediator of, or the one who revealed, the new and better covenant of the gospel. (See D&C 133:57; LDS Bible Dictionary, s.v. "Law of Moses," pp. 722-23.)

8:7    **faultless**—without weakness

8:7-8    The "second" covenant, or "new covenant," is the gospel of Jesus Christ, which Jesus brought back when he lived on earth (see D&C 133:57).

8:9    **regarded**—admired

8:10    Paul said that the gospel of Jesus Christ should be found in our hearts and in our minds. How can you get the gospel of Jesus Christ in your heart?

8:13    **decayeth**—is rotting
**vanish away**—disappear

9:1    **first covenant**—law of Moses

9:2    Like the temple, the tabernacle was a dwelling place for God. However, the tabernacle was

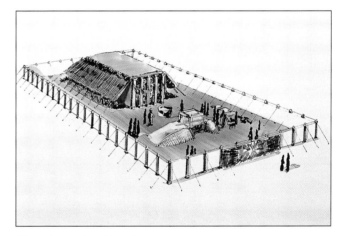

*The tabernacle of Israel*

portable, meaning it could be moved from one location to another.

9:3    **veil**—curtain used to separate rooms

4 Which had the golden censer, and the ark of the covenant overlaid round about with gold, wherein was the golden pot that had manna, and Aaron's rod that budded, and the tables of the covenant;

5 And over it the cherubims of glory shadowing the mercyseat; of which we cannot now speak particularly.

6 Now when these things were thus ordained, the priests went always into the first tabernacle, accomplishing the service of God.

7 But into the second went the high priest alone once every year, not without blood, which he offered for himself, and for the errors of the people:

8 ¶ The Holy Ghost this signifying, that the way into the holiest of all was not yet made manifest, while as the first tabernacle was yet standing:

## CHRIST IS THE HIGH PRIEST OF THE NEW COVENANT

9 Which was a figure for the time then present, in which were offered both gifts and sacrifices, that could not make him that did the service perfect, as pertaining to the conscience;

10 Which stood only in meats and drinks, and divers washings, and carnal ordinances, imposed on them until the time of reformation.

11 But Christ being come an high priest of good things to come, by a greater and more perfect tabernacle, not made with hands, that is to say, not of this building;

12 Neither by the blood of goats and calves, but by his own blood he entered in once into the holy place, having obtained eternal redemption for us.

13 For if the blood of bulls and of goats, and the ashes of an heifer sprinkling the unclean, sanctifieth to the purifying of the flesh:

14 How much more shall the blood of Christ, who through the eternal Spirit offered himself without spot to God, purge your conscience from dead works to serve the living God?

15 ¶ And for this cause he is the mediator of the new testament, that by means of death, for the redemption of the transgressions that were under the first testament, they which are called might receive the promise of eternal inheritance.

16 For where a testament is, there must also of necessity be the death of the testator.

17 For a testament is of force after men are dead: otherwise it is of no strength at all while the testator liveth.

18 Whereupon neither the first testament was dedicated without blood.

19 For when Moses had spoken every precept to all the people according to the law, he took the blood of calves and of goats, with water, and scarlet wool, and hyssop, and sprinkled both the book, and all the people,

20 Saying, This is the blood of the testament which God hath enjoined unto you.

21 Moreover he sprinkled with blood both the tabernacle, and all the vessels of the ministry.

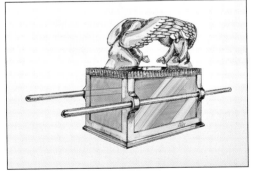

*The ark of the covenant*

9:4-5 🔎 The ark of the covenant was a chest made of wood and covered with gold. It held the stone tablets that the Ten Commandments were written on. The top of the chest was called the mercyseat. (See LDS Bible Dictionary, s.v. "Ark of the Covenant," pp. 613-14.)

9:5 📖 **cherubims**—angels

9:10-14 🔎 The drinks, washings, and ordinances of the law of Moses all pointed to Christ. Jesus Christ, through the shedding of his own blood, replaced the law of Moses with the gospel as we now have it. (See Hebrews 9:24-28.)

9:15 ⚡ The Joseph Smith Translation changes "testament" to "covenant" (see JST, Hebrews 9:15). A covenant is a two-way promise between God and man.

9:16-17 ⚡ Jesus Christ sealed his mission by the shedding of his own blood. Joseph Smith also sealed his mission and testimony with his own blood (see D&C 135:1-7).

9:19 📖 **hyssop**—plant used for religious purposes

22 And almost all things are by the law purged with blood; and without shedding of blood is no remission.

23 ¶ It was therefore necessary that the patterns of things in the heavens should be purified with these; but the heavenly things themselves with better sacrifices than these.

24 For Christ is not entered into the holy places made with hands, which are the figures of the true; but into heaven itself, now to appear in the presence of God for us:

25 Nor yet that he should offer himself often, as the high priest entereth into the holy place every year with blood of others;

26 For then must he often have suffered since the foundation of the world: but now once in the end of the world hath he appeared to put away sin by the sacrifice of himself.

27 And as it is appointed unto men once to die, but after this the judgment:

28 So Christ was once offered to bear the sins of many; and unto them that look for him shall he appear the second time without sin unto salvation.

# CHAPTER 10

*Paul pleads with the Church to remember the sacrifice of Jesus Christ. Look for the comparison he makes between the high priest of Israel and Christ.*

## JESUS WAS SACRIFICED FOR OUR SINS

1 ¶ FOR the law having a shadow of good things to come, and not the very image of the things, can never with those sacrifices which they offered year by year continually make the comers thereunto perfect.

2 For then would they not have ceased to be offered?

because that the worshippers once purged should have had no more conscience of sins.

3 But in those sacrifices there is a remembrance again made of sins every year.

4 For it is not possible that the blood of bulls and of goats should take away sins.

5 Wherefore when he cometh into the world, he saith, Sacrifice and offering thou wouldest not, but a body hast thou prepared me:

6 In burnt offerings and sacrifices for sin thou hast had no pleasure.

7 ¶ Then said I, Lo, I come (in the volume of the book it is written of me,) to do thy will, O God.

8 Above when he said, Sacrifice and offering and burnt offerings and offering for sin thou wouldest not, neither hadst pleasure therein; which are offered by the law;

9 Then said he, Lo, I come to do thy will, O God. He taketh away the first, that he may establish the second.

10 By the which will we are sanctified through the offering of the body of Jesus Christ once for all.

11 And every priest standeth daily ministering and offering oftentimes the same sacrifices, which can never take away sins:

12 But this man, after he had offered one sacrifice for sins for ever, sat down on the right hand of God;

13 From henceforth expecting till his enemies be made his footstool.

14 For by one offering he hath perfected for ever them that are sanctified.

15 Whereof the Holy Ghost also is a witness to us: for after that he had said before,

16 This is the covenant that I will make with them after those days, saith the Lord, I will put my laws into their hearts, and in their minds will I write them;

---

9:24-28 The high priest entered the tabernacle and sprinkled the blood of sacrifices on the altar. In a similar way, Jesus entered heaven and represented us to Heavenly Father through the sacrifice he performed called the Atonement in which his own blood was shed.

9:26 The Joseph Smith Translation changes the phrase "in the end of the world" to "the meridian of time" (JST, Hebrews 9:26). This was the time when Jesus Christ lived on the earth.

10:2 ***purged***—cleansed
***conscience***—awareness

10:9 God took away the first (the law of sacrifice) that he might establish the second (the atonement of Jesus Christ) (see Galatians 3:24).

10:10 "To be *sanctified* is to become clean, pure, and spotless; to be free from the blood and sins of the world. . . . *Sanctification* is a state of saintliness." (Bruce R. McConkie, *Mormon Doctrine*, p. 675.) It comes only by obedience to the commandments and through the power of the Holy Ghost.

10:10-12 Israel's high priest made a sacrifice every year for the sins of the people. Jesus Christ made his sacrifice once for all mankind (see Alma 34:9-15; JST, Hebrews 10:10).

17 And their sins and iniquities will I remember no more.

18 Now where remission of these is, there is no more offering for sin.

19 ¶ Having therefore, brethren, boldness to enter into the holiest by the blood of Jesus,

20 By a new and living way, which he hath consecrated for us, through the veil, that is to say, his flesh;

21 And having an high priest over the house of God;

22 Let us draw near with a true heart in full assurance of faith, having our hearts sprinkled from an evil conscience, and our bodies washed with pure water.

### THOSE WHO REBEL AGAINST GOD WILL BE PUNISHED

23 Let us hold fast the profession of our faith without wavering; (for he is faithful that promised;)

24 And let us consider one another to provoke unto love and to good works:

25 Not forsaking the assembling of ourselves together, as the manner of some is; but exhorting one another: and so much the more, as ye see the day approaching.

26 For if we sin wilfully after that we have received the knowledge of the truth, there remaineth no more sacrifice for sins,

27 But a certain fearful looking for of judgment and fiery indignation, which shall devour the adversaries.

28 He that despised Moses' law died without mercy under two or three witnesses:

29 Of how much sorer punishment, suppose ye, shall he be thought worthy, who hath trodden under foot the Son of God, and hath counted the blood of the covenant, wherewith he was sanctified, an unholy thing, and hath done despite unto the Spirit of grace?

30 For we know him that hath said, Vengeance belongeth unto me, I will recompense, saith the Lord. And again, The Lord shall judge his people.

31 It is a fearful thing to fall into the hands of the living God.

### THE RIGHTEOUS SHALL LIVE BY FAITH

32 But call to remembrance the former days, in which, after ye were illuminated, ye endured a great fight of afflictions;

33 Partly, whilst ye were made a gazingstock both by reproaches and afflictions; and partly, whilst ye became companions of them that were so used.

34 For ye had compassion of me in my bonds, and took joyfully the spoiling of your goods, knowing in yourselves that ye have in heaven a better and an enduring substance.

35 Cast not away therefore your confidence, which hath great recompence of reward.

36 For ye have need of patience, that, after ye have done the will of God, ye might receive the promise.

37 For yet a little while, and he that shall come will come, and will not tarry.

38 Now the just shall live by faith: but if any man draw back, my soul shall have no pleasure in him.

39 But we are not of them who draw back unto perdition; but of them that believe to the saving of the soul.

## CHAPTER 11

*Paul spoke to the Hebrews about the power of faith. Watch for what has been and can be done by those people who have faith in the Lord Jesus Christ.*

### PAUL DEFINES FAITH

1 ¶ NOW faith is the substance of things hoped for, the evidence of things not seen.

2 For by it the elders obtained a good report.

---

10:17-20 How does it make you feel to know that if you repent Jesus will remember your sins no more and will bring you back into Heavenly Father's presence?

10:20 **consecrated**—set apart as sacred

10:23 **profession**—declaration, affirmation, testimony

10:26 Learning the gospel requires us to keep more of the Lord's commandments (see D&C 82:3).

10:27 **indignation**—anger
**devour**—destroy

10:28 **despised**—rejected

10:29 **despite**—insult

10:30 **Vengeance**—Getting even with someone
**recompense**—repay

10:32 **were illuminated**—received the gospel

10:33 **gazingstock**—spectacle (something openly looked at)

10:39 **perdition**—ruin or destruction

11:1 The Joseph Smith Translation changes "substance" to "assurance" (JST, Hebrews 11:1). If you have assurance about something, you know that it is true. Another definition of faith is found in Alma 32:21.

*"By faith Abel offered unto God a more excellent sacrifice than Cain."*

3 Through faith we understand that the worlds were framed by the word of God, so that things which are seen were not made of things which do appear.

## PAUL TELLS ABOUT PEOPLE IN THE OLD TESTAMENT WHO HAD GREAT FAITH

4 ¶ By faith Abel offered unto God a more excellent sacrifice than Cain, by which he obtained witness that he was righteous, God testifying of his gifts: and by it he being dead yet speaketh.

5 By faith Enoch was translated that he should not see death; and was not found, because God had translated him: for before his translation he had this testimony, that he pleased God.

6 But without faith it is impossible to please him: for he that cometh to God must believe that he is, and that he is a rewarder of them that diligently seek him.

7 By faith Noah, being warned of God of things not seen as yet, moved with fear, prepared an ark to the saving of his house; by the which he condemned the world, and became heir of the righteousness which is by faith.

8 By faith Abraham, when he was called to go out into a place which he should after receive for an inheritance, obeyed; and he went out, not knowing whither he went.

9 By faith he sojourned in the land of promise, as in a strange country, dwelling in tabernacles with Isaac and Jacob, the heirs with him of the same promise:

10 For he looked for a city which hath foundations, whose builder and maker is God.

11 Through faith also Sara herself received strength to conceive seed, and was delivered of a child when she was past age, because she judged him faithful who had promised.

12 Therefore sprang there even of one, and him as good as dead, so many as the stars of the sky in multitude, and as the sand which is by the sea shore innumerable.

13 These all died in faith, not having received the promises, but having seen them afar off, and were persuaded of them, and embraced them, and confessed that they were strangers and pilgrims on the earth.

14 For they that say such things declare plainly that they seek a country.

15 And truly, if they had been mindful of that country from whence they came out, they might have had opportunity to have returned.

16 But now they desire a better country, that is, an heavenly: wherefore God is not ashamed to be called their God: for he hath prepared for them a city.

---

11:5 ☀ The account of the translation of Enoch is found in Moses 7:67-69.

✎ **Enoch was translated**—Enoch's body was changed so he could be taken into heaven

11:6 ➋ Faith in the Lord Jesus Christ is the first principle of the gospel (see Articles of Faith 1:4). We must have faith in order to please God. Do you have faith in Jesus? What can you do to strengthen your faith?

11:7 🔍 The account of Noah is found in Genesis 6-9.

11:9 ✎ **sojourned**—lived

11:10 ➋ The "city" Abraham looked for was the celestial kingdom (see Hebrews 11:16). How can your faith that you can get to the celestial kingdom help you make your way through life?

11:11 ✎ **conceive seed**—become pregnant

11:12 🔍 Abraham was promised that he would have posterity (children) as numerous as the stars (see Genesis 15:5).

11:13 🔍 Abraham's son Isaac and Isaac's son Jacob believed Abraham and had similar faith that they would get to the celestial kingdom (see Genesis 26:1-5; 28:1-4, 13-15).

*Noah's faith gave him courage to build the ark.*

17 By faith Abraham, when he was tried, offered up Isaac: and he that had received the promises offered up his only begotten son,

18 Of whom it was said, That in Isaac shall thy seed be called:

19 Accounting that God was able to raise him up, even from the dead; from whence also he received him in a figure.

20 By faith Isaac blessed Jacob and Esau concerning things to come.

21 By faith Jacob, when he was a dying, blessed both the sons of Joseph; and worshipped, leaning upon the top of his staff.

22 By faith Joseph, when he died, made mention of the departing of the children of Israel; and gave commandment concerning his bones.

23 By faith Moses, when he was born, was hid three months of his parents, because they saw he was a proper child; and they were not afraid of the king's commandment.

24 By faith Moses, when he was come to years, refused to be called the son of Pharaoh's daughter;

25 Choosing rather to suffer affliction with the people of God, than to enjoy the pleasures of sin for a season;

26 Esteeming the reproach of Christ greater riches than the treasures in Egypt: for he had respect unto the recompence of the reward.

27 By faith he forsook Egypt, not fearing the wrath of the king: for he endured, as seeing him who is invisible.

28 Through faith he kept the passover, and the sprinkling of blood, lest he that destroyed the firstborn should touch them.

29 By faith they passed through the Red sea as by dry land: which the Egyptians assaying to do were drowned.

30 By faith the walls of Jericho fell down, after they were compassed about seven days.

31 By faith the harlot Rahab perished not with them that believed not, when she had received the spies with peace.

32 ¶ And what shall I more say? for the time would fail me to tell of Gedeon, and of Barak, and of Samson, and of Jephthae; of David also, and Samuel, and of the prophets:

33 Who through faith subdued kingdoms, wrought righteousness, obtained promises, stopped the mouths of lions,

34 Quenched the violence of fire, escaped the edge of the sword, out of weakness were made strong, waxed valiant in fight, turned to flight the armies of the aliens.

35 Women received their dead raised to life again: and others were tortured, not accepting deliverance; that they might obtain a better resurrection:

36 And others had trial of cruel mockings and scourgings, yea, moreover of bonds and imprisonment:

37 They were stoned, they were sawn asunder, were tempted, were slain with the sword: they wandered about in sheepskins and goatskins; being destitute, afflicted, tormented;

38 (Of whom the world was not worthy:) they wandered in deserts, and in mountains, and in dens and caves of the earth.

39 And these all, having obtained a good report through faith, received not the promise:

40 God having provided some better thing for us, that they without us should not be made perfect.

---

11:17-   Abraham was commanded to sacrifice his son
19       Isaac, and had faith that if he did so, God could raise Isaac from the dead. God blessed Abraham because of his faith and Isaac was not hurt. (See Genesis 22:1-13.) What are some difficult things God has asked you to do? How can your faith help you to do them?

11:33-   These many miracles and blessings were
40       received through the power of faith. How does knowing about the miracles and blessings described in these verses help you have the faith to do all God wants you to do?

11:40    The Joseph Smith Translation changes this verse to read, "God having provided some better things for them through their sufferings, for without sufferings they could not be made perfect."

# CHAPTER 12

*The Lord sometimes scolds us so that we will be better members of the Church. Look for the blessings that come to those who listen to the Lord and do what he says.*

## GOD SCOLDS HIS CHILDREN BECAUSE HE LOVES THEM

1 ¶ WHEREFORE seeing we also are compassed about with so great a cloud of witnesses, let us lay aside every weight, and the sin which doth so easily beset us, and let us run with patience the race that is set before us,

2 Looking unto Jesus the author and finisher of our faith; who for the joy that was set before him endured the cross, despising the shame, and is set down at the right hand of the throne of God.

3 For consider him that endured such contradiction of sinners against himself, lest ye be wearied and faint in your minds.

4 ¶ Ye have not yet resisted unto blood, striving against sin.

5 And ye have forgotten the exhortation which speaketh unto you as unto children, My son, despise not thou the chastening of the Lord, nor faint when thou art rebuked of him:

6 For whom the Lord loveth he chasteneth, and scourgeth every son whom he receiveth.

7 If ye endure chastening, God dealeth with you as with sons; for what son is he whom the father chasteneth not?

8 But if ye be without chastisement, whereof all are partakers, then are ye bastards, and not sons.

9 Furthermore we have had fathers of our flesh which corrected us, and we gave them reverence: shall we not much rather be in subjection unto the Father of spirits, and live?

10 For they verily for a few days chastened us after their own pleasure; but he for our profit, that we might be partakers of his holiness.

11 Now no chastening for the present seemeth to be joyous, but grievous: nevertheless afterward it yieldeth the peaceable fruit of righteousness unto them which are exercised thereby.

12 Wherefore lift up the hands which hang down, and the feeble knees;

13 And make straight paths for your feet, lest that which is lame be turned out of the way; but let it rather be healed.

## WE CAN SEE GOD IF WE BECOME HOLY

14 Follow peace with all men, and holiness, without which no man shall see the Lord:

15 Looking diligently lest any man fail of the grace of God; lest any root of bitterness springing up trouble you, and thereby many be defiled;

16 Lest there be any fornicator, or profane person, as Esau, who for one morsel of meat sold his birthright.

17 For ye know how that afterward, when he would have inherited the blessing, he was rejected: for he found no place of repentance, though he sought it carefully with tears.

---

12:1 The "cloud of witnesses" that compassed or surrounded Church members was the many people of faith in the Old Testament that Paul listed in Hebrews 11. Their examples can inspire us to repent of our sins and patiently run "the race" for eternal life.

**beset**—surround and cling to

12:2 Our salvation depends on the atonement of Jesus Christ. He is "the author and finisher of our faith" because he was "prepared from the foundation of the world to redeem [his] people" (Ether 3:14). Jesus "finished" all that he was asked to do (see D&C 19:2).

12:3 **contradiction**—opposition

12:5 **chastening**—scolding
**rebuked**—corrected

12:5-10 The Lord chastens, or disciplines, his children because he loves them (see D&C 95:1). How can discipline help you become a better person?

12:9 God is the Father of our spirits (see Psalm 82:6; Acts 17:29).

12:15 Grace is divine help given by God through the atonement of Jesus Christ. It provides us with the power needed to repent, keep the commandments, and become like God. (See LDS Bible Dictionary, s.v. "Grace," p. 697.)

**bitterness**—hatred

12:16-17 Esau was the son of Isaac who sold his birthright blessing to his brother, Jacob, for a bowl of soup (see Genesis 25:29-34). The blessing meant little to Esau, for he lived a godless life. When he realized his mistake it was too late to get his blessing back.

## PEOPLE WHO GO TO THE CELESTIAL KINGDOM BELONG TO THE CHURCH OF THE FIRSTBORN

18 ¶ For ye are not come unto the mount that might be touched, and that burned with fire, nor unto blackness, and darkness, and tempest,

19 And the sound of a trumpet, and the voice of words; which voice they that heard intreated that the word should not be spoken to them any more:

20 (For they could not endure that which was commanded, And if so much as a beast touch the mountain, it shall be stoned, or thrust through with a dart:

21 And so terrible was the sight, that Moses said, I exceedingly fear and quake:)

22 But ye are come unto mount Sion, and unto the city of the living God, the heavenly Jerusalem, and to an innumerable company of angels,

23 To the general assembly and church of the firstborn, which are written in heaven, and to God the Judge of all, and to the spirits of just men made perfect,

24 And to Jesus the mediator of the new covenant, and to the blood of sprinkling, that speaketh better things than that of Abel.

## PAUL GIVES A WARNING AGAINST REFUSING TO LISTEN TO GOD'S VOICE

25 See that ye refuse not him that speaketh. For if they escaped not who refused him that spake on earth, much more shall not we escape, if we turn away from him that speaketh from heaven:

26 Whose voice then shook the earth: but now he hath promised, saying, Yet once more I shake not the earth only, but also heaven.

27 And this word, Yet once more, signifieth the removing of those things that are shaken, as of things that are made, that those things which cannot be shaken may remain.

28 Wherefore we receiving a kingdom which cannot be moved, let us have grace, whereby we may serve God acceptably with reverence and godly fear:

29 For our God is a consuming fire.

*God spoke to the children of Israel from Mount Sinai.*

12:18-21   In these verses Paul is describing the day that the children of Israel ran from the voice of Jehovah and refused to see him (see Exodus 19:10-11, 14-18; 20:18-19).

12:22-24   In these verses, phrases such as "mount Sion," "the heavenly Jerusalem," "innumerable . . . angels," "general assembly," and "church of the firstborn" are used to describe the celestial kingdom and those who will live there (see D&C 76:50-70).

12:24   The "new covenant" is the "everlasting covenant, even the fulness of [the] gospel" (D&C 66:2). Christ made this covenant available to us by shedding his blood as he atoned for our sins.

12:25-28   When God spoke from Mount Sinai the earth shook. In the last days, "the Lord shall utter his voice out of heaven; the heavens shall shake and the earth shall tremble. . . . And the wicked shall go away into unquenchable fire." (D&C 43:18, 33.)

12:29   When Jesus comes again his glory will be as a consuming fire. The prophet Malachi said that that day "shall burn as an oven; . . . and all that do wickedly, shall be stubble: and the day that cometh shall burn them up" (Malachi 4:1).

God will be "a consuming fire" only to the wicked. The righteous shall "walk in the light of it" (Revelation 21:24). How can you prepare to be one who walks in the light?

# CHAPTER 13

*Paul teaches the Saints that Jesus Christ should be the center of their lives. Watch for ways that you could better center your life in Christ.*

## Look for Opportunities to Serve Others

1 ¶ LET brotherly love continue.

2 Be not forgetful to entertain strangers: for thereby some have entertained angels unawares.

3 Remember them that are in bonds, as bound with them; and them which suffer adversity, as being yourselves also in the body.

## Marriage Is Pleasing to God

4 Marriage is honourable in all, and the bed undefiled: but whoremongers and adulterers God will judge.

5 Let your conversation be without covetousness; and be content with such things as ye have: for he hath said, I will never leave thee, nor forsake thee.

6 So that we may boldly say, The Lord is my helper, and I will not fear what man shall do unto me.

## Center Your Sacrifices in Christ

7 Remember them which have the rule over you, who have spoken unto you the word of God: whose faith follow, considering the end of their conversation.

8 Jesus Christ the same yesterday, and to day, and for ever.

9 Be not carried about with divers and strange doctrines. For it is a good thing that the heart be established with grace; not with meats, which have not profited them that have been occupied therein.

10 We have an altar, whereof they have no right to eat which serve the tabernacle.

11 For the bodies of those beasts, whose blood is brought into the sanctuary by the high priest for sin, are burned without the camp.

12 Wherefore Jesus also, that he might sanctify the people with his own blood, suffered without the gate.

13 Let us go forth therefore unto him without the camp, bearing his reproach.

14 For here have we no continuing city, but we seek one to come.

15 By him therefore let us offer the sacrifice of praise to God continually, that is, the fruit of our lips giving thanks to his name.

16 But to do good and to communicate forget not: for with such sacrifices God is well pleased.

## Pray for Church Leaders and Follow Their Inspired Counsel

17 Obey them that have the rule over you, and submit yourselves: for they watch for your souls, as they that must give account, that they may do it with joy, and not with grief: for that is unprofitable for you.

18 ¶ Pray for us: for we trust we have a good conscience, in all things willing to live honestly.

---

13:1-3 Paul counseled the Saints to practice brotherly love towards others. Similarly, Jesus taught that serving others was like serving him (see Matthew 25:40).

13:4 **undefiled**—not sinful
**whoremongers and adulterers**—people who use the sacred creative powers with those to whom they are not married

13:5 The Joseph Smith Translation changes the word "conversation" to "consecrations," meaning donations that you give to the Lord (see JST, Hebrews 13:5). "True saints make their contributions freely and willingly to the Lord without coveting [or wishing they kept] what they have chosen to return to Him who gave them all" (Bruce R. McConkie, *Doctrinal New Testament Commentary* 3:237).

13:8 Jesus works to provide eternal life for Heavenly Father's children and always gives the same blessings for the same obedience (see Mormon 9:7-11; D&C 130:20-21).

13:9 **divers**—different

13:11 **sanctuary**—sacred or holy place, the temple

13:11-13 Some animals were sacrificed "without," or outside, the ancient camp of Israel (see Leviticus 4:12). This was a symbol of Jesus, who would suffer for our sins outside Jerusalem. (See LDS Bible Dictionary, s.v. "Sacrifices," pp. 765-67.)

13:14 **continuing city**—heaven

13:15-16 What can you say and do to show your thanks to the Savior for what he has done for you?

13:17-18 "The children who pray for the brethren [Church leaders] will grow up loving them, speaking well of them, honoring and emulating them [following their example]" (Spencer W. Kimball, *The Teachings of Spencer W. Kimball*, p. 121).

19 But I beseech you the rather to do this, that I may be restored to you the sooner.

20 Now the God of peace, that brought again from the dead our Lord Jesus, that great shepherd of the sheep, through the blood of the everlasting covenant,

21 Make you perfect in every good work to do his will, working in you that which is wellpleasing in his sight, through Jesus Christ; to whom be glory for ever and ever. Amen.

22 And I beseech you, brethren, suffer the word of exhortation: for I have written a letter unto you in few words.

23 Know ye that our brother Timothy is set at liberty; with whom, if he come shortly, I will see you.

24 Salute all them that have the rule over you, and all the saints. They of Italy salute you.

25 Grace be with you all. Amen.

---

13:20 **everlasting covenant**—gospel of Jesus Christ

13:20-
21 Paul teaches that Jesus helps us "do his will." In what ways have you felt the Savior "working in you" to do his will and become a better person?

# THE GENERAL EPISTLE OF
# JAMES

*The author of this letter is generally thought to be the Lord's brother James, a son of Mary (see Galations 1:19). Written to the scattered tribes of Israel, the book of James tells us how God wants us to live. It stresses that doing the Lord's work will bring great blessings.*

## CHAPTER 1

*This chapter inspired young Joseph Smith to go to a grove of trees (what we now call the Sacred Grove) and pray. Look for what James teaches about finding wisdom and learning truth.*

### GOD WILL TEACH US IF WE ASK HIM

1 JAMES, a servant of God and of the Lord Jesus Christ, to the twelve tribes which are scattered abroad, greeting.

2 ¶ My brethren, count it all joy when ye fall into divers temptations;

3 Knowing this, that the trying of your faith worketh patience.

4 But let patience have her perfect work, that ye may be perfect and entire, wanting nothing.

5 If any of you lack wisdom, let him ask of God, that giveth to all men liberally, and upbraideth not; and it shall be given him.

6 But let him ask in faith, nothing wavering. For he that wavereth is like a wave of the sea driven with the wind and tossed.

7 For let not that man think that he shall receive any thing of the Lord.

8 A double minded man is unstable in all his ways.

### THE POOR AND THE RICH CAN BOTH LEARN FROM TRIALS

9 Let the brother of low degree rejoice in that he is exalted:

10 But the rich, in that he is made low: because as the flower of the grass he shall pass away.

11 For the sun is no sooner risen with a burning heat, but it withereth the grass, and the flower thereof falleth, and the grace of the fashion of it perisheth: so also shall the rich man fade away in his ways.

### WE MUST RESIST TEMPTATION

12 Blessed is the man that endureth temptation: for when he is tried, he shall receive the crown of life, which the Lord hath promised to them that love him.

---

1:2-4 Trials and suffering, while often painful, teach us valuable lessons that we would otherwise not learn (see Ether 12:6; D&C 122:7).

1:5 **giveth to all men liberally, and upbraideth not**—gives freely, and doesn't criticize or scold

1:5-6 These verses greatly impressed Joseph Smith. As a result he went to what is now known as the Sacred Grove to pray about which church was true. In answer to Joseph's prayer, Heavenly Father and Jesus Christ appeared to him and told him to join none of the churches. Joseph was chosen to restore the true Church to the earth. (See Joseph Smith—History 1:11-19.)

Heavenly Father hears and answers our prayers. What answers have you received from Heavenly Father?

1:6-7 God answers the prayers of those who pray to him in faith. The Lord may not honor the requests of those who waver or doubt his abilities. (See Mormon 9:21.)

1:9-10 The poor can rejoice in their humble circumstances. The rich who are humble can rejoice in sharing their wealth with others (see 1 Timothy 6:17-19).

1:11 **grace of the fashion of it perisheth**—beauty is lost

---

= Word Help 　 = A Closer Look

= More Light 　 = Ponder This

Words in pink are explained in the Glossary.

*"If any of you lack wisdom, let him ask of God."*

13 ¶ Let no man say when he is tempted, I am tempted of God: for God cannot be tempted with evil, neither tempteth he any man:

## FAITH WITHOUT WORKS IS DEAD

14 But every man is tempted, when he is drawn away of his own lust, and enticed.

15 Then when lust hath conceived, it bringeth forth sin: and sin, when it is finished, bringeth forth death.

16 Do not err, my beloved brethren.

17 Every good gift and every perfect gift is from above, and cometh down from the Father of lights, with whom is no variableness, neither shadow of turning.

18 Of his own will begat he us with the word of truth, that we should be a kind of firstfruits of his creatures.

19 ¶ Wherefore, my beloved brethren, let every man be swift to hear, slow to speak, slow to wrath:

20 For the wrath of man worketh not the righteousness of God.

21 Wherefore lay apart all filthiness and superfluity of naughtiness, and receive with meekness the engrafted word, which is able to save your souls.

---

1:13, 17    God is the source of all that is good. Satan is the source of all that is evil. (See Moroni 7:12-14.)

1:14    **enticed**—attracted and deceived

1:15    **when lust hath conceived**—when evil desire begins to grow

1:17    **no variableness**—no change

1:19    **wrath**—anger

1:21    This verse may be rephrased as follows: Stay away from sin and the flood of wickedness. Humbly obey the gospel, which will bring you eternal life. (See D&C 25:10.)

## WE MUST DO ALL WE CAN TO BE SAVED IN THE CELESTIAL KINGDOM

22 But be ye doers of the word, and not hearers only, deceiving your own selves.

23 For if any be a hearer of the word, and not a doer, he is like unto a man beholding his natural face in a glass:

24 For he beholdeth himself, and goeth his way, and straightway forgetteth what manner of man he was.

25 But whoso looketh into the perfect law of liberty, and continueth therein, he being not a forgetful hearer, but a doer of the work, this man shall be blessed in his deed.

26 If any man among you seem to be religious, and bridleth not his tongue, but deceiveth his own heart, this man's religion is vain.

27 Pure religion and undefiled before God and the Father is this, To visit the fatherless and widows in their affliction, and to keep himself unspotted from the world.

## CHAPTER 2

*We will be judged by the things we have done and by our faith in Jesus Christ. Note what James invites us to do and not do so that our day of judgment will be joyful.*

## WE MUST RESPECT AND JUDGE EVERYONE IN THE SAME WAY

1 ¶ MY brethren, have not the faith of our Lord Jesus Christ, the Lord of glory, with respect of persons.

2 For if there come unto your assembly a man with a gold ring, in goodly apparel, and there come in also a poor man in vile raiment;

3 And ye have respect to him that weareth the gay clothing, and say unto him, Sit thou here in a good place; and say to the poor, Stand thou there, or sit here under my footstool:

4 Are ye not then partial in yourselves, and are become judges of evil thoughts?

5 Hearken, my beloved brethren, Hath not God chosen the poor of this world rich in faith, and heirs of the kingdom which he hath promised to them that love him?

6 But ye have despised the poor. Do not rich men oppress you, and draw you before the judgment seats?

7 Do not they blaspheme that worthy name by the which ye are called?

8 ¶ If ye fulfil the royal law according to the scripture, Thou shalt love thy neighbour as thyself, ye do well:

9 But if ye have respect to persons, ye commit sin, and are convinced of the law as transgressors.

10 For whosoever shall keep the whole law, and yet offend in one point, he is guilty of all.

---

**1:22-23** President Spencer W. Kimball taught: "One cannot receive eternal life without being a 'doer of the word' (see James 1:22) and being valiant in obedience to the Lord's commandments. And one cannot become a 'doer of the word' without first becoming a 'hearer.' And to become a 'hearer' is not simply to stand idly by and wait for chance bits of information; it is to seek out and study and pray and comprehend." (*The Teachings of Spencer W. Kimball,* pp. 127–28.)

**1:26** ***bridleth not his tongue***—does not control what he says
***vain***—empty and useless

**1:26-27** What could you do to better live your religion?

**2:1** The Joseph Smith Translation explains that we "cannot have the faith of our Lord Jesus Christ" and favor one person over another (see JST, James 2:1).

**2:2** ***vile raiment***—filthy clothes

**2:4** ***partial***—showing that you favor some people over other people

**2:5** ***heirs***—those who inherit or receive the blessings of their parents

Jesus said that the poor in spirit will inherit the kingdom of heaven (see Matthew 5:3).

**2:6** ***oppress***—weigh down or trouble

**2:7** Blasphemy is the sin of claiming to be like God or speaking evil of God.

**2:8** The second great commandment God has given us is to love one another (see Leviticus 19:18; Matthew 22:39).

**2:9** ***convinced of***—found guilty by

**2:10** James explains that even if we keep all of the commandments except one, we have not kept the "whole law."

11 For he that said, Do not commit adultery, said also, Do not kill. Now if thou commit no adultery, yet if thou kill, thou art become a transgressor of the law.

12 So speak ye, and so do, as they that shall be judged by the law of liberty.

13 For he shall have judgment without mercy, that hath shewed no mercy; and mercy rejoiceth against judgment.

14 ¶ What doth it profit, my brethren, though a man say he hath faith, and have not works? can faith save him?

15 If a brother or sister be naked, and destitute of daily food,

16 And one of you say unto them, Depart in peace, be ye warmed and filled; notwithstanding ye give them not those things which are needful to the body; what doth it profit?

17 Even so faith, if it hath not works, is dead, being alone.

18 Yea, a man may say, Thou hast faith, and I have works: shew me thy faith without thy works, and I will shew thee my faith by my works.

19 Thou believest that there is one God; thou doest well: the devils also believe, and tremble.

20 But wilt thou know, O vain man, that faith without works is dead?

21 Was not Abraham our father justified by works, when he had offered Isaac his son upon the altar?

22 Seest thou how faith wrought with his works, and by works was faith made perfect?

23 And the scripture was fulfilled which saith, Abraham believed God, and it was imputed unto him for righteousness: and he was called the Friend of God.

24 Ye see then how that by works a man is justified, and not by faith only.

25 Likewise also was not Rahab the harlot justified by works, when she had received the messengers, and had sent them out another way?

26 For as the body without the spirit is dead, so faith without works is dead also.

## CHAPTER 3

*James teaches about perfection. Look for the key principle James says will lead us to perfection.*

### A MAN IS PERFECTED BY CONTROLLING HIS TONGUE

1 ¶ MY brethren, be not many masters, knowing that we shall receive the greater condemnation.

2 For in many things we offend all. If any man offend not in word, the same is a perfect man, and able also to bridle the whole body.

3 Behold, we put bits in the horses' mouths, that they may obey us; and we turn about their whole body.

---

2:13 **shewed**—This word is pronounced the same way as the word *showed* and has the same meaning; *shewed* is simply an old spelling of *showed.*

2:14 **works**—the principles and ordinances we can live

2:15 **destitute of**—totally without

2:15-17 What should we do if a person comes to us poor and hungry? How will helping the poor and needy add good works to your faith?

2:18 **shew**—This word is pronounced the same way as the word *show* and has the same meaning; *shew* is simply an old spelling of *show.*

2:20 **vain**—empty and useless

2:21 A person who is justified has had his sins forgiven. Our sins are forgiven when we exercise faith in the Savior's atonement, repent of our sins, and obey the commandments and ordinances of the gospel.

2:21-23 Abraham was willing to offer his son Isaac on an altar, showing his faith in obeying all that God asked of him (see Genesis 22). In this way Abraham became "the Friend of God" and received a promise of eternal life.

2:22 **wrought**—worked together

2:23 **imputed**—counted

2:25 The messengers that Rahab helped were Israelite spies sent to determine how to defeat the city of Jericho. Because of her help she was promised that she and her family would be spared when Israel conquered the city. (See Joshua 2.)

2:26 James taught that faith without works is dead. How are our works improved because of our faith? How can our faith grow by our doing the will of the Lord?

3:2 **in many things we offend all**—we all make mistakes in many ways
**bridle**—control

4 Behold also the ships, which though they be so great, and are driven of fierce winds, yet are they turned about with a very small helm, whithersoever the governor listeth.

5 Even so the tongue is a little member, and boasteth great things. Behold, how great a matter a little fire kindleth!

6 And the tongue is a fire, a world of iniquity: so is the tongue among our members, that it defileth the whole body, and setteth on fire the course of nature; and it is set on fire of hell.

7 For every kind of beasts, and of birds, and of serpents, and of things in the sea, is tamed, and hath been tamed of mankind:

8 But the tongue can no man tame; it is an unruly evil, full of deadly poison.

9 Therewith bless we God, even the Father; and therewith curse we men, which are made after the similitude of God.

10 Out of the same mouth proceedeth blessing and cursing. My brethren, these things ought not so to be.

11 Doth a fountain send forth at the same place sweet water and bitter?

12 Can the fig tree, my brethren, bear olive berries? either a vine, figs? so can no fountain both yield salt water and fresh.

## JAMES GIVES A DEFINITION OF A WISE MAN

13 ¶ Who is a wise man and endued with knowledge among you? let him shew out of a good conversation his works with meekness of wisdom.

14 But if ye have bitter envying and strife in your hearts, glory not, and lie not against the truth.

15 This wisdom descendeth not from above, but is earthly, sensual, devilish.

16 For where envying and strife is, there is confusion and every evil work.

17 But the wisdom that is from above is first pure, then peaceable, gentle, and easy to be intreated, full of mercy and good fruits, without partiality, and without hypocrisy.

18 And the fruit of righteousness is sown in peace of them that make peace.

## CHAPTER 4

*James cautions against pride and contention. Watch for how you can overcome pride and be better friends with your neighbors.*

### WARS BEGIN BECAUSE OF EVIL DESIRES

1 ¶ FROM whence come wars and fightings among you? come they not hence, even of your lusts that war in your members?

2 Ye lust, and have not: ye kill, and desire to have, and cannot obtain: ye fight and war, yet ye have not, because ye ask not.

3 Ye ask, and receive not, because ye ask amiss, that ye may consume it upon your lusts.

4 Ye adulterers and adulteresses, know ye not that the friendship of the world is enmity with God?

---

3:5-6   How could lying, gossiping, swearing, or speaking evil of others affect you spiritually? On the other hand, how does saying your prayers, bearing your testimony, or giving others compliments affect your spirituality?

3:6   *iniquity*—sin
*defileth*—destroys or makes unclean

3:8   James declares that the tongue can be full of deadly poison. We should be very careful with what we say to other people. Alma teaches, "For our words will condemn us . . . ; and our thoughts will also condemn us" (Alma 12:14).

3:9   *similitude*—likeness

3:13   *endued with*—blessed with, given
*conversation*—conduct
*meekness*—humility

3:14   *envying*—jealousy

3:14-16   Do you ever feel angry towards or jealous of others? How can you control those feelings? How could prayer help you overcome those feelings?

3:17   *to be intreated*—to get along with

4:1   *lusts*—evil desires

4:2   Often there is a conflict within us as we face choosing between the things of the world and the things of the Spirit. Fighting, murder, and war are among the things of the world. We are cautioned to avoid lusting after the things of the world (see 1 John 2:15-16).

4:3   *amiss*—for the wrong reasons
*consume*—waste

4:4   Paul reminds us that we cannot be friendly with worldly things and still be friends with God (see Matthew 6:19-24).

whosoever therefore will be a friend of the world is the enemy of God.

5 Do ye think that the scripture saith in vain, The spirit that dwelleth in us lusteth to envy?

### HUMILITY HELPS US OVERCOME THE WORLD

6 But he giveth more grace. Wherefore he saith, God resisteth the proud, but giveth grace unto the humble.

7 Submit yourselves therefore to God. Resist the devil, and he will flee from you.

8 Draw nigh to God, and he will draw nigh to you. Cleanse your hands, ye sinners; and purify your hearts, ye double minded.

9 Be afflicted, and mourn, and weep: let your laughter be turned to mourning, and your joy to heaviness.

10 Humble yourselves in the sight of the Lord, and he shall lift you up.

### WE ARE TAUGHT TO NOT SPEAK EVIL OF ONE ANOTHER

11 ¶ Speak not evil one of another, brethren. He that speaketh evil of his brother, and judgeth his brother, speaketh evil of the law, and judgeth the law: but if thou judge the law, thou art not a doer of the law, but a judge.

12 There is one lawgiver, who is able to save and to destroy: who art thou that judgest another?

### WE SIN WHEN WE DON'T DO WHAT WE KNOW WE SHOULD

13 Go to now, ye that say, To day or to morrow we will go into such a city, and continue there a year, and buy and sell, and get gain:

14 Whereas ye know not what shall be on the morrow. For what is your life? It is even a vapour, that appeareth for a little time, and then vanisheth away.

15 For that ye ought to say, If the Lord will, we shall live, and do this, or that.

16 But now ye rejoice in your boastings: all such rejoicing is evil.

17 Therefore to him that knoweth to do good, and doeth it not, to him it is sin.

## CHAPTER 5

*In this final chapter James gives counsel to the rich and to those who suffer affliction and sickness. Look for what he says about healing the sick and about the blessings of missionary work.*

### JAMES WARNS THOSE WHO ARE SELFISH WITH THEIR RICHES

1 ¶ GO to now, ye rich men, weep and howl for your miseries that shall come upon you.

2 Your riches are corrupted, and your garments are motheaten.

3 Your gold and silver is cankered; and the rust of them shall be a witness against you, and shall eat your flesh as it were fire. Ye have heaped treasure together for the last days.

4 Behold, the hire of the labourers who have reaped down your fields, which is of you kept back by fraud, crieth: and the cries of them which have reaped are entered into the ears of the Lord of sabaoth.

5 Ye have lived in pleasure on the earth, and been wanton; ye have nourished your hearts, as in a day of slaughter.

6 Ye have condemned and killed the just; and he doth not resist you.

---

4:6    Humility is necessary if we want to receive blessings from God (see D&C 136:32-33).

4:8    **double minded**—undecided or divided

4:9    When a member of the Church commits sin, he or she should feel sincere sorrow for the sin. This is a requirement for true repentance. (See 2 Corinthians 7:9-10.)

4:9-10    The Greek word for *repent* means "to change." How can you tell if a person has truly repented?

4:11-12    The Joseph Smith Translation clarifies the Savior's teaching about how to judge: "Judge not unrighteously, that ye be not judged: but judge righteous judgment" (JST, Matthew 7:1-2).

4:14    **vapour**—fog or mist

5:1-3    Riches are not bad if one seeks them in order to "do good—to clothe the naked, and to feed the hungry, . . . and administer [give] relief to the sick and the afflicted" (Jacob 2:19).

5:2    **corrupted**—spoiled, ruined

5:3    **cankered**—rusted, worn out

5:4    **fraud**—cheating

5:5    **wanton**—without self-control
**as in a day of slaughter**—as if every day were a day for feasting

## BE PATIENT IN SUFFERING

7 Be patient therefore, brethren, unto the coming of the Lord. Behold, the husbandman waiteth for the precious fruit of the earth, and hath long patience for it, until he receive the early and latter rain.

8 Be ye also patient; stablish your hearts: for the coming of the Lord draweth nigh.

9 Grudge not one against another, brethren, lest ye be condemned: behold, the judge standeth before the door.

10 Take, my brethren, the prophets, who have spoken in the name of the Lord, for an example of suffering affliction, and of patience.

11 Behold, we count them happy which endure. Ye have heard of the patience of Job, and have seen the end of the Lord; that the Lord is very pitiful, and of tender mercy.

12 ¶ But above all things, my brethren, swear not, neither by heaven, neither by the earth, neither by any other oath: but let your yea be yea; and your nay, nay; lest ye fall into condemnation.

## WE ARE COMMANDED TO PRAY

13 Is any among you afflicted? let him pray. Is any merry? let him sing psalms.

14 Is any sick among you? let him call for the elders of the church; and let them pray over him, anointing him with oil in the name of the Lord:

15 And the prayer of faith shall save the sick, and the Lord shall raise him up; and if he have committed sins, they shall be forgiven him.

16 Confess your faults one to another, and pray one for another, that ye may be healed. The effectual fervent prayer of a righteous man availeth much.

17 Elias was a man subject to like passions as we are, and he prayed earnestly that it might not rain: and it rained not on the earth by the space of three years and six months.

18 And he prayed again, and the heaven gave rain, and the earth brought forth her fruit.

19 Brethren, if any of you do err from the truth, and one convert him;

20 Let him know, that he which converteth the sinner from the error of his way shall save a soul from death, and shall hide a multitude of sins.

---

5:7 **husbandman**—farmer

5:9 **Grudge**—Grumble, complain

5:12 James's counsel to "swear not" refers to not using the name of God or heaven to guarantee the truth of what you have said (see Matthew 5:33-37). We should be dependable and keep our word without having to swear an oath by using God's name in the wrong way.

5:14- The Lord explained that "he that hath faith in
16 me to be healed, and is not appointed unto death, shall be healed" (see D&C 42:43-44, 48-52).

5:16 No command is repeated more often in scripture than the command to pray. Sincere prayer can make a difference. What blessings come to you when your prayers are sincere?

5:17 This Elias is the prophet Elijah from the Old Testament (see 1 Kings 17:1).

5:19- There is great joy to be found in helping others
20 repent of their sins and come unto Jesus Christ (see D&C 18:15-16). There is another blessing that comes from sharing the gospel with others. "James indicated that each good deed, each testimony, each proselyting effort, each safeguard thrown about others is like a blanket over one's own sins" (Spencer W. Kimball, *Faith Precedes the Miracle*, p. 184).

# THE FIRST EPISTLE GENERAL OF
# PETER

*This letter was written by the Apostle Peter to converts. Peter encouraged them to hold on to their faith though they were suffering severe persecution.*

## CHAPTER 1

*Through the atonement of Jesus Christ, those who endure in faith will receive eternal life. Look for the phrase "trial of your faith" and think about why it is important that our faith be tested before we receive God's greatest blessings.*

### PETER GREETS AND PRAISES THE PEOPLE

1 PETER, an apostle of Jesus Christ, to the strangers scattered throughout Pontus, Galatia, Cappadocia, Asia, and Bithynia,

2 Elect according to the foreknowledge of God the Father, through sanctification of the Spirit, unto obedience and sprinkling of the blood of Jesus Christ: Grace unto you, and peace, be multiplied.

3 ¶ Blessed be the God and Father of our Lord Jesus Christ, which according to his abundant mercy hath begotten us again unto a lively hope by the resurrection of Jesus Christ from the dead,

4 To an inheritance incorruptible, and undefiled, and that fadeth not away, reserved in heaven for you,

5 Who are kept by the power of God through faith unto salvation ready to be revealed in the last time.

### THE TRIAL OF FAITH COMES BEFORE THE BLESSINGS

6 ¶ Wherein ye greatly rejoice, though now for a season, if need be, ye are in heaviness through manifold temptations:

7 That the trial of your faith, being much more precious than of gold that perisheth, though it be tried with fire, might be found unto praise and honour and glory at the appearing of Jesus Christ:

8 Whom having not seen, ye love; in whom, though now ye see him not, yet believing, ye rejoice with joy unspeakable and full of glory:

9 Receiving the end of your faith, even the salvation of your souls.

---

1:1 The word *strangers* did not mean the same thing in Peter's day that it does today. Peter is saying that the Church members are "strangers" because they once lived with their Father in Heaven but are now on earth and find the worldliness of earth life uncomfortable. They want to see heaven again. (See Hebrews 11:13-16.)

1:2 "Elect according to the foreknowledge of God" refers to those who were chosen or called in the premortal life because they were noble and great (see Abraham 3:23). The term *sanctification* is explained by Elder Bruce R. McConkie: "To be *sanctified* is to become clean, pure, and spotless; to be free from the blood and sins of the world. . . . *Sanctification* is a state of saintliness." (*Mormon Doctrine*, p. 675.) Sanctification comes only by obedience to the commandments and through the power of the Holy Ghost.

1:4 Peter spoke of "an inheritance incorruptible, and undefiled," which means that the blessings we receive in heaven are holy and will last forever.

1:6 *ye are in heaviness through manifold temptations*—it is hard to bear your trials, temptations, and afflictions

1:7 The trial of our faith is the process by which the Lord proves us to see if we are worthy of his blessings (see D&C 98:14-15). What are you doing to show the Lord that you have faith?

1:9-10 Those who endure in faith receive the gift of eternal life, "which gift is the greatest of all the gifts of God" (D&C 14:7).

| | | | |
|---|---|---|---|
| = Word Help | | = A Closer Look | |
| = More Light | | = Ponder This | |

Words in pink are explained in the Glossary.

10 ¶ Of which salvation the prophets have enquired and searched diligently, who prophesied of the grace that should come unto you:

11 Searching what, or what manner of time the Spirit of Christ which was in them did signify, when it testified beforehand the sufferings of Christ, and the glory that should follow.

12 Unto whom it was revealed, that not unto themselves, but unto us they did minister the things, which are now reported unto you by them that have preached the gospel unto you with the Holy Ghost sent down from heaven; which things the angels desire to look into.

13 ¶ Wherefore gird up the loins of your mind, be sober, and hope to the end for the grace that is to be brought unto you at the revelation of Jesus Christ;

14 As obedient children, not fashioning yourselves according to the former lusts in your ignorance:

15 But as he which hath called you is holy, so be ye holy in all manner of conversation;

16 Because it is written, Be ye holy; for I am holy.

17 And if ye call on the Father, who without respect of persons judgeth according to every man's work, pass the time of your sojourning here in fear:

## JESUS WAS FOREORDAINED TO BE THE REDEEMER

18 Forasmuch as ye know that ye were not redeemed with corruptible things, as silver and gold, from your vain conversation received by tradition from your fathers;

19 But with the precious blood of Christ, as of a lamb without blemish and without spot:

20 Who verily was foreordained before the foundation of the world, but was manifest in these last times for you,

21 Who by him do believe in God, that raised him up from the dead, and gave him glory; that your faith and hope might be in God.

22 Seeing ye have purified your souls in obeying the truth through the Spirit unto unfeigned love of the brethren, see that ye love one another with a pure heart fervently:

23 Being born again, not of corruptible seed, but of incorruptible, by the word of God, which liveth and abideth for ever.

24 ¶ For all flesh is as grass, and all the glory of man as the flower of grass. The grass withereth, and the flower thereof falleth away:

25 But the word of the Lord endureth for ever. And this is the word which by the gospel is preached unto you.

## CHAPTER 2

*Peter invites the Saints to become more righteous even though they live in a wicked world. Watch for Peter's counsel that can help you increase in righteousness.*

### CONVERTS ARE LIKE NEWBORN BABIES

1 ¶ WHEREFORE laying aside all malice, and all guile, and hypocrisies, and envies, and all evil speakings,

---

1:11 *signify*—show, prove

1:13 *gird up the loins of your mind*—prepare yourselves to listen
*sober*—serious, calm in spirit

1:14-15 The Saints in Peter's day had at one time, before their conversion, lived according to their "lusts," or evil desires. They lived that way in "ignorance," being unaware of the gospel of Jesus Christ. Peter asked them to live in holy "conversation," or conduct. They were to, in the words of the Apostle Paul, "walk worthy of God" (1 Thessalonians 2:12).

1:15-16 We are commanded to be holy, even as Jesus is holy (see 3 Nephi 12:48). What does it mean to you to be holy?

1:17 *pass the time of your sojourning here in fear*—live your life with devotion to God

1:18-19 Salvation does not come through the "corrupt-

ible," or temporary, riches of the world. We are redeemed from our "vain conversation," or bad conduct, through the power of Jesus Christ, which is the only way "salvation can come unto the children of men" (Mosiah 3:17).

1:22 *unfeigned*—sincere

Who loves you with a pure heart? Who are some of the people you love? Who are some people you could love more than you have in the past?

1:22-25 Peter teaches that the word of the Lord is eternal and will purify us if we obey the truth (see John 17:17).

2:1-3 Jesus taught that we must "be converted, and become as little children" to be saved (Matthew 18:3). Similarly, Peter teaches that we must give up all wickedness, such as malice (hatred) and guile (dishonesty), and be as babes desiring the pure word of God.

*In the premortal life Heavenly Father chose Jesus as our Savior. Peter wrote in his first epistle that Jesus "was foreordained before the foundation of the world" to be our Redeemer.*

2 As newborn babes, desire the sincere milk of the word, that ye may grow thereby:

3 If so be ye have tasted that the Lord is gracious.

## JESUS CHRIST IS THE CHIEF CORNERSTONE OF THE GOSPEL

4 ¶ To whom coming, as unto a living stone, disallowed indeed of men, but chosen of God, and precious,

5 Ye also, as lively stones, are built up a spiritual house, an holy priesthood, to offer up spiritual sacrifices, acceptable to God by Jesus Christ.

6 Wherefore also it is contained in the scripture, Behold, I lay in Sion a chief corner stone, elect, precious: and he that believeth on him shall not be confounded.

7 Unto you therefore which believe he is precious: but unto them which be disobedient, the stone which the builders disallowed, the same is made the head of the corner,

8 And a stone of stumbling, and a rock of offence, even to them which stumble at the word, being disobedient: whereunto also they were appointed.

## CHURCH MEMBERS SHOULD BE EXAMPLES OF THE GOSPEL

9 But ye are a chosen generation, a royal priesthood, an holy nation, a peculiar people; that ye should shew forth the praises of him who hath called you out of darkness into his marvellous light:

10 Which in time past were not a people, but are now the people of God: which had not obtained mercy, but now have obtained mercy.

11 Dearly beloved, I beseech you as strangers and pilgrims, abstain from fleshly lusts, which war against the soul;

12 Having your conversation honest among the Gentiles: that, whereas they speak against you as evil-doers, they may by your good works, which they shall behold, glorify God in the day of visitation.

13 ¶ Submit yourselves to every ordinance of man for the Lord's sake: whether it be to the king, as supreme;

14 Or unto governors, as unto them that are sent by him for the punishment of evildoers, and for the praise of them that do well.

15 For so is the will of God, that with well doing ye may put to silence the ignorance of foolish men:

16 As free, and not using your liberty for a cloke of maliciousness, but as the servants of God.

17 Honour all men. Love the brotherhood. Fear God. Honour the king.

18 Servants, be subject to your masters with all fear; not only to the good and gentle, but also to the froward.

## JESUS CHRIST SET A PERFECT EXAMPLE FOR ALL PEOPLE

19 For this is thankworthy, if a man for conscience toward God endure grief, suffering wrongfully.

20 For what glory is it, if, when ye be buffeted for your faults, ye shall take it patiently? but if, when ye do well, and suffer for it, ye take it patiently, this is acceptable with God.

---

2:4 **To whom coming**—Coming unto the Lord
**disallowed**—refused

2:5-6 Members of the Church are the lively stones with which Jesus is building a spiritual house, "whose house [we are]" (Hebrews 3:6). Jesus himself is the "chief corner stone," the stone which all other stones are lined up to and built upon. His house shall never fall (see Matthew 7:24-25).

2:6 **confounded**—ashamed

2:7-8 To those who believe, the Lord is "their rock and their salvation" (1 Nephi 15:15). But those who disobey end up stumbling over the word of his gospel. They are "ashamed to take upon [them] the name of Christ" (Mormon 8:38).

2:9 **shew**—This word is pronounced the same way as the word *show* and has the same meaning; *shew* is simply an old spelling of *show*.

2:9-10 The word *peculiar* in 1 Peter comes from a Greek word that means "purchased or preserved." How did Jesus purchase us? What did it cost him to preserve us from sin?

2:11 **abstain from fleshly lusts**—stay away from evil desires of the body

2:12 *Gentiles* is a word that means "nations." It refers to those not of the family of Israel or who do not believe in the God of Israel. (See LDS Bible Dictionary, s.v. "Gentile," pp. 679-80.)

2:13 **ordinance**—law

2:16 **for a cloke of maliciousness**—to hide your evil deeds

2:18 **froward**—unfair, harsh

2:19 **endure grief, suffering wrongfully**—suffers when he has not sinned

2:20 **buffeted**—beaten, punished

21 For even hereunto were ye called: because Christ also suffered for us, leaving us an example, that ye should follow his steps:

22 Who did no sin, neither was guile found in his mouth:

23 Who, when he was reviled, reviled not again; when he suffered, he threatened not; but committed himself to him that judgeth righteously:

24 Who his own self bare our sins in his own body on the tree, that we, being dead to sins, should live unto righteousness: by whose stripes ye were healed.

25 For ye were as sheep going astray; but are now returned unto the Shepherd and Bishop of your souls.

# CHAPTER 3

*Peter teaches the importance of living the gospel. Look for different ways you can be an example.*

## WIVES AND HUSBANDS SHOULD GIVE HONOR TO EACH OTHER

1 ¶ LIKEWISE, ye wives, be in subjection to your own husbands; that, if any obey not the word, they also may without the word be won by the conversation of the wives;

2 While they behold your chaste conversation coupled with fear.

3 Whose adorning let it not be that outward adorning of plaiting the hair, and of wearing of gold, or of putting on of apparel;

4 But let it be the hidden man of the heart, in that which is not corruptible, even the ornament of a meek and quiet spirit, which is in the sight of God of great price.

5 For after this manner in the old time the holy women also, who trusted in God, adorned themselves, being in subjection unto their own husbands:

6 Even as Sara obeyed Abraham, calling him lord: whose daughters ye are, as long as ye do well, and are not afraid with any amazement.

7 Likewise, ye husbands, dwell with them according to knowledge, giving honour unto the wife, as unto the weaker vessel, and as being heirs together of the grace of life; that your prayers be not hindered.

## SAINTS SHOULD TREAT EACH OTHER BY GOSPEL STANDARDS

8 ¶ Finally, be ye all of one mind, having compassion one of another, love as brethren, be pitiful, be courteous:

9 Not rendering evil for evil, or railing for railing: but contrariwise blessing; knowing that ye are thereunto called, that ye should inherit a blessing.

10 For he that will love life, and see good days, let him refrain his tongue from evil, and his lips that they speak no guile:

11 Let him eschew evil, and do good; let him seek peace, and ensue it.

12 For the eyes of the Lord are over the righteous, and his ears are open unto their prayers: but the face of the Lord is against them that do evil.

---

2:22 📖 **guile**—dishonesty

2:23 📖 **reviled**—persecuted

2:24-25 🔄 How is the Savior like a shepherd to us? Could a bishop also be like a shepherd? How?

3:1-2 🔄 The word "conversation" is changed to "conduct" in the Joseph Smith Translation (see JST, 1 Peter 3:1-2, 16). How does our example affect others who are learning about the Church?

3:3 📖 **adorning**—adding to one's looks with something like jewelry or a hairstyle
**plaiting the hair**—arranging the hair in a showy way

3:3-4 🔄 Peter says that modest and simple clothing combined with a gentle and forgiving nature is precious to God. Why is it more important to believe in who we are rather than how we look? (See 1 Samuel 16:7.)

3:4 📖 **corruptible**—temporary, likely to change

3:7 📖 **vessel**—body

3:8 📖 **pitiful**—kind, tenderhearted

3:8-9 🔍 Jesus taught us how to treat others who may treat us poorly. He did not tell us to "get even"; rather, he said, "Love your enemies, . . . pray for them" (Matthew 5:44).

3:9 📖 **rendering**—giving
**contrariwise**—instead

3:10 📖 **guile**—dishonesty

3:11 📖 **eschew**—avoid, turn away from
**ensue**—eagerly follow

## WE MAY SUFFER FOR DOING RIGHT

13 And who is he that will harm you, if ye be followers of that which is good?

14 But and if ye suffer for righteousness' sake, happy are ye: and be not afraid of their terror, neither be troubled;

15 But sanctify the Lord God in your hearts: and be ready always to give an answer to every man that asketh you a reason of the hope that is in you with meekness and fear:

16 ¶ Having a good conscience; that, whereas they speak evil of you, as of evildoers, they may be ashamed that falsely accuse your good conversation in Christ.

17 For it is better, if the will of God be so, that ye suffer for well doing, than for evil doing.

## CHRIST VISITS THE SPIRIT WORLD

18 ¶ For Christ also hath once suffered for sins, the just for the unjust, that he might bring us to God, being put to death in the flesh, but quickened by the Spirit:

19 By which also he went and preached unto the spirits in prison;

20 Which sometime were disobedient, when once the longsuffering of God waited in the days of Noah, while the ark was a preparing, wherein few, that is, eight souls were saved by water.

21 ¶ The like figure whereunto even baptism doth also now save us (not the putting away of the filth of the flesh, but the answer of a good conscience toward God,) by the resurrection of Jesus Christ:

22 Who is gone into heaven, and is on the right hand of God; angels and authorities and powers being made subject unto him.

## CHAPTER 4

*Jesus provided the way for the gospel to be preached to the spirits of those who have died. Watch for reasons why the gospel must be preached to the dead.*

## MEMBERS OF THE CHURCH SHOULD NOT COMMIT SINS

1 ¶ FORASMUCH then as Christ hath suffered for us in the flesh, arm yourselves likewise with the same mind: for he that hath suffered in the flesh hath ceased from sin;

2 That he no longer should live the rest of his time in the flesh to the lusts of men, but to the will of God.

3 For the time past of our life may suffice us to have wrought the will of the Gentiles, when we walked in lasciviousness, lusts, excess of wine, revellings, banquetings, and abominable idolatries:

4 ¶ Wherein they think it strange that ye run not with them to the same excess of riot, speaking evil of you:

5 Who shall give account to him that is ready to judge the quick and the dead.

6 For for this cause was the gospel preached also to them that are dead, that they might be judged according to men in the flesh, but live according to God in the spirit.

7 ¶ But the end of all things is at hand: be ye therefore sober, and watch unto prayer.

---

3:15 **sanctify**—respect, revere

"Every member of the Church should be converted and have a knowledge of the gospel, including a knowledge of the scriptures. How wonderful it would be if every member of the Church could [do] as Peter of old." (David O. McKay, in Conference Report, October 1969, p. 88.)

3:18 **quickened**—made alive

3:19 The Lord has revealed a detailed account of what happened when Jesus went to the spirit world (see D&C 138).

Jesus' visit to the spirit world made it possible for many who had died to learn the gospel for the first time. How does family history and temple work help those who have died?

3:21 "Baptism does not wash away the sins of men unless they have repented" (Bruce R. McConkie, *Doctrinal New Testament Commentary* 3:314).

4:2 **lusts**—evil desires

4:3 Peter reminded the members of the Church of the many sins they had committed before they were converted.

4:5 **quick**—living

4:6 President Joseph F. Smith saw a vision of the spirit world and how the gospel is preached to the spirits in prison (see D&C 138).

*Jesus Christ in the spirit world*

## MEMBERS OF THE CHURCH SHOULD LOVE AND CARE FOR OTHER PEOPLE

8 And above all things have fervent charity among yourselves: for charity shall cover the multitude of sins.

9 Use hospitality one to another without grudging.

10 As every man hath received the gift, even so minister the same one to another, as good stewards of the manifold grace of God.

11 If any man speak, let him speak as the oracles of God; if any man minister, let him do it as of the ability which God giveth: that God in all things may be glorified through Jesus Christ, to whom be praise and dominion for ever and ever. Amen.

## TRIALS AND DIFFICULTIES HELP US LEARN IMPORTANT LESSONS

12 ¶ Beloved, think it not strange concerning the fiery trial which is to try you, as though some strange thing happened unto you:

13 But rejoice, inasmuch as ye are partakers of Christ's sufferings; that, when his glory shall be revealed, ye may be glad also with exceeding joy.

14 If ye be reproached for the name of Christ, happy are ye; for the spirit of glory and of God resteth upon you: on their part he is evil spoken of, but on your part he is glorified.

15 But let none of you suffer as a murderer, or as a thief, or as an evildoer, or as a busybody in other men's matters.

16 Yet if any man suffer as a Christian, let him not be ashamed; but let him glorify God on this behalf.

17 For the time is come that judgment must begin at the house of God: and if it first begin at us, what shall the end be of them that obey not the gospel of God?

18 And if the righteous scarcely be saved, where shall the ungodly and the sinner appear?

19 Wherefore let them that suffer according to the will of God commit the keeping of their souls to him in well doing, as unto a faithful Creator.

## CHAPTER 5

*Peter explains what leaders and members of the Church should do to be saved. Note what they are asked to do.*

## LEADERS OF THE CHURCH SHOULD WILLINGLY SERVE

1 ¶ THE elders which are among you I exhort, who am also an elder, and a witness of the sufferings of Christ, and also a partaker of the glory that shall be revealed:

2 Feed the flock of God which is among you, taking the oversight thereof, not by constraint, but willingly; not for filthy lucre, but of a ready mind;

3 Neither as being lords over God's heritage, but being ensamples to the flock.

4 And when the chief Shepherd shall appear, ye shall receive a crown of glory that fadeth not away.

5 ¶ Likewise, ye younger, submit yourselves unto the elder. Yea, all of you be subject one to another, and be clothed with humility: for God resisteth the proud, and giveth grace to the humble.

---

4:8   "Charity is the pure love of Christ" (Moroni 7:47).

The Joseph Smith Translation changes the word "cover" to "preventeth" (see JST, 1 Peter 4:8). How does having charity prevent us from committing sins?

4:9   **hospitality**—loving care
**grudging**—complaining, grumbling

4:11   **the oracles of God**—the words of God

4:12-19   What difficult challenges have you faced in life? What lessons have you learned from these trials? How do we become more like Jesus when we experience trials?

4:14   **reproached**—insulted

4:15   Why do sins cause people to suffer? (See Alma 41:11.)

4:19   **commit the keeping of their souls**—trust their souls

5:2   **constraint**—force
**filthy lucre**—money

5:2-3   Peter learned from Jesus how important it is to feed His sheep (see John 21:15-17). This includes willingly helping other people without getting paid and being a good example to others.

5:3   **heritage**—children

5:5   **resisteth**—opposes

## MEMBERS OF THE CHURCH SHOULD STRIVE TO BE MORE RIGHTEOUS

6 Humble yourselves therefore under the mighty hand of God, that he may exalt you in due time:

7 Casting all your care upon him; for he careth for you.

8 ¶ Be sober, be vigilant; because your adversary the devil, as a roaring lion, walketh about, seeking whom he may devour:

9 Whom resist stedfast in the faith, knowing that the same afflictions are accomplished in your brethren that are in the world.

10 ¶ But the God of all grace, who hath called us unto his eternal glory by Christ Jesus, after that ye have suffered a while, make you perfect, stablish, strengthen, settle you.

11 To him be glory and dominion for ever and ever. Amen.

12 By Silvanus, a faithful brother unto you, as I suppose, I have written briefly, exhorting, and testifying that this is the true grace of God wherein ye stand.

13 The church that is at Babylon, elected together with you, saluteth you; and so doth Marcus my son.

14 Greet ye one another with a kiss of charity. Peace be with you all that are in Christ Jesus. Amen.

---

5:8     **sober**—serious, calm in spirit
        **vigilant**—watchful

5:8-10   Peter knew that Satan would try to "devour," or destroy, members of the Church. Peter also knew that Jesus can strengthen us against Satan's temptations. What does Peter say we can do to be worthy of Jesus' help?

5:9     **Whom resist stedfast**—Resist him (the devil), being firm

5:11    **dominion**—authority, power

# THE SECOND EPISTLE GENERAL OF
# PETER

*Peter wrote this second epistle near the end of his life. The purpose of this letter is to show how knowing Jesus Christ better can help us become more like him.*

## CHAPTER 1

*Peter tells Church members to make their calling and election sure. Look for how Jesus Christ's example can help us obtain this blessing.*

### MEMBERS OF THE CHURCH CAN MAKE THEIR CALLING AND ELECTION SURE

1 SIMON Peter, a servant and an apostle of Jesus Christ, to them that have obtained like precious faith with us through the righteousness of God and our Saviour Jesus Christ:

2 Grace and peace be multiplied unto you through the knowledge of God, and of Jesus our Lord,

3 According as his divine power hath given unto us all things that pertain unto life and godliness, through the knowledge of him that hath called us to glory and virtue:

4 Whereby are given unto us exceeding great and precious promises: that by these ye might be partakers of the divine nature, having escaped the corruption that is in the world through lust.

5 ¶ And beside this, giving all diligence, add to your faith virtue; and to virtue knowledge;

6 And to knowledge temperance; and to temperance patience; and to patience godliness;

7 And to godliness brotherly kindness; and to brotherly kindness charity.

8 For if these things be in you, and abound, they make you that ye shall neither be barren nor unfruitful in the knowledge of our Lord Jesus Christ.

9 But he that lacketh these things is blind, and cannot see afar off, and hath forgotten that he was purged from his old sins.

10 Wherefore the rather, brethren, give diligence to make your calling and election sure: for if ye do these things, ye shall never fall:

11 For so an entrance shall be ministered unto you abundantly into the everlasting kingdom of our Lord and Saviour Jesus Christ.

### PETER IS AN EYEWITNESS OF THE LORD

12 ¶ Wherefore I will not be negligent to put you always in remembrance of these things, though ye know them, and be established in the present truth.

13 Yea, I think it meet, as long as I am in this tabernacle, to stir you up by putting you in remembrance;

---

1:4 **be partakers of the divine nature**—become Christlike
**corruption**—evil

1:4-8 The qualities Peter mentions can help us become more Christlike. Which ones are you doing well at? Which ones do you need to work on harder?

1:5 **diligence**—consistent effort
**virtue**—goodness in thought and action

1:6 **temperance**—self-control

1:8 **abound**—increase or grow
**barren**—empty

1:10 Elder Bruce R. McConkie said, "To have one's calling and election made sure is to be sealed up unto eternal life; it is to have the unconditional guarantee of exaltation in the highest heaven of the celestial world" (*Doctrinal New Testament Commentary* 3:330).

1:12 **not be negligent**—not fail or neglect

1:13 **tabernacle**—body

---

 = Word Help     = A Closer Look
 = More Light     = Ponder This
Words in pink are explained in the Glossary.

*Peter prepares to write a letter to the early Christians.*

14 Knowing that shortly I must put off this my tabernacle, even as our Lord Jesus Christ hath shewed me.
15 Moreover I will endeavour that ye may be able after my decease to have these things always in remembrance.
16 ¶ For we have not followed cunningly devised fables, when we made known unto you the power and coming of our Lord Jesus Christ, but were eyewitnesses of his majesty.
17 For he received from God the Father honour and glory, when there came such a voice to him from the excellent glory, This is my beloved Son, in whom I am well pleased.
18 And this voice which came from heaven we heard, when we were with him in the holy mount.
19 ¶ We have also a more sure word of prophecy; whereunto ye do well that ye take heed, as unto a light that shineth in a dark place, until the day dawn, and the day star arise in your hearts:

---

1:14    **put off this my tabernacle**—die
**shewed**—This word is pronounced the same way as the word *showed* and has the same meaning; *shewed* is simply an old spelling of *showed*.

Jesus Christ had told Peter that he (Peter) would be crucified (see John 21:18-19).

1:15    **endeavour**—try, make every effort
**decease**—death

1:16    **cunningly devised fables**—stories that are not true

**majesty**—glory

1:18    "In the holy mount" refers to the experience when Peter, James, and John were with Jesus on the Mount of Transfiguration (see Matthew 17:1-9).

1:19    Joseph Smith said, "The more sure word of prophecy means a man's knowing that he is sealed up unto eternal life, by revelation and the spirit of prophecy, through the power of the Holy Priesthood" (D&C 131:5).

20 Knowing this first, that no prophecy of the scripture is of any private interpretation.

21 For the prophecy came not in old time by the will of man: but holy men of God spake as they were moved by the Holy Ghost.

## CHAPTER 2

*Peter speaks of members of the Church who teach others to do wrong. Watch for the warning he gives to those who have been taught what is right but choose to do wrong.*

### FALSE TEACHERS WILL BE DESTROYED BY GOD

1 ¶ BUT there were false prophets also among the people, even as there shall be false teachers among you, who privily shall bring in damnable heresies, even denying the Lord that bought them, and bring upon themselves swift destruction.

2 And many shall follow their pernicious ways; by reason of whom the way of truth shall be evil spoken of.

3 ¶ And through covetousness shall they with feigned words make merchandise of you: whose judgment now of a long time lingereth not, and their damnation slumbereth not.

4 For if God spared not the angels that sinned, but cast them down to hell, and delivered them into chains of darkness, to be reserved unto judgment;

5 And spared not the old world, but saved Noah the eighth person, a preacher of righteousness, bringing in the flood upon the world of the ungodly;

6 And turning the cities of Sodom and Gomorrha into ashes condemned them with an overthrow, making them an ensample unto those that after should live ungodly;

7 ¶ And delivered just Lot, vexed with the filthy conversation of the wicked:

8 (For that righteous man dwelling among them, in seeing and hearing, vexed his righteous soul from day to day with their unlawful deeds;)

9 The Lord knoweth how to deliver the godly out of temptations, and to reserve the unjust unto the day of judgment to be punished:

### MEMBERS WHO WILL NOT RESIST SIN OFTEN LEAVE THE CHURCH

10 ¶ But chiefly them that walk after the flesh in the lust of uncleanness, and despise government. Presumptuous are they, selfwilled, they are not afraid to speak evil of dignities.

11 Whereas angels, which are greater in power and might, bring not railing accusation against them before the Lord.

12 But these, as natural brute beasts, made to be taken and destroyed, speak evil of the things that they understand not; and shall utterly perish in their own corruption;

13 And shall receive the reward of unrighteousness, as they that count it pleasure to riot in the day time. Spots they are and blemishes, sporting themselves with their own deceivings while they feast with you;

---

1:20   The Joseph Smith Translation changes verse 20 to read, ". . . no prophecy of the scriptures is given of any private will of man."

1:21   Scriptures come as prophets speak by the power of the Holy Ghost (see D&C 68:3–4). How have the scriptures helped you? How do you know they are from God?

2:1   **privily**—in secret
**heresies**—false teachings

2:2   **pernicious**—destructive

2:3   **covetousness**—desire to have more, greed
**feigned**—untrue, lying

  Because they are greedy, some people will lie and cheat to make money. What advertisements can you think of that make something bad look good so that it can be sold for money?

2:4-8   During Old Testament times God punished the wicked people who tried to destroy the righteous

(see Genesis 7; 19; Revelation 12).

2:6   **ensample**—example

2:7   **vexed**—troubled, bothered

2:10   **Presumptuous**—Not reverent; Daring
**dignities**—that which belongs to God

2:11   **railing accusation**—insulting or angry charge of wrongdoing

2:12   Peter's description of evil men as "natural brute beasts" is similar to the "natural man" King Benjamin spoke of. The natural man remains an enemy to God unless he listens to the promptings of the Holy Spirit and becomes a humble follower of Christ. (See Mosiah 3:19.)

2:13   **riot in the day time**—sin openly and rebel where others can see them

  Sinful members who may influence others to also sin are here compared to spots and blemishes.

14 Having eyes full of adultery, and that cannot cease from sin; beguiling unstable souls: an heart they have exercised with covetous practices; cursed children:

15 Which have forsaken the right way, and are gone astray, following the way of Balaam the son of Bosor, who loved the wages of unrighteousness;

16 But was rebuked for his iniquity: the dumb ass speaking with man's voice forbad the madness of the prophet.

17 These are wells without water, clouds that are carried with a tempest; to whom the mist of darkness is reserved for ever.

18 For when they speak great swelling words of vanity, they allure through the lusts of the flesh, through much wantonness, those that were clean escaped from them who live in error.

19 While they promise them liberty, they themselves are the servants of corruption: for of whom a man is overcome, of the same is he brought in bondage.

20 For if after they have escaped the pollutions of the world through the knowledge of the Lord and Saviour Jesus Christ, they are again entangled therein, and overcome, the latter end is worse with them than the beginning.

21 For it had been better for them not to have known the way of righteousness, than, after they have known it, to turn from the holy commandment delivered unto them.

22 But it is happened unto them according to the true proverb, The dog is turned to his own vomit again;

and the sow that was washed to her wallowing in the mire.

# CHAPTER 3

*Peter taught about Jesus Christ's second coming. Look for how you can prepare for that great day.*

## MANY PEOPLE IN THE LATTER DAYS WILL DOUBT THE REALITY OF THE SECOND COMING

1 ¶ THIS second epistle, beloved, I now write unto you; in both which I stir up your pure minds by way of remembrance:

2 That ye may be mindful of the words which were spoken before by the holy prophets, and of the commandment of us the apostles of the Lord and Saviour:

3 ¶ Knowing this first, that there shall come in the last days scoffers, walking after their own lusts,

4 And saying, Where is the promise of his coming? for since the fathers fell asleep, all things continue as they were from the beginning of the creation.

5 For this they willingly are ignorant of, that by the word of God the heavens were of old, and the earth standing out of the water and in the water:

6 Whereby the world that then was, being overflowed with water, perished:

7 But the heavens and the earth, which are now, by the same word are kept in store, reserved unto fire against the day of judgment and perdition of ungodly men.

---

2:14   The use of the sacred creative powers with someone other than your husband or wife (adultery) is a serious sin. It often leads "unstable souls" (others with weak testimonies) to sin as well (see Alma 39:11).

2:15-16   Peter uses the sad example of the Old Testament prophet Balaam to show how loving money and people's praise can lead us to sin (see Numbers 22-24).

2:17-19   Paul explains that Satan's false teachers promise happiness and freedom, but what they give is bondage, or slavery, to sin (see Alma 30:60).

2:20-21   The Lord has revealed in our own day that "he who sins against the greater light shall receive the greater condemnation" (see D&C 82:3).

2:22   The proverb about a dog and a pig describes what it is like to return to sin after we have repented (see Proverbs 26:11). When we stop a

sin, why is it so bad to start doing it again? (See D&C 82:7.)

3:3   **scoffers**—people who do not believe and who make fun of those who do
**lusts**—evil desires

3:4   "In this simple statement is summarized one of the basic reasons why the wisdom of men cannot interpret the events of creation, redemption, and salvation. The reason: It is false to assume that all things have always been the same." (Bruce R. McConkie, *Doctrinal New Testament Commentary* 3:366.)

3:5-6   Peter speaks of the flood that covered the entire earth (see Genesis 7:11-24).

3:7   "The heavens and the earth, which are now" refers to the earth in its current fallen state. Evil and wickedness are now found on the earth. At Christ's second coming the earth will be cleansed by fire and all those who do wickedly will be destroyed (see Malachi 4:1).

8 ¶ But, beloved, be not ignorant of this one thing, that one day is with the Lord as a thousand years, and a thousand years as one day.

9 ¶ The Lord is not slack concerning his promise, as some men count slackness; but is longsuffering to us-ward, not willing that any should perish, but that all should come to repentance.

## THE EARTH WILL BE CLEANSED WITH FIRE AT THE SECOND COMING

10 But the day of the Lord will come as a thief in the night; in the which the heavens shall pass away with a great noise, and the elements shall melt with fervent heat, the earth also and the works that are therein shall be burned up.

11 ¶ Seeing then that all these things shall be dissolved, what manner of persons ought ye to be in all holy conversation and godliness,

12 Looking for and hasting unto the coming of the day of God, wherein the heavens being on fire shall be dissolved, and the elements shall melt with fervent heat?

13 Nevertheless we, according to his promise, look for new heavens and a new earth, wherein dwelleth righteousness.

## PREPARE FOR THE SECOND COMING

14 Wherefore, beloved, seeing that ye look for such things, be diligent that ye may be found of him in peace, without spot, and blameless.

15 And account that the longsuffering of our Lord is salvation; even as our beloved brother Paul also according to the wisdom given unto him hath written unto you;

16 As also in all his epistles, speaking in them of these things; in which are some things hard to be understood, which they that are unlearned and unstable wrest, as they do also the other scriptures, unto their own destruction.

17 Ye therefore, beloved, seeing ye know these things before, beware lest ye also, being led away with the error of the wicked, fall from your own sted-fastness.

18 But grow in grace, and in the knowledge of our Lord and Saviour Jesus Christ. To him be glory both now and for ever. Amen.

---

3:9-10  Some may think the Lord is delaying the Second Coming, but Peter teaches that the Lord is not "slack" in His promises, meaning that all He speaks will truly come to pass (see D&C 1:38).

3:10  *as a thief in the night*—suddenly, without warning
*fervent*—intense or strong

3:11  At the second coming of Jesus Christ the righteous will be caught up to meet him and be saved (see 1 Thessalonians 4:16-17). What are you doing to prepare yourself for that great day? Why should the faithful not fear?

3:13  At the Second Coming the earth will be cleansed by fire, renewed, and receive its paradisiacal glory (see Articles of Faith 1:10).

3:16  Those who are "unlearned" and do not believe in Jesus Christ will try to "wrest" (change or twist) the scriptures to prove that there will be no Second Coming.

3:17-18  Peter warns the people to not fall away from the truth and to be ready for the Second Coming. What does this teach you about Peter's love for the Saints? What warnings do the prophets give us today? Why should we follow the counsel of the prophet?

# The First Epistle General of

# JOHN

*This letter was written by John the Beloved to members of the Church living about sixty years after the death of Jesus Christ. John wrote to warn them of false teachers who sought to lead them away from the gospel of Jesus Christ.*

## CHAPTER 1

*John testifies that he knew Jesus Christ. Look for what he tells the Saints they must do to come to know Christ.*

### THE SAINTS WALK WITH GOD THROUGH OBEDIENCE

1 THAT which was from the beginning, which we have heard, which we have seen with our eyes, which we have looked upon, and our hands have handled, of the Word of life;

2 (For the life was manifested, and we have seen it, and bear witness, and shew unto you that eternal life, which was with the Father, and was manifested unto us;)

3 That which we have seen and heard declare we unto you, that ye also may have fellowship with us: and truly our fellowship is with the Father, and with his Son Jesus Christ.

4 And these things write we unto you, that your joy may be full.

### WE MUST CONFESS OUR SINS TO GAIN FORGIVENESS

5 ¶ This then is the message which we have heard of him, and declare unto you, that God is light, and in him is no darkness at all.

6 If we say that we have fellowship with him, and walk in darkness, we lie, and do not the truth:

7 But if we walk in the light, as he is in the light, we have fellowship one with another, and the blood of Jesus Christ his Son cleanseth us from all sin.

8 ¶ If we say that we have no sin, we deceive ourselves, and the truth is not in us.

9 If we confess our sins, he is faithful and just to forgive us our sins, and to cleanse us from all unrighteousness.

10 If we say that we have not sinned, we make him a liar, and his word is not in us.

## CHAPTER 2

*John speaks about knowing God. Watch for what we must do to know God.*

---

1:1    The Joseph Smith Translation begins this chapter with: "Brethren, this is the testimony which we give of . . ." (JST, 1 John 1:1).

1:1-3    "That which was from the beginning" is Jesus Christ, "the Word of life" (see John 1:1-2, 14). John testifies that he and others had seen and touched the resurrected Savior of the world (see John 20:19–20).

1:2    **shew**—This word is pronounced the same way as the word *show* and has the same meaning; *shew* is simply an old spelling of *show*.

1:3-4    John wanted the Saints to enjoy the same fellowship with God and Jesus that he enjoyed (see D&C 93:1).

1:6    **do not the truth**—are not obedient to the gospel

1:7    Jesus shed his blood in Gethsemane to atone for the sins of all mankind. Through this atonement we can be clean from sin if we repent. The Lord declared, "My blood shall not cleanse them if they hear me not" (D&C 29:17).

1:8-10    Since we are all guilty of sin, confessing (admitting) that we have sinned is an important part of becoming clean. Whom should we confess our sins to so we can become clean?

---

= Word Help    = A Closer Look

= More Light    = Ponder This

Words in pink are explained in the Glossary.

## THE SAVIOR WILL HELP ALL PEOPLE WHO SIN AND REPENT

1 ¶ MY little children, these things write I unto you, that ye sin not. And if any man sin, we have an advocate with the Father, Jesus Christ the righteous:

2 And he is the propitiation for our sins: and not for ours only, but also for the sins of the whole world.

## JOHN EXPLAINS HOW WE CAN KNOW GOD

3 ¶ And hereby we do know that we know him, if we keep his commandments.

4 He that saith, I know him, and keepeth not his commandments, is a liar, and the truth is not in him.

5 But whoso keepeth his word, in him verily is the love of God perfected: hereby know we that we are in him.

6 He that saith he abideth in him ought himself also so to walk, even as he walked.

7 ¶ Brethren, I write no new commandment unto you, but an old commandment which ye had from the beginning. The old commandment is the word which ye have heard from the beginning.

8 Again, a new commandment I write unto you, which thing is true in him and in you: because the darkness is past, and the true light now shineth.

9 He that saith he is in the light, and hateth his brother, is in darkness even until now.

10 He that loveth his brother abideth in the light, and there is none occasion of stumbling in him.

11 But he that hateth his brother is in darkness, and walketh in darkness, and knoweth not whither he goeth, because that darkness hath blinded his eyes.

12 ¶ I write unto you, little children, because your sins are forgiven you for his name's sake.

13 I write unto you, fathers, because ye have known him that is from the beginning. I write unto you, young men, because ye have overcome the wicked one. I write unto you, little children, because ye have known the Father.

14 I have written unto you, fathers, because ye have known him that is from the beginning. I have written unto you, young men, because ye are strong, and the word of God abideth in you, and ye have overcome the wicked one.

## WE SHOULD NOT LOVE THE THINGS OF THE WORLD

15 Love not the world, neither the things that are in the world. If any man love the world, the love of the Father is not in him.

16 For all that is in the world, the lust of the flesh, and the lust of the eyes, and the pride of life, is not of the Father, but is of the world.

17 And the world passeth away, and the lust thereof: but he that doeth the will of God abideth for ever.

## ANTICHRISTS WILL COME IN THE LAST DAYS

18 ¶ Little children, it is the last time: and as ye have heard that antichrist shall come, even now are there many antichrists; whereby we know that it is the last time.

19 They went out from us, but they were not of us; for if they had been of us, they would no doubt have continued with us: but they went out, that they might be made manifest that they were not all of us.

---

2:1 John uses the phrase "my little children" as a tender way of speaking to his fellow followers of Christ (see also 1 John 2:12, 13, 18, 28). The Lord used similar language as he addressed his latter-day servants: "Fear not, little children, for you are mine" (D&C 50:41; see also D&C 50:40; 78:17-18).

The Joseph Smith Translation adds the important words "and repent" after the words "if any man sin" (JST, 1 John 2:1).

**an advocate**—a person who defends us

2:2 The Savior suffered for our sins so that if we repent they will be taken away (see Acts 5:30-32).

2:3-6 John 17:3 explains that if we wish to have eternal life we must know God the Father and his Son, Jesus Christ. What are you doing to get closer to them?

2:7-8 Though the commandments John writes are new to his readers, they are the same commandments that were given to Adam and his children (see JST, 1 John 2:7-8).

2:9-11 How can loving other people help us?

2:15-17 We cannot love the things of the world and love God at the same time (see Matthew 6:24).

2:16 **lust**—evil desires

2:18 **antichrists**—people who deny and fight against Jesus Christ and his teachings

2:19 **made manifest**—seen by others

20 ¶ But ye have an unction from the Holy One, and ye know all things.

21 I have not written unto you because ye know not the truth, but because ye know it, and that no lie is of the truth.

22 Who is a liar but he that denieth that Jesus is the Christ? He is antichrist, that denieth the Father and the Son.

23 Whosoever denieth the Son, the same hath not the Father: [but] he that acknowledgeth the Son hath the Father also.

24 Let that therefore abide in you, which ye have heard from the beginning. If that which ye have heard from the beginning shall remain in you, ye also shall continue in the Son, and in the Father.

25 And this is the promise that he hath promised us, even eternal life.

26 These things have I written unto you concerning them that seduce you.

## WE CAN LEARN TRUTH THROUGH THE HOLY GHOST

27 But the anointing which ye have received of him abideth in you, and ye need not that any man teach you: but as the same anointing teacheth you of all things, and is truth, and is no lie, and even as it hath taught you, ye shall abide in him.

28 ¶ And now, little children, abide in him; that, when he shall appear, we may have confidence, and not be ashamed before him at his coming.

29 If ye know that he is righteous, ye know that every one that doeth righteousness is born of him.

# CHAPTER 3

*John explains what we must do to gain eternal life. Look for ways you can become more Christlike in your own life.*

## THOSE WHO ARE BORN AGAIN DO NOT CONTINUE IN SIN

1 ¶ BEHOLD, what manner of love the Father hath bestowed upon us, that we should be called the sons of God: therefore the world knoweth us not, because it knew him not.

2 Beloved, now are we the sons of God, and it doth not yet appear what we shall be: but we know that, when he shall appear, we shall be like him; for we shall see him as he is.

3 And every man that hath this hope in him purifieth himself, even as he is pure.

4 ¶ Whosoever committeth sin transgresseth also the law: for sin is the transgression of the law.

5 And ye know that he was manifested to take away our sins; and in him is no sin.

6 Whosoever abideth in him sinneth not: whosoever sinneth hath not seen him, neither known him.

7 Little children, let no man deceive you: he that doeth righteousness is righteous, even as he is righteous.

8 He that committeth sin is of the devil; for the devil sinneth from the beginning. For this purpose the Son of God was manifested, that he might destroy the works of the devil.

---

2:20    The members of the Church having received an "unction from the Holy One" means "they had received the Holy Ghost so that the spirit of revelation and knowledge rested with them" (Bruce R. McConkie, *Mormon Doctrine*, p. 813).

2:23    **acknowledgeth**—testifies of

2:26    People who try to "seduce" members of the Church are "those who teach false doctrines and lead the saints away from the paths of truth and righteousness" (Bruce R. McConkie, *Doctrinal New Testament Commentary* 3:382).

2:27    This "anointing" refers to the Holy Ghost, who can teach us all things (see John 14:26).

2:28    To abide in Christ is to keep his commandments (see 1 John 2:3-6). How will keeping God's commandments give you courage and confidence when the Savior comes again?

3:1    **bestowed upon**—given as a gift to

3:2-3    Christ is our example. We ought to try very hard to be like him. As we become more and more like him we will become clean from our sins. (See 2 Nephi 31:7-10.)

3:5    **was manifested**—appeared

3:6    **abideth in**—lives in or stays close to

3:8-9    Note the important changes made to these verses in the Joseph Smith Translation (the changes appear in italic type): "He that *continueth in* sin is of the devil; for the devil sinneth from the beginning. For this purpose the Son of God was manifested, that he might destroy the works of the devil. Whosoever is born of God doth not *continue in* sin; for *the Spirit of God* remaineth in him; and he cannot *continue in* sin, because he is born of God, *having received that holy Spirit of promise*." (JST, 1 John 3:8-9.)

9 Whosoever is born of God doth not commit sin; for his seed remaineth in him: and he cannot sin, because he is born of God.

10 In this the children of God are manifest, and the children of the devil: whosoever doeth not righteousness is not of God, neither he that loveth not his brother.

## WE OUGHT TO LOVE ONE ANOTHER

11 ¶ For this is the message that ye heard from the beginning, that we should love one another.

12 Not as Cain, who was of that wicked one, and slew his brother. And wherefore slew he him? Because his own works were evil, and his brother's righteous.

13 Marvel not, my brethren, if the world hate you.

14 ¶ We know that we have passed from death unto life, because we love the brethren. He that loveth not his brother abideth in death.

15 Whosoever hateth his brother is a murderer: and ye know that no murderer hath eternal life abiding in him.

16 Hereby perceive we the love of God, because he laid down his life for us: and we ought to lay down our lives for the brethren.

17 But whoso hath this world's good, and seeth his brother have need, and shutteth up his bowels of compassion from him, how dwelleth the love of God in him?

18 My little children, let us not love in word, neither in tongue; but in deed and in truth.

19 And hereby we know that we are of the truth, and shall assure our hearts before him.

20 ¶ For if our heart condemn us, God is greater than our heart, and knoweth all things.

21 Beloved, if our heart condemn us not, then have we confidence toward God.

22 And whatsoever we ask, we receive of him, because we keep his commandments, and do those things that are pleasing in his sight.

23 ¶ And this is his commandment, That we should believe on the name of his Son Jesus Christ, and love one another, as he gave us commandment.

24 And he that keepeth his commandments dwelleth in him, and he in him. And hereby we know that he abideth in us, by the Spirit which he hath given us.

## CHAPTER 4

*John warns that there are people in the world who desire to destroy our belief in the Savior. He also teaches us how much God loves us and how we should love Him. Watch for what John says that can help you increase your love for God.*

## GOOD PEOPLE TESTIFY THAT JESUS CHRIST IS THE SAVIOR

1 ¶ BELOVED, believe not every spirit, but try the spirits whether they are of God: because many false prophets are gone out into the world.

2 Hereby know ye the Spirit of God: Every spirit that confesseth that Jesus Christ is come in the flesh is of God:

3 And every spirit that confesseth not that Jesus Christ is come in the flesh is not of God: and this is that spirit

---

3:9 To be "born of God" is to be born again, changed in your heart in such a way that you want to do good and always try to avoid evil (see Mosiah 5:2, 7; Alma 5:14).

3:12 Cain killed his brother, Abel, out of hatred and jealousy because Cain wanted to obtain his brother's flocks (see Moses 5:26, 31-33).

3:16 Jesus said that the greatest love we can have is to be willing to die for those we love (see John 15:13). This is the kind of love Jesus has for us.

3:17 **shutteth up his bowels of compassion from—** refuses to share with

3:20 **condemn us—**blames us for our mistakes

3:21 **confidence—**hope

3:22 John tells us that the Lord will give us what we pray for when we are obedient to his commandments. Have you noticed a difference in your prayers when you are doing your best to keep the commandments compared with when you are not as obedient as you could be?

3:23 Jesus taught that to love one another is the second most important commandment we could keep (see Matthew 22:37-39).

4:2 **confesseth—**says openly

4:2-3 Sometimes it is difficult to tell if something is true or false. What does John tell us to do so that we can know if something is true? (See Moroni 7:16-17.)

4:3 **antichrist—**a person who denies and fights against Jesus Christ and his teachings

of antichrist, whereof ye have heard that it should come; and even now already is it in the world.

4 ¶ Ye are of God, little children, and have overcome them: because greater is he that is in you, than he that is in the world.

5 They are of the world: therefore speak they of the world, and the world heareth them.

6 We are of God: he that knoweth God heareth us; he that is not of God heareth not us. Hereby know we the spirit of truth, and the spirit of error.

## WE SHOULD LOVE GOD AND ONE ANOTHER

7 ¶ Beloved, let us love one another: for love is of God; and every one that loveth is born of God, and knoweth God.

8 He that loveth not knoweth not God; for God is love.

9 In this was manifested the love of God toward us, because that God sent his only begotten Son into the world, that we might live through him.

10 Herein is love, not that we loved God, but that he loved us, and sent his Son to be the propitiation for our sins.

11 Beloved, if God so loved us, we ought also to love one another.

12 No man hath seen God at any time. If we love one another, God dwelleth in us, and his love is perfected in us.

13 Hereby know we that we dwell in him, and he in us, because he hath given us of his Spirit.

14 ¶ And we have seen and do testify that the Father sent the Son to be the Saviour of the world.

15 Whosoever shall confess that Jesus is the Son of God, God dwelleth in him, and he in God.

16 And we have known and believed the love that God hath to us. God is love; and he that dwelleth in love dwelleth in God, and God in him.

17 ¶ Herein is our love made perfect, that we may have boldness in the day of judgment: because as he is, so are we in this world.

18 There is no fear in love; but perfect love casteth out fear: because fear hath torment. He that feareth is not made perfect in love.

19 We love him, because he first loved us.

20 If a man say, I love God, and hateth his brother, he is a liar: for he that loveth not his brother whom he hath seen, how can he love God whom he hath not seen?

21 And this commandment have we from him, That he who loveth God love his brother also.

## CHAPTER 5

*John teaches that through the Savior we can have eternal life (which is to live forever with our Father in Heaven). Look for what we must do to be able to live with God again.*

## WE ARE BORN OF GOD THROUGH BELIEF IN CHRIST

1 ¶ WHOSOEVER believeth that Jesus is the Christ is born of God: and every one that loveth him that begat loveth him also that is begotten of him.

2 By this we know that we love the children of God, when we love God, and keep his commandments.

3 For this is the love of God, that we keep his commandments: and his commandments are not grievous.

4 For whatsoever is born of God overcometh the world: and this is the victory that overcometh the world, even our faith.

5 Who is he that overcometh the world, but he that believeth that Jesus is the Son of God?

---

4:6 The leaders of The Church of Jesus Christ of Latter-day Saints are God's servants. Inspired words from his servants' mouths are the same as words from his own mouth (see D&C 1:38).

4:10 **propitiation**—payment; one who pays or suffers for another

4:12 The Joseph Smith Translation explains that people who believe can see God (JST, 1 John 4:12).

4:17-18 What must a person do to be able to stand without fear before God in the Day of Judgment?

4:18 **hath torment**—expects punishment

4:20-21 What we do for others often shows our love for God (see Mosiah 2:17). How can you show your love for God's children?

5:1 King Benjamin taught that being born of God means that you change so much that you no longer desire "to do evil, but to do good continually" (Mosiah 5:2). This change can come only through belief in Christ.

5:3 **grievous**—hard or a burden

5:3-5 Who are the only people who overcome the world?

6 ¶ This is he that came by water and blood, even Jesus Christ; not by water only, but by water and blood. And it is the Spirit that beareth witness, because the Spirit is truth.

7 For there are three that bear record in heaven, the Father, the Word, and the Holy Ghost: and these three are one.

8 And there are three that bear witness in earth, the Spirit, and the water, and the blood: and these three agree in one.

## BELIEF IN CHRIST WILL LEAD TO ETERNAL LIFE

9 If we receive the witness of men, the witness of God is greater: for this is the witness of God which he hath testified of his Son.

10 ¶ He that believeth on the Son of God hath the witness in himself: he that believeth not God hath made him a liar; because he believeth not the record that God gave of his Son.

11 And this is the record, that God hath given to us eternal life, and this life is in his Son.

12 He that hath the Son hath life; and he that hath not the Son of God hath not life.

13 These things have I written unto you that believe on the name of the Son of God; that ye may know that ye have eternal life, and that ye may believe on the name of the Son of God.

14 ¶ And this is the confidence that we have in him, that, if we ask any thing according to his will, he heareth us:

15 And if we know that he hear us, whatsoever we ask, we know that we have the petitions that we desired of him.

16 If any man see his brother sin a sin which is not unto death, he shall ask, and he shall give him life for them that sin not unto death. There is a sin unto death: I do not say that he shall pray for it.

17 All unrighteousness is sin: and there is a sin not unto death.

18 ¶ We know that whosoever is born of God sinneth not; but he that is begotten of God keepeth himself, and that wicked one toucheth him not.

19 And we know that we are of God, and the whole world lieth in wickedness.

20 And we know that the Son of God is come, and hath given us an understanding, that we may know him that is true, and we are in him that is true, even in his Son Jesus Christ. This is the true God, and eternal life.

21 Little children, keep yourselves from idols. Amen.

---

5:9 **witness**—testimony

5:10-12 *Eternal* is a title for Heavenly Father. Eternal life is the kind of life that he lives. The Son, Jesus Christ, has eternal life. If we believe in the Son (see John 3:36), we will have that life. If we do not believe in the Son, we will live forever but not be like God.

5:14-15 According to latter-day revelation, if we pray "in the Spirit" we are praying "the will of God." Those prayers will be answered. (See D&C 46:30.)

5:16 To "sin unto death" is to turn from the light and truth of the gospel and do "evil works" as "a child of the devil" (see Alma 5:41-42).

# THE SECOND EPISTLE OF
# JOHN

*In the days of the early Church, many people taught false doctrines. Some false teachers said that Christ didn't have a body and that the Atonement was not real. In this second epistle John urges Church members to hold fast to the truth and guard against falsehood.*

## CHAPTER 1

*Both Paul and John often refer to the Church as a woman (see 2 Corinthians 11:2; Ephesians 5:25). Look for how the problems faced by the woman could actually be problems faced by the Church.*

### JOHN REJOICES OVER THOSE WHO ARE TRUE AND FAITHFUL

1 THE elder unto the elect lady and her children, whom I love in the truth; and not I only, but also all they that have known the truth;

2 For the truth's sake, which dwelleth in us, and shall be with us for ever.

3 Grace be with you, mercy, and peace, from God the Father, and from the Lord Jesus Christ, the Son of the Father, in truth and love.

4 I rejoiced greatly that I found of thy children walking in truth, as we have received a commandment from the Father.

5 ¶ And now I beseech thee, lady, not as though I wrote a new commandment unto thee, but that which we had from the beginning, that we love one another.

6 And this is love, that we walk after his command-ments. This is the commandment, That, as ye have heard from the beginning, ye should walk in it.

### JOHN TEACHES TO BEWARE OF ANTICHRIST DECEIVERS

7 ¶ For many deceivers are entered into the world, who confess not that Jesus Christ is come in the flesh. This is a deceiver and an antichrist.

8 Look to yourselves, that we lose not those things which we have wrought, but that we receive a full reward.

9 Whosoever transgresseth, and abideth not in the doctrine of Christ, hath not God. He that abideth in the doctrine of Christ, he hath both the Father and the Son.

10 ¶ If there come any unto you, and bring not this doctrine, receive him not into your house, neither bid him God speed:

11 For he that biddeth him God speed is partaker of his evil deeds.

12 ¶ Having many things to write unto you, I would not write with paper and ink: but I trust to come unto you, and speak face to face, that our joy may be full.

13 The children of thy elect sister greet thee. Amen.

---

1:1    "Elder" is an office in the Melchizedek Priesthood to which worthy male members may be ordained at the age of eighteen or older (see D&C 107:7).

     **elect**—chosen

1:6    Jesus also taught that if we love him we will keep his commandments (see John 14:15).

1:7    **an antichrist**—a person who denies and fights against Jesus Christ and his teachings

1:8    **wrought**—performed

1:9    **transgresseth**—sins

1:10    **bid him God speed**—help him or make him welcome

---

| | | |
|---|---|---|
| = Word Help | | = A Closer Look |
| = More Light | | = Ponder This |

Words in pink are explained in the Glossary.

# THE THIRD EPISTLE OF
# JOHN

*Early Church members often took traveling Church leaders and missionaries into their homes to provide for their needs. In this letter John praises Gaius for unselfishly helping God's servants.*

## CHAPTER 1

*During this trying time in the early Church, there were many faithful Church leaders. Sadly, however, there were others who tried to take over and mislead the members. Look for how John praises the good members and warns the bad.*

### FAITHFUL SAINTS ARE COMPLIMENTED AND ENCOURAGED

1 THE elder unto the wellbeloved Gaius, whom I love in the truth.

2 Beloved, I wish above all things that thou mayest prosper and be in health, even as thy soul prospereth.

3 ¶ For I rejoiced greatly, when the brethren came and testified of the truth that is in thee, even as thou walkest in the truth.

4 I have no greater joy than to hear that my children walk in truth.

5 Beloved, thou doest faithfully whatsoever thou doest to the brethren, and to strangers;

6 Which have borne witness of thy charity before the church: whom if thou bring forward on their journey after a godly sort, thou shalt do well:

7 Because that for his name's sake they went forth, taking nothing of the Gentiles.

8 We therefore ought to receive such, that we might be fellowhelpers to the truth.

### SOME MEMBERS DO NOT SUPPORT CHURCH LEADERS

9 ¶ I wrote unto the church: but Diotrephes, who loveth to have the preeminence among them, receiveth us not.

10 Wherefore, if I come, I will remember his deeds which he doeth, prating against us with malicious words: and not content therewith, neither doth he himself receive the brethren, and forbiddeth them that would, and casteth them out of the church.

11 Beloved, follow not that which is evil, but that which is good. He that doeth good is of God: but he that doeth evil hath not seen God.

12 ¶ Demetrius hath good report of all men, and of the truth itself: yea, and we also bear record; and ye know that our record is true.

13 I had many things to write, but I will not with ink and pen write unto thee:

14 But I trust I shall shortly see thee, and we shall speak face to face. Peace be to thee. Our friends salute thee. Greet the friends by name.

---

1:2 **prosper**—do well, receive blessings

1:3 **walkest in the truth**—obey the commandments

1:4 This verse speaks of the great joy felt by the Church leaders when the members are true and faithful. Why do you think they are so happy when the members choose what is right?

1:5-6 The Church leaders often traveled and met with the Saints. Some reported to John and others how well they had been treated by Gaius. This faithful member was living as Jesus taught (see Matthew 10:40-42).

1:9 **the preeminence among**—power over

1:9-11 Diotrephes, a local Church officer, was ignoring the authority and teachings of the leaders of the Church. In our day, Elder Harold B. Lee warned that "there are many clever people who are not willing to listen to the humble prophets of the Lord" (*The Teachings of Harold B. Lee*, p. 328).

1:10 **prating**—gossiping, telling lies
**malicious**—mean, hateful

---

= Word Help    = A Closer Look

= More Light    = Ponder This

Words in pink are explained in the Glossary.

# THE GENERAL EPISTLE OF
# JUDE

*Jude, like James, is generally thought to be one of the Lord's brothers. He wanted to write about salvation, but instead he had to warn about false teachers and false doctrine that had "crept in" unnoticed (Jude 1:4). (See LDS Bible Dictionary, s.v. "Jude, Epistle of," p. 719.)*

## CHAPTER 1

*From the time of the premortal life, Heavenly Father's plan and teachings have been opposed by wicked people. Look for Jude's warning against false teachings and for why it is so important that you believe the truth.*

### JUDE WARNS AGAINST FALSE TEACHERS

1 JUDE, the servant of Jesus Christ, and brother of James, to them that are sanctified by God the Father, and preserved in Jesus Christ, and called:

2 Mercy unto you, and peace, and love, be multiplied.

3 ¶ Beloved, when I gave all diligence to write unto you of the common salvation, it was needful for me to write unto you, and exhort you that ye should earnestly contend for the faith which was once delivered unto the saints.

4 For there are certain men crept in unawares, who were before of old ordained to this condemnation, ungodly men, turning the grace of our God into lasciv-

iousness, and denying the only Lord God, and our Lord Jesus Christ.

5 I will therefore put you in remembrance, though ye once knew this, how that the Lord, having saved the people out of the land of Egypt, afterward destroyed them that believed not.

6 And the angels which kept not their first estate, but left their own habitation, he hath reserved in everlasting chains under darkness unto the judgment of the great day.

7 Even as Sodom and Gomorrha, and the cities about them in like manner, giving themselves over to fornication, and going after strange flesh, are set forth for an example, suffering the vengeance of eternal fire.

8 ¶ Likewise also these filthy dreamers defile the flesh, despise dominion, and speak evil of dignities.

9 Yet Michael the archangel, when contending with the devil he disputed about the body of Moses, durst not bring against him a railing accusation, but said, The Lord rebuke thee.

10 But these speak evil of those things which they know not: but what they know naturally, as brute beasts, in those things they corrupt themselves.

---

1:1    "To be *sanctified* is to become clean, pure, and spotless; to be free from the blood and sins of the world" (Bruce R. McConkie, *Mormon Doctrine*, p. 675). Sanctification comes only by obedience to the commandments and through the power of the Holy Ghost.

1:3    Jude speaks of a "common salvation," or salvation that is available to everyone. Similarly, the third article of faith states: "All mankind may be saved, by obedience to the laws and ordinances of the Gospel" (Articles of Faith 1:3).

   **earnestly contend for**—diligently defend, work hard for

1:4    These evil men who "crept in unawares" (came in unnoticed) said that it was all right to be lascivious (immoral) because God would forgive all our sins.

1:6    These angels are likely the spirits who followed Satan when we lived in heaven before we came to earth. Abraham called the pre-earth life our "first estate." (See Abraham 3:27-28.)

1:7    **fornication, and going after strange flesh**—misuse of the sacred procreative powers

1:9    Joseph Smith taught that Michael the archangel is "our Father Adam" (*The Teachings of Joseph Smith*, p. 19).

---

| | |
|---|---|
| = Word Help | = A Closer Look |
| = More Light | = Ponder This |

Words in pink are explained in the Glossary.

*"The Lord cometh with ten thousands of his saints."*

11 Woe unto them! for they have gone in the way of Cain, and ran greedily after the error of Balaam for reward, and perished in the gainsaying of Core.

12 These are spots in your feasts of charity, when they feast with you, feeding themselves without fear: clouds they are without water, carried about of winds; trees whose fruit withereth, without fruit, twice dead, plucked up by the roots;

13 Raging waves of the sea, foaming out their own shame; wandering stars, to whom is reserved the blackness of darkness for ever.

14 And Enoch also, the seventh from Adam, prophe-sied of these, saying, Behold, the Lord cometh with ten thousands of his saints,

15 ¶ To execute judgment upon all, and to convince all that are ungodly among them of all their ungodly deeds which they have ungodly committed, and of all their hard speeches which ungodly sinners have spoken against him.

16 These are murmurers, complainers, walking after their own lusts; and their mouth speaketh great swelling words, having men's persons in admiration because of advantage.

---

1:11-16   Jude uses six comparisons to describe wicked people. For example, he says they are like clouds without water, or in other words, they are selfish and empty. What do you learn from Jude's other comparisons?

1:14-15   Enoch's prophecies and writings will come forth in the last days (see D&C 107:53-57). Joseph Smith taught that Enoch personally visited Jude and said the words recorded in Jude 1:14-15 (see *The Teachings of Joseph Smith*, p. 221).

## JUDE PLEADS WITH THE SAINTS TO REMAIN FIRM IN THE FAITH

17 But, beloved, remember ye the words which were spoken before of the apostles of our Lord Jesus Christ;

18 How that they told you there should be mockers in the last time, who should walk after their own ungodly lusts.

19 These be they who separate themselves, sensual, having not the Spirit.

20 But ye, beloved, building up yourselves on your most holy faith, praying in the Holy Ghost,

21 Keep yourselves in the love of God, looking for the mercy of our Lord Jesus Christ unto eternal life.

22 And of some have compassion, making a difference:

23 And others save with fear, pulling them out of the fire; hating even the garment spotted by the flesh.

24 Now unto him that is able to keep you from falling, and to present you faultless before the presence of his glory with exceeding joy,

25 To the only wise God our Saviour, be glory and majesty, dominion and power, both now and ever. Amen.

---

1:19 **sensual**—worldly

1:22-23 Compassion is love and understanding. How do you think having compassion on someone could make "a difference" and help pull that person "out of the fire," meaning out of sin?

# THE REVELATION
## OF ST. JOHN THE DIVINE*

*Jesus Christ commanded the Apostle John to write the book of Revelation. It was a message of hope to the Saints who lived in a very dangerous time of apostasy and persecution. Heavenly Father wanted the faithful members to know that one day Jesus Christ would return and defeat Satan and destroy all wickedness.*

## CHAPTER 1

*John was imprisoned on the Isle of Patmos at the time he received this glorious vision of the Lord. Look for what Jesus revealed to John about Himself and the future.*

### JESUS CHRIST REVEALS THE FUTURE TO JOHN

1 THE Revelation of Jesus Christ, which God gave unto him, to shew unto his servants things which must shortly come to pass; and he sent and signified it by his angel unto his servant John:

2 Who bare record of the word of God, and of the testimony of Jesus Christ, and of all things that he saw.

3 ¶ Blessed is he that readeth, and they that hear the words of this prophecy, and keep those things which are written therein: for the time is at hand.

4 John to the seven churches which are in Asia: Grace be unto you, and peace, from him which is, and which was, and which is to come; and from the seven Spirits which are before his throne;

---

\*   The book of Revelation makes use of many symbols. A symbol is something that represents, or stands for, something else (for example, a nation's flag represents, or is a symbol for, that nation). Explanations for many of the symbols used in Revelation are found in the study helps that follow. In fact, some of the "Word Help" entries in this section are more like "Symbol Help" entries. For example, the "Word Help" at Revelation 1:12 indicates that the "seven golden candlesticks" stand for the seven churches in Asia.

1:1   The Joseph Smith Translation indicates that this book is "the Revelation of John, a servant of God, which was given unto him of Jesus Christ" (JST, Revelation 1:1).

**shew**—This word is pronounced the same way as the word *show* and has the same meaning; *shew* is simply an old spelling of *show*.
**signified it**—made it known by giving him a sign

1:3   The "time . . . at hand" refers to "the coming of the Lord" (JST, Revelation 1:3).

John said that those who read, understand, and keep this prophecy would be blessed. How can keeping in mind this promise help you as you read Revelation?

1:4   The phrase "which is, and which was, and which is to come" describes Jesus Christ, who knows all things. Jesus said, "I am the Spirit of truth" (D&C 93:26); "truth is knowledge of things as they are, and as they were, and as they are to come" (D&C 93:24). The Joseph Smith Translation identifies the "seven Spirits" as "the seven servants who are over the seven churches" (JST, Revelation 1:4). They were like bishops over wards or presidents over stakes.

*Isle of Patmos as it appears today*

| | |
|---|---|
| = Word Help | = A Closer Look |
| = More Light | = Ponder This |
| Words in pink are explained in the Glossary. | |

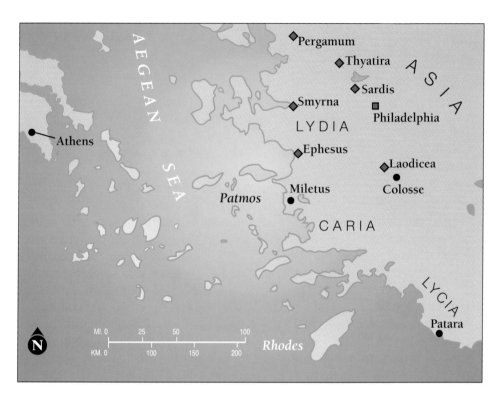

*This map shows Patmos and the seven cities mentioned in Revelation 2 and 3.*

5 And from Jesus Christ, who is the faithful witness, and the first begotten of the dead, and the prince of the kings of the earth. Unto him that loved us, and washed us from our sins in his own blood,

6 And hath made us kings and priests unto God and his Father; to him be glory and dominion for ever and ever. Amen.

## JOHN IS IMPRISONED ON THE ISLE OF PATMOS

7 Behold, he cometh with clouds; and every eye shall see him, and they also which pierced him: and all kindreds of the earth shall wail because of him. Even so, Amen.

8 I am Alpha and Omega, the beginning and the ending, saith the Lord, which is, and which was, and which is to come, the Almighty.

9 ¶ I John, who also am your brother, and companion in tribulation, and in the kingdom and patience of Jesus Christ, was in the isle that is called Patmos, for the word of God, and for the testimony of Jesus Christ.

## JOHN SEES THE RISEN LORD IN VISION

10 I was in the Spirit on the Lord's day, and heard behind me a great voice, as of a trumpet,

11 Saying, I am Alpha and Omega, the first and the last: and, What thou seest, write in a book, and send it unto the seven churches which are in Asia; unto Ephesus, and unto Smyrna, and unto Pergamos, and unto Thyatira, and unto Sardis, and unto Philadelphia, and unto Laodicea.

---

1:5     Jesus Christ was the "first begotten of the dead," meaning the first to be resurrected from the dead (see 1 Corinthians 15:20).

1:7     The Joseph Smith Translation reveals that at the Second Coming, Jesus will come "in the clouds with ten thousands of his saints" (JST, Revelation 1:7; see also Jude 1:14-15).

1:10     *the Lord's day*—Sunday

12 And I turned to see the voice that spake with me. And being turned, I saw seven golden candlesticks;

13 And in the midst of the seven candlesticks one like unto the Son of man, clothed with a garment down to the foot, and girt about the paps with a golden girdle.

14 His head and his hairs were white like wool, as white as snow; and his eyes were as a flame of fire;

15 And his feet like unto fine brass, as if they burned in a furnace; and his voice as the sound of many waters.

16 And he had in his right hand seven stars: and out of his mouth went a sharp twoedged sword: and his countenance was as the sun shineth in his strength.

17 And when I saw him, I fell at his feet as dead. And he laid his right hand upon me, saying unto me, Fear not; I am the first and the last:

18 I am he that liveth, and was dead; and, behold, I am alive for evermore, Amen; and have the keys of hell and of death.

19 Write the things which thou hast seen, and the things which are, and the things which shall be hereafter;

20 The mystery of the seven stars which thou sawest in my right hand, and the seven golden candlesticks. The seven stars are the angels of the seven churches: and the seven candlesticks which thou sawest are the seven churches.

# CHAPTER 2

*Revelation 2 and 3 contain messages for members of the Church in seven cities. Look for what the Lord teaches (as revealed to John by the angel) concerning how the Saints can receive eternal life.*

## JOHN WRITES TO THE CHURCH IN EPHESUS

1 ¶ UNTO the angel of the church of Ephesus write; These things saith he that holdeth the seven stars in his right hand, who walketh in the midst of the seven golden candlesticks;

2 I know thy works, and thy labour, and thy patience, and how thou canst not bear them which are evil: and thou hast tried them which say they are apostles, and are not, and hast found them liars:

3 And hast borne, and hast patience, and for my name's sake hast laboured, and hast not fainted.

4 Nevertheless I have somewhat against thee, because thou hast left thy first love.

5 Remember therefore from whence thou art fallen, and repent, and do the first works; or else I will come unto thee quickly, and will remove thy candlestick out of his place, except thou repent.

6 But this thou hast, that thou hatest the deeds of the Nicolaitans, which I also hate.

---

*John saw seven golden candlesticks.*

1:12 **seven golden candlesticks**—seven churches (see verse 20)

1:13 **paps**—chest

1:16 **seven stars**—seven leaders of the churches (see JST, verse 20)

Jesus speaks only truth and "the guilty taketh the truth to be hard." Jesus' words cut the guilty "to the very center" like "a sharp twoedged sword." (See 1 Nephi 16:2.)

1:18 Jesus died and is now "alive for evermore." How can this knowledge help you when someone you love dies?

2:1 The Joseph Smith Translation uses the word "servant" in place of "angel" in this chapter (see JST, Revelation 2:1, 8, 12, 18).

Jesus Christ holds the seven stars (servants) and is in the midst of the seven candlesticks (churches) (see Revelation 1:13, 16, 20).

2:3 **hast borne, and hast patience**—have endured patiently

2:6 Nicolaitans were a group who used false beliefs as an excuse to do evil (see LDS Bible Dictionary, s.v. "Nicolaitans," p. 738).

7 He that hath an ear, let him hear what the Spirit saith unto the churches; To him that overcometh will I give to eat of the tree of life, which is in the midst of the paradise of God.

## JOHN WRITES TO THE CHURCH IN SMYRNA

8 ¶ And unto the angel of the church in Smyrna write; These things saith the first and the last, which was dead, and is alive;

9 I know thy works, and tribulation, and poverty, (but thou art rich) and I know the blasphemy of them which say they are Jews, and are not, but are the synagogue of Satan.

10 Fear none of those things which thou shalt suffer: behold, the devil shall cast some of you into prison, that ye may be tried; and ye shall have tribulation ten days: be thou faithful unto death, and I will give thee a crown of life.

11 He that hath an ear, let him hear what the Spirit saith unto the churches; He that overcometh shall not be hurt of the second death.

## JOHN WRITES TO THE CHURCH IN PERGAMOS

12 ¶ And to the angel of the church in Pergamos write; These things saith he which hath the sharp sword with two edges;

13 I know thy works, and where thou dwellest, even where Satan's seat is: and thou holdest fast my name, and hast not denied my faith, even in those days wherein Antipas was my faithful martyr, who was slain among you, where Satan dwelleth.

14 But I have a few things against thee, because thou hast there them that hold the doctrine of Balaam, who taught Balac to cast a stumblingblock before the children of Israel, to eat things sacrificed unto idols, and to commit fornication.

15 So hast thou also them that hold the doctrine of the Nicolaitans, which thing I hate.

16 Repent; or else I will come unto thee quickly, and will fight against them with the sword of my mouth.

17 He that hath an ear, let him hear what the Spirit saith unto the churches; To him that overcometh will I give to eat of the hidden manna, and will give him a white stone, and in the stone a new name written, which no man knoweth saving he that receiveth it.

## JOHN WRITES TO THE CHURCH IN THYATIRA

18 ¶ And unto the angel of the church in Thyatira write; These things saith the Son of God, who hath his eyes like unto a flame of fire, and his feet are like fine brass;

19 I know thy works, and charity, and service, and faith, and thy patience, and thy works; and the last to be more than the first.

20 Notwithstanding I have a few things against thee, because thou sufferest that woman Jezebel, which calleth herself a prophetess, to teach and to seduce my servants to commit fornication, and to eat things sacrificed unto idols.

21 And I gave her space to repent of her fornication; and she repented not.

22 Behold, I will cast her into a bed, and them that

---

2:7    The words "He that hath an ear, let him hear" are used several times in chapters 2 and 3. They mean, "Only those whose souls are enlightened by the power of the Holy Spirit can hear the word of God. The hearing ear is the ear of faith." (Bruce R. McConkie, *Doctrinal New Testament Commentary* 3:447.)

**overcometh**—stays faithful even when tempted and persecuted

2:9    John records the Lord's words that though these Saints were suffering and poor, they were rich. In what way could poor members of the Church be rich?

2:9-10    Those who rejected Christ and were persecuting the Saints were "part of the Church of the Devil [synagogue of Satan]" (Bruce R. McConkie, *Doctrinal New Testament Commentary* 3:448).

2:11    Those receiving the punishment of the second death will not be resurrected in the first resurrec-

tion and will be separated from the Lord after their resurrection (see D&C 63:17-18).

2:13    **martyr**—person killed because of what he believes

2:14-16    The "doctrine of Balaam" is "to divine [prophesy] for hire; to give counsel contrary to the divine will; to pervert the right way of the Lord— all with a view to gaining wealth and the honors of men" (Bruce R. McConkie, *Doctrinal New Testament Commentary* 3:450; see also Numbers 22-25; 31:15-16; 2 Peter 2:15-16; Jude 1:11-12).

2:17    Manna was a food that the Lord miraculously gave the children of Israel while they traveled forty years in the wilderness (see Exodus 16:11-15).

The white stone will be an aid for people who go to the celestial kingdom (see D&C 130:10-11).

2:22    The Joseph Smith Translation changes "a bed" to "hell" (JST, Revelation 2:22).

commit adultery with her into great tribulation, except they repent of their deeds.

23 And I will kill her children with death; and all the churches shall know that I am he which searcheth the reins and hearts: and I will give unto every one of you according to your works.

24 But unto you I say, and unto the rest in Thyatira, as many as have not this doctrine, and which have not known the depths of Satan, as they speak; I will put upon you none other burden.

25 But that which ye have already hold fast till I come.

26 And he that overcometh, and keepeth my works unto the end, to him will I give power over the nations:

27 And he shall rule them with a rod of iron; as the vessels of a potter shall they be broken to shivers: even as I received of my Father.

28 And I will give him the morning star.

29 He that hath an ear, let him hear what the Spirit saith unto the churches.

## CHAPTER 3

*As revealed through John, the Lord counsels the Saints to hold on to the good and repent of their sins. As you read, notice the difference between what the wicked are told and what the righteous are told.*

### JOHN WRITES TO THE CHURCH IN SARDIS

1 ¶ AND unto the angel of the church in Sardis write; These things saith he that hath the seven Spirits of

God, and the seven stars; I know thy works, that thou hast a name that thou livest, and art dead.

2 Be watchful, and strengthen the things which remain, that are ready to die: for I have not found thy works perfect before God.

3 Remember therefore how thou hast received and heard, and hold fast, and repent. If therefore thou shalt not watch, I will come on thee as a thief, and thou shalt not know what hour I will come upon thee.

4 Thou hast a few names even in Sardis which have not defiled their garments; and they shall walk with me in white: for they are worthy.

5 He that overcometh, the same shall be clothed in white raiment; and I will not blot out his name out of the book of life, but I will confess his name before my Father, and before his angels.

6 He that hath an ear, let him hear what the Spirit saith unto the churches.

### JOHN WRITES TO THE CHURCH IN PHILADELPHIA

7 ¶ And to the angel of the church in Philadelphia write; These things saith he that is holy, he that is true, he that hath the key of David, he that openeth, and no man shutteth; and shutteth, and no man openeth;

8 I know thy works: behold, I have set before thee an open door, and no man can shut it: for thou hast a little strength, and hast kept my word, and hast not denied my name.

9 Behold, I will make them of the synagogue of Satan, which say they are Jews, and are not, but do lie; behold, I will make them to come and worship before thy feet, and to know that I have loved thee.

10 Because thou hast kept the word of my patience,

---

2:23 **reins and hearts**—thoughts and feelings

2:26-27 The Lord promises that those who faithfully keep his commandments will be made rulers over "many kingdoms." They will rule "with the word of God" and govern "by faith, with equity [fairness] and justice." (JST, Revelation 2:26-27.)

2:28 The morning star is the Savior (see Revelation 22:16).

3:1 The "angel of the church in Sardis" refers to "the presiding officer of the Church in Sardis" (Bruce R. McConkie, *Doctrinal New Testament Commentary* 3:454).

The seven "Spirits" and "stars" are the seven leaders of the churches to whom John wrote (see Revelation 1:20; JST, Revelation 4:5).

3:4 **not defiled their garments**—not become wicked

3:4-5 White is a symbol of being spiritually clean. We become clean through repentance and living righteously. (See Isaiah 1:18.)

3:5 The book of life "is the record kept in heaven which contains the names of the faithful and an account of their righteous . . . deeds" (Bruce R. McConkie, *Doctrinal New Testament Commentary* 3:455).

3:7-8 "The *key of David* is the absolute power resident in Christ whereby his will is expressed in all things" (Bruce R. McConkie, *Mormon Doctrine*, p. 409).

3:9 **of the synagogue of Satan**—who are Satan's followers

I also will keep thee from the hour of temptation, which shall come upon all the world, to try them that dwell upon the earth.

11 Behold, I come quickly: hold that fast which thou hast, that no man take thy crown.

12 Him that overcometh will I make a pillar in the temple of my God, and he shall go no more out: and I will write upon him the name of my God, and the name of the city of my God, which is new Jerusalem, which cometh down out of heaven from my God: and I will write upon him my new name.

13 He that hath an ear, let him hear what the Spirit saith unto the churches.

### JOHN WRITES TO THE CHURCH IN LAODICEA

14 ¶ And unto the angel of the church of the Laodiceans write; These things saith the Amen, the faithful and true witness, the beginning of the creation of God;

15 I know thy works, that thou art neither cold nor hot: I would thou wert cold or hot.

16 So then because thou art lukewarm, and neither cold nor hot, I will spue thee out of my mouth.

17 Because thou sayest, I am rich, and increased with goods, and have need of nothing; and knowest not that thou art wretched, and miserable, and poor, and blind, and naked:

18 I counsel thee to buy of me gold tried in the fire, that thou mayest be rich; and white raiment, that thou mayest be clothed, and that the shame of thy nakedness do not appear; and anoint thine eyes with eyesalve, that thou mayest see.

19 As many as I love, I rebuke and chasten: be zealous therefore, and repent.

20 Behold, I stand at the door, and knock: if any man hear my voice, and open the door, I will come in to him, and will sup with him, and he with me.

21 To him that overcometh will I grant to sit with me in my throne, even as I also overcame, and am set down with my Father in his throne.

22 He that hath an ear, let him hear what the Spirit saith unto the churches.

## CHAPTER 4

*John sees Heavenly Father sitting on his throne surrounded by many of his creations. Look for how those who are near Heavenly Father feel about him.*

### JOHN SEES HEAVENLY FATHER SITTING ON HIS THRONE

1 ¶ AFTER this I looked, and, behold, a door was opened in heaven: and the first voice which I heard was as it were of a trumpet talking with me; which said, Come up hither, and I will shew thee things which must be hereafter.

2 And immediately I was in the spirit: and, behold, a throne was set in heaven, and one sat on the throne.

3 And he that sat was to look upon like a jasper and a sardine stone: and there was a rainbow round about the throne, in sight like unto an emerald.

4 And round about the throne were four and twenty seats: and upon the seats I saw four and twenty elders sitting, clothed in white raiment; and they had on their heads crowns of gold.

---

3:11    *hold that fast*—hold on to that

3:12, 21   The blessings of eternal life come to those who "endure to the end" (D&C 14:7).

3:12    The "new Jerusalem" is the city of God that will come down "out of heaven" after the earth becomes a celestial kingdom (see Revelation 21:1-2; see also Bruce R. McConkie, *Mormon Doctrine*, s.v. "New Jerusalem," pp. 531-33).

3:15-16   Too many people in the world try to keep one foot on the Lord's side and one foot on Satan's side. "There is safety for us only on the Lord's side of the line" (George Albert Smith, *Sharing the Gospel with Others*, p. 43).

3:16    *spue*—spit

3:19    *rebuke and chasten*—correct and discipline

3:20    *sup*—visit and eat

The Savior knocks on the door; but who must answer and open the door to receive him? What does this verse mean to you?

4:3    Ezekiel, an Old Testament prophet, had a similar vision, and in recording it he also used bright colors and a rainbow to describe or represent "the glory of the Lord" (see Ezekiel 1:26-28).

4:4    These twenty-four elders were faithful leaders of the Church who had lived in John's day (see D&C 77:5; see also Revelation 6:9-11).

John likely knew the twenty-four elders who sat around the throne of God. What might it mean to John to see his former friends now with God in heaven?

*raiment*—clothing

5 And out of the throne proceeded lightnings and thunderings and voices: and there were seven lamps of fire burning before the throne, which are the seven Spirits of God.

6 And before the throne there was a sea of glass like unto crystal: and in the midst of the throne, and round about the throne, were four beasts full of eyes before and behind.

7 And the first beast was like a lion, and the second beast like a calf, and the third beast had a face as a man, and the fourth beast was like a flying eagle.

## THOSE NEAR HEAVENLY FATHER GIVE HIM HONOR AND PRAISE

8 ¶ And the four beasts had each of them six wings about him; and they were full of eyes within: and they rest not day and night, saying, Holy, holy, holy, Lord God Almighty, which was, and is, and is to come.

9 And when those beasts give glory and honour and thanks to him that sat on the throne, who liveth for ever and ever,

10 The four and twenty elders fall down before him that sat on the throne, and worship him that liveth for ever and ever, and cast their crowns before the throne, saying,

11 Thou art worthy, O Lord, to receive glory and honour and power: for thou hast created all things, and for thy pleasure they are and were created.

## CHAPTER 5

*The Savior has different names and titles that represent his power. Watch for the three names or titles Christ is represented by in this chapter.*

### JOHN SEES THE OPENING OF THE BOOK WITH SEVEN SEALS

1 ¶ AND I saw in the right hand of him that sat on the throne a book written within and on the backside, sealed with seven seals.

2 And I saw a strong angel proclaiming with a loud voice, Who is worthy to open the book, and to loose the seals thereof?

3 And no man in heaven, nor in earth, neither under the earth, was able to open the book, neither to look thereon.

4 And I wept much, because no man was found worthy to open and to read the book, neither to look thereon.

5 And one of the elders saith unto me, Weep not: behold, the Lion of the tribe of Juda, the Root of David, hath prevailed to open the book, and to loose the seven seals thereof.

---

4:5    The Joseph Smith Translation explains that the "seven Spirits of God" were actually the "seven servants of God" (JST, Revelation 4:5), who were the leaders of the churches in Asia.

4:6    The earth will be like a "sea of glass" in its celestial condition (see D&C 77:1; 130:6-9).

4:6-7    The four beasts were actual individual creatures that prove God can and will save all his worthy creations (see D&C 77:2-4; *The Teachings of Joseph Smith*, pp. 71-72, 38-39).

4:8    The Prophet Joseph Smith learned that the beasts' eyes represented their knowledge. The wings represented their power "to move" and "to act." (D&C 77:4.)

5:1    According to a revelation to Joseph Smith, the sealed book contains "the works of God" during the seven thousand years of the earth's existence (see D&C 77:6).

5:5    Jesus Christ is the Lion of the Tribe of Judah as well as the Root of David (see Revelation 22:16; Bruce R. McConkie, *Mormon Doctrine*, p. 449).

*The book in John's vision may have been like an ancient scroll made of animal skins or papyrus and wrapped around sticks.*

6 ¶ And I beheld, and, lo, in the midst of the throne and of the four beasts, and in the midst of the elders, stood a Lamb as it had been slain, having seven horns and seven eyes, which are the seven Spirits of God sent forth into all the earth.

7 And he came and took the book out of the right hand of him that sat upon the throne.

## PRAISE IS GIVEN TO GOD AND THE LAMB

8 And when he had taken the book, the four beasts and four and twenty elders fell down before the Lamb, having every one of them harps, and golden vials full of odours, which are the prayers of saints.

9 And they sung a new song, saying, Thou art worthy to take the book, and to open the seals thereof: for thou wast slain, and hast redeemed us to God by thy blood out of every kindred, and tongue, and people, and nation;

10 And hast made us unto our God kings and priests: and we shall reign on the earth.

11 And I beheld, and I heard the voice of many angels round about the throne and the beasts and the elders: and the number of them was ten thousand times ten thousand, and thousands of thousands;

12 Saying with a loud voice, Worthy is the Lamb that was slain to receive power, and riches, and wisdom, and strength, and honour, and glory, and blessing.

13 And every creature which is in heaven, and on the earth, and under the earth, and such as are in the sea, and all that are in them, heard I saying, Blessing, and honour, and glory, and power, be unto him that sitteth upon the throne, and unto the Lamb for ever and ever.

14 And the four beasts said, Amen. And the four and twenty elders fell down and worshipped him that liveth for ever and ever.

## CHAPTER 6

*John sees the Lamb (Jesus Christ) open the first six seals of the book. Look for what happens in connection with each of the six seals as they are opened.*

## THE FIRST FIVE SEALS ARE OPENED

1 ¶ AND I saw when the Lamb opened one of the seals, and I heard, as it were the noise of thunder, one of the four beasts saying, Come and see.

2 And I saw, and behold a white horse: and he that sat on him had a bow; and a crown was given unto him: and he went forth conquering, and to conquer.

---

5:6    The Joseph Smith Translation changes "seven" horns and eyes to "twelve" horns and eyes, "which are the twelve servants," or Apostles, "of God" (see JST, Revelation 5:6).

   Christ is also referred to as the Lamb of God who takes away the sins of the world (see John 1:29, 36).

5:8    *odours*—incense or perfume

5:9    *redeemed us to God*—paid for our sins and brought us back into God's presence

   The "new song" is like a testimony of the redemption that comes to all mankind through the atonement of Jesus Christ. A similar "new song," or testimony, says, "The Lord hath brought again Zion; The Lord hath redeemed his people" (D&C 84:98-99).

5:9-14    These verses speak of thousands of God's creations worshiping God and the Lamb. How do you show your respect and appreciation for Heavenly Father and his Son?

6:1    From modern revelation we learn "that the first seal contains the things of the first thousand years, and the second also of the second thousand years, and so on until the seventh" (D&C 77:7).

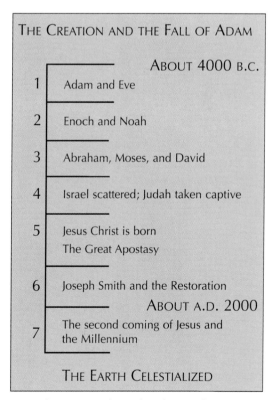

THE CREATION AND THE FALL OF ADAM

ABOUT 4000 B.C.

1   Adam and Eve

2   Enoch and Noah

3   Abraham, Moses, and David

4   Israel scattered; Judah taken captive

5   Jesus Christ is born
    The Great Apostasy

6   Joseph Smith and the Restoration

ABOUT A.D. 2000

7   The second coming of Jesus and the Millennium

THE EARTH CELESTIALIZED

*The seven seals (each a thousand years)*

3 ¶ And when he had opened the second seal, I heard the second beast say, Come and see.

4 And there went out another horse that was red: and power was given to him that sat thereon to take peace from the earth, and that they should kill one another: and there was given unto him a great sword.

5 And when he had opened the third seal, I heard the third beast say, Come and see. And I beheld, and lo a black horse; and he that sat on him had a pair of balances in his hand.

6 And I heard a voice in the midst of the four beasts say, A measure of wheat for a penny, and three measures of barley for a penny; and see thou hurt not the oil and the wine.

7 And when he had opened the fourth seal, I heard the voice of the fourth beast say, Come and see.

8 And I looked, and behold a pale horse: and his name that sat on him was Death, and Hell followed with him. And power was given unto them over the fourth part of the earth, to kill with sword, and with hunger, and with death, and with the beasts of the earth.

9 ¶ And when he had opened the fifth seal, I saw under the altar the souls of them that were slain for the word of God, and for the testimony which they held:

10 And they cried with a loud voice, saying, How long, O Lord, holy and true, dost thou not judge and avenge our blood on them that dwell on the earth?

11 And white robes were given unto every one of them; and it was said unto them, that they should rest yet for a little season, until their fellowservants also and their brethren, that should be killed as they were, should be fulfilled.

## THE SIXTH SEAL IS OPENED

12 And I beheld when he had opened the sixth seal, and, lo, there was a great earthquake; and the sun became black as sackcloth of hair, and the moon became as blood;

13 And the stars of heaven fell unto the earth, even as a fig tree casteth her untimely figs, when she is shaken of a mighty wind.

14 And the heaven departed as a scroll when it is rolled together; and every mountain and island were moved out of their places.

15 And the kings of the earth, and the great men, and the rich men, and the chief captains, and the mighty men, and every bondman, and every free man, hid themselves in the dens and in the rocks of the mountains;

16 And said to the mountains and rocks, Fall on us, and hide us from the face of him that sitteth on the throne, and from the wrath of the Lamb:

17 For the great day of his wrath is come; and who shall be able to stand?

## CHAPTER 7

*John's vision continues. He sees some events that take place before the opening of the seventh seal. Look for how he describes the restoration of the gospel in the last days and for what he says will happen to people who are saved in the celestial kingdom.*

---

6:6   A "penny" was an average day's wage (see Matthew 20:2). A "measure of wheat" was less than a quart or a liter. In other words, because of famine, a day's worth of food for one person cost a day's wage.

6:9-11   The fifth seal represents the events of the earth's fifth thousand-year period (see D&C 77:7). Therefore the souls John saw were those early Christians who were killed from the time of Christ to about A.D. 1000. The "white robes" they were given represent their righteousness (see Revelation 19:8).

6:12   "Sackcloth of hair" is a rough cloth often made from the hair of black goats. The roughness of sackcloth is symbolic of sadness and mourning, but in this case the dark color pointed to an event prior to the Second Coming when the sun would be darkened. (See *Vine's Complete Expository Dictionary*, s.v. "Sackcloth," p. 543.)

6:12-17   The time in which we live is near the end of the sixth seal. Elder Joseph Fielding Smith said, "We are living in the Saturday Evening of Time" (*Doctrines of Salvation* 3:1).

6:14   The Joseph Smith Translation changes the first part of this verse to read, "And the heavens opened as a scroll is opened when it is rolled together."

6:15-17   At the second coming of the Savior, why will some people be so afraid that they will want the mountains to fall on them to hide them from God?

## John Sees the Gospel Restored and 144,000 Righteous People Sealed Up to Eternal Life

1 ¶ AND after these things I saw four angels standing on the four corners of the earth, holding the four winds of the earth, that the wind should not blow on the earth, nor on the sea, nor on any tree.

2 And I saw another angel ascending from the east, having the seal of the living God: and he cried with a loud voice to the four angels, to whom it was given to hurt the earth and the sea,

3 Saying, Hurt not the earth, neither the sea, nor the trees, till we have sealed the servants of our God in their foreheads.

4 And I heard the number of them which were sealed: and there were sealed an hundred and forty and four thousand of all the tribes of the children of Israel.

5 Of the tribe of Juda were sealed twelve thousand. Of the tribe of Reuben were sealed twelve thousand. Of the tribe of Gad were sealed twelve thousand.

6 Of the tribe of Aser were sealed twelve thousand. Of the tribe of Nepthalim were sealed twelve thousand. Of the tribe of Manasses were sealed twelve thousand.

7 Of the tribe of Simeon were sealed twelve thousand. Of the tribe of Levi were sealed twelve thousand. Of the tribe of Issachar were sealed twelve thousand.

8 Of the tribe of Zabulon were sealed twelve thousand. Of the tribe of Joseph were sealed twelve thousand. Of the tribe of Benjamin were sealed twelve thousand.

## John Sees a Multitude of People from All Nations Who Are Exalted

9 After this I beheld, and, lo, a great multitude, which no man could number, of all nations, and kindreds, and people, and tongues, stood before the throne, and before the Lamb, clothed with white robes, and palms in their hands;

10 And cried with a loud voice, saying, Salvation to our God which sitteth upon the throne, and unto the Lamb.

11 And all the angels stood round about the throne, and about the elders and the four beasts, and fell before the throne on their faces, and worshipped God,

12 Saying, Amen: Blessing, and glory, and wisdom, and thanksgiving, and honour, and power, and might, be unto our God for ever and ever. Amen.

13 ¶ And one of the elders answered, saying unto me, What are these which are arrayed in white robes? and whence came they?

14 And I said unto him, Sir, thou knowest. And he said to me, These are they which came out of great tribulation, and have washed their robes, and made them white in the blood of the Lamb.

15 Therefore are they before the throne of God, and serve him day and night in his temple: and he that sitteth on the throne shall dwell among them.

---

7:1 The Lord told Joseph Smith that these four angels "have the everlasting gospel to commit to every nation, kindred, tongue, and people" (D&C 77:8).

7:2 The Prophet Joseph Smith was told that the angel mentioned in verse 2 was "Elias," who is to "gather together the tribes of Israel and restore all things" to the earth (see D&C 77:9).

7:3 These servants of God receiving a seal in their foreheads symbolizes their taking the name of God upon themselves by covenant (see Revelation 22:4).

7:4-8 "John here sees 144,000 of these kings and priests, 12,000 from each tribe, converted, baptized, endowed, married for eternity, and finally sealed up unto eternal life" (Bruce R. McConkie, *Doctrinal New Testament Commentary* 3:491).

7:5-8 The name "twelve tribes of Israel" refers to the twelve sons of Jacob (whose name was changed to Israel) and all of their posterity or family (see Genesis 29:32 to 30:24; 35:16-20).

7:9 *the Lamb*—Jesus Christ

The multitude's wearing white robes shows worthiness and purity. Their having palm leaves in their hands is a reminder of Jesus' triumphal entry into Jerusalem when the people recognized him as their king (see Matthew 21:1-11).

7:10-12 Why do you think being in the presence of Jesus and Heavenly Father would make a person sing praises, worship, and bow?

7:13 *arrayed*—dressed

7:14 *tribulation*—trials, struggles

Our sins are forgiven us, or our garments are made white, through the atonement of Jesus Christ.

16 They shall hunger no more, neither thirst any more; neither shall the sun light on them, nor any heat.

17 For the Lamb which is in the midst of the throne shall feed them, and shall lead them unto living fountains of waters: and God shall wipe away all tears from their eyes.

# CHAPTER 8

*John saw fire and destruction poured out upon the earth after the seventh seal was opened and before the second coming of Jesus Christ. Notice the signs that will be given to help us prepare for the coming of Christ.*

## THE SEVENTH SEAL IS OPENED

1 ¶ AND when he had opened the seventh seal, there was silence in heaven about the space of half an hour.

2 And I saw the seven angels which stood before God; and to them were given seven trumpets.

3 And another angel came and stood at the altar, having a golden censer; and there was given unto him much incense, that he should offer it with the prayers of all saints upon the golden altar which was before the throne.

4 And the smoke of the incense, which came with the prayers of the saints, ascended up before God out of the angel's hand.

5 And the angel took the censer, and filled it with fire of the altar, and cast it into the earth: and there were voices, and thunderings, and lightnings, and an earthquake.

6 And the seven angels which had the seven trumpets prepared themselves to sound.

## THE FIRST TRUMPET IS SOUNDED

7 ¶ The first angel sounded, and there followed hail and fire mingled with blood, and they were cast upon the earth: and the third part of trees was burnt up, and all green grass was burnt up.

## THE SECOND TRUMPET IS SOUNDED

8 And the second angel sounded, and as it were a great mountain burning with fire was cast into the sea: and the third part of the sea became blood;

9 And the third part of the creatures which were in the sea, and had life, died; and the third part of the ships were destroyed.

## THE THIRD TRUMPET IS SOUNDED

10 And the third angel sounded, and there fell a great star from heaven, burning as it were a lamp, and it fell upon the third part of the rivers, and upon the fountains of waters;

11 And the name of the star is called Wormwood: and the third part of the waters became wormwood; and many men died of the waters, because they were made bitter.

## THE FOURTH TRUMPET IS SOUNDED

12 And the fourth angel sounded, and the third part of the sun was smitten, and the third part of the moon, and the third part of the stars; so as the third part of them was darkened, and the day shone not for a third part of it, and the night likewise.

---

7:16-17   The celestial kingdom will be a place where there is joy, peace, and eternal happiness. Which blessings listed in these verses would you appreciate most? Why?

8:1   "What is meant by the half hour of silence has not yet been revealed" (Bruce R. McConkie, *Doctrinal New Testament Commentary* 3:498).

8:2   Anciently the trumpet announced important events and gave signals during wars. These trumpets announce plagues to come upon the people of the earth that prepare the way for the coming of the Lord (see D&C 77:12).

8:3   censer—container used to burn incense

8:6   sound—blow their trumpets

8:7   This plague is similar to the seventh plague Moses pronounced upon the Egyptians (see

Exodus 9:23-25).

8:8   This plague is like the first plague Moses pronounced upon the Egyptians (see Exodus 7:20-21).

8:11   Wormwood is a plant with a strong, bitter taste. In the scriptures the word *wormwood* is often used to suggest great sorrow (see Proverbs 5:4; Amos 5:7).

8:12   In the ninth plague Moses pronounced on Egypt, a thick darkness covered the earth for three days (see Exodus 10:21-23).

8:12-13   The plagues described in Revelation 8 are similar to the plagues poured out upon Egypt during the days of Moses. The children of Israel were freed from slavery as a result of the plagues. Why do you think similar plagues will be used in the last days?

13 And I beheld, and heard an angel flying through the midst of heaven, saying with a loud voice, Woe, woe, woe, to the inhabiters of the earth by reason of the other voices of the trumpet of the three angels, which are yet to sound!

# CHAPTER 9

*Because people will become more wicked, many frightening events will occur before the second coming of Jesus Christ. Note who will be protected during this time.*

## THE FIFTH TRUMPET IS SOUNDED

1 ¶ AND the fifth angel sounded, and I saw a star fall from heaven unto the earth: and to him was given the key of the bottomless pit.

2 And he opened the bottomless pit; and there arose a smoke out of the pit, as the smoke of a great furnace; and the sun and the air were darkened by reason of the smoke of the pit.

3 And there came out of the smoke locusts upon the earth: and unto them was given power, as the scorpions of the earth have power.

4 And it was commanded them that they should not hurt the grass of the earth, neither any green thing, neither any tree; but only those men which have not the seal of God in their foreheads.

5 And to them it was given that they should not kill them, but that they should be tormented five months: and their torment was as the torment of a scorpion, when he striketh a man.

6 And in those days shall men seek death, and shall not find it; and shall desire to die, and death shall flee from them.

7 And the shapes of the locusts were like unto horses prepared unto battle; and on their heads were as it were crowns like gold, and their faces were as the faces of men.

8 And they had hair as the hair of women, and their teeth were as the teeth of lions.

9 And they had breastplates, as it were breastplates of iron; and the sound of their wings was as the sound of chariots of many horses running to battle.

10 And they had tails like unto scorpions, and there were stings in their tails: and their power was to hurt men five months.

11 And they had a king over them, which is the angel of the bottomless pit, whose name in the Hebrew tongue is Abaddon, but in the Greek tongue hath his name Apollyon.

12 One woe is past; and, behold, there come two woes more hereafter.

## THE SIXTH TRUMPET IS SOUNDED

13 ¶ And the sixth angel sounded, and I heard a voice from the four horns of the golden altar which is before God,

14 Saying to the sixth angel which had the trumpet, Loose the four angels which are bound in the great river Euphrates.

15 And the four angels were loosed, which were prepared for an hour, and a day, and a month, and a year, for to slay the third part of men.

16 And the number of the army of the horsemen were two hundred thousand thousand: and I heard the number of them.

---

9:1 The star that fell "from heaven" who "was given the key of the bottomless pit" describes Lucifer, who was cast out of heaven to earth and had power over his followers (see Revelation 12:9).

9:2-3 Smoke is a symbol of "evil influence," and the locusts are symbols of wicked men influenced by the devil (see Bruce R. McConkie, *Doctrinal New Testament Commentary* 3:501).

9:4 Those protected have "the seal of God in their foreheads." Joseph Smith said this refers to those who have kept sacred temple covenants (see *The Teachings of Joseph Smith*, p. 616).

9:5 **tormented**—given great pain or misery

9:7-10 John sees in vision a war fought with weapons that didn't exist in his day. Which modern-day weapons and war machines do you think he is describing?

9:11 **Abaddon, Apollyon**—Destroyer (Satan)

9:12 **woe**—trouble, disaster

9:14-15 The Joseph Smith Translation changes "great river Euphrates" to "bottomless pit" (JST, Revelation 9:14). Four of Satan's angels influence men into a war that kills one of every three people.

9:16 **two hundred thousand thousand**—two hundred million

17 And thus I saw the horses in the vision, and them that sat on them, having breastplates of fire, and of jacinth, and brimstone: and the heads of the horses were as the heads of lions; and out of their mouths issued fire and smoke and brimstone.

18 By these three was the third part of men killed, by the fire, and by the smoke, and by the brimstone, which issued out of their mouths.

19 For their power is in their mouth, and in their tails: for their tails were like unto serpents, and had heads, and with them they do hurt.

20 And the rest of the men which were not killed by these plagues yet repented not of the works of their hands, that they should not worship devils, and idols of gold, and silver, and brass, and stone, and of wood: which neither can see, nor hear, nor walk:

21 Neither repented they of their murders, nor of their sorceries, nor of their fornication, nor of their thefts.

## CHAPTER 10

*This chapter describes part of John's mission. Look for what John is asked to do in the last days.*

### A MIGHTY ANGEL APPEARS TO JOHN WITH A LITTLE BOOK

1 ¶ AND I saw another mighty angel come down from heaven, clothed with a cloud: and a rainbow was upon his head, and his face was as it were the sun, and his feet as pillars of fire:

2 And he had in his hand a little book open: and he set his right foot upon the sea, and his left foot on the earth,

3 And cried with a loud voice, as when a lion roareth: and when he had cried, seven thunders uttered their voices.

4 And when the seven thunders had uttered their voices, I was about to write: and I heard a voice from heaven saying unto me, Seal up those things which the seven thunders uttered, and write them not.

5 And the angel which I saw stand upon the sea and upon the earth lifted up his hand to heaven,

6 And sware by him that liveth for ever and ever, who created heaven, and the things that therein are, and the earth, and the things that therein are, and the sea, and the things which are therein, that there should be time no longer:

7 But in the days of the voice of the seventh angel, when he shall begin to sound, the mystery of God should be finished, as he hath declared to his servants the prophets.

### JOHN EATS THE LITTLE BOOK

8 ¶ And the voice which I heard from heaven spake unto me again, and said, Go and take the little book which is open in the hand of the angel which standeth upon the sea and upon the earth.

9 And I went unto the angel, and said unto him, Give me the little book. And he said unto me, Take it, and eat it up; and it shall make thy belly bitter, but it shall be in thy mouth sweet as honey.

10 And I took the little book out of the angel's hand, and ate it up; and it was in my mouth sweet as honey:

---

9:17 **jacinth**—reddish brown stone
**brimstone**—yellow mineral, sulphur

9:20-21 This is like the final destructions recorded in the Book of Mormon. The wicked will not repent, even though they suffer plagues, destruction, and war. (See Mormon 3:11-13; Ether 15:19.)

Why do you think many people will not turn to the Lord, even when they suffer serious problems?

9:21 The Greek word for *sorceries* in this verse can also mean "drugs" (see *Vine's Complete Expository Dictionary*, s.v. "Sorcery," p. 587).

10:2, 8 The little book is the mission given to John to teach the gospel to the lost tribes of Israel in the last days (see D&C 77:14; *The Teachings of Joseph Smith*, p. 356).

10:6 **sware by him that liveth for ever and ever**—made a promise in the name of the Lord

10:6-7 The references to "time no longer" and "the days of the voice of the seventh angel" have to do with the beginning of the Millennium (see Bruce R. McConkie, *Doctrinal New Testament Commentary* 3:505).

10:7 The term "mystery of God" pertains to the truths God keeps "hidden" from the world (see D&C 77:6). During the Millennium all the mysteries of God will be revealed to us (see D&C 101:25, 32-34).

10:9-10 John eats the little book to show his willingness to fulfill the mission given by the Lord. The sweet taste in his mouth represents the joy of doing the work of the Lord. The bitter belly represents the warnings of destruction contained in the book. (See Ezekiel 3:1-3.)

and as soon as I had eaten it, my belly was bitter.

11 And he said unto me, Thou must prophesy again before many peoples, and nations, and tongues, and kings.

## CHAPTER 11

*John sees what happens in Jerusalem before the Savior comes again. In this chapter, watch for how the Lord shows his power.*

### JOHN IS COMMANDED TO MEASURE THE TEMPLE AND THOSE WHO WORSHIP THERE

1 ¶ AND there was given me a reed like unto a rod: and the angel stood, saying, Rise, and measure the temple of God, and the altar, and them that worship therein.

2 But the court which is without the temple leave out, and measure it not; for it is given unto the Gentiles: and the holy city shall they tread under foot forty and two months.

### TWO PROPHETS WILL TESTIFY IN JERUSALEM FOR THREE AND A HALF YEARS

3 ¶ And I will give power unto my two witnesses, and they shall prophesy a thousand two hundred and threescore days, clothed in sackcloth.

4 These are the two olive trees, and the two candlesticks standing before the God of the earth.

5 And if any man will hurt them, fire proceedeth out of their mouth, and devoureth their enemies: and if any man will hurt them, he must in this manner be killed.

6 These have power to shut heaven, that it rain not in the days of their prophecy: and have power over waters to turn them to blood, and to smite the earth with all plagues, as often as they will.

7 And when they shall have finished their testimony, the beast that ascendeth out of the bottomless pit shall make war against them, and shall overcome them, and kill them.

### THE TWO PROPHETS WILL BE RESURRECTED AND TAKEN INTO HEAVEN

8 And their dead bodies shall lie in the street of the great city, which spiritually is called Sodom and Egypt, where also our Lord was crucified.

9 And they of the people and kindreds and tongues and nations shall see their dead bodies three days and an half, and shall not suffer their dead bodies to be put in graves.

10 And they that dwell upon the earth shall rejoice over them, and make merry, and shall send gifts one to another; because these two prophets tormented them that dwelt on the earth.

11 And after three days and an half the Spirit of life from God entered into them, and they stood upon their feet; and great fear fell upon them which saw them.

12 And they heard a great voice from heaven saying unto them, Come up hither. And they ascended up to heaven in a cloud; and their enemies beheld them.

---

11:1    A reed was a long stick, approximately 10$\frac{1}{2}$ to 11 feet in length (see Ezekiel 40:5; see also Merrill F. Unger, *The New Unger's Bible Dictionary*, s.v. "Metrology," p. 842).

John's assignment to measure people who come to the temple may be symbolic of their being judged to see if they are worthy. What must a person do to be worthy to worship in the temple?

11:2    *Gentiles* is a word that means "nations." It refers to those not of the family of Israel or who do not believe in the God of Israel. (See LDS Bible Dictionary, s.v. "Gentile," pp. 679-80.)

The "holy city" is Jerusalem (see Nehemiah 11:1; Revelation 11:8).

11:3    Doctrine and Covenants 77:15 explains that the "two witnesses" are two prophets (see also Revelation 11:10). "No doubt they [the two witnesses] will be members of the Council of the Twelve or of the First Presidency of the Church" (Bruce R. McConkie, *Doctrinal New Testament Commentary* 3:509).

11:5    *devoureth*—destroys

11:7    The beast coming out of the bottomless pit represents the great army that will gather to attack the Jews (see Revelation 9:2-19).

11:8    Jerusalem, where "our Lord was crucified," is described as being as wicked as Sodom (see Genesis 18:20-21) and Egypt.

11:9    *kindreds*—families or tribes
*suffer*—allow

11:10    *dwelt*—lived

11:12    *ascended*—rose

13 And the same hour was there a great earthquake, and the tenth part of the city fell, and in the earthquake were slain of men seven thousand: and the remnant were affrighted, and gave glory to the God of heaven.

14 ¶ The second woe is past; and, behold, the third woe cometh quickly.

## THE SEVENTH TRUMPET IS SOUNDED

15 And the seventh angel sounded; and there were great voices in heaven, saying, The kingdoms of this world are become the kingdoms of our Lord, and of his Christ; and he shall reign for ever and ever.

16 And the four and twenty elders, which sat before God on their seats, fell upon their faces, and worshipped God,

17 Saying, We give thee thanks, O Lord God Almighty, which art, and wast, and art to come; because thou hast taken to thee thy great power, and hast reigned.

18 And the nations were angry, and thy wrath is come, and the time of the dead, that they should be judged, and that thou shouldest give reward unto thy servants the prophets, and to the saints, and them that fear thy name, small and great; and shouldest destroy them which destroy the earth.

19 And the temple of God was opened in heaven, and there was seen in his temple the ark of his testament: and there were lightnings, and voices, and thunderings, and an earthquake, and great hail.

## CHAPTER 12

*In this chapter John speaks about the devil and the War in Heaven, which continues here on earth. Look for how the faithful overcame Satan.*

## THE CHURCH AND KINGDOM OF GOD ARE ESTABLISHED

1 ¶ AND there appeared a great wonder in heaven; a woman clothed with the sun, and the moon under her feet, and upon her head a crown of twelve stars:

2 And she being with child cried, travailing in birth, and pained to be delivered.

3 And there appeared another wonder in heaven; and behold a great red dragon, having seven heads and ten horns, and seven crowns upon his heads.

4 And his tail drew the third part of the stars of heaven, and did cast them to the earth: and the dragon stood before the woman which was ready to be delivered, for to devour her child as soon as it was born.

5 And she brought forth a man child, who was to rule all nations with a rod of iron: and her child was caught up unto God, and to his throne.

6 And the woman fled into the wilderness, where she hath a place prepared of God, that they should feed her there a thousand two hundred and threescore days.

---

11:13 This earthquake will be so strong it will cause the fish in the sea and the birds in the heaven to shake (see Ezekiel 38:19-20).

**slain**—killed
**the remnant**—those who were not killed

11:15 The prophet Daniel also saw that in the last days God's kingdom would roll forth like a great stone and crush everything in its way, including all of the kingdoms of the world (see Daniel 2:26-45).

11:18 **wrath**—anger, punishment

11:19 The "ark of his testament" is also called the "ark of the covenant" (see Hebrews 9:4-5).

12:1 The Joseph Smith Translation teaches that the "woman" in this chapter represents the "church of God" (JST, Revelation 12:7).

12:2 **travailing in birth**—experiencing the physical hardships just before giving birth

12:3 The red dragon is defined later in this chapter as the devil, or Satan. The heads, horns, and crowns represent his kingdom here on the earth. (See Revelation 12:9.)

12:4 The "third part of the stars of heaven" are those who were cast out of Heavenly Father's presence and followed Satan (see D&C 29:36). The child in this chapter represents the kingdom of God (see JST, Revelation 12:7).

**devour her child**—kill or destroy the kingdom of God

12:5 The "rod of iron" represents the word of God (see 1 Nephi 11:25).

12:6 The fleeing of the woman, or the Church, into the wilderness represents the Apostasy (see Bruce R. McConkie, *Doctrinal New Testament Commentary* 3:517). Furthermore, in the Joseph Smith Translation the woman remains in the wilderness a thousand two hundred and threescore (1,260) *years,* not days (see JST, Revelation 12:5).

## Satan Is Cast Out of Heaven and into the Earth

7 And there was war in heaven: Michael and his angels fought against the dragon; and the dragon fought and his angels,

8 And prevailed not; neither was their place found any more in heaven.

9 And the great dragon was cast out, that old serpent, called the Devil, and Satan, which deceiveth the whole world: he was cast out into the earth, and his angels were cast out with him.

10 And I heard a loud voice saying in heaven, Now is come salvation, and strength, and the kingdom of our God, and the power of his Christ: for the accuser of our brethren is cast down, which accused them before our God day and night.

11 And they overcame him by the blood of the Lamb, and by the word of their testimony; and they loved not their lives unto the death.

12 ¶ Therefore rejoice, ye heavens, and ye that dwell in them. Woe to the inhabiters of the earth and of the sea! for the devil is come down unto you, having great wrath, because he knoweth that he hath but a short time.

13 And when the dragon saw that he was cast unto the earth, he persecuted the woman which brought forth the man child.

14 And to the woman were given two wings of a great eagle, that she might fly into the wilderness, into her place, where she is nourished for a time, and times, and half a time, from the face of the serpent.

15 And the serpent cast out of his mouth water as a flood after the woman, that he might cause her to be carried away of the flood.

16 And the earth helped the woman, and the earth opened her mouth, and swallowed up the flood which the dragon cast out of his mouth.

17 And the dragon was wroth with the woman, and went to make war with the remnant of her seed, which keep the commandments of God, and have the testimony of Jesus Christ.

## CHAPTER 13

*In this chapter John sees fierce-looking beasts that represent earthly kingdoms controlled by Satan. Look for images John used to describe those kingdoms.*

## Satan Governs Earthly Kingdoms

1 ¶ AND I stood upon the sand of the sea, and saw a beast rise up out of the sea, having seven heads and ten horns, and upon his horns ten crowns, and upon his heads the name of blasphemy.

2 And the beast which I saw was like unto a leopard, and his feet were as the feet of a bear, and his mouth as the mouth of a lion: and the dragon gave him his power, and his seat, and great authority.

---

12:7-9 "The war that is now going on among men, the war between good and evil, is but a continuation of the war that began in heaven" (Bruce R. McConkie, *The Millennial Messiah*, p. 667).

12:10 **the accuser of our brethren**—Satan

12:11 We overcame Satan once because of our testimony of "the blood of the Lamb," or the atonement of Jesus Christ. How can your testimony of Jesus Christ help you overcome Satan now?

12:13 **man child**—kingdom of God (see JST, Revelation 12:7)

12:14 The phrase "a time, and times, and half a time" is a reference to three and a half years. One Latter-day Saint commentator has explained: "The period of her [the woman's] rest would be one thousand two hundred and sixty days, or three-and-one-half years. (Verse five of the JST changes 'days' to 'years,' probably to suggest that the stay in the wilderness would be of long duration.)" (Richard D. Draper, *Opening the Seven Seals*, p. 138.)

12:17 The devil continues to war against the remnant of the woman's seed. In latter-day revelation the seed are "the saints of God" (D&C 76:28-29).

13:1 The Joseph Smith Translation teaches that this beast was a "likeness of the kingdoms of the earth" (JST, Revelation 13:1). Also, note that the Prophet Joseph Smith, speaking to missionaries, said: "Declare the first principles, and let mysteries alone, lest ye be overthrown. Never meddle with the visions of beasts and subjects you do not understand." (*The Teachings of Joseph Smith*, p. 432.)

Blasphemy is the sin of claiming to be like God or speaking evil of God.

13:2 **the dragon**—Satan

3 And I saw one of his heads as it were wounded to death; and his deadly wound was healed: and all the world wondered after the beast.

4 And they worshipped the dragon which gave power unto the beast: and they worshipped the beast, saying, Who is like unto the beast? who is able to make war with him?

5 And there was given unto him a mouth speaking great things and blasphemies; and power was given unto him to continue forty and two months.

6 And he opened his mouth in blasphemy against God, to blaspheme his name, and his tabernacle, and them that dwell in heaven.

7 And it was given unto him to make war with the saints, and to overcome them: and power was given him over all kindreds, and tongues, and nations.

8 And all that dwell upon the earth shall worship him, whose names are not written in the book of life of the Lamb slain from the foundation of the world.

9 If any man have an ear, let him hear.

10 He that leadeth into captivity shall go into captivity: he that killeth with the sword must be killed with the sword. Here is the patience and the faith of the saints.

### THE CHURCH OF THE DEVIL WORKS MIRACLES

11 ¶ And I beheld another beast coming up out of the earth; and he had two horns like a lamb, and he spake as a dragon.

12 And he exerciseth all the power of the first beast before him, and causeth the earth and them which dwell therein to worship the first beast, whose deadly wound was healed.

13 And he doeth great wonders, so that he maketh fire come down from heaven on the earth in the sight of men,

14 And deceiveth them that dwell on the earth by the means of those miracles which he had power to do in the sight of the beast; saying to them that dwell on the earth, that they should make an image to the beast, which had the wound by a sword, and did live.

15 And he had power to give life unto the image of the beast, that the image of the beast should both speak, and cause that as many as would not worship the image of the beast should be killed.

16 And he causeth all, both small and great, rich and poor, free and bond, to receive a mark in their right hand, or in their foreheads:

17 And that no man might buy or sell, save he that had the mark, or the name of the beast, or the number of his name.

18 Here is wisdom. Let him that hath understanding count the number of the beast: for it is the number of a man; and his number is Six hundred threescore and six.

## CHAPTER 14

*John sees in vision Jesus Christ appearing on Mount Zion, the restoration of the gospel, and the destruction of the wicked at the Second Coming. Watch for what is promised to those who die in righteousness.*

---

13:4-6 In the last days many will be deceived and follow false prophets. Elder Bruce R. McConkie said: "Most of the worship in the world is *false worship* because it . . . does not cling to Christ and his gospel standards" (*Mormon Doctrine*, p. 849).

13:8 The book of life "is the record kept in heaven which contains the names of the faithful and an account of their righteous covenants and deeds" (Bruce R. McConkie, *Mormon Doctrine*, p. 97).

13:11 Satan seeks "to destroy the souls of men" in the last days by deceiving and leading them to believe in false teachings (see D&C 10:25-27, 33). The beast in this verse looked "like a lamb" (Christ) but "spake as a dragon" (Satan).

13:13-14 How can Satan's servants do miracles? Just as Pharaoh's magicians copied some of Moses' miracles (see Exodus 7:10-12; 8:6-7, 17-19), Satan's servants have power to perform some "miracles" that deceive those who are spiritually weak (see Matthew 24:24).

13:14 *image*—figure or idol

13:16 *bond*—slave

13:16-17 Elder Bruce R. McConkie said, "As the servants of God have their calling and election made sure when they are 'sealed. . . in their foreheads' (Rev. 7:2-8), so the Great Imitator places a mark in the right hand or foreheads of those who follow him" (*Doctrinal New Testament Commentary* 3:524).

13:18 *threescore*—sixty

## CHRIST APPEARS ON MOUNT SION (ZION)

1 ¶ AND I looked, and, lo, a Lamb stood on the mount Sion, and with him an hundred forty and four thousand, having his Father's name written in their foreheads.

2 And I heard a voice from heaven, as the voice of many waters, and as the voice of a great thunder: and I heard the voice of harpers harping with their harps:

3 And they sung as it were a new song before the throne, and before the four beasts, and the elders: and no man could learn that song but the hundred and forty and four thousand, which were redeemed from the earth.

4 These are they which were not defiled with women; for they are virgins. These are they which follow the Lamb whithersoever he goeth. These were redeemed from among men, being the firstfruits unto God and to the Lamb.

5 And in their mouth was found no guile: for they are without fault before the throne of God.

## ANGELS WILL BE SENT TO RESTORE THE GOSPEL IN THE LATTER DAYS

6 ¶ And I saw another angel fly in the midst of heaven, having the everlasting gospel to preach unto them that dwell on the earth, and to every nation, and kindred, and tongue, and people,

7 Saying with a loud voice, Fear God, and give glory to him; for the hour of his judgment is come: and worship him that made heaven, and earth, and the sea, and the fountains of waters.

8 And there followed another angel, saying, Babylon is fallen, is fallen, that great city, because she made all nations drink of the wine of the wrath of her fornication.

9 And the third angel followed them, saying with a loud voice, If any man worship the beast and his image, and receive his mark in his forehead, or in his hand,

10 The same shall drink of the wine of the wrath of God, which is poured out without mixture into the cup of his indignation; and he shall be tormented with fire and brimstone in the presence of the holy angels, and in the presence of the Lamb:

11 And the smoke of their torment ascendeth up for ever and ever: and they have no rest day nor night, who worship the beast and his image, and whosoever receiveth the mark of his name.

12 Here is the patience of the saints: here are they that keep the commandments of God, and the faith of Jesus.

13 ¶ And I heard a voice from heaven saying unto me, Write, Blessed are the dead which die in the Lord from henceforth: Yea, saith the Spirit, that they may rest from their labours; and their works do follow them.

## RIGHTEOUS PEOPLE ARE GATHERED AND WICKED PEOPLE ARE CUT DOWN AT THE FINAL HARVEST

14 And I looked, and behold a white cloud, and upon the cloud one sat like unto the Son of man, having on his head a golden crown, and in his hand a sharp sickle.

---

14:1 **a Lamb**—Jesus Christ

"All of the references to Mount Zion which talk of the Second Coming and related latter-day events appear to have in mind the new Mount Zion in Jackson County, Missouri" (Bruce R. McConkie, *Doctrinal New Testament Commentary* 3:525-26).

Who are these 144,000? See for Revelation 7:4-8.

14:3 **redeemed**—saved

14:4 **defiled**—made unclean
**firstfruits**—first saved

14:5 **guile**—deception, dishonesty

14:6-9 These verses testify that angels would be sent to restore the gospel. Some of these angels include the following: Moroni (see D&C 20:6-8); John the Baptist (see D&C 13:1); Peter, James, and John (see D&C 27:12); and Moses, Elias, and Elijah (see D&C 110:11-16).

14:8 Babylon is a symbol for the wickedness of the world (see D&C 1:16; 133:14).

14:9-11 These verses explain that a person cannot serve the world and its wickedness (the beast) and still be saved by God.

14:12-13 What does a righteous person gain if he or she dies while serving the Lord? (See Mark 8:35; D&C 59:2.)

14:14 "In the language of Adam, Man of Holiness is [Heavenly Father's] name, and the name of his Only Begotten is the Son of Man, even Jesus Christ" (Moses 6:57).

15 And another angel came out of the temple, crying with a loud voice to him that sat on the cloud, Thrust in thy sickle, and reap: for the time is come for thee to reap; for the harvest of the earth is ripe.

16 And he that sat on the cloud thrust in his sickle on the earth; and the earth was reaped.

17 And another angel came out of the temple which is in heaven, he also having a sharp sickle.

18 And another angel came out from the altar, which had power over fire; and cried with a loud cry to him that had the sharp sickle, saying, Thrust in thy sharp sickle, and gather the clusters of the vine of the earth; for her grapes are fully ripe.

19 And the angel thrust in his sickle into the earth, and gathered the vine of the earth, and cast it into the great winepress of the wrath of God.

20 And the winepress was trodden without the city, and blood came out of the winepress, even unto the horse bridles, by the space of a thousand and six hundred furlongs.

# CHAPTER 15

*John sees the celestial kingdom. Notice how John describes the joy and happiness of those who live there.*

## EXALTED SAINTS PRAISE GOD FOREVER

1 ¶ AND I saw another sign in heaven, great and marvellous, seven angels having the seven last plagues; for in them is filled up the wrath of God.

2 And I saw as it were a sea of glass mingled with fire: and them that had gotten the victory over the beast, and over his image, and over his mark, and over the number of his name, stand on the sea of glass, having the harps of God.

3 And they sing the song of Moses the servant of God, and the song of the Lamb, saying, Great and marvellous are thy works, Lord God Almighty; just and true are thy ways, thou King of saints.

4 Who shall not fear thee, O Lord, and glorify thy name? for thou only art holy: for all nations shall come and worship before thee; for thy judgments are made manifest.

## SEVEN PLAGUES ARE PREPARED TO BE POURED OUT ON THE WICKED

5 ¶ And after that I looked, and, behold, the temple of the tabernacle of the testimony in heaven was opened:

6 And the seven angels came out of the temple, having the seven plagues, clothed in pure and white linen, and having their breasts girded with golden girdles.

7 And one of the four beasts gave unto the seven angels seven golden vials full of the wrath of God, who liveth for ever and ever.

8 And the temple was filled with smoke from the glory of God, and from his power; and no man was able to enter into the temple, till the seven plagues of the seven angels were fulfilled.

# CHAPTER 16

*Sometimes God disciplines his children to help them repent. Look for what God will do in the last days to give the wicked a chance to repent.*

---

14:15-20 To "reap" means to harvest the crops. "First, as recorded in verses 14-16, [John] sees the Son of Man harvest his saints. This is now in process. . . . Then, as recorded in verses 17-20, he sees the harvest-havoc wrought among the wicked and ungodly." (Bruce R. McConkie, *Doctrinal New Testament Commentary* 3:535.)

14:20 ***a thousand and six hundred furlongs***—about 184 miles

15:1 These plagues on the wicked are described in Revelation 16-18.

 ***wrath***—anger

15:2 The earth, when it is glorified, will become the celestial kingdom. It is sometimes described as being like a sea of glass. (See D&C 130:6-9.)

The beast, his image, and his mark are representations for Satan and his followers (see Revelation 13:11-18).

15:3-4 "All the righteous saints of all the ages shall sing this song in celestial glory forevermore [see D&C 133:56]" (Bruce R. McConkie, *Doctrinal New Testament Commentary* 3:538). Would you like to take part in this heavenly choir? Why?

15:5 John sees a temple in heaven like the tabernacle that existed in Old Testament times (see Numbers 1:50).

15:6 ***having their breasts girded with golden girdles***—wearing golden sashes

15:7 ***vials***—bowls, small containers for liquid

## GOD CAUSES PLAGUES THAT THE WICKED MIGHT REPENT

1 ¶ AND I heard a great voice out of the temple saying to the seven angels, Go your ways, and pour out the vials of the wrath of God upon the earth.

2 And the first went, and poured out his vial upon the earth; and there fell a noisome and grievous sore upon the men which had the mark of the beast, and upon them which worshipped his image.

3 And the second angel poured out his vial upon the sea; and it became as the blood of a dead man: and every living soul died in the sea.

4 And the third angel poured out his vial upon the rivers and fountains of waters; and they became blood.

5 And I heard the angel of the waters say, Thou art righteous, O Lord, which art, and wast, and shalt be, because thou hast judged thus.

6 For they have shed the blood of saints and prophets, and thou hast given them blood to drink; for they are worthy.

7 And I heard another out of the altar say, Even so, Lord God Almighty, true and righteous are thy judgments.

8 ¶ And the fourth angel poured out his vial upon the sun; and power was given unto him to scorch men with fire.

9 And men were scorched with great heat, and blasphemed the name of God, which hath power over these plagues: and they repented not to give him glory.

10 And the fifth angel poured out his vial upon the seat of the beast; and his kingdom was full of darkness; and they gnawed their tongues for pain,

11 And blasphemed the God of heaven because of their pains and their sores, and repented not of their deeds.

12 ¶ And the sixth angel poured out his vial upon the great river Euphrates; and the water thereof was dried up, that the way of the kings of the east might be prepared.

## NATIONS GATHER FOR THE BATTLE OF ARMAGEDDON

13 And I saw three unclean spirits like frogs come out of the mouth of the dragon, and out of the mouth of the beast, and out of the mouth of the false prophet.

14 For they are the spirits of devils, working miracles, which go forth unto the kings of the earth and of the whole world, to gather them to the battle of that great day of God Almighty.

15 Behold, I come as a thief. Blessed is he that watcheth, and keepeth his garments, lest he walk naked, and they see his shame.

16 And he gathered them together into a place called in the Hebrew tongue Armageddon.

---

16:1 **vials**—bowls, small containers for liquid
**wrath**—anger and punishments

16:2 **noisome and grievous**—bad and painful
**men which had the mark of the beast**—people identified as followers of Satan

16:4 Moses turned the waters of Egypt into blood (see Exodus 7:20).

16:8-9 One plague will apparently include increased heat from the sun. This could hurt people and all living things. If this happened in your day, whom could you turn to for help?

16:10 **seat**—throne

16:11 **blasphemed**—cursed

16:13-16 Jesus prophesied that in the last days false prophets would arise showing "signs and wonders" to "deceive the very elect" (Matthew 24:24). In this way Satan will lead the kings of the earth to gather their armies for the last battle.

Valley of Armageddon

16:16 Armageddon is located in a valley fifty miles north of Jerusalem and will be the scene of a "great and final conflict taking place at the second coming of the Lord" (LDS Bible Dictionary, s.v. "Armageddon," p. 614; see also Zechariah 14:2).

## DESTRUCTION COMES WITH THE SECOND COMING OF JESUS CHRIST

17 ¶ And the seventh angel poured out his vial into the air; and there came a great voice out of the temple of heaven, from the throne, saying, It is done.

18 And there were voices, and thunders, and lightnings; and there was a great earthquake, such as was not since men were upon the earth, so mighty an earthquake, and so great.

19 And the great city was divided into three parts, and the cities of the nations fell: and great Babylon came in remembrance before God, to give unto her the cup of the wine of the fierceness of his wrath.

20 And every island fled away, and the mountains were not found.

21 And there fell upon men a great hail out of heaven, every stone about the weight of a talent: and men blasphemed God because of the plague of the hail; for the plague thereof was exceeding great.

## CHAPTER 17

*John sees symbols representing the devil's kingdom. Watch for why following Jesus is the only way to overcome the beast and his wickedness.*

## THE CHURCH OF THE DEVIL BRINGS GREAT WICKEDNESS

1 ¶ AND there came one of the seven angels which had the seven vials, and talked with me, saying unto me, Come hither; I will shew unto thee the judgment of the great whore that sitteth upon many waters:

2 With whom the kings of the earth have committed fornication, and the inhabitants of the earth have been made drunk with the wine of her fornication.

3 So he carried me away in the spirit into the wilderness: and I saw a woman sit upon a scarlet coloured beast, full of names of blasphemy, having seven heads and ten horns.

4 And the woman was arrayed in purple and scarlet colour, and decked with gold and precious stones and pearls, having a golden cup in her hand full of abominations and filthiness of her fornication:

5 And upon her forehead was a name written, MYSTERY, BABYLON THE GREAT, THE MOTHER OF HARLOTS AND ABOMINATIONS OF THE EARTH.

6 And I saw the woman drunken with the blood of the saints, and with the blood of the martyrs of Jesus: and when I saw her, I wondered with great admiration.

---

16:21 **about the weight of a talent**—somewhere between 57 and 130 pounds

17:1 **vials**—bowls, small containers for liquid

"John the Revelator saw the same vision that was given to Nephi. To John, an angel—perhaps the same one who conversed with Nephi—called the great and abominable church 'the great whore that sitteth upon many waters.'" (Bruce R. McConkie, *The Millennial Messiah*, p. 52.)

She "sitteth upon many waters" means Satan's influence is among all people and nations (see Revelation 17:15). "The judgment of the great whore" refers to the fall of Babylon, meaning the end of wickedness (see Revelation 18).

17:2 **kings of the earth**—governments of different countries

The kings of all nations become "drunk with the wine" of the church of the devil by making wicked choices and ignoring the prophets' warnings (see Isaiah 29:9-10).

17:4 **arrayed**—clothed
**decked**—decorated

17:5 "BABYLON THE GREAT" is the church of the devil, with all its false teachings and wickedness (see D&C 133:14). The phrase "THE MOTHER OF HARLOTS" suggests that "false churches beget [create more] false churches" (Bruce R. McConkie, *Doctrinal New Testament Commentary* 3:554).

The false woman (church) has a name on her forehead. By contrast, the true followers of the Lord are sealed by the priesthood (see Revelation 7:3).

17:6 **admiration**—amazement

## THE BEAST CARRIED THE WOMAN

7 ¶ And the angel said unto me, Wherefore didst thou marvel? I will tell thee the mystery of the woman, and of the beast that carrieth her, which hath the seven heads and ten horns.

8 The beast that thou sawest was, and is not; and shall ascend out of the bottomless pit, and go into perdition: and they that dwell on the earth shall wonder, whose names were not written in the book of life from the foundation of the world, when they behold the beast that was, and is not, and yet is.

9 And here is the mind which hath wisdom. The seven heads are seven mountains, on which the woman sitteth.

10 And there are seven kings: five are fallen, and one is, and the other is not yet come; and when he cometh, he must continue a short space.

11 And the beast that was, and is not, even he is the eighth, and is of the seven, and goeth into perdition.

12 And the ten horns which thou sawest are ten kings, which have received no kingdom as yet; but receive power as kings one hour with the beast.

13 These have one mind, and shall give their power and strength unto the beast.

14 ¶ These shall make war with the Lamb, and the Lamb shall overcome them: for he is Lord of lords, and King of kings: and they that are with him are called, and chosen, and faithful.

15 And he saith unto me, The waters which thou sawest, where the whore sitteth, are peoples, and multitudes, and nations, and tongues.

16 And the ten horns which thou sawest upon the beast, these shall hate the whore, and shall make her desolate and naked, and shall eat her flesh, and burn her with fire.

17 For God hath put in their hearts to fulfil his will, and to agree, and give their kingdom unto the beast, until the words of God shall be fulfilled.

18 And the woman which thou sawest is that great city, which reigneth over the kings of the earth.

# CHAPTER 18

*In Revelation 17, John describes the wickedness of "Babylon." In chapter 18, he describes Babylon's fall. As you read, think of things in this world that are similar to what John describes in this chapter.*

## THE WICKEDNESS OF THE WORLD WILL END AT THE SECOND COMING OF JESUS CHRIST

1 ¶ AND after these things I saw another angel come down from heaven, having great power; and the earth was lightened with his glory.

2 And he cried mightily with a strong voice, saying, Babylon the great is fallen, is fallen, and is become the habitation of devils, and the hold of every foul spirit, and a cage of every unclean and hateful bird.

3 For all nations have drunk of the wine of the wrath of her fornication, and the kings of the earth have committed fornication with her, and the merchants of the earth are waxed rich through the abundance of her delicacies.

4 And I heard another voice from heaven, saying, Come out of her, my people, that ye be not partakers of her sins, and that ye receive not of her plagues.

5 For her sins have reached unto heaven, and God hath remembered her iniquities.

---

17:7-
18       Much of the meaning of this chapter has not been explained by the Lord. Joseph Smith said, "Whenever God gives a vision of an image, or beast, or figure of any kind, He always holds Himself responsible to give a revelation or interpretation of the meaning thereof, otherwise we are not responsible or accountable for our belief in it" (*The Teachings of Joseph Smith*, p. 72).

17:8     **perdition**—final destruction or ruin

         The book of life contains a record of all the works of the righteous (see D&C 128:6-7).

17:16-
17       Part of the destruction in the last days will come as wicked nations "war among themselves" and shall "fall into the pit which they digged to ensnare the people of the Lord" (1 Nephi 22:13-14).

18:2     *Babylon* stands for everything that is wicked in the world (see LDS Bible Dictionary, s.v. "Babylon," p. 618).

18:2-3   John sees a time when most of the world has accepted the wickedness of Babylon (see 2 Timothy 3:1-5).

18:3     In this chapter the words *her* and *she* refer to Babylon.

18:4     **plagues**—terrible disasters

18:5     **iniquities**—sins

6 Reward her even as she rewarded you, and double unto her double according to her works: in the cup which she hath filled fill to her double.

7 How much she hath glorified herself, and lived deliciously, so much torment and sorrow give her: for she saith in her heart, I sit a queen, and am no widow, and shall see no sorrow.

8 Therefore shall her plagues come in one day, death, and mourning, and famine; and she shall be utterly burned with fire: for strong is the Lord God who judgeth her.

## THE WICKED WILL BE VERY SAD WHEN WICKEDNESS ENDS

9 ¶ And the kings of the earth, who have committed fornication and lived deliciously with her, shall bewail her, and lament for her, when they shall see the smoke of her burning,

10 Standing afar off for the fear of her torment, saying, Alas, alas, that great city Babylon, that mighty city! for in one hour is thy judgment come.

11 And the merchants of the earth shall weep and mourn over her; for no man buyeth their merchandise any more:

12 The merchandise of gold, and silver, and precious stones, and of pearls, and fine linen, and purple, and silk, and scarlet, and all thyine wood, and all manner vessels of ivory, and all manner vessels of most precious wood, and of brass, and iron, and marble,

13 And cinnamon, and odours, and ointments, and frankincense, and wine, and oil, and fine flour, and wheat, and beasts, and sheep, and horses, and chariots, and slaves, and souls of men.

14 And the fruits that thy soul lusted after are departed from thee, and all things which were dainty and goodly are departed from thee, and thou shalt find them no more at all.

15 The merchants of these things, which were made rich by her, shall stand afar off for the fear of her torment, weeping and wailing,

16 And saying, Alas, alas, that great city, that was clothed in fine linen, and purple, and scarlet, and decked with gold, and precious stones, and pearls!

17 For in one hour so great riches is come to nought. And every shipmaster, and all the company in ships, and sailors, and as many as trade by sea, stood afar off,

18 And cried when they saw the smoke of her burning, saying, What city is like unto this great city!

19 And they cast dust on their heads, and cried, weeping and wailing, saying, Alas, alas, that great city, wherein were made rich all that had ships in the sea by reason of her costliness! for in one hour is she made desolate.

## THE SAINTS WILL REJOICE WHEN BABYLON IS DESTROYED

20 Rejoice over her, thou heaven, and ye holy apostles and prophets; for God hath avenged you on her.

21 And a mighty angel took up a stone like a great millstone, and cast it into the sea, saying, Thus with violence shall that great city Babylon be thrown down, and shall be found no more at all.

22 And the voice of harpers, and musicians, and of pipers, and trumpeters, shall be heard no more at all in thee; and no craftsman, of whatsoever craft he be, shall be found any more in thee; and the sound of a millstone shall be heard no more at all in thee;

23 And the light of a candle shall shine no more at all in thee; and the voice of the bridegroom and of the bride shall be heard no more at all in thee: for thy merchants were the great men of the earth; for by thy sorceries were all nations deceived.

24 And in her was found the blood of prophets, and of saints, and of all that were slain upon the earth.

---

18:6    Jesus taught that the way we treat other people is the way the Lord will treat us (see Matthew 7:2).

18:7    Even though Satan would like us to think that sin is fun, we know that "wickedness never was happiness" (Alma 41:10). Why would Satan like us to think that wickedness is fun?

18:8    At the Second Coming, "Babylon," or the wicked people of the earth, will be burned (see Malachi 4:1).

        **plagues**—terrible disasters

18:9    **bewail her, and lament for her**—cry for her, and be sad over her

18:11   **merchants**—business people
        **their merchandise**—the goods that they sold

18:14   **lusted after**—had evil desires for

18:17   **is come to nought**—is worthless

18:19   **made desolate**—destroyed or made empty

18:20   What do you think life would be like in a world where there is no wickedness?

18:21-  These verses show how complete the destruc-
18:23   tion of Babylon will be, "for in one hour is she made desolate" (Revelation 18:19).

18:23   **sorceries**—deceptions through magic or tricks

# CHAPTER 19

*John sees the second coming of the Savior and his victory over evil. Look for what will happen to all that is wicked in the world when the Savior comes to earth.*

## ALL WHO ARE IN HEAVEN PRAISE THE LORD

1 ¶ AND after these things I heard a great voice of much people in heaven, saying, Alleluia; Salvation, and glory, and honour, and power, unto the Lord our God:

2 For true and righteous are his judgments: for he hath judged the great whore, which did corrupt the earth with her fornication, and hath avenged the blood of his servants at her hand.

3 And again they said, Alleluia. And her smoke rose up for ever and ever.

4 And the four and twenty elders and the four beasts fell down and worshipped God that sat on the throne, saying, Amen; Alleluia.

5 ¶ And a voice came out of the throne, saying, Praise our God, all ye his servants, and ye that fear him, both small and great.

6 And I heard as it were the voice of a great multitude, and as the voice of many waters, and as the voice of mighty thunderings, saying, Alleluia: for the Lord God omnipotent reigneth.

## RIGHTEOUS SAINTS ARE LIKE THE BRIDE WHO IS READY FOR HER MARRIAGE WITH THE LAMB (JESUS CHRIST)

7 Let us be glad and rejoice, and give honour to him: for the marriage of the Lamb is come, and his wife hath made herself ready.

8 And to her was granted that she should be arrayed in fine linen, clean and white: for the fine linen is the righteousness of saints.

9 And he saith unto me, Write, Blessed are they which are called unto the marriage supper of the Lamb. And he saith unto me, These are the true sayings of God.

10 And I fell at his feet to worship him. And he said unto me, See thou do it not: I am thy fellowservant, and of thy brethren that have the testimony of Jesus: worship God: for the testimony of Jesus is the spirit of prophecy.

## CHRIST WILL COME TO RULE ON THE EARTH AS THE KING OF KINGS AND THE LORD OF LORDS

11 ¶ And I saw heaven opened, and behold a white horse; and he that sat upon him was called Faithful and True, and in righteousness he doth judge and make war.

12 His eyes were as a flame of fire, and on his head were many crowns; and he had a name written, that no man knew, but he himself.

13 And he was clothed with a vesture dipped in blood: and his name is called The Word of God.

14 And the armies which were in heaven followed him upon white horses, clothed in fine linen, white and clean.

15 And out of his mouth goeth a sharp sword, that with it he should smite the nations: and he shall rule them with a rod of iron: and he treadeth the winepress of the fierceness and wrath of Almighty God.

16 And he hath on his vesture and on his thigh a name written, KING OF KINGS, AND LORD OF LORDS.

---

19:1 **Alleluia**—Praise the Lord

19:2 **corrupt**—cause great evil in

God will destroy "the great whore" to punish her for having killed and led away many of his children (see Revelation 6:9-11).

19:6 **omnipotent**—all-powerful **reigneth**—rules

19:7-9 Worthy members of the Church will be invited to the "marriage supper of the Lamb." How can you be ready and willing to come?

19:8 **arrayed**—clothed

19:10 What can you do to strengthen your testimony of Jesus Christ?

19:13 **vesture**—clothing

The Savior is the Word (see D&C 93:8-10).

19:15 The Joseph Smith Translation explains that "out of his [the Savior's] mouth proceedeth the word of God," with which he will defeat and rule the nations (JST, Revelation 19:15). Doctrine and Covenants 133:46-53 says that Jesus treaded the winepress alone. The symbol of the winepress shows that the Savior had to complete the Atonement by himself.

## BIRDS ARE INVITED TO THE SUPPER OF THE GREAT GOD

17 And I saw an angel standing in the sun; and he cried with a loud voice, saying to all the fowls that fly in the midst of heaven, Come and gather yourselves together unto the supper of the great God;

18 That ye may eat the flesh of kings, and the flesh of captains, and the flesh of mighty men, and the flesh of horses, and of them that sit on them, and the flesh of all men, both free and bond, both small and great.

19 And I saw the beast, and the kings of the earth, and their armies, gathered together to make war against him that sat on the horse, and against his army.

20 And the beast was taken, and with him the false prophet that wrought miracles before him, with which he deceived them that had received the mark of the beast, and them that worshipped his image. These both were cast alive into a lake of fire burning with brimstone.

21 And the remnant were slain with the sword of him that sat upon the horse, which sword proceeded out of his mouth: and all the fowls were filled with their flesh.

## CHAPTER 20

*Christ's second coming is described in Revelation 19. In Revelation 20, watch for events that will happen following Christ's second coming.*

## SATAN IS BOUND DURING THE MILLENNIUM

1 ¶ AND I saw an angel come down from heaven, having the key of the bottomless pit and a great chain in his hand.

2 And he laid hold on the dragon, that old serpent, which is the Devil, and Satan, and bound him a thousand years,

3 And cast him into the bottomless pit, and shut him up, and set a seal upon him, that he should deceive the nations no more, till the thousand years should be fulfilled: and after that he must be loosed a little season.

4 And I saw thrones, and they sat upon them, and judgment was given unto them: and I saw the souls of them that were beheaded for the witness of Jesus, and for the word of God, and which had not worshipped the beast, neither his image, neither had received his mark upon their foreheads, or in their hands; and they lived and reigned with Christ a thousand years.

5 But the rest of the dead lived not again until the thousand years were finished. This is the first resurrection.

6 Blessed and holy is he that hath part in the first resurrection: on such the second death hath no power, but they shall be priests of God and of Christ, and shall reign with him a thousand years.

## SATAN IS LOOSED FOR A LITTLE SEASON

7 And when the thousand years are expired, Satan shall be loosed out of his prison,

---

19:17-18 🔥 The Joseph Smith Translation explains that at "the supper of the great God," birds will eat the flesh of all "who fight against the Lamb" (JST, Revelation 19:18; see also Ezekiel 39:17-20; D&C 29:20).

19:19 🔍 This beast is a symbol for the military and political leaders of the wicked (see JST, Revelation 13:1-8).

19:20 🔍 The false prophet is the "beast coming up out of the earth" and is a symbol for false religions that exist in the last days (see Revelation 13:11-15). The mark and the image (statue) of the beast are described in Revelation 13:14-18.

*wrought*—performed

🔥 The "lake of fire burning with brimstone" represents the endless torment that the wicked will endure because of "an awful view of their own guilt and abominations [sins]" (see Mosiah 3:25-27).

19:21 *the remnant*—those that were left

🔥 The Joseph Smith Translation explains that it is the "word" that comes out of the Lord's mouth that will kill the wicked (see JST, Revelation 19:21).

20:2 *bound*—imprisoned

20:3 🔍 The "thousand years" is called the Millennium. During the Millennium there will be peace and righteousness upon the whole earth (see Isaiah 65:17-25; D&C 101:26-35).

20:6 🔥 The resurrection of Jesus Christ brings all people "back into the presence of the Lord." Those who have not repented of their sins experience a "second death" and are cut off again from the presence of God forever. (Helaman 14:17-18.)

20:7 *expired*—ended
*loosed*—released

20:7-9 🔥 This battle is called "the battle of the great God" (see D&C 88:110-115).

8 And shall go out to deceive the nations which are in the four quarters of the earth, Gog and Magog, to gather them together to battle: the number of whom is as the sand of the sea.

9 And they went up on the breadth of the earth, and compassed the camp of the saints about, and the beloved city: and fire came down from God out of heaven, and devoured them.

10 And the devil that deceived them was cast into the lake of fire and brimstone, where the beast and the false prophet are, and shall be tormented day and night for ever and ever.

## THERE WILL BE A FINAL JUDGMENT

11 ¶ And I saw a great white throne, and him that sat on it, from whose face the earth and the heaven fled away; and there was found no place for them.

12 And I saw the dead, small and great, stand before God; and the books were opened: and another book was opened, which is the book of life: and the dead were judged out of those things which were written in the books, according to their works.

13 And the sea gave up the dead which were in it; and death and hell delivered up the dead which were in them: and they were judged every man according to their works.

14 And death and hell were cast into the lake of fire. This is the second death.

15 And whosoever was not found written in the book of life was cast into the lake of fire.

## CHAPTER 21

*John sees the earth become a celestial kingdom. Notice who will be able to live there and what it will be like for them.*

## THOSE WHO OVERCOME SHALL INHERIT ALL THINGS AND BE THE CHILDREN OF GOD

1 ¶ AND I saw a new heaven and a new earth: for the first heaven and the first earth were passed away; and there was no more sea.

2 And I John saw the holy city, new Jerusalem, coming down from God out of heaven, prepared as a bride adorned for her husband.

3 And I heard a great voice out of heaven saying, Behold, the tabernacle of God is with men, and he will dwell with them, and they shall be his people, and God himself shall be with them, and be their God.

4 And God shall wipe away all tears from their eyes; and there shall be no more death, neither sorrow, nor crying, neither shall there be any more pain: for the former things are passed away.

5 And he that sat upon the throne said, Behold, I make all things new. And he said unto me, Write: for these words are true and faithful.

6 And he said unto me, It is done. I am Alpha and Omega, the beginning and the end. I will give unto him that is athirst of the fountain of the water of life freely.

7 He that overcometh shall inherit all things; and I will be his God, and he shall be my son.

8 But the fearful, and unbelieving, and the abominable, and murderers, and whoremongers, and sorcerers, and idolaters, and all liars, shall have their part in the lake which burneth with fire and brimstone: which is the second death.

## THE HOLY JERUSALEM COMES DOWN OUT OF HEAVEN

9 ¶ And there came unto me one of the seven angels which had the seven vials full of the seven last

---

20:8    *deceive*—trick, lie to

20:9    *compassed*—circled around

20:10   The lake of fire and brimstone is a symbolic description of the place where the devil and his followers will spend eternity (see 🔥 for Revelation 19:20).

20:12-  The resurrection will bring all men to Christ to
13      be judged (see Alma 11:44). The books represent, among other things, the records kept on the earth of men's works. That which is recorded on earth is also recorded in heaven. (See D&C 128:6-8.)

        What will the books record about your life?

21:3    *tabernacle*—house

21:6    *Alpha* and *Omega* are the first and last letters of the Greek alphabet. They are also titles for Jesus Christ and symbolize that he is "the beginning and the end." (See LDS Bible Dictionary, s.v. "Alpha," p. 606, s.v. "Omega," p. 740.)

21:8    *abominable*—dreadful, horrible
        *whoremongers*—people who abuse the sacred creative power

# A Ω

*Alpha and Omega*

*An angel shows John "that great city, the holy Jerusalem, descending out of heaven."*

plagues, and talked with me, saying, Come hither, I will shew thee the bride, the Lamb's wife.

10 And he carried me away in the spirit to a great and high mountain, and shewed me that great city, the holy Jerusalem, descending out of heaven from God,

11 Having the glory of God: and her light was like unto a stone most precious, even like a jasper stone, clear as crystal;

12 And had a wall great and high, and had twelve gates, and at the gates twelve angels, and names written thereon, which are the names of the twelve tribes of the children of Israel:

13 On the east three gates; on the north three gates; on the south three gates; and on the west three gates.

14 And the wall of the city had twelve foundations, and in them the names of the twelve apostles of the Lamb.

15 And he that talked with me had a golden reed to measure the city, and the gates thereof, and the wall thereof.

16 And the city lieth foursquare, and the length is as large as the breadth: and he measured the city with the reed, twelve thousand furlongs. The length and the breadth and the height of it are equal.

17 And he measured the wall thereof, an hundred and forty and four cubits, according to the measure of a man, that is, of the angel.

18 And the building of the wall of it was of jasper: and the city was pure gold, like unto clear glass.

19 And the foundations of the wall of the city were garnished with all manner of precious stones. The first foundation was jasper; the second, sapphire; the third, a chalcedony; the fourth, an emerald;

20 The fifth, sardonyx; the sixth, sardius; the seventh, chrysolite; the eighth, beryl; the ninth, a topaz; the tenth, a chrysoprasus; the eleventh, a jacinth; the twelfth, an amethyst.

21 And the twelve gates were twelve pearls; every several gate was of one pearl: and the street of the city was pure gold, as it were transparent glass.

22 And I saw no temple therein: for the Lord God Almighty and the Lamb are the temple of it.

23 And the city had no need of the sun, neither of the moon, to shine in it: for the glory of God did lighten it, and the Lamb is the light thereof.

24 And the nations of them which are saved shall walk in the light of it: and the kings of the earth do bring their glory and honour into it.

25 And the gates of it shall not be shut at all by day: for there shall be no night there.

26 And they shall bring the glory and honour of the nations into it.

27 And there shall in no wise enter into it any thing that defileth, neither whatsoever worketh abomination, or maketh a lie: but they which are written in the Lamb's book of life.

# CHAPTER 22

*The final chapter of Revelation is a testimony of Jesus Christ. Look for the promises given to those who worship and follow Jesus.*

## RIGHTEOUS SAINTS WILL REIGN IN THE CELESTIAL KINGDOM AS GODS

1 ¶ AND he shewed me a pure river of water of life, clear as crystal, proceeding out of the throne of God and of the Lamb.

2 In the midst of the street of it, and on either side of the river, was there the tree of life, which bare twelve manner of fruits, and yielded her fruit every month: and the leaves of the tree were for the healing of the nations.

3 And there shall be no more curse: but the throne of

---

21:10-
21  These verses tell of the day when, in the words of Elder Bruce R. McConkie, "the earth becomes a celestial sphere, with its capital city coming down from celestial spheres." There are no human words to describe this city's true beauty. (See *Doctrinal New Testament Commentary* 3:586, 588.)

21:10  **shewed**—This word is pronounced the same way as the word *showed* and has the same meaning; *shewed* is simply an old spelling of *showed*.

21:19  **garnished**—decorated

21:27  What is "the Lamb's book of life"? (See for Revelation 3:5.)

What do you think it would be like to live in this heavenly city?

22:1  **the Lamb**—Jesus Christ

22:2  The tree of life is where the faithful partake of the fruit of eternal life (see 1 Nephi 8:10-12; Revelation 2:7).

22:3  "In the beginning the Lord cursed the ground [see Genesis 3:17-24]. . . . Now the curse is removed; all men who attain celestial glory have free access to the tree of life and partake of all the goodness of God." (Bruce R. McConkie, *Doctrinal New Testament Commentary* 3:589.)

God and of the Lamb shall be in it; and his servants shall serve him:

4 And they shall see his face; and his name shall be in their foreheads.

5 And there shall be no night there; and they need no candle, neither light of the sun; for the Lord God giveth them light: and they shall reign for ever and ever.

## CHRIST COMES AND REWARDS THE FAITHFUL

6 ¶ And he said unto me, These sayings are faithful and true: and the Lord God of the holy prophets sent his angel to shew unto his servants the things which must shortly be done.

7 Behold, I come quickly: blessed is he that keepeth the sayings of the prophecy of this book.

8 And I John saw these things, and heard them. And when I had heard and seen, I fell down to worship before the feet of the angel which shewed me these things.

9 Then saith he unto me, See thou do it not: for I am thy fellowservant, and of thy brethren the prophets, and of them which keep the sayings of this book: worship God.

10 And he saith unto me, Seal not the sayings of the prophecy of this book: for the time is at hand.

11 He that is unjust, let him be unjust still: and he which is filthy, let him be filthy still: and he that is righteous, let him be righteous still: and he that is holy, let him be holy still.

12 And, behold, I come quickly; and my reward is with me, to give every man according as his work shall be.

13 I am Alpha and Omega, the beginning and the end, the first and the last.

14 Blessed are they that do his commandments, that they may have right to the tree of life, and may enter in through the gates into the city.

15 For without are dogs, and sorcerers, and whoremongers, and murderers, and idolaters, and whosoever loveth and maketh a lie.

16 I Jesus have sent mine angel to testify unto you these things in the churches. I am the root and the offspring of David, and the bright and morning star.

## COME UNTO CHRIST

17 And the Spirit and the bride say, Come. And let him that heareth say, Come. And let him that is athirst come. And whosoever will, let him take the water of life freely.

18 For I testify unto every man that heareth the words of the prophecy of this book, If any man shall add unto these things, God shall add unto him the plagues that are written in this book:

19 And if any man shall take away from the words of the book of this prophecy, God shall take away his part out of the book of life, and out of the holy city, and from the things which are written in this book.

20 ¶ He which testifieth these things saith, Surely I come quickly. Amen. Even so, come, Lord Jesus.

21 The grace of our Lord Jesus Christ be with you all. Amen.

---

22:4 The phrase "his name shall be in their foreheads" teaches that the Saints will become like God, for "when he shall appear, we shall be like him" (1 John 3:2).

22:5 What do you imagine it will be like to dwell forever in heaven, where there will be no wickedness?

22:7 What do you think it means to keep "the sayings of the prophecy of this book [book of Revelation]"? What has this book "said" to you as you have studied it?

22:10 John was commanded not to seal the contents of this book. The Lord wants everyone to be able to read the prophecies found inside the book of Revelation.

22:14 Those who keep the commandments and endure to the end are blessed. They receive eternal life. (See D&C 14:7.)

22:15 *sorcerers*—evil magicians
*idolaters*—those who worship false gods

22:18-
19 "Moses issued the same decree relative to his teachings . . . [see Deuteronomy 4:2; 12:32]. God alone can add or diminish from holy writ. What he has spoken, he has spoken, and none but he can alter. When a prophet speaks by the power of the Holy Ghost, it is the voice of God; and none can change it without suffering the penalty prescribed for perverting the pronouncements of Deity." (Bruce R. McConkie, *Doctrinal New Testament Commentary* 3:593.)

22:21 How has studying the scriptures changed your life?

# GLOSSARY

**Blaspheme, Blasphemy.** These words refer to the sin of falsely claiming to be like God or of speaking evil of God.

**Chief priests.** Jewish religious leaders and teachers.

**Christ.** A Greek word meaning "the Anointed One"; the Hebrew word with the same meaning is *Messiah* (see LDS Bible Dictionary, s.v. "Christ," p. 633).

**Circumcise, Circumcision.** The law of circumcision was first given to Abraham (see Genesis 17). Circumcision was an ordinance for boys who were eight days old to show they were God's covenant children. The Joseph Smith Translation indicates that it was also to remind the Lord's people that baptism was not necessary until the age of eight (see JST, Genesis 17:11-12). By the time of Paul's writings, circumcision had come to represent the Jews and the law of Moses.

**David.** One of Israel's greatest kings. David was promised that the Messiah would be born into his family. Because Jesus Christ was a son of David, he was a rightful king of Israel.

**Elders.** Jewish religious leaders and teachers. This term is also used to refer to priesthood holders in the Church of Jesus Christ (see James 5:14-15).

**Election.** The process by which people were chosen by God in the premortal life and given the opportunity to be saved. While they are on the earth, the elect must prove their worthiness to be saved. (See LDS Bible Dictionary, s.v. "Election," pp. 662-63.)

**Elias.** The Greek word for *Elijah*. Elias is also a title for someone who prepares the way for another person. John the Baptist prepared the way for Jesus Christ, and so he was an Elias. (See LDS Bible Dictionary, s.v. "Elias," p. 663.)

**Fornication, Fornicators.** Misuse of the sacred creative powers; that is, use of these powers between people who are not married.

**Gentiles.** A word that means "nations." It refers to those not of the family of Israel or who do not believe in the God of Israel. (See LDS Bible Dictionary, s.v. "Gentile," pp. 679-80.)

**Grace.** Divine help given by God through the atonement of Jesus Christ. It provides us with the power needed to repent, keep the commandments, and become like God. (See LDS Bible Dictionary, s.v. "Grace," p. 697; 2 Nephi 25:23.)

**High priest.** The leading officer in the Aaronic Priesthood under the law of Moses. The office was passed down through the firstborn among the family of Aaron. During New Testament times, apostate high priests were appointed by King Herod and the Romans. (See LDS Bible Dictionary, s.v. "High Priest," pp. 702-3.)

**Hypocrisy, Hypocrites.** Hypocrites are people who pretend to be good when they are not.

**Israel.** A word that means "one who prevails with God," or "let God prevail." The name *Israel* is used several ways in the scriptures. It may refer to (1) the man Jacob, whose name was changed to Israel; (2) the family, children, or tribes of Israel; (3) the land of Israel; or (4) the true believers in Christ, no matter what their family or where they live. (See LDS Bible Dictionary, s.v. "Israel," p. 708.)

**Jew.** The word *Jew* comes from a Hebrew word meaning "one belonging to Judah." As such, it identifies those who are of the tribe of Judah. However, the term is also used to identify citizens of the kingdom of Judah, no matter what their tribe (see Acts 21:37-39; 22:3; Romans 11:1; Philippians 3:5; 2 Nephi 30:4; 33:8). The word *Jew* also distinguished those who belonged to the religion of the Jews. Christ, a Jew, taught that "salvation is of the Jews" (John 4:22), meaning that through the Jews "had come the prophets, the priesthood, and the Redeemer himself" (Bruce R. McConkie, *Mormon Doctrine*, p. 393).

**Justification.** A person who is "justified" has had his sins forgiven and stands approved of God. Our sins can be forgiven because of the Savior's atonement and when we exercise faith in Christ, repent of our sins, and obey all of the commandments and ordinances of the gospel.

**Kingdom of God, Kingdom of heaven.** The phrases "kingdom of God" and "kingdom of heaven" are

used several ways in the scriptures. Often they mean the celestial kingdom. Sometimes they refer to the Lord's true church on the earth. Other times they refer to the government over which Jesus Christ will reign during the Millennium. (See Bruce R. McConkie, *Mormon Doctrine*, pp. 415-18.)

**Law.** "The law" is the law of Moses, which the children of Israel were commanded to follow from the days of Moses until the time of Jesus Christ (see LDS Bible Dictionary, s.v. "Law of Moses," pp. 722-23).

**Lepers, Leprosy.** In the New Testament the term *leprosy* is used to refer to many different skin diseases and infections.

**Offence, Offend.** An offence is a stumbling block, meaning anyone or anything that blocks someone from doing what is right or causes them to sin. To "be offended" is to stumble spiritually and turn away from the truth.

**Palsy.** Persons described as being "sick of the palsy" or "taken with a palsy" were physically disabled.

**Parables.** Stories about things on earth that are told to help explain heavenly or spiritual things.

**Passover.** The Feast of the Passover was an important Jewish celebration. It was a reminder to the children of Israel that the angel of death "passed over" their firstborn children when the firstborn children of Egypt all died. (See LDS Bible Dictionary, s.v. "Feasts," pp. 672-74.)

**Pharisees.** Religious and political leaders of the Jews.

**Publicans.** Tax collectors.

**Sadducees.** Religious and political leaders of the Jews.

**Samaritans.** People who lived in Samaria and were part Israelite and part Gentile. The Samaritans' religion was a mixture of the religion of Israel and idol worship. They were hated by the Jews. (See LDS Bible Dictionary, s.v. "Samaritans," p. 768.)

**Sanctification, Sanctify.** "To be *sanctified* is to become clean, pure, and spotless" (Bruce R. McConkie, *Mormon Doctrine*, p. 675). A person can become sanctified only through the atonement of Jesus Christ and by obedience to the laws, ordinances, and commandments of the gospel of Jesus Christ.

**Sanhedrin.** Often called "the council," the Sanhedrin was a group of seventy-one men who ruled the Jews. It was made up of Pharisees, Sadducees, and scribes, and was led by the high priest. (See LDS Bible Dictionary, s.v. "Sanhedrin," p. 769.)

**Scribes.** Men who taught the scriptures. They were sometimes called lawyers. (See LDS Bible Dictionary, s.v. "Scribe," p. 770.)

**Seed.** Children, members of a family, or descendants.

**Sepulchre.** Burial place for the dead (comes from the same Greek word as *tomb*).

**Son of man.** "In the language of Adam, Man of Holiness is [Heavenly Father's] name, and the name of his Only Begotten is the Son of Man, even Jesus Christ" (Moses 6:57).

**Synagogues.** Jewish places of worship.

# PRONUNCIATION GUIDE

There are many words in the New Testament that are difficult to pronounce because they come from Hebrew or Greek or even old English. The following guide will help you with the most common way of pronouncing these words in modern English.

## Key

Whenever you see a syllable in the pronunciation guide that is CAPITALIZED, it is the part of the word that should be emphasized (for example, BETH-le-hem). The sounds for the syllables listed below will help you pronounce the words correctly. (This key is drawn in large part from William O. Walker, Jr., ed., *The HarperCollins Bible Pronunciation Guide,* as well as from James Strong's *Exhaustive Concordance of the Bible.*)

| | | | | | |
|---|---|---|---|---|---|
| a | c**a**t | er | **er**ror | or | **for** |
| ah | f**a**ther | eye | bird's-**eye** | ou | h**ow** |
| air | c**are** | i | **it** | sh | **s**ure |
| ar | **ar**e | ie | p**ie** | u, uh | **a**go |
| aw | j**aw** | ihr | **ear** | ur | h**er** |
| ay | p**ay** | o | h**o**t | us | b**us** |
| ch | **ch**ew | ock | **lock** | x | ve**x** |
| e, eh | p**e**t | oh | g**o** | zh | mea**s**ure |
| ee | s**ee**m | oo | b**oo**t | | |

**Abiathar** = uh-BIE-uh-thar

**Agabus** = AG-uh-bus

**Agrippa** = uh-GRIP-uh

**Alphaeus** = al-FEE-us

**Ananias** = an-uh-NIE-us

**Antioch** = AN-tee-ock

**Apollos** = uh-POL-lohs

**Aquila** = ak-WIL-uh

**Areopagus** = air-ee-OP-uh-gus

**Arimathaea** = air-uh-muh-THEE-uh

**Armageddon** = ar-muh-GED-un


**Babylon** = BAB-uh-lon

**Barabbas** = buh-RAB-us

**Barnabas** = BAR-nuh-bus

**Bartholomew** = bar-THOL-uh-myoo

**Bartimaeus** = bar-tuh-MEE-us

**Beelzebub** = bee-EL-zi-bub

**Berea** = bi-REE-uh

**Bethabara** = beth-AB-ruh

**Bethany** = BETH-uh-nee

**Bethesda** = buh-THEZ-duh

**Bethlehem** = BETH-le-hem

**Bethphage** = BETH-fuh-jee

**Bethsaida** = beth-SAY-duh

**Boanerges** = boh-uh-NUR-jeez


**Caesar** = SEE-zur

**Caesarea** = ses-uh-REE-uh

**Caesarea Philippi** = ses-uh-REE-uh fi-LIP-eye

**Caiaphas** = KIE-uh-fus

**Calvary** = KAL-vuh-ree

**Capernaum** = kuh-PUR-nay-um

**Cephas** = SEE-fus

**Cherubim** = CHAIR-uh-bim

**Chorazin** = kor-uh-ZIN

**Claudius** = KLAW-dee-us

**Colossians** = koh-LOSH-uns

**Corban** = KOR-bahn

**Corinth** = KOR-inth

**Corinthians** = koh-RIN-thee-uns

**Cornelius** = kor-NEEL-yus

**Cyprus** = SIE-prus

**Cyrenian** = sie-REE-nee-un


**Dalmanutha** = dal-muh-NOO-thuh

**Damascus** = duh-MAS-kus

**Decapolis** = di-KAP-uh-lis

**Demetrius** = di-MEE-tree-us

**Egypt** = EE-jipt

**Elias** = i-LIE-us

**Eli Eli lama sabachthani** = EE-lie EE-lie LAH-muh suh-BAHK-thuh-nee

**Elymas** = EL-uh-mus

**Emmaus** = em-MAY-us

**Enoch** = EE-nuk

**Ephesians** = i-FEE-zhuns

**Ephesus** = EF-uh-sus

**Ephphatha** = EF-uh-thuh

**Esaias** = i-ZAY-us

**Ethiopia** = ee-thee-OH-pee-uh

**Eunuch** = YOO-nuk

**Eutychus** = YOO-tuh-kus


**Felix** = FEE-lix

**Festus** = FES-tus


**Gabriel** = GAY-bree-ul

**Gadarenes** = GAD-uh-reens

**Gaius** = GAY-yus

**Galatia** = guh-LAY-shuh

**Galatians** = guh-LAY-shuns

**Galilee** = GAL-uh-lee

**Gamaliel** = guh-MAY-lee-el

**Gennesaret** = gi-NES-uh-ret

**Gentile** = JEN-tile

**Gergesenes** = GER-guh-seens

**Gethsemane** = geth-SEM-uh-nee

**Golgotha** = GOL-guh-thuh

**Gomorrha** = guh-MOR-uh


**Hebrews** = HEE-broos

**Herod** = HAIR-ud

**Herodias** = hi-ROH-dee-us

**Herodians** = hi-ROH-dee-uns

**Hosanna** = hoh-ZAN-uh


**Isaac** = EYE-zik

**Issachar** = IS-uh-kar


**Jairus** = jay-EYE-rus

**Jeremias** = jer-uh-MIE-us

**Jerusalem** = ji-ROO-suh-lum

**Jonas** = JOH-nus

**Joppa** = JOP-uh

**Juda** = JOO-duh

**Judaea** = joo-DEE-uh

**Judas Iscariot** = JOO-dus is-KAIR-ee-ut

**Laodicea** = lay-od-i-SEE-uh
**Lazarus** = LAZ-uh-rus
**Legion** = LEE-jun
**Levi** = LEE-vie

**Macedonia =** Mas-uh-DOH-nee-uh
**Magog** = MAY-gog
**Malchus** = MAL-kus
**Manasses** = muh-NAS-eez
**Mary Magdalene** = MAIR-ee MAG-duh-leen
**Melchisedec** = mel-KES-eh-deck

**Nazareth** = NAZ-uh-reth
**Nicodemus** = nik-uh-DEE-mus
**Nicolaitans** = nik-oh-LAY-uh-tuns
**Nineveh** = NIN-uh-vuh

**Onesimus** = oh-NES-uh-mus

**Pentecost** = PEN-ti-kost
**Pergamos** = PUR-guh-mus
**Pharaoh** = FAIR-oh
**Pharisees** = FAIR-uh-sees
**Philadelphia** = fil-uh-DEL-fee-uh
**Philemon** = fie-LEE-mun
**Philippi** = fi-LIP-eye
**Philippians** = fi-LIP-ee-unz
**Pontius Pilate** = PON-shus PIE-lut
**Praetorium** = pri-TOR-ee-um
**Priscilla** = pri-SIL-uh
**Publius =** PUB-lee-us

**Rabbi** = RAB-eye
**Raca** = RAHK-ah
**Rama** = RAY-muh
**Reuben** = ROO-bin

**Sadducees** = SAD-joo-sees
**Salome** = suh-LOH-mee

**Samaria** = suh-MAIR-ee-uh
**Samaritan** = suh-MAIR-uh-tun
**Sapphira** = suh-FIE-ruh
**Sardis** = SAR-dis
**Saul** = SAWL
**Sepulchre** = SEP-ul-kur
**Sidon** = SIE-dun
**Silas** = SIE-lus
**Siloam** = sie-LOH-um
**Simeon** = SIM-ee-un
**Simon Bar-jona** = SIE-mun bar-JOH-nuh
**Smyrna** = SMUR-nuh
**Sodom** = SOD-um
**Synagogue** = SIN-uh-gog
**Syria** = SIHR-ee-uh
**Syrophenician** = sie-roh-fi-NEE-shun

**Tabernacle** = TAB-ur-nak-ul
**Talitha cumi** = TAL-uh-thuh KOO-mie
**Tarsus** = TAR-sus
**Thaddaeus** = THAD-ee-us
**Theophilus** = thee-OFF-uh-lus
**Thessalonians** = thes-uh-LOH-nee-uhns
**Thessalonica** = thes-uh-luh-NIE-kuh
**Thyatira**= thi-uh-TIE-ruh
**Tiberias** = tie-BIHR-ee-us
**Timaeus** = tie-MEE-us
**Timotheus** = ti-MOH-thee-us
**Timothy** = TIM-oh-thee
**Titus** = TIE-tus
**Tyre** = TIRE

**Zabulon** = ZAB-yuh-lon
**Zacchaeus** = za-KEE-us
**Zacharias** = zak-uh-RIE-us
**Zebedee** = ZEB-uh-dee

# Sources Cited

Benson, Ezra Taft. *The Teachings of Ezra Taft Benson.* Salt Lake City: Bookcraft, 1988.

———. "Think on Christ." *Ensign* 14 (April 1984): 9–13.

Conference Reports. Salt Lake City: The Church of Jesus Christ of Latter-day Saints. October 1969; April 1988; October 1997.

Draper, Richard D. *Opening the Seven Seals: The Visions of John the Revelator.* Salt Lake City: Deseret Book Co., 1991.

Dummelow, J. R., ed. *A Commentary on the Holy Bible.* New York: Macmillan, 1936.

*Encyclopedia of Mormonism.* Edited by Daniel H. Ludlow. 5 vols. New York: Macmillan, 1992.

Farrar, Frederic W. *The Life of Christ.* 1874. Reprint, Salt Lake City: Bookcraft, 1994.

Faust, James E. "A Crown of Thorns, a Crown of Glory." *Ensign* 21 (May 1991): 68–70.

First Presidency. Letter to Members of The Church of Jesus Christ of Latter-day Saints, 15 May 1997.

*For the Strength of Youth* [pamphlet]. Salt Lake City: The Church of Jesus Christ of Latter-day Saints, 1990.

Groberg, John H. "The Beauty and Importance of the Sacrament." *Ensign* 19 (May 1989): 38–40.

Hinckley, Gordon B. " 'Be Not Afraid, Only Believe.' " *Ensign* 26 (February 1996): 2–5.

———. "He Is at Peace." *Ensign* 15 (December 1985): 41.

———. "Messages of Inspiration from President Hinckley." *Church News,* 6 December 1997, p. 2.

———. "Stand Strong Against the Wiles of the World." *Ensign* 25 (November 1995): 98–101.

———. *Teachings of Gordon B. Hinckley.* Salt Lake City: Deseret Book Co., 1997.

Hunter, Howard W. *The Teachings of Howard W. Hunter.* Edited by Clyde J. Williams. Salt Lake City: Bookcraft, 1997.

Kimball, Spencer W. *Faith Precedes the Miracle.* Salt Lake City: Deseret Book Co., 1972.

———. *Humility.* Brigham Young University Speeches of the Year. Provo, Utah, 16 January 1963.

———. *The Miracle of Forgiveness.* Salt Lake City: Bookcraft, 1969.

———. *The Teachings of Spencer W. Kimball.* Edited by Edward L. Kimball. Salt Lake City: Bookcraft, 1982.

Lee, Harold B. *Stand Ye in Holy Places.* Salt Lake City: Deseret Book Co., 1974.

———. *The Teachings of Harold B. Lee.* Edited by Clyde J. Williams. Salt Lake City: Bookcraft, 1996.

Maxwell, Neal A. *"But for a Small Moment."* Salt Lake City: Bookcraft, 1986.

———. *Meek and Lowly.* Salt Lake City: Deseret Book Co., 1987.

———. *Sermons Not Spoken.* Salt Lake City: Bookcraft, 1985.

———. "Some Thoughts on the Gospel and the Behavioral Sciences." *BYU Studies* 16 (Summer 1976): 589–602.

McConkie, Bruce R. *Doctrinal New Testament Commentary.* 3 vols. Salt Lake City: Bookcraft, 1965–73.

———. *The Millennial Messiah.* Salt Lake City: Deseret Book Co., 1982.

———. *Mormon Doctrine.* 2d ed. Salt Lake City: Bookcraft, 1966.

———. *The Mortal Messiah.* 4 vols. Salt Lake City: Deseret Book Co., 1979–81.

———. *A New Witness for the Articles of Faith.* Salt Lake City: Deseret Book Co., 1985.

———. *Sermons and Writings of Bruce R. McConkie.* Edited by Mark L. McConkie. Salt Lake City: Bookcraft, 1998.

McKay, David O. *Gospel Ideals.* Salt Lake City: Improvement Era, 1953.

Metzger, Bruce M. *The Canon of the New Testament: Its Origin, Development, and Significance.* New York: Oxford University Press, 1987.

Packer, Boyd K. "Teach the Scriptures." Address to religious educators, 14 October 1977, Salt Lake City.

———. *"That All May Be Edified."* Salt Lake City: Bookcraft, 1982.

Perry, L. Tom. "Father—Your Role, Your Responsibility." *Ensign* 17 (November 1977): 62–64.

Richards, LeGrand. *A Marvelous Work and a Wonder.* Rev. ed. Salt Lake City: Deseret Book Co., 1966.

Roberts, B. H. *The Seventy's Course in Theology.* 5 vols. 1907–12. Reprint (5 vols. in 1), Orem, Utah: Grandin Book Co., 1994.

Smith, George Albert. *Sharing the Gospel with Others.* Salt Lake City: Deseret Book Co., 1948.

Smith, Joseph. *The Teachings of Joseph Smith.* Edited by Larry E. Dahl and Donald Q. Cannon. Salt Lake City: Bookcraft, 1997.

Smith, Joseph F. *Gospel Doctrine.* Salt Lake City: Deseret Book Co., 1939.

Smith, Joseph Fielding. *Answers to Gospel Questions.* Compiled by Joseph Fielding Smith, Jr. 5 vols. Salt Lake City: Deseret Book Co., 1957–66.

———. *Doctrines of Salvation.* Compiled by Bruce R. McConkie. 3 vols. Salt Lake City: Bookcraft, 1954–56.

———. *The Way to Perfection.* Salt Lake City: Genealogical Society of The Church of Jesus Christ of Latter-day Saints, 1958.

Sperry, Sydney B. *Paul's Life and Letters.* Salt Lake City: Bookcraft, 1955.

Strong, James. *The Exhaustive Concordance of the Bible.* Nashville, Tenn.: Abingdon Press, 1973.

Talmage, James E. *Jesus the Christ.* 3rd ed. Salt Lake City: The Church of Jesus Christ of Latter-day Saints, 1916.

Unger, Merrill F. *The New Unger's Bible Dictionary.* Edited by R. K. Harrison. Chicago: Moody Press, 1988.

*Vine's Complete Expository Dictionary of Old and New Testament Words.* Nashville, Tenn.: Thomas Nelson, 1985.

Walker, William O., Jr., ed. *The HarperCollins Bible Pronunciation Guide.* San Francisco: HarperCollins, 1994.

# ILLUSTRATION AND PHOTO CREDITS

All color illustrations by Robert T. Barrett.

All color illustrations © Robert T. Barrett except for those on pages 6, 34, 73, 114, 326, 433, and 462, which are © The Church of Jesus Christ of Latter-day Saints.

All maps by Tom Child.

The following provided photographs for inclusion in this book (names are followed by the pages on which the photos appear):

Church Educational System—55, 121, 197, 215, 241, 245, 400, 421, 422, 429, 466, 470

Randall C. Bird—60

Richard O. Christensen—50, 168

David H. Garner—8, 18, 27, 65, 70, 80, 93, 120, 134, 143, 153, 163, 169, 200, 216, 234, 262, 264, 304, 324, 338, 341, 345, 361, 401, 483

Paul Johnson—372

George R. Sims—52, 101, 193, 208, 247, 248, 276, 403

Dennis Q. Taylor—371, 464

Thomas R. Valletta—37, 85, 88, 115, 175